Finance

for Non-Financial Managers

Fourth Edition

Pierre G. Bergeron

University of Ottawa

THOMSON

NELSON

Australia   Canada   Mexico   Singapore   Spain   United Kingdom   United States

Finance for Non-Financial Managers
Fourth Edition
by Pierre G. Bergeron

Editorial Director and Publisher:
Evelyn Veitch

Executive Editor:
Veronica Visentin

Senior Marketing Manager:
Don Thompson

Senior Developmental Editor:
Joanne Sutherland

Managing Production Editor:
Susan Calvert

Copy Editor/Proofreader:
Karen Rolfe

Indexer:
Edwin Durbin

Senior Production Coordinator:
Hedy Sellers

Creative Director:
Angela Cluer

Interior Design:
Sarah Battersby

Cover Design:
Peter Papayanakis

Cover Image:
David Buffington/Photodisc Red/
Getty Images

Compositor:
Nelson Gonzalez

Printer:
Transcontinental

National Library of Canada Cataloguing in Publication

Bergeron, Pierre G.
   Finance for non-financial managers: the quickest way to the bottom line / Pierre G. Bergeron. –4th ed.

Includes index.
ISBN 0-17-622466-1

1. Business enterprises–Finance.
I. Title.

HG4026.B46 2003   658.15
C2003-903328-7

To the memory of my beloved father

Paul E. Bergeron

a friend
a tutor
a motivator

who started me on the trail that
has led to this book, among others,
and introduced me to the measures
of excellence.

Contents

About the Author

Pierre G. Bergeron is Professor at the School of Management, University of Ottawa. He was formerly Secretary, Associate Dean (External Relations), and Assistant Dean (Undergraduate Programs) at the same university. He is President of Budgeting Concepts Inc., an Ottawa-based corporate financial planning consulting firm. He is a highly skilled educator with more than 25 years of experience.

Mr. Bergeron has occupied the position of Director in federal government agencies, such as Industry Canada (Incentives Division) and Human Resources Canada (Financial Planning Division). In the private sector, he worked at Imperial Oil Limited in the Quebec Marketing Region and at the company's head office in Toronto in market analysis and capital project evaluation. He was also Director, Corporate Financial Planning, at Domtar Limited.

Mr. Bergeron is the author of seven books: *Modern Management in Canada; Introduction aux affaires; Gestion dynamique: concepts, méthodes et applications; Finance for Non-Financial Managers; Gestion Moderne: Théorie et Cas; Planification, Budgétisation et Gestion par Objectifs;* and *Capital Expenditure Planning for Growth and Profit.* The third edition of *Finance for Non-Financial Managers* was so successful that it was adapted by an American publishing company under the title *Survivor's Guide to Finance.* Mr. Bergeron has written extensively on finance, planning, budgeting, and capital budgeting for professional journals including *CAmagazine, CMA Magazine, CGA Magazine, Banker and ICB Review,* the *Financial Post,* and *Optimum.* He is the recipient of the Walter J. MacDonald award for his series of articles on capital budgeting decisions, which appeared in *CAmagazine.*

Mr. Bergeron developed the Canadian Tourism Commission's Web site component *The ABC of Financial Performance Measures and Benchmarks for Canada's Tourism Sector* (www.canadatourism.com). This is a six-guide financial analysis program supplemented with a software program designed to help small and medium-sized tourism businesses assess their financial performance and compare themselves to their respective sectors and financial benchmarks.

He also collaborated with Industry Canada in developing its *Strategis* Web site component called *Steps to Growth Capital* (strategis.ic.gc.ca/growth), a program designed to help entrepreneurs raise risk capital funds from venture capital markets. He also participated in producing *Tourism is Your Business: A Financial Management Program* for Canada's Lodging Industry, a manual and a series of video elements on the subject of finance. In addition, he created a two-segment financial planning program (profitplanning.com) to help managers gauge the impact of business strategies, plans, and budgets on financial statements, and to make business decisions using the more sophisticated time-value-of-money investment yardsticks. A unique feature of this finance software is that it can perform just about any financial statement analysis and decision-making calculation included in the book *Finance for Non-Financial Managers.*

Mr. Bergeron is a graduate of the University of Ottawa and the University of Western Ontario.

Preface

Over the past 25 years, many managers and executives taking my seminars on *Finance for Non-Financial Managers* have expressed the need for a simple and basic financial management book, one that would easily clarify financial terms, concepts, and techniques, and help them apply the theory of finance to solve business problems. The intent of this book is to respond to that need.

This book is written for managers, executives, and business students who have little experience in the field of finance. It is aimed primarily at readers who wish to broaden their understanding of financial analysis, improve their decision-making skills, or upgrade old skills in the field of financial management and accounting.

I have written this book with the conviction that finance is a function that is far too important to be left only to financial specialists. Financial activities should be practised by non-financial managers who are responsible for resources and interested in improving the financial performance and destiny of their organizations.

This book will be particularly useful to (1) managers in all types of organizations who currently work in various non-financial functions such as marketing, production, human resources, engineering, or research and development; (2) financial analysts who want to adopt more rigid methodologies for solving financial problems; (3) accountants who want to learn how to analyze financial statements in a more comprehensive way and use them as decision-making instruments; (4) entrepreneurs of small and medium-sized businesses who feel the need to develop fundamental skills in financial control and financial planning; and (5) independent professionals, such as lawyers, engineers, and medical practitioners, who want to develop the financial side of their profession.

The various financial topics are presented in a format appropriate for both groups, e.g., those who supply financial information (accountants) and those who use it (non-financial managers and financial analysts). One of the most important objectives of this book is to make the various topics presented in each chapter intelligible to all readers at different levels of education and experience.

In addition to managers and executives, business students will find this book instrumental in learning the essentials of financial statement analysis and capital budgeting techniques. It can be used for a one-semester course at colleges, at universities for continuing education courses in finance, in business courses for nonbusiness majors, and in small business management and entrepreneurship courses.

Readers will find *Finance for Non-Financial Managers* informative and enjoyable. There is no need to present finance as an abstract or obtuse subject. Properly explained and presented, finance can be easily understood and, more importantly, applied to business situations so that non-financial managers and executives can be more effective. I have presented various financial management concepts and techniques in a simple way, using a common-sense approach, supported by many tables, figures, examples, and illustrations.

Finance for Non-Financial Managers is an attempt to translate my seminars, which are a source of joy and challenge, into another medium. I continue to be most gratified by the positive responses from the many users of the book, at all levels of businesses, who have found it very helpful. I wish every reader good luck and hope that you will be able to find these financial tools helpful for improving your decisions and, in the process, bring growth and financial affluence to your business.

New to this edition

This fourth edition has been written to improve the clarity of many finance techniques and the relationship between the various concepts covered in the book. The explanation of the financial concepts and techniques, supported by numerous practical examples, is a result of many questions and discussions that I have had with managers and executives during my seminars. I have to point out, however, that while revising this book, I have not lost sight of its primary focus, which is to be an executive briefing instrument that will help managers and executives grasp the more important financial relationships and issues.

The fourth edition maintains the unique and distinct features that were introduced in the third edition. First, each chapter begins with a list of well-defined learning objectives to help readers identify what they can expect to understand after reading the chapter. These objectives are important because they provide some form of a checklist of the more important topics that will be covered in the chapter. The objectives are linked directly to the end-of-chapter questions, exercises, and cases. The learning objectives are also directly keyed to the Chapter Summary. Second, each chapter is introduced by an Opening Case that presents the more important financial topics covered in the chapter and ends with insightful exercises related to that particular case. This helps readers understand more completely the link between the theory and its applications. Third, and of equal importance, all introductory Opening Cases are connected. This unique feature enables the reader to visualize how all concepts covered in the book can be logically linked to analyze financial statements and to make decisions to improve a company's bottom line. Fourth, each chapter ends with different types of questions, exercises, and cases to help readers comprehend more fully all chapter themes and concepts through personal reflection in addition to testing their comprehension and sharpening their analytical and decision-making abilities. Over 200 new questions have been added to this edition.

Supplementary Material

The supplement package to accompany the fourth edition of *Finance for Non-Financial Managers* has been significantly expanded from previous editions.

- The *instructor's manual* now includes answers to the review and discussion questions found at the end of each chapter in the text.
- There are over 200 new *Microsoft® PowerPoint slides* that summarize the text's key concepts.

- A new test bank is now available that contains over 1900 multiple-choice, true/false, and fill-in-the-blank questions as well as questions related to the exercises.
- *Microsoft® Excel spreadsheet templates* will once again accompany this edition. The purpose of the spreadsheets is to help users of *Finance for Non-Financial Managers* perform most financial calculations in the fourth edition of the book, allowing students to devote more time on the analytical and decision-making activities and less on "number crunching." The spreadsheet program includes two segments. The first helps to analyze financial statements and the second helps make business decisions related to the exercises and cases contained in the book. After taking just a few moments to input numbers drawn from financial statements onto the spreadsheet program, which contains more than 30 different financial analytic tools (e.g., 25 financial ratios, economic value added, Z-score, sustainable growth rate, internal rate of return), readers can now focus on interpretation of financial statements and decisions and less on calculations. The spreadsheets will be available on the new Web site for the book
- www.bergeron4e.nelson.com will also feature the PowerPoint slides and additional quiz questions.

Acknowledgments

Although I am the author of this book, the inspiration for the book's structure, content, and style emerged from the questions and discussions that I have had with many executives and managers. They have helped me immensely in writing a pragmatic book in plain language that will surely help many readers understand more thoroughly the intricate discipline of financial management.

At Nelson, I am indebted to Herb Hilderley who, some 25 years ago, recognized the need for this type of book and provided me with the opportunity to make the first edition a reality. I also want to thank Veronica Visentin, Executive Editor; Joanne Sutherland, Senior Developmental Editor; and Susan Calvert, Managing Production Editor, Higher Education, who kept things moving smoothly and promptly. Thanks also to Karen Rolfe, who diligently edited the manuscript and made many suggestions for improving accuracy and clarity and whose sharp eye found further corrections to make at proofreading.

I want to extend my gratitude to the reviewers who provided me with constructive suggestions for this fourth edition: Harold J. Keller, The College of the Rockies; Dr. M. Nauman Farooqi, Mount Allison University, and John Cavaliere, Sault College.

Finally, *un gros merci* to my wife Pierrette, for having put up with the demands and sacrifices of such an undertaking. As with previous books, Pierrette is always there giving assistance, encouragement, empathy, and support.

Pierre G. Bergeron
Ottawa, Ontario

Finance
for Non-Financial Managers

1

Overview of Financial Management

Learning Objectives

After reading this chapter, you should be able to:

1. Define the meaning of financial management.

2. Identify the individuals responsible for the finance function.

3. Explain the four financial objectives.

4. Comment on the three major types of business decisions.

Chapter Outline

OPENING CASE

After spending ten years with different organizations, Len and Joan Miller decided to open their own retail business, CompuTech Sales and Services. While Len had worked for several computer retail stores, Joan was employed as a sales representative for a multinational computer organization. Both felt that their combined experience would prove an asset for succeeding in their new venture.

However, before making their final decision, they decided to speak to a long-term friend and entrepreneur, Bill Murray, who had operated his own very successful retail business for the past 25 years to obtain advice before launching their business. The following summarizes Bill's comments:

> The two most important factors for any business to be successful are products/services and management. There must be a demand for the products or services that you want to sell, and you must possess management (e.g., planning, organizing, leading, controlling) and business (e.g., merchandising, pricing, sales, promotion) skills if you are to realize your vision and objectives. You will also need operating and financial information to gauge the results of your ongoing business decisions. Although an accountant will help you set up your bookkeeping and accounting systems, you have to ensure that you have the ability to analyze your financial statements. Not being able to read financial statements is much like being a racing car driver who is unable to read the instruments on his dashboard. Like these instruments, financial statement analysis will help you see how well your business has done and, most importantly, what decisions you need to make to improve the financial performance of your retail operations.
>
> To succeed, your business will have to generate a healthy profit (efficiency) and be able to pay its bills on time (liquidity). In addition, your business must show signs of continuous growth in all segments such as sales and profit (prosperity). Be sure that you do not overburden your business with too much debt (stability).
>
> You will always be faced with three types of business decisions. The first type is *investing decisions,* such as the one that will help you launch your business. If your business prospers, you will face a series of investing decisions such as expanding your business, opening new retail outlets, buying equipment for your business, etc.
>
> *Operating decisions* are the second type of business decision. They affect your day-to-day operations. You will continually face decisions such as pricing, advertising, hiring new employees, office expenses, etc. Through your budgeting exercise, you will have to ensure that you keep your operating costs as low as possible in order to maximize your profit (efficiency).
>
> The third type is *financing decisions.* Once you know exactly how much it will cost you to start your business, you must approach investors such as lenders for financial support. These different sources of financing bear a cost. You must ensure that your business generates enough profit (return) to pay for financing your business (cost).

Len and Joan were enlightened by Bill Murray's comments and were convinced that if they put his suggestions into practice, they would stand a good chance of realizing their dream.

This chapter examines in more detail the recommendations made by Bill Murray. In particular, it focuses on four key topics:

- Why is financial management so important for business owners and managers?
- Who is really responsible for the finance function of a business?
- What are the more important financial objectives for owners and managers?
- Which categories of business decisions are usually faced by managers?

Introduction

Financial management has undergone major changes during recent decades. Initially, finance consisted mainly of raising funds to purchase the assets needed by a business. When finance emerged as an organizational function back in the 1920s, financial management focused almost exclusively on legal matters: acquisitions, corporate offerings, mergers, formation of new businesses, reorganizations, recapitalizations, bankruptcies, and business consolidations. Finance concentrated mostly on the external activities of a business, such as raising funds, rather than on internal activities, such as finding methods to allocate funds effectively within a business. Originally, activities such as cost accounting, credit and collection, budgeting, financial planning, financial accounting, and management of working capital were not an important part of the manager's "tool kit." Only in the past several decades has attention turned to developing analytical and decision-making techniques to assist managers in improving the effectiveness of their investing, operating, and financing decisions. Put simply, in the beginning, more attention was paid to managing the right-hand side of the balance sheet (raising funds from lenders and shareholders).

Today, although the management of the right-hand side of the balance sheet is still considered important, financial management focuses increasingly on the left-hand side of the balance sheet (finding ways to manage more efficiently all assets of a business, such as cash, accounts receivable, and inventories, and on improving the productivity of capital assets). Finance has assumed unprecedented importance as a management function. Today, improving a company's bottom line is a major managerial challenge. Here are some of the reasons.

First, on the economic front, many economists considered the recessions of the early 1980s and the early 1990s as deeper and broader than any other downturns experienced since the Great Depression. As a result, the cost of operating businesses came under intense scrutiny. During the 1980s, managers began to realize that the North American economy was not only undergoing another shift in the business cycle but also had reached a certain level of maturity. Managers began to downsize their organizations in an effort to make them more efficient, responsive, and productive.

Second, on the political side, governments began to open their national borders and push industrial strategies to make their companies and industries leaders on world markets. Both the *Free Trade Agreement*, which was implemented in 1989, and the *North American Free Trade Agreement*, which took effect in 1994, forced managers to rethink their cost structure, improve their manufacturing capabilities, and sharpen their international marketing strategies.

Third, with more global and open world economies, companies were forced to make structural changes to their organizations (removing organizational layers and introducing cross-functional teams and network organizations) in order to make them more responsive to market demand. For example, Wal-Mart has certainly changed the cost structure of Canadian retailers!

Fourth, technological changes compelled managers to alter their company's operations dramatically by producing new and/or better products or services, reducing their operating costs, modifying the size of their plants, and integrating operating activities. Technological change is taking place in all sectors of organizations, such as manufacturing (e.g., reengineering), administration (e.g., office automation), communication (e.g., information technology), and the increasing use of the Internet (e.g., Web sites to advertise and sell products and services).

Fifth, the product life cycle is now measured not in years, but in months. Whenever a company introduces a product or service into the market, "time risk," that is, the number of months or years it should take a company to recover its investment, has to be measured in order to determine a price structure that is acceptable.

Sixth, on the manufacturing side, managers not only had to find more innovative ways to produce their goods and provide services more efficiently but also had to be concerned about quality objectives. Many Canadian firms have turned to total quality management and measuring the quality of their products and services against world standards. For example, getting certification from the International Standards Organization (ISO) enables a company to improve its chance of success on world markets.

All these changes affected the company's bottom line. Now, when operating managers make investing, operating, and financing decisions, they have to gauge how these decisions affect their bottom line.

Objective 1 ➡️

What Is Financial Management?

Financial management ensures that a company uses its resources in the most efficient and effective way: maximizing the income generated by a business, which ultimately increases the value of a business (its net worth or shareholders' equity). What was called "finance" in the past is now referred to as "financial management," reflecting the current emphasis on the importance of having all operating managers in a business participate in making important decisions that affect the financial destiny of their respective organizational units and the company as a whole.

Financial management deals with two things: first, raising funds, and, second, buying and utilizing assets in order to gain the highest possible return. An important objective of financial management is to ensure that the assets used in business produce a return higher than the cost of borrowing. It would be pointless for a business to raise funds from investors at a cost of 10% and invest them in assets that generate only 7%. As shown in Figure 1.1, the objective of financial management is to ensure that the return on assets generated by a business (here, 15%) is higher than the cost of money borrowed from investors—that is, lenders and shareholders (here, 11%).

FIGURE 1.1   RELATIONSHIP BETWEEN ROA AND COST OF FINANCING

Balance Sheet	
Assets	Investors
Return on assets	Cost of financing
15%	11%

Each year, *Fortune* lists companies as the largest wealth creators (out of a pool of 1,000 large companies). The ranking is based on market-value added (MVA), defined as the difference between the amount of funds that capital investors have put into a company and the money that they can take out. The article also shows companies with the highest economic value added (EVA), which is defined as the after-tax net operating profit minus the cost of capital.

Financial management focuses on five important questions:

How are we doing? Managers, short- and long-term lenders, shareholders, suppliers, etc. want to know about a company's financial performance: Is the company profitable? What is the return on its investment? Is the company efficient and keeping its costs under control? Is the company adding value for its shareholders? The company's financial statements provide answers to these questions and help managers find ways to maximize profits.

How much cash do we have on hand? Knowing how much cash a company has on hand is important to determine its liquidity. Can it meet its payroll? Pay its suppliers on time? Service its debt? How much cash can be generated internally, that is, from operations within the next months or years? Managers must know how much cash the company now has on hand and how much it will have in the future in order to determine how much it will want to borrow from external sources such as lenders and shareholders.

What should we spend our funds on? Money can be spent on (1) operating activities such as salaries, advertising, freight, supplies, insurance, etc.; (2) working capital assets such as inventories, accounts receivable; and (3) capital assets such as machinery and equipment. Managers must determine if operating costs are efficient and whether the money that will be spent on capital assets for automation and expansion will generate a return that is higher than the cost of capital and, equally important, will compensate for the risk. Since money can be invested in different projects bearing different risk levels, the return to be earned from various investments must show different economic values.

Where will our funds come from? Once managers have identified how much money the company needs and how much cash it now has on hand, they have to determine where the funds can be obtained in the future. Suppliers? Bankers? Long-term investors such as shareholders, venture capitalists, or insurance companies?

How will our business be protected? The most important responsibility of managers is to protect the investors' interests and, equally importantly, maximize their share value (MVA). It is important to recognize that managers are employed by shareholders and should therefore act on their behalf. However, managers have to reconcile the legitimate and sometimes conflicting objectives of various interest groups (e.g., unions, lenders, employees, customers, suppliers, communities, and government agencies). Since shareholders have a unique and legal status, managers must ensure that their interests are not compromised, not like the dramatic drop in the value of shares at companies such as Enron and WorldCom where billions of dollars were lost due to accounting errors.

Who Is Responsible for the Finance Function?

Objective 2 ▶▶

As shown in Figure 1.2, responsibility for financial activities is shared between the treasurer, the controller, and operating managers.

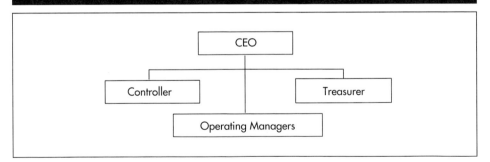

FIGURE 1.2   RESPONSIBILITY OF FINANCIAL MANAGEMENT

Controller

Controller

Person responsible for establishing the accounting and financial reporting policies and procedures.

The **controller** establishes the accounting and financial reporting policies and procedures; maintains the accounting, auditing, and management control mechanisms; and analyzes financial results. Together with operating managers, the controller prepares annual budgets and financial plans and determines financial objectives and standards to ensure efficiency and adequate returns. This controllership function affects how funds are expensed and invested to satisfy consumer needs and shareholders' interests.

Treasurer

The **treasurer**—that is, the person responsible for raising funds—looks after investors, plans investment strategies, analyzes tax implications, and gauges the impact of internal and external events on a firm's capital structure, or the relationship between long-term debts and shareholders' equity. The treasurer also regulates the flow of funds, determines dividend payments, recommends short- and long-term financing strategies, and cultivates relations with investors. In short, the treasurer is responsible for the accounts shown on the right side of the balance sheet: debt and owners' equity.

Table 1.1 shows a list of typical activities of the finance function under the jurisdiction of the controller (controllership functions) and the treasurer (treasury functions).

Treasurer

Person responsible for raising funds and regulating the flow of funds.

TABLE 1.1   THE FUNCTIONS OF THE CONTROLLER AND THE TREASURER

Functions of the Controller	Functions of the Treasurer
• General accounting	• Raising capital
• Cost accounting	• Investor relations
• Credit and collection	• Short-term financing
• Management information system	• Dividend and interest payments
• Accounts payable	• Insurance
• Corporate accounting	• Analysis of investment securities
• Internal auditing	• Retirement funds
• Budgets and analysis	• Property taxes
• Payroll	• Investment portfolio
• Systems and procedures	• Cash-flow requirements
• Planning	• Actuarial
• Controlling	• Underwriting policy and manuals
• Interpreting financial reports	• Tax administration

Operating Managers

Financial management is also practised by **operating managers** (or line managers) in various organizational units such as marketing, manufacturing, research and development, and general administration. These managers are responsible for analyzing operating and financial data, making decisions about asset acquisitions, and improving the operating performance of their respective organizational units and of the company as a whole.

People often think of finance as a function performed by accountants, bookkeepers, treasurers, controllers, or financial analysts. Although these people play

Operating manager

Person in charge of organizational units such as marketing, manufacturing, human resources, and responsible for making operating and investing decisions.

a key role in financial management and in the financial planning process, all managers are accountable for their decisions since they may impact, directly or indirectly, the financial performance of their business unit or organization.

A business is much like an aircraft; someone has to pilot it. In an aircraft, a pilot is responsible for analyzing various instruments on the dashboard to make sure that the flight will run smoothly, from takeoff to landing. For a business establishment, an operating manager is responsible for managing or piloting it, and the instruments used to steer the business are financial statements. These financial statements reflect how well a business has done in the past and, based on objectives and plans, how well it will perform in the future.

Many business decisions cut across all business functions such as marketing, operations, manufacturing, administration, human resources, research and development, and after-sales services. To be sure, operators of businesses make many of these decisions on a daily basis. For example, some of these types of decisions may include hiring an employee, increasing the selling price of one or two product lines or services, cutting back on some operating expenses, adding a bigger share of the budget to promotion and advertising, buying new equipment in order to make the business more efficient, and providing a better service to customers. These decisions have one thing in common: they impact on a business establishment's financial performance (profit and loss statement) and financial structure (balance sheet). These two financial documents inform operators of business establishments about the outcome of their decisions. Operating managers who have difficulty reading or interpreting financial statements are not able to effectively gauge how well their business has done, is currently doing, or how it will do in the future.

An aircraft pilot is in the best position to control his airplane (whether a Concord or a Cesna) for three reasons. He:

- understands his operating environment;
- knows exactly where he wants to go; and
- has an appreciation about what needs to be done in order to reach his destination.

Objective 3 ➡

Financial Objectives

The four most important financial objectives of a firm include efficiency, liquidity, prosperity, and stability.

Efficiency

Efficiency
The relationship between profits (outputs) generated and assets employed (inputs).

Efficiency means the productivity of assets, which is the relationship between profits generated and assets employed (i.e., return on assets, return on equity, and return on sales). The objective is to ensure that a company's assets are used efficiently to produce an acceptable rate of return. High profits satisfy investors and indicate that the assets of a business are working hard. The more profit a company earns, the more cash it can invest in the business to finance its growth and to purchase capital assets. For example, Figure 1.3 shows a company that earns $0.08 on every dollar's worth of sales revenue (return on sales, or ROS). This profit can be reinvested in the business through retained earnings ($0.05). With this money, the firm invests $0.02 in working capital such as accounts receivable and inventory (for day-to-day operating purposes) and $0.03 in capital assets to purchase equipment and machinery (for long-term growth purposes). The balance of the money ($0.03) can be used for external uses. Here, the shareholders will receive $0.02 to compensate for the investment they have made in the business, and $0.01 will be used to repay the principal on the debt. If the $0.08 return on sales begins to shrink, the company will have less internally generated funds to help its growth, invest in capital assets, and satisfy its shareholders.

FIGURE 1.3   RETURN ON SALES OBJECTIVE

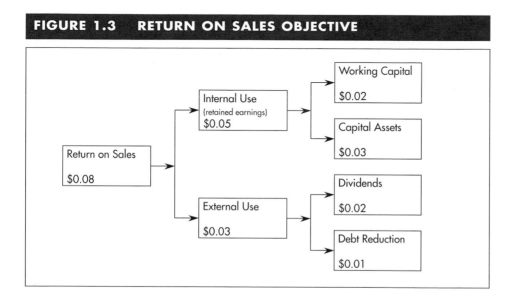

Liquidity

Liquidity is a company's ability to meet its short-term financial commitments. If a business increases its sales, it will inevitably increase its working capital accounts such as inventory, accounts receivable, and cash required to pay its employees, suppliers, and creditors on time (as shown in Figure 1.3, $0.02 is invested in working capital accounts). If a company wants to grow but shows a reduction in its return on sales performance, it will have less cash from internal operations to invest in working capital accounts, and may have to rely on short-term borrowing in order to keep growing. Too much borrowing reduces a company's profit (because of interest charges) and contributes to reducing its return on sales.

Prosperity

Prosperity means growth in all segments of a business: sales volume, profits, dividend payments, capital assets, shareholders' equity, and working capital. If a company's return on sales deteriorates, the company may not be able to finance its growth through internally generated funds. Consequently, it would have difficulty investing in capital assets such as equipment and machinery in order to expand its operations and improve its productivity (as shown in Figure 1.3, an amount of $0.03 is invested in capital assets). If the company wants to invest in these types of assets, it may have to borrow (if internally generated cash is insufficient) from long-term lenders and shareholders to finance the purchase of new capital assets.

Stability

Stability refers to the financial structure of a business. Here, financial management ensures equilibrium between the funds provided by creditors and those provided by shareholders (relationship between debt and shareholders' equity). If a business continues to borrow from lenders, it may have a high debt-to-equity ratio and as a result may not be able to meet its short- and long-term debt obligations, particularly if there is a slowdown in business activities caused by economic conditions. If the company's return on sales is adequate, it will have enough cash (as shown in Figure 1.3, an amount of $0.03 is used for external activities) to pay dividends to its shareholders ($0.02) and reduce the principal on its debt ($0.01). If the company does not produce an adequate return on sales, it may have to borrow more from lenders and consequently produce a negative effect on its stability.

The bottom line is this: If a company wants to maintain or improve its stability, it must never lose sight of the first objective, to earn a suitable return on sales. If successful, profits (or retained earnings) can be used to increase working capital and to purchase capital assets (if required), to pay dividends, and to reduce debt without relying too extensively on debt financing.

Business Decisions

Figure 1.4 shows the three types of decisions made by managers: investing decisions, operating decisions, and financing decisions.[1] For example, if managers want to invest $1.0 million in capital assets (investing decisions), the funds required to purchase these assets would come from two sources: internal and external. First, internal funds are generated by the business (managers) through operating decisions (through the improvement in the management of working capital accounts and in the income statement); second, shareholders and lenders,

---

1   Much of the arithmetic done in the rest of this chapter may be overwhelming for some readers. However, it is included here to show how business decisions can be calculated. These calculations will be explained in more detail in later chapters.

through financing decisions, provide external funds. As shown in the figure, if the company generates $500,000 from internal sources and is able to obtain the rest ($500,000) from investors, the $1,000,000 in assets would be financed equitably.

The ideal situation is to finance, to the maximum, the purchase of capital assets with internally generated funds. For example, if the company purchases the assets ($1.0 million) with $800,000 of internal funds, it would rely less on external funding and be able to enhance its financial stability.

Internal financing is obtained from retained earnings—that is, the profits generated by the business, depreciation, and amortization that appear on the income statement as noncash expenses—and by reducing working capital accounts such as accounts receivable and inventories. In Figure 1.4, the box representing working capital is shaded because managers can obtain funds only if they are able to reduce accounts such as accounts receivable and inventory. An increase in these accounts would be considered a use or an application of funds. To illustrate, suppose that a plant manager wants to buy a $50,000 machine; it could be financed by a $50,000 reduction in inventory.

FIGURE 1.4   SOURCES OF FUNDS

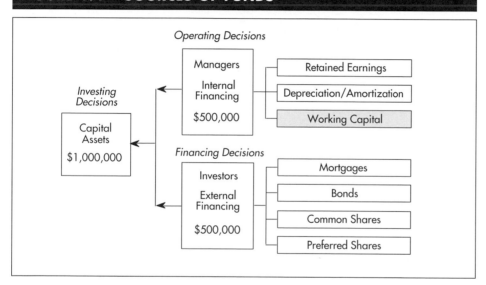

Figure 1.5 illustrates how the three types of business decisions appear on the balance sheet. On the left side are investments in accounts receivable and inventories (current assets); capital assets such as buildings, machinery, and equipment; and other assets or intangible assets such as research and development, goodwill, and patents. Operating managers are responsible for investing decisions.

The right side of the balance sheet shows the external financing decisions related to the acquisition of funds from long-term lenders and shareholders. Borrowing funds from investors is the responsibility of the chief executive officer (CEO), the chief financial officer (CFO), or the treasurer.

FIGURE 1.5   BUSINESS DECISIONS

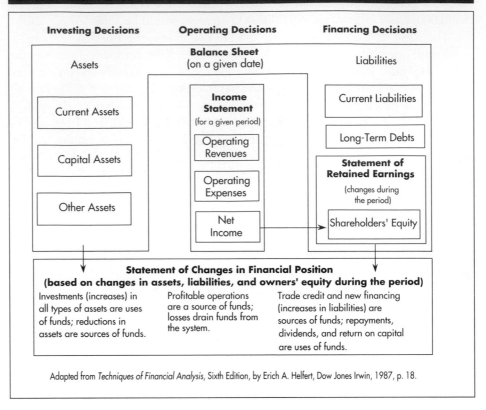

Adapted from *Techniques of Financial Analysis*, Sixth Edition, by Erich A. Helfert, Dow Jones Irwin, 1987, p. 18.

The centre of the balance sheet shows to what extent operating decisions affect the balance sheet.[2] Operating decisions are the responsibility of all managers and include decisions that affect every account shown on the income statement. If managers make prudent operating decisions in marketing, manufacturing, production, administration, human resources, etc., they will help generate higher profit levels and ultimately improve the return on sales performance. As mentioned earlier, higher income enables management to pay dividends and to reinvest the rest in the business through retained earnings (shareholders' equity).

Figure 1.5 also shows how the three types of business decisions affect a company's cash position. For instance, a decrease in the asset accounts (e.g., through selling an asset such as a truck or by reducing inventories) would be considered a source of funds. An increase in liability and equity accounts (through borrowing from banks or the injection of additional funds from shareholders) would also be considered a source of funds, as is income (or profit) generated by a business.

This book will explore in detail these three types of business decisions. After studying the structure and analysis of financial statements in Chapters 2, 3, and 4, we will discuss investing decisions in Chapters 7, 8, 11, and 12; financing decisions in Chapters 6 and 10; and operating decisions in Chapters 5 and 9.

---

2   The income statement is presented at the centre of the balance sheet in Figure 1.5 strictly for presentation purposes. It shows how net income (or profit) increases the shareholders' equity on the balance sheet.

Here is a brief overview of how these three types of business decisions can favourably affect the financial performance (income statement) and financial structure (balance sheet) of a business.

Investing Decisions

As mentioned earlier, **investing decisions** deal with the accounts appearing on the left side of the balance sheet—that is, working capital accounts (cash, accounts receivable, and inventory) and capital assets (e.g., machinery, equipment). As shown in Figure 1.5, investing decisions have an impact on a company's cash flow. Investing funds in working capital and capital assets is a drain on a company's cash position since it is considered a use of cash or application of funds. However, a reduction in such assets, achieved by lowering inventory or accounts receivable or by selling unproductive capital assets, is a source of funds.

Let's now examine how current asset and capital asset decisions affect a company's cash-flow performance.

Managing working capital means accelerating the movement of cash in a business. This movement of cash is referred to as the cash-conversion cycle. The faster accounts receivable are collected or inventory is turned over, the more cash and profit a firm earns.

Current assets are not productive assets, but they are necessary for a business to operate; it must sell on credit and carry a certain amount of inventory. However, it is necessary to determine the right amount of working capital that should be maintained. The faster working capital assets are transformed into cash, the faster the cash can be invested into more productive assets such as equipment and machinery; this ultimately improves a company's profit performance.

Decisions related to managing cash determine the minimum level of cash that will satisfy business needs under normal operating conditions. Cash reserves (including marketable securities) should be sufficient to satisfy daily cash expenditures (e.g., salaries, suppliers, etc.).

Cash reserve decisions are usually based on planning assumptions such as:

- the practical minimum level of cash balance required to meet ongoing operating conditions;
- an amount necessary to absorb unforeseen expenditures; and
- the level of cash required to take advantage of profitable business opportunities (e.g., special discounts on purchases or anticipation of an increase in the price of raw materials).

It is important to keep cash at a minimum since investment securities yield only about 6% interest before tax (3% after tax if a company is in a 50% tax bracket). It would therefore be more economically advantageous to invest excess cash into investment opportunities in order to earn a more attractive return.

Decisions related to accounts receivable deal with collecting receivables from customers as quickly as possible. For example, if a business has slow-paying customers (say 90 days), management may decide to offer cash discounts off the orig-

Investing decisions

Decisions related to the acquisition of assets (current and capital).

inal sale price to accelerate the cash flow and shorten the collection period (say, a 2% discount if the customer pays within ten days). Before offering such discounts, however, management will want to analyze the cost of offering the discount versus the interest earned in the bank as a result of receiving payment from the customers more quickly. Management will want to get answers to the following questions:

- What is the status of our accounts receivable (e.g., aging of the accounts receivable)?
- What are our competitors' credit policies?
- How much will we lose in profit if we offer, say, a 2%, net 30 day discount?
- How much interest can be earned from the bank on the additional cash flow?

Let's take the example of a business that has $300,000 in accounts receivable on sales of $1,825,000 and is experiencing a 60-day average collection period. If management is able to reduce its receivables to, say, 30 days, the company would have an extra $150,000 in cash that could be invested in term deposits at, say, 10%, and earn an extra $15,000 a year in profit. The following shows the calculation:

	Current performance	Targeted performance
Sales	$1,825,000	$1,825,000
Average daily sales	$5,000	$5,000
Average collection period	60 days	30 days
Investment in accounts receivable	$300,000	$150,000
Reduction in accounts receivable	$150,000	
Incremental profit (@ 10%)	$ 15,000	

Decisions related to inventories deal with lowering the amount of raw materials, unfinished goods, and finished goods. Turning inventory rapidly can also improve a company's cash position and, ultimately, its profitability and return on investment. Several techniques can be used to make such decisions, including:

- the just-in-time inventory management process, which is a supply system that attempts to reduce working inventories; and
- the economic ordering quantity system, which determines the optimal number of units that should be ordered each time goods are purchased from suppliers.

As with managing accounts receivable, the intent here is to invest as little as possible in inventory since it is also considered a nonproductive asset. To illustrate, let's take the example of a business that buys $1,000,000 a year in raw materials and supplies and holds $250,000 in inventory. This means that the company's inventory turns four times a year. If management can reduce its inventory to $200,000 (turnover of five times a year) by using the just-in-time approach or the economic ordering quantity method, the company will benefit from an extra

$50,000 in cash. If this amount is invested in securities bearing a 10% interest rate, the company would earn an additional $5,000 in profit. The following shows the calculation:

	Current performance	Targeted performance
Cost of goods sold	$1,000,000	$1,000,000
Inventory turnover	4 times	5 times
Inventory level	$250,000	$200,000
Reduction in inventory		$ 50,000
Incremental profit (@ 10%)		$ 5,000

Decisions dealing with **capital (or fixed) assets** involve the purchase of equipment or machinery, and the more complicated decisions such as plant expansion, plant modernization to increase productivity, or investment in new facilities. These types of decisions are usually made during the capital budgeting exercise. Here, management must examine the relationship between the cash invested in such assets and the anticipated cash that can be generated in the future by these assets. For example, if someone invests $100,000 in Canada Savings Bonds and earns $10,000 in interest, that person earns 10%. The same applies when managers invest in capital assets. They want to measure two things: the expected return on assets and how it compares to the cost of capital.

Here is an example of how investment decisions in capital assets are calculated. Let's say that a company invests $1.0 million in the following assets:

Capital assets

Balance sheet accounts such as land, buildings, equipment, machinery.

Land	$ 100,000
Buildings	400,000
Machinery & equipment	400,000
Working capital	100,000
Total investments	$1,000,000

Let's also assume that this investment produces $120,000 in after-tax profit each year. The following shows the calculation:

Sales revenue	$2,000,000
Cost of goods sold	1,200,000
Gross margin	800,000
Operating expenses	560,000
Profit before taxes	240,000
Income taxes	120,000
Profit after taxes	$ 120,000

Several capital budgeting techniques are used to gauge the economic desirability of such investments. For example, there is the return on assets calculation that relates profit after taxes to investment in assets. It is calculated as follows:

$$\frac{\text{Profit after taxes}}{\text{Investment in assets}} = \frac{\$120,000}{\$1,000,000} = 12\%$$

This means that the $1.0 million investment generates a 12% after-tax return. Managers must also consider whether the investment is worth the risk. Before making a decision, they would have to relate the return of that particular investment to both the cost of capital and the inherent risks associated with the project. For example, if the company borrows the entire amount from lenders at a before-tax cost of 10%, it means that the after-tax cost of capital would be 5% (assuming that the firm is in a 50% tax bracket). In this particular instance, the company would earn 7% more than the cost of borrowed funds.

The project's risk would also be considered. Managers would have to gauge whether a 12% return on this particular investment is worth the risk. If this investment was in the high-risk category, such as an investment in an untried product, management may want to earn at least 35% to 40% to justify the investment. However, if the project is low risk, such as the expansion of an existing plant, it could require a much lower return on its investment (say, around 15%).

Financing Decisions

Financing decisions

Decisions related to borrowing from lenders and shareholders.

As shown in Figure 1.5, **financing decisions** deal with the accounts listed on the right side of the balance sheet—that is, funds borrowed from short-term lenders, long-term lenders, and shareholders. Financing decisions examine the best way funds can be raised from investors (lenders and shareholders). Financing decisions deal with four elements: matching principle, sources and forms of financing, cost of financing, and financing mix.

THE MATCHING PRINCIPLE Essentially, the matching principle explores the selection of the most appropriate financing source when buying an asset. This means that short-term funds should be used to finance current assets while long-term funds should buy the more permanent assets such as capital assets. For example, it would not make much sense to buy a house on a credit card such as MasterCard or Visa! Simply put, the matching principle calls for relating the maturity of the sources of funds and the maturity of the uses of funds.

SOURCES AND FORMS OF FINANCING A business can obtain money from a wide range of sources and in different forms. *Sources* are institutions that provide funds and include commercial banks, investment bankers, equipment vendors, government agencies, private venture capital companies, suppliers, trust companies, life insurance companies, mortgage companies, individuals, and shareholders. *Forms* are the financing instruments used to buy the assets. They include short-term loans (secured or unsecured), term or installment loans, revolving loans, lease financing, mortgages, bonds, and preferred or common shares.

COST OF BORROWED FUNDS Another important element in financing decisions is determining the **cost of borrowed funds** when raising funds from different sources. This is critical because borrowed funds are used to purchase assets, and managers want to ensure that the return generated by the assets exceeds the cost of capital. Determining the cost of capital usually precedes the capital budgeting exercise.

Cost of borrowed funds

Effective after-tax cost of raising funds from different sources (lenders and shareholders).

Cost of capital deals with the accounts shown on the lower portion of the balance sheet. It involves the more permanent forms of financing such as mortgages, bonds (long-term debts), and preferred and common shares (shareholders' equity). These are referred to as "capital funds"; thus, their cost is known as cost of capital. In the earlier example of a $1.0 million investment in capital assets, managers would have to determine the cost of each loan and the weighted cost of capital. For instance, if the business borrows $400,000 from a mortgage company at 12%, $300,000 from bondholders at 13%, and the rest ($300,000) from shareholders at, say, 15%,[3] the composite weighted after-tax cost of capital would be 8.8%. Since interest charges on mortgage and bond financing are tax-deductible and the company is in a 50% tax bracket, such financing options are more attractive than shareholder financing since dividends are paid with after-tax profits. The calculation is as follows:

Sources	Amount ($)	Before-tax cost (%)	After-tax cost (%)	Proportion	Weighted cost of capital (%)
Mortgage	400,000	12.0	6.0	.40	2.4
Bonds	300,000	13.0	6.5	.30	1.9
Shares	300,000	15.0	15.0	.30	4.5
Weighted cost of capital	1,000,000			1.00	8.8

FINANCING MIX Another important component of financing decisions is determining the proportion of funds that should be raised from lenders versus owners (the **financing mix**). As shown above, it would be advantageous to borrow as much as possible from lenders because that is the least expensive option (6.0%). However, since lenders do not want to take all the risks related to the investment decisions, they will insist that an appropriate amount of funds be provided by shareholders. Equally important in financing decisions is a firm's ability to repay its debt obligation. If both the economy and the industry sectors are in a strong growth position, the company will generate healthy profits, be able to repay its loan without difficulty, and borrow more funds from lenders rather than shareholders. However, if the economic indicators and the marketplace indicate slow growth, a low leveraged position (meaning less money borrowed from lenders) would be more advantageous and less risky.

Financing mix

Proportion of funds raised from lenders and shareholders.

---

3   This percentage is equivalent to what the shareholders could earn if they were to invest these funds elsewhere; it is sometimes called the opportunity cost.

Operating Decisions

As shown in Figure 1.5, **operating decisions** deal with many accounts appearing on the income statement, as we will see in later chapters. These accounts include sales revenue, cost of goods sold, and selling and administrative expenses. Effective operating decisions improve net income, which in turn enhances shareholders' equity position.

Profit can be improved in a number of ways. First, as discussed earlier, investment and financing decisions can have a positive impact on a company's profit performance. There is interplay between investing, financing, and operating decisions. Let's look at one example. If management decides to purchase a $50,000 forklift (investment decision) that will have a ten-year life span, the treasurer will have to determine how this truck will be financed (financing decision). Financing $30,000 of it by debt bearing a 10% interest charge and the rest through equity will reduce the company's before-tax profit by $8,000 (annual depreciation charge of $5,000 plus $3,000 in interest charges). This cost would have to be compared to any operating savings generated by the forklift.

BUDGETING TECHNIQUES Operating decisions can also increase a company's income in many ways. Some decisions cut across all organizational functions and activities affecting the income statement, such as improving employee productivity, reducing waste, and eliminating useless activities. Here are a few budgeting approaches used by managers that can help improve profitability.

Demassing is a recession-driven technique that was used widely during the sharp economic downturn in the early 1980s. The purpose of this approach was to remove headquarters' staff and entire management layers and professional positions from organizational charts. Organizations were simply flattened. It has been reported that more than a third of U.S. middle-management positions were eliminated in 1981–82 as a result of demassing exercises.

Planned downsizing is similar to demassing except that it is a more systematic way of cutting overhead costs. Guidelines used in planned downsizing include:[4]

- matching organizational structure with strategies;
- pinpointing excess staff in the control and support organizational units;
- evaluating the effectiveness of organizational units;
- performing a zero-based evaluation by questioning everything;
- introducing norms and ratios such as allowing one support staff position per 100 employees or maintaining computer-related expenses below 1%;
- using strategic concepts such as product life cycles and value added to determine staff size;
- enforcing sunset laws by closing down, decentralizing, or contracting out mature or aging activities before starting new ones; and

---

4   For interesting reading on this subject, see Tomasso, Robert, M., *Downsizing: Reshaping the Corporation for the Future*, New York: AMACOM, 1987.

- flattening organizational pyramids by asking pertinent questions such as How many management layers are really necessary? How many people can one manager manage? How can a manager's span of control be increased?

Productivity measures[5] are essential for measuring the performance of organizational units. Productivity indicators must first be identified for each organizational unit before the units can be made more productive. If organizational efficiencies and effectiveness for the most important activities performed by managers and employees are measured and used as goals, they can improve productivity and ultimately the bottom line because:

Productivity measures
Ways of measuring organizational performance (i.e., return on assets).

- productivity is more likely to improve when expected results are measured;

- productivity increases rapidly when expected benefits are shared with those who will produce them;

- the greater the alignment of employee expectations (needs) with organizational objectives (targets), the greater the motivation to accomplish both; and

- when productivity objectives are placed on a time scale, there is a greater likelihood of achieving the objectives.

Rewarding simplification instead of needless complication can also produce positive financial effects. Jack Welch was an advocate of keeping things simple at General Electric. As he pointed out, "The leader's unending responsibility must be to remove every detour, every barrier, to ensure that vision is first clear, and then real. The leader must create an atmosphere in the organization where people feel not only free to, but obliged to demand clarity and purpose from their leaders."[6] In the process, GE was able to improve its operating efficiencies and improve the bottom line by billions of dollars.

Cutting back useless activities and replacing them with productive work adds value to financial statements. For instance, the Dallas-based oil and gas producer Oryx is estimated to have saved $70 million in operating costs by eliminating rules, procedures, reviews, reports, and approvals that had little to do with the company's real objective of finding more hydrocarbons.

Focusing on quality work instead of fast work can also increase operating margins and the bottom line. Doing work too quickly and too cheaply often inadvertently becomes costly because quality suffers. Several of the payoffs of improving quality include lower costs, increased productivity, worker pride, and customer loyalty. One tool that has produced positive benefits on the bottom line through cost reduction, productivity improvement, customer retention, cycle-time reduction, defect reduction and product/service development is Six Sigma.

---

5   For interesting reading on this subject, see Giuliani, Rudolph W., *Leadership*, (particularly Chapter 4, Everyone's Accountable All the Time), New York: Miramax Books, 2002.

6   Welch, Jack, *Jack: Straight from the Gut*, New York: Warner Business Books, 2001, p. 336. For interesting readings on the subject of Six Sigma, refer to Peter Pandre, Robert Neuman, and Roland Cavanagh, *The Six Sigma Way*, New York: McGraw-Hill, 2000, and George, Michael L., *Lean Six Sigma*, New York: McGraw-Hill, 2002.

The Six Sigma four-step process includes measure, analyze, improve and control, and has been adapted by companies such as GE, Motorola, Black & Decker, Bombardier, Dupont, Dow Chemical, and Federal Express. At GE for example, Six Sigma expected to generate $1.5 billion in 1999 while operating margins went from 14.8% in 1996 to 18.9% in 2000.

Empowering workers through team building and communication can also produce synergistic effects on a company's operating performance. Empowerment is more than a trendy slogan; it has produced positive financial results. Working in teams creates a great sense of interdependence. Some plants have increased productivity substantially just by giving workers the option to decide how to perform their work. Workers learned to inspect their own work, management listened more actively to their suggestions, and employee dignity was greatly elevated.

Gross margin

Difference between sales revenue and cost of goods sold.

GROSS MARGIN Decisions that affect the **gross margin** are the revenue and cost of goods sold accounts. Revenue comprises decisions affecting output (number of units) and selling price. Decisions regarding the marketing variables determine, to a large extent, sales output and market share performance. Effective marketing decisions can improve a company's sales performance and, ultimately, its revenue. There are a number of ways management can determine the most appropriate selling price. These are mark-up percentages, cost-plus pricing, suggested retail price, psychological pricing, discounts, and geographic price policies.

For manufacturing businesses, cost of goods sold represents a substantial percentage (as much as 80%) of a company's total expenses. For this reason, a great deal of attention is devoted to making a company's manufacturing operations more efficient by modernizing its plants (through mechanization or automation), reducing waste, improving employee morale, and empowering workers.

Operating income

Difference between gross margin and operating expenses.

OPERATING INCOME Decisions affecting **operating income** are found in two categories of expenses: selling and administration. Many of the operating budgeting techniques explained earlier, such as planned downsizing, cutting useless activities, and empowering workers, are examples of how profit can be improved. In the past, incremental or traditional budgeting was used to prepare budgets for overhead units. To justify the amount of budget or funds to be allocated to such units, input-oriented budgeting techniques (emphasis on activities and functions or on objects of expenditures such as salaries, telephone, travel, and training) were frequently used. Today, more businesses are using results-oriented budgeting techniques where productivity measures or some form of standards are applied to help justify and approve budget proposals. When preparing operating budgets for most overhead units, two broad operating decisions are often explored: economy and levels of service.

These types of decisions deal with cost–benefit analysis, and the focus is on doing a job in the most economical manner. Here are some common issues relating to such decisions: Should we have this job done by our staff or should it be contracted outside? Should we lease or buy this equipment? Should we automate our office? Should we rearrange the work flow?

Zero-base budgeting, popularized in the early 1970s, places the burden on managers to justify their budgets. Today, we talk about reengineering and activity-based budgeting. This budgeting process calls for identifying different levels of service that can be offered by overhead units such as finance, human resources, engineering, accounting, and administration and pinpointing a cost for each. When unit managers have identified each level of service, they are in a much better position to identify the cost of each. This approach makes it easier for management to link budget proposals to corporate priorities and objectives.

INCOME AFTER TAXES Other accounts that affect **income after taxes** are interest earned and interest charges. Here, the treasurer has the responsibility of making decisions regarding the most appropriate sources and forms of financing and investing funds in investment securities that offer the highest yield.

Income after taxes

Difference between operating income and other expenses (e.g., interest charges), including income taxes.

✱ Decision-Making in Action

The management committee of Flint Ltd. is considering investing $1.0 million in capital assets for expansion purposes, and an additional $200,000 for working capital requirements (e.g., accounts receivable, inventory). Currently, the profit after taxes generated by the company is $500,000, which represents a 5.0% return on sales of $10.0 million. The investment proposal was presented to the board of directors for consideration and approval.

To finance the $1.2 million investment, Flint's CFO explained that a certain portion of the expansion would be financed by internal sources. He indicated that (1) the sales revenue for the budget year would show a 10% increase over the current year, and that (2) the return on sales (as a result of cost-cutting activities, particularly in manufacturing) would be increased to 7.0%. He also indicated that the allowance for depreciation would be $50,000.

The CFO explained that the profit after taxes was to be allocated as follows:

• 60% for internal use (half of the funds would be allocated toward working capital and the rest to the new capital project); and
• 40% for external purposes, of which 60% would be used to pay dividends and the rest to reduce the principal on the debt.

Based on the feasibility study prepared by the controller's department, he explained that the capital expansion would generate $200,000 a year in profit after taxes (income tax rate is at 50%). However, in order to finance the purchase of these assets, he would have to raise capital funds from a lending institution at a cost estimated at 10% (before tax). The shareholders were prepared to invest $200,000 toward the capital project, and an amount of $100,000 would be obtained from the bank for financing the working capital requirements. The shareholders seek at least a 12% return on their investment.

The members of the board of directors indicated that if the project generated 15%, they would consider approving it. However, before approval, they wanted answers to the following questions:

1. How much cash would be generated internally (operating activities)?
2. How much cash would have to be raised from external sources (financing activities)?
3. How would the return on assets of the project (investing activities) compare to the cost of capital (financing activities)?
4. Should the board of directors approve the investment proposal?
5. On the basis of the above information, what is the breakdown of the financing package?

The CFO provided the following explanation to these questions:

ANSWER TO QUESTION 1:

An amount of **$462,000** would be generated internally based on the following:

- Sales revenue for the budget year will be $11,000,000 (a 10% increase over the current year);
- A 7% return on sales would generate $770,000 in profit after taxes;
- An amount of 60% or $462,000 would be reinvested in the business in the form of retained earnings and the remaining 40% (or $308,000) would be used for external use: $184,800 (or 60%) for the payment of dividends, and $123,200 (or 40%) for the payment of the debt.

ANSWER TO QUESTION 2:

External financing would be as follows: $200,000 from shareholders and $388,000 from long-term lenders. Below is the calculation.

a. Funds generated from operating activities:

After-tax profit (retained earnings)		+$ 462,000
Depreciation		+ 50,000
Subtotal		+ 512,000
Working capital requirements	− $200,000	
Working capital loan	+ 100,000	− 100,000
Funds generated from operating activities		+$ 412,000

b. Investing activities

Capital assets	− $1,000,000
Shortfall	− $ 588,000

c. Financing activities

Shareholders	+ $200,000	
Long-term debt	+ $388,000	+$ 588,000
		$ 000

ANSWER TO QUESTION 3:

Return on assets is 16.7%, and cost of capital is 7.38%. The calculations are as follows:

a. Return on assets:

$$\frac{\text{Profit}}{\text{Total assets}} = \frac{\$200,000}{\$1,200,000} = 16.7\%$$

b. Cost of capital

Source	Amount	Proportion		After-tax cost		Weighted Cost
Owners' equity	$200,000	.34	×	12.0%	=	4.08%
Long-term debt	388,000	.66	×	5.0%	=	3.30%
Total capital raised	$588,000	1.00				7.38%

Chapter Summary

The role of financial management is not limited to raising capital dollars; it also extends to finding ways to use funds more effectively within a business. It focuses on issues dealing with the following questions: How are we doing? How much cash do we have on hand? What should we spend our funds on? Where will our funds come from? How will our business be protected?

◀◀ Objective 1

The finance functions are usually divided between the controller, who is responsible for the internal financial activities of a business, and the treasurer, who is responsible for the external financial activities. If financial management is to be effective, operating managers should also perform this function.

◀◀ Objective 2

Financial management focuses on four basic objectives: efficiency (productivity of assets); liquidity (ability to meet current debt obligations); prosperity (improvement of the financial health of the business); and stability (appropriate balance between the funds provided by the owners and the creditors).

◀◀ Objective 3

Business decisions can be grouped under three broad categories: investing decisions, financing decisions, and operating decisions. (1) *Investing decisions* deal with the accounts appearing on the left side of the balance sheet; that is, the management of the working capital accounts (e.g., cash, accounts receivable, and inventory) and the acquisition of capital assets (e.g., equipment). Investing decisions have an impact on a company's funds flow. Investments in working capital or in capital assets are a drain on a company's cash position. However, reductions in such assets, achieved by either reducing inventory or accounts receivable or selling unproductive capital assets, are sources of funds. (2) *Financing decisions* deal with the accounts appearing on the right side of the balance sheet: funds bor-

◀◀ Objective 4

rowed from short-term lenders, long-term lenders, and shareholders. Financing decisions look at the best way to raise funds from different investors. (3) *Operating decisions* deal with the accounts appearing on the income statement, such as revenue, cost of goods sold, and selling and administration expenses. Effective operating decisions can only improve net income and in turn, enhance a firm's equity position and return on investment.

KEY TERMS

Capital assets
Controller
Cost of borrowed funds
Demassing
Efficiency
Financial management
Financing decisions
Financing mix
Gross margin
Income after taxes

Investing decisions
Operating decisions
Operating income
Operating managers
Planned downsizing
Productivity indicators
Prosperity
Stability
Treasurer

REVIEW QUESTIONS

1. Define financial management.

2. Why is it important for managers to ask questions such as How are we doing and How will our business be protected?

3. Differentiate between the role of the treasurer and the role of the controller.

4. What are the four financial objectives? What do they mean?

5. Differentiate between internal financing and external financing.

6. What are investing decisions and financing decisions?

7. What are capital assets?

8. What are working capital assets?

9. What do we mean by the "matching principle"?

10. What is the "cost of capital"?

11. What is an operating decision? Give some examples.

12. How can "productivity indicators" and "rewarding quality work" improve the bottom line?

13. Why is it important for operating managers to understand the fundamentals of financial management?

DISCUSSION QUESTIONS

1. Will the finance function be more important in the future than it was in the past? Discuss.

2. Comment on the importance of the "return on sales" financial objective.

3. Who is responsible for the business decisions in a business?

TESTING YOUR COMPREHENSION

True/False Questions

_____ 1. An important objective of financial management is to ensure that the cost of borrowing is higher than the return on assets.

_____ 2. Efficiency means the ability of a firm to meet its short-term financial obligations.

_____ 3. The treasurer is responsible for raising funds.

_____ 4. Looking after the accounts payable and corporate accounting is a responsibility of the controller.

_____ 5. Return on sales is used for two reasons: to pay expenses and to reinvest funds in working capital.

_____ 6. The stability objective is related to the financial structure of a business.

_____ 7. Investing decisions have to do with the type of analysis that shareholders or investors perform before investing their money in a business.

_____ 8. Internal financing is obtained from two basic sources: retained earnings and depreciation.

_____ 9. Operating decisions deal with better utilization of accounts receivable and inventory.

_____ 10. A business that reduces its level of inventory and maintains the level of its cost of goods sold increases its cash flow.

_____ 11. Just-in-time inventory is a technique used by managers to improve the collection of accounts receivable.

_____ 12. Essentially, "matching" means selecting the most appropriate financing source when buying an asset.

_____ 13. Two popular ways to improve the bottom line are the use of productivity indicators and planned downsizing.

Multiple-Choice Questions

1. The ultimate objective of financial management is to:
   a. make sure that ROA is higher than ROS
   b. ensure that the outputs (profits) are higher than assets.
   c. ensure that ROA is higher than the cost of financing
   d. secure more funds from lenders than shareholders
   e. ensure that sales revenue grow faster than profits

2. The controller is responsible for:
   a. investor relations
   b. analyzing investment securities
   c. tax administration
   d. general accounting
   e. analyzing short-term and long-term financing

3. The treasurer is responsible for:
   a. raising capital
   b. interpreting financial reports
   c. budget and analysis
   d. cost accounting
   e. credit and collection

4. The following is considered an "efficiency" financial objective:
   a. cost of borrowed funds
   b. return on sales
   c. ability to meet short-term financial commitments
   d. return on accounts receivable
   e. relationship between equity and debt

5. Income after taxes is used to:
   a. pay employee salaries
   b. pay dividends
   c. pay executive bonuses
   d. pay off interest on debt
   e. reinvest in training and development

6. Internal financing can be obtained from:
   a. short-term loans
   b. depreciation
   c. sales revenue
   d. shareholder investments
   e. mortgages

7. Investment decisions have to do with:
   a. cash management
   b. cost of borrowed funds
   c. financing mix
   d. planned downsizing
   e. cutting back useless activities

8. The matching principle explores:
   a. the best solution for mixing long-term financing sources
   b. the most appropriate financing source when buying an asset
   c. the optimization of dividend payments versus debt reduction
   d. whether funds should be obtained from suppliers or commercial banks
   e. the maximization between current assets and current liabilities

9. The purchase of equipment is:
   a. a financing decision
   b. a working capital decision
   c. an investing decision
   d. an operating decision
   e. a leverage decision

10. Average collection period is a tool that measures:
    a. accounts payable
    b. accounts receivable
    c. inventory
    d. discounts on cash sales
    e. bank loans

11. The company's cash flow improves when the:
    a. average collection period is increased
    b. inventory increases faster than cost of goods sold
    c. inventory increases faster than accounts receivable
    d. accounts receivable increases faster than sales revenue
    e. inventory turnover is reduced

12. Gross margin is the difference between:
    a. operating profit and selling expenses
    b. sales revenue and operating expenses
    c. operating profit and cost of goods sold
    d. sales revenue and cost of goods sold
    e. profit before taxes and income taxes

Fill-in-the-Blanks Questions

1. The _____ is the person responsible for establishing the accounting and financial reporting policies and procedures of a company.

2. The _____ is the person responsible for raising funds and regulating the flow of funds.

3. The four financial objectives of a firm include efficiency, _____, prosperity, and stability.

4. Internal financing can be obtained from retained earnings, _____, and a reduction in the working capital accounts.

5. There are three types of business decisions, financing decisions, _____ decisions, and investing decisions.

6. _____ assets shown on the balance sheet include accounts such as accounts receivable and inventory.

7. _____ of financing are institutions that provide funds (e.g., commercial banks).

8. _____ margin shown on the income statement is the difference between sales revenue and cost of goods sold.

Learning Exercises

Exercise 1(a)

Len and Joan intend to invest $200,000 in a business to launch their CompuTech Sales and Services retail store. Their financial projections show that during the first year of operations CompuTech would generate $25,000 in profit after taxes with substantial increments during the following years. To finance their business, Len and Joan would obtain a $100,000 loan from the bank at 8% (after taxes) and invest part of their $100,000 savings into their business. The Millers are currently earning 8% (after taxes) on their savings.

1. With the above information, calculate CompuTech's return on assets and its cost of financing.

2. Should the Millers start the company? Why or why not?

Exercise 1(b)

With the following information, calculate the company's return on assets and the cost of financing.

Current assets	$ 250,000
Capital assets	1,260,000
Income after taxes	170,000
Cost of debt (after tax)	12%
Cost of equity	12%

1. If managers want to earn a 12% return on assets, how much income after taxes must the company generate?

2. If managers want to earn a 15% return on assets, how much income after taxes must the company generate?

Exercise 2(a)

Len and Joan want to reinvest at least 70% of their profit after taxes (see Exercise 1(a)) in their business and use the rest to pay the principal on their loan. They expect to invest 50% of the reinvested earnings in working capital and 50% in capital assets. CompuTech's first-year sales revenue is estimated to be $350,000.

On the basis of the above information, calculate, as a percentage of sales, how much the Millers would keep in the business for growth purposes (i.e., working capital and the purchase of capital assets), and how much would be used to pay off the principal on their loan.

Exercise 2(b)

Assume that a company earns $280,000 after taxes on $3 million of sales revenue. The board of directors decides to keep half of the amount to pay for dividends and reinvest the rest in the company. Forty percent of the retained earnings is invested in working capital for growth, and the rest is used for buying capital assets.

1. On the basis of the above information, calculate, as a percentage of sales, how much would be kept in the company for growth purposes (i.e., working capital and capital assets), and how much would be used to pay dividends.

2. Explain who is responsible for making the split between the amount of funds to be retained in the business and the amount to be paid to the shareholders.

3. What do you think the board of directors would do if income after taxes increased to $350,000?

Exercise 3(a)

On the basis of CompuTech's estimated sales revenue of $350,000, Len and Joan expect to have $35,000 in accounts receivable for sales made to commercial and government accounts.

1. Calculate CompuTech's average collection period.

2. If CompuTech's sales increase by 20% in the following year, what would be the level of accounts receivable if Len and Joan are able to achieve a 30-day average collection period?

3. What would CompuTech's accounts receivable have been if the company had maintained its current average collection period?

Exercise 3(b)

A company has sales of $2,500,000 a year and has, in accounts receivable, a total of $550,000.

1. Calculate the company's average collection period.

2. If sales are to increase by 10% the following year, what would be the level of accounts receivable if management achieves the objective of a 40-day average collection period?

Exercise 4(a)

CompuTech buys $175,000 worth of goods each year and holds $50,000 in inventory.

1. Calculate CompuTech's inventory turnover.

2. Calculate CompuTech's inventory if it turned over five times per year.

Exercise 4(b)

A firm buys $5,500,000 worth of materials and supplies each year and holds $1,240,000 in inventory.

1. Calculate the company's inventory turnover.

2. If management wants to improve its inventory turnover by two times, how much would the company have to hold in stock?

Exercise 5(a)

With the following information, calculate CompuTech's weighted cost of borrowing and its weighted cost of capital. Assume that the company's income tax rate is 33%.

Source	Amount
Accounts payable	$ 17,000
Short-term loan	35,000
Mortgage	60,000
Common shares	100,000

The bank charges 12.0% (before tax) for the term loan and 11.0% for the mortgage. The Millers expect to earn 8% on their savings.

1. Calculate the company's after-tax cost of borrowing.

2. Calculate the company's after-tax cost of capital.

Exercise 5(b)

With the following information, calculate the company's weighted cost of borrowing and the company's weighted cost of capital. Assume that the company's income tax rate is 50%.

Source	Amount
Accounts payable	$200,000
Short-term loan	250,000
Mortgage	500,000
Long-term loan	250,000
Common shares	300,000
Retained earnings	800,000

The before-tax bank charges are 11.0% for the term loan, 10.0% for the long-term loan, and 10.5% on the mortgage. The shareholders expect to earn 16%.

1. Calculate the company's after-tax cost of borrowing.

2. Calculate the company's after-tax cost of capital.

Case

Packard Industries Inc.

In 2004, the management committee of Packard Industries Inc. is considering investing $800,000 for the purchase of machinery and equipment in order to increase the productivity of the company's plant. In 2003, the company's sales revenue amounted to $2,800,000, goods purchased from suppliers totalled $600,000, and income after taxes was $280,000. The company's 2003 balance sheet is as follows:

PACKARD INDUSTRIES INC.
BALANCE SHEET
FOR THE PERIOD ENDING DECEMBER 31, 2003

Assets

Current assets

Cash	$	20,000
Accounts receivable		400,000
Inventory		300,000
Total current assets	$	720,000
Capital assets (net)		1,000,000
Total assets		**$1,720,000**

Liabilities and equity

Current liabilities

Accounts payable	$	170,000
Working capital loan		150,000
Total current liabilities	$	320,000
Long-term debts		500,000
Shareholders' equity		
Common shares		200,000
Retained earnings		700,000
Total shareholders' equity		900,000
Total liabilities and equity		**$1,720,000**

In 2004, management expects sales revenue to increase by 10% and, with cutbacks in different segments of operations, return on sales is expected to improve to 12%. Cost of goods sold as a percentage of sales revenue is expected to show an improvement and reach 20%. Depreciation is expected to total $100,000.

Management also expects improvements in the working capital accounts. The company's objective is to improve accounts receivable by eight days, and turn inventory around 0.2 times faster.

1. Calculate the company's return on total assets for 2003.

2. How much cash will be generated from operations in 2004, in particular from:

   a) retained earnings?

   b) depreciation?

   c) accounts receivable?

   d) inventory?

3. How much will management have to raise from external activities (shareholders and lenders) to proceed with an $800,000 investment in capital assets?

From Scorekeeping to Financial Statements

Learning Objectives

After reading this chapter, you should be able to:

1. Understand the bookkeeping and accounting process.

2. Explain the activities related to bookkeeping.

3. Comment on three financial statements.

4. Discuss the content of the auditor's report.

5. Explain the meaning of analysis in financial management.

6. Discuss the meaning of decision-making in financial management.

7. Differentiate between cash accounting and accrual accounting.

8. Give an overview of corporate taxation in Canada.

9. Differentiate between depreciation methods, capital cost allowance, and amortization.

10. Explain the meaning of deferred taxes.

11. Differentiate between net income after taxes and cash flow.

12. Discuss the meaning of working capital.

Chapter Outline

OPENING CASE

After their discussion with Bill Murray, Len and Joan did some additional homework in light of Bill's comments. They felt that Bill's advice about pinpointing operational and financial objectives was critical for formulating operational plans that would help them succeed.

Len and Joan also felt that it was important for them to learn how to set up a book-keeping and accounting system. They knew that relevant and timely information was critical for analyzing all aspects of their retail operations and making key decisions. They asked Bill if he knew an accountant. He suggested May Ogaki, a chartered accountant with experience in counselling small businesses.

During their first meeting, Len and Joan indicated to May that they were looking for an integrated information system that would provide them with different types of operational and financial data. They would need a cash register that could generate reports about their sales, purchases, inventory, costs, etc. Len made the following comments:

> As far as I'm considered, the cash register should be considered the most important information instrument in our business. It should provide us with operational daily, weekly, and monthly data. Anything that we buy and sell will go through the cash register. With a good software program integrated to our cash register, we should be able to know exactly what product is moving and when, the amount of inventory we have in stock at all times, when we should be ordering goods from suppliers, how much profit we make on each product line, how many sales each salesperson in the store makes, etc. In addition, we need an accounting software program that will provide us with financial statements such as balance sheets, income statements, and statements of cash flow. This software should also help us prepare our monthly operating budget.

May recommended accounting software programs such as Simply Accounting and Quicken, which would provide the type of financial information they needed. May indicated that she would investigate further and meet with them to recommend specifically, on the basis of their requirements, the type of programs they should get.

However, before leaving, May asked Len and Joan to think about the type of accounts or ledgers that they would like to see on their financial statements. As May pointed out:

This is the first step that you have to go through in the bookkeeping and accounting process. Once you know the information that you want to analyze to help you make your decisions, it will be easy for me to determine the type of operational and financial reports that should be produced.

May also recommended a basic course in accounting to understand some of the fundamentals of accounting and financial terms and concepts. Although it was important to have an accountant prepare the financial statements annually for income tax purposes, Len and Joan should be able to read and analyze their own financial statements. Just like a pilot who reads aircraft instruments, owners and managers should be able to understand and interpret their own financial statements. This point simply validated what Bill Murray told them during their first meeting.

This chapter examines in detail some of the points made by May Ogaki. In particular, it focuses on three key topics:

- important accounting terms and concepts;
- key steps involved in the bookkeeping and accounting process; and
- information that should be included in financial statements such as the income statement, the statement of retained earnings, and the balance sheet.

Introduction

Managers, owners, lenders, investors, and short-term creditors want to know the financial health of the firms they deal with, and, to do this, they may want to analyze reports that summarize the financial condition of the business. The financial performance is presented in a report called the income statement, also known as the "statement of operations," "profit and loss statement," or "statement of earnings." The financial structure of a business is presented in another report called the balance sheet, also referred to as the "statement of financial condition" or "statement of financial position."

The term **"financial statements"** is generally used to reflect the fact that several financial reports such as the income statement and the balance sheet are included in annual reports. This chapter examines the meaning of these financial statements, what they contain, and their structure. Chapter 3 looks at a fourth financial statement called the statement of changes in financial position.

Accounting is considered the language of business; it is used to present financial information about business activities. It shows the results of managerial decisions dealing with all segments of a business such as marketing, manufacturing, administration, engineering, human resources, and distribution. Accounting is the methodology that gives data about the financial structure and financial performance of a business.

Financial statements
Financial reports, which include the income statement, the statement of retained earnings, the balance sheet, and the statement of changes in financial position.

Every day, hundreds or even thousands of activities take place in a business: goods are sold on a cash or credit basis; materials are purchased; salaries, rent, and hydro bills are paid; customers pay their accounts; and goods that were purchased on credit are paid for. If managers want to know, on a daily, monthly, or yearly basis, the financial results of all these transactions, they must have them collected and recorded in a logical and methodical manner. For example, if managers want to know:

- the profit position of their business, they will refer to the income statement;
- how much the business owns or owes, they will refer to the balance sheet;
- how much money the business has accumulated and the amount of dividends that was paid to their shareholders this year, they will look at the statement of retained earnings;
- how much cash was generated or used by the business, they will look at the statement of changes in financial position (also known as statement of cash flows).

These reports give financial results of all transactions that have taken place in a business between two calendar dates also known as accounting periods or fiscal periods.

Managers who want to know how their business performed in the past, how it is doing now, and what decisions they should make to improve its financial position, must refer to a variety of reports. For example, they will refer to the operational reports, produced by a management information system, and the financial reports, produced by bookkeeping and accounting systems. This chapter gives an overview of the methodology used by accountants for preparing these financial statements. The ultimate objective of financial management is to help managers analyze financial statements and to make sound financial decisions.

Financial management embraces four broad activities: bookkeeping, accounting, analysis, and decision-making. Let's briefly examine each.

Bookkeeping involves collecting, classifying, and recording information that arises from the multitude of transactions taking place in a business. As will be discussed later in this chapter, these transactions are first recorded in books of original entry, known as journals, and are subsequently recorded in books of final entry, known as ledgers.

Accounting is the activity that arranges the information into separate and distinct financial statements, such as the balance sheet and the income statement. Since these financial statements are structured in a standardized format, they can be easily read, understood, and analyzed. For instance, if you want to know what a business owns, you look at the asset component of the balance sheet; if you want to know how much a business owes and the nature of its liabilities, you look at the liability and shareholders' components of the statement. These financial statements are prepared on the basis of **generally accepted accounting principles (GAAP).** Accounting is a profession, with certain requirements and standards of education, accreditation, and conduct. In order to measure the financial affairs of a business, accountants must follow established rules, procedures, and standards.

Generally Accepted Accounting Principles (GAAP)

A broad set of rules delineating how various transactions will be reported on financial statements.

These rules govern how accountants measure, process, and communicate financial information.

Analysis consists of interpreting financial statements. The data presented on the financial statements should be considered not merely as statistics, but as information that should be examined carefully to see how well (or badly) a business is doing. For example, the reader may want to know about a company's:

- profit position (How much profit is the company generating? What is the ROA?);
- accounts receivable and inventories (Are they at reasonable levels?);
- relationship between the current assets and current debts (Is it acceptable?);
- long-term debt (Is it in line with the amount of money the owners have put into the business?).

Finally, there is *decision-making*. It is not enough to record, arrange, and analyze data. To make decisions to improve the financial performance and financial structure of their businesses, managers must use financial information. For example, the information will help to:

- set the right price;
- establish the most appropriate credit policy;
- maintain an optimal inventory level;
- assess the financial viability of capital investments for new plants or the expansion or modernization of existing ones; and
- determine the most appropriate source of funds needed to finance operations.

This chapter discusses bookkeeping and accounting; financial statement analysis and decision-making will be examined in later chapters.

The Bookkeeping and Accounting Process

◀ Objective 1

Bookkeeping and accounting are the touchstones of business information. Managers need information to plan and control their operations. Once managers have formulated their operational and financial objectives, and prepared their strategic and operational plans, the next logical step in the management process is to implement the plans and compare performance with projections.

Operating and financial data that are presented clearly and logically make it easy for managers to review and analyze performance and make decisions to solve problems or exploit opportunities. The planning and controlling management functions cannot be performed effectively if managers are deprived of such basic operational and financial information. Therefore, the purpose of bookkeeping and accounting activities is to ensure that managers are provided with the right kind of information at the right time.

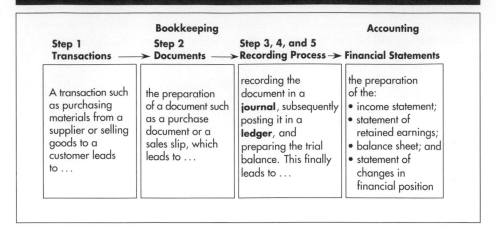

FIGURE 2.1   THE BOOKKEEPING AND THE ACCOUNTING PROCESS

	Bookkeeping		Accounting
Step 1 **Transactions** →	**Step 2** **Documents** →	**Step 3, 4, and 5** **Recording Process** →	**Financial Statements**
A transaction such as purchasing materials from a supplier or selling goods to a customer leads to ...	the preparation of a document such as a purchase document or a sales slip, which leads to ...	recording the document in a **journal**, subsequently posting it in a **ledger**, and preparing the trial balance. This finally leads to ...	the preparation of the: • income statement; • statement of retained earnings; • balance sheet; and • statement of changes in financial position

Let's first examine the activities involved in bookkeeping and accounting. As shown in Figure 2.1, *bookkeeping* is the clerical activity aimed at systematically recording financial transactions incurred by a business, on a day-by-day basis, in different sets of books such as journals and ledgers. *Accounting,* on the other hand, involves the preparation of financial statements such as the income statement, the statement of retained earnings, the balance sheet, and the statement of changes in financial position. Accounting is a more specialized, creative, and comprehensive activity because accountants must present data in financial statements to inform managers, creditors, shareholders, and government agencies about the financial performance of a business.

Bookkeeping

Objective 2 ➥

Chart of accounts

A set of categories by which accounting transactions are recorded.

Bookkeeping

Activity that involves collecting, classifying, and reporting accounting transactions.

Bookkeeping begins with the preparation of a **chart of accounts,** which establishes the categories by which transactions of the business are recorded. These are much like the accounts that an individual has at home such a bankbook, car, house, trailer, credit card, clothing, food, insurance, salary, holidays, etc. The number of accounts that a business sets up depends largely on the needs and desires of management.

Bookkeeping involves collecting, classifying, and reporting transactions taking place each day in different departments of a business. Some transactions take place in the sales department, others in the accounts receivable department or manufacturing plant. All business transactions are recorded under five major groupings or accounts:

- assets, or what a business owns;
- liabilities, or what it owes to creditors;
- equity, or what it owes to shareholders;

- revenue, or how much it earned as a result of selling its goods or services; and

- expenses, or how much it cost to produce and sell its goods or services.

The Accounting Equation

To understand how the accounting system works, it is important to see the interplay between these five accounts. Each time a business transaction takes place, at least two accounts are affected. This is referred to as **double-entry bookkeeping**, meaning that every business transaction results in two account entries. For example, when a business buys a truck with borrowed funds from a banker, both the asset and liability accounts are affected. If a business pays its mortgage with cash, both its asset and liability accounts are also affected. If shareholders invest money in a business, and the funds are used to buy a truck, two accounts are also affected, assets and equity.

In its simplest form, the financial picture of a business can be expressed by the following equation, referred to as the **accounting equation**:

Assets = Liabilities + Equity

It can also be expressed in the following way:

Assets − Liabilities = Equity

For the moment, we'll assume that both the revenue and the expense accounts are part of the equity account. Let's examine several transactions to see how this equation works. If a person invests $100,000 in a start-up operation, this money would first be deposited in a bank account, and the business would owe that amount to the owner. After this first transaction, the financial position of the business would be as follows:

Assets   = Liabilities + Equity
$100,000 = $ 0   + $100,000

Let's assume that the next day the business buys a $30,000 truck and pays $10,000 in cash and borrows $20,000 from the bank. This means that the company would increase its asset accounts to $120,000 (the truck account would show an increase of $30,000 and the bank account would be reduced by $10,000, down to $90,000); the business would also owe $20,000 to a creditor (the bank). After this second transaction, the accounting equation would read as follows:

Assets   = Liabilities + Equity
$120,000 = $20,000 + $100,000

Double-entry bookkeeping

System for posting financial transactions so that the accounting equation remains in balance.

Accounting equation

Assets = Liabilities + Equity or Assets − Liabilities = Equity

There are some basic rules that determine whether a transaction should be a debit or a credit. These rules are summarized below:

	Assets	*Liabilities*	*Owners' equity*
Debit	Increases	Decreases	Decreases
Credit	Decreases	Increases	Increases

Owners' equity will be increased or decreased, respectively, if a business makes a profit or incurs a loss. There are two types of accounts—revenues and expenses—that determine whether a business finds itself in a profit or a loss situation. Any change in the revenue and expense accounts also affects the accounting equation. For example, if a business sells $1,000 worth of goods on a cash basis to a customer, its financial worth—that is, the equity account (through the revenue account)—would be increased by $1,000 since it would be "wealthier" by that amount. If the money is deposited in the bank account, the asset side would be increased accordingly. However, in order to produce the goods, raw materials would have to be purchased from suppliers, and expenses such as salaries would also have to be paid to employees. If the purchase of raw materials amounts to $700, and the payment for salaries is $100, it means that the company took $800 from its bank account (asset) and reduced its financial worth or equity (through the expense accounts) accordingly. The effect of these transactions on the financial position of the business would be as follows:

$$\text{Assets} = \text{Liabilities} + \text{Equity}$$
$$\$120,200 = \$20,000 + \$100,200$$

As shown, debits and credits can also be registered in revenue and expense accounts. For this reason, the credit and debit rules can be expanded to apply to these two accounts and can be read as follows:

	Revenues	*Expenses*
Debit	Decreases	Increases
Credit	Increases	Decreases

As shown in Figure 2.2, a credit in equity or revenue accounts increases the wealth of a business. Conversely, a debit in the expense or capital accounts reduces the wealth of a business.

The Accounting Cycle

Accounting cycle

Steps involved in processing financial transactions for preparing financial statements.

There are several steps involved from the time that a transaction is processed in a business to the time that it is reported in one of the financial statements. This bookkeeping and **accounting cycle** includes five steps. As shown in Figure 2.1, step 1 has to do with transactions, step 2 with the preparation of documents and steps 3 to 5 with recording and posting, and preparation of the trial balance.

FIGURE 2.2   DEBITS AND CREDITS

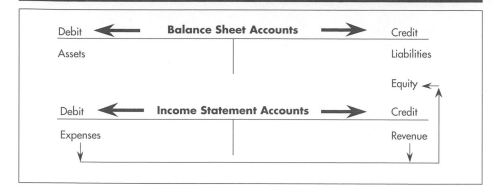

STEP 1 The first step is a business transaction (e.g., investing money in a business, buying a truck, selling goods, paying salaries).

STEP 2 Each transaction is accompanied by a document (e.g., a deposit slip from the bank, a sales slip, a purchase document, a cheque stub).

STEP 3 Through the bookkeeping system, each transaction is recorded in different sets of books: journals and ledgers. As indicated earlier, each business transaction (e.g., cash, truck, loan) affects at least two accounts. Accountants call the recording process double-entry accounting. The most significant virtue of this double-entry system is that all accounts must always be in balance, and an arithmetical error is automatically brought into the open by a lack of balance. Since some transactions are recorded on the left side of the books and others on the right, each side is given a name. The word **debit** refers to entries recorded on the left side of an account; the word **credit** to entries recorded on the right. As shown in Figure 2.2, when all accounts are closed at the end of an accounting period, the asset and expense accounts have debit balances and the liability, equity, and revenue accounts have credit balances.

To illustrate, here is how the previously mentioned bookkeeping transactions would be debited and credited in their respective accounts.

A debit takes place when there is:

- an increase in an asset account (e.g., a deposit of $100,000 in the bank account or the acquisition of a $30,000 truck);
- a decrease in a liability, or equity, account;
- a decrease in a revenue account; or
- an increase in an expense account (e.g., purchase of $700 worth of materials and payment of $100 in salaries).

A credit takes place when there is:

- a decrease in an asset account (e.g., withdrawal of $10,000 from the bank);
- an increase in a liability or equity account (e.g., borrowing $20,000 from the bank);

Debit

Accounting entries recorded on the left side of an account.

Credit

Accounting entries recorded on the right side of an account.

- an increase in a revenue account (e.g., selling $1,000 worth of goods); or
- a decrease in an expense account.

As mentioned earlier, the books used to record accounting transactions are journals and ledgers. Journals, sometimes referred to as the books of original entry, are used to record transactions in a chronological order—that is, as they happen. Table 2.1 shows how the journal entries of the four transactions mentioned previously would be recorded.

Journalizing

Process of recording transactions in a journal (e.g., sales journal, salaries journal).

The process of recording transactions in the journal is called **journalizing**. As shown in the table, the total of all debit entries amounts to $131,800, which equals the sum of all credit entries.

STEP 4 The fourth step in the process is to transfer the amounts recorded in the journals into ledgers. Journals do not show the outstanding balance of each account after each transaction has been recorded. For this purpose, a second set of books called ledgers, or the books of final account, are created. A ledger is very much like a chequebook. It shows all amounts debited and credited in each account, including its running balance. As mentioned earlier, ledgers for a home would include hydro, credit card, mortgage, salary, and food accounts. If a person wants to know how much she owns or owes, how much income she earned, or the expenses incurred for telephone, grocery, or entertainment during a given year, the outstanding balance for each of these accounts would give the answer.

Posting

Process of transferring recorded transactions from the journals to the appropriate ledger accounts (e.g., sales revenue, accounts receivable).

All transactions recorded in journals are subsequently transferred to the appropriate ledger accounts; this process is called **posting**. Figure 2.3 shows how each of the four journal transactions mentioned previously would be posted in their respective ledgers (sometimes referred to as T-accounts). Ledger accounts are usually given a number to facilitate the process of recording the transactions, whether the recording is done manually or electronically.

TABLE 2.1	THE JOURNALS		Debit	Credit
Transaction 1	Cash		$100,000	
		Equity		$100,000
Transaction 2	Truck		$ 30,000	
		Cash		$ 10,000
		Bank loan		$ 20,000
Transaction 3	Cash		$ 1,000	
		Revenue		$ 1,000
Transaction 4	Purchases		$ 700	
	Salaries		$ 100	
		Cash		$ 800
Total			$131,800	$131,800

Chapter 2: From Scorekeeping to Financial Statements

FIGURE 2.3   THE LEDGERS

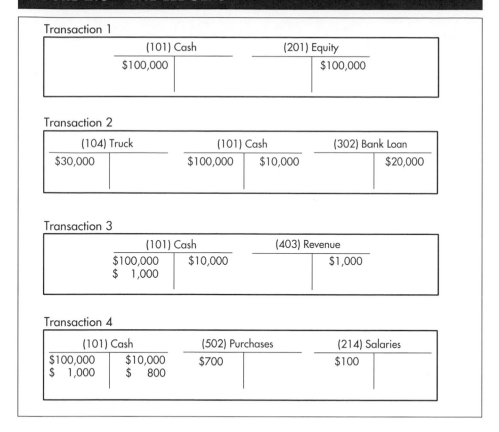

Transaction 1

(101) Cash		(201) Equity	
$100,000			$100,000

Transaction 2

(104) Truck		(101) Cash		(302) Bank Loan	
$30,000		$100,000	$10,000		$20,000

Transaction 3

(101) Cash		(403) Revenue	
$100,000	$10,000		$1,000
$ 1,000			

Transaction 4

(101) Cash		(502) Purchases		(214) Salaries	
$100,000	$10,000	$700		$100	
$ 1,000	$ 800				

The Trial Balance

STEP 5 The fifth and final step in the bookkeeping and accounting cycle is called "closing the books." It is done at the end of an accounting period (i.e., the end of a month or the end of a fiscal year). To ensure that all transactions recorded during the period are error-free—that is, the sum of all debits equals the sum of all credits—the outstanding account balances are listed under their appropriate column in the **trial balance**.

As shown in Table 2.2, the trial balance is done by listing, in parallel columns, the total of all debit balances and the total of all credit balances for each account appearing in the ledgers. Once this has been done, the debit and credit columns of the trial balance are added. If the debit column equals the credit column, it means that there should be no arithmetical errors; all accounts are in balance. Since the ledger accounts are used to prepare the financial statements (i.e., the income statement and the balance sheet), it is preferable, before commencing this exercise, to do a trial balance.

Trial balance

Statement that ensures that the general ledger is in balance (debit transactions = credit transactions).

TABLE 2.2 THE TRIAL BALANCE

	Debit	Credit
Cash	$ 90,200	
Truck	30,000	
Bank loan		$ 20,000
Equity		100,000
Sales revenue		1,000
Purchases	700	
Salaries	100	
Total	$121,000	$121,000

Some of the most common errors that will cause inequality in trial balance totals are:

- One of the columns of the trial balance was added incorrectly.
- One amount of an account balance was improperly recorded on the trial balance.
- A debit balance that was recorded on the trial balance as a credit (or vice versa) was omitted entirely.
- One side of an account was computed incorrectly.
- An erroneous amount was posted as a debit or as a credit in an account.
- A debit entry was recorded as a credit, or vice versa.
- A debit or a credit entry was omitted.

With some other errors, the debit column will still be equal to the credit column in the trial balance. These errors include:

- failure to record an entire transaction;
- recording the same erroneous amount for both the debit and the credit;
- recording the same transaction more than once; or
- recording one part of a transaction in the wrong account.

Objective 3 ▶

Accounting

Process of recording and summarizing business transactions on a company's financial statements.

Income statement

Financial statement that shows a summary of revenues and expenses for a specified period of time.

Accounting

The function of **accounting** governs the way the four financial statements shown in Figure 2.4 are prepared. The Canadian Institute of Chartered Accountants provides some generally accepted accounting principles (GAAP) regarding the way in which the accounts should be presented on the income statement, the statement of retained earnings, the balance sheet, and the statement of changes in financial position. Here is an overview of these four financial statements.

The **income statement** is much like a "movie" of the business. It shows the flow of revenues and expenses incurred by a business during a given period (e.g., one month, that is from, say, June 1 to June 30, or one year, say from January 1 to

December 31). As shown in Figure 2.4, the income statement shows income (profit[1]) at four levels:

- The first level is gross margin, which is calculated by deducting the cost of producing the goods sold from sales revenue.
- The second level is operating income, which is calculated by deducting operating expenses such as selling and administrative expenses from the gross margin.
- The third level, income before taxes, is computed by adding other income to the operating income, and by deducting interest charges from this balance.
- The fourth level is the income after taxes. It is also often referred to as the "owners' section," since income after taxes actually belongs to the shareholders, to be paid in dividends or to be retained in the business for reinvestment purposes or reducing debt.

As shown in Figure 2.4, the **statement of retained earnings** shows the amount of income retained in a business since it was started. This statement also identi-

Statement of retained earnings

Financial statement that shows the amount of income retained in a business since it was started.

FIGURE 2.4   FINANCIAL STATEMENTS

The Income Statement

| Sales revenue |
| – Cost of goods sold |
| 1. = Gross Margin |
| – Selling and general expenses |
| 2. = Operating income |
| – Interest expenses |
| + Other revenue |
| 3. = Income before taxes |
| – Income taxes |
| 4. = Income after taxes |

The Statement of Retained Earnings

| 1. Retained Earnings (Beginning Balance) |
| 2. Current-Year Earnings |
| 3. Dividends |
| 4. Retained Earnings (Ending Balance) |

The Balance Sheet

1. Current Assets	4. Current Liabilities
2. Capital Assets	5. Long-Term Debts
3. Intangible Assets	6. Shareholders' Equity

The Statement of Changes in Financial Position

| 1. Operating Activities |
| 2. Financing Activities |
| 3. Investing Activities |
| 4. Cash Balance |

---

1 Managers will use the term "profit and loss statement" for the income statement for reporting purposes in internal documents, but not in external documents such as the annual report for a simple reason: the word "profit" is considered by many to symbolize greed. Also, the word "profit" suggests a surplus on top of what is really needed for the business to operate.

Balance sheet

Financial statement that shows a "snapshot" of a company's financial condition (assets, liabilities, and equity).

fies the income earned and dividends paid during a current operating year and the amount of earnings remaining in the business at the end of the period.

The **balance sheet** is a "snapshot" of a company's financial position or financial condition. As shown in Figure 2.4, this statement is divided into six sections. The left side shows what the business owns, or its assets. Asset accounts are grouped under three headings:

- *Current assets* are accounts that are more liquid or can be converted into cash quickly (e.g., accounts receivable, inventory, marketable securities, and prepaid expenses).
- *Capital assets* (also referred to as fixed assets) include accounts such as land, buildings, machinery, and equipment, which are illiquid and used by the business over an extended period of time.
- *Intangible assets*, such as goodwill and patents, would also appear on the asset side of the balance sheet.

The right side shows what a business owes to its creditors (lenders) and shareholders (owners). Debts are also grouped under two headings:

- *Current liabilities* are loans that come due within a 12-month period and include accounts such as accounts payable, term loans, and accrued expenses.
- *Long-term debts* such as long-term loans, bonds, and mortgages are loans that are to be paid beyond the current accounting period.

The right side of the balance sheet also shows the *shareholders' equity* account, which is funds provided by the shareholders to a business.

The statement of changes in financial position shows where funds came from and where they went between two accounting periods. Figure 2.4 shows how this statement is divided into four sections:

- The first, *operating activities*, shows the sources and uses of funds generated by the business itself (e.g., income after taxes).
- The second, *financing activities*, includes items such as long-term loans and shareholders' participation.
- The third, *investing activities*, includes transactions such as the purchase or sale of assets.
- The fourth, *cash balance*, shows the effects that all changes (sources or uses of funds) registered under the three activities have had on the cash account.

Figure 2.5 gives a comparison of the relationship between the balance sheet and the income statement. As indicated earlier, the income statement is much like a movie of what went on during an operating period (say from January 1 to December 31) of a business. This is the reason the income statement reads "for the period ended December 31." On the other hand, the balance sheet shows a "picture" of the financial position of a business at a given point in time (say December 31). For this reason, the balance sheet reads "as at December 31."

FIGURE 2.5   RELATIONSHIP BETWEEN THE INCOME STATEMENT AND THE BALANCE SHEET

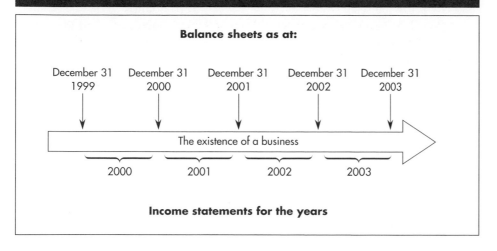

There is a parallel between an individual and a business in terms of growth (in the first case, the weight, in the second, the wealth). Supposing that both John Pound and ABC Inc. were born and started, respectively, in 1960. At the end of the first year, John weighed 20 pounds and ABC Inc. had accumulated $100,000 in income after taxes. Each year during the next 43 years, John's daily activities included eating (intake of food and drinks) and exercising (burning of calories). On the other hand, ABC Inc. made sales revenue and incurred expenses. For both John and ABC, 43 (one for each year) 12-month movies were produced. This would be the information recorded on the income statement. Also, at the end of each year, John could have weighed himself to find out how many pounds he had gained (or lost) and would record the results in his diary. In the case of ABC Inc., the accumulated gains would be recorded in the balance sheet. The number of pounds that John gained (or lost) each year would be added to (or subtracted from) the previous year's weight. In the case of ABC Inc., each time it generated a profit (or loss), that number would also be added or subtracted from the previous year's balance sheet.

Now, assuming that on January 1, 2003, John's weight was 170 pounds and on December 31, 2003, his weight had increased by 10 pounds. However, during the 12-month period, suppose he actually gained 15 pounds, but five pounds was removed through liposuction just before he stepped on the scale. The removal of excess pounds would be equivalent to what is paid in dividends and recorded in the statement of retained earnings. Similar to the evolution of John's weight pattern, ABC Inc.'s earnings and dividends would also be recorded in the same fashion on the three financial statements. This information would be recorded as follows:

	John Pound	ABC Inc.
Beginning of year (January 1, 2003)		
On the scale	170 pounds	
Last year's balance sheet		$1,000,000
Change during the year		
Changes in weight	+ 15 pounds	
Income statement (income)		+$ 200,000
Adjustment during the year		
Removal of excess fat	− 5 pounds	
Net change	+ 10 pounds	
Statement of retained earnings (dividends)		−$ 100,000
Statement of retained earnings (net change)		+$ 100,000
End of year (December 31, 2003)		
On the scale	180 pounds	
This year's balance sheet		$1,100,000

Let's now examine these three financial statements in more detail. Tables 2.3, 2.4, and 2.5 show Eastman Technologies Inc.'s income statement, statement of retained earnings, and balance sheet respectively. Eastman's statement of changes in financial position will be examined in Chapter 3.

The Income Statement

Everyone associated with a business wants to know if it is making a profit and, if so, how much. This financial statement summarizes the sales revenue and expenses for a period of time (one month, six months, or a year). The income statement for Eastman Technologies Inc. for the year ending December 31, 2003, is to be read in a step-down fashion. As shown in Table 2.3, the income statement shows four levels of profitability: (1) the gross margin, (2) the operating income, (3) the income before taxes, and (4) the income after taxes. The accounts shown on the income statement can be grouped in three distinct sections:

1. the operating section, which shows the gross margin and the operating income;

2. the nonoperating section, which shows income before taxes; and

3. the owners' section, which shows the income after taxes or the amount left to the owners.

Operating section

Section of the income statement that shows a company's gross margin and operating income.

OPERATING SECTION This section includes the gross margin and the operating income.

TABLE 2.3 THE INCOME STATEMENT

Eastman Technologies Inc.
Income Statement for the Year Ended
December 31, 2003

1. Operating Section

Net sales		$2,500,000	
Cost of goods sold		1,900,000	
Gross margin		**600,000**	Level 1
Operating expenses			
Selling expenses:			
Sales salaries	$140,000		
Advertising expenses	20,000		
Total selling expenses	160,000		
Administrative expenses:			
Office salaries	170,000		
Lease	20,000		
Depreciation	40,000		
Total administration expenses	230,000		
Total operating expenses		390,000	
Operating income		**210,000**	Level 2

2. Non-Operating Section

Other income	20,000		
Other expenses (interest)	35,000	15,000	
Income before taxes		**195,000**	Level 3

3. Owners' Section

Income taxes		97,500	
Income after taxes		**$ 97,500**	Level 4

GROSS MARGIN The gross margin (also referred to as gross profit) is calculated by subtracting the cost of goods sold from net sales or revenues.

Net sales	$2,500,000
Less cost of goods sold	1,900,000
Equals gross margin	$ 600,000

Net sales or sales revenue is what a business earns for the sale of its products and/or services. It represents items actually delivered or shipped to customers during the fiscal period. The terms "net sales" or "net revenue" are used because allowances for sales discounts and sales returns have been adjusted from gross sales. Net sales are the amount a company has received or expects to receive after allowing for these adjustments and for discounts off list prices, sales returns, prompt-payment discounts, and other deductions from the original sales prices. Sales taxes (provincial or GST) are not included in the net sales revenue amount. Essentially, net sales are the amount that a business receives in order to cover all operating expenses and to generate a profit.

Net sales
What a business earns for the sale of its products and/or services.

Cost of goods sold

Cost incurred in making or producing goods that are sold.

Cost of goods sold (also known as cost of sales) is the cost incurred in making or producing the goods that were sold. It is by far the largest expense in the income statement for a manufacturing enterprise (in many cases, it may represent as much as 80% of a company's total expenses). It includes three major items: materials purchased from suppliers, transportation cost or freight-in for goods shipped from suppliers to the company's plant, and all expenses associated with the manufacturing process to make the goods, such as wages and depreciation on the plant's equipment and machinery.

Gross margin is the difference between net sales and cost of goods sold. It is the profit a business makes after paying for the cost of making the goods. It is called gross margin because no other types of expenses have been deducted, and it represents the amount of money left over to pay for other general expenses such as selling and administration. Gross margin is the starting point for earning an adequate income after taxes.

OPERATING INCOME Operating income is sometimes called operating earnings or earnings before interests and taxes (EBIT). Deducting operating expenses, such as selling and administration expenses, from the gross margin gives the operating income. Generally, operating expenses include every expense other than the cost of goods sold, interest, and income tax. There are sometimes hundreds of operating expenses included in this category, ranging from salaries (a large amount) to legal fees (usually a small amount).

Selling expenses

Cost incurred by a organization to promote, sell, and distribute its goods and services.

Selling expenses are incurred by a marketing organization to promote, sell, and distribute its goods and services. These expenses include advertising, sales salaries, sales commissions, trade shows, sales supplies, delivery expenses, and sales promotions.

Administrative expenses

Expenses that are not directly related to producing and selling goods or services.

Administrative expenses are all other expenses that are not directly related to producing and selling goods. They include expenses incurred by organizational units, such as human resources, accounting, legal, finance, computers, consultants, insurance, and depreciation (a noncash expense) on office equipment. When it was first purchased, office equipment was considered a capital expenditure. For such purchases, a useful life is usually estimated as before it would wear out or have to be replaced by new technology. It would then be depreciated over its useful life, and the cost would therefore be amortized, or spread, over that same time period (perhaps five or six years). Typical assets that are capitalized include factory equipment, computers, tools, machinery, buildings, etc.

By subtracting these operating expenses from the gross margin, we obtain the second level of profit, operating income. This level of profitability is directly affected by decisions made by operating managers (e.g., cost of goods sold, and selling and administrative expenses); therefore, managers are directly accountable for the "operating income" performance.

Gross margin	$600,000
Less operating expenses	390,000
Equals operating income	$210,000

NONOPERATING SECTION This section deals with income and expenses that are not directly connected to the principal operating activities of a firm.

INCOME BEFORE TAXES The **nonoperating section** determines the level of income before taxes of a business. It includes three types of items: (1) interest income and interest charges, (2) extraordinary items, and (3) nonrecurring items.

- Interest income includes interest earned on investments (e.g., short-term deposits), and interest charges, which are interest paid for funds borrowed.

- Extraordinary items are unusual and infrequent gains (revenue) or losses (expenses) for a given year. They are occurrences unrelated to the usual activities of the business and not expected to occur again. An example is a loss from a fire.

- Nonrecurring items are unusual or infrequent. For example, a business may sell a major capital asset and record a gain. Or a business may record a restructuring charge for the cost of laying off employees who will receive severance packages. These unusual gains or losses are therefore reported separately from the ongoing, continuing operations of a business. The logical reason for this is that irregular gains or losses would complicate the analysis and forecasting of the financial performance of a business.

Operating income		$210,000
Plus other income	$ 20,000	
Less other expenses	35,000	15,000
Equals income before taxes		$195,000

As shown, the company's expenses exceed the other income by $15,000 and consequently reduce the operating profit to $195,000. This amount, called income before taxes, is used for three purposes: to pay income taxes, pay dividends to shareholders, and reinvest in the business.

OWNERS' SECTION The **owner's section** deals with the amount of money left to the shareholders; that is, "the bottom line."

INCOME AFTER TAXES This is the profit that belongs to the shareholders. In this case, Eastman Technologies Inc. earned $97,500 in income. It is the responsibility of the board of directors to decide how much of this amount will be paid to the shareholders in dividends and how much will be left in the business in the form of retained earnings. The portion of the income after taxes paid to shareholders and retained in the business appears on the next statement, called the statement of retained earnings.

Income taxes are the total amount of taxes due to federal and provincial governments on the taxable income earned by the business during the current fiscal accounting period. Income taxes are calculated by multiplying the taxable income for the period by the appropriate tax rate (in this case, 50%). Income tax expense

Nonoperating section
This section of the income statement shows income or expenses that are not directly related to the principal activities of a business (e.g., interest income, extraordinary expenses, nonrecurring items).

Owners' section
Section of the income statement that shows the amount of money left to the shareholders (i.e., income after taxes).

does not include other types of taxes, such as payroll and property taxes that are included in cost of goods sold and operating expenses.

Income before taxes	$195,000
Less income taxes	97,500
Equals income after taxes	$ 97,500

The Statement of Retained Earnings

The statement of retained earnings (used in the case of corporations) is relatively simple to prepare. It is an important statement because it links the income statement and the balance sheet. **Retained earnings** represent the amount of money kept by a company after it pays dividends to its shareholders. This statement shows:

1. the amount of accumulated earnings at the start of the fiscal or accounting period (that is, the money that was not distributed to the shareholders) (this amount should agree with the retained earnings figure appearing in the previous year's balance sheet);

2. the total net income (or loss) after taxes for the current operating year;

3. any amount paid to the shareholders in the form of dividends, which is drawn from the current year's income statement; and

4. the amount left in retained earnings at the end of the fiscal year (this amount determines the retained earnings figure that will appear in the company's current year's balance sheet).

Table 2.4 shows Eastman's statement of retained earnings for 2003. It should be noted that the net earnings figure of $97,500 for the year was obtained from the income statement in Table 2.3, and the $255,000 retained earnings as at December 31, 2003 is the same as the amount shown on the balance sheet (see Table 2.5).

TABLE 2.4	THE STATEMENT OF RETAINED EARNINGS

Eastman Technologies Inc.
Retained Earnings Statement for the Year Ended
December 31, 2003

Retained earnings (beginning balance)		$205,000
Net earnings for the year	$97,500	
Dividends	47,500	50,000
Retained earnings (ending balance)		$255,000

The Balance Sheet

Table 2.5 shows Eastman's balance sheet; it gives a "position statement" of the company as at December 31, 2003, and 2002. The balance sheet is like a photograph in that it gives a picture of the size of each major account of a business at a particular moment; it does not show changes in each account from the previous year's financial statement. And, like an X-ray, the balance sheet gives a report

TABLE 2.5 THE BALANCE SHEET		
Eastman Technologies Inc. **Balance Sheet as at December 31**		
Assets	**2003**	**2002**
Current assets		
Cash	$ 22,000	$ 18,000
Prepaid expenses	60,000	55,000
Accounts receivable	300,000	280,000
Inventory	218,000	185,000
Total current assets	**600,000**	**538,000**
Capital assets (at cost)	1,340,000	1,050,000
Accumulated depreciation	140,000	100,000
Capital assets (net)	**1,200,000**	**950,000**
Total assets	$1,800,000	$1,488,000
Liabilities		
Current liabilities		
Accounts payable	$ 195,000	$ 175,000
Notes payable	150,000	135,000
Accrued expenses	20,000	18,000
Taxes payable	80,000	70,000
Total current liabilities	**445,000**	**398,000**
Long-term debts	**800,000**	**600,000**
Common shares	300,000	285,000
Retained earnings	255,000	205,000
Shareholders' equity	**555,000**	**490,000**
Total liabilities and equity	$1,800,000	$1,488,000

about the health of a business at the close of an accounting period. Each separate item reported on the balance sheet is called an account. Every account has a name and a dollar amount, which is called its balance reported at the end of the accounting period.

The balance sheet comprises assets, liabilities, and shareholders' equity (also known as net worth). As shown on Eastman's balance sheet (Table 2.5), the total of all assets ($1,800,000), equals the liability and equity side of the balance sheet. Usually, the balance sheet's assets, liabilities, and equity accounts are grouped under several sub-accounts, namely current assets, capital assets, investments, intangible assets, current liabilities, long-term debts, and shareholders' equity.

Assets

Resources that a business owns to produce goods and services (e.g., cash, accounts receivable, buildings).

Current assets

Assets such as accounts receivable and inventory expected to be turned into cash (usually in one year or less).

ASSETS **Assets** are the physical items (tangible) or rights (intangible) owned by a business. Assets have a monetary value attached to them and usually appear under two headings: current assets and capital assets. Some businesses with other assets, such as investments and intangible assets, will show them separately.

CURRENT ASSETS **Current assets** are defined as cash or other assets expected to be turned into cash, usually in one year or less; that is, during the operating cycle. Current assets include cash, marketable securities, accounts receivable, notes receivable, inventories, and prepaid expenses. It is common to list these assets on the balance sheet in order of liquidity. For instance, since cash is more liquid than marketable securities, it will be listed first. Similarly, since notes receivable can typically be converted into cash more quickly than inventory, they will be listed before inventory.

Cash includes all funds such as bills, coins, and cheques that are on hand or readily available from the bank account. A certain reservoir of cash is usually kept on hand in order to pay current bills and to take advantage of specific opportunities, such as cash discounts.

Marketable securities include items, such as term deposits or shares, that can be readily converted into cash (in less than one year), and are regarded as an added reservoir of cash. Since the company will obtain a greater return on these types of assets than on its bank account, the company will buy securities.

Accounts receivable represents money owed to the company by its regular business customers for the purchase of goods or services, which can be collected within a reasonable time period (usually between 30 and 90 days). To reduce the size of the cash tied up in this account, some businesses formulate credit policies and collection procedures to minimize the time it takes to turn receivables into cash.

Notes receivable are written promises that have a specific maturity date. A note receivable may be the result of the settlement of an account by a customer who does not have the cash to pay the account according to the company's credit terms. If a company believes that some accounts will not be collected, it will open an account called "allowance for doubtful receivables." Since this account is a "negative" asset account, it will be deducted from the regular accounts receivable to reflect the true value of that account.

Prepaid expenses are payments made for services that have not yet been received. A prepaid expense is an operating expense that is recorded before services were received. Rent, insurance, office supplies, or property taxes are typical examples of such items. For example, Eastman may pay $8,000 for its insurance premium on June 30. If this is a one-year insurance policy and Eastman's accounting cycle closes on December 31, half of the premium, $4,000, will be registered as a prepaid expense. This amount will be charged to the next year's accounting period. If Eastman decides to cancel its policy on December 31, the insurance company will owe Eastman $4,000. This is why such items are regarded as assets. Another example is office and computer supplies bought in bulk and then gradually used up over several months. Annual property taxes may be paid at the start of the taxation year, and these amounts should be allocated over all the months covered by the property taxes.

The *inventory* account describes the monetary value a company places on the material it has purchased or goods it has manufactured. Usually, a manufacturer has three types of accounts under inventory:

- raw materials, which represent the goods purchased from various suppliers to be used for manufacturing purposes;
- work-in-process, which includes the goods or materials tied up in various stages of the production process, somewhere between raw materials and finished goods; and
- finished goods, which are the products ready for sale.

Since inventory is not a source of income, management makes an effort to keep it at low levels or to move it as quickly as possible. Inventory is recorded at cost, not the price at which the firm hopes to sell it.

CAPITAL ASSETS Capital assets (also called fixed assets) are items that are considered permanent and are to be used over an extended period of time (many years). The word "used" is important because it characterizes the major difference between current assets and capital assets. Such assets have a limited life span (building, equipment, machinery) or an unlimited one (land). They are usually listed on the balance sheet at the price they were purchased for, at "book value" (historical costs less accumulated depreciation, which is the sum of all annual depreciation since the purchase of the capital asset). However, a company may experience significant changes in the value of some assets and will consequently "write up," or increase, their value. In other instances, the company will "write down" an asset (decrease its value). If this is done, the financial reports will explain, in a footnote, the difference between the original cost and the new value. For example, a write-up would take place when the value of a piece of land appreciates significantly, while a write-down would be done when a capital asset suddenly becomes obsolete.

Capital assets (other than land) have a finite life span and wear out over a number of years. Therefore, a company will allocate a certain amount of the total value of the capital asset over many years; this allocated amount is called depreciation. For example, if a building with an original cost of $2,000,000 has a 20-

year physical life span, $100,000 will be allocated as an expense each year. Although this $100,000 is not a cash outlay, it is considered an expense and registered as such (as was indicated earlier) in the income statement. If the building has been used for four years, the balance sheet will show an accumulated depreciation of $400,000 deducted from the gross (also called original or purchase price) capital asset. The difference between the gross capital assets and the accumulated depreciation is called "net capital assets" or "book value."

INVESTMENTS **Investments** are similar to marketable securities, except that they are invested for a longer period. They include items such as bonds and shares purchased from other companies.

Investments
Assets such as bonds and shares purchased from other businesses.

INTANGIBLE ASSETS **Intangible assets** represent values of trademarks, goodwill, franchises, and patents. These items are not tangible but represent some value to the owners of a business. Goodwill, for example, arises when a firm purchases another firm for a price that is higher than the value of the tangible assets. This difference represents the potential earning power resulting from its name or reputation. Also, company trademarks such as Coca-Cola, McDonald's, and Microsoft are worth millions of dollars.

Intangible assets
Items that are not tangible but represent some value to a business (e.g., trademarks, patents).

LIABILITIES **Liabilities** represent the debts of a business. They are the credit that persons or other businesses (other than the shareholders) have extended to a business in order to provide some financial assistance for purchasing the assets. Liabilities are also divided into two distinct groups: current liabilities and long-term debts.

Liabilities
The debts of a business.

CURRENT LIABILITIES **Current liabilities** are what a business has to pay its creditors, monies that are owed to them within a short time (less than one year). Normally, such debts are used to finance the current assets. Current liabilities include accounts payable, notes payable, accrued expenses, and taxes.

Accounts payable usually represent the most current debts of a business. This is the money owed to suppliers of goods or services that were purchased on credit.

Notes payable are written promises to repay a specified sum of money within a short period time (less than one year).

Accrued liability accounts represent what a company owes for services it has received and for which it has not yet paid or an expense that has been incurred but not recorded. Normally a business records expenses as soon as the invoice is received for operating costs, even though it doesn't pay the invoice until several weeks later. However, certain unpaid expenses must be identified when a business closes its books. For instance, if employees are paid every second week, and the company closes its books on December 31, it would have to record that it owes (as a liability) to its employees salaries for the week prior to December 31. The following are typical examples of accrued liabilities:

Current liabilities
Debts that a business must pay within one year (i.e., accounts payable).

- accumulated vacation and sick leave pay;
- interest on debt that hasn't come due by year-end;

- property taxes that should be charged for the year but have not been paid yet; and

- warranty and guarantee work that will be done during the following year on products already sold.

Accrued expenses are the opposite of prepaid expenses. Accrued expenses are services that have been received, but not paid for, and are not included in the accounts payable.

LONG-TERM DEBTS Long-term debts include accounts that are not due for at least one year. They include items such as mortgages, contracts, or long-term notes and loans, such as bonds. These items are used to finance the purchase of capital assets. A mortgage is a long-term obligation for which a company has pledged certain capital assets (land and buildings) to serve as collateral. This assures lenders that the value of some assets will be made available to them if the company ceases to operate or if it is sold or liquidated. A long-term note is similar to notes payable (current liabilities) except that this item is to be repaid beyond a one-year period.

SHAREHOLDERS' EQUITY Shareholders' equity is another way of financing a business. This money comes from the owners of a business in the form of a capital account (if it is a sole proprietorship), partners' account (if it is a partnership), or capital shares (if it is a corporation).

Capital shares represent the amount of money put into the business by the shareholders. These could be common shares (certificates of ownership in a company) or preferred shares (shares that rank ahead of common shares in their claims on dividends and in their claim on assets in the event of liquidation).

Retained earnings represent the profits or income generated by the business not claimed by the owners in the form of dividends. This represents the profits that have been accumulated and reinvested into the business to finance the purchase of current or capital assets or to pay off debts. If a company makes a profit during a given year, the amount in the retained earnings account shown on the current year's balance sheet is greater than the amount shown on the previous year's balance sheet. Conversely, if it incurs a loss, the retained earnings account drops accordingly.

Long-term debts
Debts that are not due for at least one year.

Shareholders' equity
Funds provided in a business by its shareholders (i.e., shares, retained earnings).

The Auditor's Report

◀■ Objective 4

Canadian federal corporate law requires that every federally incorporated limited company appoint an auditor to represent shareholders and report to them annually on the company's financial statements. In Canada, the **auditor's report** includes:

1. the auditor's opinion on the financial statements;
2. a statement that the financial statements are prepared in accordance with generally accepted accounting principles applied on a basis consistent with that of the preceding year; and

Auditor's report
Report prepared by an independent accounting firm that is presented to a company's shareholders.

3. a description of the scope of the examination (the audit itself). It usually comments on the accounting procedures and any tests made to support the accounting records and presents evidence to show that they were made in accordance with generally accepted auditing standards.

The following is a typical auditor's statement that appears in annual reports.

> We have audited the balance sheets of ABC Ltd. as at December 31, 2002, and December 31, 2003, and the income statements, the statement of retained earnings, and the statement of changes in financial position for the years then ended. These financial statements are the responsibility of the company's management. Our responsibility is to express an opinion on these financial statements based on our audits.
>
> We conducted our audits in accordance with generally accepted auditing standards. Those standards require that we plan and perform an audit to obtain reasonable assurance whether the financial statements are free of material misstatement. An audit includes examination, on a test basis, of evidence supporting the amounts and disclosures in the financial statements. An audit also includes assessing the accounting principles used and significant estimates made by management, as well as evaluating the overall financial statement presentation.
>
> In our opinion, these financial statements present fairly, in all material respects, the financial position of the company as at December 31, 2003, and December 31, 2002, and the results of its operations and the changes in its financial position for the years then ended in accordance with generally accepted accounting principles.

A typical annual report contains more than financial statements. It also includes additional information in the form of footnotes to financial statements. These footnotes are essential to financial statements; in fact, they are an integral, inseparable part of an annual report. Without footnotes, financial statements would be incomplete since the footnotes provide adequate disclosure about relevant information so the shareholders can make informed decisions and at the same time protect their interests. The two types of footnotes disclose:

- the main accounting methods used by the business; and
- information that cannot be incorporated in the main body of the financial statements (e.g., details regarding stock ownership, long-term operating leases, maturity dates, interest rates, collateral or other security provisions, legal lawsuits, employees' retirement, and pension plans).

Writing the footnotes is a necessary but difficult task since the auditors have to explain sometimes-complex issues in a relatively small space.

Objective 5 ➡️

Analysis

Once the financial statements have been drawn up, the information can be analyzed and interpreted. Many techniques exist for analyzing financial statements. What is important, however, is ensuring that the right type of information has been gathered and presented in a way that will assist managers, creditors, and shareholders to analyze the data in a meaningful way.

Here are typical analytical techniques that will be examined in Chapters 3 and 4:

- Statement of changes in financial position, which gives a picture of the changes taking place between two consecutive balance sheets; that is, where the funds came from and where they went.

- Horizontal analysis, which gives a picture of the company's historical growth pattern regarding its financial structure and profit.

- Vertical analysis, which helps financial analysts compare different numbers on a balance sheet and income statement (through ratios) in a more meaningful way.

- Ratio analysis, which expresses different sets of numbers contained in financial statements as ratios: liquidity ratios, debt-coverage ratios, asset-management ratios, and profitability ratios.

- Break-even analysis, which shows the relationship between revenues, expenses (fixed and variable), and profits.

- Operational analysis, which uses information contained in financial statements and management information reports to evaluate the efficiency, effectiveness, and productivity of a business.

Decision-Making

◄ Objective 6

This last activity of financial management gets to the heart of the management process—decision-making. Bookkeeping, accounting, and analysis are the key steps in financial management because they provide important information to management, which will assist in making prudent decisions. Decision-making techniques will also be reviewed in subsequent chapters. The information contained in financial statements and the analysis of this data provide answers to the following questions:

- How much money should we borrow?
- Should we borrow on a short-term or a long-term basis?
- How much inventory should be kept on hand?
- Should we buy or lease an asset?
- Should we invest in this project? Expand this operation? Modernize our plant?
- How much credit should we extend?
- How quickly should our company grow?
- What size of capital commitments should our company tackle this year? Next year?
- What level of risk does this project present?

Chapter 2: From Scorekeeping to Financial Statements

- How should we administer our working capital assets?
- What is the optimal level of capital structure?
- What price should we set for our products?
- How can we compare the financial viability of different projects coming from various divisions, and how can we rate them?

These are typical questions managers ask, and they will be discussed throughout this book. Before moving on to the analysis and decision-making chapters, a few important concepts associated with financial statements should be reviewed and understood. They are:

- the accounting methods (cash method versus accrual method);
- an overview of taxation in Canada;
- the depreciation methods, capital cost allowance, and amortization;
- deferred taxes;
- income after taxes (or profit) versus cash flow; and
- working capital.

Objective 7 ➡️

Accounting Methods

There are two ways of reporting financial statements: the cash method and the accrual method.

The **cash method** keeps a record of cash receipts from sales and from disbursements of expenses. In this case, the business recognizes revenue when cash or its equivalent is received, irrespective of when the goods or services are delivered. Expenses are treated in a similar way. At the end of an accounting period, the expenses are deducted from revenues, and the excess gives the net income or loss for the period. This accounting method is limited to small businesses (such as variety stores) where most transactions are done on a cash basis. For this reason, all financial reports or statements discussed in this book, unless otherwise stated, use the accrual method.

The **accrual method** disregards the receipt and disbursement of cash. It records revenue when goods are sold or services rendered. For example, if a business makes a sale, whether on a cash or credit basis, or buys goods, also on either a cash or credit basis, it assumes that the revenues and the expenses have been incurred. Although a sale is made on credit (and cash has not been received) or goods are purchased from suppliers on credit (and payment has not been made), the income statement shows the respective revenue and expense transactions in the appropriate accounts. The most important accounts that differentiate cash basis from accrual basis are the accounts receivable and accounts payable.

The main purpose of the accrual method is to obtain a measure of the results of business operations by allocating, to each fiscal period, the appropriate revenue and expense items. In accounting, this process is called "matching expenses with revenues." This concept is important in order to reflect, in a realistic way, the

Cash method

Accounting method of recording business transactions when sales are made and expenses incurred.

Accrual method

Accounting method that considers sales when made and expenses when incurred, regardless of when the transactions take place.

true income or profit generated by a business during a particular operating period.

Overview of Corporate Taxation in Canada

◀◼ Objective 8

Taxation is a topic that is far too complex to be addressed in just a few pages. The intent here is to provide some general understanding of corporate taxation in Canada related to corporate income tax rates, small business deductions, business expenses and deductions, business losses, and capital cost allowance.

In view of the fact that the *Income Tax Act* stipulates different treatment for public, private, and Canadian-controlled corporations, it is important to make the distinction between them. Essentially, a *public corporation* is one resident in Canada, with at least one class of its shares publicly traded in Canada. A *private corporation* is a corporation resident in Canada that is neither a public corporation nor controlled by one. Finally, a *Canadian-controlled private corporation* is a private corporation that meets two basic conditions. First, it was at one time a resident corporation and was either incorporated in Canada or resident here after June 18, 1971. Second, it is not controlled directly or indirectly by nonresident persons or by one or more public corporations or by any combination of nonresidents and public corporations.

Corporate Income Tax Rates

When calculating the combined federal and provincial taxes, several variations must be noted; any general figure applied arbitrarily can prove to be misleading. Provincial tax rates on corporate income vary significantly, and a number of abatements or special deductions exist. For instance, the deductions are particularly significant in the taxation of small business income, income derived from manufacturing and process operations in Canada, and income from production of minerals, oil, and gas.

Putting aside capital gains taxes, investment income, and temporary surtaxes, the general rate of corporate tax in Canada in the 48% range. When calculating taxes, businesses consider that the federal government grants an abatement of 10% to accommodate varying taxes imposed by each province. Thus, the combined federal and provincial tax is computed as follows:

Total tax payable = general tax rate of 39.12% on taxable income

Less: 10% of the corporation's taxable income earned in each province (abatement)

Plus: provincial taxes, with various rates applied against taxable income earned in particular provinces or territories.

Small Business Deductions

The net federal tax rate on eligible for small businesses is around 13%. Consider a small business that has the federal income rate reduced to 7% for qualifying small-business income in a particular province. A Canadian-controlled private corporation operating in that province would pay the following tax rate on its first $225,000 (eligible limit for 2003, which will increase to $300,000 by 2006) of taxable income:

General federal tax rate (including surtax)	39.12%
Less: Abatement for provincial tax	10.00
Net federal tax	29.12
Less: Small business deductions	16.00
Total federal tax	13.12
Assumed provincial tax	7.00
Total tax	20.12%

Note that the tax savings apply only on the first $225,000 of annual taxable income to active businesses in Canada.

BUSINESS EXPENSES AND DEDUCTIONS All operating expenses incurred by a business, such as salaries, purchases, advertising, etc., can be claimed against gross income, thereby reducing a business's taxable income.

Also, interest on debt is considered a business expense, and hence is generally deductible in calculating taxable business income. Rent and lease payments are also considered deductible business expenses. However, repayment of principal on a loan, and dividends on both common and preferred shares, are not deductible and are paid with after-tax income.

Business Losses

Business losses that took place during prior years are also tax deductible. For example, a company that incurred losses during the previous three years can carry forward that loss and deduct it from the income of the next seven years (through the filing of an amended return). The *Income Tax Act* provides detailed explanation of such tax-deductible losses.

A Noncash Tax-Deductible Expense

As will be covered in the following section, in arriving at taxable income, businesses may deduct capital cost allowances (CCA) on depreciable assets. Through capital cost allowances, provision is made for businesses to recover, over some time frame, the original amount invested without having to pay tax on the portion of the investments.

As a general rule, depreciable assets fall into one of over 30 asset classes defined for tax purposes. Maximum capital cost allowance rates, ranging from 4 to 100% per year, are prescribed for each class. For example, the CCA rate for general machinery, which falls in class 8, has a maximum rate of 20%, while buildings, which fall in class 1, show a maximum CCA rate of 4%. As the following section explains, these rates are applied against declining asset balances in each class.

Depreciation Methods, Capital Cost Allowance, and Amortization

◀ Objective 9

Depreciation is used to spread the cost of using a capital asset over a period of years, whereas capital cost allowance is used to calculate the amount of tax that should be paid in a given year. Amortization, like depreciation, is used for spreading the cost of an intangible asset over a period of years.

Depreciation

Depreciation is the estimated decrease in the book value of a capital asset, fixed asset, or long-lived asset, computed annually, for accounting purposes, over the estimated useful life of the asset. It has nothing to do with the market value of the asset. For example, a truck may last seven years; a building, 40 years; and furniture, 15 years. Although a truck may be purchased on a cash basis during a particular year, since it will be used for seven years, the business will apportion the cost over the useful life of that asset.

There are different ways of calculating depreciation. The two most widely used methods are the straight-line method and the sum-of-the-years'-digits method. Let's examine how these two depreciation methods are calculated.

Depreciation

Estimated decrease in the value of capital assets due to wear and tear and/or obsolescence.

Straight-Line Method

This method is the most widely used and the simplest to calculate. It allocates an equal portion of the capital asset to be depreciated each year over its estimated useful life. It is calculated as follows:

$$\text{Depreciation} = \frac{\text{Purchase cost} - \text{scrap/salvage value}}{\text{Estimated useful life in years}}$$

For example, if an asset costs $100,000 and has a useful life of five years and no salvage value, the yearly depreciation amount would be $20,000.

$$\text{Depreciation} = \frac{\$100,000}{5} = \$20,000$$

The yearly depreciation, the net asset book value, and the percentage-depreciated value of an asset are presented as follows:

Year	Depreciation	Net asset book value	% Depreciated
0	—	$100,000	0%
1	$ 20,000	80,000	20%
2	20,000	60,000	40%
3	20,000	40,000	60%
4	20,000	20,000	80%
5	20,000	—	100%
Total	$100,000		

Sum-of-the-Years'-Digits Method

This method is an accelerated way of calculating depreciation. It is based on the sum of the digits of the estimated life of an asset, which is used as the common denominator. The numerators of the fractions are the years in the asset's life. Using the same $100,000 cost to illustrate this method of calculation, the arithmetic works this way:

1. If the life of the asset is five years, each individual year would be listed as follows: 1, 2, 3, 4, and 5; if it is 10 years, the list would go from 1 to 10.
2. The sum-of-the-digits for each year would be added as follows: $1 + 2 + 3 + 4 + 5 = 15$.
3. A fraction is identified for each year as follows: 1/15, 2/15, 3/15, 4/15, and 5/15.

Each fraction, starting with the last year, is multiplied by the original $100,000 investment. The calculation to find the depreciation is therefore done in the following way:

$$\text{Cost} \times \frac{\text{Number of years of depreciation remaining}}{\text{Sum of total digits of the asset's useful life}}$$

Year	Fraction		Cost of the assets		Depreciation	Net book value	% Depreciated
1	5/15	×	$100,000	=	$ 33,333	$ 66,667	33.3%
2	4/15	×	100,000	=	26,667	40,000	60.0%
3	3/15	×	100,000	=	20,000	20,000	80.0%
4	2/15	×	100,000	=	13,333	6,667	93.3%
5	1/15	×	100,000	=	6,667	—	100.0%
Total					$100,000		

Capital cost allowance

A tax deduction that Canadian tax laws allow a business to claim for the loss in value of capital assets due to wear and tear and/or obsolescence.

Capital Cost Allowance

Whereas depreciation is a usage rate established by each individual business operator for the purpose of calculating income, **capital cost allowance (CCA)** is

Chapter 2: From Scorekeeping to Financial Statements

a rate established by Canada Customs and Revenue Agency that is used by all businesses for different categories of assets for the purpose of calculating income tax. The income tax regulations stipulate that all businesses must use these rates to calculate their income taxes, even though the same asset may become obsolete after five years in one business, but last 20 years in another business.

Irrespective of the rate of depreciation and method of depreciation used to calculate the income of a business, Canada Customs and Revenue Agency establishes a set of percentages for different categories or groups of capital assets. For example, automotive equipment falls under class 10, with a current rate of 30%. The calculation of the CCA is done on a declining basis similar to the sum-of-the-years'-digits method (CCA never brings down the value of the asset to zero.) The CCA allowance for each year is obtained by multiplying the maximum rate allowed (e.g., 50%) by the undepreciated balance. Using the $100,000 example, the capital cost allowance is calculated as follows:

Year	Value at beginning of year	CCA rate	CCA	Value at end of year
1	$ 100,000	50% ÷ 2*	$ 25,000	$ 75,000
2	75,000	50%	37,500	37,500
3	37,500	50%	18,750	18,750
4	18,750	50%	9,375	9,375
5	9,375	50%	4,687	4,688

* Income tax regulations allow only half of the CCA rate for the first year.

Amortization

Amortization is also a tax-deductible expense. It applies to intangible assets such as goodwill, patents, franchise fees, trademarks, legal and architectural fees, and research and development. Basically, amortization is to intangible assets what depreciation is to capital assets. The calculation is the same as CCA—that is, the declining method. For example, if a company buys another business that includes a $100,000 goodwill amount, the income tax regulations allow the amortization of this intangible asset over a period of years.

Amortization

A tax-deductible expense that applies to intangible assets such as goodwill and trademarks.

Deferred Taxes

◀ Objective 10

Because companies use depreciation rates that are different from the capital cost allowance rate allowed by governments to calculate income taxes, in many instances businesses pay less tax than they should, particularly during the first several years of the asset utilization. This means that the company owes taxes (liability) to the government. These are referred to as **deferred taxes.**

Deferred taxes

Future tax liability resulting from the difference between depreciation and capital cost allowance.

Using the $100,000 example, the five-year straight-line depreciation rate (equivalent to 20%), and the 50% CCA rate, the deferred taxes would be calculated as follows:

Years	CCA @ 50%	Internal depreciation @ 20%	Difference between CCA and depreciation	Difference in annual deferred taxes (tax rate @ 50%)	Difference in cumulative deferred taxes
1	$25,000	$20,000	$ 5,000	$2,500	−$ 2,500
2	$37,500	$20,000	$17,500	$8,750	−$11,250
3	$18,750	$20,000	−$ 1,250	−$ 625	−$10,625
4	$ 9,375	$20,000	−$10,625	−$5,312	−$ 5,313
5	$ 4,687	$20,000	−$15,313	−$7,656	—

With the above depreciation and CCA rates, let's now produce the first year's income statement. As shown in Table 2.6, depreciation is used as an expense. The first column, including CCA, is used to calculate the company's income taxes. Column 3 shows the company's "profit and loss statement" for the year when using the company's five-year depreciation rate (or 20%), while column 2 shows the company's "income statement." The depreciation expense, the income taxes paid in that year, and the amount of deferred taxes that the company owes to the government all appear in the statement. The income after taxes in columns 2 and 3 are the same ($40,000); the only difference between the two columns is the timing of payment of the taxes. The company paid $2,500 less in taxes this year due to a higher CCA rate. Therefore, the company owes this amount to the government in the form of deferred taxes. It is like an interest-free loan.

TABLE 2.6 THE INCOME STATEMENT AND THE PROFIT AND LOSS STATEMENT

	1 Accountant's Worksheet	2 Income Statement	3 P & L Statement
Revenue	$300,000	$300,000	$300,000
Cost of sales	150,000	150,000	150,000
Gross margin	150,000	150,000	150,000
Operating expenses	50,000	50,000	50,000
CCA/Depreciation	25,000	20,000 ←	20,000
Total expenses	75,000	70,000	70,000
Income before taxes	75,000	80,000	80,000
Taxes—Current (50%)	37,500 →	37,500	
—Deferred	2,500 →	2,500	40,000
	40,000	40,000	40,000
Income/profit after taxes	$ 35,000	$ 40,000	$ 40,000

Chapter 2: From Scorekeeping to Financial Statements

Income after Taxes versus Cash Flow

◀◀ Objective 11

We have defined **income** (or profit) as the excess of revenues over expenses. Income tells how efficient a business is. On the other hand, **cash flow** is the result of the income after tax plus depreciation. The calculation is relatively simple. If we refer to Table 2.3, Eastman's Income Statement, the cash flow calculation is done as follows:

Net income after taxes	$ 97,500
Depreciation	40,000
Cash flow	$137,500

Income

The excess of revenues over expenses.

Cash flow

Result of the income after taxes plus depreciation.

Depreciation is added to net income after taxes because it is the only expense item on the income statement that is not a cash outlay. Depreciation is nothing more than an accounting or book entry; it is not a cheque made out to "Depreciation Inc." or cash paid to someone called "Ms. Depreciation." Since depreciation is regarded as a book entry and not a cash outlay, it should be added to the net income after taxes to determine the true amount of cash that was generated by a business. In the case of Eastman, the cash inflow from operations in 2003 is $137,500.

Cash flow is important because it provides business operators and investors an idea of the debt repayment ability of the business. Sometimes cash flow can be even more important to a business than income; while the business may be losing money (income- or profit-wise), the owner may still have money or cash to pay its debts.

Some businesses make the mistake of paying for their current expenses with the cash generated by depreciation. Then, when the time comes to replace worn-out capital assets, there is not enough money to pay for them, and the business finds itself in trouble.

Different depreciation methods will result in different reported amounts of net income after tax and may, in some cases, produce different cash flows. As noted, there are different ways of calculating depreciation, and each method gives different amounts of depreciation for each year.

Working Capital

◀◀ Objective 12

Working capital includes the current accounts listed on the top of the balance sheet—current assets and current liabilities. Every account shown on the balance sheet labelled "current," such as cash, accounts receivable, notes receivable, accounts payable, and notes payable, is part of working capital. People often think of a business in terms of land, buildings, equipment, and machinery—its "hard assets"—but, in many industries, close to 50% of the assets are current assets. Many businesses go under because of poor working capital management— for example, carrying an inventory that is too large or financed at too high an interest rate. Working capital represents the focal point of the "operating cycle" of a business. Goods are sold for cash or on credit, and when the company

Working capital

Total current assets and total current liabilities.

collects its receivables from its customers, the cycle ends. For many businesses the control of working capital is the key to successful and profitable operation. The objective is to shorten the working capital cycle. By and large, the faster the cycle, the more profitable the business. Referring to Eastman's balance sheets in Table 2.5, working capital accounts include the following items:

Eastman Technologies Inc.
Working Capital for Period Ended December 31, 2003

Current assets		*Current liabilities*	
Cash	$ 22,000	Accounts payable	$195,000
Prepaid expenses	60,000	Notes payable	150,000
Accounts receivable	300,000	Accrued expenses	20,000
Inventory	218,000	Taxes payable	80,000
Total current assets	$600,000	Total current liabilities	$445,000

Net working capital is defined as the difference between current assets and current liabilities. Eastman's net working capital is computed as follows:

Current assets	$600,000
Current liabilities	445,000
Net working capital	$155,000

Working capital management means the management of individual current asset and current liability accounts to ensure that there is a good interrelationship between them. Because of the importance of working capital management, Chapter 11 is devoted entirely to this topic.

✳ Decision-Making in Action

The CEO of Oxford Manufacturing Inc. was reviewing the December 31, 2003, financial statements prepared by his controller. The controller confirmed that these financial statements were prepared in accordance to generally accepted accounting principles in order to make it easy for managers, lenders, owners, etc. to analyze and interpret their content to make enlightened decisions.

The CEO noticed that the income statement contained three levels of income: gross margin, operating income, and income after taxes. The first level of income (gross margin) shows how much profit was earned by Oxford after paying for the cost of manufacturing: that is, purchases, freight-in, and all other expenses related to producing goods. The second level

of income (operating income) shows the amount of profit that Oxford made after deducting, from sales revenue, all operating expenses (cost of goods sold and operating expenses). This is the level of income for which managers are accountable since they are directly responsible for making decisions related to sales revenue and operating expenses. These two income levels deal with the operating section of the income statement.

The third level of income (income after taxes) is in two sections. The first is referred to as the nonoperating section and shows how much other income and other expenses were added to (or deducted from) the operating income. Essentially, this section deals with all interest earned (or interest charges), nonrecurrent expenses, and extraordinary expenses. After deducting this amount from the operating income, the company is left with income before taxes. The second section of income is the owners' section, which shows how much income tax is deducted from income before taxes. The shareholders then decide what to do with this third level of income: pay dividends or reinvest it in the business in the form of retained earnings.

The CEO noticed that although Oxford earned a profit of $260,000, it generated $315,000 in cash ($260,000 + $55,000 for depreciation, which is a noncash expense).

OXFORD MANUFACTURING INC.
INCOME STATEMENT
FOR THE PERIOD ENDING DECEMBER 31, 2003

Sales revenue	$4,500,000		
Cost of goods sold	3,500,000		
Gross margin		**$1,000,000**	**Level 1**
Operating expenses			
Selling expenses	300,000		
Administrative expenses	200,000		
Depreciation	55,000		
Total operating expenses		555,000	
Operating income		**445,000**	**Level 2**
Other income	20,000		
Other expenses	35,000	15,000	
Income before taxes		430,000	
Income taxes		170,000	
Income after taxes		**$ 260,000**	**Level 3**

He also noticed that the second financial statement, the statement of retained earnings, had little value to his managers but showed important information about the amount of profit that had been invested back into Oxford since it was started. He noticed that as of January 1, 2003, a total of $1,100,000 had been reinvested in Oxford. During the operating year, $50,000 was paid out in dividends to shareholders and deducted from the $260,000 earnings (or income after taxes), and the balance of $210,000 was reinvested in Oxford. At the end of the operating year, Oxford had accumulated $1,310,000 in retained earnings. This same amount also appears in the current year's balance sheet under the heading Shareholders' Equity.

OXFORD MANUFACTURING INC.
STATEMENT OF RETAINED EARNINGS
FOR THE PERIOD ENDING DECEMBER 31, 2003

Retained earnings (beginning balance)		$1,100,000
Earnings for the year	$260,000	
Dividends	50,000	210,000
Retained earnings (ending balance)		$1,310,000

The third financial statement is the balance sheet. The CEO noticed that this financial statement was divided into two sections: what Oxford owns (assets) and what it owes to its creditors (liabilities) and shareholders (equity).

The asset section was further subdivided into three sections. The first grouping of accounts are current assets or those assets that can be converted into cash within the operating year. The second grouping of accounts are capital assets or those that are tangible, such as land, buildings, machinery, and equipment. Since these assets are used over an extended period of years, the original cost of the assets can be amortized (accumulated depreciation) over their respective useful lives. The worth of these tangible assets in the company books is recorded as net capital assets. The third grouping of accounts is intangible assets and includes goodwill, patents, etc.

Two groups of individuals finance the assets listed on the company's books: creditors and shareholders; hence the division of the liability and shareholders' side of the balance sheet into two sections: liabilities and shareholders' equity. The liability section also contains two subgroups, the first being current liabilities, which help finance current assets. These liabilities must be paid within the next operating year

OXFORD MANUFACTURING INC.
BALANCE SHEET
AS AT DECEMBER 31, 2003

Current assets		
Cash	$ 35,000	
Marketable securities	50,000	
Prepaid expenses	30,000	
Accounts receivable	450,000	
Inventory	750,000	
Total current assets		$1,315,000
Capital assets (at cost)	2,450,000	
Accumulated depreciation	650,000	
Capital assets (net)		1,800,000
Intangible assets		65,000
Total assets		**$3,180,000**
Current liabilities		
Accounts payable	$ 130,000	
Accrued expenses	50,000	
Current portion of long-term debt	40,000	
Working capital loan	350,000	
Total current liabilities		570,000
Long-term debts		900,000
Total liabilities		**1,470,000**
Shareholders' equity		
Capital shares	400,000	
Retained earnings	1,310,000	
Total shareholders' equity		**1,710,000**
Total liabilities and shareholders' equity		**$3,180,000**

Chapter Summary

Bookkeeping and accounting are the touchstones of business information, which is essential for managers to plan and control their operations. Bookkeeping and accounting activities provide managers with the right kind of information at the right time.

◀◀ Objective 1

Bookkeeping involves collecting, classifying, and reporting transactions taking place each day in different departments of a business. Each time a business transaction takes place, at least two accounts are affected; this is referred to as double-entry bookkeeping. In its simplest form, the financial picture of a business can be expressed by the following formula:

◀◀ Objective 2

Assets = Liabilities + Equity

The chapter reviewed three key financial statements. The *income statement* presents the operating results; that is, revenues and expenses and income for a given period of time. The *statement of retained earnings* shows the changes that take place in retained earnings during a given fiscal period. It shows the income that was added to the earnings, the dividends paid, and the retained earnings at the end of the fiscal period. The *balance sheet*, which describes a company's financial position at a given moment in time, contains a list of the assets (what a company owns), liabilities (creditors that have a claim on the assets), and owners' equity (owners who also have a claim on the assets).

◀◀ Objective 3

Canadian federal corporate law requires that every federally incorporated limited company appoint an auditor to represent shareholders and report to them annually on the company's financial statements.

◀◀ Objective 4

Once the financial statements have been drawn up, the information can be analyzed and interpreted. Some of the more popular analytical tools include the statement of changes in financial position, horizontal and vertical analysis, ratio analysis and break-even analysis.

◀◀ Objective 5

Decision-making is the process of using information for the purpose of improving the financial performance of a business. Some of the more important decisions

◀◀ Objective 6

made by managers include the following: How much money should we borrow? Should we buy or lease? Should we invest in this project? What level of risk does this project present?

Objective 7 ▶ There are two accounting methods: the *cash method*, which recognizes revenue and expenses when cash or its equivalent is received or disbursed; and the *accrual method*, which records revenue when goods are sold or services rendered, and when expenses are incurred.

Objective 8 ▶ Corporate income tax rates, small business deductions, business expenses and deductions, business losses, and capital cost allowance are all important to businesses.

Objective 9 ▶ *Depreciation* is an estimated decrease in the value of capital or long-lived assets. There are several ways of calculating depreciation, and the chapter presented two: the straight-line method and the sum-of-the-years'-digits method. These methods are used by individual business operators for the purpose of calculating income. *Capital cost allowance* is the rate of depreciation established by Canada Customs and Revenue Agency and is used by all businesses for calculating their income taxes. *Amortization* is a rate used for allocating the cost of an intangible asset over a period of years.

Objective 10 ▶ Because companies use depreciation rates that are different from the capital cost allowance rate allowed by governments to calculate income taxes, in many instances businesses pay less tax than they should, particularly during the first several years of the asset utilization. This means that the company owes taxes (liability) to the government. These are referred to as deferred taxes.

Objective 11 ▶ Income after taxes (or profit) is defined as the excess of revenues over expenses. Income after taxes tells you how efficient a business is. Cash flow is the result of the income after taxes plus depreciation.

Objective 12 ▶ Working capital includes all items in the current asset and current liability accounts of a balance sheet. Net working capital is the difference between current assets and current liabilities.

Key Terms

Accounting	Auditor's report
Accounting cycle	Balance sheet
Accounting equation	Bookkeeping
Accrual method	Capital cost allowance
Administrative expenses	Cash flow
Amortization	Cash method
Assets	Chart of accounts

Cost of goods sold

Credit

Current assets

Current liabilities

Debit

Deferred taxes

Depreciation

Double-entry bookkeeping

Financial statements

Generally accepted accounting principles (GAAP)

Income

Income statement

Intangible assets

Investments

Journalizing

Liabilities

Long-term debts

Net sales

Nonoperating section

Operating section

Owners' section

Posting

Retained earnings

Selling expenses

Shareholders' equity

Statement of retained earnings

Trial balance

Working capital

Review Questions

1. What are financial statements and what do they include?

2. What activities are involved in bookkeeping?

3. Explain the accounting equation.

4. What are journals and ledgers?

5. What is the purpose of a trial balance?

6. Explain the different sections of the income statement.

7. What does the statement of retained earnings show?

8. What is the connection between the statement of retained earnings and the balance sheet?

9. What is the basic structure of the balance sheet?

10. Differentiate between current assets and capital assets.

11. What are the four sections included in the statement of changes in financial position?

12. What is the purpose of the auditor's report?

13. Differentiate between cash accounting and accrual accounting.

14. What are deferred taxes?

15. Differentiate between income after taxes and cash flow.

16. Explain the meaning of working capital.

17. What is the difference between depreciation and capital cost allowance?

Discussion Questions

1. Is there a difference between the book value of accounts shown on the balance sheet and market value? Explain.

2. Why is the management of working capital so important to the success of a business?

3. Why do you think auditors write in a company's annual report the following statement: "These consolidated financial statements are the responsibility of the company's management. Our responsibility is to express an opinion on these consolidated financial statements based on our audits"?

Testing Your Comprehension

True/False Questions

_F_ 1. Business transactions are first recorded in the ledgers.

_T_ 2. The accounting equation reads as follows: A = L + E

_F_ 3. The word "debit" refers to an entry recorded on the right side of an account.

_T_ 4. A debit takes place when there is an increase in an asset account.

_T_ 5. Journals are sometimes referred to as the books of original entry.

_F_ 6. The trial balance shows only the balance sheet accounts.

_F_ 7. The function of bookkeeping governs the way the four financial statements will be prepared.

_T_ 8. The gross margin is the difference between sales revenue and cost of goods sold.

_F_ 9. Interest earned from investment in securities is recorded in the sales revenue account.

_T_ 10. Operating income is calculated by deducting operating expenses from the gross margin.

_F_ 11. Dividends are recorded as an expense in the nonoperating section of the income statement.

_T_ 12. Retained earnings shows the amount of funds that have been retained in the business since it started.

_T_ 13. Assets can be tangible or intangible.

_F_ 14. Intangible assets are accounts appearing as current assets in the balance sheet.

_T_ 15. Prepaid expenses are payments made on accounts for which services have not yet been received.

_F_ 16. Capital assets usually appreciate in a company's balance sheet.

_T_ 17. Current liabilities include accounts such as accounts payable and accrued liability.

_F_ 18. Canadian federal corporate law requires that every limited company appoint a controller to represent shareholders and report to them annually on the company's financial statements.

___T___ 19. Accrual accounting methods disregard the receipt and disbursements of cash.

___F___ 20. Capital cost allowance is an internal method used to spread the cost of using a capital asset over its useful life.

___T___ 21. Capital cost allowance is usually calculated on a declining basis.

___F___ 22. A deferred tax is usually shown on the balance sheet as an asset.

___F___ 23. You can calculate a company's cash flow by adding depreciation to income before taxes.

___T___ 24. Net working capital is the difference between current assets and current liabilities.

Multiple-Choice Questions

1. The accounting equation reads as follows:
   a. A = L − E
   b. L = E + A
   c. A = L − E
   d. A = L + E
   e. E = A + L

2. The following is considered a debit transaction:
   a. increase in the accounts receivable account
   b. decrease in the accounts receivable account
   c. decrease in the inventory account
   d. increase in the revenue account
   e. decrease in the selling expense account

3. Gross margin is the difference between:
   a. net sales and operating expenses
   b. operating income and operating expenses
   c. gross margin and operating expenses
   d. net sales and cost of goods sold
   e. operating income and cost of goods sold

4. Operating income is calculated by deducting:
   a. cost of goods sold from operating income
   b. cost of goods sold from income before taxes
   c. operating expenses from income before taxes
   d. operating expenses from gross margin
   e. operating expenses from sales revenue

5. Dividends are deducted from:
   a. income after taxes
   b. sales revenue
   c. operating income
   d. income before taxes
   e. accumulated retained dividends

6. The following is considered a current asset:
   a. prepaid liability
   b. prepaid expenses
   c. accrued asset
   d. prepaid income
   e. accrued liability

7. Marketable securities are usually part of the:
   a. current liability accounts
   b. retained earnings accounts
   c. revenue accounts
   d. current asset accounts
   e. capital asset accounts

8. The following is a current liability account:
   a. mortgage
   b. accrued expenses
   c. prepaid expenses
   d. investment securities
   e. intangible liability

9. Payments made on accounts for which services have not yet been received are called:
   a. prepaid liabilities
   b. deferred liabilities
   c. accrued liabilities
   d. accrued expenses
   e. prepaid expenses

10. Goodwill is considered:
    a. a fixed asset
    b. a deferred asset
    c. an intangible asset
    d. a current asset
    e. a prepaid asset

11. Retained earnings represent:
    a. current assets
    b. fixed assets
    c. income generated by a business
    d. deferred income reinvested in current assets
    e. earnings paid to shareholders

12. Capital cost allowance is:
    a. Canada Custom and Revenue Agency's equivalent of accumulated depreciation
    b. used to calculate the book value of capital assets
    c. used to calculate the residual value of fixed assets

    d. Canada Custom and Revenue Agency's equivalent of depreciation
    e. used to calculate retained earnings

13. Deferred taxes is a result of the difference between:
    a. CCA and current assets
    b. accumulated depreciation and depreciation
    c. CCA and accumulated depreciation
    d. revenue and accumulated earnings
    e. CCA and depreciation

14. You can calculate a company's cash flow by adding:
    a. accumulated depreciation to income after taxes
    b. depreciation to income after taxes
    c. income from operations to interest income
    d. depreciation to income before taxes
    e. depreciation expense to gross margin

15. The difference between current assets and current liabilities is called:
    a. fixed assets
    b. operating assets
    c. intangible assets
    d. working capital
    e. operating profit

Fill-in-the-Blanks Questions

1. _____ is the process of transferring recorded transactions from the journals to the appropriate ledger accounts (e.g., sales revenue, accounts receivable).

2. The _____ balance is a statement that ensures that the general ledger is in balance (debit transactions = credit transactions).

3. The _____ section of the income statement shows a company's gross margin and operating income.

4. The _____ section of the income statement shows income or expenses that are not directly related to the principal activities of a business (e.g., interest income).

5. _____ listed on the balance sheet are resources that a business owns to produce goods and services.

6. The shareholders' equity of the balance sheet generally shows two basic accounts: common shares and _____.

7. _____ liabilities are debts that a business must pay within one year.

8. _____ assets are items shown on a balance sheet such as trademarks, goodwill, franchises, and patents.

9. An _____ liability account represents what a company owes for services it has received and not yet paid or an expense that has been incurred but not recorded.

10. The _____ report is prepared by an independent accounting firm and then presented to a company's shareholders.

Learning Exercises

Exercise 1(a)

After opening their computer sales and services store, the Millers went through the following four transactions. They:

1. invested $100,000 in cash in the business;

2. purchased on credit $10,000 worth of goods from several suppliers;

3. sold on a cash basis $13,000 worth of products and services; and

4. paid $3,000 for salaries.

    With the above information, prepare the following:

1. the journal entries;

2. the ledgers; and

3. the trial balance.

Exercise 1(b)

Jim Benson opens a retail store called The Bead Shop. During the first month of operation, Jim goes through the following accounting transactions:

1. invests $100,000 in cash in the business;

2. buys $50,000 worth of equipment on credit he obtained from the bank;

3. buys $60,000 worth of goods from different suppliers, pays $30,000 in cash, and puts the rest on credit;

4. spends $5,000 in cash for advertising;

5. sells $20,000 worth of goods on credit;

6. pays $15,000 in cash for salaries;

7. pays $10,000 to the bank toward the loan;

8. pays $5,000 to a supplier;

9. pays $13,000 for some merchandise that he had purchased on credit; and

10. pays a salary of $3,000.

Chapter 2: From Scorekeeping to Financial Statements

With the above transactions, prepare the following:

1. the journal entries;

2. the ledgers; and

3. the trial balance.

Exercise 2(a)

At the end of December 31, 2003, CompuTech's accounts are as follows:

Purchases	$ 175,000
Salaries	80,000
Advertising	3,000
Travelling	2,000
Sales revenue	350,000
Interest charges	10,000
Freight-in	2,000
Income taxes	13,000
Sales commissions	2,000
Depreciation	38,000

With the above accounts, prepare CompuTech's income statement for the period ending December 31, 2003.

Exercise 2(b)

At the end of December 31, 2003, Cougar Inc.'s accounts are as follows:

Office salaries	$ 30,000
Interest expenses	3,000
Depreciation (administration)	2,000
Cost of goods sold	300,000
Income taxes	35,000
Sales salaries	40,000
Interest income	6,000
Gross sales revenue	520,000
Advertising	10,000
Office supplies	3,000
Promotional expenses	2,000
Sales discounts	20,000
Travel expenses	3,000
Rental charges	5,000

With the above accounts, prepare Cougar's income statement for the period ending December 31, 2003.

Exercise 3(a)

At the end of December 31, 2003, CompuTech's accounts are as follows:

Accounts receivable	$35,000
Cash	10,000
Term loan	35,000
Capital shares	100,000
Long-term debt	60,000
Marketable securities	5,000
Gross capital assets	170,000
Prepaid expenses	5,000
Retained earnings	25,000
Accumulated depreciation	38,000
Accounts payable	17,000
Inventory	50,000

With the above accounts, prepare CompuTech's balance sheet as at December 31, 2003.

Exercise 3(b)

At the end of December 31, 2003, Cougar Inc.'s accounts are as follows:

Accumulated depreciation	$ 100,000
Taxes payable	5,000
Bank loan (long-term)	25,000
Inventory	90,000
Accounts receivable	60,000
Capital assets (at cost)	300,000
Accounts payable	40,000
Mortgage	130,000
Accrued expenses	10,000
Deferred taxes	5,000
Common shares	100,000
Prepaid expenses	10,000
Intangible assets	20,000
Cash	25,000
Retained earnings	80,000
Term loan	10,000

With the above accounts, prepare Cougar Inc.'s balance sheet as at December 31, 2003.

Exercise 4(a)

On its balance sheet, CompuTech shows equipment purchased for $125,000 and a vehicle purchased for $35,000.

The rate of depreciation and capital cost allowance for the above capital assets are as follows:

	Depreciation	Capital cost allowance
1. Equipment	25%	40%
2. Vehicle	20%	30%

For the first five years of operation, calculate the amount of depreciation and capital cost allowance for the above-mentioned capital assets.

Exercise 4(b)

On its balance sheet, Singh's Auto Centre shows buildings purchased for $700,000, equipment purchased for $350,000, and machinery purchased for $170,000.

The rate of depreciation and capital cost allowance for the above capital assets are as follows:

	Depreciation	Capital cost allowance
1. Buildings	5%	7%
2. Equipment	20%	25%
3. Machinery	15%	30%

For the first five years of operation, calculate the amount of depreciation and capital cost allowance for the above-mentioned capital assets.

Exercise 5(a)

By using the information contained in exercises 2(a) and 4(a) calculate CompuTech's:

1. deferred taxes during the first five years; and

2. income statement using year 2 of the CCA and depreciation rates.

Exercise 5(b)

ABC Inc.'s sales revenue and expenses for 2003 amounted to the following:

Sales revenue	$500,000
Cost of goods sold	300,000
Gross margin	200,000
Operating expenses	100,000

The company's balance sheet shows the gross value of a capital asset worth $100,000. The company's depreciation rate for the asset is 15%, and Canada Customs and Revenue Agency's capital cost allowance is 30%. The company's income tax rate is 50%.

On the basis of the above information:

1. Calculate the company's deferred taxes during the first five years.

2. Prepare the income statement using year 2 of the CCA and depreciation rates.

Exercise 6

An accountant employed by Zimmerman's Electronics Inc. was reviewing the following balances shown in the company's ledgers:

Mortgage	$80,000	Interest charges	$10,000
Prepaid insurance	2,000	Land	25,000
Marketable securities	5,000	Office salaries	70,000
Sales returns	50,000	Common shares	15,000
Cash	5,000	Supplies	20,000
Advertising	50,000	Insurance	10,000
Accounts receivable	15,000	Depreciation	20,000
Gross sales	650,000	Income taxes	10,000
Accounts payable	12,000	Dividend payments	10,000
Buildings (net)	100,000	Interest income	15,000
Cost of goods sold	300,000	Inventory	20,000
Notes payable	10,000	Sales salaries	100,000
Retained earnings (December 31, 2002)	40,000		

1. With the above account balances, prepare the following financial statements:
   a) income statement;
   b) statement of retained earnings; and
   c) balance sheet.

2. Calculate the company's cash flow for the year.

3

Analyzing Changes in Financial Statements

Learning Objectives

After reading this chapter, you should be able to:

1. Explain why it is important to examine the changes in the flow of funds in financial statements.

2. Identify the key elements of funds flow.

3. Analyze funds flow by comparing two consecutive balance sheets.

4. State the basic rules that can be used to identify funds flow.

5. Explain the statement of changes in financial position.

Chapter Outline

OPENING CASE

In February 2003, Len and Joan started their computer retail business. During the first several months of operations, sales objectives were realized, and operating expenses were in line with their budget. As part of their original plans, Len and Joan considered opening up a new retail outlet. In fact, the Millers were thinking of opening several retail outlets in different cities over the next ten years. They understood, however, that in any start-up venture, business survival was critical. They realized that any cash invested in CompuTech had to "return a suitable level of profit." They understood that some of the cash required to open new retail stores would have to come from their existing business. They remembered Bill Murray's comments that in order to maintain stability, they should not only rely on cash from lenders as a source of growth funds but also generate cash from internal operations (profit). As far as the Millers were concerned, the key was to minimize expenses during the first few years of operations and put a reasonable amount of cash into products and services in order to generate profitable sales revenue.

The Millers' goal for 2003 and 2004 was to develop a good understanding of the computer retail business in terms of customer needs, supplier arrangements, and day-to-day operating activities. They understood the importance of cash flow. They had often heard from course instructors and long-time business entrepreneurs that "cash is king." They remembered their instructor's comment that having the money when you need it is as important as being able to predict when you'll get it.

In line with their cash flow philosophy, the Millers did not want to open a new retail outlet until 2005. They realized after speaking with various lenders that financing choices to expand their business quickly, particularly for a successful business venture, were extensive, and the terms and conditions could be varied. Their cash flow strategy was to generate as much cash as possible from CompuTech during 2003 and 2004, invest a minimal amount of funds for the purchase of equipment during these two years, and reduce their debt in order to prepare themselves for future growth.

The Millers' longer-term plan was to open a new retail outlet in 2005, estimated to cost around $350,000. In light of their investment plan, they had to implement a cash flow strategy that could lead them successfully toward their expansion program. They wanted to ensure that they had a balanced financing package for their goal of a 20%

increase in sales revenue for 2004 and 90% in 2005. The following summarizes CompuTech's key financial figures. As shown, the investment in capital assets is expected to be minimal in 2004 (only $40,000) with a substantial increase ($350,000) in 2005. To pay for these investments, the Millers would have to obtain cash from their operations. Part of the cash would come from income after taxes and depreciation in the amount of $73,000 and $157,000 for the years 2004 and 2005 respectively, and lenders would fund $150,000 in 2005. Appendix A (at the end of the book) presents CompuTech's financial statements, the income statements, the statements of retained earnings and the balance sheets for the years 2003 to 2005.

(in $000s)	2003	2004	2005
Sales revenue	$350	$420	$800
Income after taxes and depreciation	63	73	$157
Investment in capital assets	$170	40	350
Long-term loans	$ 60	−$ 10	$150

This chapter examines the concepts related to the management of cash flow. In particular, it focuses on three key topics:

1. What do we mean by cash (or funds) flow?

2. What is considered a source of funds and a use of funds?

3. What is the meaning of the statement of changes in financial position, and how can it be read?

Introduction

The previous chapter examined the contents and structure of the income statement, the statement of retained earnings, and the balance sheet. As indicated:

- The *income statement* is like a movie in that it shows the amount of revenue earned and expenses incurred between two dates or during a given time period.

- The *statement of retained earnings* tells how much profit or income has been accumulated by a business since it began its operations, the income it earned (drawn from the income statement) during the current operating year, the amount of dividends paid to its shareholders (also during the current operating year), and the amount of income retained in the business.

- The *balance sheet*, like a snapshot, gives a picture of what a business owns as well as what the business owes to creditors and to the owner(s) at a given point in time.

These three financial statements have a specific purpose, giving important information about the financial performance and financial condition of a business. However, they do not show the funds flow or cash flow that takes place between two consecutive accounting periods; the *statement of changes in financial position* (also called the statement of cash flows) does that.

To illustrate the meaning of change, let's examine six accounts drawn from, say, Judy's balance sheets for 2002 and 2003. As shown, the two columns give a picture of what Judy owns and what she owes at the end of these two accounting periods. You cannot tell what changes took place if you look at only one column or one year. But if you place the accounts of two consecutive balance sheets side by side, you can readily observe the changes. That is why this financial statement is called the statement of *changes* in financial position.

	2003	*2002*	*Sources*	*Uses*
1. Bank loan	$ 20,000	$ 5,000	$15,000	—
2. Mortgage	140,000	100,000	40,000	—
3. Visa	2,000	1,000	1,000	—
4. Watch	1,000	—	—	1,000
5. Car	30,000	5,000	—	25,000
6. House	$180,000	$150,000	—	$30,000
Total			$56,000	$56,000

Let's examine the meaning and the significance of these changes. As shown, in 2002 Judy owed $5,000 to the bank; in 2003, she owed $20,000. This change means that Judy borrowed an additional $15,000 from the bank in 2003. Because she borrowed money, this is a change called a **source of funds**. To find out what she did with the money, we have to look at other balance sheet accounts; these will be identified later. Also, the mortgage account shows a $40,000 increase between the two accounting periods (from $100,000 to $140,000). This means that Judy borrowed an additional amount from a mortgage company. This loan is also considered a source. Again, we're not sure yet what Judy did with these funds. Furthermore, Judy's Visa account shows a $1,000 increase. Again, Judy borrowed an extra $1,000 on her credit card. The changes in these three accounts show that Judy pocketed or took in $56,000 in cash. Now, let's see what she did with this cash.

By examining the other balance sheet accounts, we see that Judy purchased a $1,000 watch because the 2002 watch account on the balance sheet had a nil balance, and a $1,000 amount is shown in 2003. This acquisition is considered a purchase and therefore a **use of funds**. We can assume that Judy took the $1,000 amount borrowed from Visa to make that purchase. Also in 2003, Judy's car account increased by $25,000. In 2002 this account showed $5,000, which increased to $30,000 in 2003. This means that Judy purchased a car. We can assume that she used the bank loan ($15,000) and some of the mortgage money ($40,000) to buy the car. Also in 2003, Judy had a $30,000 solarium installed in her house. As shown, in 2002, Judy's house account was $150,000; it increased to

Source of funds

Cash that is obtained from different sources (e.g., obtaining a loan, selling an asset).

Use of funds

Cash that is disbursed or expended for buying or paying something (e.g., paying a mortgage, buying a car).

Chapter 3: Analyzing Changes in Financial Statements

$180,000 in 2003. In order to make this addition to her house, she must have used what was left over from the mortgage funds after the car purchase.

We can see from these simple examples the changes in various accounts that took place between Judy's two accounting periods; that is, where she got the money from and where it went. Judy obtained $56,000 from three different sources (bank loan, mortgage, and Visa) and used it to buy a watch and a car, and to add a solarium to her house.

Why Examine Change in the Flow of Funds?

◀ Objective 1

Financial analysts, lenders, investors, and managers are interested in changes taking place in business activities from year to year. They want to know where funds are coming from and what they are being spent on. More importantly, they want to know how much the company will spend in future years and from which sources it will secure the funds.

This type of analysis and decision-making process brings management to the heart of financial management: the procurement and allocation of funds, also known as the management of **funds flow**. Changes in various balance sheet accounts indicate the net flow of funds resulting from management decisions. The fourth financial statement (statement of changes in financial position) shows the amount of funds invested (uses or application of funds) in working capital accounts and capital asset accounts and where these funds are coming from (sources of funds).

Funds flow

The procurement (source) or allocation (use) of funds.

Figure 1.4 in Chapter 1 illustrates this point. It shows that a business purchased $1 million worth of assets (investing activities). Half of the funds used to finance these investments came from internal sources (operating activities) and the other half from external sources (financing activities) such as shareholders and long-term lenders.

To understand, let's examine two consecutive balance sheets (as at December 31) of two individuals, John Goodboy (Table 3.1) and John Badboy (Table 3.2). Table 3.1 shows that John Goodboy obtained $21,000 from different sources and used $21,000 to purchase different assets and to pay several loans.

On the "source" or "came from" side, it shows that John cashed in a term deposit and borrowed a little from The Bay, Sears, and the Royal Bank. However, the major portion ($16,400) of his "source money" came from equity. This is the surplus (like profit) that John had left over from his salary after paying off the living expenses he incurred during the year. For example, he could have earned $60,000 in salary and spent $43,600 for living expenses (e.g., rent, food, entertainment, hydro).

On the "use" or "went" side, John deposited money in his savings account, bought some furniture, a car, and a trailer, and made some small renovations to his house. In addition, he paid off part of his debts to MasterCard, his brother-in-law, and Royal Trust.

TABLE 3.1   BALANCE SHEET OF JOHN GOODBOY

	2003	2002	Where the money Came from	Where the money Went
Assets				
Cash in bank	$ 3,000	$ 1,000	—	$ 2,000
Term deposits	1,000	2,000	$ 1,000	—
Furniture	4,000	2,000	—	2,000
Car	9,000	6,000	—	3,000
House	70,000	68,000	—	2,000
Trailer	8,000	—	—	8,000
Total Assets	**$95,000**	**$79,000**		
Liabilities				
MasterCard	$ 1,000	$ 2,000	—	1,000
The Bay	1,000	500	500	—
Sears	900	800	100	—
Brother-in-law	1,000	2,000	—	1,000
Royal Bank	5,000	2,000	3,000	—
Royal Trust	48,000	50,000	—	2,000
Total Liabilities	**56,900**	**57,300**		
Equity	**38,100**	**21,700**	16,400	—
Total Liabilities and Equity	**$95,000**	**$79,000**	**$21,000**	**$21,000**

TABLE 3.2   BALANCE SHEET OF JOHN BADBOY

	2003	2002	Where the money Came from	Where the money Went
Assets				
Cash in bank	$ 100	$ 1,000	$ 900	—
Term deposits	—	2,000	2,000	—
Furniture	4,000	2,000	—	$ 2,000
Car	12,000	6,000	—	6,000
House	78,000	68,000	—	10,000
Trailer	10,000	—	—	10,000
Total Assets	**$104,100**	**$79,000**		
Liabilities				
MasterCard	$ 6,000	$ 2,000	4,000	—
The Bay	2,000	500	1,500	—
Sears	3,000	800	2,200	—
Brother-in-law	3,000	2,000	1,000	—
Royal Bank	4,000	2,000	2,000	—
Royal Trust	63,400	50,000	13,400	—
Total Liabilities	**81,400**	**57,300**		
Equity	**22,700**	**21,700**	1,000	—
Total Liabilities and Equity	**$104,100**	**$79,000**	**$28,000**	**$28,000**

FIGURE 3.1   JOHN GOODBOY'S SOURCES AND USES OF
              FUNDS

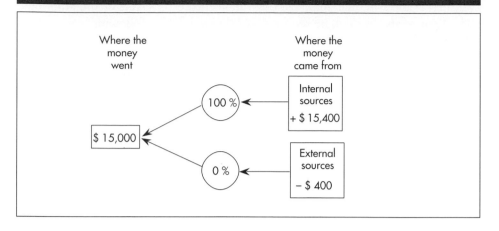

As shown in Table 3.1, John actually spent $15,000 to buy different assets: some furniture ($2,000), a car ($3,000), renovations to his house ($2,000), and a trailer ($8,000).

Figure 3.1 and the following show what John Goodboy had to do to finance the purchase of these four assets valued at $15,000. An amount of $15,400 came from his personal funding, called internal sources, such as cash in the bank and the surplus he had left over from his salary after paying off his living expenses. Even though John was able to purchase $15,000 worth of assets, he had enough to reduce his overall outstanding debt by $400.

Internal financing	Sources	Uses	Difference
Cash in the bank	—	$2,000	
Term deposits	$ 1,000	—	
Equity	16,400	—	
Total	$17,400	$2,000	+$15,400
External financing (Debt)			
MasterCard	—	1,000	
The Bay	500	—	
Sears	100	—	
Brother-in-law	—	1,000	
Royal Bank	3,000	—	
Royal Trust	—	2,000	
Total	$ 3,600	$4,000	−$ 400
Sources—Grand Total			+$15,000

John Badboy's financial position, shown in Table 3.2, gives a different picture. The asset accounts show an increase of $25,100 between 2003 and 2002, to $104,100, with a corresponding total increase in the liability and equity accounts.

This is $9,100 ($104,100 − $95,000 or $25,100 − $16,000) more than John Goodboy's $95,000 amount in total assets for 2003. The main difference, however, lies in the way that John Badboy financed the purchase of the additional $25,100 in assets. In total, he required $28,000 to buy the following: some furniture ($2,000), a car ($6,000), installation of new windows in his house ($10,000), and a trailer ($10,000).

As shown, John Badboy's sources of funds to buy these different assets were obtained from creditors such as MasterCard, The Bay, Sears, his brother-in-law, Royal Bank, and Royal Trust.

The following shows what John Badboy had to do to finance these four assets valued at $28,000. As shown, $3,900 came from his own personal funding while $24,100 came from external sources or lenders.

Internal financing	Sources	Uses	Difference
Cash in the bank	$ 900	—	
Term deposits	2,000	—	
Equity	1,000	—	
Total	$ 3,900	—	+$ 3,900
External financing (Debt)			
MasterCard	$ 4,000	—	
The Bay	1,500	—	
Sears	2,200	—	
Brother-in-law	1,000	—	
Royal Bank	2,000	—	
Royal Trust	13,400	—	
Total	$24,100		+$24,100
Sources—Grand Total			+$28,000

As shown above and in Figure 3.2, in order to buy these assets John Badboy obtained almost all ($24,100, or 86.1%) of the funds from external sources. Only $3,900 was generated internally, by withdrawing money from his bank and term deposits, and a small amount of equity from a surplus between his salary and living expenses. John Badboy is spending almost every dollar he earns! If he continues this practice, he will soon find himself in a severe financial crunch.

Objective 2 ➠

Key Elements of Funds Flow

As shown in Table 3.3, the more important sources of funds are income from operations, sale of capital assets, sale of investment securities, increase in long-term debts, increase in capital shares, and decrease in working capital such as accounts receivable and inventory. Uses or application of funds take place when a company experiences an operating loss, purchases capital assets, buys investment securities, reduces its long-term debt, decreases its capital shares, increases its working capital (e.g., accounts receivable or inventory), and pays dividends.

FIGURE 3.2   JOHN BADBOY'S SOURCES AND USES OF FUNDS

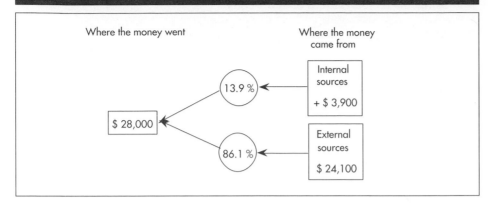

TABLE 3.3   KEY ELEMENTS OF FUNDS FLOW

Sources of Funds	Uses of Funds
• Income from operations	• Loss from operations
• Sale of capital assets	• Purchase of capital assets
• Sale of investment securities	• Purchase of investment securities
• Increase in long-term debts	• Decrease in long-term debts
• Increase in capital shares	• Decrease in capital shares
• Decrease in working capital	• Increase in working capital
	• Pay dividends

Comparing Consecutive Balance Sheets

Table 3.4 presents Eastman Technologies Inc.'s **consecutive balance sheets** for 2003 and 2002 (as at December 31). By placing these two balance sheets side by side, we can analyze Eastman's sources and uses of funds, or the changes that took place between these two accounting periods.

Table 3.4 presents a list of all sources and uses of funds in Eastman's major accounts listed under assets, liabilities, and equity. The table shows how the changes in financial condition emerged in Eastman's consecutive balance sheets. Eastman obtained $352,000 from different sources and used the same amount to purchase assets and increase some of the working capital accounts (these current asset and current liability accounts are shaded). In the next section we will analyze the significance and meaning of each change in cash flow shown in Eastman's financial statements. First, however, let's look at how the changes between two consecutive balance sheets can be interpreted just by following some simple guidelines.

◀ Objective 3

Consecutive balance sheets

Balance sheets from consecutive periods show whether a change in each account is a source or a use.

TABLE 3.4   COMPARATIVE BALANCE SHEETS FOR 2003 AND 2002

Eastman Technologies Inc.
Statement of Sources and Uses of Funds

Assets	2003	2002	Sources	Uses
Current assets				
Cash	$ 22,000	$ 18,000	—	$ 4,000
Prepaid expenses	60,000	55,000	—	5,000
Accounts receivable	300,000	280,000	—	20,000
Inventory	218,000	185,000	—	33,000
Total current assets	600,000	538,000		
Capital assets (at cost)	1,340,000	1,050,000	—	290,000
Accumulated depreciation	140,000	100,000	40,000	—
Capital assets (net)	1,200,000	950,000		
Total assets	$1,800,000	$1,488,000		
Liabilities				
Current liabilities				
Accounts payable	$ 195,000	$ 175,000	20,000	—
Notes payable	150,000	135,000	15,000	—
Accrued expenses	20,000	18,000	2,000	—
Taxes payable	80,000	70,000	10,000	—
Total current liabilities	445,000	398,000		
Long-term debts	800,000	600,000	200,000	—
Common shares	300,000	285,000	15,000	—
Retained earnings	255,000	205,000	50,000	—
Owners' equity	555,000	490,000		
Total liabilities and equity	$1,800,000	$1,488,000	$352,000	$352,000

Rules That Can Be Used to Identify Funds Flow

Objective 4 ➡

Rules of sources of funds

A source of funds takes place when there is a decrease in an asset account or an increase in a liability or equity account.

Rules of uses of funds

A use of funds takes place when there is an increase in an asset account or a decrease in a liability or equity account.

Sources of funds and uses (or applications) of funds are associated with specific types of changes in a balance sheet. Figure 3.3 shows the **rules** to follow to determine whether an asset, liability, or equity account is a source or a use.

Sources of funds take place when there is:

- a decrease in asset accounts;
- an increase in liability accounts; or
- an increase in the owners' equity accounts (capital or retained earnings increase due to income from operations).

Chapter 3: Analyzing Changes in Financial Statements

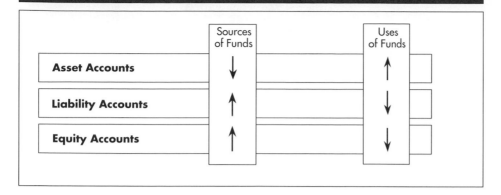

FIGURE 3.3   RULES FOR IDENTIFYING WHETHER AN ACCOUNT IS A SOURCE OR A USE OF FUNDS

Uses of funds take place when there is:

- an increase in asset accounts;
- a decrease in liability accounts; or
- a decrease in owners' equity (dividends paid or retained earnings decrease due to loss from operations).

By applying these rules to Eastman Technologies Inc.'s financial statements, we can easily determine the company's sources and uses of funds (see Table 3.4). The sources and uses of these accounts are listed in Table 3.5. As shown, the source and use rules identified earlier have been applied. The table shows that Eastman obtained $352,000 worth of funds from eight different accounts (funds from operations, accounts payable, etc.) and used or applied funds against five different accounts (prepaid expenses, accounts receivable, etc.).

Now that we have a basic understanding of the meaning of sources and uses of funds, and how they can be identified, let's turn to the structure of the statement of changes in financial position and see how it is prepared.

The Statement of Changes in Financial Position

◀◀ Objective 5

Let's begin by saying that cash flow can be examined at two levels: micro and macro. At the *micro level,* cash flow looks at short-term operating statements such as the monthly cash receipts and disbursements incurred by a business. The financial tool used to determine cash flow at this level is called the **cash budget.** This is one aspect of the treasury function. The objective is to ensure that the company has enough cash on hand to pay the company's ongoing bills (e.g., salaries, purchases, advertising, etc.) and debts as they come due. On the other hand, if the company has enough cash reserve, the treasurer would invest the surplus in short-

Cash budget

A treasury function that determines the cash flow of business at the micro level to determine the level of liquidity.

TABLE 3.5   THE STATEMENT OF SOURCES AND USES OF FUNDS

Eastman Technologies Inc.
for the Year Ended 2003

Sources of Funds

Funds from operations	
Increase in retained earnings	$ 50,000
Increase in depreciation	40,000
Increase in accounts payable	20,000
Increase in notes payable	15,000
Increase in accrued expenses	2,000
Increase in taxes payable	10,000
Increase in long-term debts	200,000
Increase in common shares	15,000
Total sources of funds	$352,000

Uses of Funds

Increase in cash	$ 4,000
Increase in prepaid expenses	5,000
Increase in accounts receivable	20,000
Increase in inventory	33,000
Increase in capital assets	290,000
Total uses of funds	$352,000

term securities. This type of analysis and decision-making determines the business's level of liquidity.

At the *macro level*, cash flow deals with solvency and the ability of a business to:

1. generate cash from its operations (profit plus depreciation and the management of working capital accounts);

2. pay all of its debts (both short- and long-term) and dividends; and

3. purchase capital assets (capital budget).

While the operating cash receipts and disbursements show the liquidity performance of a business, the information dealing with solvency appears in the **statement of changes in financial position.** That information involves operating activities, investing activities, and financing activities.

Preparing the statement of changes in financial position is a relatively complex task, but interpreting it is fairly simple and critical to stakeholders. To prepare this statement, the financial information has to be drawn from (1) the balance sheet, (2) the income statement, and (3) the statement of retained earnings.

Three key steps comprise the process of preparing this statement for Eastman Technologies Inc.:

• First, the sources and uses of funds must be identified. These was already done and presented in tables 3.4 and 3.5.

Statement of changes in financial position

A financial statement that reveals the level of solvency of a business. It looks at the macro level of the cash flow of a business.

- Second, the list of accounts affecting the net change in noncash working capital accounts must also be prepared (these are the current asset and current liability accounts shaded in Table 3.4 and listed in Table 3.8).
- Third, by using the information obtained in steps 1 and 2, the statement of changes in financial position can be prepared (see Table 3.6). The table identifies from which statement (income statement, statement of retained earnings, and balance sheet) the accounts producing a source and a use of funds are drawn.

The statement of changes in financial position presented in Table 3.6 lists these sources and uses of funds under three main headings:

- operating activities;
- financing activities; and
- investing activities.

TABLE 3.6   THE STATEMENT OF CHANGES IN FINANCIAL POSITION

Eastman Technologies Inc.
for the Year Ended 2003

Operating activities

Income after taxes	$ 97,500	Income Statement
Add: Depreciation	40,000	Income Statement
Net change in non-cash working capital accounts	−11,000*	Balance Sheet
Total	$126,500	

Financing activities

Payment of dividends	−$ 47,500	Statement of Retained Earnings
Long-term debt	200,000	Balance Sheet
Common shares	15,000	Balance Sheet
Total	$167,500	

Investing activities

Purchase of capital assets	$290,000	Balance Sheet

Cash balance

Increase in cash	−$ 4,000	Balance Sheet
Cash at beginning of year	$ 18,000	
Cash at end of year	$ 22,000	

* The number with a minus sign signifies a use of cash.

Operating Activities

Operating activities deal with the flow of funds generated by the business itself (internally generated funds). There are three important funds-generated items in this section: income after taxes, depreciation, and net change in noncash working capital accounts.

INCOME AFTER TAXES AND DEPRECIATION Eastman Technologies Inc. earned $97,500 in income after taxes in 2003 (see Table 3.7).

DEPRECIATION By adding back $40,000 in depreciation to this figure, the company generated $137,500 in cash. Depreciation is added back to income after taxes since this account is a book entry and does not represent a cash outflow.

NET CHANGE IN NONCASH WORKING CAPITAL ACCOUNTS The statement of changes in financial position does not usually give a detailed listing of the cash flow generated by a company's individual working capital accounts. However, since working capital accounts are an important element in the management of a company's cash flow, the company will produce a detailed statement called the **net change in noncash working capital accounts** (see Table 3.8). This statement shows whether individual working capital accounts are generating cash (a source) or present an application of funds (a use). Although a company's net increase in working capital may not change dramatically, this does not mean that all accounts are under control. Noncash working capital accounts include all current assets (excluding cash), and all current liability accounts. These accounts are all drawn from the balance sheet.

The seven working capital accounts drawn from the balance sheet (see the shaded portion of the balance sheet in Table 3.4) show a net use of $11,000 (see the shaded portion of the balance sheet in Table 3.4, or Table 3.8). This means that the business used $11,000 over the past 12-month period to carry on its day-

TABLE 3.7 THE INCOME STATEMENT	
Eastman Technologies Inc. **for the Year Ended 2003**	
Net sales	$2,500,000
Cost of goods sold	1,900,000
Gross margin	**600,000**
Operating expenses	350,000
Depreciation	40,000
Total operating expenses	390,000
Operating income	**210,000**
Other income/expenses (net)	15,000
Income before taxes	195,000
Taxes	97,500
Income after taxes	**$ 97,500**

TABLE 3.8   NET CHANGE IN NONCASH WORKING CAPITAL ACCOUNTS

Eastman Technologies Inc.
for the Year Ended 2003

Sources

Increase in accounts payable	$20,000		
Increase in notes payable	15,000		
Increase in accrued expenses	2,000		
Increase in deferred taxes	10,000	$47,000	Drawn from working capital accounts in the balance sheet, that is current assets and current liabilities

Uses

Increase in accounts receivable	$20,000	
Increase in inventory	33,000	
Increase in prepaid expenses	5,000	58,000
Net increase (decrease) in noncash working capital accounts		$11,000

to-day business operations. In this particular case, by adding back depreciation ($40,000) to the income after taxes ($97,500),the income statement generated $137,500 in cash (see Table 3.7), and the working capital accounts shown on the balance sheet produced an $11,000 outflow. As shown in the upper portion of the statement of changes in financial position under the heading "Operating Activities" in Table 3.6, the total funds generated from the business's operations amount to $126,500.

Financing Activities

Financing activities involve the flow of funds registered in the sale of shares, repayment of long-term debts, borrowing of long-term debts, and payment of dividends. With the exception of the payment of dividends, which is obtained from the statement of retained earnings, this information is drawn from the balance sheet. Sources and uses of funds under financing activities deal with the "big ticket accounts," that is, those appearing on the lower portion of the balance sheet under the heading "Long-term debts and owners' equity." As shown in Table 3.6 under the heading "Financing Activities," Eastman Technologies Inc. obtained a total of $167,500. First, the company paid $47,500 in dividends (see Table 3.9); second, it borrowed $200,000 from its long-term lenders; and finally, the shareholders invested $15,000 in the business.

All accounts appearing under operating and financing activities generated $294,000 in cash. What did Eastman do with this money? The next section answers this question.

Financing activities

That portion of the statement of changes in financial position that shows how much cash was provided (or used) from external sources (e.g., sale of shares, borrowing or repaying a mortgage, payment of dividends).

TABLE 3.9 THE STATEMENT OF RETAINED EARNINGS

Eastman Technologies Inc.
for the Year Ended 2003

Retained earnings (beginning balance)		$205,000
Earnings for the year	$ 97,500	
Dividends	47,500	50,000
Retained earnings (ending balance)		$255,000

Investing activities

That portion of the statement of changes in financial position that shows how much cash was provided (or used) to buy or sell assets (e.g., purchase or sale of a building).

Investing Activities

Investing activities deal with the other "big-ticket items" shown in the balance sheet under the heading "Capital assets." This section shows the source or use of funds for buying or selling capital assets. As shown in Table 3.6, Eastman invested $290,000 in capital assets.

As indicated above, operating and financing activities generated $294,000 and used $290,000 for buying the capital assets shown in the investing activities section. In total, the net amount from these three activities gives a surplus of $4,000 for an increase in the company's bank account. Therefore, Eastman used $4,000 for a bank deposit. As shown in the company's 2003 and 2002 balance sheets, the cash account increased from $18,000 to $22,000.

✳ Decision-Making in Action

The CEO of Oxford Manufacturing is contemplating the possibility of investing $1.0 million in capital assets in 2003. Before presenting the capital budget plan to the board of directors, he wants to know how much money would be generated internally, before pinpointing the amount of funds that would have to be raised from investors (e.g., lenders and shareholders).

To do this, the controller had to go through the following seven steps:

1. All operating managers prepared their respective operating budgets (e.g., manufacturing, marketing, human resources, engineering, etc.);
2. The controller then consolidated these operating budgets and prepared:
   – the company's overall operating budget; and
   – a pro-forma income statement for 2003 (see Table 3.10).

3. The controller also prepared a detailed listing of all capital projects estimated to total $1.0 million (e.g., acquisitions, purchase of equipment or machinery, plant expansion and/or modernization, etc.) that would be acquired or undertaken during the budget year (capital budget).
4. The treasurer identified the additional external sources of financing (in addition to internal sources) that would be required to finance:
   – the $1.0 million capital budget;
   – the working capital accounts (e.g., accounts receivable, inventory); and
   – dividends to shareholders (an amount of $155,674 shown in Table 3.11) during 2003.
5. The controller then prepared the company's monthly cash budget and the pro-forma balance sheet for 2003.

TABLE 3.10   THE PRO FORMA INCOME STATEMENT

Oxford Manufacturing Inc.
for the Year Ended 2003

Sales revenue		$5,100,000
Cost of goods sold		3,800,000
Gross margin		**1,300,000**
Operating expenses		
Selling		270,000
Administrative expenses		270,000
Depreciation		60,000
Total operating expenses		600,000
Operating income		**700,000**
Other income/expenses		
Other income	22,000	
Other expenses	50,000	28,000
Income before taxes		672,000
Taxes		260,000
Income after taxes		**$ 412,000**

TABLE 3.11   THE PRO FORMA STATEMENT OF RETAINED EARNINGS

Oxford Manufacturing Inc.
for the Year Ended 2003

Retained earnings (beginning balance)		$1,310,000
Earnings for the year	$ 412,000	
Dividends	155,674	
		256,326
Retained earnings (ending balance)		$1,566,326

6. The controller also compared individual accounts shown on the company's pro-forma balance sheet for 2003 to the 2002 balance sheet accounts. This information identified various sources and uses of funds for each account. (This information is shown on the right in Table 3.12).

– operating activities:	source of	$ 367,000 +
– financing activities:	source of	$ 644,326 +
– investing activities:	use of	$1,000,000 –
– change in the cash account:	use of	$ 11,326 –
– net change:		0

As shown, approximately 37% of the capital budget will be financed by Oxford's operations and the rest by external sources.

By using the information contained in Table 3.13, the CEO will be able to inform the board of directors how much cash (or funds) will be generated from the business itself (internally generated funds) versus externally generated funds (investors) to finance the $1.0 million purchase of capital assets.

To many stakeholders, businesses pivot around cash. The statement of changes in financial position shows a company's cash flow performance. It shows how well Oxford performed in the past in terms of cash flow and how much cash the company should generate in the future to buy the capital assets listed in the capital budget.

By looking at Table 3.13, the board of directors will have enough information to determine whether the business should go ahead with the purchase of the $1.0 million worth of capital assets. The CEO should therefore be prepared to answer the following questions:

7. Finally the controller prepared the statement of changes in financial position (Table 3.13). The funds flow changes between the two accounting periods generated from each activity are as follows:

- Should operating managers redo their operating budgets in order to squeeze more cash from the business (more than the $412,000)?
- Should operating managers examine whether more cash could be squeezed from working capital (e.g., accounts receivable and inventory), where there is a net outflow of $105,000?
- Should Oxford pay less than the $155,674 in dividends to the shareholders? What impact will this have on the shareholders' views about Oxford?
- Will Oxford be able to raise the $700,000 from the long-term lenders? What's the cost of capital?
- Will Oxford be able to raise the $100,000 from the shareholders? Should the company perhaps ask for more or less?
- If Oxford is not able to obtain the cash from internal or external sources, should the company then cut back its $1.0 million amount in the capital budget? If so, where should the cuts take place? What impact will these cuts have on the business?

TABLE 3.12 COMPARATIVE BALANCE SHEETS FOR 2003 AND 2002

Oxford Manufacturing Inc.
Statement of Sources and Uses of Funds

Assets	Pro Forma 2003	Year-end 2002	Sources	Uses
Current Assets				
Cash	$ 46,326	$ 35,000	—	$ 11,326
Marketable securities	50,000	50,000	—	—
Prepaid expenses	25,000	30,000	5,000	—
Accounts receivable	550,000	450,000	—	100,000
Inventory	850,000	750,000	—	100,000
Total current assets	1,521,326	1,315,000		
Capital assets (at cost)	3,450,000	2,450,000	—	1,000,000
Accumulated depreciation	710,000	650,000	60,000	—
Captial assets (net)	2,740,000	1,800,000		
Intangible assets	65,000	65,000		
Total Assets	$4,326,326	$3,180,000		

Liabilities				
Current liabilities				
Accounts payable	$ 170,000	$ 130,000	40,000	—
Accrued expenses	50,000	50,000	—	—
Current portion of long-term debt	40,000	40,000	—	—
Working capital loan	400,000	350,000	50,000	—
Total current liabilities	660,000	570,000		
Long-term debts	1,600,000	900,000	700,000	—
Total liabilities	2,260,000	1,470,000		

Shareholders' equity				
Common shares	500,000	400,000	100,000	—
Retained earnings	1,566,326	1,310,000	256,326	—
Total shareholders' equity	2,066,326	1,710,000		
Total liabilities and shareholders' equity	$4,326,326	$3,180,000	$1,211,326	$1,211,326

TABLE 3.13   THE STATEMENT OF CHANGES IN FINANCIAL POSITION

Oxford Manufacturing Inc.
for the Year Ended 2003

Operating activities

Income after taxes	$ 412,000	
Depreciation	60,000	
Net change in noncash working capital accounts	(105,000)	
Total		$ 367,000

Financing activities

Payment of dividends	$ (155,674)	
Long-term debt	700,000	
Common shares	100,000	
Total		$ 644,326

Investing activities

Purchase of capital assets	$1,000,000	$1,000,000
Increase in cash		$ 11,326
Cash at beginning of year	$ 35,000	
Cash at end of year	$ 46,326	

Changes in noncash working capital accounts

Sources

Prepaid expenses	$ 5,000	
Accounts payable	40,000	
Working capital loan	50,000	$95,000

Uses

Accounts receivable	100,000	
Inventory	100,000	200,000
Net increase in noncash working capital accounts		$ 105,000

Chapter Summary

Since the income statement shows only the amount of revenue earned and expenses incurred between two dates and the balance sheet gives a picture only of the financial condition of a business at a particular point in time, managers, owners, and creditors will want to examine consecutive balance sheets to have a better picture of the business's financial performance in terms of cash flow.

◀◀ Objective 1

The more important sources of funds are income from operations, sale of capital assets, sale of investment securities, increase in long-term debts, increase in capital shares, and decrease in working capital such as accounts receivable and inventory. Use or application of funds take place when a company experiences an operating loss, purchases capital assets, buys investment securities, reduces its long-term debt, decreases its capital shares, increases its working capital (e.g., accounts receivable or inventory) and pays dividends.

◀◀ Objective 2

In order to identify funds flow (sources and uses of funds), the first step in the process of preparing the statement of changes in financial position, two consequence balance sheets must be placed side by side in order to see where the changes in funds flow for each individual account.

◀◀ Objective 3

The following are basic rules that can be applied to identify funds flow. *Sources of funds* take place when there is a decrease in asset accounts, an increase in liability accounts or an increase in the owners' equity accounts (capital or retained earnings increase due to income from operations). *Uses of funds* take place when there is an increase in asset accounts, a decrease in liability accounts, or a decrease in owners' equity (dividends paid or retained earnings decrease due to loss from operations).

◀◀ Objective 4

The statement of changes in financial position gives a complete picture of the sources and uses of funds of a business under three distinct headings: operating activities, financing activities, and investing activities.

◀◀ Objective 5

Key Terms

Cash budget
Consecutive balance sheets
External financing
Financing activities
Funds flow
Internal financing
Investing activities

Net change in noncash working capital accounts
Operating activities
Rules of sources of funds
Rules of uses of funds
Source of funds
Statement of changes in financial position
Use of funds

Review Questions

1. Why is it important for managers to analyze changes in the flow of funds between two consecutive accounting periods?

2. Differentiate between a "source" of funds and a "use" of funds.

3. What do we mean by internal sources of financing?

4. What do we mean by external sources of financing?

5. Identify some of the key sources and uses of funds.

6. Why is depreciation considered a source of funds?

7. Why is working capital accounts part of the operating activities shown on the statement of changes in financial position?

8. Comment on the key rules that can be used to identify whether a change in the accounts shown on a balance sheet between two consecutive accounting periods is considered a source of funds or a use of funds.

9. Identify the basic structure of the statement of changes in financial position.

10. What is the purpose of the statement of net change in noncash working capital accounts?

11. Comment on the more important items that are usually shown under operating activities in the statement of changes in financial position.

12. What financial statements are used to prepare the statement of changes in financial position?

13. Comment on the more important items that are usually shown under financing activities in the statement of changes in financial position.

14. Comment on the more important items that are usually shown under investing activities in the statement of changes in financial position.

Discussion Questions

1. How does the statement of changes in financial position complement the other financial statements, that is, the income statement and the balance sheet?

2. How can managers use the statement of changes in financial position to make important business decisions?

Testing Your Comprehension

True/False Questions

___T___ 1. The sale of investment securities would be considered a source of funds.

___F___ 2. The purchase of capital assets would be considered a source of funds.

___T___ 3. An increase in net working capital accounts would be considered a use of funds.

F 4. To make an analysis of the changes in the flow of funds, we have to compare two consecutive income statements.

F 5. A decrease in an asset account between two consecutive accounting periods is considered a use of funds.

T 6. A decrease in a liability account between two consecutive accounting periods is considered a use of funds.

T 7. An increase in an equity account between two consecutive accounting periods is considered a source of funds.

F 8. An increase in the prepaid expense account between two consecutive accounting periods is considered a source of funds.

T 9. A decrease in the accounts payable account between two consecutive accounting periods is considered a use of funds.

T 10. The depreciation account is part of the operating activities in the statement of changes in financial position.

F 11. The prepaid expense account is part of the financing activities in the statement of changes in financial position.

F 12. The short-term-loan account is part of the financing activities in the statement of changes in financial position.

T 13. The common share account is part of the financing activities in the statement of changes in financial position.

F 14. Dividends are usually shown as an operating activity in the statement of changes in financial position.

Multiple-Choice Questions

1. The following is considered a source of funds:
   a. purchase of investment securities
   b. sale of investment securities
   c. increase in a working capital account
   d. increase in a capital asset account
   e. decrease in a mortgage account

2. The following statements are used to prepare the statement of changes in financial position:
   a. balance sheet
   b. income statement
   c. statement of retained earnings
   d. net change in noncash working capital accounts
   e. all of the above

3. The following is considered a use of funds:
   a. increase in the mortgage account
   b. decrease in the salaries accounts
   c. increase in the inventory account
   d. increase in the mortgage account
   e. decrease in the cost of goods sold account

4. The following is considered a source of funds:
   a. increase in the dividends account
   b. decrease in an asset account
   c. decrease in a liability account
   d. decrease in an equity account
   e. increase in the sales revenue account

5. The following account appears as an operating activity in the statement of changes in financial position:
   a. long-term debt
   b. common shares
   c. purchase of assets
   d. purchase of another business
   e. depreciation

6. Depreciation is considered:
   a. an operating activity
   b. an investing activity
   c. a financing activity
   d. a noncash working capital account
   e. none of the above

7. The following account appears as a financing activity in the statement of changes in financial position:
   a. working capital loan
   b. accounts receivable
   c. mortgage
   d. term deposits
   e. accounts payable

8. The following account appears as an investing activity in the statement of changes in financial position:
   a. purchase of equipment
   b. purchase of raw materials
   c. purchase of investment securities
   d. purchase of common shares
   e. sale of products

9. The cash in the bank account is usually considered:
   a. an operating activity
   b. an investing activity
   c. a financing activity
   d. a noncash working capital account
   e. none of the above

10. The net change in noncash working capital accounts include the following:
    a. cash account
    b. sales revenue account
    c. accounts receivable account
    d. deferred income tax account
    e. income statement account

11. One way to calculate the cash generated from operations is by adding:
    a. interest earned to income before taxes
    b. depreciation to income before taxes
    c. dividends to common shares
    d. depreciation to sales revenue
    e. depreciation to income after taxes

12. The purchase of another business would be considered:
    a. a noncash working capital transaction
    b. an operating activity
    c. a financing activity
    d. an investing activity
    e. a source of funds

Fill-in-the-Blanks Questions

1. _____ of funds, which are considered cash inflows, can be obtained from different accounts (e.g., obtaining a loan, selling an asset).

2. _____, which is considered a noncash expense, is included in the operating section of the statement of changes in financial position.

3. As a rule, when an asset account decreases from one period to the next, it is considered a _____ of funds.

4. The cash _____ is a treasury function that determines the cash flow of a business at the micro level to determine the level of liquidity.

5. There are three types of activities included in the statement of changes in financial position: _____ activities, financing activities, and investing activities.

6. The only item drawn from the statement of retained earnings to prepare the statement of changes in financial position is the _____ _____.

7. The three major items included as operating activities in the statement of changes in financial position are _____, income after taxes, and the net change in noncash working capital accounts.

8. _____ activities included in the statement of changes in financial position show how much cash was provided (or used) to buy or sell assets.

Learning Exercises

Exercise 1(a)

Using CompuTech's financial statements, identify whether the following changes are considered a source of funds or a use of funds.

	2004	2003	Source	Use
Cash in the bank	$ 16,000	$ 10,000		_none_
Accounts receivable	45,000	35,000		10,000
Capital assets	210,000	170,000		40,000
Term loan	40,000	35,000	5000	
Long-term debt	50,000	60,000		10,000
Total			$5000	$60,000

Exercise 1(b)

Identify, under the appropriate heading, whether the following changes are considered a source of funds or a use of funds.

	This year	Last year	Source	Use
Cash in the bank	$ 3,000	$ 2,000		_none_
Marketable securities	12,000	10,000		2000
Loan made to a friend	—	5,000	5000	
Car loan	12,000	8,000	4000	
Mortgage	75,000	60,000	15,000	
House	134,600	130,000		4600
Trailer	12,000	—		12,000
Visa	1,250	600	650	
Furniture	5,600	4,000		1600
The Bay	—	450		450
RRSP	23,000	20,000		3000
Total			$	$

Exercise 2(a)

On the basis of Len and Joan Miller's personal balance sheets shown below, identify whether each account is a source or a use.

	2003	2002	Source	Use
Assets				
Short-term deposits	$ 2,000	$ 2,000	_____	_____
Savings bonds	5,000	4,000	_____	_____
RRSP	30,000	20,000	_____	_____
Furniture	8,500	7,000	_____	_____
House	205,000	136,000	_____	_____
Car	22,000	6,000	_____	_____
Total assets	$272,500	$175,000		
Liabilities				
Amex	$ 4,500	$ 2,000	_____	_____
Car loan	24,000	3,000	_____	_____
TD Canada Trust	21,000	11,000	_____	_____
Mortgage	112,000	79,000	_____	_____
Total liabilities	161,500	95,000	_____	_____
Equity	111,000	80,000	_____	_____
Total liabilities and equity	$272,500	$175,000	$_____	_____

Exercise 2(b)

On the basis of Vicky Deshpande's balance sheets shown below, identify whether each account is a source or a use.

	2003	2002	Source	Use
Assets				
Cash	$ 2,000	$ 4,000	_____	_____
Savings bonds	5,000	4,000	_____	_____
RRSP	20,000	16,000	_____	_____
Computers	7,500	3,000	_____	_____
House	145,000	136,000	_____	_____
Cottage	65,000	—	_____	_____
Land	—	40,000	_____	_____
Car	12,000	6,000	_____	_____
Total assets	$256,500	$209,000		

Liabilities

Visa	$ 1,500	$ 2,000	_____	_____
Sears	3,000	2,000	_____	_____
Bank loan	14,000	3,000	_____	_____
Bank of Montreal	21,000	11,000	_____	_____
Mortgage	112,000	99,000	_____	_____
Total liabilities	151,500	117,000	_____	_____
Equity	105,000	92,000	_____	_____
Total liabilities and equity	$256,500	$209,000	$_____	_____

Exercise 3(a)-

Indicate under which activity (operating, financing, investing) the following accounts belong in the statement of changes in financial position:

	Activity
Notes receivable (short-term)	_____
RRSP	_____
Computer	_____
Long-term loan	_____
Income after taxes	_____
Notes payable (short-term)	_____
Amortization	_____
Inventory	_____
Car	_____

Exercise 3(b) –

Indicate under which activity (operating, financing, investing) the following accounts belong in the statement of changes in financial position:

	Activity
Accounts receivable	_____
Land	_____
Mortgage	_____
Income after taxes	_____
Accounts payable	_____
Depreciation	_____
Inventory	_____
Prepaid expenses	_____
Common shares	_____
Buildings	_____
Accrued expenses	_____
Taxes payable	_____
Equipment	_____
Long-term loan	_____
Purchase of a company	_____
Dividends	_____
Preferred shares	_____

Exercise 4(a)-

With the following accounts drawn from CompuTech's balance sheet, identify those that are considered working capital accounts and prepare the net change in noncash working capital accounts statement.

Accounts	2004	2003
Accounts payable	$ 20,000	$ 17,000
Retained earnings	58,000	25,000
Long-term debts	50,000	60,000
Accounts receivable	45,000	35,000
Gross capital assets	210,000	170,000
Inventory	65,000	50,000
Cash	16,000	10,000
Accumulated depreciation	78,000	38,000
Term loan	40,000	35,000
Prepaid expenses	5,000	5,000

Exercise 4(b) -

With the following accounts, identify those that are considered working capital accounts and prepare the net change in noncash working capital accounts statement.

Accounts	This year	Last year
Accounts receivable	$230,000	$210,000
Capital assets	550,000	450,000
Inventory	350,000	290,000
Prepaid expenses	50,000	40,000
Accumulated depreciation	210,000	180,000
Dividends	40,000	32,000
Accounts payable	240,000	190,000
Revolving loan	90,000	100,000
Mortgage	120,000	110,000
Accrued expenses	20,000	30,000
Common shares	50,000	40,000
Term loan	82,000	34,000
Income after taxes	48,000	39,000

Exercise 5(a)

With the following financial statements, prepare CompuTech's:

1. net change in noncash working capital accounts; and

2. statement of changes in financial position.

COMPUTECH SALES AND SERVICES
INCOME STATEMENT
FOR THE YEAR ENDED 2004

Sales revenue	$420,000
Cost of goods sold	209,000
Gross margin	211,000
Operating expenses	151,000
Operating income	60,000
Interest charges	14,000
Income before taxes	46,000
Income taxes	13,000
Income after taxes	$ 33,000

COMPUTECH SALES AND SERVICES
BALANCE SHEETS
AS AT DECEMBER 31

	2004	2003
Current assets		
Cash	$ 16,000	$ 10,000
Marketable securities	5,000	5,000
Prepaid expenses	5,000	5,000
Accounts receivable	45,000	35,000
Inventory	65,000	50,000
Total current assets	136,000	105,000
Capital assets		
Capital assets (gross)	210,000	170,000
Accumulated depreciation	78,000	38,000
Capital assets (net)	132,000	132,000
Total assets	$268,000	$237,000
Current liabilities		
Accounts payable	$ 20,000	$ 17,000
Term loan	40,000	35,000
Total current liabilities	60,000	52,000
Long-term loans	50,000	60,000
Shareholders' equity		
Common shares	100,000	100,000
Retained earnings	58,000	25,000
Total shareholders' equity	158,000	125,000
Total liabilities and shareholders' equity	$268,000	$237,000

Exercise 5(b)

With the following financial statements, prepare:

1. the net change in noncash working capital accounts; and

2. the statement of changes in financial position.

INCOME STATEMENT
FOR THE YEAR ENDED 2003

Net sales	$550,000
Cost of goods sold	200,000
Gross margin	350,000
Operating expenses	210,000
Operating income	140,000
Other income	10,000
Income before taxes	150,000
Income taxes	60,000
Income after taxes	$ 90,000

STATEMENT OF RETAINED EARNINGS
FOR THE YEAR ENDED 2003

Retained earnings (beginning balance)		$210,000
Income from operations	$90,000	
Dividends	70,000	20,000
Retained earnings (ending balance)		$230,000

BALANCE SHEETS
AS AT DECEMBER 31

	2003	2002
Current assets		
Cash	$ 3,000	$ 4,000
Accounts receivable	250,000	200,000
Inventory	300,000	230,000
Total current assets	553,000	434,000
Capital assets		
Capital assets (gross)	400,000	350,000
Accumulated depreciation	100,000	65,000
Capital assets (net)	300,000	285,000
Total assets	$853,000	$719,000
Current liabilities		
Accounts payable	$200,000	$178,000
Accrued expenses	32,000	38,000
Term loan	120,000	100,000
Total current liabilities	352,000	316,000
Long-term loans	200,000	122,000
Shareholders' equity		
Common shares	71,000	71,000
Retained earnings	230,000	210,000
Total shareholders' equity	301,000	281,000
Total liabilities and shareholders' equity	$853,000	$719,000

Case

Austin Industries Inc.

The management committee of Austin Industries Inc. would like to invest $75,000 in capital assets in 2004. The board of directors wants to approve the decision, but first they must find out how much cash will be generated by the operations in 2004. The board also may raise more funds from shareholders and increase long-term borrowing.

On the basis of the information shown on Austin Industries Inc.'s 2004 projected balance sheet, identify the sources and uses of funds for 2004.

AUSTIN INDUSTRIES INC.
BALANCE SHEETS
(000s)

	2004	2003
Current assets		
Cash	$ 7	$ 15
Term deposits	—	11
Accounts receivable	30	22
Inventory	75	53
Total current assets	112	101
Capital assets		
Capital assets (gross)	150	75
Less: accumulated depreciation	(41)	(26)
Total capital assets (net)	109	49
Total assets	$221	$150
Current liabilities		
Accounts payable	$ 18	$ 15
Notes payable	3	15
Other current liabilities	15	7
Total current liabilities	36	37
Long-term debt		
Mortgage	26	8
Shareholders' equity		
Common shares	64	38
Retained earnings	95	67
Total owners' equity	159	105
Total liabilities and shareholders' equity	$221	$150

In 2004, management of Austin Industries Inc. expects to generate $38,000 in income after taxes. The board of directors will pay $10,000 in dividends to the shareholders.

1. On the basis of this information, prepare the following statements:

   a) the statement of accounts affecting the net change in noncash working capital accounts for 2004; and

   b) the statement of changes in financial position for 2004.

4

Financial Statement Analysis

Learning Objectives

After reading this chapter, you should be able to:

1. Explain why ratios are used to analyze financial statements.

2. Analyze financial statements by using meaningful ratios.

3. Evaluate a company's balance sheet and income statement by using common-size statement analysis.

4. Evaluate a company's balance sheet and income statement by using horizontal statement analysis.

5. Describe how financial benchmarks can be used to measure and improve a company's financial performance.

6. Examine financial statements by using the Du Pont financial system.

7. Comment on the limitations of financial ratios.

Chapter Outline

Opening Case

Since CompuTech Sales and Services started, the Millers have received their company's financial statements from accountant May Ogaki each month.

As May pointed out, the information presented on the various financial statements is critical to gauge the results of past decisions and to determine what has to be done in the future. The Millers vividly remembered Bill Murray's points regarding the requirements needed to keep a business liquid, stable, productive, and profitable. The Millers consider these points when analyzing their financial statements. CompuTech Sales and Services' financial statements for 2004 are presented in Exercise 4 at the end of this chapter and in more detail in Appendix A.

The first requirement was to pay their current bills on time and to be "liquid." In 2004, CompuTech bought approximately $200,000 worth of goods from different suppliers. The Millers always paid their invoices on time. They believed this was important if CompuTech was to maintain a healthy working relationship with its suppliers. Also, being in a favourable liquid position, the business could benefit from cash and trade discounts. The business had $90,000 in bank loans (short and long term). In order to maintain a reputation of "trustworthiness" with their banker, the Millers ensured that all debt commitments were honoured each month.

The second requirement was "stability," maintaining a level of debt that CompuTech could afford. The Millers did not want to overextend themselves into too much debt for two reasons. First, the more debt that the business had to carry, the more costly it was. They realized that a heavy debt load would adversely affect profit performance, particularly if interest charges increased, even by 1% or 2%. Also, the Miller's strategy for 2005 was to keep their level of debt as low as possible (even reducing it) to allow them more leverage to finance the opening of a new store in 2005.

The third requirement was "productivity." To the Millers, productivity meant getting the "biggest bang for each invested dollar." Productivity meant generating the highest level of revenue with the least amount of resources (assets). For example, they realized that dollars invested in accounts receivable ($45,000) and inventory ($65,000), although necessary, did not generate any profit. For this reason, they wanted the investment level in working capital accounts as low as possible. In total CompuTech had

$268,000 invested in assets, and each dollar generated $1.57 in sales revenue ($420,000/$268,000). To find out whether CompuTech was productive or not, the Millers had to obtain information from different sources (e.g., banks, industry associations, Dun & Bradstreet) to compare their firm's performance against the industry and other competing firms. This information was used as benchmarks for decision-making.

The last requirement for long-term growth and success was "profitability." This involved the level of profit CompuTech would generate compared to sales revenue, assets, and equity. The Millers realized the importance of making effective investment and operating decisions in order to maximize profitability. High profit level is a sign of efficiency. In 2004, for example, the Millers expect to earn 7.8 cents for every sales revenue dollar ($33,000/$420,000). As far as they were concerned, return on sales was one of their most important financial objectives. Improving profitability would be achieved by increasing sales revenue and being vigilant in spending budget dollars (e.g., cost of goods sold and operating expenses). They knew that the more profit the business earned, the more expansion could be funded by internally generated funds, requiring less from external sources (i.e., lenders).

This chapter examines the more important financial ratios used by businesses to measure a company's financial performance. In particular, it focuses on three key topics:

1. Why are financial ratios important to measure a company's success?
2. What financial ratios can be used to measure liquidity, debt, productivity, and profitability?
3. How can benchmarks be used to measure financial performance?

Introduction

Financial statement analysis is not limited to assessing sources and uses of funds. Another important tool used to gauge the financial health of a business is ratio analysis. A financial ratio is the comparison or relationship between different numbers appearing on a balance sheet and/or an income statement. This relationship is usually expressed in terms of a ratio or a percentage.

Business managers, suppliers, investors, and market analysts do not look only at the makeup of financial statements, that is, the "cosmetics." Just because a balance sheet balances or is prepared by a renowned accounting firm does not mean that a business is in a healthy financial position.

After reading this chapter, you will be able to analyze financial statements, and gauge the financial soundness and profitability of any business.

Ratio analysis
The analysis of calculations that help readers of financial statements to assess the financial structure and performance of a business.

Ratio analysis helps readers of financial statements assess the financial structure and profitability performance of businesses by exploring answers to the following questions:

- Is this company able to meet its current debt obligations?
- Are the company's assets being managed effectively?
- Are the business's accounts receivable and inventory at suitable levels?
- Will the company be able to meet its long-term debt commitments?
- Can the company service its debt comfortably?
- Is the company profitable?
- Is this business using its assets or resources efficiently?
- How does the company's financial structure and profitability compare with those of others in the same industry?
- Is the shareholders' return on investment satisfactory?
- Do investors have a high regard for the company?

This chapter analyzes financial statements, showing how to meaningfully compare numbers appearing on balance sheets and income statements. Here are a few examples of how numbers shown on financial statements can be compared and for what reasons:

Why compare …	To see whether …
• Current liabilities to current assets	• the company is able to meet its payroll and pay its suppliers on time
• Accounts receivable to sales	• the company is collecting its receivables quickly enough
• Inventory to cost of goods sold	• the company's inventory is turning over quickly enough
• Fixed charges to income	• the business can service its debt
• Total debt to total assets	• the company has too much debt
• Total assets to sales	• the company's assets are productive
• Net income to sales	• the company as a whole is efficient

Objective 1 ▶▶

Why Use Ratios to Analyze Financial Statements?

Managers analyze financial statements for two key reasons. First, to examine the past in order to gauge how well a business performed in terms of meeting its financial objectives of efficiency, liquidity, prosperity, and stability (see Chapter 1). Second, to formulate goals and strategies that will help improve the company's future financial performance. One important characteristic of good business goals is the element of precision and meaningfulness. Financial ratios are considered vital instruments that can make financial analysis and decision-making useful and unambiguous.

Analyzing financial statements through ratios helps managers, market analysts, or investors find out what is good or bad about a business. While ratios give only signals about what is wrong or right, they can easily trigger a process that can help managers dig a little deeper in order to find answers to questions, solve problems, or improve performance.

Financial statements become valuable instruments when managers or analysts are able to make the connection between different accounts or groups of accounts shown on income statements and balance sheets. Furthermore, this information can be quite revealing when compared to competitors and industry norms that can be used as **benchmarks**. Only when the analysis is completed can corrective measures be taken to improve financial performance.

The real value of financial statement analysis lies in the fact that it can be used to help predict a company's future financial performance. If the analysis is done effectively, managers can anticipate future conditions and, more importantly, make decisions that will improve the future for their business.

The importance of analyzing financial statements can be grouped under four headings: (1) to maximize return, (2) to ensure liquidity, (3) to maintain solvency, and (4) to secure long-term prosperity. Let's briefly examine each.

Benchmarks
Excellent industry norms to which one's own financial ratios can be compared.

Maximizing Return

In business, the word "return" is synonymous with survival. To survive, a business must earn adequate profit and cash flow that will earn a suitable **return** for investors, and provide adequate funds to finance both the business's working capital requirements and capital assets. Ratios such as return on sales, return on assets, and return on invested capital can readily show whether a business is generating enough profit to satisfy its day-to-day operating needs and longer-term financial aspirations.

Return
Adequate funds to finance a company's growth.

Profitability can be improved by a combination of the following:

- increasing sales volume and/or unit selling price;
- reducing operating expenses (e.g., cost of goods sold, selling, or administration);
- reducing the use of borrowed capital (interest charges); and
- cutting back nonproductive assets (e.g., working capital and capital assets).

As will be covered later in this chapter, the use of financial ratios through the common-size statement analysis technique of the income statement can help set the stage for improved profitability and return performance. As shown on the following page, the first step is to convert all numbers in the income statement from dollar figures to percentages (or ratios). To do this, each line on the income statement is compared to sales revenue. Once the percentages or ratios have been calculated, they can be used to analyze past performance and can be compared to specific competitors and to industry-wide statistics. This analysis can readily help managers pinpoint operating efficiencies (or inefficiencies) and profitability.

% of sales revenue	2002	2003	2004
Sales revenue	100.0%	100.0%	100.0%
Cost of goods sold	80.0	81.0	79.0
Gross margin	20.0	19.0	21.0
Operating expenses	15.0	16.0	15.0
Income before taxes	5.0%	3.0%	6.0%

As shown above, return on sales (or for every dollar's worth of sales) was reduced from 5 cents to 3 cents between 2002 and 2003. Managers must determine the reasons for this deterioration in operating efficiencies. More importantly, they must formulate financial goals for each operating line on the income statement (e.g., 79 cents in cost of goods sold and 15 cents in operating expenses). Also, they must determine strategies and plans that will help realize the 2004 goals in order to improve their gross margin and income before tax performance. To illustrate the importance of this simple analysis, if the sales revenue objective for 2004 is $10 million, a 6% return on sales would generate $600,000 in income before taxes. If the return on sales performance is maintained at the 2003 operating efficiency level (3.0%), the income level would be reduced to $300,000. Common-size statement analysis helps to pinpoint what should be done for each account on the income statement in order to improve profitability (here, by an extra $300,000) and return.

Ensuring Liquidity

Liquidity

Ability of a firm to meet its short-term financial obligations.

In business, being liquid is just as important as generating an adequate return. No business activity is more important than being able to transact daily with customers and pay employees, bills, and debt on time. To operate with some degree of comfort, a business must have enough cash (**liquidity**) to pay its day-to-day operating expenses and retire other liabilities on schedule. It is usually possible to defer a payment of some financial obligations (e.g., accounts payable or bank loan) because of a temporary cash shortage; however, exploiting that privilege can quickly lead to financial downfall. An important ratio that can test a company's liquidity position is the relationship between all current asset accounts such as accounts receivable and inventories shown on the balance sheet to all current liability accounts that must be paid within a reasonable time period (e.g., a year) such as accounts payable and accrued expenses.

Stakeholders such as short-term lenders, suppliers, employees, and owners are interested in measuring liquidity.

Businesses that want to improve their profit performance (maximize return) must implement effective cash management strategies such as:

- accelerating cash receipts by speeding billing and collection processes;
- delaying disbursements to maximize the use of cash;

- reducing working capital requirements (e.g., inventories and accounts receivable);
- monitoring the operating cycle that can help gauge cash goals (i.e., number of days it takes from the purchase of inventory to collecting receivables from customers).

Some of the financial ratios that can provide answers to these concerns include the cash ratio, the current ratio, the quick ratio, and the cash conversion cycle.

Maintaining Solvency

Solvency can be defined as a company's ability to pay its debts. Solvency ratios attempt to determine whether a business is overextended in debt. This analysis helps to pinpoint whether a firm has (or will have) the ability to pay its principal and interest obligations as they become due. Cash flow performance and capital structure (proportion of debt to equity) can help determine the solvency prospects of a company in order to avoid financial trouble. Maintaining solvency is essential for any business; defaulting on debt obligations can lead to legal proceedings that could easily put a strain on a business's day-to-day operations and even derail its operations.

Both managers and investors are always on the alert for the threat of insolvency that applies to both current and longer-term operating conditions. When a business is insolvent, its liabilities exceed assets, and it is operating with a negative equity. Nevertheless, if a company operates with a positive equity structure, it can still be insolvent if it has difficulty servicing its debt payments. For this reason, financial measures are used to test whether a business is financially solvent. Solvency can be examined from two angles:

1. financial structure, which examines whether a company has too much debt compared to the owners' investment in the business (equity); and
2. debt-paying ability, which examines whether a business has the ability to service its debt with relative ease. Here, solvency is analyzed from two angles:
   - *short-term solvency* tests, which were discussed earlier (i.e., quick ratio, current ratio),
   - *long-term solvency* tests (i.e., debt-service coverage, fixed-charges coverage).

Testing the solvency of a business is of prime interest to market analysts, investment portfolio managers, private investors, investment bankers, and other stakeholders. They will usually test a firm's solvency performance before deciding whether to make or renew a loan. These financial ratios can determine the financial profile of a firm in terms of its creditworthiness and be used to judge whether it will have enough cash to pay its loans, interest, and dividends on time.

As will be covered later in this chapter, the use of financial ratios through the common-size statement analysis of the balance sheet can be used as a platform for improving a business's financial structure. As shown on the following page,

Solvency
Ability to service or pay all debts (short and long term).

converting all figures in the balance sheet from dollar figures to percentages (or ratios) is the first step. Here, every line on the balance sheet is compared to total liabilities and equity. Once the ratios have been calculated, they can be used to analyze performance over time and to compare the company to specific competitors and to industry-wide statistics.

% of liabilities and equity	2002	2003 (projected)	2004
Current liabilities	20.0%	23.0%	21.0%
Long-term debt	40.0	42.0	39.0
Total debt	60.0	65.0	60.0
Shareholders' equity	40.0	35.0	40.0
Liabilities and equity	100.0%	100.0%	100.0%

Common-size ratios

Method of reducing (a) all numbers on the balance sheet to a percentage of total assets and (b) all numbers on the income statement to a percentage of sales revenue.

As shown, by using the **common-size ratio** analysis, the company's leverage structure changed between 2002 and 2003. More debt as compared to shareholders' equity was used to finance the purchase of assets (65% compared to 60%). Management must therefore determine whether this financial structure should be maintained or altered. Detailed analysis would give answers regarding the level of margin of safety for owners' equity against the claims of creditors, and whether there will be enough funds available from operations to pay the interest owed to lenders and other fixed charges such as lease payments.

Securing Long-Term Prosperity

Prosperity, the ability of a business to grow smoothly, is always a concern for stakeholders. Growth funds come from several sources:

- internally generated funds (cash from operations);
- externally generated funds (lenders and shareholders);
- reduced dividends; and
- reduced amount of funds invested in capital assets.

Certainly, the size of the market, a company's yearly growth rate, and the aggressiveness of management to increase the business's share of the market or launch new products and operate in different markets will determine, to a large extent, how quickly a business's sales revenue will increase. However, sales revenue is only one piece of the puzzle. Sales revenue increments impact all lines shown on the income statement (e.g., cost of goods sold, selling expenses, administrative expenses, etc.) and the balance sheet (e.g., accounts receivable, inventory, working capital loans, long-term debts, etc.).

Typical questions that stakeholders usually ask are:

- Do we have sufficient resources (physical, financial, human) to grow?
- Where will growth funds come from? Internal sources? External sources? How much?

- Do we have enough borrowing power to finance our growth?
- Will we have enough cash to service the new debt and equity (interest charges and dividends)?
- Will the incremental return on sales and earnings before interest and taxes (EBIT) be positive? If yes, to what extent?

As shown below, the use of financial ratios or percentages through the horizontal analysis of the income statement and the balance sheet shows the proportion of growth patterns in all components of the financial statements between two consecutive fiscal periods. This comparison could be done between:

- this year's month and last year's month;
- this year's quarter and last year's quarter; or
- this year's 12-month operating results and last year's 12-month operating results.

% change over previous year	2002	2003	2004
Income statement accounts			
Sales revenue	11.5%	25.0%	25.3%
Cost of goods sold	12.1	19.5	10.4
Operating expenses	8.8	12.6	17.5
Income after taxes	10.4	93.2	81.4
Balance sheet accounts			
Current assets	9.5	17.8	3.2
Capital assets	21.3	38.2	32.4
Total assets	14.3	26.3	17.0
Current liabilities	8.5	14.4	2.4
Long-term debt	14.6	41.0	−14.0
Total debt	12.1	24.8	−5.4
Shareholders' equity	15.3	27.8	40.9
Total liabilities and equity	14.3%	26.3%	17.0%

As shown, horizontal analysis gives a clear indication of the growth patterns (past and future) for various accounts appearing on financial statements. It reveals, for example, that a 25.3% increase in sales revenue for the forecast period (2004) will generate an 81.4% increase in income after taxes. It will also require a 17% increase in total assets whereby most of the growth funds will come from shareholders' equity (new capital from shareholders or increase in retained earnings). These numbers provide managers and investors with the opportunity to query whether the growth rate for each element on the financial statements is feasible.

Now that we understand why ratios are important to analyze financial statements and to help make important operating, financing, and investing decisions, let's now examine the more commonly used financial ratios, what they measure, and how they are calculated.

Financial Ratios

As discussed in Chapter 2, the purpose of the initial two steps in financial management (bookkeeping and accounting) is to prepare financial statements. The next two steps involve the analysis of business performance for the purpose of assessing financial strengths and weaknesses, and making investing, financing, and operating decisions.

When looking at a balance sheet or an income statement, it is relatively easy to gauge how much profit a business has made, how much debt it owes to its creditors, or the amount of funds owners have invested in it. However, in order to evaluate business performance in more depth and with more precision, managers and business investors use **financial ratios** to gauge liquidity, debt, coverage, asset management, profitability, and market value.

Financial ratio

Comparison or relationship between numbers shown on financial statements.

Hundreds of ratios can be used to gauge financial performance and management competence. Using a proliferation of ratios for evaluating financial performance of a business can, however, confuse more than enlighten. Some ratios are deficient because they (1) can mislead, (2) do not give a complete picture of a financial situation, (3) do not have a practical application, and (4) show in a roundabout manner what other ratios show more clearly. For example, what would be the point of comparing current liabilities to owners' equity, or selling expenses to capital assets? The real objective of ratio analysis is to reduce the large number of accounts (or items) contained in financial statements to a relatively small number of meaningful relationships. Important relationships (ratios) depend to a large measure on the purpose of the ratios selected and should relate components in which a logical decision-making relationship exists between the two elements.

Ratios are diagnostic tools. Just as a doctor measures various characteristics of the blood, someone evaluating a company measures the various relationships of numbers shown on financial statements. Just as a blood test can show symptoms of a disease, the study of numbers on financial statements reveals symptoms of problems or of management errors that require correction.

As indicated earlier, a ratio is simply a comparison of one account to another to express the size of an item in relation to the other. For instance, if you wanted to express how sunny a month was, you could calculate the ratio of sunny days to rainy days. Dividing the number of sunny days (say 15) by the number of rainy days (say 15) gives a ratio of 1. Alternatively, you could work out the ratio of sunny days to total days. In this case, you divide the number of sunny days in the month (15) by the total number of days in the month (30) to give .50 or 50%.

Categories of ratios

Balance sheet ratios, income statement ratios, combined ratios.

This chapter examines 16 ratios that can be grouped under three **categories:**

1. balance sheet ratios, which relate two accounts shown on the balance sheet;

2. income statement ratios, which show the relationship between two accounts on the income statement; and

3. combined ratios, which relate numbers on the balance sheet to the numbers on the income statement.

Balance sheet, income statement, and combined ratios can also be regrouped under five other categories (**ratio measures**) in order to measure a company's financial performance.

Ratio measures

Liquidity, debt/coverage, asset-management, profitability, and market value.

1. *Liquidity ratios* measure the ability of a firm to meet its short-term cash obligations.

2. *Debt/coverage ratios* are used to evaluate the capital structure, the proportion of funds a business borrows from creditors and owners to finance the purchase of assets, and the firm's ability to service its debt.

3. *Asset-management ratios* evaluate how efficiently managers use the assets of a business.

4. *Profitability ratios* measure the overall operating effectiveness of a business by comparing profit level to sales, assets, and equity.

5. *Market-value ratios* are used to assess the way investors and stock markets react to a company's performance.

This chapter examines these five groups of financial ratios. The 16 ratios identified in Table 4.1 will be defined and examined within the context of Eastman Technologies Inc.'s income statement and balance sheet, shown in Tables 2.3 and 2.5 respectively in Chapter 2.

TABLE 4.1   COMMONLY USED FINANCIAL RATIOS

A. Liquidity Ratios
    1. Current ratio (times)
    2. Quick ratio (times)

B. Debt/Coverage Ratios
    3. Debt-to-total assets (%)
    4. Debt-to-equity (times)
    5. Times-interest-earned (times)
    6. Fixed charges coverage (times)

C. Asset-Management Ratios
    7. Average collection period (days)
    8. Inventory turnover (times)
    9. Capital assets turnover (times)
    10. Total assets turnover (times)

D. Profitability Ratios
    11. Profit margin on sales (%)
    12. Return on sales (%)
    13. Return on total assets (%)
    14. Return on equity (%)

→ not given

some

Liquidity Ratios

Liquidity ratios examine the current accounts shown on the balance sheet—that is, the relationship between current assets and current liabilities. These two groupings of accounts are referred to as working capital. By referring to Table 2.5, we can calculate Eastman's net working capital in 2003 as follows:

Liquidity ratios

Ratios that measure the ability of a firm to meet its cash obligations.

Current assets	$600,000
Current liabilities	445,000
Net working capital	$155,000

These ratios measure the short-term solvency and help judge the adequacy of liquid assets for meeting short-term obligations as they come due. The $155,000 in net working capital is the level of funds Eastman has to operate with on a day-to-day basis—that is, to pay on time its accounts payable, short-term bank loans, and weekly operating expenses such as wages and salaries. Businesses experience financial difficulty because they cannot pay obligations as they come due and not merely because they are not profitable.

The most commonly used liquidity ratios are the current ratio and the quick ratio.

Current ratio

A ratio that gauges general business liquidity.

CURRENT RATIO The **current ratio,** also referred to as the working capital ratio, is calculated by dividing current assets by current liabilities. It is an excellent way to gauge business liquidity because it measures to what extent current assets exceed current liabilities. A common rule of thumb suggests that an acceptable current ratio should be around 2 to 1; that is, every dollar's worth of current liabilities should be backed up by at least two dollars' worth of current assets. This makes sense because if the firm could realize only one-half of the values stated in the balance sheet, if liquidating current assets, it would still have adequate funds to pay all current liabilities. Nevertheless, a general standard for this ratio is not useful because it fails to recognize that an appropriate current ratio is a function of the nature of a company's business and would vary with different operating cycles of different businesses. It is more pertinent to use industry averages than overall standards. Eastman's current ratio is computed as follows:

$$\frac{\text{Current assets}}{\text{Current liabilities}} = \frac{\$600,000}{\$445,000} = 1.35 \text{ times}$$

This means that Eastman has $1.35 of current assets for every dollar of current liabilities. This ratio falls short of the 2 to 1 acceptable ratio. However, the current ratio has a general weakness in that it ignores the *composition* of the current asset accounts, which may be as important as their relationship to current liabilities. Therefore, before judging the liquidity position of a business, it is always prudent to examine other factors, such as the ratio of the industry in which it operates, the composition of the company's current assets, and the season of the year. For example, a business that has a 2 to 1 current ratio with, say, 80% of its current assets in inventory would not be as liquid as a company in the same industry that has a 1.5 to 1 ratio with only 30% of its current assets comprising inventory. Therefore, current ratio analysis must be supplemented by other working capital ratios such as the quick ratio.

Quick ratio

The relationship between the more liquid current assets and all current liabilities.

QUICK RATIO The **quick ratio,** also called the acid-test ratio, measures the relationship between the more liquid current asset accounts such as cash, marketable securities, and accounts receivable and the current liability accounts. This ratio complements the current ratio because the problem in meeting current liabilities may rest on delays or even in the inability to convert inventories into cash to meet current obligations, particularly in periods of economic disturbance. This is a more rigorous measure of the short-term liability-paying ability of a business since the least-liquid current asset, inventory, is not included in the calculation because this account takes more time to be converted into cash. The quick ratio does assume that receivables are of good quality and will be converted into cash over the next 12 months.

Eastman's quick ratio, which includes cash ($22,000), prepaid expenses ($60,000), and accounts receivable ($300,000), is calculated as follows:

$$\frac{\text{Quick assets}}{\text{Current liabilities}} = \frac{\$382,000}{\$445,000} = 0.86 \text{ times}$$

An acceptable quick ratio is close to 1 to 1; this means that Eastman's second liquidity position also does not appear to be acceptable. However, before passing final judgment on Eastman's liquidity position, it would be preferable to evaluate the company's historical working capital performance and compare it to industry standards or norms.

Debt/Coverage Ratios

Debt/coverage ratios deal with debt, the funds borrowed by a business to finance the purchase of its assets. Two questions are usually asked when gauging indebtedness. First, what would be the best mix of funds provided by lenders and the owner to buy assets (debt ratios)? Second, will the business be able to service its contractual loan agreement—that is, pay the interest and principal each month (coverage ratios)? The most commonly used debt/coverage ratios are debt-to-total-assets ratio, debt-to-equity ratio, times-interest-earned ratio and fixed-charges coverage ratio.

Debt/coverage ratios

A ratio that measures the capital structure of a business and its debt-paying ability.

DEBT-TO-TOTAL-ASSETS RATIO The **debt-to-total-assets ratio** (also called debt ratio) measures the proportion of all debts (current liabilities and long-term debts listed on the balance sheet) injected into a business by lenders to all assets shown on the balance sheet. The more debt employed by a firm, the more highly leveraged it is. This ratio is calculated by dividing total debts by total assets.

Debt-to-total-assets ratio

A ratio that measures how much debt a business uses to finance all assets.

This ratio is important to lenders because they want to ensure that shareholders invest a sufficient amount of funds in the business in order to spread the risk more equitably. For Eastman, the ratio is computed as follows:

$$\frac{\text{Total debt}}{\text{Total assets}} = \frac{\$1,245,000}{\$1,800,000} = 69\%$$

This means that 69% of Eastman's assets are financed by debt, and thus lenders bear the greatest portion of risk. This suggests that creditors may have difficulty in collecting their loan from the business in the event of bankruptcy or liquidation. Usually when this ratio exceeds 50%, creditors may be reluctant to provide more debt financing. However, as with all other ratios, it is important to assess the type or nature of the assets owned by the business, since that may very well influence how far lenders will go in funding the operations. The assets of the business appearing in the books, for example, may be worth much less than their market value. For example, a business may obtain more funds from lenders to construct a plant in an industrial park located in a large metropolitan area than for one located in an economically depressed region.

Debt-to-equity ratio

A ratio that measures the proportion of debt used compared to equity to finance all assets.

DEBT-TO-EQUITY RATIO The **debt-to-equity ratio** is actually redundant if the debt-to-total assets ratio is used, as the two ratios convey the same information. The debt-to-equity ratio is explained here because financial publications that provide industry average ratios for comparison purposes often cite the debt-to-equity ratio instead of the debt-to-total assets ratio. Therefore, it is important to be familiar with this measure. This ratio also shows whether a company is using debts prudently or has gone too far and is overburdened with debt that may cause problems. It is important to show the relative proportion of lenders' claims compared to ownership claims since this proportion (or percentage) is used as a measure of debt exposure. Companies with debt-to-equity ratios above 1 are probably relying too much on debt.

In the case of Eastman, the ratio works out to:

$$\frac{\text{Total debt}}{\text{Total shareholders' equity}} = \frac{\$1,245,000}{\$555,000} = 2.24 \text{ times}$$

Eastman uses over two dollars in borrowed funds compared to each dollar provided by shareholders. The debt-to-equity ratio shows that a considerable amount of funds is being financed by debt rather than by equity and that the company would find it difficult to borrow additional funds without first raising more equity capital. Management would probably be subjecting the firm to the risk of bankruptcy if it sought to increase the debt-to-equity ratio any further by borrowing additional funds. For this reason, it would be advantageous for Eastman to start thinking about trying to lower its total debt and/or increase owners' equity over the next year in an effort to improve its financial structure.

Times-interest-earned ratio

A ratio that measures to what extent a business can service its interest on debt.

TIMES-INTEREST-EARNED RATIO The **times-interest-earned ratio (TIE)** measures to what extent a business can service its debt, or the business's ability to pay back the loan as per agreement. Take the example of a potential homeowner who is seeking a loan to buy a $200,000 house. Here, the bank would be interested not only in the value of the house in relation to how much the home buyer is prepared to put into the house, but also the buyer's ability to repay the loan on a month-to-month basis. An acceptable ratio is around 30%; that is, for every dollar's worth of gross salary, the loan repayment should not exceed 30 cents. For example, if a home buyer earns $5,000 a month and is in the 40% tax bracket, $1,500 (or 30%) would go against the loan, $2,000 would be used to pay income taxes, and the remaining $1,500 would be left for monthly living expenses. The higher the loan repayment in proportion to the buyer's gross salary, the less he would have left to pay for ongoing living expenses.

This is what the times-interest-earned ratio reveals. It is determined by dividing earnings before interest and taxes (EBIT) by interest charges. The ratio measures the extent to which operating income can decline before the business is unable to meet its annual interest costs.

This ratio shows the number of dollars of income (earnings) before interest and taxes that is available to pay each dollar of interest expense. Adding the income before taxes ($195,000) and interest charges ($35,000) and dividing the sum by interest charges makes the calculation. This $230,000 would be equivalent to the homebuyer's $5,000 gross salary. A higher ratio adds more certainty to the estimate of the business's ability to pay all interest charges as agreed.

The calculation is always done on a before-tax basis, because interest charges are a tax-deductible expense. Referring to Table 2.3, Eastman's ratio is computed as follows:

$$\frac{\text{Income before taxes} + \text{Interest charges}}{\text{Interest charges}} = \frac{\$195,000 + \$35,000}{\$35,000} = 6.57 \text{ times}$$

This means that the company has $6.57 of earnings before interest and taxes (EBIT) available per dollar of interest charges to pay interests and taxes. Since interest and taxes amount to only $3.78 (sum or $97,500 + $35,000 or $132,500/$35,000), the rest is profit. Here is another way of describing this ratio:

EBIT	$6.57
Interest charges	1.00 (ratio)
EBT	5.57
Income taxes	2.78 ($97,000/$35,000)
EAIT	$2.79

With each $6.57 earnings before interest and taxes, Eastman pays $1.00 toward interest and is left with $5.57 in earnings before taxes. Since the company is in the 50% tax bracket, Eastman pays $2.78 in income taxes and is therefore left with $2.79 to:

- pay dividends;
- pay the principal on the loan; and
- reinvest the rest in the business as retained earnings.

The lower the ratio, the riskier it is. To illustrate, if the times-interest-earned ratio is reduced to 3.0, it means that the company would be left with only $2.00 (after paying the interest charges) to pay income taxes, the principal on the loan, and dividends, and to reinvest profit in the business (i.e., retained earnings). A comfortable times-interest-earned ratio is in the 4.0 to 5.0 range. An acceptable ratio is around 3.0 to 4.0 times.

This ratio complements the debt ratios in providing additional information about the company's ability to meet debt obligations. However, it still does not present a complete picture. The ultimate question is one of whether or not the company can meet its commitments to all creditors. Thus, a ratio based on all fixed charges is helpful.

FIXED-CHARGES COVERAGE RATIO This ratio is similar to the times-interest-earned ratio. However, it is more inclusive in that it recognizes that many firms

Fixed-charges coverage ratio

A ratio that measures to what extent a business can service all its fixed charges (e.g, interest, leases).

incur long-term obligations under scheduled rental or lease payments. The cumulative total of those obligations, lease payments plus interest charges, comprise a firm's total annual fixed charges. The **fixed-charges coverage ratio** is calculated by dividing the product of the income before taxes and all fixed charges by fixed charges. Fixed charges can include items such as lease payments, interest on debt, principal repayment, and sinking funds (or the annual payment required to amortize a bond). These types of outlays are regarded as unavoidable. The Eastman ratio is computed as follows:

$$\frac{\text{Income before taxes} + \text{Interest charges} + \text{Lease}}{\text{Interest charges} + \text{Lease}} = \frac{\$195,000 + \$35,000 + \$20,000}{\$35,000 + \$20,000} = 4.54 \text{ times}$$

Other fixed charges such as lease payments, which are included in Eastman's operating results, reduces the times-interest-earned ratio from 6.57 to 4.54. This ratio is being used more often because of the increasing popularity of long-term lease agreements. It shows how much income before taxes is left to pay for all fixed charges.

Asset-Management Ratios

Asset-management ratio

A ratio that evaluates how efficiently managers use the assets of a business.

Asset-management ratios, sometimes referred to as activity ratios, operating ratios, or management ratios, measure the efficiency with which a business uses its corporate assets or resources (i.e., inventories, accounts receivable, capital assets) to earn a profit. These ratios answer one basic question: Does the amount of each category of asset shown on the balance sheet seem too high or too low in view of what the firm has accomplished or wants to realize in the future? The more commonly used asset-management ratios are the average collection period, the inventory turnover, the capital assets turnover, and the total assets turnover.

Average collection period

How many days it takes for customers to pay their bills.

AVERAGE COLLECTION PERIOD The **average collection period (ACP)** measures how long a firm's average sales dollar remains in the hands of its customers. A longer collection period automatically creates a larger investment in assets and may even indicate that the firm is extending credit terms that are too generous. However, management must be aware of competitive credit practices in order to offer similar credit terms so as not to lose sales as a result of too-stringent credit policies. The main point is that investment in accounts receivable has a cost, and excess accounts receivable means that too much debt or shareholders' equity is being used by the business. If this is the case, the business would not be as capital-efficient as it could be.

The average collection period is calculated in two steps. The first step is calculating the average daily sales, which is done by dividing the total annual net sales by 365 days. Eastman's average daily sales is $6,849 ($2,500,000 ÷ 365). The second step is dividing the average daily sales into accounts receivable. Eastman's average collection period is 44 days and is calculated as follows:

$$\frac{\text{Accounts receivable}}{\text{Average daily sales}} = \frac{\$300,000}{\$6,849} = 44 \text{ days}$$

134   Chapter 4: Financial Statement Analysis   NEL

If Eastman were able to collect its receivables within 30 days, the company would reduce its accounts receivable by $95,886 ($6,849 ×14 days) and thus add this amount to the company's treasury to be invested in more productive assets. The question for Eastman is: How long should sales credit be? The accounts receivable manager responsible has to decide whether the average collection period is getting out of hand. If so, actions would have to be taken to shorten credit terms, shut off credit to slow payers, or step up collection efforts.

INVENTORY TURNOVER Inventory turnover (also called inventory utilization ratio) measures the number of times a company's investment in inventory is turned over during a given year. An inventory item "turns" each time a firm buys or repurchases another similar item for stock. The number of times that cycle recurs during the year represents that product's annual turnover rate. Of course, a company's balance sheet does not show individual items. For this reason and for practical purposes, this ratio looks at the total average annual turnover rate. The higher the turnover ratio the better, since a company with a high turnover requires a smaller investment in inventory than one producing the same level of sales with a low turnover rate. Company management has to be sure, however, to keep inventory at a level that is just right in order not to miss sales.

> **Inventory turnover**
> The number of times a year a company turns over its inventory.

While both sales and cost of goods sold are used in the calculation, they give different results because sales exceed cost of goods sold by the amount of the gross margin. Nevertheless, cost of goods sold (not sales revenue) should be used as the numerator for calculating the inventory turnover ratio since the denominator (inventory) is valued at cost, and the purpose is to assess the adequacy of the physical turnover of that inventory.

Another point to remember is that since a company's sales revenue takes place over a 12-month period (moving-picture concept) while inventory level is computed at a specific point in time (still-photography concept), it would be more appropriate to use the average inventory for the year. Usually this is done by taking the beginning plus ending inventory and dividing it by two. Quarterly and even monthly inventory can also be used.

This ratio indicates the efficiency in turning over inventory and can be compared with the experience of other companies in the same industry. It also provides some indication as to the adequacy of a company's inventory for the volume of business being handled. If a company has an inventory turnover rate that is above the industry average, it means that a better balance is being maintained between inventory and cost of goods sold. As a result, there will be less risk for the business of being caught with top-heavy inventory in the event of a decline in the price of raw materials or finished products. Here is how Eastman's ratio is calculated:

$$\frac{\text{Cost of goods sold}}{\text{Inventory}} = \frac{\$1,900,000}{\$218,000} = 8.7 \text{ times}$$

Eastman turns the average item carried in its inventory 8.7 times during the year. Of course, not every item in the company's stock turns at the same rate. Nevertheless, the overall average provides a logical starting point for positive inventory management. If Eastman were able to turn over its inventory faster, say up to 10 times a year, it would reduce its inventory from $218,000 to $190,000 ($1,900,000 ÷ 10) and thus add an extra $28,000 to the company's treasury.

Capital assets turnover

A measurement of how intensively a firm's capital assets are used to generate sales.

CAPITAL ASSETS TURNOVER The **capital (or fixed) assets turnover ratio** (also called fixed assets utilization ratio) measures how intensively a firm's capital assets such as land, buildings, and equipment are used to generate sales. A low capital assets turnover implies that a firm has too much investment in capital assets relative to sales; the ratio is basically a measure of productivity. The following shows how Eastman's capital assets turnover ratio is calculated:

$$\frac{\text{Sales}}{\text{Capital assets}} = \frac{\$2,500,000}{\$1,200,000} = 2.1 \text{ times}$$

This means that the company generates $2.10 worth of sales for every dollar invested in capital assets. If a competing firm has a 3.00 ratio, it implies that it is more productive since every dollar invested in capital assets produces an extra $0.90 in sales. If a business shows a weakness in this ratio, its plant may be operating below capacity, and managers should be looking at the possibility of selling the less-productive assets.

There is one problem with the use of capital assets turnover for comparison purposes. If the capital-assets turnover ratio of a firm with assets that were acquired many years ago is compared to a company that has recently automated its operations to make them more efficient or productive, the more modern firm will have a much lower ratio than the old and less productive company.

Total assets turnover

How intensively a firm's total assets are used to generate sales.

TOTAL ASSETS TURNOVER The **total assets turnover** ratio measures the turnover or utilization of all of a firm's assets, both capital assets and current assets. It also gives an indication of the efficiency with which assets are used; a low ratio means that excessive assets are employed to generate sales and/or that some assets (capital or current assets) should be liquidated or reduced. This ratio is very useful as an initial indicator of a problem with sales or an excessive accumulation of assets. When managers see that this ratio is too low, they may have to modify their sales objectives and plans, examine the growth in the marketplace and competitors, or determine if their asset base is too large. Eastman's total assets turnover is as follows:

$$\frac{\text{Sales}}{\text{Total assets}} = \frac{\$2,500,000}{\$1,800,000} = 1.4 \text{ times}$$

In this case, the company produces $1.40 worth of sales for every dollar invested in total assets. If Eastman is able to reduce its investment in accounts receivable and inventory and/or sell a division or capital assets that are a burden on the company's operating performance, it would increase the total assets turnover ratio and thus would be more productive.

Profitability Ratios

Profitability ratios deal with bottom-line performance and measure the extent to which a business is successful in generating profit relative to sales, investment in assets, and equity. These ratios show the level of business efficiency and effectiveness and reflect the results of a large number of policies and decisions. Therefore, profitability ratios show the combined effects or operating results of liquidity, asset management, and debt management. The most commonly used profitability ratios are profit margin on sales, return on sales, return on total assets, and return on equity.

Profitability ratio
A ratio that measures the overall effectiveness of a business.

PROFIT MARGIN ON SALES **Profit margin on sales** or net operating margin (operating income, or earnings before interest and taxes or EBIT) is computed by dividing net operating income by sales. This ratio is an excellent measure of a firm's ability to make any financial gains since the calculation excludes nonoperating items, such as interest and other income, which are not part of the mainstream operating activities of a business. The main purpose of this ratio is to assess the effectiveness of management in generating operating income. Eastman's profit margin on sales is as follows:

Profit margin on sales
The operating efficiency of a business.

$$\frac{\text{Operating income}}{\text{Sales}} = \frac{\$210,000}{\$2,500,000} = 8.4\%$$

In the case of Eastman, the company generates 8.4 cents in operating income for every dollar's worth of sales.

RETURN ON SALES **Return on sales** represents an important measure of a company's financial performance after recognizing its interest charges and income tax obligation. This ratio gauges the firm's overall ability to squeeze profits from each sales dollar. This ratio measures the overall profitability of a business and is calculated by dividing income after taxes by sales. Profit-seeking businesses are keenly interested in maximizing their return on sales, since this bottom-line figure represents funds either distributed to shareholders in the form of dividends or retained and reinvested in the business. Eastman's return on sales is calculated as follows:

Return on sales
A company's overall ability to generate profit from each sales dollar.

$$\frac{\text{Income after taxes}}{\text{Sales}} = \frac{\$97,500}{\$2,500,000} = 3.9\%$$

For every dollar's worth of sales, Eastman earns 3.9 cents in income after taxes. The higher the ratio, the more beneficial it is to the wealth of the business and to its shareholders. For effective analysis, this ratio should also be compared to historical company performance, used as a platform for planning purposes, and compared to the industry average or specific firms competing in the industry.

The return on sales ratio has a limitation in that it is based on income after deduction of interest expenses. If the company has increased its debt substantially, the result may be a decrease in income after taxes because of the interest expense deduction, even if the return on the shareholders' investment has actually increased. The profit margin on sales overcomes this problem and provides another view of profitability.

RETURN ON TOTAL ASSETS This ratio measures profit performance in relation to all assets invested in the business. **Return on total assets** might be viewed as a measure of the efficiency of total asset usage. It is calculated by dividing net income after taxes by total assets. Eastman's return on total assets is computed as follows:

Return on total assets
The performance of assets employed in a business.

$$\frac{\text{Income after taxes}}{\text{Total assets}} = \frac{\$97,500}{\$1,800,000} = 5.4\%$$

To have any meaning, this ratio should also be compared to the industry average or to competing firms. Another way of measuring the effectiveness of this ratio is by comparing it to the company's cost of capital. The difference between these two numbers would identify the economic value added (EVA).

RETURN ON EQUITY This ratio relates the income after taxes to owners' equity. **Return on equity** is critical to shareholders since it shows the yield they earn on their investments. It also allows shareholders to judge whether the return made on their investment is worth the risk. Eastman's return on equity ratio is calculated as follows:

Return on equity
The yield shareholders earn on their investment.

$$\frac{\text{Income after taxes}}{\text{Owners' equity}} = \frac{\$97,500}{\$555,000} = 17.6\%$$

This means that for every dollar invested in the business by the shareholders, 17.6 cents is earned. By most standards, this profit performance would be judged as relatively good.

Market-Value Ratios

Up to this point, we have examined financial statement ratios, which are calculated by using information drawn from financial statements. The next two ratios are **market-value ratios,** which are used to analyze the way investors and stock markets react to a company's performance.

Market-value ratios
Measurement tools to gauge the way investors react to a company's market performance.

These ratios would be impossible to calculate for Eastman or any company whose stock is not actively traded on the stock market (e.g., Toronto or Vancouver stock exchange). Only public companies have to report market-value ratios at the bottom of their financial statements. If a company's liquidity, asset management, debt management, and profitability ratios are all good, the chances for its market ratios would be excellent, and its share price would also be on the high side.

Market-value ratios relate the data presented on a company's financial statements to financial market data and provide some insight into how investors perceive a business as a whole, including its strength on the securities markets. The more commonly used market-value ratios are earnings per share and price/earnings ratio.

EARNINGS PER SHARE **Earnings per share** is calculated by dividing the net income after preferred dividends—that is, net income available to common shareholders—by the number of common shares outstanding. Assuming that Eastman has 40,000 outstanding shares in 2003, the calculation would be as follows:

Earnings per share

Measures how much net income is available to each outstanding share.

$$\text{Earnings per share} = \frac{\text{Income after taxes}}{\text{Number of shares outstanding}} = \frac{\$97,500}{40,000} = \$2.44$$

Earnings per share is a measure that both management and shareholders value because it is widely used in the valuation of common shares, and is often the basis for setting specific strategic goals and plans. Normally, market analysts do not have to calculate the results since they are readily available in financial pages of daily newspapers.

PRICE EARNINGS RATIO **Price/earnings ratio (P/E)** is one of the most used ratios in share value and securities analysis. The P/E ratio shows how much investors are willing to pay per dollar of reported profits. The P/E ratio is the market price of common shares divided by the earnings per common share. In the case of Eastman, we assume here that in 2003, the company's common share market price was $30.00. Daily newspaper stock market pages include EPS and the P/E ratio, which are considered primary stock valuation criteria. The price/earnings ratio is calculated as follows:

Price/earnings ratio (P/E)

A ratio that indicates how much investors are willing to pay per dollar of reported profits.

$$\text{Price/earnings ratio} = \frac{\text{Price per common share}}{\text{Earnings per common share}} = \frac{\$30.00}{\$2.44} = 12.3 \text{ times}$$

Eastman's 12.3 P/E ratio is more meaningful when compared to the P/E ratios of other companies. If a competitor is generating a P/E ratio of 10, Eastman's P/E ratio is above the competitor, suggesting that it could be regarded as somewhat less risky, or having better growth prospects, or both.

Table 4.2 summarizes Eastman's 16 most important financial ratios.

TABLE 4.2 EASTMAN TECHNOLOGIES INC.'S FINANCIAL RATIOS

Liquidity Ratios

1. Current Ratio

$$\frac{\text{Current assets}}{\text{Current liabilities}} = \frac{\$\,600,000}{\$\,445,000} = 1.35 \text{ times}$$

2. Quick Ratio

$$\frac{\text{Quick assets}}{\text{Current liabilities}} = \frac{\$\,382,000}{\$\,445,000} = 0.86 \text{ times}$$

Debt/Coverage Ratios

3. Debt-to-Total-Assets Ratio

$$\frac{\text{Total debt}}{\text{Total assets}} = \frac{\$\,1,245,000}{\$\,1,800,000} = 69\%$$

4. Debt-to-Equity Ratio

$$\frac{\text{Total debt}}{\text{Total shareholders' equity}} = \frac{\$\,1,245,000}{\$\,555,000} = 2.24 \text{ times}$$

5. Times-Interest-Earned Ratio

$$\frac{\text{Income before taxes + interest charges}}{\text{Interest charges}} = \frac{\$\,195,000 + \$\,35,000}{\$\,35,000} = 6.57 \text{ times}$$

6. Fixed-Charges Coverage Ratio

$$\frac{\text{Income before taxes + interest charges + lease}}{\text{Interest charges + lease}} = \frac{\$\,195,000 + \$\,35,000 + \$20,000}{\$\,35,000 + \$20,000} = 4.54 \text{ times}$$

Asset-Management Ratios

7. Average Collection Period

$$\frac{\text{Accounts receivable}}{\text{Average daily sales}} = \frac{\$\,300,000}{\$\,6,849} = 44 \text{ days}$$

8. Inventory Turnover

$$\frac{\text{Cost of goods sold}}{\text{Inventory}} = \frac{\$\,1,900,000}{\$\,218,000} = 8.7 \text{ times}$$

9. Capital Assets Turnover

$$\frac{\text{Sales}}{\text{Capital assets}} = \frac{\$\,2,500,000}{\$\,1,200,000} = 2.1 \text{ times}$$

10. Total Assets Turnover

$$\frac{\text{Sales}}{\text{Total assets}} = \frac{\$\,2,500,000}{\$\,1,800,000} = 1.4 \text{ times}$$

Profitability Ratios

11. Profit Margin on Sales

$$\frac{\text{Operating income}}{\text{Sales}} = \frac{\$\,210,000}{\$\,2,500,000} = 8.4\%$$

12. Return on Sales

$$\frac{\text{Income after taxes}}{\text{Sales}} = \frac{\$\,97,500}{\$\,2,500,000} = 3.9\%$$

13. Return on Total Assets

$$\frac{\text{Income after taxes}}{\text{Total assets}} = \frac{\$\,97,500}{\$\,1,800,000} = 5.4\%$$

14. Return on Equity

$$\frac{\text{Income after taxes}}{\text{Owners' equity}} = \frac{\$\,97,500}{\$\,555,000} = 17.6\%$$

Market-Value Ratios

15. Earnings per share

$$\frac{\text{Income after taxes}}{\text{Number of shares outstandings}} = \frac{\$\,97,500}{40,000} = \$2.44$$

16. Price/Earnings Ratio

$$\frac{\text{Price per common share}}{\text{Earnings per common share}} = \frac{\$\,30.00}{\$\,2.44} = 12.3 \text{ times}$$

Common-Size Statement Analysis

◀ Objective 3

One of the most frequently used approaches in probing a balance sheet and an income statement is to list the individual items between two successive years by converting the numbers on the financial statements to comparable percentages. This is called "**common-size statement analysis,**" "common-size ratios" or "vertical analysis."

As shown in Table 4.3, each component of Eastman's balance sheet related to assets is expressed as a percentage of total assets, and each component related to liabilities and shareholders' equity is expressed as a percentage of total liabilities and shareholders' equity. Common-size statement analysis is useful for comparing the performance of one business to another or one division to another, because it ignores the difference in the size of the individual accounts. All elements are converted on comparable terms—a percentage.

Common-size statement analysis

Method of converting (1) all numbers on the balance sheet to a percentage of total assets and (2) all numbers on the income statement to a percentage of sales revenue.

TABLE 4.3 COMMON-SIZE STATEMENT ANALYSIS OF THE BALANCE SHEET

Eastman Technologies Inc.
Balance Sheets as at December 31

Assets	2003	%	2002	%
Current assets				
Cash	$ 22,000	1.22	$ 18,000	1.21
Prepaid expenses	60,000	3.33	55,000	3.69
Accounts receivable	300,000	16.67	280,000	18.82
Inventory	218,000	12.11	185,000	12.44
Total current assets	**600,000**	**33.33**	**538,000**	**36.16**
Capital assets (at cost)	1,340,000	74.44	1,050,000	70.56
Accumulated depreciation	140,000	7.77	100,000	6.72
Capital assets (net)	**1,200,000**	**66.67**	**950,000**	**63.84**
Total Assets	$1,800,000	100.00	$1,488,000	100.00
Liabilities				
Current liabilities				
Accounts payable	$ 195,000	10.83	$ 175,000	11.76
Notes payable	150,000	8.33	135,000	9.07
Accrued expenses	20,000	1.11	18,000	1.21
Taxes payable	80,000	4.45	70,000	4.71
Total current liabilities	**445,000**	**24.72**	**398,000**	**26.75**
Long-term debts	**800,000**	**44.44**	**600,000**	**40.32**
Common shares	300,000	16.67	285,000	19.15
Retained earnings	255,000	14.17	205,000	13.78
Shareholders' equity	**555,000**	**30.84**	**490,000**	**32.93**
Total liabilities and equity	$1,800,000	100.00	$1,488,000	100.00

Common-size statement analysis also reveals the change in mix between several elements of a balance sheet and between two consecutive balance sheets. For example, Table 4.3 shows that, in 2002, current assets represented 36.16% out of every asset dollar of the company. In 2003, this ratio was reduced to 33.33%. This is evidenced by the fact that prepaid expenses dropped from 3.69% to 3.33%. In addition, the ratio shows that accounts receivable and inventory, which represent a greater percentage of the total assets, were also reduced. The same analysis can be performed for each component in the liability and shareholders' equity accounts.

Common-size ratio analysis of the income statement provides the same type of information. As shown in Table 4.4, each component of Eastman's income statement is converted to a percentage of total sales. Eastman's income performance improved over the accounting period; in 2003, for every dollar sale, it made 3.9% (or cents) compared to 3.3% (or cents) in 2002. Although the overall profitability performance of the company improved, it is evident that some accounts improved and others deteriorated. For example, the cost of goods sold went from 77.5% to 76.0%, which improved the company's margin from 22.5% to 24.0%. Salary and rent accounts improved, while depreciation showed an increase.

TABLE 4.4 COMMON-SIZE STATEMENT ANALYSIS OF THE INCOME STATEMENT

Eastman Technologies Inc.
Income Statements for the Years Ended December 31

	2003	% of sales	2002	% of sales
Net sales	$ 2,500,000	100.0	$ 2,250,000	100.0
Cost of goods sold	1,900,000	76.0	1,743,000	77.5
Gross margin	**600,000**	**24.0**	**507,000**	**22.5**
Operating expenses				
Selling expenses:				
Sales salaries	$140,000	5.6	128,000	5.7
Advertising expenses	20,000	0.8	19,000	0.9
Total selling expenses	160,000	6.4	147,000	6.6
Administrative expenses:				
Office salaries	170,000	6.8	155,000	6.9
Lease	20,000	0.8	20,000	0.9
Depreciation	40,000	1.6	30,000	1.3
Total administration expenses	230,000	9.2	205,000	9.1
Total operating expenses	390,000	15.6	352,000	15.6
Operating income	**210,000**	**8.4**	**155,000**	**6.8**
Other income	20,000	0.8	18,000	0.8
Other expenses (interest)	35,000	1.4	23,000	1.0
	15,000	0.6	5,000	0.2
Income before taxes	195,000	7.8	150,000	6.6
Income taxes	97,500	3.9	75,000	3.3
Income after taxes	**$ 97,500**	**3.9**	**$ 75,000**	**3.3**

Chapter 4: Financial Statement Analysis

Common-size statement analysis not only enables management to compare financial statements from one year to the next, between companies or operating divisions, but also can reveal sufficient information for management to answer the following types of questions:

- Is our company's capital structure in line with that of the industry?
- Is the ratio of the company's current assets to total assets favourable?
- Is the investment in capital assets in the right proportion?
- Are the manufacturing costs too high?
- Are the operating expenses too high?
- Is the ratio of income after taxes to sales adequate?

Horizontal Statement Analysis

Horizontal statement analysis is performed by reviewing two consecutive financial statements and then comparing the differences between the two periods. The comparison shows the growth or decline in each component of a financial statement, both in absolute dollars and as a percentage. For example, if the income statements show figures of $900,000 in 2002 and $990,000 in 2003, horizontal analysis will show the $90,000 increase and a 10% growth.

Tables 4.5 and 4.6 show horizontal analysis for Eastman's balance sheet and income statement respectively. In Table 4.5, Eastman's balance sheets show significant changes in certain accounts. For example, current assets show an 11.5% growth while total net capital assets increased by 26.3%. The lower part of the balance sheet shows an increase of 11.8% in Eastman's current liabilities, an increase of 33.3% in its long-term debts, and a 13.9% increase in total shareholders' equity.

Table 4.6 shows a 30% increase in income after taxes. Individual components that have contributed to this significant increase are registered in sales, which show a larger increase than the cost of goods sold (11.1% versus 9.0%). Although salaries increased by only 9.4%, this was offset by a hefty 52.2% increase in interest expenses.

Horizontal statement analysis
The percentage change of accounts shown on two consecutive financial statements.

Chapter 4: Financial Statement Analysis

143

TABLE 4.5   HORIZONTAL ANALYSIS OF THE BALANCE SHEET

Eastman Technologies Inc.
Balance Sheets as at December 31

Assets	2003	2002	Amount of change	% of change
Current Assets				
Cash	$ 22,000	$ 18,000	$ 4,000	22.2
Prepaid expenses	60,000	55,000	5,000	9.1
Accounts receivable	300,000	280,000	20,000	7.1
Inventory	218,000	185,000	33,000	17.8
Total current assets	**600,000**	**538,000**	**62,000**	**11.5**
Capital assets (at cost)	1,340,000	1,050,000	290,000	27.6
Accumulated depreciation	140,000	100,000	40,000	40.0
Capital assets (net)	**1,200,000**	**950,000**	**250,000**	**26.3**
Total assets	$1,800,000	$1,488,000	312,000	21.0
Liabilities				
Current liabilities				
Accounts payable	$ 195,000	$ 175,000	20,000	11.4
Notes payable	150,000	135,000	15,000	11.1
Accrued expenses	20,000	18,000	2,000	11.1
Taxes payable	80,000	70,000	10,000	14.3
Total current liabilities	**445,000**	**398,000**	**47,000**	**11.8**
Long-term debts	**800,000**	**600,000**	**200,000**	**33.3**
Common shares	300,000	285,000	15,000	5.2
Retained earnings	255,000	205,000	50,000	24.4
Shareholders' equity	**555,000**	**490,000**	**65,000**	**13.9**
Total liabilities and equity	$1,800,000	$1,488,000	$312,000	21.0

| TABLE 4.6 | HORIZONTAL ANALYSIS OF THE INCOME STATEMENT |

Eastman Technologies Inc.
Income Statement for the Years Ended December 31

	2003	2002	Amount of Change	% of Change
Net sales	$2,500,000	$2,250,000	$250,000	11.1
Cost of goods sold	1,900,000	1,743,000	157,000	9.0
Gross margin	**600,000**	**507,000**	**93,000**	**18.3**
Operating expenses				
Selling expenses:				
Sales salaries	$ 140,000	128,000	12,000	9.4
Advertising expenses	20,000	19,000	1,000	5.3
Total selling expenses	160,000	147,000	13,000	8.8
Administrative expenses:				
Office salaries	170,000	155,000	15,000	9.7
Lease	20,000	20,000	—	—
Depreciation	40,000	30,000	10,000	33.3
Total administration expenses	230,000	205,000	25,000	12.2
Total operating expenses	390,000	352,000	38,000	10.8
Operating income	**210,000**	**155,000**	**55,000**	**35.4**
Other income	20,000	18,000	2,000	11.1
Other expenses (interest)	35,000	23,000	12,000	52.2
	15,000	5,000	10,000	30.0
Income before taxes	195,000	150,000	45,000	30.0
Income taxes	97,500	75,000	22,500	30.0
Income after taxes	**$ 97,500**	**$ 75,000**	**$ 22,500**	**30.0**

Using Benchmarks to Analyze Financial Statements

◀ Objective 5

An effective way to learn from others is benchmarking. **Benchmarking** is the process of searching for the best practices among competitors or noncompetitors that have led to their superior performance. It is looking for companies that are doing "something excellent," learning about their best practices, and then adapting them for your own company. By aspiring to be as good as the best in the industry, managers can set their own ambitions and use this tool as a way to at least catch up if not to become better than the benchmarked company.

Benchmarking is a management technique that was pioneered by Xerox Corporation during the late '70s as part of an effort to respond to international competition in the photocopier industry. Benchmarking is recognized as an effective tool that can help business operators identify and solve problems, formulate strategic plans to achieve specific targets, and implement processes geared for improving their operations. It can help operators better understand their industry in terms of innovative practices and creative solutions that have been applied in different businesses.

Benchmarking

Process of searching for the best practices by comparing oneself to a competitor's excellent performance.

Benchmarks can be grouped under four categories. *Process benchmarks* focus on discrete work processes and operating systems. These benchmarks focus, for example, on the effectiveness of a customer's operating service, customer billing, the way orders are filled and goods received, employee recruitment programs, or even management's planning process. They can help managers to focus on improving efficiencies, lowering costs, or increasing revenues that can all lead to improving the bottom line.

Performance benchmarks focus on product and service comparisons to help pinpoint the effectiveness of a business establishment's strategies related to prices, technical quality, product or services features, speed, and reliability.

Strategic benchmarks (also called outside-of-industry benchmarks) give notice to operators on how effective their business establishment is able to compete within their industry by using excellent norms achieved by businesses that operate outside their own industry (e.g., hotel versus restaurant). Since they are not industry related, they can help managers analyze winning strategies or best practices used by businesses operating in different sectors. These benchmarks help to influence the long-term competitive patterns of a business, and the benefits can accrue over the long term.

Internal benchmarks look at excellent operating systems within a company's own establishments for the purpose of applying processes and systems uniformly throughout its operations. For example, a business that has five restaurants located in different locations will make comparisons amongst all of them to determine the one that shows the best operating results so that others can learn from these organizational units. These excellent business units are referred to as "champions." This method can also be used for comparing similar operating systems employed in different operating functions, such as in the marketing department versus the human resources department.

The following are the steps involved when introducing a benchmarking process[1]:

1. Pinpoint what needs to be benchmarked (e.g., a service, a process).

2. Pinpoint the organization or organizations that will be used as leaders or the "best-in-class" in the activity or field to be benchmarked.

3. Research and examine the data that needs to be collected. The data must provide meaningful comparison.

4. Identify your own current operating performance and gauge the gaps (if any) that exist with the benchmarking organization or business establishment.

5. Formulate the performance levels that you want to achieve within the planning period (short, medium, and long term).

6. Obtain agreement from senior management and communicate to all levels of management and employees what needs to be done to implement the process.

7. Pinpoint realistic objectives to be achieved and the strategies needed to reach them.

---

1 For further reading on this subject, refer to Robert Camp, *Benchmarking: The Search for Industry Best Practices That Lead to Superior Performance*, New York: Quality Press, 1989.

8. Put in place an action plan that will help achieve each objective.

9. Implement the action plans and monitor the process to determine achievement levels and find solutions if goals are not realized.

10. Re-evaluate and update the benchmarks based on more recent performance data.

Financial Benchmarks

Financial benchmarks are financial performance ratios that can be calculated by using dollar figures shown on financial statements (income statement and balance sheet) for the purpose of pinpointing excellent financial performance. These points of reference are recognized as the standard of excellence against which a business can compare performance measures.

Financial benchmarks can also be grouped under four categories: liquidity, debt coverage, asset management, and profitability. However, certain financial benchmarks should be interpreted with some degree of caution. For example, what is an excellent return on sales or debt-to-total assets performance for a particular business operating in a specific industry could be marginal to others operating in a different industry. Because of this, financial benchmarks will be categorized here in three groups: hard financial benchmarks, soft financial benchmarks, and self-regulated financial benchmarks. Table 4.7 shows under which of these three categories the 14 financial ratios described in this chapter fall under and why.

Hard financial benchmarks are financial targets that can be applied to just about any business and industry to gauge financial performance. For example, the ability to service debt can be applied as a measurement tool in any sector or business establishment. To illustrate, a person who is looking for a mortgage to finance his house must demonstrate that he is able to pay (or service) the monthly payments. Banks calculate this ratio for anyone applying for a mortgage, whether the person works for a small or large business establishment, a government organization, or a retail store.

Soft financial benchmarks are financial targets (most financial benchmarks fall in this category) that should be used with some degree of interpretation for two reasons. First, these financial benchmarks vary from industry to industry (depending on the nature of the operation). For example, liquidity ratios for manufacturers would be different from service establishments where inventory is not an important component of working capital. Second, liquidity ratios can vary from business to business depending on the nature or composition of certain accounts shown on a business' financial statements. Here are two examples.

- A business that sells perishable goods, such as a food store or restaurant, will want to collect its bills more quickly than one selling durable goods such as computers and VCRs to wholesalers or retailers. The average collection period would be different.

Financial benchmarks
Financial performance ratios that can be calculated by using dollar figures shown on financial statements (income statement and balance sheet) for the purpose of pinpointing excellent financial performance.

Hard financial benchmarks
Financial targets that can be applied to any business or industry to gauge financial performance.

Soft financial benchmarks
Most financial benchmarks fall in this category and should be used with some degree of interpretation.

TABLE 4.7   FINANCIAL BENCHMARKS

Financial Ratios	Category	Benchmark	Reasons
A. Liquidity Ratios			
1. Current ratio (times)	S SR	1.5 times	S • Aging of accounts receivable and nature of inventory (i.e., perishable) • Composition of working capital accounts (e.g., inventory versus accounts receivable) SR Depends on cash needs, credit policies, and agreement with suppliers
2. Quick ratio (times)	S SR	1.0 times	S Aging of accounts receivable SR Depends on cash needs and credit policies
B. Debt/Coverage Ratios			
3. Debt to total assets (%)	S	50%	Type of assets and location of business
4. Debt to equity (times)	S	1 to 1	Type of assets and location of business
5. Times interest earned (times)	H	4–5 times	
6. Fixed-charges coverage (times)	H	4–5 times	
C. Asset-Management Ratios			
7. Average collection period (days)	SR	30 days	Depends on credit policies
8. Inventory turnover (times)	S	N/A	Level of profit margin and type of inventory (i.e., perishable)
9. Capital assets turnover (times)	S SR	N/A	S Nature of industry, age of capital assets SR Automated versus labour-intensive plant
10. Total assets turnover (times)	S	N/A	S Nature of industry, age of capital assets SR Depends on cash needs, credit policies agreement with suppliers, and automated versus labour-intensive plant
D. Profitability Ratios			
11. Profit margin on sales (%)	S	N/A	Nature of business
12. Return on sales (%)	S	N/A	Nature of business
13. Return on total assets (%)	SR	N/A	SR Depends on cost of capital
14. Return on equity (%)	S	N/A	S Level of risk

S = Soft   H = Hard   SR = Self-regulated

• A business that operates with depreciated assets will show a higher level of productivity (related to sales revenue) than a manufacturing plant that is highly automated and only two or three years old.

Self-regulated financial benchmarks are financial ratios that are contingent on (1) a company's own policies and practices and/or (2) other financial performance measures. For example, a business that offers a 2%/10-day net 30 will probably show a better average collection than a business with a different credit policy. Also, a company that has a high cost of capital (more equity and/or higher interest rates) would require a higher return-on-assets ratio in order to obtain a superior economic value added (EVA) compared to another business that is able to finance most of its assets with debt.

Reading industry and trade journals, and attending trade shows and public symposia helps to keep managers and employees aware of what others are doing and gives them ideas for how to improve their own company's practices.

Benchmarking can be used in three ways: comparing one company to specific competitors, comparing a company to industry, and using trend analysis.

Self-regulated financial benchmark

Financial targets that are determined by a business's own policies, practices, and other financial measures.

Comparing a Company to Specific Competitors

As indicated earlier, the first step in benchmarking is to select, from trade journals or periodicals, the companies that are showing the best financial results in their respective industries for managing their resources (e.g., current assets, accounts receivable, capital assets turnover, etc.). For example, teams in various sectors of a company could embark on benchmarking journeys and try to find solutions to improve various aspects of the company's financial statements.

For example, Standard & Poor's Compustat Services, Inc. produces all types of historical and current financial ratios about individual firms and industries. If a company wants to improve its working capital accounts, debt structure, or profit performance, it should refer to the Report Library and look for companies that excel in these specific areas. The next logical step would be to analyze and ask questions about why that company's performance is superior.

Table 4.8 shows a partial list of the type of financial information that can be drawn from the Compustat Report Library on a company and industry-wide basis.

As shown in the table, there is certainly no lack of information that can be drawn from annual financial reports for comparative purposes. If a business is in the food industry, information can be drawn for all public corporations in that industry, while focusing on the ratios of those companies that are considered excellent.

Comparing a Company to Industry

To be of any value, the ratio of a particular operation or business should be compared to the sector or industry in which the business operates. To illustrate how ratios can be used as measurement tools, let us examine Table 4.9 and compare Eastman's 16 ratios to those of the industry in general.

By looking at Table 4.9, it is possible to see whether Eastman's management should be satisfied or concerned about the financial structure and profitability position of the business.

TABLE 4.8   BENCHMARKING THE CORPORATION

PARTIAL LIST OF FINANCIAL INFORMATION THAT CAN BE DRAWN FROM STANDARD & POOR'S COMPUSTAT SERVICES, INC., LIBRARY REPORT

Income Statement Reports
- Annual Income Statement—11 Years
- Comparative Income Statement
- Comparative Composite Income Statement
- Trend Income Statement
- Common-Size Income Statement
- Quarterly Common-Size Income Statement
- 12-Month Moving Income Statement

Balance Sheet Reports
- Annual Balance Sheet—11 Years
- Annual Balance Sheet—With Footnotes
- Composite Historical Annual Balance Sheet
- Trend Balance Sheet
- Common-Size Balance Sheet
- Quarterly Trend Balance Sheet

Statement of Cash Flows
- Statement of Cash Flows (Annual and Quarterly)
- Cash Statement by Source and Use (Annual and Quarterly)
- 12-Month Moving Statement of Cash Flows
- Working Capital Statement (Annual and Quarterly)

Ratio Reports
- Annual Ratio
- Quarterly Ratio
- Comparative Annual Ratio

Market Reports
- Daily Market Date—Seven Days
- Daily Adjusted Prices

Summary Reports
- Profitability
- Trend—Five Years

Earnings Estimate Reports
- Standardized Unexpected Earnings—Current
- Analysts' Coverage

Graphics Library
- Fundamental Financial Data
- Six-Month and One-Year Daily Price
- Company Segment Pie Chart
- Geographic Segment Pie Chart
- Ten-Year Monthly Price/Earnings

TABLE 4.9 COMPARATIVE RATIO ANALYSIS OF EASTMAN TECHNOLOGIES INC. WITH INDUSTRY

Eastman Technologies Inc.
with Industry

Ratios	Eastman Technologies Inc.	Industry
A. Liquidity Ratios		
1. Current ratio (times)	1.35	2.00
2. Quick ratio (times)	0.86	1.25
B. Debt/Coverage Ratios		
3. Debt-to-total-assets (%)	69	55
4. Debt-to-equity (times)	2.24	1.52
5. Times-interest-earned (times)	6.6	6.0
6. Fixed-charges coverage (times)	4.5	4.12
C. Asset-Management Ratios		
7. Average collection period (days)	44	53
8. Inventory turnover (times)	8.7	6.3
9. Capital assets turnover (times)	2.1	4.3
10. Total assets turnover (times)	1.4	2.1
D. Profitability Ratios		
11. Profit margin on sales (%)	8.4	6.2
12. Return on sales (%)	3.9	2.4
13. Return on total assets (%)	5.4	4.4
14. Return on equity (%)	17.6	14.3
E. Market-Value Ratios		
15. Earnings per share ($)	2.44	2.11
16. Price/earnings ratio (times)	12.3	10.0

On *liquidity*, Eastman appears to be in a difficult position compared to the industry. Maybe there is no reason for concern if the company is able to meet its current commitments on time. If the current ratio were too high, say 3.5 or 4.0, it could mean that the company had money tied up in assets that had low earning power, since cash or marketable securities are low-profit generators. A high liquidity ratio could also mean that management should reduce inventories and accounts receivable and put the proceeds into more productive uses.

On *debt/coverage*, the company appears to be in a more precarious position than industry. This means that the creditors are more exposed; that is, they bear a greater amount of risk. Although Eastman has a higher debt ratio, its fixed debt commitments are slightly better than industry (6.6 compared to 6.0). Nevertheless, the high debt-to-total-assets ratio and debt-to-equity ratio suggests that Eastman has reached, if not exceeded, its borrowing capacity.

On *asset-management*, Eastman is doing a good job with the management of its current assets, but shows signs of weakness in the administration of the capital and total assets. Both the average collection period and the inventory turnover indicate that management is keeping the accounts receivable and inventory at minimum levels. These ratios are also in line with the liquidity ratios that deal with the current portion of the assets shown on the balance sheet. The capital assets turnover and total assets turnover indicate that, overall, the business has too many assets (mainly capital assets) for the level of sales. It also means that the capital assets are not working hard enough. The only way to correct this situation is by increasing sales or by liquidating (if possible) some of its capital assets.

On *profitability*, Eastman is doing well on all counts. Profit margin and income after taxes in relation to sales, assets, and equity is healthy. The profit level is particularly encouraging, despite the fact that capital assets and debt burden are higher than industry.

On *market value,* Eastman is also doing well. Both the earnings per share and price/earnings ratio exceed those of the industry.

Trend Analysis

Comparing one set of figures for a given year to those of the industry gives a good picture of the financial structure and profitability level of a particular business. However, this analysis does not give a full picture of the situation, since it does not take into account the element of time. Comparative analysis gives a snapshot view of the financial statements at a given point in time—like still photography. For a more complete picture, ratios of one company should be compared to those of industry over a period of several years, like a motion picture; this would show whether the financial statements are improving or deteriorating.

Trend analysis is illustrated in Figure 4.1. Four of Eastman's ratios are compared with industry over a four-year period (from 2000 to 2003); they are the current ratio, debt-to-total-assets, capital assets turnover, and return on total assets.

Eastman's *current ratio* has always been inferior to that of industry. The gap widened between 2000 and 2003, and reached a 0.65 spread in 2003 (1.35 versus 2.00). This means that the company decreased the level of receivables and inventory, or increased its current liabilities. Although the current ratio is a good indicator of current asset management, management and creditors may want to learn more about individual current asset accounts by looking at average collection period and inventory turnover.

The *debt-to-total-assets* ratio has deteriorated over the years. While Eastman finances 69 cents of each asset by debt, the industry is at only 55 cents. The debt-ratio position started to weaken in 2000 and continued to deteriorate. The company probably invested large sums of money in capital assets that, as can be seen in the capital assets turnover, are not being very productive in relation to industry.

Eastman's *capital assets* turnover followed the same trend as that of the debt ratio. Although the management of current assets has been good over the last four years, the acquisition of capital assets during the 2000–03 period indicates that Eastman has a surplus of nonproductive capital assets. This means that Eastman management should closely examine all capital asset accounts to see what can be done to improve the ratio. If management sees a growth trend in sales, it might not want to change anything; however, if sales are projected to improve only marginally, it may have to sell some of the capital assets in order to make all assets work at full capacity.

Trend analysis

Analyzing a company's performance over a number of years.

FIGURE 4.1   TREND ANALYSIS

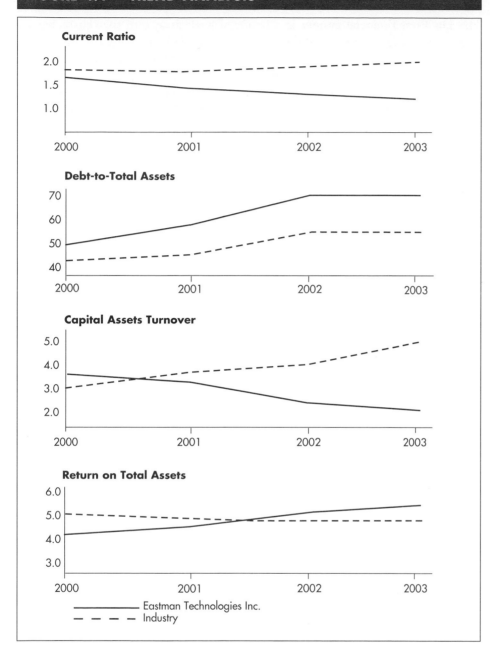

Return on total assets shows a strong position for Eastman. It is operating at a level one point higher than industry (5.4 versus 4.4). The profitability position of Eastman surpassed that of industry in 2002; industry's trend declined over the four-year period, while Eastman's profit position during the same period improved considerably. In short, Eastman's profitability position is healthy despite the fact that the debt ratio and the capital assets turnover are weaker than industry.

The Du Pont Financial System

Du Pont financial system

Presentation of financial ratios in a logical way to measure return on investment (ROI).

The **Du Pont financial system** is a financial analysis system that has achieved international recognition. Du Pont brought together the key financial ratios in a logical presentation to assist management in measuring their return on investment (ROI). The system shows the various components affecting ROI, such as net income, capital and current assets, and the most important figures appearing on the income statement and the balance sheet. Figure 4.2 shows a modified and simplified version of the Du Pont financial system.

The numbers in the upper portion of the diagram deal with balance sheet items, and show how current assets, such as cash, inventory, accounts receivable and capital assets, are employed. To obtain the total assets turnover, sales are divided by total assets.

The numbers in the lower portion of the diagram deal with income statement items. They give the income performance in relation to sales. By multiplying the total assets turnover by the income as a percentage of sales, we obtain the return on investment figures.

Eastman's ROA was calculated by multiplying the 1.4 total assets turnover by the 8.4 profit margin on sales. This gives an 11.7% *before-tax* ROA performance.

FIGURE 4.2 THE DU PONT FINANCIAL SYSTEM

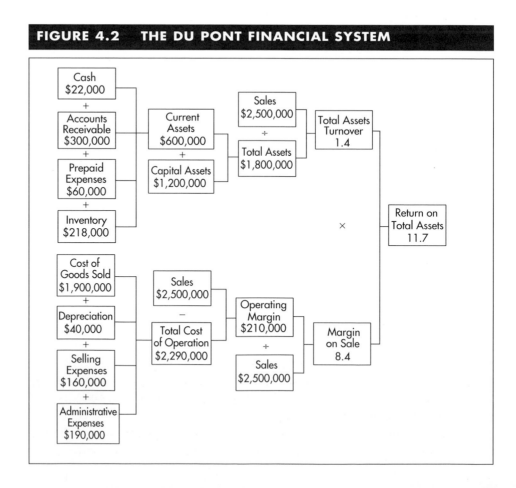

If the company wants to increase this ratio, it will have to improve the capital assets turnover ratio and/or the profit margin on sales.

Limitations of Financial Ratios

◀ Objective 7

Although financial ratios can be effective tools for gauging financial performance and managerial effectiveness, they should not be used blindly. First, they should be used as only one instrument in the management tool kit. Essentially, a financial ratio gives an indication of the weak and strong points in a business. Ratios will not say why something is going wrong and what to do about a particular situation; they pinpoint only where a problem exists. For example, the inventory turnover may have gone from 10 to 7 over a period of three years, and the industry average may be at 9; this means that management will have to investigate further to see what is going wrong and what to do about it.

A second limitation of ratios emerges when a particular set of ratios in a business is compared to other businesses or industry averages. Although there are accepted accounting principles and conventions for constructing financial statements, several different numbers can be used to calculate a ratio. For example, for calculating the inventory turnover, one business may use the cost of goods sold as the numerator, while another may wish to use its sales figures. Even though both companies are part of the same industry, and are equally efficient in the management of inventory, they will show different ratios. In another situation, a business may use the operating profit to calculate its total assets turnover, while another may use the net income after taxes. It is important to remember that before ratios are compared some of the numbers on the financial statements may have to be adjusted for comparison purposes.

Third, the fact that different operating methodologies can be used to run a business may render the comparison of financial ratios irrelevant. For instance, one business may lease most of its assets while another may own them. If this is the case, some of the ratios, such as debt-to-total assets, fixed-charges coverage, total assets turnover, and return on total assets would be irrelevant.

A fourth limitation is the inflation factor. Inflation can make the ratio of a particular business look good or bad over time, when trends are examined. For example, inventory turnover may have deteriorated over a three-year period; the problem here may not be due to the increase in physical inventory but, rather, to a substantial increase in the cost of the goods. Also, an increase in return on total assets may not mean that the company is more efficient; it may reflect the fact that sales prices (and not volume) have increased rapidly and that the capital assets, which are shown on the financial statements at book costs, have remained unchanged.

Finally, since balance sheets reflect the financial situation of a business at a particular point in time, usually at the end of a fiscal period (e.g., as at December 31), this may result in a weak ratio, which might not be the case if the same calculation were done using the June figures.

Although financial ratios have limitations, a business operator should not shy away from using them. As long as a manager knows how to use them, understands their limitations, and accepts the fact that they are used as indicators and as one of many management tools, she will be in a better position to use them wisely, effectively, and with some degree of caution.

❋ Decision-Making in Action

We have covered quite a few financial concepts and techniques, such as ratios, common-size statement analysis, horizontal analysis, internal and external financing, sources and uses of funds, and depreciation as a source of cash. Let's now see how these financial concepts and techniques can be used to analyze financial information and, most importantly, to make decisions that will improve a company's bottom line and cash flow performance.

Referring to Eastman Technologies' financial statements, let's assume that management is formulating its financial objectives for 2004 and making the following projections:

Income statement objectives

- Sales will show a 15% growth.
- Cost of goods sold as a percentage of sales revenue will improve to 75%.
- Operating expenses as a percentage of sales revenue (excluding depreciation) will improve to 13.2%.
- Depreciation expense will be $56,000.

Balance sheet objectives

- Accounts receivable will be reduced to 37 days.
- Inventory turnover will be improved to 10 times.
- Shareholders will invest $100,000 in common shares in the company.
- Capital budget is estimated at $400,000.

Retained earnings statement objectives

- The board of directors wants to pay $50,000 in dividends.

If management wants to invest $400,000 in capital assets such as equipment and machinery, how much money will the company have to borrow from lenders? As shown in Table 4.10, the company will have to borrow $148,974. The following shows how this number was calculated.

- A 15% increase over the $2,500,000 sales in 2003 will bring in $2,875,000 in sales revenue.
- A 75% efficiency performance (as a percentage of sales) at the production level (versus 76% in 2003) will produce $2,156,250 in cost of goods sold.
- Operating expenses, as a percentage of sales, will decrease to 13.2 (versus 14.0 in 2003), or an estimated $379,500.
- Depreciation expense will reach $56,000 in 2004. Total operating expenses as a percentage of sales revenue are therefore estimated at $435,500 and will be reduced to 15.2% of sales (versus 15.6% in 2003).
- The average collection period target of 37 days (compared to 44 days in 2003) will produce $8,551 in cash despite the 15% sales revenue increase. The calculation is as follows:

2003	accounts receivable	$300,000
2004	target of 37 days (average daily sales of $7,877 × 37)	$291,449
Net change		$ 8,551

The projected balance sheet also shows inventory to generate an extra $2,350 in cash (turnover will improve to 10 times compared to 8.7 times). The calculation is as follows:

2003	inventory	$218,000
2004	target of 10 times (cost of goods sold $2,156,500 ÷ 10)	$215,650
Net change		$ 2,350

As shown in the lower portion of Table 4.10, a total of $201,026 will be generated internally from operating activities. As shown under "Investing Activities," the company will invest $400,000 in its capital budget. Since the operating activities will generate $201,026, the company will have to borrow

$148,974 from long-term lenders; shareholders will invest $100,000 in the business and be paid $50,000 in dividends. This means that to finance its capital budget, Eastman will generate 50% of the funds internally and the rest from external sources.

TABLE 4.10 DECISION-MAKING IN ACTION

	2003	2004 (projected)	% of sales	Objectives
Income statement assumptions				
Sales revenue	$2,500,000	$2,875,000	100.0	15% growth
Cost of goods sold	1,900,000	2,156,250	75.0	
Gross margin	600,000	718,750	25.0	
Selling and administration expenses	350,000	379,500	13.2	
Depreciation	40,000	56,000	2.0	
Total operating expenses	390,000	435,500	15.2	
Operating income	210,000	283,250	9.8	
Other expenses/revenue	15,000	15,000	0.5	
Income before taxes	195,000	268,250	9.3	
Income taxes	97,500	134,125	4.6	
Income after taxes	$ 97,500	$ 134,125	4.6	

Balance sheet assumptions related to working capital accounts				
Accounts receivable	44 days	$ 291,449	37 days	
Inventory turnover	8.7 times	$ 215,650	10 times	

Operating activities

Income from operations	$ 134,125	
Depreciation	56,000	
Accounts receivable	8,551	
Inventory	2,350	
Total operating activities		$ 201,026

Financing activities

Common shares	$100,000	
Dividends	(50,000)	
Long-term borrowing	148,974	
Total financing activities		$ 198,974
Investing activities		$ 400,000

Chapter Summary

Financial statements should be analyzed in order to maximize a company's return, ensure its liquidity, maintain its solvency, and secure its long-term prosperity.

◀ Objective 1

Financial ratios can be grouped under five main categories. *Liquidity ratios*, such as current ratio and quick (or acid test) ratio, measure a company's ability to meet

◀ Objective 2

its short-term debts. Second, the *debt/coverage ratios*, such as debt-to-total assets, debt-to-equity, times-interest-earned, and fixed-charges coverage, can be used to measure the extent to which a business is financed by debt as opposed to equity and how it is able to service its debt. Third, the *asset-management ratios*, such as average collection period, inventory turnover, capital assets turnover, and total assets turnover, measure how effectively managers utilize the assets or resources of a business. Fourth, the *profitability ratios*, such as profit margin on sales, return on sales, return on total assets, and return on equity, gauge management's overall effectiveness. Finally, *market-value ratios* compare the data presented on a company's financial statements to financial market data and include earnings per share and price/earnings ratio.

Objective 3 ▶ Analysts who constantly examine financial statements will look at them from different angles. To enhance their financial statement analysis, analysts will go through the common-size statement analysis and horizontal analysis. Common-size-ratio analysis converts all the elements on the financial statements to percentages.

Objective 4 ▶ Horizontal analysis compares the financial results of a particular period to those of the previous period or to the budget.

Objective 5 ▶ In order to derive the most value from financial ratios, management should compare its standards of performance to other companies in the same industry, or to industry averages. Financial benchmarks, that is, businesses that show superior financial performance, should be examined closely to see how well they are doing for the purpose of applying similar practices in a business's own operations. Also, since financial statements give the financial picture of a company at a particular point in time, financial trends should be assessed to see if financial structure and profitability are improving or deteriorating.

Objective 6 ▶ The Du Pont financial system provides an effective way of measuring the overall financial performance of a business. The system measures a company's return on total assets, taking into account the capital assets turnover and the operating margin.

Objective 7 ▶ Although financial ratios are important management tools for assessing the performance of a business, they should be used with caution. Ratios tell where a particular operation is or is not doing well; they do not say why, or what to do about a specific situation.

Key Terms

Asset-management ratios

Average collection period

Benchmarking

Benchmarks

Capital assets turnover

Categories of ratios

Common-size ratios

Common-size statement analysis

Current ratio

Debt/coverage ratios

Debt-to-equity ratio

Debt-to-total-assets ratio

Du Pont financial system

Earnings per share

Financial benchmark

Financial ratio

Fixed-charges coverage ratio

Hard financial benchmark

Horizontal statement analysis

Inventory turnover

Liquidity

Liquidity ratios

Market-value ratios

Price/earnings ratio (P/E)

Profit margin on sales

Profitability ratios

Quick ratio

Ratio analysis

Ratio measures

Return

Return on equity

Return on sales

Return on total assets

Self-regulated financial benchmark

Soft financial benchmark

Solvency

Times-interest-earned ratio

Total assets turnover

Trend analysis

Review Questions

1. Why is it important to use ratios to analyze financial statements?

2. What does management want to achieve when they try to "ensure liquidity" and "maintain solvency"?

3. What do liquidity ratios reveal?

4. Differentiate between the current ratio and the quick ratio.

5. Is it possible for a firm to have a high current ratio and still have difficulty paying its current bills? Why?

6. Is the inventory ratio more important to a grocery store than to a hardware store? Why?

7. What is the purpose of the debt/coverage ratios?

8. What is the purpose of the times-interest-earned ratio?

9. What is the purpose of the asset-management ratios?

10. Explain the purpose of the inventory turnover ratio.

11. Profitability ratios try to indicate the financial performance of a business in terms of sales, total assets, and equity. Explain.

12. What is a financial benchmark and what is it used for?

13. What is the purpose of common-size statement analysis? Horizontal analysis?

14. Explain what the Du Pont financial system tries to reveal.

15. Why should managers examine trends when looking at financial statements?

16. What are the limitations of financial ratios?

Discussion Questions

1. Why are financial ratios so critical to managers when evaluating business performance?

2. Explain why some companies can influence many of their ratios simply by choosing their fiscal year-end. In what type of industries do you think this might be a particular problem?

3. Financial ratios are analyzed by four groups of individuals: managers, short-term lenders, long-term lenders, and equity investors. What is the primary emphasis of each group in evaluating ratios?

Testing Your Comprehension

True/False Questions

___F___ 1. The current ratio is an excellent way to gauge profitability.

___F___ 2. The only current asset account not included in calculating the quick ratio is accounts receivable.

___F___ 3. The debt-to-total-assets ratio measures the proportion of long-term debt to all assets.

___T___ 4. The times-interest-earned ratio measures the extent to which a business can service its debt.

___F___ 5. Calculating the average collection period is done by dividing total sales revenue by the average daily sales.

___T___ 6. The higher the inventory turnover is, the better it is.

___T___ 7. A profitability ratio can be considered an effectiveness ratio.

___F___ 8. Return on total assets is calculated by dividing capital assets by income after taxes.

___T___ 9. Vertical analysis is also called common-size statement analysis.

___T___ 10. The Du Pont financial system shows a company's return on assets by multiplying total assets turnover by the operating margin on sales ratio.

___F___ 11. Increasing the average collection period can increase cash flow.

___T___ 12. Inventory turnover is calculated by dividing operating margin by inventory.

___T___ 13. A times-interest-earned ratio of 6.0 is better than 4.0.

___F___ 14. Return on sales is calculated by dividing sales revenue by the operating margin.

Multiple-Choice Questions

1. Net working capital is the difference between:
   a. current assets and long-term liabilities
   b. current assets and current liabilities
   c. operating assets and operating expenses
   d. current revenues and current expenses
   e. net margin and net capital

2. Maximizing return has to do with the relationship between:
   a. current assets and current liabilities
   b. income after taxes and total assets
   c. earnings before interest and taxes and interest
   d. income after taxes and sales revenue
   e. total assets and total debts

3. The account removed from current assets to calculate the quick ratio is:
   a. cash
   b. accounts receivable
   c. inventory
   d. prepaid expenses
   e. intangible assets

4. The following is a debt-coverage ratio:
   a. quick ratio
   b. inventory turnover
   c. earnings per share
   d. return on equity
   e. fixed-charges coverage ratio

5. The times-interest-earned ratio is calculated by dividing income before interest and taxes, and interest charges by:
   a. income after taxes
   b. income before taxes
   c. interest charges less income taxes
   d. interest charges
   e. operating income

6. The following is an asset-management ratio:
   a. current ratio
   b. average collection period
   c. times-interest-earned ratio
   d. return on assets
   e. quick ratio

7. Inventory turnover is calculated by dividing inventory into:
   a. operating expenses
   b. gross margin
   c. cost of goods sold
   d. total assets
   e. working capital

8. Total assets turnover is calculated by dividing total assets into:
   a. gross margin
   b. operating income
   c. cost of goods sold
   d. income after taxes
   e. sales revenue

9. Profit margin on sales measures performance related to:
   a. capital assets
   b. gross margin
   c. working capital
   d. operating income
   e. income after taxes

10. The following is a profitability ratio:
    a. return on sales ratio
    b. quick ratio
    c. inventory ratio
    d. times-interest-earned ratio
    e. total assets turnover

Chapter 4: Financial Statement Analysis

11. The Du Pont financial system measures a company's return on:
    a. sales
    b. assets
    c. equity
    d. gross margin
    e. current assets

12. The common-size income statement analysis technique uses:
    a. sales revenue as the numerator
    b. sales revenue as the denominator
    c. profit after taxes as the denominator
    d. profit after taxes as the numerator
    e. gross margin as the denominator

Fill-in-the-Blanks Questions

1. _____ ratios measure the ability of a firm to meet its cash obligations.

2. The _____ ratio gauges the business's general liquidity.

3. The _____ ratio shows the relationship between the more liquid current assets and all current liabilities.

4. The _____ ratio measures to what extent a business can service its interest on debt.

5. _____ ratios evaluate how efficiently managers use the assets of a business.

6. To calculate the average collection period, you have to divide accounts receivable by the _____.

7. Total assets turnover makes the relationship between _____ and total assets.

8. Profit margin on sales makes the relationship between _____ and sales revenue.

9. _____ ratios are measurement tools used to gauge the way investors react to a company's market performance.

10. _____ analysis shows the percentage change of accounts shown on two consecutive financial statements.

11. _____ is the process of searching for the best practices by comparing oneself to a competitor's excellent performance.

12. The _____ financial system presents financial ratios in a logical way to measure return on investment (ROI).

Learning Exercises

Exercise 1(a)-

The Millers are trying to find ways to improve their cash flow situation during 2004. After looking closely at their working capital accounts, they believe that additional cash could be generated internally if the accounts receivable and inventory were managed more efficiently. With the following information, calculate how much cash CompuTech could generate within the next six months if the Millers were able to improve the average collection period to 30 days and the inventory turnover to 4.5 times.

Sales revenue	$420,000
Cost of goods sold	$209,000
Accounts receivable	$ 45,000
Inventory	$ 65,000

Exercise 1(b)–

Mary Pascal is having some problems with her cash flow. She asks her accountant to find a solution that would generate more cash from her working capital. The accountant indicates that if Mary were to manage her accounts receivable and inventory more efficiently, she would be able to improve her cash flow performance. With the following information, calculate how much cash Mary could generate within the next four months if she were able to improve her average collection period to 35 days and the inventory turnover to six times.

Sales revenue	$2,500,000
Cost of goods sold	1,700,000
Accounts receivable	300,000
Inventory	400,000

Exercise 2(a) –

In 2004, the Millers will be approaching a bank to determine the possibility of increasing their term loan. Bankers will analyze CompuTech's ability to service its debt. With the following information, calculate CompuTech's times-interest-earned ratio and fixed-charges coverage ratio for 2004. If you were the banker, would you feel comfortable with the company's ability to service its debt? Why or why not?

INCOME STATEMENT
FOR THE PERIOD ENDING DECEMBER 31, 2004

Sales revenue		$420,000
Cost of goods sold		209,000
Gross margin		211,000
Operating expenses		
Salaries	$93,000	
Lease payment	7,000	
Depreciation	40,000	
Other expenses	11,000	
Total operating expenses		151,000
Operating income		60,000
Interest charges		14,000
Income before taxes		46,000
Income taxes		13,000
Income after taxes		$ 33,000

Exercise 2(b)–

Helen Wiseman, owner of a convenience store, is going to meet her banker and is hoping for an increase in her working capital loan. She figures that an additional loan would increase her interest charges by an extra $10,000. Before seeing her banker, she asks her accountant to determine whether she would have difficulty in servicing her debt with the additional interest charges.

With the following information, calculate the company's times-interest-earned ratio and fixed-charges coverage ratio. If you were the banker, would you consider approving the loan? Why or why not?

INCOME STATEMENT

Sales revenue		$600,000
Cost of goods sold		200,000
Gross margin		400,000
Operating expenses		
Sales salaries	150,000	
Rent	20,000	
Office salaries	90,000	
Advertising	23,000	
Total operating expenses		283,000
Operating income		117,000
Interest charges		30,000
Income before taxes		87,000
Income taxes		25,000
Income after taxes		$ 62,000

Exercise 3(a) –

By using the information contained in Exercise 1(a) and Exercise 2(a), calculate the amount of cash that CompuTech could generate between January 1 and December 31, 2004.

Exercise 3(b) -

After being in business for six years, Graham Mason, owner of a small retail store, is considering buying a new information system that would provide him with better operating and financial information. Graham feels that the new system would help him have much better control over his inventory so that he would be able to manage his purchases more wisely. He is also interested in making major renovations to his store.

After going through some detailed calculations, he calculates that he would have to invest around $250,000 to have his plans completed by December 31, 2004. Graham is considering borrowing money from the bank. However, before meeting his banker, he asks his accountant to figure out how much cash he would be able to squeeze from his operations (internally) to help finance his two projects.

Graham feels that he would be able to improve his average collection period to 40 days and turn his inventory around three times a year by December 31, 2004. With the following information, calculate how much cash Graham could raise internally between January 1 and December 31, 2004.

BALANCE SHEET
AS AT DECEMBER 31, 2004

Cash	$ 25,000	Accounts payable	$150,000
Accounts receivable	100,000	Notes payable	50,000
Inventory	200,000	Deferred taxes	50,000
Total	$325,000	Total	$250,000

INCOME STATEMENT
FOR THE PERIOD ENDING DECEMBER 31, 2004

Revenue	$500,000
Cost of goods sold	300,000
Gross margin	200,000
Other expenses	135,000
Depreciation	15,000
	150,000
Income before taxes	50,000
Income taxes	25,000
Income after taxes	$ 25,000

Exercise 4

By using CompuTech's financial statements for 2004, calculate the following ratios:

1. current ratio

2. quick ratio

3. debt-to-total-assets ratio

4. debt-to-equity ratio

5. times-interest-earned ratio

6. fixed-charges coverage ratio

7. average collection period

8. inventory turnover ratio

9. capital assets turnover ratio

10. total assets turnover ratio

Chapter 4: Financial Statement Analysis

11. profit margin on sales ratio

12. return on sales ratio

13. return on total assets ratio

14. return on equity ratio

COMPUTECH SALES AND SERVICES
BALANCE SHEET AS AT DECEMBER 31, 2004

Current assets		Current liabilities	
Cash	$ 16,000	Accounts payable	$ 20,000
Marketable securities	5,000	Term loan	40,000
Prepaid expenses	5,000		
Accounts receivable	45,000		
Inventory	65,000		
Total current assets	136,000	Total current liabilities	60,000
		Long-term debts	50,000
Capital assets		Shareholders' equity	
Capital assets (cost)	210,000	Capital shares	100,000
Less: acc. depreciation	78,000	Retained earnings	58,000
Capital assets (net)	132,000	Shareholders' equity	158,000
Total assets	$268,000	Total liabilities and equity	$268,000

COMPUTECH SALES AND SERVICES
INCOME STATEMENT FOR THE PERIOD ENDING 2004

Net sales revenue		$420,000
Cost of goods sold		209,000
Gross margin		211,000
Operating expenses		
Sales expenses	$66,000	
Leasing	7,000	
Administrative expenses	38,000	111,000
Operating income (without depreciation)		100,000
Depreciation		40,000
Operating income		60,000
Other expenses (interest)		14,000
Net income before taxes		46,000
Income taxes		13,000
Net income after taxes		$ 33,000

Cases

Case 1: Tasty Restaurants

Jaclyn Hargrove is the owner of six Tasty Restaurants. For the past 10 years, she has always relied on her accountant to provide the analysis of her financial statements. Jaclyn feels that if she were able to read her financial statements, she would be able to improve the analysis of her financial performance. More importantly, she would be able to improve the decisions that touch on all aspects of her business from the management of working capital to making investments.

Jaclyn has just purchased accounting software that would provide her with monthly, quarterly, and yearly financial statements and all types of ratios that would help her improve her analysis and decisions.

To help her understand the meaning of her financial statements, Jaclyn asks you for some advice. She shows you her December 31, 2003, balance sheet and income statement and asks you to calculate and explain the meaning of the more important financial ratios.

To help Jaclyn understand financial ratios, calculate the 2003 financial ratios by using the 2003 balance sheet and income statement, and explain to her the meaning and significance of each ratio.

a) current ratio

b) quick ratio

c) debt-to-total-assets ratio

d) debt-to-equity ratio

e) times-interest-earned ratio

f) fixed-charges coverage ratio

g) average collection period

h) inventory turnover ratio

i) capital assets turnover ratio

j) total assets turnover ratio

k) profit margin on sales ratio

l) return on sales ratio

m) return on total assets ratio

n) return on equity ratio

BALANCE SHEET
AS AT DECEMBER 31, 2003

Current assets		Current liabilities	
Cash	$ 90,000	Accounts payable	$ 710,000
Term deposits	120,000	Notes payable	250,000
Accounts receivable	900,000	Accruals	260,000
Inventory	1,100,000	Deferred taxes	90,000
Total current assets	2,210,000	Total current liabilities	$1,310,000
		Long-term debt	1,640,000
Capital assets		Shareholders' equity	
Capital assets (cost)	2,600,000	Preferred shares	100,000
Less: acc. depreciation	700,000	Common shares	500,000
		Retained earnings	560,000
Capital assets (net)	1,900,000	Shareholders' equity	1,160,000
Total assets	$4,110,000	Total liabilities and equity	$4,110,000

Chapter 4: Financial Statement Analysis

INCOME STATEMENT
FOR THE PERIOD ENDING DECEMBER 31, 2003

Net sales revenue		$4,500,000
Cost of goods sold		3,300,000
Gross margin		1,200,000
Operating expenses		
Sales expenses	$350,000	
Rent	100,000	
Administrative expenses	345,000	795,000
Operating income (without depreciation)		405,000
Depreciation		50,000
Operating income		355,000
Other income	20,000	
Other expenses (interest)	120,000	100,000
Net income before taxes		255,000
Income taxes		127,500
Net income after taxes		$ 127,500

Case 2: Imperial Electronics Ltd.

Imperial Electronics Ltd. is a publicly owned company with 100,000 common shares outstanding. At the last executive committee meeting, Sandra Redgrave, CEO of the company, informed the board members of the economic slowdown that she anticipated during the next several years. She also told them that several U.S. firms were considering becoming more aggressive in the industry, particularly in the Canadian market.

Because of these external threats, management of Imperial Electronics Ltd. anticipates more difficult times ahead. For this reason, company management is now trying to watch its financial ratios more closely in order to keep the firm under control as it grows.

On the basis of the information contained in the company's financial statements, calculate and comment on Imperial Electronics Ltd.'s December 31, 2003, financial ratios by comparing them to the industry average. The common shares are valued on the stock market at $120.00.

a) current ratio
b) quick ratio
c) debt-to-total-assets ratio
d) debt-to-equity ratio
e) times-interest-earned ratio
f) fixed-charges coverage ratio
g) average collection period
h) inventory turnover ratio

i) capital assets turnover ratio
j) total assets turnover ratio
k) profit margin on sales ratio
l) return on sales ratio
m) return on total assets ratio
n) return on equity ratio
o) earnings per share ratio
p) price/earnings ratio

In July 2004, management of Imperial Electronics Ltd. is planning to invest substantial sums of money ($3,000,000) in capital assets for modernization and expansion purposes. The management committee is considering the possibility of borrowing funds from external sources. However, before meeting the investors, members of the management committee want to examine the amount that could be generated internally between January 1 and June 30, 2004.

Industry financial ratios are as follows:

a)	current ratio	1.95	times
b)	quick ratio	1.03	times
c)	debt-to-total-assets ratio	55	percent
d)	debt-to-equity ratio	1.21	times
e)	times-interest-earned ratio	6.43	times
f)	fixed-charges coverage ratio	4.51	times
g)	average collection period	35.00	days
h)	inventory turnover ratio	7.00	times
i)	capital assets turnover ratio	5.10	times
j)	total assets turnover ratio	2.90	times
k)	profit margin on sales ratio	9.10%	
l)	return on sales ratio	2.10%	
m)	return-on-total-assets ratio	6.00%	
n)	return on equity ratio	21.00%	
o)	earnings per share	$8.50	
p)	price/earnings ratio	10.3	times

Assuming that the company is just as efficient as industry in managing its inventory and accounts receivable, calculate the amount of cash it could generate between January 1 and June 30, 2004. Also, assume that in 2004 sales will increase by 9%, after-tax return on sales will be 5%, depreciation will increase to $400,000, and cost of goods sold in relation to sales revenue will improve to 72%.

Chapter 4: Financial Statement Analysis

IMPERIAL ELECTRONICS LTD.
INCOME STATEMENT
FOR THE PERIOD ENDED DECEMBER 31, 2003

Net sales		$30,000,000
Cost of goods sold		23,000,000
Gross margin		7,000,000
Operating expenses		
Selling expenses	$2,500,000	
Lease	125,000	
Administrative expenses	1,700,000	
Total operating expenses		4,325,000
Operating income (without depreciation)		2,675,000
Depreciation		300,000
Operating income		2,375,000
Other expenses (interest)		400,000
Net income before taxes		1,975,000
Income taxes		900,000
Net income after taxes		$ 1,075,000

IMPERIAL ELECTRONICS LTD.
BALANCE SHEET
AS AT DECEMBER 31, 2003

Current assets		*Current liabilities*	
Cash	$ 150,000	Accounts payable	$ 2,500,000
Term deposits	200,000	Notes payable	1,600,000
Prepaid expenses	250,000	Accruals	220,000
Accounts receivable	3,500,000	Income tax payable	80,000
Inventory	4,100,000	Total current liabilities	4,400,000
Total current assets	$ 8,200,000	Long-term debt	4,200,000
Capital assets		*Shareholders' equity*	
Capital assets (gross)	$ 8,200,000	Common shares	2,500,000
Less: depreciation	2,000,000	Retained earnings	3,300,000
Total capital assets (net)	6,200,000	Total net worth	5,800,000
Total assets	$14,400,000	Total liabilities and equity	$14,400,000

5

Profit Planning and Decision-Making

Learning Objectives

After reading this chapter, you should be able to:

1. Explain the relevance of break-even analysis.

2. Differentiate between cost behaviour: fixed, variable, and semi-variable costs.

3. Make the connection between the anatomy of profit: the relationship between revenue and costs.

4. Explain the break-even analysis in terms of the contribution margin, the relevant range, and the relevant costs.

5. Draw the break-even chart.

6. Calculate the break-even point, the cash break-even point, and the profit break-even point.

7. Show where the break-even point can be applied in different organizations.

8. Indicate how the break-even wedge can be used to analyze a company's profit performance.

9. Differentiate between different types of cost concepts such as committed and discretionary costs, controllable and noncontrollable costs, and direct and indirect costs.

Chapter Outline

OPENING CASE

Now that the Millers have been in business for close to two years, they are continuously faced with operating and investment decisions such as:

- Should we increase our advertising budget? By how much?
- Should we hire more part-time or full-time sales clerks? Should we let some go? If so, how many?
- Should we introduce a new product line?
- Should we open a new retail outlet?
- Should we reduce our selling price for a product line? Increase it? By how much?
- Should we introduce a new service?

The Millers realize that the key element that will determine whether or not they should go ahead with some of these decisions is whether the increase in sales revenue will be adequate to generate sufficient profit. For example, if an additional $2,000 in advertising is spent, how much more revenue should be generated in order to pay for this cost and to generate a profit? Although the Millers had been making some of these decisions by using their instinct and good judgment, they were looking for a decision-making tool that could help validate their feelings. Len had heard that break-even analysis is an effective tool that could be used for that purpose. He therefore decided to meet with May Ogaki, his accountant, to learn more about how this tool could be used to improve the quality of his decisions. During the meeting, May made the following comments:

> Break-even analysis is an excellent and effective decision-making tool and very easy to apply. Before using this tool, however, you need to carefully differentiate your store's costs in terms of what is fixed and what is variable. You will surely have to draw on your cost-accounting knowledge and skills if you want to use the break-even technique as a reliable decision-making instrument. As you are fully aware, some of your costs are relatively easy to classify between fixed and variable. For example, costs such as the goods you buy from suppliers and sales commissions vary directly with sales revenue and, for this reason, they are considered "variable." The more you sell, the more you buy goods from suppliers. However, costs such as leasing and office salaries do not vary with the level of sales activities (sales revenue). For that reason, they are considered "fixed."
>
> Other costs, however, are more difficult to differentiate; for example, you may want to classify some of your sales clerks' salaries as fixed and some as variable. Advertising could also be considered fixed or variable. It all depends

on how you look at these costs. For instance, should you set a "fixed budget" for advertising a product line, or should you increase your advertising budget if you sell more of a certain product line? Once you have determined exactly how each item (e.g., advertising, sales salaries, etc.) shown on your operating budget should be considered (fixed or variable), doing the break-even calculation can be quick and easy.

The allocation of your store's overhead costs to each department is also an important element to consider when calculating the break-even point for different product lines. For example, how will you want to distribute your interest charges, your depreciation expense, and office salaries against each product line? You will have to go through this cost-accounting allocation process if you want to get the full benefit of the break-even technique.

Len felt that the break-even calculation would be an excellent tool and considered investing some time and effort in understanding cost accounting in order to improve the effectiveness of his decisions.

This chapter examines how break-even analysis can be used as a decision-making instrument. In particular, it focuses on the following two topics:

1. the interplay between the various cost elements (fixed versus variable) involved in decision-making; and

2. how break-even analysis can be used as an effective decision-making tool.

Introduction

If a business were operated without fixed costs (e.g., rent, salaries), its managers would not have to be concerned about incurring a loss. In fact, managers of this unusual type of business would not have to go through detailed calculations to set prices for different products nor evaluate the level of risk associated with the business. If variable costs (e.g., purchases, sales commission) were the only element to be deducted from sales revenue to arrive at a profit, profit planning would be relatively simple. In this instance, all that would be required would be to deduct, say, a $5.00 variable cost from a $7.00 unit selling price and obtain a $2.00 profit. Irrespective of whether a business sold 20 or 100,000 widgets, it would make a $2.00 profit on each unit. The absence of fixed costs would not only facilitate the preparation of profit plans and detailed operating budgets but also allow the business to operate at minimal or no risk. Under these operating conditions, chances for incurring a loss would be virtually nonexistent.

However, businesses do not operate under such favourable conditions. The fact that businesses have to pay ongoing fixed costs creates an element of the unknown. Recognizing the fact that fixed costs must be paid, managers must have a complete knowledge of the number of widgets that should be sold. In addition, they should know at what price each product should be sold, the exact costs that will be incurred in producing each widget, and the total costs that will be generated by the business if x or y widgets are sold.

If managers are to plan their profit in a proficient manner, and measure precisely the risk they are prepared to take, they should be able to calculate, analyze, and compare the projected sales volume, the unit selling price for each product, and all costs associated with running the business. If, on the other hand, managers are unable to forecast their costs and revenues with reasonable accuracy, the chances of aiming at a favourable profit level are minimized.

Objective 1 ➡

Relevance of Break-Even Analysis

Break-even analysis is a straightforward yet very powerful financial technique that can help managers make a wide range of important decisions that touch on all types of business activities.

For *pricing decisions,* break-even analysis helps to analyze the effect of changing prices and volume relationships on levels of profit. For example, if a software company decides to increase its unit selling price by 5% with no change in variable costs and fixed costs, break-even analysis would make it easy for managers to determine whether the change will have a positive or negative impact on profitability. Nevertheless, the most difficult variable element to pin down in this particular analysis is the reaction of the competitors.

Whether to take on a *new product, new plant, new sales representative, new sales office,* or *new advertising campaign* are typical decisions that break-even analysis can help with. For example, break-even analysis can help determine the incremental sales volume level that is required in order to justify an investment, given the projected unit selling price and operating costs.

Modernization or *automation* decisions can be made more clearly with break-even analysis since it can disclose profit implications. The break-even analysis framework simply requires a determination to what extent variable costs (e.g., direct labour, etc.) can be substituted by fixed costs (e.g., interest charges or depreciation of capital assets). For example, if management wants to invest $1.0 million to automate a plant, additional costs (presumably most of them fixed) associated with the automation program would replace the use of workers and the reduction of wages (variable costs). Break-even analysis helps to study the interplay between the various types of costs affecting a business and the impact they have on profit performance.

Expansion decisions involve the study of the impact that incremental volume has on profitability. When a business reaches full operating capacity at one of its plants, management must decide whether to use its resources to expand the existing plant or to build a new one. The key question is this: Will the incremental volume and cost levels have a positive (or negative) effect on profitability? Because expansion programs impact variable costs, fixed costs, economies of scale, and profitability, break-even analysis helps to analyze the interplay between each of these variables.

Profit decisions deal with what a company needs to do in order to achieve a certain level of profitability. For example, if a company is operating at a loss or below-profit performance and wants to achieve a profit objective, say 10% return on investment, the break-even analysis tool will help company management decide on the following in order to achieve the objective.

- How many units should we sell?
- At what price should we sell our product or service?
- What should our fixed costs be?
- What should each unit cost?
- Which product or service should we push?

Cost Behaviour: Fixed, Variable, and Semi-Variable Costs

◀ Objective 2

Calculating the profit generated by a product at different levels of production requires a total awareness of how volume, price, product mix, and product costs relate to one another. The tool used for analyzing the behaviour of these different variables, how they relate to one another, and how they affect profit levels, is called **cost-volume-profit analysis.** The major advantage to understanding the cost-volume-profit concept is that it helps managers to determine the interrelationships among all costs affecting profits.

To prepare profit and operating budgets, managers must classify all costs into two distinct groups: fixed costs and variable costs.

Cost-volume-profit analysis

Tool used for analyzing how volume, price, product mix, and product costs relate to one another.

Fixed Costs

Costs that remain constant at varying levels of production are called **fixed costs,** also known as period costs, time costs, constant costs, or standby costs. Although there are subtle variations between each of these terms, they all have an element of "fixedness," and all must be paid eventually. Such costs do not change as a result of variations in levels of production. Some of these costs are inescapable because they are essential for operating purposes. The following are typical examples of fixed costs:

Fixed costs

These are costs that remain constant at varying levels of production.

- rent;
- interest on mortgage;
- property insurance;
- property taxes;
- office salaries;
- depreciation;
- protection service;
- telephone; and
- professional fees.

Figure 5.1 shows the relationship between fixed costs and volume.

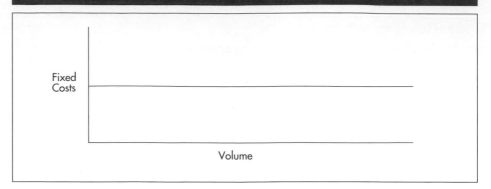

FIGURE 5.1 RELATIONSHIP OF FIXED COSTS TO VOLUME

Variable Costs

Costs that vary directly with fluctuations in production levels are referred to as **variable costs,** also known as direct costs, out-of-pocket costs, or volume costs. As the volume of a business increases, so do these costs. For example, if a business produces 100 widgets at a per-unit cost of $0.10 for material A and $0.20 for material B, the firm would therefore incur a total variable cost of $30. If the firm sells 1,000 units, the costs would increase to $300.

The reason such costs are called variable is because they vary almost automatically with volume. The following are typical examples of variable costs:

- sales commission;
- direct labour;
- packing materials;
- electricity;
- overtime premiums;
- equipment rentals;
- materials;
- freight-out; and
- fuel.

Figure 5.2 shows the relationship between variable costs and volume.

Semi-Variable Costs

While some costs vary directly and proportionately with volume, others have some characteristics of both fixed and variable costs; in other words, they possess different degrees of variability, or they change in a disproportionate way with changes in output levels. For this reason, these types of costs are considered **semi-variable** (or semi-fixed).

Variable costs

Costs that fluctuate directly with changes in volume of production.

Semi-variable costs

Costs that change disproportionately with changes in output levels.

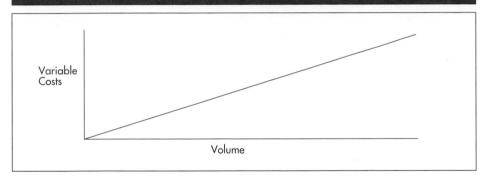

FIGURE 5.2 RELATIONSHIP OF VARIABLE COSTS TO VOLUME

Let us take four examples. First, electricity in a house is a typical example. House owners have to pay a basic fixed cost each month (say $50.00) even if they don't use any electricity; in fact, the owner could be away on holidays for a month and still receive a $50.00 bill from the hydro company. However, the owners would have to pay additional costs if they were at home using electrical equipment (e.g., stove, toasters, heaters, dryers, etc.). This cost would vary according to the number of people living in the house and the extent to which electrical appliances are used.

Second, a business owner may pay a fixed rent to operate a business up to a certain volume level. When that level is reached, the owner may have no choice but to increase the space in order to meet increased production. If this is the case, these costs would be considered fixed for a specific period or up to a certain capacity or range of production.

Third, a business owner may pay x dollars for raw material at y level of production, but when that level of operation is exceeded, less may be paid because of increased purchase discounts.

Fourth, if a business owner wants to produce an extra volume of units with the same production crew, after regular hours, time-and-a-half or double time may have to be paid. These direct or variable costs would not vary proportionately with volume increments, and would surely not fit the linear cost pattern.

As shown in Figure 5.3, it is important to separate fixed and variable costs for different levels of volume. This helps to prepare operating budgets in a more proficient manner. Once the costs are identified under their respective categories, they can be related to specific levels of volume. One way of separating costs is by percentage of capacity. As shown in Figure 5.4, an owner may incur a total cost of $10.00 per unit (fixed and variable costs between periods A and B) up to 40% of capacity. At that point (B to C), costs will be increased by $2.00 per unit in order to exceed the 40% level of production capacity; this would bring total unit cost to $12.00. Between points C and D (up to 60% of capacity), costs remain the same (fixed costs will not change, while variable costs per unit can still vary proportionately with volume). Again, in order to go beyond the 60% capacity level,

FIGURE 5.3   RELATIONSHIP OF SEMI-VARIABLE AND SEMI-FIXED COSTS TO VOLUME

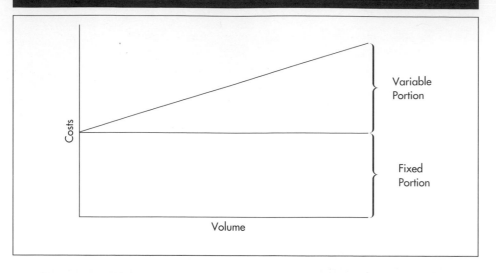

FIGURE 5.4   RELATIONSHIP OF COSTS TO CHANGES IN LEVEL OF PRODUCTION

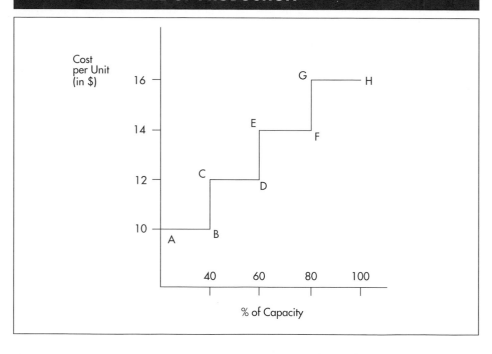

the owner may increase costs from $12.00 to $14.00. As shown on the chart, costs move from $14.00 to $16.00 (F to G) at the 80% capacity level and remain at that point (G to H) up to 100% capacity.

The Anatomy of Profit: Relationship between Revenue and Costs

◀ Objective 3

If operating costs changed in the same proportion as that of revenue, or if profits had a linear relationship with costs or revenue, this chapter would be irrelevant. However, as indicated earlier, costs behave in a variety of ways with respect to revenue. If budgets and profit plans are to be prepared in a meaningful way, it is important for management to be completely familiar with the way costs change within specific time periods, at different levels of production, and even with changes in methods of operation.

Knowing the structure of costs and how they affect profits when volume changes enables management to make well-informed decisions. The cost-volume-profit analysis helps managers to establish prices in a more prudent way. Establishing accurate prices for a business is the key to achieving profit goals and, ultimately, to determining the success of a business.

The factors that affect profit levels are:

- volume of production;
- prices;
- costs (fixed and variable); and
- changes in product mix.

Managers who understand the interrelationships among the above factors and how they each affect profit can more readily realign their operations to changing market conditions. They can identify the relative profitability levels of different product lines, establish prices more effectively, have a better product mix, and, most importantly, be in a better position to make operating changes that will best optimize the use of financial, physical, material, and human resources.

Specifically, analyzing the relationships among costs, volume, and profit enables an operator to answer fundamental questions, such as:

- How much volume do we need to sell before hiring another employee?
- At what sales volume should we change our method of operation; for example, should we maintain the existing warehouse or should we move to a larger one?
- Which products require streamlining, from a cost point of view, if we are to improve our profit performance?
- Should we change our product mix?
- When should we purchase another piece of equipment?
- Should we reduce the level of output of product A and increase that of product B?

One of the most effective techniques used in profit planning, solving problems, and making rational decisions is called break-even analysis.

Break-Even Analysis

Cost behaviour can be understood more easily in a cost-volume-profit relationship when break-even analysis is used. The importance of break-even analysis is that it projects the impact of management decisions made today on future profit levels. This technique helps management to see, well in advance, profit performance resulting from changes in methods of operations. The break-even method gives a picture of the effect that changes in price, costs, and volume have on profit.

Break-even point

Level of production where sales revenue equals total costs.

Break-even analysis deals with the **break-even point,** which can be defined as that point where, at a specific level of revenues, a business ceases to incur losses and begins to make a profit. In other words, it is at that level of operation where profit levels stand at zero, or where total revenues equal total costs. Before examining the break-even chart, let's examine several important concepts, namely, the contribution margin, relevant range, and relevant costs. These concepts will help us to further understand the mechanics of break-even analysis.

Contribution Margin Analysis

So far, fixed, variable, and semi-variable costs have been explained. These concepts suggest that every time a business produces a unit, it increases its revenue and reduces the loss up to a point where total revenues equal total costs. If sales continue to climb past the break-even point, profits are realized. There is another way of looking at this. Each time a business produces a unit, the sales generated on each unit "contribute" to paying for fixed costs. Simply put, when variable costs are deducted from revenues, we are left with an amount that will be used to pay off fixed costs and then realize a desired profit level. The difference between the revenue generated and the variable cost is called the **contribution margin.** The contribution margin is the level of profit that contributes to paying for fixed costs and, eventually, realizing a profit. For example, assume that John's monthly fixed expenses for his house (e.g., mortgage, hydro, insurance, etc.) are $2,500. Let's also assume that John works on a commission basis (say a job in direct marketing) and earns, on average, $25 an hour. It would take 100 hours for John to pay all his fixed expenses ($2,500 ÷ 25 hours). In other words, every hour of work (or $25) contributes toward the fixed expenses. If John works 101 hours, the money that he would earn during the last hour would contribute toward a surplus (profit). If John works 40 hours a week (or 160 hours a month), he would make a $1,500 surplus (160 hours × $25 = $4,000 − $2,500). Contribution margin is also known as marginal contribution, profit pick-up, cash margin, or margin income.

Contribution margin

The difference between sales revenue and variable costs.

Rearranging information shown on an income statement can help identify (or calculate) the contribution margin. Table 5.1 shows how contribution margin relates to revenue, fixed and variable costs, and profit.

TABLE 5.1 THE INCOME STATEMENT AND THE CONTRIBUTION MARGIN

Revenue		$1,000,000
Less variable costs:		
Direct material	$500,000	
Direct labour	250,000	
Total variable costs		750,000
Contribution margin		250,000
Less fixed costs:		
Manufacturing	150,000	
Administration	50,000	
Total fixed costs		200,000
Operating profit		$ 50,000

The contribution margin can also be expressed on a per-unit basis, as the difference between unit selling price and unit variable cost. This information becomes extremely valuable for decision-making purposes. If the contribution margin is positive, management knows how much money is earned on each unit sold, which will contribute to meeting fixed costs and realizing a profit. The contribution can also be expressed by a ratio called the marginal contribution ratio, marginal contributional ratio, contribution ratio, or marginal income ratio. The term that will be used in this chapter is **profit-volume (PV) ratio.**

Table 5.2 shows how to compute the contribution by using the PV ratio for varying volume levels. As shown in the table, the difference between revenues and variable costs gives a contribution of $250,000 or a PV ratio of 0.25 ($250,000 ÷ $1,000,000). If revenue increases by 25%, to $1,250,000, the contribution becomes $312,500 and the PV ratio still remains at 0.25 ($312,000 ÷ $1,250,000). If revenue drops to $600,000 and produces a contribution of $150,000, as shown, the PV ratio is still 0.25 ($150,000 ÷ $600,000).

The contribution margin approach offers significant benefits for examining pricing alternatives. Management can readily determine the impact each increase

PV ratio

Profit-volume ratio; the contribution margin expressed on a per-unit basis.

TABLE 5.2 CALCULATING THE CONTRIBUTION USING THE PV RATIO

	Base Case	Ratio	Increased Revenues	Decreased Revenues
Revenue	$1,000,000		$1,250,000	$600,000
Variable cost	750,000	.75	937,500	450,000
Contribution margin	250,000	.25 (PV)	312,500	150,000
Fixed costs	200,000		200,000	200,000
Operating profit (loss)	$ 50,000		$ 112,500	$ (50,000)

or decrease in price has on volume, revenues, and profit; this analysis helps streamline production operations in order to reach optimum cost levels.

Relevant Range

Relevant range

Costs (fixed and variable) that apply to a certain level of production.

Relevant range has to do with specific fixed and variable costs that apply to a certain level of production. Changes in the operating variable costs alter the PV ratio, which in turn affects the profit level. As was indicated earlier, fixed costs can change from period to period, or from one level of output to another. These costs must therefore be budgeted as accurately as possible, since they have a direct impact on the profitability level of a firm in both the short term and the long term. Cost analysis for costs incurred within a specific period must be considered within a designated range of volume levels. As indicated earlier, if the management of a business decides to increase its manufacturing capacity, more additional costs (fixed costs) will be incurred, or overtime (variable costs) at time-and-a-half or double time will have to be taken into account. Figure 5.5 shows graphically an example of relevant range. In this particular case, the cost information used to budget for a particular year would be relevant for volume of production within the 0 to 1,000 range ($5,000) and the 1,000 to 2,000 range ($10,000). If volume exceeds the 2,000 limit, different cost information ($15,000) would have to be integrated into the profit analysis.

Relevant Costs

Relevant costs

Cost alternatives that managers can choose from to operate a business.

Relevant costs arise when management has the option of choosing among several cost alternatives to operate a business. Cost variations among the options are called differential costs. For example, if management is currently spending $20,000 in operating costs for selling $50,000 worth of goods, two cost options

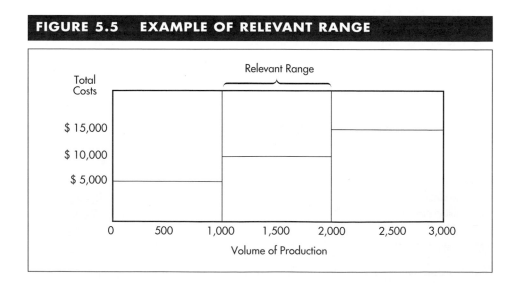

FIGURE 5.5   EXAMPLE OF RELEVANT RANGE

Chapter 5: Profit Planning and Decision-Making

TABLE 5.3 DIFFERENTIAL COSTS BETWEEN TWO COST OPTIONS

	Option A	Option B	Differential
Sales revenue	$50,000	$50,000	—
Current costs	20,000	20,000	—
Variable cost	10,000	14,000	$ 4,000
Fixed cost	15,000	13,000	(2,000)
Total relevant cost	25,000	27,000	2,000
Total cost	45,000	47,000	2,000
Profit	$ 5,000	$ 3,000	$ 2,000

The net cost or profit advantage of choosing option A is $2,000.

may be analyzed for making a plant more cost-efficient and increasing profitability. As shown in Table 5.3, option A shows that an additional $10,000 in variable costs and $15,000 in fixed costs would have to be incurred. Option B shows an additional $14,000 in variable costs (less efficient than option A) and $13,000 in fixed costs (more efficient than option A). The table shows the differential between the two options. The $20,000 that is already spent for selling the $50,000 worth of goods is not taken into account in this analysis since it has already been spent. (These costs are sometimes referred to as sunk costs.) The only costs that are relevant for the purpose of this analysis are the uncommitted or unspent costs, which are $25,000 for option A and $27,000 for option B. These options should be analyzed because of the $2,000 cost differential. As shown in the table, option A gives a $5,000 profit compared to $3,000 for option B.

The Break-Even Chart

◀◀ Objective 5

The **break-even chart** is a relatively simple way of picturing the effect of change in both revenue and cost on profitability. Figure 5.6 shows the break-even chart for a firm that sells widgets. As shown, there are different parts in a break-even chart. They are:

Break-even chart
Graphic that shows the effect of change in both revenue and costs on profitability.

- sales revenue   line OD
- revenue zone   area OED
- fixed-cost line   line AB
- fixed-cost zone   area AOEB
- total-cost line   line AC
- total-cost zone   area AOEC
- profit zone   area ZCD
- loss zone   area AOZ

FIGURE 5.6 THE BREAK-EVEN CHART

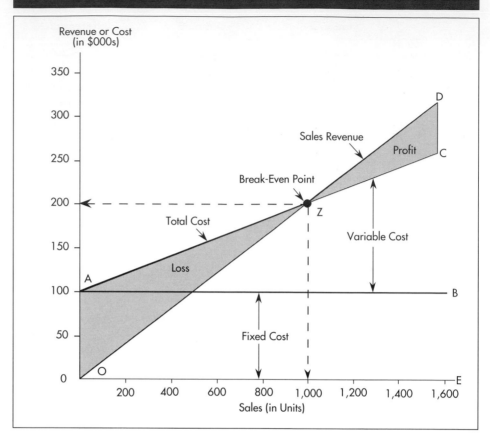

As shown in the figure, the horizontal axis represents the number of units sold, while the vertical axis represents total sales revenue and total costs.

Fixed costs (line AB) are shown parallel to the volume-in-units line. Fixed costs are $100,000 and remain unchanged, whether at 0, 600, or 1,600 units.

Sales revenue (line OD) slopes upward at an angle. As the company sells more units, sales revenue increases proportionately.

Total-cost line (line AC) portrays a gradual slope that intersects the sales revenue line at the 1,000-unit mark. The line begins at $100,000 (fixed cost), and slopes at an angle that is less steep than the revenue line.

The loss zone (area AOZ) represents losses if the company sells less than 1,000 units. If the company's unit selling price is maintained at $200 and fixed costs and variable costs are kept at the stated levels, losses range from $100,000, at zero unit sales, to $100 at 999 units.

The profit zone (area ZCD) represents the profits made by the company. Any volume of sales made over the 1,000-mark (horizontal axis) or $200,000 sales revenue (vertical axis) represents a profit to the company.

The profit and cost schedule shown in Table 5.4 was used to construct the break-even chart shown in Figure 5.6. The table shows numerically the change in

TABLE 5.4   THE PROFIT AND COST SCHEDULE

Sales Units	Unit Price	Sales Revenue	Fixed Cost	Variable Cost	Total Cost	Profit (Loss)
0	$200	0	$100,000	0	$100,000	$(100,000)
200	200	$ 40,000	100,000	$ 20,000	120,000	(80,000)
400	200	80,000	100,000	40,000	140,000	(60,000)
600	200	120,000	100,000	60,000	160,000	(40,000)
800	200	160,000	100,000	80,000	180,000	(20,000)
1,000	200	200,000	100,000	100,000	200,000	—
1,200	200	240,000	100,000	120,000	220,000	20,000
1,400	200	280,000	100,000	140,000	240,000	40,000
1,600	200	320,000	100,000	160,000	260,000	60,000

profit at varying levels of sales units—from 200 to 1,600. For example, at 200 widgets with an average unit selling price of $200, the company's sales revenue amounts to $40,000. At any level of sales volume, the company's fixed costs remain unchanged at $100,000. If the unit variable cost is $100, the total variable cost is $20,000 at the 200-unit volume level. At that level, total costs (fixed and variable) amount to $120,000 and the company realizes a loss in the amount of $80,000.

At 400 units, the loss is reduced to $60,000; at 1,000 units, sales revenue is at $200,000, fixed costs remain at $100,000, and variable costs reach a level of $100,000, for a total cost of $200,000. At that point, the company is showing neither a loss nor a profit, since costs equal sales revenue. It is at this particular sales-volume level that break-even takes place. Additional volume will improve the company's profit position. With sales units reaching levels of 1,400 and 1,600, the company generates profits of $40,000 and $60,000 respectively.

Finding the Break-Even Point by Formula

◄◄ Objective 6

The break-even chart gives a visual presentation of the different variables affecting profitability. However, if the intent is to establish the quantity and revenue break-even points, and the variables, such as sales units, fixed costs, and unit variable costs are known, the graph can be formulated algebraically. The following information is needed for an algebraic solution:

SP = selling price per unit

VC = variable cost per unit

FC = fixed cost

N = quantity of units sold at break-even

By definition, we know that, at break-even, total revenue equals total cost. If:

total revenue = $SP \times N$

and total cost = $(VC \times N) + FC$

Chapter 5: Profit Planning and Decision-Making

therefore break-even is:

$$(SP \times N) = (VC \times N) + FC$$

The above formula can also be presented in the following way:

$$N (SP - VC) = FC$$
$$\text{or} \quad N = FC/(SP - VC)$$

By using the information from Table 5.4, we get:

$$FC = \$100,000$$
$$SP = \$200$$
$$VC = \$100$$

The contribution margin (SP − VC) is $100 (that is, $200 minus $100).

By applying the above information to the break-even algebraic formula, we get the following break-even results for quantity and for revenue.

Unit break-even point is:

Unit break-even point

Number of units that must be sold in order to cover total costs.

$$BEP = \frac{\text{Fixed Cost}}{\text{Price per unit} - \text{Variable cost per unit}}$$
$$\text{(or Unit contribution)}$$

$$BEP = \frac{\$100,000}{\$200 - \$100} = \frac{\$100,000}{\$100} = 1,000 \text{ units}$$

Revenue break-even point

Sales revenue that must be reached in order to cover total costs.

Revenue break-even point is calculated in two steps:

STEP 1 Find the PV ratio or unit contribution

$$PV = \frac{\text{Unit contribution}}{\text{Unit selling price}} = \frac{\$100}{\$200} = 0.50$$

STEP 2 Find the revenue break-even point

$$BEP = \frac{\text{Fixed cost}}{PV} = \frac{\$100,000}{0.50} = \$200,000$$

If the break-even volume is multiplied by the unit selling price, the same answer is obtained: 1,000 units × $200 = $200,000.

Cash Break-Even Point

The break-even model can also be applied to solve cash-management problems. Most costs, such as rent, salaries, hydro, insurance, raw materials, or telephone, are cash outlays. There are, however, other costs that are noncash items, such as depreciation; even though they are treated as expenses, they do not entail an actual outflow of cash.

If we refer to the revenue and cost information in Table 5.4, and assume that the $100,000 fixed cost includes an amount of $25,000 for depreciation, the fixed cash disbursements would therefore be $75,000.

In this case, the **cash break-even point** for both quantity and revenue would be calculated as follows:

Quantity (or unit) break-even point is:

$$\text{Cash BEP} = \frac{\text{Fixed cost} - \text{Depreciation}}{\text{Price per unit} - \text{Variable cost per unit}}$$

$$= \frac{\$100,000 - \$25,000}{\$200 - \$100} = \frac{\$75,000}{\$100} = 750 \text{ units}$$

Revenue break-even point is:

$$\text{Revenue cash BEP} = \frac{\text{Fixed cost} - \text{Depreciation}}{\text{PV}}$$

$$= \frac{\$75,000}{0.50} = \$150,000$$

Cash break-even point
Number of units or sales revenue that must be reached in order to cover total cash fixed costs (total fixed costs less depreciation).

Profit Break-Even Point

Companies are interested in more than just breaking even. Some establish profit objectives to determine the sales units that should be sold in order to reach the stated objective. To do this, they modify the break-even formula. Referring to our base data shown in Table 5.4, and assuming that $10,000 is the objective, we can calculate the **profit break-even points** for both quantity and revenue as follows:

Quantity (or unit) break-even point is:

$$\text{Profit BEP} = \frac{\text{Fixed cost} + \text{Profit objective}}{\text{Price per unit} - \text{Variable cost}}$$

$$= \frac{\$100,000 + \$10,000}{\$200 - \$100} = 1,100 \text{ units}$$

Revenue break-even point is:

$$\text{Revenue profit BEP} = \frac{\text{Fixed cost} + \text{Profit}}{\text{PV}} = \frac{\$110,000}{0.50} = \$220,000$$

Profit break-even point
Number of units or sales revenue that must be reached in order to cover total costs plus a profit objective.

The various quantity and revenue break-even points are summarized below:

	Quantity (in units)	Revenue
Regular break-even	1,000	$200,000
Cash break-even	750	$150,000
Profit break-even	1,100	$220,000

Sensitivity Analysis

Any change in sales revenue, whether it comes from increased unit selling price, change in product mix, or a reduction in fixed or variable costs, will have favourable or unfavourable effects on a company's profitability. For example, referring to the base data in Table 5.4, a reduction of $20,000 in fixed costs (to $80,000) would reduce the break-even point to 800 units or $160,000 in sales revenue. Similarly, reducing variable costs to $80 (assuming that fixed costs are at the original level of $100,000) would reduce the break-even point to 833 units [($100,000 ÷ ($200 − $80)]. A simultaneous decline of both costs would improve the company's profitability substantially and reduce the break-even point to 666 units [($80,000 ÷ ($200 - $80)]. The opposite takes place if fixed and variable costs are increased. A change in unit selling price would also have an effect on profitability. If, for instance, the company faces a $20 per unit variable cost increase, and it wishes to maintain its break-even point at the 1,000 mark, the company would have to increase the unit selling price by $20 to $220. Obviously, this assumes that the increase in unit selling price would have no adverse effect on units sold.

Before deciding to make changes in the methods of operation, or to purchase new equipment, it is important to make a **sensitivity analysis** of different break-even points representing changes in unit sales, selling price, unit variable cost, and fixed cost.

Sensitivity analysis
Technique that shows to what extent a change in one variable (e.g., selling price, fixed costs) impacts on the break-even point.

Objective 7 ➡

Where the Break-Even Point Can Be Applied

The break-even system can be used in just about any type of business or any area of a company's operations where variable and fixed costs exist and where products or services are offered. For example, a break-even chart can be applied in any of the following areas: company-wide, district or sales territory, service centre, retail store, plant, production centre, department, product division, or machine operation.

Let us examine how the break-even points can be presented for four of the above operations: company-wide, district or sales territory, service centre, and retail store.

Company-Wide

Figure 5.7 shows a company-wide break-even chart. It indicates the various components of all elements entering into the total cost line. For example, the chart shows the total company fixed costs (which include production, sales, general, and administrative expenses) and the variable costs (which include direct material and direct labour for various company operations), and income taxes and the net profit after income taxes. The break-even point is shown for both cash and profit, both before and after taxes.

District or Sales Territory

The break-even chart is also useful for analyzing whether it is economically attractive to open a sales office in a particular area. In this case, the fixed costs are rental charges, clerical staff, hydro, depreciation of office equipment, etc. Fixed costs would also include a portion of head office fixed expenses. The variable costs would consist of sales commissions, travel, and living allowances. The break-even chart for a district or sales territory is shown in Figure 5.8.

FIGURE 5.7 COMPANY-WIDE BREAK-EVEN CHART

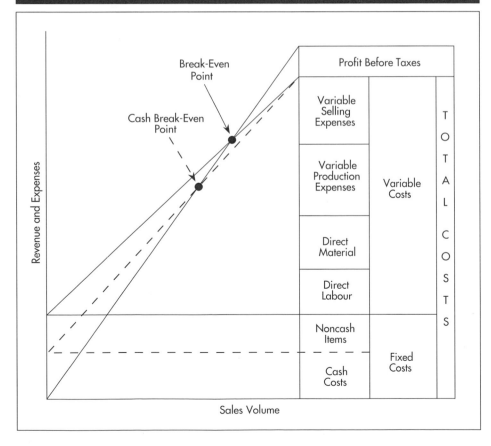

FIGURE 5.8   DISTRICT OR SALES TERRITORY BREAK-EVEN CHART

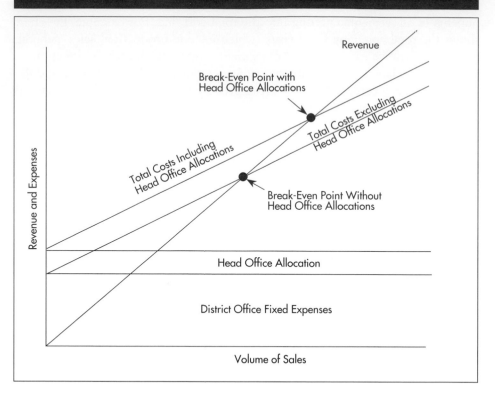

The break-even analysis may become useful for determining whether a sales office should be located in the centre core of the business district, where high fixed costs would be incurred and variable costs would be minimized, or in an area remote from the city core, where fixed costs are lower and variable costs higher. In weighing the two possibilities, the marketing manager would have to consider the market potential, the market share objectives, and the sales revenue for the short and medium term.

Service Centre

Break-even analysis works exceptionally well for activities that produce specific units of output. Here, fixed costs and direct costs can be related to specific levels of operation. Like a retail store, a service centre does not produce specific production units; while fixed costs can be readily identified, variable costs cannot be related to a specific level of operation. The break-even concept can be applied to service operations but with subtle differences. The break-even chart for a service centre is shown in Figure 5.9. The vertical axis represents sales revenue and expenses; the horizontal axis represents sales revenue. The dollar scale of the horizontal and vertical lines is identical since the break-even chart deals with dollar measurements in both instances. The fixed-costs line is parallel to the horizontal

FIGURE 5.9 SERVICE CENTRE BREAK-EVEN CHART

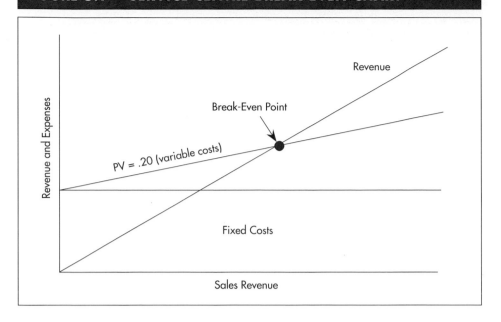

line, while the revenue line can have a 45 degree slant. Variable costs vary not with the quantity of units sold, but with the dollar amount, with the slope of the line determined by the PV ratio. For example, if the variable costs represented 20% of sales revenue, variable costs would increase by a factor of 0.20 every time a dollar sale is made.

Retail Store

As shown in Table 5.5, the break-even point can also be calculated for a retail store. First, we must determine the number of products that would be sold, and the unit-selling price for each. As shown in the table, the total revenue amounts to $500,000. Based on that forecast, variable costs, which include purchases and commissions, amount to $275,000 and $25,000 respectively. By deducting total variable costs from total sales revenue, we find that the store's contribution margin is $200,000. This margin contributes to pay for the $100,000 in fixed costs; the remaining $100,000 is profit. As indicated in the table, the store breaks even at $250,000, or 50% of its sales estimates.

TABLE 5.5 RETAIL STORE BREAK-EVEN POINT

	Suits	Jackets	Shirts	Ties	Socks	Overcoats	Total
No. of units	800	200	700	900	2,400	500	
Unit price	$300	$150	$50	$30	$17.50	$300	
Revenue							$500,000
Variable costs							
Purchases							$275,000
Commissions							25,000
Total variable costs							$300,000
Contribution margin							$200,000
Fixed costs							$100,000
Profit							$100,000

$$\frac{\text{Contribution margin}}{\text{Sales revenue}} = \frac{\$200,000}{\$500,000} = .40 \text{ or } \$0.40$$

$$\frac{\text{Fixed costs}}{\text{PV ratio}} = \frac{\$100,000}{.40} = \$250,000$$

Break-even wedge

Method that helps managers determine the most appropriate way of structuring operating costs (fixed versus variable).

Break-Even Wedges

Break-even wedges help managers look at different ways of structuring the cost profile of their businesses. They make their decisions based on two major factors: the level of risk they are prepared to take, and the level of expected sales volume. Some managers may favour a high volume and a low PV ratio; others, a low volume and high PV ratio. Some may prefer high fixed costs and low variable costs while others prefer low fixed costs and high variable costs. Figure 5.10 shows different possibilities.

For example, with an extremely high and stable level of sales, it would be preferable for Company A to build a highly automated plant with high fixed costs and low unit variable costs. Management of Company B is not as optimistic about sales levels; it would therefore go for a plant that is not as highly automated (lower fixed costs), but it would have to pay higher unit variable costs (direct labour). Company A would therefore have a competitive advantage over B if the economy is strong and there is a large demand for the product. Profits are amplified when Company A has reached its break-even point. If, however, the economy is weak and production levels are low, Company B would have a distinct competitive advantage over Company A because its fixed costs would be lower.

The figure shows four companies with different cost structures and PV ratios. Each company shows a different profit wedge. As indicated earlier, Company A and Company B have the same break-even points, but Company A has higher fixed costs and a higher PV ratio than Company B. Although Company A's profits are amplified after the break-even point, it is more vulnerable if sales volume falls short of the break-even point. As shown, the loss zone is more pronounced for Company A than for Company B.

FIGURE 5.10   BREAK-EVEN WEDGES

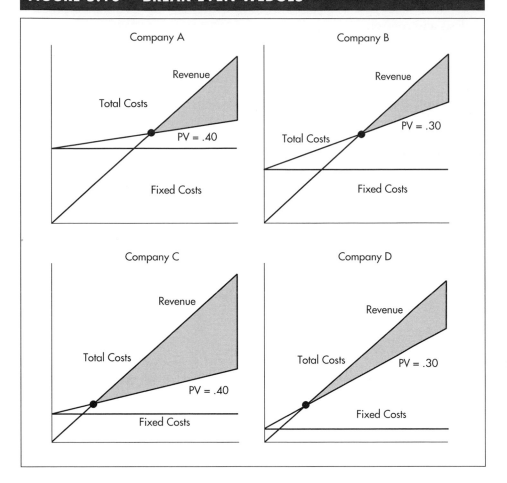

Companies C and D have lower fixed costs. The sales revenue line is the same as those of Companies A and B, but the profit levels are reached earlier. For example, Company C's profit structure (PV ratio) is similar to that of Company A, but, Company C generates a profit on each sales dollar at a lower level of production. Profits generated by Companies B and D follow a similar pattern.

The major advantage of Companies A and C is that profits amplify faster once they have reached the break-even point (producing a wider wedge or bigger PV ratio). These companies are, however, more vulnerable to losses in a slow economy. Companies B and D have similar revenue and variable-cost patterns (the slope of the lines are identical), which produce a similar wedge in the profit zone.

Other Cost Concepts

◀ Objective 9

Managers classify costs in different categories. So far, we have made the distinction between fixed and variable costs and have shown that there are also costs that can be classified as semi-fixed or semi-variable. Costs must be classified in separate and distinct categories when preparing a cost-volume-profit analysis. Let us examine other cost concepts and see how they can be used for purposes of analysis and control.

Committed versus Discretionary Costs

Fixed costs can be grouped in two distinct categories: committed and discretionary.

Committed fixed costs are those that cannot be controlled and that must be incurred in order to operate a business. They include depreciation on buildings and equipment and salaries paid to managers.

Discretionary fixed costs are those that can be controlled by managers from one period to another if necessary. For example, expenditures on research and development, training programs, advertising, and promotional activities can be increased or decreased from one period to the next.

It is important to recognize the difference between committed and discretionary fixed costs for cost-volume-profit analysis purposes. As shown in Figure 5.11, for a difficult anticipated planning period, management may decide to cut back some discretionary fixed costs in order to bring the break-even point from B to A.

Controllable versus Noncontrollable Costs

Accountability is important in the management process. For this reason, it is vital to separate all costs that are within the jurisdiction of a manager from those that are not.

Budgets are allocated to individual managers, and the managers are monitored to see whether they operate within budget ceilings. If certain costs over

Committed fixed costs

Costs that must be incurred in order to operate a business.

Discretionary fixed costs

Costs that can be controlled by managers.

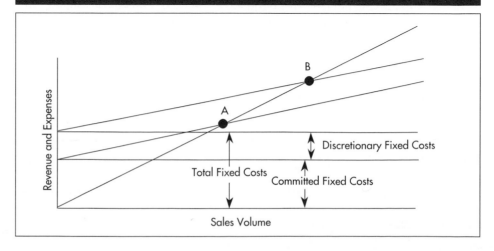

FIGURE 5.11   COMMITTED VERSUS DISCRETIONARY FIXED COSTS

Chapter 5: Profit Planning and Decision-Making

which managers have control exceed the budget, the managers must explain why. Typical **controllable costs** for plant managers are maintenance, production supplies, overtime, waste, and equipment. Certain other costs are incurred over which they have no control; typical **noncontrollable costs** are depreciation, insurance, supervisors' salaries, and other overhead costs.

It is important to distinguish between these two types of costs for reporting purposes. On the manager's budget reports, costs should be grouped under these two categories, and managers should be expected to account only for variances over which they have control.

Controllable costs

Costs that operating managers are accountable for.

Noncontrollable costs

Costs that are not under the direct control of operating managers.

Direct versus Indirect Costs

Costs may be direct or indirect. **Direct costs** are directly related to a specific activity, product, program, project, or objective. These costs would be avoided if an activity was eliminated or incurred if the activity was performed.

Indirect costs are not associated with a specific activity, product, program, project, or objective. Typical indirect costs include overhead, which is usually apportioned among different operating or production units. For example, Table 5.6(a) shows a company that produces three different products, each generating identifiable direct costs. A total of $90,000 in indirect costs or overhead costs is allocated equally ($30,000) to the products. As shown, products A and B are producing positive net results while product C is showing a $5,000 loss. Under these circumstances, management may contemplate the possibility of abandoning product C. If this is the case, the absorption of the $90,000 overhead (if these costs cannot be reduced with the abandonment of product C) would therefore have to be split between products A and B. As shown in Table 5.6(b), this would reduce the profit position of these two products, and even produce a negative result for product B. In addition to apparently losing money on product B, the company would reduce its overall profitability from $45,000 to $20,000. The company would, therefore, be in a better position if it continued to manufacture product C.

Direct costs

Materials and labour expenses that are directly incurred when making a product.

Indirect costs

Costs that are necessary in the production cycle but that cannot be clearly allocated to specific products or services.

TABLE 5.6 (a)	DIRECT AND INDIRECT COSTS			
	Product A	**Product B**	**Product C**	**Total**
Sales	$100,000	$90,000	$75,000	$265,000
Direct costs	25,000	55,000	50,000	130,000
Indirect costs	30,000	30,000	30,000	90,000
Total costs	55,000	85,000	80,000	220,000
Profit	$ 45,000	$ 5,000	$ (5,000)	$ 45,000

TABLE 5.6 (b)   DIRECT AND INDIRECT COSTS

	Product A	Product B	Total
Sales	$100,000	$ 90,000	$190,000
Direct costs	25,000	55,000	80,000
Indirect costs	30,000 *45,000*	45,000	90,000
Total costs	70,000	100,000	170,000
Profit	$ 30,000	$ (10,000)	$ 20,000

❋ Decision-Making in Action

Let's now examine how the break-even concept can be applied within the context of decision-making. The left side of Table 5.7 shows the income statement of Widget Inc. As indicated, the company needs to earn $100,000 before tax profit. Management is considering the following questions:

1. Should we increase our selling price by 5%?
2. Should we increase our advertising budget by $30,000?
3. Should we hire a new sales representative? Cost is estimated at $60,000.
4. What would our break-even sales revenue be if we were to reduce our variable costs by 3%?
5. How much sales revenue must we achieve to earn an extra $20,000 before tax profit?

To answer these questions, the Widget Inc. managers must first rearrange the profit-and-loss statement by putting under two distinct groupings all variable costs and all fixed costs. As shown under the rearranged profit and loss statement in the middle section of Table 5.7, it is assumed that the company's variable costs amount to $1,700,000 and generate $800,000 in contribution margin. Total fixed costs amount to $700,000. By regrouping the variable and fixed costs, it is possible to calculate the PV ratio. As shown, the PV ratio is .32, calculated by dividing the $800,000 contribution margin by the $2,500,000 sales revenue. This means that for every dollar's worth of sales, the company is generating $0.32 in contribution margin. The PV ratio is required to quickly answer the above-mentioned questions. For example, dividing

fixed costs by the PV ratio shows that the company would have to sell $2,187,500 or 87.5% of its sales revenue objective.

The right side of Table 5.7 presents the number of units sold and, for each unit, the selling price, variable cost, and contribution margin. The contribution is maintained at .32, or $3.20 per unit.

Now, let's answer the five questions referred to earlier.

QUESTION 1: SHOULD WE INCREASE OUR SELLING PRICE BY 5%?

If the selling price is increased by 5%, the unit selling price would therefore be $10.50, increasing the contribution margin to $3.70 or 37%. Dividing the fixed costs ($700,000) by the new contribution margin shows that the company's new break-even point would be $1,891,892 or 75.7% of its sales revenue objective. But before increasing its selling price, the company would have to consider the effect of a change in the selling price on sales volume; that is, how many customers would be lost as a result of this change. The same arithmetic could be done for a 3% increase, a 2% decrease, etc.

QUESTION 2: SHOULD WE INCREASE OUR ADVERTISING BUDGET BY $30,000?

If the advertising budget is increased by $30,000, total fixed costs would be increased to $730,000. Dividing these fixed costs by PV ratio (.32) shows that the break-even point would be increased to $2,281,250 (instead

TABLE 5.7   DECISION-MAKING IN ACTION

Profit and Loss Statement		Rearranged Profit and Loss Statement		Average Unit Selling Price and Cost
Sales revenue	$2,500,000	Sales revenue	$2,500,000	250,000
Cost of goods sold	1,900,000	Variable costs		
Gross margin	600,000	Cost of goods sold	1,600,000	$10.00
		Selling	50,000	6.80
		Administration	50,000	
Selling expenses	300,000	Total variable costs	1,700,000	
Administration	200,000			
Subtotal	500,000	Contribution margin	800,000	$ 3.20
		Fixed costs		
Profit before taxes	$ 100,000	Cost of goods sold	300,000	
		Selling	250,000	
		Administration	150,000	
		Total fixed costs	700,000	
		Profit before taxes	$ 100,000	
		PV ratio	.32	.32

of $2,187,500), a difference of $93,750. Before increasing the advertising budget, management would have to determine whether the extra $30,000 expenditure would be able to generate an additional $93,750 in sales revenue. If it is estimated that the $30,000 would generate, say, an extra $175,000 in sales revenue, the higher advertising budget could be justified.

QUESTION 3: SHOULD WE HIRE A NEW SALES REPRESENTATIVE? COST IS ESTIMATED AT $60,000.

The arithmetic here is similar to that of question 2. Fixed costs would increase to $760,000 and the new break-even point would rise to $2,375,000 (compared to the existing $2,500,000). This would require an additional $125,000 in sales revenue. Could the new sales representative generate this much revenue within the first year? If not, how about the second or third year?

QUESTION 4: WHAT WOULD OUR BREAK-EVEN SALES REVENUE BE IF WE WERE TO REDUCE OUR VARIABLE COSTS BY 3%?

A 3% reduction would bring the total variable costs to $1,649,000 and increase the PV ratio to .34. The arithmetic is done as follows:

Sales revenue	$2,500,000
Variable costs	1,649,000
Contribution margin	$ 851,000
PV ratio	.34

Here, the break-even point would be reduced to $2,058,823 (from $2,187,500) or 82.3% of the sales revenue objective (instead of 87.5%).

QUESTION 5: HOW MUCH SALES REVENUE MUST WE BRING IN TO EARN AN EXTRA $20,000 BEFORE TAX PROFIT?

If management wants to realize a $120,000 profit objective, sales revenue would have to be $2,562,500 ([$700,000 + $120,000] ÷ .32). This means that the company's sales revenue would have to be increased by 2.5% ($2,562,500 ÷ $2,500,000).

Chapter Summary

Objective 1 ➠   Break-even analysis can be used in business to make different types of decisions such as pricing decisions, new product decisions, modernization decisions, and expansion decisions. However, in order to make the right decision, management must have a complete knowledge of its business's operating-cost structure.

Objective 2 ➠   Cost-volume-profit analysis consists of analyzing the interrelationships among volume of production, fixed costs, and variable costs. *Fixed costs* remain constant and do not vary with different levels of production. *Variable costs* vary in direct proportion to changes in level of output. There are also *semi-fixed or semi-variable costs* that vary at different levels of production.

Objective 3 ➠   The factors that affect profit are volume of production, prices, costs (fixed and variable costs), and changes in product mix. Managers who understand the connection between these three variables can readily pinpoint how each of these affect the level of profitability.

Objective 4 ➠   The contribution margin is the difference between the selling price of a product and the variable costs. This difference is used to pay for fixed costs, and to earn a profit. Relevant range has to do with costs (fixed and variable) that apply to a certain level of production. Relevant costs are alternative ways that managers can choose to operate a business.

Objective 5 ➠   The break-even chart gives a visual presentation of the interrelationships between revenues, variable costs, fixed costs, and total costs.

Objective 6 ➠   The *break-even point* can be calculated by using this formula:

$$N = FC/(SP - VC)$$

The *cash break-even point* determines how many units a business must sell in order to pay for its cash expenses. The *profit break-even* point determines the number of units a business must sell in order to achieve a targeted profit objective. *Sensitivity analysis* is used to gauge the various break-even points when there are changes in any one of the variables, such as unit selling price, volume of production, fixed costs, or variable costs.

Objective 7 ➠   Break-even analysis can be applied in many areas, including sales territories, retail stores, plants, departments, product divisions, production centres, service centres, and machine operations.

Objective 8 ➠   The break-even wedge analysis can help managers determine the most appropriate way to structure their operating costs (fixed versus variable). The PV ratio, that is the relationship between the contribution margin and revenue, can determine to what extent a business will want to structure its costs such as more fixed and less variable or less fixed and more variable.

Costs can also be broken down into under other categories. *Committed fixed costs* are those that must be incurred by a business while *discretionary fixed costs* are those that can be controlled by managers. Also, managers are accountable for *controllable costs* while *noncontrollable costs* are not under the direct influence of operating managers. Finally, there are *direct costs,* which include labour and material expenses, which can be lined to making a product or providing a service while *indirect costs* cannot be clearly allocated to specific products or services.

◀ Objective 9

Key Terms

Break-even chart	Indirect costs
Break-even point	Noncontrollable costs
Break-even wedge	Profit break-even point
Cash break-even point	PV ratio
Committed fixed costs	Relevant costs
Contribution margin	Relevant range
Controllable costs	Revenue break-even point
Cost-volume-profit analysis	Semi-variable costs
Direct costs	Sensitivity analysis
Discretionary fixed costs	Unit break-even point
Fixed costs	Variable costs

Review Questions

1. What is the relevance of break-even analysis?

2. Differentiate between fixed and variable costs.

3. Why are some costs called "semi-fixed"?

4. Explain the meaning and the significance of the contribution margin.

5. Comment on the more important elements that affect profit levels.

6. What do we mean by relevant range?

7. What do we mean by relevant costs?

8. Draw a hypothetical break-even chart.

9. What is a PV ratio?

10. Why would someone use the PV ratio instead of the unit contribution margin?

11. Why should managers be interested in calculating the profit break-even point?

12. How can the contribution margin be calculated?

13. Differentiate between the break-even point and the cash break-even point.

14. What is the significance of calculating the cash break-even point?

15. What is the usefulness of sensitivity analysis?

16. Differentiate between committed fixed costs and discretionary fixed costs.

Chapter 5: Profit Planning and Decision-Making

17. What is the difference between a direct cost and an indirect cost? Give an example for each.

18. What is the significance of using the break-even wedge analysis when analyzing the break-even point?

Discussion Questions

1. How can the break-even analysis help managers make pricing decisions? Give an example.

2. "The major factor that will underlie the cost structure of a business is the level of risk that managers are prepared to take, and the level of expected sales volume." Explain.

Testing Your Comprehension

True/False Questions

___T___ 1. Fixed costs remain constant at varying levels of production.

___F___ 2. Sales commission is considered a semi-variable cost.

___F___ 3. The break-even point is reached when sales revenue equals variable costs.

___T___ 4. The contribution margin is calculated by subtracting variable costs from sales revenue.

___F___ 5. The PV ratio is calculated by dividing the contribution margin by the variable costs.

___T___ 6. The higher the PV ratio, the better it is.

___T___ 7. Changes in the operating variable costs can alter the PV ratio.

___F___ 8. The break-even point is calculated by dividing total costs by the unit contribution margin.

___F___ 9. The profit break-even point can be calculated by dividing profit by the unit contribution margin.

___T___ 10. Discretionary costs are those that can be controlled by managers.

___F___ 11. The break-even wedge helps managers determine the most appropriate way of structuring committed versus discretionary costs.

___T___ 12. A direct cost is closely associated with an objective.

___F___ 13. A change in the level of fixed costs can influence the contribution margin.

___T___ 14. A change in product mix can affect the break-even point.

Multiple-Choice Questions

1. The following is considered a fixed cost:
   a. direct labour
   b. packing materials
   c. freight
   d. sales commission
   e. insurance

2. The following can affect the break-even point:
   a. change in volume mix
   b. change in selling price
   c. change in fixed costs
   d. change in variable costs
   e. all of the above

3. The following is considered a variable cost:
   a. professional fees
   b. overtime
   c. depreciation
   d. interest charges
   e. taxes

4. The contribution margin is the difference between:
   a. sales revenue and cost of goods sold
   b. sales revenue and fixed costs
   c. sales revenue and variable costs
   d. sales revenue and operating income
   e. sales revenue and income before taxes

5. To calculate the PV ratio, you:
   a. divide the contribution margin by sales revenue
   b. divide sales revenue by the contribution margin
   c. multiply sales revenue by the unit contribution margin
   d. multiply the contribution margin by the unit sales revenue
   e. add the contribution margin to sales revenue

6. The break-even point is reached when:
   a. sales revenue covers all fixed costs
   b. sales revenue covers all costs
   c. sales revenue covers all variable costs
   d. all costs are deducted from fixed and variable costs
   e. fixed costs are deducted from the variable costs

7. The revenue break-even point can be calculated by dividing the PV ratio into:
   a. sales revenue
   b. all operating costs
   c. cost of goods sold
   d. fixed costs
   e. variable costs

8. The item that is not considered a noncash expense is:
   a. prepaid expenses
   b. depreciation
   c. fixed costs
   d. electricity
   e. semi-variable costs

9. The profit break-even point can be calculated by dividing the unit contribution margin into:
   a. profit
   b. fixed costs
   c. profit plus fixed costs
   d. profit plus variable costs
   e. sales revenue plus profit

10. To calculate the new break-even point if a company wants to invest more money in its advertising budget, the additional advertising expense should be added to the:
    a. sales revenue
    b. existing variable costs
    c. existing profit objective
    d. existing fixed costs
    e. existing total costs

11. Committed fixed costs are those costs that:
    a. can be controlled
    b. cannot be controlled
    c. can be changed with the volume of production
    d. should be eliminated if a company experiences a loss
    e. should be increased in order to generate more volume

12. The break-even wedge is a method that helps managers determine the relationship between:
    a. fixed and variable costs
    b. revenue and the contribution margin
    c. committed and discretionary fixed costs
    d. contribution margin and fixed costs
    e. semi-variable costs and sales revenue

Fill-in-the-Blanks Questions

1. _____ variable costs change disproportionately with changes in output levels.

2. The _____ is the difference between sales revenue and variable costs.

3. If you divide the contribution margin by sales revenue, you get the _____ ratio.

4. _____ range is defined as costs (fixed and variable) that apply to a certain level of production.

5. The break-even chart shows the effect of change in both revenue and costs on _____.

6. The break-even point is defined as the level of production where sales revenue equals total _____.

7. To calculate the unit break-even point, you need to divide _____ by the unit contribution margin.

8. To calculate the revenue break-even point, you need to divide fixed costs by the _____.

9. _____ analysis is a technique that shows to what extent a change in one variable (e.g., selling price, fixed costs) impacts on the break-even point.

10. Operating managers are accountable for _____ costs such as production supplies, overtime, waste, and equipment.

Learning Exercises

Exercise 1(a)

The Millers are thinking of introducing a new product line in their store. On the basis of the following information:

- total fixed costs allocated to the department are estimated at $15,000;
- total number of units expected to be sold are 10,000 based on a market study;
- total variable costs are $20,000; and
- unit selling price is $4.50

calculate the:

1. break-even point in units; and

2. break-even point in revenue.

Should they go ahead with their plan?

Exercise 1(b)

With the following information:

- total fixed costs are estimated at $100,000;
- total units expected to be sold are 50,000;
- total variable costs are $300,000; and
- unit selling price is $8.00

calculate the:

1. break-even point in units; and

2. break-even point in revenue.

Exercise 2(a)

The Millers have been approached by a supplier to sell a new product line. Based on the supplier's estimates, CompuTech could sell as many as 1,500 units. The suggested retail price for each unit is $14.50. The purchase price for each unit is $7.00. The amount of fixed costs allocated to that particular department is $6,000. On the basis of this information calculate the:

1. contribution margin;

2. PV ratio;

3. revenue break-even by using the PV ratio; and

4. profit generated.

Exercise 2(b)

A company expects to sell 75,000 widgets at a price of $10.00. The unit variable cost is estimated at $8.00 and the fixed costs at $125,000. On the basis of this information calculate the:

1. contribution margin;

2. PV ratio;

3. revenue break-even by using the PV ratio; and

4. profit generated.

Exercise 3(a)

Using the information contained in Exercise 1(a), if fixed costs were increased by $5,000 and variable costs and unit selling price remained unchanged, what would be the new PV ratio and break-even point in units and in revenue?

Exercise 3(b)

Using the information contained in Exercise 1(b), if rent were increased by $25,000 and variable costs and unit selling price remained unchanged, what would be the new PV ratio and break-even point in units and in revenue?

Exercise 4(a) *HW*

With the following information, calculate the break-even point for CompuTech's product lines A, B, and C.

- Sales revenue

  Product line A $45,000

  Product line B $21,750

  Product line C $35,000

- Cost of goods sold for the three product lines is 45%, 50%, and 52% of sales revenue respectively.

- Fixed costs are estimated at $32,000.

Exercise 4(b) *HW*

With the following information, calculate the break-even point for a retail store.

- Sales revenue

  Product line A $100,000

  Product line B $200,000

  Product line C $600,000

- Cost of goods sold for the three product lines is 50%, 45%, and 55% of sales revenue respectively.

- Fixed costs are estimated at $350,000.

Exercise 5(a)

With the following information, calculate CompuTech's:

1. profit;

2. break-even point in revenue; and

3. cash break-even point.

Purchases	$205,000	Office salaries	$ 35,000
Freight in	4,000	Sales revenue	420,000
Salaries (selling)	55,000	Depreciation	40,000
Sales commission	3,000	Leasing	7,000
Travelling	3,000	Interest charges	14,000
Advertising	5,000	Office supplies	3,000

Exercise 5(b) *HW*

With the following information, calculate the:

1. profit;

2. break-even point in revenue; and

3. cash break-even point.

Depreciation	$ 30,000	Office supplies	$ 3,000
Plant direct wages	100,000	Sales revenue	550,000
Plant supervision	60,000	Overtime	30,000
Advertising	30,000	Rent	35,000
Plant insurance	20,000	Property taxes	10,000
Sales commission	100,000	Raw materials	100,000

Cases

Case 1: Quick Photo Ltd.

Tony Kasabian was just about ready to put the finishing touches to a business plan that he was to present to a local banker for financing his new venture, Quick Photo Ltd. The investment proposal contained a marketing plan designed to capture a good share of the Southern Ontario photo finishing market. Tony was interested in buying several new high-technology film processors manufactured in Germany and capable of processing top-quality prints from films within 15 minutes. His retailing plan consisted of operating photo processors in kiosks in several Ontario high-traffic malls including locations in Don Mills, Ottawa, Windsor, London, and Kingston. He felt that his business concept was in line with the trend of developing high-quality films quickly.

However, he realized that his banker would be asking him many questions about the market size, his competitors, his sales revenue targets for the next several years, and, most important, his marketing assumptions backing up his sales forecast. Therefore, before finalizing his business plan, Tony asked his friend, a recent commerce graduate, to help him calculate the number of rolls of film that he would have to process each year in order to cover his fixed costs and earn a reasonable profit.

On average, Tony figured out that he would charge $8.00 per roll of film developed, a price consistent with competitors' charges for work of similar quality; his rapid service would be a bonus. Quick Photo's income statement for the first year of operations is as follows:

Number of rolls of films developed		200,000
Sales revenue		$1,600,000
Cost of goods sold		
Direct materials	$250,000	
Direct labour	265,000	
Depreciation	78,000	
Supervision	80,000	
Total cost of goods sold		673,000
Gross margin		$927,000
Operating expenses		
Selling expenses		
Salaries	$230,000	
Sales commission	110,000	
Advertising	25,000	
Subtotal	365,000	
Administration expenses		
Salaries	185,000	
Insurance	20,000	
Rent	60,000	
Depreciation	33,000	
Subtotal	298,000	
Total operating expenses		663,000
Operating income		264,000
Interest charges		35,000
Income before taxes		229,000
Income taxes		101,000
Income after taxes		$ 128,000

1. Calculate Tony's break-even point in revenue and the cash break-even point in revenue.

2. How many rolls of films a year and what level of sales revenue must Tony reach if he wants to realize an objective of $275,000 in income before tax?

3. Calculate Tony's annual revenue break-even point by using the PV ratio if he is to realize the $275,000 income before-tax objective.

4. If he increases his advertising budget by $20,000, what would be Tony's new yearly break-even point in rolls of films and in revenue? How many additional rolls of films must Tony develop in order to increase his sales revenue and cover the incremental advertising budget?

5. If Tony reduces his direct material costs for processing the rolls of films by $25,000, what would be his new break-even point in units and in revenue?

Case 2: V & A Carpet Cleaning Services *HW.*

In March 1992, Vincent and Anne-Marie Finney started their carpet-cleaning business in Toronto. The business was geared primarily at married couples, a market that they felt was growing rapidly. Vincent and Anne-Marie had worked during the previous ten years as salaried employees for different types of organizations and were frustrated with the fact that their future was in the hands of employers. They decided to start V & A Carpet Cleaning Services, a residential carpet-cleaning service located in the Toronto area. After ten years of tremendous success in the business, the couple decided to launch a franchise operation.

They decided to place advertisements in different daily newspapers across Canada promoting the franchise business. Bill and Jill Robinson of Ottawa saw the advertisement and called V & A Carpet Cleaning Services to obtain information about the economics and advantages of managing a carpet-cleaning franchise operation. The Finneys provided the following information:

- Average revenue for cleaning carpets in each household is $120.
- A 20% sales commission per contract is secured by a sales representative.
- Machine operators receive $30 for cleaning the carpets in each household.
- Average cost for gas and maintenance for trucks for each household is $5.50.
- Maintenance charge is $400 per machine for each 100 houses cleaned.
- Monthly rental charge for office and small warehouse for inventory is $1,200.
- Annual depreciation for the equipment is $500.
- Monthly salary paid to both Bill and Jill totals $3,500.
- A $1,400 monthly salary for office employees.
- A $500 yearly expense for various insurance policies.
- A $125 monthly expense for utilities and telephone.
- A yearly $10,000 fee for the franchise.
- A $5.00 franchise fee for each household cleaned.

On the basis of the above information, calculate the following:

1. How many households would Bill and Jill have to clean each year in order to start making a profit?
2. How much sales revenue would they have to earn each year in order to break even?
3. How many households would they have to clean each year if they want to earn a yearly profit of $45,000?
4. Prepare a profit and loss statement on the basis of earning $45,000 in profit.

Chapter 5: Profit Planning and Decision-Making

6

Cost of Capital and Capital Structure

Learning Objectives

After reading this chapter, you should be able to:

1. Define the meaning of financial structure and capital structure.

2. Explain the meaning of cost of financing and how it is calculated.

3. Explain the meaning of the economic value added concept and how it is calculated.

4. Calculate the cost of capital and explain the leverage concept.

5. Explain the interdependence of the major areas of finance.

6. Calculate the cost of capital for publicly owned companies and the characteristics of the long-term financing sources.

7. Make the connection between the marginal cost of capital and investment decisions.

8. Explain the importance of leverage analysis and how it is calculated.

Chapter Outline

OPENING CASE

By the end of 2004, the Millers were pleased with CompuTech Sales and Services' financial performance. In fact, they exceeded their financial expectations. During that year, they decided to incorporate their business. It is now called CompuTech Inc. The Millers were entering an important phase in their business development to further expand their retail business. The one determining factor that limited the number of outlets they hoped to open was how much financing they would be able to obtain from lenders. They were also considering asking a few friends to invest in their business as shareholders.

The quality of the collateral and the company's ability to service its debt would be important elements that could encourage lenders to invest in CompuTech. On the other hand, the factor that would entice potential shareholders to invest in the company is its ability to grow in terms of sales and earnings. The Millers would have to prove to potential shareholders that they have the ability to manage the company extraordinarily well and demonstrate that CompuTech would be able to generate substantial earnings.

The Millers began to prepare an investment proposal to be presented to different investors. They wanted to expand the working capital of their existing retail outlet and open another retail outlet in 2005. The amount of the required investment was estimated at $350,000. The following shows how the Millers proposed to finance their expansion program.

	Uses	Sources
Working capital requirements	$ 99,000	
Short-term financing		$ 72,000
Capital assets	350,000	
Internal financing		157,000
Capital shares		70,000
Long-term debts		150,000
Total	$449,000	$449,000

The Millers remembered their initial conversation with entrepreneur Bill Murray when he said, "You must ensure that your business generates enough profit to pay for financing your business." Now that the Millers were facing growth and expansion, they began to realize the significance of Bill's statement. They had to ensure that sufficient cash would be available from the business to pay the interest and dividends to the shareholders. They also had to ensure that earnings from their business would be sufficient to reinvest into their business for working capital requirements and for the purchase of capital assets (new store, equipment, etc.).

A quick analysis of their projected financial statements for 2005 indicated that CompuTech would generate a 12.1% return on assets. The Millers had to make sure that the cost of the borrowed funds from different financing sources would be less than that. In order to encourage other shareholders to invest in CompuTech, they had to demonstrate a positive economic value added (EVA).

The Millers had more ambitious objectives for the longer term. They wanted to go public by 2012. This meant that they had six to seven years to demonstrate that CompuTech had real growth potential with powerful earnings. They were thinking of approaching venture capitalists by 2007 to invest substantial sums of money in their business in the form of equity. They realized, however, that these types of investors were looking for 25% to 35% (if not more) return on their investment. If they wanted to entice these types of investors by 2007 the Millers had to show that CompuTech had substantial growth and earnings potential.

This chapter examines two key concepts:

1. how cost of capital is calculated and used as a management tool; and
2. the significance of leverage analysis and how it can be used to maximize return.

Introduction

This chapter examines two distinct but related topics: cost of capital and leverage. Let's begin by explaining the meaning and the significance of these two concepts.

Cost of capital deals with the cost of borrowing funds to finance a business. For example, someone who obtains a mortgage from the bank at 7.0% to finance a house would have a 7.0% cost of capital. Similarly, if an entrepreneur wants to start a business that requires $500,000 in capital, first she will determine how much it will cost to raise these funds from various investors. These long-term investors could be lenders or shareholders. As shown on the following balance sheet, in this example the cost to raise the $500,000 from investors to buy the assets is 13.1%. Also, assuming that the entrepreneur earns $100,000 in profit on a $500,000 investment in assets, the business would generate a 20.0% return on assets (ROA). As shown on the balance sheet, there is a positive 6.9% difference between the cost of borrowed funds (13.1%) and the amount that the entrepreneur expects to earn from the business (20.0%).

Cost of capital

The cost of borrowing funds from investors (lenders and shareholders) to finance a business.

We compare ROA to the cost of capital to ensure that the return generated from a particular investment justifies the cost of borrowed funds. This is how banks operate: they borrow money at a cost, and lend it for a return; they refer to the difference between the two as the "spread."

Balance Sheet	
Assets	Investors
Return on assets	Cost of capital
20.0%	13.1%

The following shows how the cost to raise funds from different investors is calculated. For example, the $100,000 amount borrowed from source A represents 20% of the $500,000 amount and accounts for 2.0% of the total weighted cost of borrowing. This 13.1% is referred to as cost of capital.

Sources	Amount	Cost		Proportion		Weight
Source A	$100,000	10%	×	.20	=	2.0%
Source B	$250,000	15%	×	.50	=	7.5%
Source C	$150,000	12%	×	.30	=	3.6%
Total	$500,000			1.00		13.1%

Leverage

Technique used to determine the most suitable operating and financial structure that will help amplify financial performance.

Leverage, on the other hand, involves determining the most suitable operating and financial structure that will help amplify financial performance. It focuses on the following questions: Should a business have more fixed costs than variable costs? What would be the right proportion? Should the business have more debt than equity? Again, what would be the best proportion?

Sales volume is the important element that helps to decide on the most suitable operating and financing mix (or structure). The more volume a business generates, the more management will be inclined to have a higher proportion of fixed costs to variable costs. For example, this was particularly critical when free trade agreements were signed with the United States and Mexico that gave wider access to markets for Canadian businesses. With expanded markets, many businesses restructured their operating and financial structures in order to maximize both profitability and the wealth to their shareholders.

Finding the most suitable operating structure can help amplify profitability. For example, if a business generates an increase in profit of 20% with a 10% increase in sales revenue, the business has a 2.0 (or 2 to 1) operating leverage; that is, each time sales revenue increases by 10%, profitability is amplified by 20%. If management decides to change the composition of its operating cost structure and obtains a leverage of 3.0 (meaning that a 10% increase in sales generates a 30% increase in profit), it simply means greater profit maximization. The importance of calculating operating leverage is this: if Company A operates with a 3.0 leverage and Company B with a 2.0 leverage, the former has a better competitive advantage.

This chapter explains these two financial concepts, cost of capital and financial structure (or leverage analysis). But first, let's distinguish between the meaning of financial structure and capital structure.

Financial Structure and Capital Structure

◄◄ Objective 1

As shown in Figure 6.1, **financial structure** means the way a company's total assets are financed by the "entire right-hand side of the balance sheet" (current liabilities, long-term debts, and shareholders' equity). **Capital structure**, on the other hand, represents the more permanent forms of financing such as long-term debts and equity (common shares, preferred shares, and retained earnings) that are normally used to finance capital (or fixed) assets. The shaded portion in the figure represents this portion of the financing package. Capital structure therefore accounts for only a portion of a company's total financial structure. As shown, it excludes current liabilities.

Here is the significance of analyzing the cost of financing and the cost of capital.

Financial structure

The way a company's assets are financed by the entire right-hand side of the balance sheet (short-term and long-term financing).

Capital structure

The permanent financing sources used to buy capital assets.

Cost of Financing

Cost of financing calculates how much a business is charged to finance the assets that are shown on a company's balance sheet. As shown in Figure 6.1, let's assume that a company borrows funds from different financial institutions, which cost 8.6%, and earns 12.0% return on its assets (ROA); in this case, the company's cost of financing is less than what it earns. This produces positive results and

Cost of financing

Represents how much it costs (%) a business to finance all assets shown on a company's balance sheet.

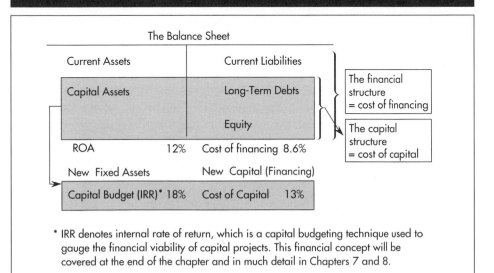

FIGURE 6.1   FINANCIAL STRUCTURE AND CAPITAL STRUCTURE

The Balance Sheet

Current Assets	Current Liabilities
Capital Assets	Long-Term Debts
	Equity

The financial structure = cost of financing

The capital structure = cost of capital

ROA 12%   Cost of financing 8.6%

New Fixed Assets   New Capital (Financing)

Capital Budget (IRR)* 18%   Cost of Capital 13%

* IRR denotes internal rate of return, which is a capital budgeting technique used to gauge the financial viability of capital projects. This financial concept will be covered at the end of the chapter and in much detail in Chapters 7 and 8.

undoubtedly makes good business sense. However, if the cost of financing a business is more than its ROA, the shareholders would not be earning enough to justify the investments in capital assets.

Cost of Capital

Cost of capital is a different concept, but it is calculated in a similar way. As indicated earlier, it deals with only the permanent forms of financing and has to do with the raising of new long-term capital to buy new capital assets. As shown in Figure 6.1, the company raises new capital funds from different financing sources (long-term debts and equity) at a cost of 13% (cost of capital). These funds are invested in new capital assets and generate an 18% return (IRR). This means that the cost of the newly acquired capital or permanent financing is less than the return expected to be earned on newly acquired capital assets. Again, this would make good business sense. In fact, the decision to borrow the capital funds at 13% in order to earn 18% would be considered favourable.

Cost of capital is associated with capital budgets since both have long-term implications. Bonds and mortgages, for example, are borrowed on a long-term basis (say 15 years) and are used to finance capital projects that also have long life spans (say 15 years). Referring to Figure 6.1, if the company's cost of capital is 13%, and it earns 18% return on assets, this means that the business would have a 5.0% positive spread every year during the next 15 years. If the spread were negative, the shareholders would make less on their investments. If this were the case, management would surely not go ahead with the investment decision.

Objective 2 ▶

The Importance of the Cost of Financing

Let's now examine the importance of cost of financing and how it is calculated. Table 6.1 shows a company that raises $1,200,000 from seven different sources. Short-term financing or current liabilities account for $250,000 (or 20.8%) of the total financing package, long-term debts account for $500,000 (or 41.6%), and equity accounts for $450,000 (or 37.6%). The table also presents the cost of financing for each amount raised, on a before- and after-tax basis. For example, management raised $50,000 from Source A at a cost of 10.2% on a before-tax basis. Assuming that the company is in a 50% tax bracket, the after-tax cost of borrowing from source A would be half, that is, 5.1%. The same arithmetic is done for calculating all other short- and long-term loans. However, the cost of raising funds from shareholders is 15%, whether before or after tax, because dividends are paid to shareholders with after-tax income. The last two columns in Table 6.1 present the weighted cost of financing. As shown, based on that particular financing structure, it would cost the company 11.53% before tax to raise funds from different sources, and 8.57% after tax.

The weighted cost of financing, however, is somewhat irrelevant unless it is compared to the return that the company earns on its assets. Table 6.2 gives us this comparison. As shown in the table on the left side of the balance sheet, the

TABLE 6.1 CALCULATING THE COST OF FINANCING

	Amounts	Proportion %	Cost of Financing Before Tax	After Tax	Weighted Cost of Financing Before Tax	After Tax
Current liabilities						
Source A	$ 50,000	4.2 ×	10.2%	5.1% =	.43%	.21%
Source B	100,000	8.3 ×	11.2%	5.6% =	.93%	.46%
Source C	100,000	8.3 ×	9.6%	4.8% =	.80%	.40%
Subtotal	250,000	20.8			2.16%	1.07%
Long-term debts						
Mortgage	200,000	16.6 ×	9.2%	4.6% =	1.53%	.76%
Bond	300,000	25.0 ×	8.8%	4.4% =	2.20%	1.10%
Subtotal	500,000	41.6			3.73%	1.86%
Total debt	750,000	62.4			5.89%	2.93%
Equity						
Common shares	150,000	12.6 ×	15.0%	15.0% =	1.89%	1.89%
Retained earnings	300,000	25.0 ×	15.0%	15.0% =	3.75%	3.75%
Subtotal	450,000	37.6			5.64%	5.64%
Total sources	$1,200,000	100.00				
Weighted cost of financing					11.53%	8.57%

TABLE 6.2 COMPARING COST OF FINANCING TO ROA

Balance Sheet						
Assets		**Liabilities**		**Before Tax**	**After Tax**	
Current	$ 400,000	Current	$ 250,000	@ 2.16%	1.07%	
Capital	800,000	Long-term	500,000	@ 3.73%	1.86%	
		Equity	450,000	@ 5.64%	5.64%	
Total	$1,200,000	Total	$ 1,200,000	11.53%	8.57%	

	ROA	Cost
Before tax	14.2 %	11.53 %
After tax	7.1%	8.57 %

Before tax

Debt $ 750,000 × 14.2% (ROA) = $ 106,500

Debt $ 750,000 × 9.4% (cost) = $ 70,500

Financial leverage = $ 36,000

After tax

Debt financing 4.71% × .624 = 2.94%

Equity financing 15.64% × .376 = 4.16%

Return on assets = 7.10%

Chapter 6: Cost of Capital and Capital Structure

company earns 14.2% (return) on its assets on a before-tax basis and 7.1% after tax. The before-tax return is based on the assumption that the company generated $170,400 ($1,200,000 × 14.2%) in income before taxes on total assets worth $1,200,000.

The after-tax return is also based on the assumption that the company is in a 50% tax bracket (14.2% ÷ 2 = 7.1%). As shown in the table, the spread is positive using the before-tax calculation because the company's assets are generating more than the cost of borrowed funds (14.2% versus 11.53%). However, the spread is negative on an after-tax basis (7.1% versus 8.57%). After-tax comparison is the common approach used for comparing cost of financing to return on assets.

Let's push this analysis a little further and calculate how much the company is earning on borrowed funds. This is what the lower portion of Table 6.2 presents. The company borrowed $750,000 ($250,000 from short-term lenders and $500,000 from long-term lenders) and earned 14.2% (ROA) or $106,500. As shown below, the weighted cost to borrow the funds from both short- and long-term sources is 9.42%. These amounts are drawn from different sources of financing that appear in Table 6.1.

Sources	Amounts	Proportion (%)		Before-tax cost		Weighted cost
Source A	$ 50,000	6.67	×	10.2%	=	0.68%
Source B	100,000	13.33	×	11.2	=	1.49
Source C	100,000	13.33	×	9.6	=	1.28
Mortgage	200,000	26.67	×	9.2	=	2.45
Bond	300,000	40.00	×	8.8	=	3.52%
Total	$750,000	100.00				9.42%

This means that there is a 4.8% spread (14.2% − 9.4%) on a before-tax basis between the cost of debt financing and the ROA. As shown in Table 6.2, the company's financial leverage—that is, the amount of money the owners earn by using other people's money—is $36,000.

The lower portion of Table 6.2 shows how the company's shareholders' return can be amplified as a result of the company's profit performance and financial structure. Since the cost of debt financing is 9.4% on a before-tax basis, the after-tax cost of financing (assuming the company is in a 50% tax bracket) would be 4.71%. Also, the proportion of the $1,200,000 raised from debt is $750,000, or 62.4%, and the balance, $450,000 or 37.6%, was obtained from shareholders' equity. As shown, instead of earning a 15.0% return, the shareholders are actually getting slightly more, 15.64%.

Here is how this number is calculated. Debt financing is constant; that is, irrespective of what happens, the company has to pay the interest—here, 4.71%, which represents 2.94% of the total cost of financing. As shown in the table, the company earns a 7.1% after-tax return on assets. By subtracting the 2.94% portion of the debt financing from the total cost, we get 4.16%. In this particular situation, the shareholders are actually earning 15.64% (.376 ×4.16) by using other people's money.

Economic Value Added

◀ Objective 3

A new term that has gained prominence in the business community to measure after-tax net operating profit relative to cost of capital is the **economic value added (EVA)**. Each year, *Fortune* magazine lists companies with the highest EVAs in one of its November issues under the title "America's Wealth Creators." EVA measures the wealth a company has created for its investors. Specifically, EVA is an attempt to measure how profitable a company truly is. Calculating the economic value added begins with the company's sales, and then subtracts the expenses incurred in running the business, which results in net operating profits after taxes (NOPAT). Then it subtracts one more expense—the cost of all the capital employed to produce the NOPAT. Capital includes elements such as buildings, heavy equipment, computers, and vehicles as well as working capital.

In effect, EVA charges the company for the use of those assets at a rate that compensates the lenders and the shareholders for providing those funds. What is left is EVA, and it measures profits after all costs are covered—including the cost of using assets shown on the balance sheet.

EVA has become the financial tool of choice at leading companies such as Coca-Cola, AT&T, Wal-Mart Stores, Eli Lilly, and Quaker Oats. At Eli Lilly, for example, EVA was linked to the company's bonus-plan pay system.

The reasons for the increasing popularly of this performance measurement are:

- it more closely reflects the wealth created for shareholders;
- it promotes management accountability; and
- it helps management make better decisions.

Table 6.3 shows an example of how EVA is calculated. As shown, the company's net operating profit before tax (NOPBT) is $1.0 million. On an after-tax basis, the net operating profit after tax (NOPAT) is $650,000. (It is assumed here that the company is in a 45% income tax bracket.) The company's cost of capital of 10.9% (after tax) to finance the $4,500,000 worth of capital funds (accounts payable is excluded from this calculation because suppliers do not charge

Economic value added (EVA)

Tool that measures the wealth a company creates for its investors. It is calculated by deducting a company's cost of capital from its net operating profits after taxes (NOPAT).

TABLE 6.3 CALCULATING THE ECONOMIC VALUE ADDED (EVA)

	Net Operating Profit	Minus	Cost of Capital	Equals	EVA
NOPBT	$1,000,000	Weighted cost of capital	10.9%*		
Minus taxes	450,000		×		
		Total capital	$4,500,000		
NOPAT	$ 650,000	MINUS	$ 490,500	EQUALS	$159,500

handwritten: 550,000 above 650,000; 59,500 below EVA

* 10.9% equals 60% of equity @ 14.5% or 8.7%
and 40% of equity @ 5.5% or 2.2%

---

interest) produces $490,500 in financing charges. The difference between the NOPAT and the cost of capital gives a $159,500 positive EVA.

These calculations show the importance of comparing the cost of debt financing to return on assets. If the return on assets is less than the cost of capital, management must either increase the return on its assets or restructure its financing package differently in order to improve either the economic value added or the wealth to its shareholders.

Objective 4 ▶

Cost of Capital and the Leverage Concept

The rest of this chapter deals with decisions related to raising new capital. Here, we are looking at the relationship between the cost of raising new permanent funds (and the most suitable capital mix), and comparing it to the return expected on the investment in new capital assets. Two important concepts that influence the choice and mix of one source of capital financing over another are cost of capital and leverage.

Cost of Capital for Privately Owned Companies

Cost of capital is a critical element in financing decisions. It is defined as the average rate of return shareholders and lenders expect to earn on the money they invested in their business. To calculate the weighted cost of capital, the costs of individual financing sources must be brought together. Finding the weighted cost of capital is an important calculation since it is used in determining the "hurdle rate"—that is, the level of return a project should generate before management will approve it in the capital budgeting process.

Here is how the concept works. Let's assume that Zylox Inc. (a privately owned company) has the opportunity to invest $100,000 in a risk-free project that will generate a 14% return, or $14,000. If the company has $50,000 of its own money (let's say retained earnings) and wishes to raise another $50,000 from external sources, the cost of raising the new capital dollars will determine, to a large extent, whether Zylox will proceed with the project. As shown on the following page, let's assume that the owners are able to raise $20,000 from source A at 9%, $20,000 from source B at 8%, and $10,000 from source C at 9.5%. They also expect to earn at least 12% on their own money (equity), since this is what they would expect to earn had they invested the $50,000 in investment certificates (sometimes referred to as **opportunity cost**). Should the company go ahead with this project? To answer this question, we have to calculate the weighted cost of capital and determine whether the risk is worth taking. The following is a simplified way of calculating the cost of capital.

Opportunity cost

The income sacrificed by not pursuing the next best alternative.

Source of capital	Amount	Proportion of total		Cost of capital		Proportion of cost
Personal	$ 50,000	0.50	×	12.0%	=	6.00%
Source A	20,000	0.20	×	9.0%	=	1.80%
Source B	20,000	0.20	×	8.0%	=	1.60%
Source C	10,000	0.10	×	9.5%	=	0.95%
	$100,000	1.00				10.35%

In this case, the weighted cost of capital is 10.35%. This project is expected to generate 14% (equivalent to ROA) or $14,000 in profit, while the total cost of borrowing is estimated at 10.35%, or $10,350. After looking at these figures, management at Zylox Inc. would be inclined to proceed with the project. If the project is considered risk-free, the chances of making a $3,650 net profit ($14,000 less $10,350) are virtually assured.

Leverage

Leverage is the percentage of debt a firm uses to finance the purchase of assets. For instance, the $100,000 asset referred to in the Zylox Inc. example is financed by a $50,000 debt, which means that the company has a 50% leverage factor.

Management can enhance profits and value by using leverage effectively. For example, with a 50% leverage factor, Zylox Inc. made a profit of $3,650. Profitability can be increased (or amplified) substantially if all funds are obtained from Source B, at a cost of only 8%. If Zylox Inc. were able to raise all funds from that single source, the profit generated would increase to $6,000, since the cost of financing would be only $8,000 and the return on the investment would remain at $14,000. The higher leverage would therefore produce an incremental $2,350 in profit ($6,000 less $3,650).

Interdependence of the Major Areas of Finance

◀ Objective 5

There is an important relationship between the major areas of finance, namely capital structure, cost of capital, and capital budgeting.

As shown in Figure 6.2, one of the first steps in planning capital projects (or capital budgeting) is to determine how much funds should be borrowed, from whom, and at what cost. If the treasurer is asked to raise, say, $1 million, the cost of raising the new funds will first have to be calculated. The capital structure largely determines the cost of capital. As shown on the following page, since raising capital from lenders costs less than from equity, it would be more attractive to obtain capital funds from lenders than from shareholders.

Different capital structures may influence the decision to proceed with a capital project or not. To illustrate, let's assume that a company has a $1 million capital investment (capital budget), which produces a 10% ROA. As shown below,

Chapter 6: Cost of Capital and Capital Structure

FIGURE 6.2   INTERDEPENDENCE OF THE MAJOR AREAS OF FINANCE

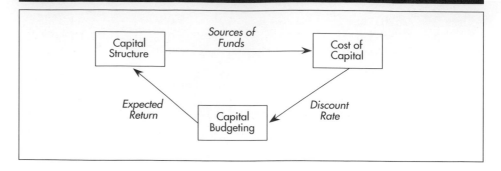

raising capital funds through option A gives a 12% weighted cost of capital, while option B gives only 8.0%. With a 10% ROA, management would not proceed with this particular project with the option A financing structure, since the company would be losing 2%. With option B, the company would be earning 2%, and management would (depending on the project's risk) probably approve the project.

Option A

	Debt		Equity		Total
Amount	$300,000	+	$700,000	=	$1,000,000
After-tax cost	5.0%		15.0%		
Proportion	× .30	+	× .70	=	1.00
Cost of capital	1.50% +		10.50%	=	12%

Option B

	Debt		Equity		Total
Amount	$700,000	+	$300,000	=	$1,000,000
After-tax cost	5.0%		15.0%		
Proportion	× .70	+	× .30	=	1.00
Cost of capital	3.50% +		4.50%	=	8.00%

The more it costs a business to raise funds, the more difficult it is for the business to go forward with its capital projects—unless, of course, the capital projects are exceptionally viable. As we will see in Chapter 8, the cost of capital is often used as the discount rate to compare the present value of a project's future cash inflow to the initial cash outflow.

Cost of Capital for Publicly Owned Companies

◀◼ Objective 6

To this point, much of the discussion related to raising funds has focused on privately owned businesses. Let's now turn to raising funds for publicly owned businesses.

The cost of capital (from external sources) incurred by publicly owned companies is set out in contractual agreements made between a borrowing company and different borrowers. The key issues are (1) the amount of interest the company will pay to lenders, (2) the dividends it will pay to preferred shareholders, and (3) the dividends and growth potential expected by the common shareholders.

In this chapter, we will calculate the cost of capital for a hypothetical publicly owned company called Wildwood Inc. Let's assume that Wildwood's management wants to raise $20 million to invest in different capital projects. We will calculate the cost of capital of four financing sources, namely:

a. long-term debts;

b. preferred shares;

c. common shares; and

d. retained earnings.

Afterward, we will define the meaning marginal cost of capital. But first, let's examine the characteristics of each of these major sources of financing.

Characteristics of Long-Term Capital Sources

Debt, preferred share, and common share financing have one important common characteristic: they are all obtained from external sources. Retained earnings (that is, profit generated by a business) is the only internal financing source. Table 6.4 summarizes the basic **characteristics of long-term financing sources** as seen from an issuing company's point of view.

These major long-term financing sources are examined in terms of payout, risk, voting rights or control, cost of capital, tax cost, and cost of issue.

Payout means the money that a business must pay to its stakeholders in exchange for funds. Payout ranges from compulsory payment (debt) of principal and interest to nonobligatory payments, such as dividends on common shares.

Risk refers to the impact each source of financing has on a business if the business is unable to meet its contractual agreement. Debt financing is the riskiest choice, particularly when economic or business conditions are difficult to predict, since bondholders may demand that interest be paid as per agreement and, if it is not, force the business into receivership.

Voting rights refer to the control that different stakeholders have over a business. Those who have the ultimate control of a company are the common shareholders. The issue of a new bond or preferred shares does not take away the rights of existing shareholders, but the issue of new common shares dilutes common

Characteristics of long-term financing sources

Factors to consider when raising funds from long-term sources are payout, risk, voting rights, cost of capital, tax cost, and cost of issue.

TABLE 6.4 CHARACTERISTICS OF THE MAJOR SOURCES OF LONG-TERM FINANCING

	Debt	Preferred Shares	Common Shares	Retained Earnings
Payout	Interest and principal must be paid as per contractual agreement. Bondholders do not participate in superior earnings.	Same as debt; amount is specified by agreement. Dividends can be cumulated from year to year.	Common share dividends are paid after debt and preferred dividends. Company is not forced to make payment.	Reduced payment of dividends puts more funds into a business; may be unfavourable in the short term but favourable in the long term.
Risk	If lenders are not paid according to agreement, they can force a business into receivership.	Have maturity and are usually callable. Have prior claim over common shareholders for receiving dividends, and other assets if company is liquidated.	Do not carry fixed maturity date.	Increases value and worth of a business.
Voting Rights (Control)	Have no say in business unless bond goes into default.	Have limited voting privileges; if they do, it is for minority representation on board of directors.	New issue creates change in ownership structure (extends voting rights). Legal right to make major decisions (elect board of directors).	When earnings are retained in a business, existing owners do not lose ownership right.
Cost of Capital	Easy to calculate and determinable since interest rate is stipulated.	Easy to calculate since it has a maturity date and a stated dividend rate and price of a share.	Rate is more difficult to ascertain since external factors and growth potential of a business form part of the cost.	Not easily determinable because of unpredictable growth trends.
Tax Cost	Interest charges are tax-deductible.	Preferred dividends are not tax-deductible.	Common dividends are not tax-deductible.	Taxed before payment is made to shareholders.
Cost of Issue	Underwriting cost is less expensive than other alternatives.	Flotation cost is expensive.	Underwriting and distribution costs are usually higher than preferred share and debt financing.	Avoids cost of issue.

shareholders' voting control. Also, additional shareholders can force a company to spread earnings more widely and thinly (see the figures in Table 6.5 for the spread of income to new and existing shareholders).

Cost of capital includes factors associated with the borrowing of money, such as payment of interest on debt, dividends for common or preferred shares, underwriting and distribution costs, and taxes. All these elements must be weighted to determine the costs associated with each source of financing. Costs related to debt and preferred shares are more easily determinable and relatively more certain than common share financing.

Tax cost plays an important part in deciding whether to go the route of debt or share financing. Common or preferred share dividends are not deductible as an expense for calculating a business's income tax; interest on bonds is. Taxes are a real cost that must be examined carefully. Table 6.5 gives an example of the impact taxes have on debt and share financing, at a certain level of income. As

TABLE 6.5 IMPACT OF DEBT AND SHARE FINANCING ON INCOME

	A Debt	B Common Shares	C Preferred Shares
Before-tax income	$500,000	$500,000	$500,000
Interest on debt	50,000	0	0
Taxable income	450,000	500,000	500,000
Taxes (at 50%)	225,000	250,000	250,000
Income after taxes	225,000	250,000	250,000
Preferred dividends	0	0	60,000
Income to common shareholders	225,000	250,000	190,000
Income to new shareholders	—	112,500	—
Income to existing shareholders	$225,000	$112,500	$190,000

Financing assumptions:
A. *Debt financing* of $500,000 raised from lenders with interest rate of 10%.
B. *Common share financing* of $500,000 raised from new shareholders in exchange for 50% of the company's shares.
C. *Preferred share financing* of $500,000 raised from investors with a dividend rate of 12%.

shown in the table, alternative A (debt financing) is the least attractive form of financing because the income after taxes is $225,000 compared to $250,000 for alternatives B and C. However, alternative A is the most lucrative for the existing shareholders, since they earn $112,500 more than common share financing offers, and $35,000 over preferred share financing.

Cost of issue includes charges associated with the underwriting and distribution of a new issue. Costs of issuing common shares are usually higher because the investigation is more detailed than debt and preferred share financing. A company that wants to raise funds will examine all the advantages and disadvantages of each source of financing and select the one that best meets its specific needs at the time of the issue.

The main factors that are taken into consideration when raising funds are:

- the nature of a company's cash flow;
- the company's annual burden of payments (existing debts);
- the cost of financing each type of capital;
- the control factor;
- the expectations of the existing common shareholders;
- the flexibility of future financing decisions;
- the pattern of the capital structure in the industry;
- the stability of the company's earnings;
- the desire to use financial leverage; and
- the market conditions that can easily dictate the use of one form of capital source over another.

Calculating the Cost of Long-Term Capital Sources

Let's now calculate the cost of long-term capital sources, namely debt, preferred shares, common shares, and retained earnings.

Cost of debt

Interest charges less income taxes.

DEBT Cost of debt financing is relatively easy to calculate. For example, if a company borrows $100,000 for one year at 10%, the lenders would receive $10,000 in interest. Ignoring income tax for the moment, the cost of capital for that particular source would be 10%.

Debt financing considers two fundamental questions. First, how should the cost be calculated when there are several different types of bonds? Second, since interest is a tax-deductible item, how does income tax affect the cost of debt?

First, if there are several bonds with different interest rates, we have to calculate the average rate of interest for that particular financing source. For example, let's assume that Wildwood Inc. decides to issue two bonds, a senior bond (like a first mortgage on a house) for $5 million at 10%, and a $2 million subordinated bond (like a second mortgage; it is paid only if the senior bonds are paid) at 12%. The average interest rate is calculated as follows:

$$\text{Average cost of bonds} = \frac{(\$5,000,000 \times 10\%) + (\$2,000,000 \times 12\%)}{\$7,000,000}$$
$$= 10.57\%$$

Second, we must deal with the impact of income taxes on the cost of debt. Since interest is tax-deductible, we must find the income tax rate in order to calculate the effective cost of debt. The higher the income tax rate, the lower the effective cost of debt will be. For example, if a company has a 50% income tax rate, the effective cost of borrowing the aforementioned $7 million in bonds is 5.28% [10.57% × (1 − .50)] or $369,600. If the income tax rate is 25%, the effective cost of borrowing would be 7.9% [10.57% × (1.0 − .25)] or $553,000. If no taxes are paid, the effective cost of debt would be 10.57% or $739,900 annually.

The formula used for calculating the after-tax cost of debt is:

$$\text{Effective cost of debt} = (\text{before-tax cost}) \times (1.0 - \text{tax rate})$$

By applying this formula to the $7 million bond issue, and assuming that Wildwood Inc.'s tax rate is 50%, the effective cost of the debt would be 5.28%, calculated as follows:

$$\text{Effective cost of debt} = 10.57\% \times (1.0 - .50) = 5.28\%$$

PREFERRED SHARES Preferred shares are a hybrid of debt and common shares. Like debt, preferred shares carry a fixed contractual commitment for a company to pay—in this case, the dividends due to the preferred shareholders. In the event of liquidation, preferred shareholders take precedence over common shareholders. Also, dividends are paid to preferred shareholders before the common dividends are paid.

Calculating the **cost of preferred shares** is just as easy as calculating the debt cost, since preferred shares carry a maturity date and a stated dividend rate with a current price. For example, if Wildwood Inc. issues preferred shares with a value of $1 million bearing 12%, the cost of this issue to the company would be $120,000 annually. If, one year from now, the preferred shares are sold in the market for 90% of their value, say $900,000, the interest rate to be earned by the new preferred shareholders would be 13.33% (12% ÷ 90%). The factors that may influence a decline in the market value of such shares are:

Cost of preferred shares

Includes fixed dividends paid to shareholders and the flotation costs.

- the general rise of the interest rate, which forces the price of the shares to drop;
- a renewed fear of rampant inflation; and
- a decline in the general value of the business as an investment opportunity.

Also, Wildwood Inc. would have to pay a commission to the investment dealers, and such flotation costs would be incorporated in the calculation.

Assuming that Wildwood Inc. sells 10,000 preferred shares at $100 each, bearing a 12% dividend rate, and the investment dealers charge a selling and distribution commission of $4 a share, Wildwood Inc. would net $96 a share. The formula used for calculating the cost of preferred shares is as follows:

$$\text{Cost of preferred shares} = \frac{\text{Dividend on preferred shares}}{\text{Market value of shares} - \text{Flotation costs}}$$

Wildwood Inc.'s cost of the preferred share issue would be 12.5% or $125,000. The calculation is as follows:

$$\text{Cost of preferred shares} = \frac{\$12}{\$100 - \$4} = 12.5\%$$

So far, we have calculated the cost of raising $8 million of the $20 million that Wildwood Inc. wants to raise. The remaining $12 million would have to come from common shares and retained earnings. If we assume that the company expects to reinvest $2 million in earnings into the business, Wildwood would have to raise $10 million from a common share issue.

COMMON SHARES As seen in the previous paragraphs, both debt and preferred share costs are easily calculated, quite determinable, and certain. They are contractual agreements signed by the company and the bondholders or preferred shareholders.

Finding the **cost of common shares** is more complicated. The common shareholders know what they want, but it is difficult for the treasurer of a company to estimate the future expected values of the business in terms of growth, retained earnings, etc., all of which are incorporated in the calculation. There are two different approaches used for calculating the cost of common shares.

The first approach is based on past performance. By looking at trends related to common share prices and dividend payments, the treasurer can put a price tag on a new issue. For instance, if, during the past five years, the selling price of

Cost of common shares

Includes dividends paid to shareholders, flotation costs, and growth rate.

common shares has been $25, and dividends paid were in the $2.50 range, the average investor's rate of return is therefore 10% ($2.50 divided by $25). If there are no significant changes in shareholders' expectations, in the interest rates, or in investors' attitudes toward risk, the treasurer can assume that the future cost of common shares will be 10%.

The second approach is based on forecasts. Here, the treasurer takes into consideration three factors: (1) annual dividends to be paid, (2) price of the common shares, and (3) expected growth in earnings and dividends. The formula to calculate the cost of common shares is as follows:

$$\text{Cost of common shares} = \frac{\text{Dividend yield shares}}{\text{Market price of the share} - \text{Issue costs}} + \text{Growth rate}$$

Let us refer to Wildwood Inc.'s financing package. The company intends to raise $10 million from common shares. Also, the common share market price is $100 and the company's current annual dividend payout is 10% or $10 per share. Historically, the company's growth performance in earnings, dividends, and share price has been 4% a year, which is a growth that is assumed to continue during the next few years. Using the above formula, Wildwood Inc.'s cost of common shares would be 14%:

$$\text{Cost of common shares} = \frac{\$10}{\$100} + 4\% = 14\%$$

The other factor taken into account is the flotation cost or the cost of selling a new issue. If Wildwood Inc.'s flotation costs are 10% on a $100 common share issue, the company would net $90. If we take this factor into consideration, the cost of the new shares would be 15.11%:

$$\text{Cost of common shares} = \frac{\$10}{\$100\,(1 - .10)} + 4\% = 15.11\%$$

The company is showing growth because a portion of the retained earnings are plowed back into investment opportunities. These investments would generate additional earnings and produce a favourable effect on the growth potential of the company. For example, if Wildwood Inc. earns 20% on its investments, and half of each dollar earned is paid in dividends and the other half retained in the business, this means that each new reinvested dollar produces ten cents ($0.50 × 20%). Suppose, instead of reinvesting half of the earnings into the business, management decides to pay all its earnings in dividends; this may force a company to bring its growth to a halt. In this case, the market price of the share may remain at $100, since the investors would still receive a 14% return. Here is how this rate is calculated:

$$\text{Cost of common shares} = \frac{\$14}{\$100} + 0 = 14\%$$

Cost of retained earnings

Includes dividends and growth rate.

RETAINED EARNINGS The remaining $2 million is expected to be generated by Wildwood Inc. through its earnings. Calculating the **cost of retained earnings** is similar to the common share calculation, except that issue costs are not incurred. If the company expects to earn $20 a share and pay $10 in dividends during the coming year, and the growth pattern is also 4%, the company's cost of retained earnings will be 14%.

Weighted Cost of Capital

We have now calculated the individual cost of capital for debt, preferred shares, common shares, and retained earnings. With this information, we can calculate Wildwood Inc.'s weighted cost of capital; the arithmetic is simple. All that is required is to (1) compute the proportion of each source of capital relative to the total capital structure and (2) multiply this number by the appropriate cost of that specific source of capital. As shown in Table 6.6, Wildwood Inc.'s weighted cost of capital is 11.428%. This rate would be the approximate value that would be used as the hurdle rate when reviewing potential capital investment projects.

MARGINAL COST OF CAPITAL Let's assume that, during the year, Wildwood Inc. wants to raise an extra $2 million in order to invest in more capital projects. It also wants to keep its capital structure in the same proportion. For the purpose of this exercise, let's assume that debt and preferred shares are raised at the same cost, while the cost for raising common shares is higher. By using the common share dividend yield, say 12%, a 10% flotation charge, and a 4% growth rate, the new cost of common share issue would be 17.33%.

The calculation is as follows:

$$\text{Cost of common shares} = \frac{12.00\%}{.90} + 4\% = 17.33\%$$

As shown in Table 6.7, the calculation of Wildwood Inc.'s new cost of capital is 12.973%. The additional dollars raised above the $20 million figure mean that Wildwood Inc. would have a new average cost of capital of 12.97%; this is referred to as the **marginal cost of capital (MCC).** This means that Wildwood Inc.'s MCC, which was 11.4% to raise the $20 million, is now increased to 13% to raise $22 million (an extra $2 million).

Marginal cost of capital

The increased level of average cost resulting from having borrowed new funds at higher rates than those previously borrowed.

TABLE 6.6	CALCULATING THE WEIGHTED AVERAGE COST OF CAPITAL						
Source of Capital	Amount of Capital	Percent of Total		After-tax Cost of Capital		Proportion of Cost
Debt	$ 7,000,000	.35	×	5.28%	=	1.848%
Preferred shares	1,000,000	.05	×	12.50%	=	.625%
Common shares	10,000,000	.50	×	15.11%	=	7.555%
Retained earnings	2,000,000	.10	×	14.00%	=	1.400%
	$20,000,000	1.00				11.428%

Chapter 6: Cost of Capital and Capital Structure

TABLE 6.7 CALCULATING THE NEW WEIGHTED AVERAGE COST OF CAPITAL

Source of Capital	Amount of Capital	Percent of Total		After-Tax Cost of Capital		Proportion of Cost
Debt	$ 7,000,000	.318	×	5.28%	=	1.679%
Preferred shares	1,000,000	.045	×	12.50%	=	.562%
Common shares	12,000,000	.545	×	17.33%	=	9.444%
Retained earnings	2,000,000	.092	×	14.00%	=	1.288%
	$22,000,000	1.00				12.973%

Figure 6.3 shows graphically the relationship between the original $20 million capital structure and that of the new $22 million. The graph shows that the cost curve is flat up to the point where it reaches $22 million; at that point, it moves up gradually and continues to rise. The reason for the rise is that Wildwood Inc. may find it difficult to raise new securities within a short time span. If it finds new sources of capital, they will be more expensive because of the higher risk to be borne by the stakeholders and the corresponding higher return they will demand from the company.

FIGURE 6.3 MARGINAL COST OF CAPITAL

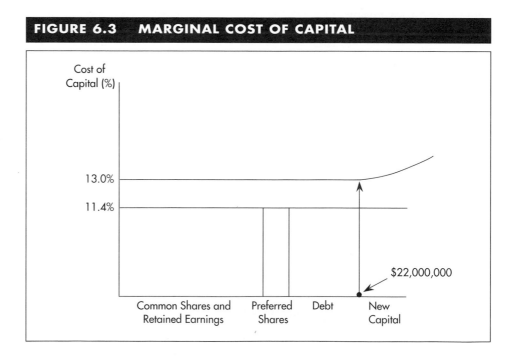

The Marginal Cost of Capital and Investment Decisions

◀◀ Objective 7

The purpose of calculating the marginal cost of capital is to ensure that the cost of borrowing does not exceed the return that will be earned from capital projects. For example, if it costs 15.0% to borrow capital dollars from different sources, the company will have to be assured that the aggregate return of all projects is at least equal to 15.0%; if it is less, the company would be in a negative return position. Let us examine how this works.

Once the marginal cost of capital is calculated, the next step is to relate it to capital projects. Using the Wildwood Inc. example, if the company intends to invest $20 million in capital projects giving an 11.4% return, all projects would be accepted. However, if managers submit capital projects that exceed the $20 million level, management would then have to examine all investment opportunities and accept a mix of projects that will maximize the overall value of the business. The procedure is as follows.

The first step is to find the marginal cost of capital, such as the one shown in Figure 6.4.

Second, projects are evaluated, and the rate of return of each project is determined. The capital budgeting technique used to assess the economic attractiveness of capital projects is called internal rate of return (IRR). This technique will be explained in Chapter 8. Using the IRR technique, the aggregate cash flow of all projects is discounted. The idea is to find the net present value of all projects

FIGURE 6.4 MARGINAL COST OF CAPITAL AND INTERNAL RATE OF RETURN

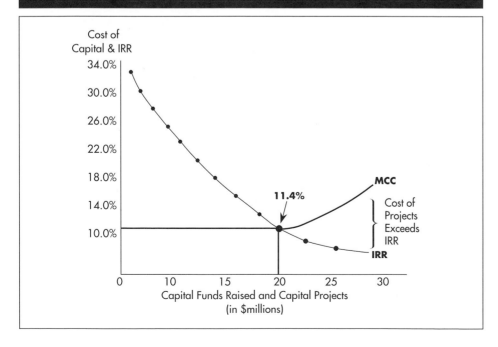

that will give a zero figure. This happens when the total cash inflow of all projects equals the total cash outflow. In Wildwood Inc.'s case, management can approve a mix of projects that, when discounted by a rate of 11.4%, gives a total that amounts to $20 million. If the company's aggregate IRR does not equal the cost of capital, we have to proceed to the next step.

In this step, the discounted present values of the cash flows of all projects are calculated at varying discount rates (say 35% down to 5%) and the result is plotted on a graph (see Figure 6.4). If the company raises $20 million at a cost of 11.4%, it will approve $20 million worth of capital projects. If more projects are approved, the aggregate IRR will fall below the 11.4% point, and Wildwood Inc. would be in a negative return position.

Leverage Analysis

Objective 8 ➡

Leverage analysis is used to determine the financing package or cost structure that will optimize the worth of a business. The purpose of leverage analysis is to answer one fundamental question: What is the best financing mix or capital structure to use to finance our assets? An example will illustrate how leverage analysis works. Let us assume that a firm borrows $400,000 at 12% (or 6% after tax) to finance projects that cost $500,000 and earn 16% (after tax). Here, the owners earn $56,000 (after-tax profit of $80,000 less interest cost of $24,000) on their $100,000 investment, a return on equity of 56%. This compares favourably to the project's return of only 16%. Under these circumstances, where there is a wide spread between the rate of return and the rate of interest, management would use debt rather than equity funds. As mentioned before, debt is less expensive than equity financing.

This example is relatively simple; it is usually more complex to determine the leverage factor that produces the greatest financial benefits. To understand the mechanics of leverage, we have to examine the behaviour of sales revenue, fixed and variable operating costs, earnings before taxes and interest, debt charges, and earnings per share. As shown in Figure 6.5, there are three types of leverage: operating leverage, financial leverage, and total or combined leverage.

Operating Leverage

Operating leverage

Financial technique used to determine to what extent fixed costs are used relative to variable costs.

Operating leverage deals with the behaviour of costs at the operating level (e.g., company or plant); it does not take financing charges into consideration. This approach determines the most suitable cost (fixed versus variable costs) that will maximize profit before interest or dividend charges. Leverage is important because operating costs have a direct impact on total corporate charges, which, in turn, affect financial leverage.

Operating leverage is based on the break-even analysis concept, which was examined in Chapter 5. It involves the relationship between three elements: sales revenue, fixed costs, and variable costs. The idea is to select the most appropriate cost mix that will maximize profits under a set of economic or industry consider-

FIGURE 6.5   THE LEVERAGE CONCEPT

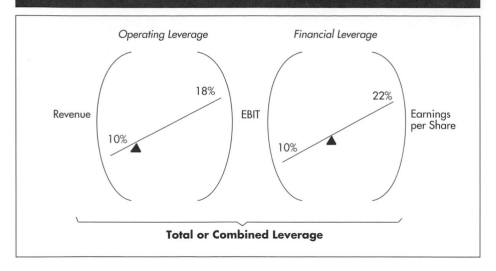

Operating Leverage

Financial Leverage

Revenue — 10% ... 18% — EBIT — 10% ... 22% — Earnings per Share

Total or Combined Leverage

ations. A favourable operating leverage is achieved when a change in revenue generates a larger change in earnings before interest and taxes (EBIT). As shown in Figure 6.5, a 10% increase in sales revenue produces an 18% increase in EBIT. The element that amplifies the earnings is the relationship between fixed costs and total operating costs.

Here is an example of how operating leverage works. Let's assume that management contemplates modernizing a manufacturing plant that will require a $700,000 capital expenditure. To decide whether to modernize or not, management will have to identify the level of sales volume and sales revenue that will be achieved in the future and the impact that the new technology will have on the company's fixed and variable cost structure.

As shown in Table 6.8, the new technology will bring about changes to the company's operating cost structure. Under the present cost structure, the company's fixed costs amount to $200,000, and it also earns a $5.00 contribution. If the company decides to modernize, the cost structure would change, and the new fixed costs would be increased to $300,000 (an increment of $100,000 over existing operations). However, the unit variable costs will be reduced to $8.00 (from $10.00) because of the decreased variable costs due to higher productivity. The new contribution margin would be increased to $7.00. In other words, the company would earn an extra $2.00 in contribution to pay for the $100,000 fixed cost increment. The question is this, is the expansion worth the investment? To answer the question, the company would have to estimate the sales volume that it expects to achieve in the next year or two. Table 6.8 shows that if the level of sales is at 40,000 units, the company would break even with the existing facility, but, if management modernizes its plant, the company would incur a $20,000 loss. However, if the company expects to sell 100,000 units, this new sales level would certainly justify the investment because it would generate a $400,000 profit instead of $300,000 for the present production methods.

TABLE 6.8 OPERATING LEVERAGE

	Present Production Methods			Proposed Production Methods		
Fixed costs		$200,000			$300,000	
Selling price		$ 15.00			$ 15.00	
Variable costs		$ 10.00			$ 8.00	
Contribution		$ 5.00			$ 7.00	
	High	**Expected**	**Low**	**High**	**Expected**	**Low**
No. of units	100,000	70,000	40,000	100,000	70,000	40,000
(in $000s)						
Revenue	$1,500	$1,050	$ 600	$1,500	$1,050	$ 600
Variable costs	1,000	700	400	800	560	320
Fixed costs	200	200	200	300	300	300
Total costs	1,200	900	600	1,100	860	620
Profit	$ 300	$ 150	$ 00	$ 400	$ 190	– $ 20

Essentially, operating leverage measures how much the operating cost structure amplifies profit performance before interest and taxes. As shown in Table 6.9, a 10% increase in sales revenue (at the proposed production methods) generates a 17.5% increase in profit before interest and taxes (EBIT) or a leverage of 1.75.

TABLE 6.9 CALCULATING THE OPERATING LEVERAGE

For the Proposed Production Methods (High)

Sales revenue	$ 1,500,000	$ 1,650,000	10.0%
Variable costs	800,000	880,000	10.0%
Contribution margin	700,000	770,000	10.0%
Fixed costs	300,000	300,000	—
Profit (EBIT)	$ 400,000	$ 470,000	17.5%

$$\frac{\text{Contribution margin}}{\text{Contribution margin} - \text{Fixed costs}} = \frac{\$ 700,000}{\$ 400,000} = 1.75$$

Financial Leverage

Financial leverage

Financial technique used to determine the most favourable capital structure (debt versus equity).

Financial leverage is used to choose the most favourable capital structure—the one that will generate the greatest financial benefits to the shareholders. It is reasonable to assume that shareholders will favour projects with return rates exceeding the cost of borrowed funds. Since debt is the least costly source of funds, shareholders will prefer to borrow the maximum amount possible from this particular source (provided that the projects can generate enough cash to pay off the debt).

TABLE 6.10 CALCULATING THE FINANCIAL LEVERAGE

For the Proposed Production Methods (High)

EBIT	$400,000	$440,000	10.0%
Interest	150,000	150,000	—
Income before taxes	$250,000	$290,000	16.0%

$$\frac{EBIT}{EBIT - Interest} = \frac{\$400,000}{\$250,000} = 1.6$$

Financial leverage can be gauged by looking at only one alternative and changing its capital structure mix to determine how much the leverage can enhance the earnings per share position for each option. Table 6.10 shows that a 10% increase in EBIT produces a 16% increase in income before taxes (or after tax since we are dealing with a 50% income tax rate). Here, the financial leverage is 1.6.

Combined Leverage

Combined leverage simply calculates both the operating and financial leverage. As shown in Table 6.11, when sales increase by 10%, income after taxes shows a 28% increase or a leverage of 2.8.

Combined leverage

Financial technique used to calculate both operating and financial leverage.

TABLE 6.11 CALCULATING THE COMBINED LEVERAGE

For the Proposed Production Methods (High)

Sales revenue	$1,500,000	$1,650,000	10.0%
Variable costs	800,000	880,000	10.0%
Contribution margin	700,000	770,000	10.0%
Fixed costs	300,000	300,000	—
Profit (EBIT)	400,000	470,000	17.5%
Interest	150,000	150,000	—
Income before taxes	250,000	320,000	—
Income taxes	125,000	160,000	—
Income after taxes	$ 125,000	$ 160,000	28.0%

$$\frac{Contribution\ margin}{EBIT - Interest} = \frac{\$700,000}{\$250,000} = 2.8$$

or

$$1.75 \times 1.6 = 2.8$$

✳ Decision-Making in Action

Management of National Electronics Ltd. is in the process of reviewing its operational plans and capital budgets. Prior to making important decisions, members of the management committee wanted some information to determine whether they should approve or reject some of the capital expenditure projects.

National Electronics Ltd.'s 2003 income statement and balance sheet are shown below.

NATIONAL ELECTRONICS LTD.
INCOME STATEMENT
FOR THE PERIOD ENDING DECEMBER 31, 2003

Sales revenue	$5,000,000
Cost of goods sold	2,900,000
Gross margin	2,100,000
Operating expenses	800,000
Operating income	1,300,000
Interest charges	100,000
Income before taxes	1,200,000
Income taxes	600,000
Income after taxes	$ 600,000

NATIONAL ELECTRONICS LTD
BALANCE SHEET
AS AT DECEMBER 31, 2003

Current assets		Current liabilities	
Accounts receivable	$1,000,000	Accounts payable	$ 500,000
Inventory	1,000,000	Working capital loan	500,000
Total current assets	2,000,000	Total current liabilities	$1,000,000
Capital assets	3,000,000	Long-term debts	
		Mortgage	$1,500,000
		Bond	500,000
		Total long-term debts	2,000,000
		Shareholders' equity	
		Retained earnings	1,000,000
		Capital shares	1,000,000
		Total shareholders' equity	2,000,000
Total assets	$5,000,000	Total debt and equity	$5,000,000

The treasurer indicated to the members of the committee that the before-tax costs of financing the working capital loan, mortgage, and bond were 13%, 10%, and 12% respectively. He also pointed out that the shareholders expect to earn 15% on their equity.

The total company's capital budget was estimated at $2.0 million. The treasurer said that the financing of the total capital budget would come from debt in the amount of $1.2 million and equity for $800,000. The cost of financing the debt would be 12% and equity, 15%.

One important project that the committee was considering was the modernization of a small manufacturing plant. At the meeting, the plant manager indicated that the project would cost $200,000 and earn an 18% internal rate of return. The plant manager indicated that the $200,000 modernization program would make significant changes in the operating cost structure. As he pointed out, the plant currently produces $450,000 in sales revenue with variable costs estimated at 80% of sales revenue and $100,000 in fixed costs. He stated that the modernization program would reduce the variable costs to 75% of sales revenue but increase the fixed costs to $115,000. The sales manager indicated that he expected sales revenue to reach $500,000 by the end of the current year and attain the $600,000 objective by the end of the following year.

The treasurer also indicated that the interest charges that were to be allocated to finance the plant's modernization program would be $8,000.

The CEO asked the following questions:

1. What is National Electronics Ltd.'s cost of financing?
2. What is National Electronics Ltd.'s cost of capital for modernizing the plant?
3. What is National Electronics Ltd.'s economic value added?
4. Should the modernization program be approved? Why? To answer this question, the controller has to produce a profit and loss statement for the plant's three levels of sales revenue ($450,000, $500,000, and $600,000) for both current operations and the modernization program.
5. If the modernization program is approved, what is the plant's operating leverage using the $600,000 sales revenue objective?
6. What is the company's financial leverage, also using the $600,000 sales revenue objective, if the modernization program is approved?
7. What is the plant's combined leverage?

As evidenced by the discussion at the management committee, several managers (e.g., treasurer, plant manager, sales manager, etc.) are involved in the decision-making process. Table 6.12 shows the calculations related to the questions raised by the CEO.

QUESTION 1: What is National Electronics Ltd.'s cost of financing?

As shown in the table, first the controller must determine the weighted cost before and after tax for each source of financing. The company is in a 50% tax bracket, which is evidenced by the amount of tax that the company pays ($600,000 in taxes deducted from the $1,200,000 income before taxes). As shown in the table, the cost of financing National Electronics Ltd. as an ongoing entity is 8.75%. The only account that does not bear an interest charge is accounts payable, that is the financing provided by suppliers.

QUESTION 2: What is National Electronics Ltd.'s cost of capital for modernizing the plant?

National Electronics Ltd.'s capital budget shows that $200,000 will be invested in a modernization program for a small manufacturing plant. By using the same financing proportion for the entire company (40% for equity and 60% for debt) as shown in the calculation for the first question, $120,000 will be financed by debt and $80,000 by equity. The cost for equity and debt is 15% and 12% on a before-tax basis and 15% and 6% after tax. As shown in the table, the cost of capital for financing the project is 9.6%.

QUESTION 3: What is National Electronics Ltd.'s economic value added?

As shown, National Electronics Ltd. produces a net operating profit before taxes (NOPBT) in the amount of $1.3 million. On the investors' side of the balance sheet (liabilities and shareholders' equity), the company raised $4.5 million from lenders and shareholders with a weighted cost of financing of 8.75%. By

Chapter 6: Cost of Capital and Capital Structure

TABLE 6.12   DECISION-MAKING IN ACTION

Question 1. Cost of Financing

	Sources	Cost Before Tax (%)	Cost After Tax (%)	Proportion	Weighted Cost of Financing (%)
Accounts payable	$ 500,000	0.0	0.0	.10	0.00
Working capital loan	500,000	13.0	6.5	.10	0.65
Mortgage	1,500,000	10.0	5.0	.30	1.50
Bond	500,000	12.0	6.0	.10	0.60
Equity	2,000,000	15.0	15.0	.40	6.00
Total	$5,000,000			1.00	8.75

Question 2: Cost of Capital for Financing the Modernization Program

	Sources	Cost Before Tax (%)	Cost After Tax (%)	Proportion	Weighted Cost of Capital (%)
Debt	$120,000	12.0	6.0	.60	3.60
Equity	$ 80,000	15.0	15.0	.40	6.00
Total	$200,000			1.00	9.60

Question 3: Economic Value Added

Net operating profit before taxes	$1,300,000	Capital	$4,500,000
Income taxes (50%)	650,000	Cost of capital	× 8.75%
Net operating profit after taxes	650,000	Cost of financing	$ 393,750
Cost of financing	393,750		
Economic value added	$ 256,250		

Question 4: The Modernized Plant's Profit and Loss Statement at the Three Sales Revenue Levels

	Before Modernization			After Modernization		
Sales revenue	$600,000	$500,000	$450,000	$600,000	$500,000	$450,000
Variable costs	480,000	400,000	360,000	450,000	375,000	337,500
Contribution margin	120,000	100,000	90,000	150,000	125,000	112,500
Fixed costs	100,000	100,000	100,000	115,000	115,000	115,000
Profit before taxes	$ 20,000	$ 000	−$ 10,000	$ 35,000	$ 10,000	−$ 2,500

TABLE 6.12   DECISION-MAKING IN ACTION (continued)

Question 5: Operating Leverage Using the Modernization Option at $600,000 Sales Revenue Level

			Increase
Sales revenue	$600,000	$660,000	10.0%
Variable costs	450,000	495,000	10.0%
Contribution margin	150,000	165,000	10.0%
Fixed costs	115,000	115,000	—
EBIT	$ 35,000	$ 50,000	42.8%

$$\frac{\$150,000}{\$ 35,000} = 4.28$$

Question 6: Financial Leverage

			Increase
Profit	$35,000	$38,500	10.0%
Interest	8,000	8,000	—
EBT	$27,000	$30,500	13.5%

$$\frac{\$35,000}{\$27,000} = 1.30$$

Question 7: Combined Leverage

			Increase
Sales revenue	$600,000	$660,000	10.0%
Variable costs	450,000	495,000	10.0%
Contribution margin	150,000	165,000	10.0%
Fixed costs	115,000	115,000	—
EBIT	35,000	50,000	42.8%
Interest	8,000	8,000	—
EBT	$ 27,000	$ 42,000	55.6%

$$4.28 \times 1.3 = 5.56$$

deducting from the NOPBT the 50% income tax charge of $650,000 and the $393,750 financing charges, the company is left with an economic value added in the amount of $256,250.

QUESTION 4: Should the modernization program be approved? Why?

A profit and loss statement for the plant's three levels of sales revenue ($450,000, $500,000 and $600,000) for both current operations and the modernization program is shown in Table 6.12.

On the basis of the information provided by the plant manager and the sales manager, the management committee should approve the modernization program. This can be looked at from two angles. First, as shown in the table, the modernized plant would generate $35,000 in profit versus $20,000 at the $600,000 sales revenue level. The existing plant shows a ratio of 80% in variable costs ($360,000/$450,000), leaving a 20% contribution margin ($90,000/$450,000) to pay for the $100,000 fixed costs. The modernization program would reduce the variable costs to 75% ($112,5000/$337,000) but increase fixed cost by an extra $15,000, up to $115,000. The determining factor that will influence the management committee to approve (or not approve) the project is the sales estimates provided by the sales manager. Even at the $450,000 sales level, it would be economically attractive for the company to modernize. Nevertheless, the most probable estimate based on the sales manager's input is in the $600,000 range.

Second, the plant manager indicated that the modernization program would earn an 18% internal rate of return. This compares favourably to the 9.6% cost of capital (an 8.4% positive difference). This is a good result in view of the fact that the modernization program would not be considered a high-risk investment.

QUESTION 5: If the modernization is approved, what is the plant's operating leverage using the $600,000 sales revenue objective?
The operating leverage is very attractive at the $600,000 sales revenue level for the modernization option. As shown in Table 6.12, a 10% increase in sales revenue would generate a 42% increase in earnings before interest and taxes (EBIT). The operating leverage is 4.28. Since National Electronics is in the 50% tax bracket, the leverage on an after-tax basis would be the same. The after-tax profit level for a 10% increase in sales revenue would also produce a 42% increase in earnings after interest and taxes ($17,500 versus $25,000).

QUESTION 6: What is the company's financial leverage, also using the $600,000 sales revenue objective, if the modernization program is approved?
The financial leverage is not as attractive, but still good. A 10% increase in earnings before taxes produces a 13.5% increase in earnings after taxes. The financial leverage is 1.3. Here, it is estimated that an $8,000 interest charge will be paid to finance the modernization program.

QUESTION 7: What is the plant's combined leverage?
The combined leverage is very positive. A 10% increase in sales revenue generates a 55.5% increment in earnings before (or after) taxes, or a combined leverage of 5.56 (4.28 × 1.3).

Chapter Summary

Objective 1 ➡️   Financing decisions consider not only sources and forms of financing but also cost of capital and capital structure. *Financial structure* means the way a company's total assets are financed by the entire right-hand side of the balance sheet, as well as short-term and long-term financing. *Capital structure* represents the permanent forms of financing, such as long-term debt, common shares, preferred shares, and retained earnings.

Objective 2 ➡️   Cost of financing represents how much it cost (%) a business to finance all assets shown on a company's balance sheet. To calculate this cost, all sources of financing, that is debt (short-term and long-term) and equity are weighted and the proportion of each cost is multiplied by its respective cost of borrowing. To make the cost of financing relevant, it should be compared to the return that the company earns on its assets.

The economic value added (EVA) is a performance tool that measures how profitable a company truly is. It is calculated by deducting the cost of using the assets (interest charges) from the net operating profit after taxes.

◀◼ Objective 3

Cost of capital means the weighted rate of return a business must provide to its investors in exchange for the money they have placed in a business. *Cost of capital* is a critically important element in the financing decision process, since it is the basis for determining the capital expenditure investment portfolio. To illustrate, if the average cost of capital is 10%, management of a company will approve a capital expenditure portfolio that will earn 10% or more. Leverage involves determining the most suitable operating and financial structure that will help amplify financial performance.

◀◼ Objective 4

The major areas of finance are the capital structure, the cost of capital, and the capital budget. The capital structure determines the proportion of the sources of financing (debt versus equity). The proportion of sources of financing is then multiplied by their appropriate cost to give the weighted cost of capital. The weighted cost of capital is then used to determine whether capital projects will be approved or not during the capital budgeting project review.

◀◼ Objective 5

The key elements to consider when calculating the cost of capital of publicly owned companies are (a) the amount of funds obtained from each financing source (lenders and shareholders), (b) the proportion of each source, (c) the after-tax cost of each source, and (d) the weighted cost of capital, which is arrived at by multiplying each amount calculated in (b) by each cost listed in (c). The most important factors to consider when determining a permanent financing scenario are payout, risk, voting rights, cost of capital, tax cost, and cost of issue.

◀◼ Objective 6

There is a connection between the marginal cost of capital and investment decisions. Cost of capital tells management how much it costs to raise funds from long-term sources while techniques in capital budgeting, such as the internal rate of return, tell management how much each project generates. If a project earns less than the cost of capital, it will likely be rejected.

◀◼ Objective 7

Leverage analysis is used to determine the financing package or cost structure that will maximize the worth of a business. There are two types of leverages: operating leverage and financial leverage. *Operating leverage* deals with the cost behaviour of an operating unit; it determines the most appropriate cost mix (fixed versus variable) that will maximize profitability under a given set of economic and industry conditions. *Financial leverage* is used to determine the most favourable capital structure—that is, the one that will generate the greatest financial benefits to the shareholders.

◀◼ Objective 8

Key Terms

Capital structure
Characteristics of long-term financing sources
Combined leverage
Cost of capital
Cost of common shares
Cost of debt
Cost of financing
Cost of preferred shares

Cost of retained earnings
Economic value added (EVA)
Financial leverage
Financial structure
Leverage
Marginal cost of capital
Operating leverage
Opportunity cost

Review Questions

1. What do we mean by financial structure?

2. What is the objective of using the leverage analysis techniques?

3. What is the purpose of calculating the cost of capital?

4. What is the meaning of the economic value added? What does it measure? Why is it important?

5. What are the major elements of the cost of capital?

6. What is the relationship between cost of capital and the internal rate of return?

7. Define "opportunity costs."

8. What major characteristics should be explored when considering the major sources of long-term financing?

9. Explain the meaning of leverage.

10. Comment on the major areas of finance.

11. Differentiate between debt financing and common share financing.

12. What does the "growth" factor represent when calculating the cost of common shares?

13. What do we mean by "marginal cost of capital"?

14. What is the purpose of operating leverage analysis?

15. What is the purpose of financial leverage analysis?

16. What is the usefulness of the combined leverage?

Discussion Questions

1. How can leverage analysis be used to determine whether a plant should be modified or not?

2. What is the connection between the management of capital structure and the management of capital assets?

Testing Your Comprehension

True/False Questions

_T_ 1. The purpose of comparing ROA to the cost of capital is to ensure that the return generated from a particular investment justifies the cost and risk.

_F_ 2. Capital structure means the way a company's total assets are financed by the entire right-hand side of the balance sheet (all liability and all equity accounts).

_T_ 3. The cost of financing calculation includes accounts such as working capital loans, mortgages, and common shares.

_T_ 4. Cost of financing can be compared to return on assets.

_F_ 5. Cost of capital can be compared to the price-earnings ratio.

_T_ 6. The capital structure largely determines the cost of capital.

_F_ 7. Debt, preferred share, and common share financing have one common characteristic: they are all obtained from "internal sources."

_F_ 8. An important disadvantage of common share financing is that it has to carry a fixed maturity date.

_T_ 9. Dividends paid to shareholders are paid with income after taxes.

_T_ 10. The calculation of the preferred share cost does not include a growth factor.

_F_ 11. Cost of issue is part of calculating the cost of retained earnings.

_T_ 12. Cost of capital usually reflects the after-tax cost.

_T_ 13. Usually the cost of capital is compared to the internal rate of return.

_F_ 14. Operating leverage deals with the behaviour of costs at the financing level.

_T_ 15. Operating level analysis is an excellent analytical tool to determine whether a plant should be modernized or not.

_T_ 16. Financial leverage deals with the relationship between debt financing and equity financing.

Multiple-Choice Questions

1. Financial structure means the way a company's total assets are financed by:
   a. short-term funds
   b. permanent funds
   c. short-term and permanent funds
   d. growth funds
   e. equity funds

2. The objective of the leverage analysis technique is to:
   a. get the most out of capital assets
   b. reduce costs
   c. optimize liquidity
   d. amplify financial performance
   e. ensure an optimal capital structure

3. The economic value added (EVA) is arrived at by subtracting the:
   a. cost of capital from the net operating profit before taxes
   b. dividends from the net operating profit before taxes
   c. interest from the cost of capital
   d. cost of capital from the net operating profit after taxes
   e. dividends from the net operating profit after taxes

4. Cost of financing is usually compared to:
   a. return on equity
   b. return on fixed assets
   c. return on sales
   d. internal rate of return
   e. return on assets

5. Cost of capital is usually compared to:
   a. return on equity
   b. return on fixed assets
   c. return on sales
   d. internal rate of return
   e. return on assets

6. The financing source that usually costs the most is:
   a. preferred share
   b. common share
   c. mortgage
   d. bond
   e. trade credit

7. The more important characteristics of long-term financing deal with:
   a. cost of issue, break-even point, and voting rights
   b. risk, liquidity, and return on investment
   c. tax cost, cost of issue, and working capital
   d. operating leverage, financial leverage, and combined leverage
   e. payout, risk, and cost of capital

8. Investors who get paid first are:
   a. common shareholders
   b. preferred shareholders
   c. unsecured bondholders
   d. mortgage holders
   e. members of the board of directors

9. The cheapest source of financing is through:
   a. a preferred share issue
   b. a common share issue
   c. retained earnings
   d. shareholders
   e. a bond issue

10. The average cost of capital takes into consideration:
    a. short-term lenders only
    b. long-term lenders only
    c. long-term lenders and shareholders
    d. trade creditors
    e. short-term and long-term lenders

11. Operating leverage deals with:
    a. fixed costs and variable costs
    b. dividends and interest
    c. (a) and (b)
    d. external financing
    e. mix of internal and external financing

12. Financial leverage deals with:
    a. fixed costs and variable costs
    b. dividends and interest
    c. (a) and (b)
    d. internal financing
    e. mix of internal and external financing

Fill-in-the-Blanks Questions

1. _____ structure is the way a company's assets are financed by the entire right-hand side of the balance sheet (short-term and long-term financing).

2. The _____ is a tool that measures the wealth a company creates for its investors.

3. The _____ cost can be explained as the income sacrificed by not pursuing the next best alternative.

4. _____ structure has to do with permanent financing sources (e.g., common shares, mortgage) used to buy capital assets.

5. _____ charges is the cost associated with debt financing.

6. Cost of preferred shares includes _____ _____ dividends paid to shareholders and the flotation costs.

7. The cost of common shares includes dividends paid to shareholders, flotation costs, and the _____ rate.

8. The _____ cost of capital is defined as the increased level of average cost resulting from having borrowed new funds at higher rates than those previously borrowed.

9. _____ leverage is a financial technique used to determine to what extent fixed costs are used relative to variable costs.

10. _____ leverage is a financial technique used to calculate both operating and financial leverage.

Learning Exercises

Exercise 1(a)

Len and Joan are considering buying a cottage valued at $175,000. They have combined savings of $40,000, and the bank approved a $120,000 first mortgage. Len's father agreed to provide them with a $10,000 loan. Also, Joan was lucky enough to win $5,000 at a casino. If Len and Joan invested their money in short-term deposits, they would be able to earn 4.5%. The interest rate that was offered by the bank on the first mortgage was 10%. Len's father agreed to lend the money at only 5%.

On the basis of this information, calculate Len's and Joan's cost of capital.

Exercise 1(b)

Daniel and Evelyn are considering buying a house valued at $250,000. They have combined savings of $20,000, and the bank approved a $200,000 first mortgage. Another financial institution agreed to provide them with a $20,000 second mortgage. Also, Daniel has just won $10,000 from a lottery. If Daniel and Evelyn invested their money in guaranteed certificates, they would be able to earn 9%. The interest rates offered by the bank were 12% for the first mortgage and 14% for the second.

On the basis of this information, calculate Daniel and Evelyn's cost of capital.

Exercise 2(a)

Len and Joan are toying with the idea of investing $1.0 million to open up two other retail outlets in different cities. After reviewing the financial projections with their accountant, May Ogaki, the Millers determined that the two retail outlets showed a combined 8.5% return on investment. After several meetings with different financial institutions, the Millers would be able to obtain the following amounts:

1st mortgage	$ 500,000
2nd mortgage	150,000
Common shares	250,000
Retained earnings	100,000
Total	$1,000,000

The cost of capital for each source of financing is:

- first mortgage, 10.0%;
- second mortgage, 13.0%;
- common shares, 14.0%; and
- retained earnings, 14.0%.

The company's corporate income tax rate is 33%.

On the basis of the above information, calculate the cost of capital for raising the $1 million. Should Len and Joan go ahead with the two stores? Why or why not?

Exercise 2(b)

One of the capital expenditure projects included in a company's capital budget was a $10 million investment for the construction of a new manufacturing facility in South America. The preliminary information provided by the financial analysis section of the company indicated that the project would earn 10% return on investment. The treasurer met several investors who showed an interest in the project and were prepared to provide the following:

Bonds	$ 5,000,000
Preferred shares	1,000,000
Common shares	3,500,000
Retained earnings	500,000
Total	$10,000,000

The cost of capital for each source of financing is:

- bonds, 11.5%;
- preferred shares, 14.0%;
- common shares, 15.0%; and
- retained earnings, 15.0%.

The company's corporate income tax rate is 50%.

The members of the management committee reviewed all projects contained in the capital project. When they examined the $10 million manufacturing facility, several showed some concern about the project's viability and were not sure whether it should be approved.

Ignoring flotation costs or brokers' fees, calculate the cost of capital for raising the $10 million. Should the management committee approve this project? Why or why not?

Exercise 3(a)

The Millers' vision was to eventually go public with their business. They knew that if CompuTech Inc. continued to grow, they would have to approach an investment dealer who would work out the issue arrangements. Their plan was to expand their business as a privately owned company for at least ten years, after which they would approach an investment dealer to raise funds. They knew that if they wanted to grow quickly they would need large sums of money, and the only way to obtain these funds was from the general public.

Len and Joan asked one of their friends, Jennifer Harris, who graduated with Joan and was now working with an investment dealer, to evaluate the cost and process of initiating a public issue. After spending several hours discussing the type of information required by investment dealers and the process, she explained how the cost would be calculated. Let's assume that the prospectus would show an expansion plan that would costs $20 million, and the Millers wished to raise funds from the following sources:

a) $8 million from a mortgage at a cost of 9%;

b) $2 million from a second mortgage at a cost of 11%;

c) $1 million from preferred shares. The expected selling price would be $10, and the flotation costs would be $0.50 per share. An amount of $1 in dividends per share would be paid to the preferred shareholders;

d) $8 million from common shares. Each share would be sold for $15 and yield $2 in dividends. The flotation costs would be 10%; and

e) $1 million from CompuTech through retained earnings.

CompuTech's corporate tax rate was estimated at that time to be 45%, and the prospectus would show CompuTech's growth rate to be 10% per year.

On the basis of the above information, calculate CompuTech's cost of capital.

Exercise 3(b)

Silverado Inc. is contemplating spending $25 million to expand its mining operation. Based on some initial analysis, the project would expand operation's production output by 20% and provide a 23% return on investment.

Prior to deciding whether to proceed with the venture, the CEO asks the treasurer to determine where the financing would come from and how much each source will cost. The treasurer finds the following:

Chapter 6: Cost of Capital and Capital Structure

a) $4 million will be funded by the selling of bond A and $6 million by the selling of bond B. The cost of bond A is estimated at 10% and the cost of bond B at 12%.

b) $1 million will be generated from preferred shares. The expected selling price is $100, and the flotation costs will be $5 per share. An amount of $11 in dividends per share will be paid to the preferred shareholders.

c) $11 million will be funded from common shares. Each share will be sold for $50, yielding $6 in dividends. The flotation costs will be 10%.

d) $3 million will be provided from internal sources (retained earnings).

The company's corporate tax rate is 50%. The treasurer expects the common shares to continue to grow at a rate of 6% per year.

1. Calculate the company's cost of capital.

2. Should the CEO approve the expansion program? Why or why not?

Exercise 4(a)

By using CompuTech's 2005 financial statements, calculate the company's economic value added.

COMPUTECH SALES AND SERVICES
INCOME STATEMENT
FOR THE PERIOD ENDING DECEMBER 31, 2005

Sales revenue		$800,000
Cost of goods sold		406,000
Gross margin		394,000
Operating expenses		
Selling	$135,000	
Administration	110,000	
Total operating expenses		245,000
Operating income		149,000
Interest charges		30,000
Income before taxes		119,000
Income taxes		42,000
Income after taxes		$ 77,000

The company's three major sources of financing will be from short-term lenders for an amount of $85,000, a long-term debt for an amount of $200,000, and equity for $305,000. The equity portion was split as follows: capital shares in the amount of $170,000 and retained earnings for $135,000.

The cost of capital for these three sources of financing is:

- short-term loans, 13.0%;

- long-term debt, 11.0%; and
- common share equity, 14.0%.

Exercise 4(b)

Oscar Lewitt, CEO of Ingram Corporation, had just read in a recent issue of *Fortune* magazine an article entitled "America's Wealth Creators" and noticed several names of corporations he was familiar with, such as Microsoft, General Electric, Intel, Wal-Mart Stores, Coca-Cola, Merck, and Pfizer. These top wealth creators were listed in terms of their market value added (MVA) and economic value added (EVA). Although he recognized that some of the MVA and EVA were in the billions of dollars, he noticed in the article two numbers, return on capital and cost of capital. He believed that if these corporations, despite their size, were able to determine how much value they were adding to the wealth of their shareholders, it would be possible to calculate the EVA for Ingram Corporation.

At his next management committee meeting, Mr. Lewitt asked his controller to determine the EVA for Ingram Corporation and to report the information to the management committee at their next meeting.

After some research about this new financial technique, the controller knew that he had to refer to his financial statements to calculate the EVA. He had to draw several numbers from the income statement and the balance sheet in order to calculate the cost of capital and return on assets. The company's most recent income statement and different sources of financing are shown below:

INGRAM CORPORATION
INCOME STATEMENT
FOR THE PERIOD ENDING DECEMBER 31, 2003

Sales revenue		$1,200,000
Cost of goods sold		650,000
Gross margin		550,000
Operating expenses		
Selling	$150,000	
Administration	125,000	
Depreciation	50,000	
Total operating expenses		325,000
Operating income		225,000
Interest charges		45,000
Income before taxes		180,000
Income taxes		67,500
Income after taxes		$ 112,500

The company's three major sources of financing are from short-term lenders for an amount of $100,000, a mortgage for an amount of $325,000, and equity for

$430,000. The equity portion was split as follows: capital shares in the amount of $130,000 and retained earnings for $300,000.

The cost of capital for these three sources of financing is:

- short-term loans, 12.0%;
- long-term debt, 10.0%; and
- shareholders' equity, 15.0%.

Based on the above information:

1. Calculate Ingram Corporation's economic value added.

2. Comment on the economic value added. How could EVA be improved?

Exercise 5(a)

Using the following information, calculate CompuTech's operating leverage, financial leverage, and combined leverage.

Sales revenue	$420,000
Variable costs	$212,000
Fixed costs	$148,000
Interest charges	$ 14,000
Corporate income tax rate	33%

Exercise 5(b)

Using the following information, calculate the company's operating leverage, financial leverage, and combined leverage.

Sales volume	100,000 units
Price per unit	$11.30
Variable costs (per unit)	$8.30
Fixed costs	$100,000
Interest charges	$ 25,000
Corporate income tax rate	50%

Exercise 6(a)

Using the data contained in Exercise 5(a), assume that the Millers want to make the company more automated and are able to reduce the variable costs to $165,000, increase the fixed costs by $20,000 (that is, to $168,000), and increase the financing charges from $14,000 to $18,000.

Calculate the new operating leverage, financial leverage, and combined leverage.

Exercise 6(b)

Using the data in Exercise 5(b), assume that a company wants to make its plant more automated and are able to reduce the variable costs to $7.30 per unit, increase the fixed costs by $100,000 (that is, to $200,000), and increase the financing charges from $25,000 to $35,000.

Calculate the new operating leverage, financial leverage, and combined leverage.

Case

Sharco Systems Inc.

Sharco Systems Inc., a manufacturer of auto parts, wants to make inroads in the European and Asian markets. Sharco's executives know that it will be a difficult task because of the strongly entrenched existing competitors in those markets. However, the company executives believe that if they formulate effective business goals and strategies and raise the resources required to implement their plans, they could become viable competitors in these markets.

The company's income statement and balance sheet are presented below. As shown, in 2003, the company earned $160 million in income after taxes on assets worth $2.0 billion.

SHARCO SYSTEMS INC.
INCOME STATEMENT
FOR THE PERIOD ENDING DECEMBER 31, 2003
(IN $MILLIONS)

Sales revenue		$2,500
Cost of goods sold		1,610
Gross margin		890
Operating expenses		
Selling	$260	
Administration	120	
Depreciation	100	
Total operating expenses		480
Operating income		410
Interest charges		90
Income before taxes		320
Income taxes		160
Income after taxes		$ 160

The before-tax cost of financing the liabilities and shareholders' equity as shown on the balance sheet is as follows:

- bank loans, 14.0%;
- current portion of long-term debt, 11.0%;
- mortgage, 11.0%;
- debentures 12.0%; and
- shareholders' equity, 16%.

Chapter 6: Cost of Capital and Capital Structure

SHARCO SYSTEMS INC.
BALANCE SHEET
AS AT DECEMBER 31, 2003
(IN $MILLIONS)

Assets

Current assets

Cash and equivalents	$ 50	
Accounts receivable	350	
Inventories	290	
Prepaid expenses	10	
Total current assets		$700

Capital assets

Buildings and equipment (at cost)	1,800	
Less: accumulated depreciation	500	
Net capital assets		1,300
Total assets		$2,000

Liabilities

Current liabilities

Bank loans	$ 100	
Accounts payable	60	
Income taxes payable	130	
Current portion of long-term debt	10	
Total current liabilities		$ 300
Long-term debts		
Mortgage	500	
Debentures	300	
Total long-term debts		800
Total liabilities		$1,100

Shareholders' equity

Preferred shares	15	
Common shares	135	
Retained earnings	750	
Total shareholders' equity		900
Total liabilities and equity		$2,000

The company had to prepare a prospectus in order to raise $350 million from the following sources:

	In millions
Debt	$150
Preferred shares	30
Common shares	100
Retained earnings	70
Total	$350

These funds would be used almost exclusively to expand operations in Europe and Asia, which would generate a return of 22% on the company's investments. The company's vice-president of finance provided the following information:

- cost of new debt is expected to be 11%;
- preferred shares would be sold at $75 and bear a 10% yield;
- internal funding from retained earnings is estimated at $70 million; and
- common share dividend yield is estimated at 7% and growth rate during the past five years has been 8.5% (this rate is expected to continue).

With the above financial statements, calculate Sharco's:

1. Before- and after-tax cost of financing for 2003.
2. Before- and after-tax cost of financing compared with the company's before- and after-tax return on assets.
3. Economic value added for 2003.
4. Cost of capital to raise funds from:
   - long-term debt only;
   - preferred shares only;
   - common shares only; and
   - all four sources.
5. Should the company proceed with the project?

7

Time Value of Money

Learning Objectives

After reading this chapter, you should be able to:

1. Discuss why money has a time value.

2. Differentiate between time value of money and inflation.

3. Differentiate between time value of money and risk.

4. Explain how to use time and cash in investment decisions.

5. Comment on using interest tables to calculate investment decisions.

6. Apply interest tables when making capital investment decisions.

Chapter Outline

OPENING CASE

The Millers are currently examining several investment options. Even though they are interested in investing money in CompuTech Inc., they also want to make sure that they will invest enough in RRSPs and educational funds for their two children, Vincent and Takara. To evaluate their needs, the Millers knew that they had to become knowledgeable in the language of the banking and investment community and in concepts dealing with compounding and discounting. They realized that if they were to invest money in RRSPs and educational funds today, the element of time would make their investment grow. They therefore had to learn how to use interest tables and financial calculators capable of performing "time value of money" calculations.

The Millers also realized that if they were to communicate knowledgeably with bankers, insurance agents, and financial advisors they had to understand financial concepts such as the notion that a "dollar earned today is worth more tomorrow." For example, if the Millers were to deposit $1,000 in the bank today for one year at 10%, time is the only factor that would make their investment grow to $1,100. Similarly, if Len Miller wanted a $100,000 life insurance policy, the insurance agent would determine the amount of premium he would have to pay each year for a certain number of years (depending on average life expectancy). Similarly, financial advisors who want to recommend to clients how much they need to save each year in different investments such as RRSPs or guaranteed investment certificates have to have a good understanding of these time-value-of-money concepts.

Bankers, insurance agents, and financial advisors are also familiar with the concept that a "dollar earned tomorrow is worth less today." This is referred to as discounting. For example, if the Millers wanted to have $60,000 for both children by the time each child turns 20, they know that they would have to invest a much lesser amount today.

The Millers also recognized that the time-value-of-money concept was important not only for personal financing but also for business decisions. The application, however, would focus almost exclusively on "discounting." Because insurance companies pay death benefits in the future, the future values of the premium payments have to be compounded (future value) or brought into the future for comparison purposes (death benefit and premium payments). Conversely, businesses make a different calculation. Since business investments are made today (purchase of assets, opening of a new retail store, or the expansion of an existing one), all cash flows that would be earned in the future would be discounted in order to find their present value, then compared to the initial investment.

The Millers understood that they had to make all types of personal and business decisions and, in order to make prudent and insightful decisions, they had to learn the time-value-of-money techniques.

This chapter examines the time-value-of-money concept. In particular, if focuses on three key topics:

1. What we mean by time value of money, and why it is important to businesses.
2. How compound and discount interest tables can be used.
3. How time-value-of-money concepts can be applied to business decisions.

Introduction

The next chapter, "Capital Investment Decisions," deals with capital budgeting decisions such as the purchase of equipment or machinery; construction, modernization or expansion of a plant; and research and development. These kinds of decisions involve outflows of money, which take place during the year a decision is made, and inflows of money, which may be generated years after the initial funds are disbursed. To make effective decisions in capital budgeting, it is important to understand why money has a time value.

This chapter focuses on three key objectives:

- to understand why money has a time value and to differentiate it from the concepts related to inflation and risk;
- to learn how to use compound and discount interest tables; and
- to get acquainted with basic capital budgeting terms and concepts such as present value, net present value, and internal rate of return.

The first part of this chapter explains how interest tables can be used both on a personal basis and in business. It touches on the meaning of compounding, discounting, and annuity. The second part of the chapter serves as a brief introduction to the application of interest tables (time value of money) when making business decisions. In particular, investment decision tools such as net present value (NPV) and internal rate of return (IRR) will be explained only briefly because Chapter 8 "Capital Investment Decisions" explains them in more detail. Therefore, the objective of the second part of this chapter makes the link between the time-value-of-money concept and investment decision-making.

Why Money Has a Time Value

If a company invests $1,000 this year in a capital asset that will generate a one-time inflow of cash of $1,050 (the original $1,000 plus a profit of $50, or 5%) next year, we can ask a fundamental question: Should the asset be purchased? These numbers tell us that the asset is totally paid for by the end of the first year and produces a $50 profit. If money could be obtained from a bank interest-free to finance the capital asset, and the company contemplated no other investments, the capital decision would be justified, as it earned 5%. However, we know that money cannot be obtained interest-free from banks and that there is always a cost attached to any sort of financing. A business may borrow $1,000 for, say, 12%; if this is the case, the $1,000 purchase of the capital asset would not be justified since the cost of borrowing would exceed the 5% return generated by the investment. After the cost of financing, the company would have a 7% negative return.

The fact that there is a cost (interest) associated with the borrowing of money, whether provided by shareholders or lenders, confirms the fact that money has a **time value.** The old saying that reminds us "not to count our cash before it is discounted" is still valid today.

If you have a choice between receiving $100 today or $110 a year from now, which option would you prefer? If money is worth 10%, it does not matter which option you select. You could invest the $100 in a term deposit, which would give you 10% interest and increase your initial $100 to $110 one year from now. Time is the only element that would have earned $10 or 10% for you. Conversely, we can say that the $110 you would receive one year from now equals today's $100.

This illustration shows that a dollar earned today is worth more tomorrow (compounded). Or, a dollar earned tomorrow is worth less today (discounted). In capital budgeting, if a company invests money in a long-term producing asset and wants to calculate the return on the investment of that asset, the company must also take into account the fact that money has a time value. The reason is simple; the company invests cash today in exchange for cash that it will earn in future years. In order to respect the time-value-of-money notion, all monies, whether spent today or earned next year or five years from now, must be placed on an equal footing. That is why it is important to understand the fundamentals of the mathematics of interest, compounding, and discounting.

Sometimes, businesses simply avoid the use of the more sophisticated capital budgeting techniques to calculate the return on capital projects. Their managements believe that the mathematics of interest, which is the foundation of time-value capital budgeting techniques, is complicated and cumbersome, and that they have to use complex mathematical compound and discount formulas. This is not so. Knowing how to read interest tables is all that is required. Once this is understood, it is easy to use the more effective capital budgeting techniques such as internal rate of return and the net present value method and assess the economic viability of capital projects in a more meaningful way. Today, spreadsheets and finance software can help financial analysts perform complex financial calculations easily and quickly.

Time value of money

Rate at which the value of money is traded off as a function of time.

Time Value of Money and Inflation

◀◀ Objective 2

People often believe that money has a time value because of inflation. This is not the case. However, **inflation** is taken into consideration when capital decisions are considered. For example, if you invest $100 in a term deposit bearing a 10% interest rate at a time when inflation is running at 5%, the purchasing power of the $110 would be reduced to $105. Time value and inflation should not be confused, particularly in capital investment decisions, since the calculation of inflation is a separate exercise.

Let us examine a capital asset that generates a multi-year funds flow. The revenues and expenses generated by the investment during the entire economic life of the asset include two elements. First, there are the revenues that are calculated on the basis of the expected volume increments, and second, the anticipated increase in unit selling price, which should include the element of inflation. Expenses also take into consideration increments in wages and the costs of material, utilities, etc., due to inflation. The difference between the projected revenues and projected expenses gives a net profit level that incorporates the inflationary factor. Once the profit projections are calculated (which includes the built-in factor for inflation), the time-value calculation of the future cash flows (compounding or discounting) begins.

Inflation
Represents a price-rise characteristic of periods of prosperity.

Time Value of Money and Risk

◀◀ Objective 3

People also confuse time value and risk. It is not because risks are inherent in capital projects that money has a time value. Nevertheless, it is important to consider the risk factor when contemplating capital investment decisions. A $1,000 investment in Canada Savings Bonds with a 10% interest rate bears little **risk.** The chances of recovering the $1,000 amount and the interest are virtually assured. However, if $1,000 is invested in an untried product, risk is paramount. Because of the relative inherent risk involved in these types of investment opportunities, the investor would be comfortable with the 10% interest rate for the Canada Savings Bonds but would probably want to earn a 40% return on a high-tech product that is on the verge of being researched and not yet commercially tested.

Risk
Represents the level of probable expectations (good or bad) that something will happen in the future.

Although risk and capital decisions are closely related, it is important to note that interest and risk are two distinct concepts. While interest implies time value, risk suggests a chance that a business takes with a particular investment.

Using Time and Cash in Investment Decisions

◀◀ Objective 4

As shown in Figure 7.1, investment decisions deal with two key concepts: time and cash. Time is important because, as mentioned earlier, when managers invest money in capital assets today, they expect to earn money from these assets over an extended number of years. For example, when a company invests $100,000 to modernize a plant that has a ten-year life span, that initial cash outflow must be

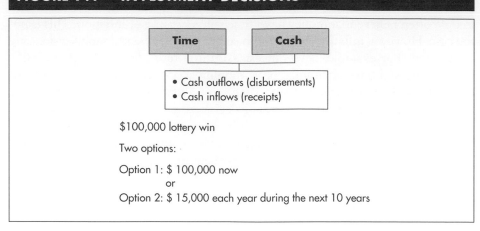

FIGURE 7.1 INVESTMENT DECISIONS

Time **Cash**

- Cash outflows (disbursements)
- Cash inflows (receipts)

$100,000 lottery win

Two options:

Option 1: $ 100,000 now

or

Option 2: $ 15,000 each year during the next 10 years

compared to all the cash inflows that will be generated through the savings in the future. There is no question that a $100,000 investment that generates $50,000 in savings during a three-year period (for a total of $150,000) would be more financially attractive than one that generates $15,000 a year during a ten-year period (also for a total of $150,000).

The second critical element is cash. If a company invests money in equipment, machinery, or research and development, it invests cash. Such an investment is commonly referred to as a **cash outflow** or cash disbursement. Management will want to compare cash invested with cash generated by the investment. The cash (not profit) that a project generates is commonly referred to as **cash inflow** or cash receipts. The common element that ties a project together is cash. Therefore, when preparing a project's pro-forma income statement, the profit figure shown at the bottom of the profit and loss statement must be converted into cash (e.g., by adding back depreciation) since time-value yardsticks use cash, not profit, to calculate a project's viability. The bottom line is this: to make capital budgeting decisions meaningful, one has to compare apples (cash outflow) with apples (cash inflow).

The following illustrates the significance of time and cash in capital budgeting. Assume that you have won a $100,000 lottery and are given the following options:

- Option 1: to receive the $100,000 lump-sum amount today; or
- Option 2: to receive $10,000 each year during the next ten years (also for a total of $100,000).

There is no question that you will go for the first option. In both options, we are dealing with cash and with time. It would be absurd to accept the $10,000 despite the fact that the total receipts equal $100,000. The fact that you could invest the $100,000 in term deposits at, say, 10% would make option 1 more economically attractive. However, if you were offered $12,000 a year instead, would you go for it? How about $15,000? Or $20,000? Well, how about $25,000 during the next six years (for a total $150,000) instead of only $100,000? As you can see,

Cash outflow

Represents cash disbursements for the purchase of assets.

Cash inflow

Represents the receipt of money (profit plus depreciation) generated by a project.

different time factors and varying amounts call for an analysis to determine the most lucrative option.

The same applies in capital budgeting. If you were to invest $100,000 in a capital asset that has a ten-year life span, how much should that asset generate in cash in order to make it economically attractive?

At the end of this chapter, once we have understood the time-value-of-money concept and how interest tables are used, we will calculate exactly how much cash you should agree to receive each year (and for how long) in preference to a lump sum. We will also be able to determine how much cash an investment in capital assets should generate each year (and for how long) in order to make a $100,000 investment worthwhile.

Using Interest Tables to Calculate Investment Decisions

◄◼ Objective 5

Let's now turn to interest tables and examine how they can be used as capital investment decision-making instruments to calculate:

- the future (compounding) and present (discounting) values of a single sum of money received or paid out at a given point in time; and

- a constant flow of money (an annuity) received or paid out over a given time period.

Algebraic Notations

Algebraic notations are introduced for two reasons. First, to show how the interest tables appearing at the end of this book are calculated and, second, to explain the makeup of the various financial equations used in calculating future and present value amounts.

It is not necessary to understand the roots of the various algebraic formulas used to calculate future and present values. It is important, however, to grasp how interest tables are used to calculate the future value of a sum received today and the present value of a sum received in the future.

Algebraic formulas are made up of symbols and letters. The symbols that you should be familiar with are:

P The principal, which is the amount available today, or the present value of a single sum. This is expressed in dollars.

F The future value of the principal or a sum. This is also expressed in dollars.

i The rate of interest. This can be expressed on an annual, semi-annual, quarterly, or monthly basis.

n The number of periods over which funds are borrowed. This is expressed in years or months.

R	A constant stream of funds to be received or spent over a number of periods. This is commonly referred to as an annuity. This flow of funds is expressed in dollars.

B	The present value of a constant stream of funds to be received or spent over a number of periods. It is the present value of an annuity. This figure is expressed in dollars.

W	The future sum of a stream of funds to be received or spent over a number of periods. It is the future value of an annuity and is expressed in dollars.

Let us now calculate, step by step, the:

• future value of a single sum (compounding);
• present value of a single sum (discounting);
• future value of a stream of sums (compounding); and
• present value of a stream of sums (discounting).

Calculating the Future Value of a Single Sum

We said earlier in this chapter that money has a time value because of the existence of interest. This means that if you deposit $1,000 in the bank today at 10%, you will collect $1,100 at the same date next year. If you keep your original amount in the bank for an indefinite period of time, interest will continue to accumulate, and as we will see later in the chapter, your $1,000 will grow year after year. This future amount is referred to as the **future value** of a single sum.

Interest can be paid in two ways. First, it can be paid by means of simple interest, which is the simplest form. Here, the banker calculates the interest only on the original $1,000 amount. If the original amount is kept in the bank for, say, three years, you would then earn $300 in interest. This is not, however, the conventional way that interest is paid. Usually, when money is deposited in a bank, the banker pays interest on both the original amount (the principal) and the accumulated balance, which increases each succeeding period as a result of the period interest that is added to the new balance. This form of interest is called **compound interest.**

Let us examine how the compound value of $1,000, deposited in the bank today at 10%, would grow at the end of three years. Table 7.1 shows that, at the end of the first year, the investor earns $100 and the ending amount is $1,100. During the second year, $110 in interest will be earned, which is made up of $100

Future value

The amount to which a payment or series of payments will grow by a given future date when compounded by a given interest rate.

Compound interest

Interest rate that is applicable on the initial principal and the accumulated interest of prior periods. Compounding is the process of determining the final value of payments when compound interest is applied.

TABLE 7.1	CALCULATING THE FUTURE VALUE OF A SINGLE SUM				
Year	Beginning Amount	Interest Rate	Amount of Interest	Beginning Amount	Ending Amount
1	$1,000	.10	$100	$1,000	$1,100
2	1,100	.10	110	1,100	1,210
3	1,210	.10	121	1,210	1,331

on the original $1,000 and $10 on the interest earned during the first year. The balance at the end of the second year is $1,210.

The same arithmetic is done for calculating the interest earned during the third year; the value of the amount at the end of that period is $1,331.

An investor does not have to go through these calculations to determine the value of the initial investment for a specific period. This would be extremely cumbersome, particularly when one deals with a ten-, 20-, or 25-year time span. That is why interest tables come in handy. Here is how these tables are used. Table 7.2 shows interest factors for interest rates ranging from 9% to 20% covering 25 years. By looking at the 10% column, you can readily see that the future value of $1,000 at the end of the third year amounts to $1,331 ($1,000 × 1.331), the same amount that was calculated in Table 7.1. Table A in Appendix B contains factors for interest rates from 1% to 36% for a 25-year period.

The algebraic equation used to calculate the future value of a single sum is as follows:

$$F_n = P (1 + i)^n$$
$$F_3 = \$1,000 (1.10)^3$$
$$F_3 = \$1,000 \times 1.331$$
$$F_3 = \$1,331$$

THE RULE OF 72 There is a quick and easy way to calculate the approximate number of years it takes for an investment to double when compounded annually at a particular rate of interest. It is called the **Rule of 72.** To find the answer, divide 72 by the interest rate of the invested principal. Here is how it works. If you want to know how many years it takes for an investment to double at, say, 10% interest compounded annually, as shown below, you divide this figure into 72 and obtain 7.2 years.

Rule of 72

Calculation that shows the approximate number of years it takes for an investment to double when compounded annually.

$$\frac{72 \text{ (rule)}}{10(\%)} = 7.2 \text{ (approximate number of years)}$$

To verify this answer, look at Table 7.2. If we go down the 10% interest column, we see that the $1.00 amount reaches $2.00 between year 7 (1.949) and year 8 (2.144).

Calculating the Present Value of a Single Sum

The opposite of compounding is discounting. Compounding means that when money is invested today, it appreciates in value because compound interest is added. The opposite takes place when money is to be received in the future; in this case, the future amount is worth less today. By referring to our previous example, because of the existence of the 10% interest rate, both amounts, $1,000 in year 1 and $1,331 ($1,000 × 1.331) in year 3, have equal values today. This, therefore, supports the argument that the $1,331 to be received in three years from now has a $1,000 value today. Since discounting is the opposite of

TABLE 7.2 COMPOUND INTEREST FACTORS TO CALCULATE THE FUTURE VALUE OF A SINGLE SUM

N	9%	10%	11%	12%	14%	16%	18%	20%
1	1.090	1.100	1.110	1.120	1.140	1.160	1.180	1.200
2	1.188	1.210	1.232	1.254	1.300	1.346	1.392	1.440
3	1.295	1.331	1.368	1.405	1.482	1.561	1.643	1.728
4	1.412	1.464	1.518	1.574	1.689	1.811	1.939	2.074
5	1.539	1.611	1.685	1.762	1.925	2.100	2.288	2.488
6	1.677	1.772	1.870	1.974	2.195	2.436	2.700	2.986
7	1.828	1.949	2.076	2.211	2.502	2.826	3.185	3.583
8	1.993	2.144	2.305	2.476	2.853	3.278	3.759	4.300
9	2.172	2.358	2.558	2.773	3.252	3.803	4.435	5.160
10	2.367	2.594	2.839	3.106	3.707	4.411	5.234	6.192
11	2.580	2.853	3.152	3.479	4.226	5.117	6.176	7.430
12	2.813	3.138	3.498	3.896	4.818	5.936	7.288	8.916
13	3.066	3.452	3.883	4.363	5.492	6.886	8.599	10.699
14	3.342	3.798	4.310	4.887	6.261	7.988	10.147	12.839
15	3.642	4.177	4.785	5.474	7.138	9.266	11.974	15.407
16	3.970	4.595	5.311	5.130	8.137	10.748	14.129	18.488
17	4.328	5.054	5.895	6.866	9.276	12.468	16.672	22.186
18	4.717	5.560	6.544	7.690	10.575	14.463	19.673	26.623
19	5.142	6.116	7.263	8.613	12.056	16.777	23.214	31.948
20	5.604	6.728	8.062	9.646	13.744	19.461	27.393	38.338
21	6.109	7.400	8.949	10.804	15.668	22.575	32.324	46.005
22	6.659	8.140	9.934	12.100	17.861	26.186	38.142	55.206
23	7.258	8.954	11.026	13.552	20.362	30.376	45.008	66.247
24	7.911	9.850	12.239	15.179	23.212	35.236	53.109	79.497
25	8.623	10.835	13.586	17.000	26.462	40.874	62.669	95.396

compounding, all we need to do is to reverse the compound algebraic equation as follows:

$$P = F \left[\frac{1}{(1 + i)^n} \right]$$

$$P = \$1,000 \times \frac{1}{(1 + .10)^3}$$

$$P = \$1,000 \times \frac{1}{1.331}$$

$$P = \$1,000 \times .75131$$

$$P = \$751.31$$

This means that the $1,000 to be received three years from now at 10% is worth $751.31 today; or, to reverse the process, if you invest $751.31 in the bank today at a 10% interest rate, it would appreciate to $1,000 in three years' time ($751.31 × 1.331).

Like the compound interest calculation, calculating the present value of a promised future sum would be time-consuming. To avoid this chore, we can use present value tables. Table 7.3 shows present-value factors for interest rates ranging from 9% to 16% between one and 25 years. Looking at the appropriate interest column (10%) and at year 3, we find factor .75131. This means that by

TABLE 7.3 PRESENT VALUE FACTORS TO CALCULATE THE VALUE OF A SINGLE SUM

N	9%	10%	11%	12%	13%	14%	15%	16%
1	0.91743	0.90909	0.90090	0.89286	0.88496	0.87719	0.86957	0.86207
2	.84168	.82645	.81162	.79719	.78315	.76947	.75614	.74316
3	.77218	.75131	.73119	.71178	.69305	.67497	.65752	.64066
4	.70843	.68301	.65873	.63552	.61332	.59208	.57175	.55229
5	.64993	.62092	.59345	.56743	.54276	.51937	.49718	.47611
6	.59627	.56447	.53464	.50663	.48032	.45559	.43233	.41044
7	.54703	.51316	.48166	.45235	.42506	.39964	.37594	.35383
8	.50187	.46651	.43393	.40388	.37616	.35056	.32690	.30503
9	.46043	.42410	.39092	.36061	.33288	.30751	.28426	.26295
10	.42241	.38554	.35218	.32197	.29459	.26974	.24718	.22668
11	.38753	.35049	.31728	.28748	.26070	.23662	.21494	.19542
12	.35553	.31863	.28584	.25667	.23071	.20756	.18691	.16846
13	.32618	.28966	.25751	.22917	.20416	.18207	.16253	.14523
14	.29925	.26333	.23199	.20462	.18068	.15971	.14133	.12520
15	.27454	.23939	.20900	.18270	.15989	.14010	.12289	.10793
16	.25187	.21763	.18829	.16312	.14150	.12289	.10686	.09304
17	.23107	.19784	.16963	.14564	.12522	.10780	.09293	.08021
18	.21199	.17986	.15202	.13004	.11081	.09456	.08080	.06914
19	.19449	.16351	.13768	.11611	.09806	.08295	.07026	.05961
20	.17843	.14864	.12403	.10367	.08678	.07276	.06110	.05139
21	.16370	.13513	.11174	.09256	.07680	.06383	.05313	.04430
22	.15018	.12285	.10067	.08264	.06796	.05599	.04620	.03819
23	.13778	.11168	.09069	.07379	.06014	.04911	.04017	.03292
24	.12640	.10153	.08170	.06588	.05322	.04308	.03493	.02838
25	.11597	.09230	.07361	.05882	.04710	.03779	.03038	.02447

multiplying the promised $1,000 future sum by .75131, we obtain a $751.31 present value. A more complete present value table appears at the end of the book, in Table B.

We now have two interest factors to keep track of, the compound interest factor and the present value factor. In the former case, factors are used to make a sum grow (compound), while in the latter case, factors are used to depreciate (discount) a sum expected to be received in the future.

Figure 7.2 shows graphically the impact that 10%, 20%, and 30% compound and discount factors have on a $1,000 amount over a 12-year period. For example, on the left side of the figure, a $1,000 investment at 10% grows to $3,138 in 12 years, while the same investment grows to $23,298 at 30%. The right side of the figure shows that $1,000 received 12 years from now is worth $319 today at 10%, and only $43 at 30%.

The Meaning of Annuity

Up to this point, we have talked about the growth and discount values of single sums. In capital budgeting, projects have multi-year economic life spans and, as a result, generate a flow of funds over many years. A series of periodic income payments of equal amounts is referred to as an **annuity**. A mortgage repayment, family allowances, RRSPs, whole-life insurance premiums, and even salaries and wages are considered typical annuities. If a company modernizes its plant at a cost

Annuity

A series of payments (or receipts) of fixed amount for a specified number of years.

FIGURE 7.2 GRAPHIC VIEW OF THE COMPOUNDING AND DISCOUNTING PROCESS

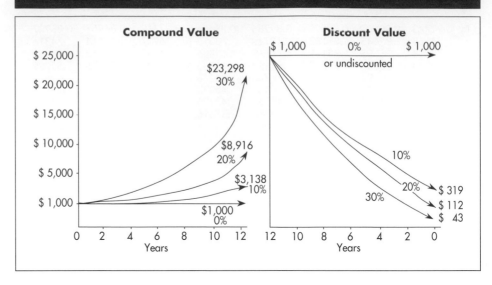

of $100,000 and produces a "fixed yearly $25,000 savings," that would also be considered an annuity.

Since capital budgeting deals with multi-year funds flow situations, it is also important to understand how to calculate the future growth and the present value of annuities.

Calculating the Future Value of an Annuity

Let's calculate the future growth of a five-year $1,000 yearly annuity bearing a 10% interest factor. There are two ways to do this calculation. First, we can go to the compound interest table in Table 7.2 and compute the growth of each $1,000 individually. As shown in Table 7.4, the sum of all future receipts amounts to $6,105, made up of $5,000 in receipts and $1,105 in interest. The calculation is done as follows. It is assumed that the annuity is paid at the end of each period—that is, on December 31—starting at the end of year 1. In four years, the $1,000

TABLE 7.4 CALCULATION OF THE COMPOUND VALUE OF AN ANNUITY

Year	Amount Received	Interest Factor	Interest	Future Sum
1	$1,000	1.464	$464	$1,464
2	1,000	1.331	331	1,331
3	1,000	1.210	210	1,210
4	1,000	1.100	100	1,100
5	1,000	0.000	—	1,000
Total	$5,000		$1,105	$6,105

amount will grow to $1,464. Since the fifth payment is received on December 31 of the last year, this receipt does not produce any interest.

However, this is a very complicated and tedious way to calculate the future value of an annuity.

The second approach is to use annuity tables. Table 7.5 shows annuity factors for interest rates ranging from 9% to 20% for periods ranging from one to 25 years. By going down the 10% interest rate column to year 5, we find factor 6.105. If we multiply this factor by the $1,000 amount representing the fixed annuity receipts, we obtain $6,105. This is a much easier way to calculate future values. Table C at the end of the book gives annuity factors for interest rates ranging from 1% to 32%.

The algebraic formula used to calculate the future value of an annuity is as follows:

$$W = R\left[\frac{(1+i)^n - 1}{i}\right]$$

$$W = \$1,000 \times 6.105$$

$$W = \$6,105$$

TABLE 7.5	COMPOUND INTEREST FACTORS TO CALCULATE THE FUTURE VALUE OF AN ANNUITY							
N	9%	10%	11%	12%	14%	16%	18%	20%
1	1.000	1.000	1.000	1.000	1.000	1.000	1.000	1.000
2	2.090	2.100	2.110	2.120	2.140	2.160	2.180	2.200
3	3.278	3.310	3.342	3.374	3.440	3.506	3.572	3.640
4	4.573	4.641	4.710	4.779	4.921	5.066	5.215	5.368
5	5.985	6.105	6.228	6.353	6.610	6.877	7.154	7.442
6	7.523	7.716	7.913	8.115	8.536	8.977	9.442	9.930
7	9.200	9.487	9.783	10.089	10.731	11.414	12.142	12.916
8	11.029	11.436	11.859	12.300	13.233	14.240	15.327	16.499
9	13.021	13.580	14.164	14.776	16.085	17.519	19.086	20.799
10	15.193	15.937	16.722	17.549	19.337	21.322	23.521	25.959
11	17.560	18.531	19.561	20.655	23.045	25.733	28.755	32.150
12	20.141	21.384	22.713	24.133	27.271	30.850	34.931	39.581
13	22.953	24.523	26.212	28.029	32.089	36.786	42.219	48.497
14	26.019	27.975	30.095	32.393	37.581	43.672	50.818	59.196
15	29.361	31.773	34.405	37.280	43.842	51.660	60.965	72.035
16	33.003	35.950	39.190	42.753	50.980	60.925	72.939	87.442
17	36.974	40.545	44.501	48.884	59.118	71.673	87.068	105.931
18	41.301	45.599	50.396	55.750	68.394	84.141	103.740	128.117
19	46.019	51.159	56.940	63.440	78.969	98.603	123.413	154.740
20	51.160	57.275	64.203	72.052	91.025	115.380	146.628	186.688
21	56.765	64.003	72.265	81.699	104.768	134.840	174.021	225.026
22	62.873	71.403	81.214	92.503	120.436	157.415	206.345	271.031
23	69.532	79.543	91.148	104.603	138.297	183.601	244.487	326.237
24	76.790	88.497	102.174	118.155	158.659	213.977	289.494	392.404
25	84.701	98.347	114.413	133.334	181.871	249.214	342.603	471.981

Calculating the Present Value of an Annuity

Discounting

The process of finding the present value of a series of future cash flows.

Calculating the present value of an annuity is the reverse of compounding an annuity. Compounding gives the future growth of a series of fixed receipts or payments; **discounting** gives the present value of a series of receipts or payments. Let us calculate the present value of a $1,000 amount received at the end of each year during a five-year period that bears a 10% interest factor. This calculation can also be done two ways. First, we can multiply yearly receipts by their respective present-value interest factors. We must therefore refer to Table 7.3 and compute the present value of each receipt. As shown in Table 7.6, the present value of the $1,000 five-year annuity totals $3,790.

However, there is no reason to go through this long process to calculate the present value of an annuity. By referring to Table 7.7, which contains a series of present-value interest factors for annuities for varying interest rates, we can find the answer quickly and easily. Looking at the 10% interest column at the line for year 5, we find factor 3.7908. The more simplified approach is, therefore, to multiply this factor by $1,000; this gives us $3,790. Table D at the end of the book gives a more complete set of interest factors for annuities ranging from one to 25 years.

The algebraic formula used to calculate the present value of an annuity is as follows:

$$B = R \left[\frac{1 - (1+i)^{-n}}{i} \right]$$

Using our example,

$$B = \$1,000 \times 3.7908$$
$$B = \$3,790$$

TABLE 7.6	CALCULATION OF THE PRESENT VALUE OF AN ANNUITY		
Year	Amount Received	Interest Factor	Present Value
1	$1,000	.9091	$ 909
2	1,000	.8264	826
3	1,000	.7513	751
4	1,000	.6830	683
5	1,000	.6209	621
Total	$5,000		$3,790

TABLE 7.7 PRESENT VALUE FACTORS TO CALCULATE THE PRESENT VALUE OF AN ANNUITY

N	9%	10%	11%	12%	13%	14%	15%	16%
1	0.9174	0.9091	0.9009	0.8929	0.8850	0.8772	0.8696	0.8621
2	1.7591	1.7355	1.7125	1.6901	1.6681	1.6467	1.6257	1.6052
3	2.5313	2.4868	2.4437	2.4018	2.3612	2.3216	2.2832	2.2459
4	3.2397	3.1699	3.1024	3.0373	2.9745	2.9137	2.8550	2.7982
5	3.8896	3.7908	3.6959	3.6048	3.5172	3.4331	3.3522	3.2743
6	4.4859	4.3553	4.2305	4.1114	3.9976	3.8887	3.7845	3.6847
7	5.0329	4.8684	4.7122	4.5638	4.4226	4.2883	4.1604	4.0386
8	5.5348	5.3349	5.1461	4.9676	4.7988	4.6389	4.4873	4.3436
9	5.9852	5.7590	5.5370	5.3282	5.1317	4.9464	4.7716	4.6065
10	6.4176	6.1446	5.8892	5.6502	5.4262	5.2161	5.0188	4.8332
11	6.8052	6.4951	6.2065	5.9377	5.6869	5.4527	5.2337	5.0286
12	7.1607	6.8137	6.4924	6.1944	5.9176	5.6603	5.4206	5.1971
13	7.4869	7.1034	6.7499	6.4235	6.1218	5.8424	5.5831	5.3423
14	7.7861	7.3667	6.9819	6.6282	6.3025	6.0021	5.7245	5.4675
15	8.0607	7.6061	7.1909	6.8109	6.4624	6.1422	5.8474	5.5755
16	8.3125	7.8237	7.3792	6.9740	6.6039	6.2651	5.9542	5.6685
17	8.5436	8.0215	7.5488	7.1196	6.7291	6.3729	6.0472	5.7487
18	8.7556	8.2014	7.7016	7.2497	6.8399	6.4674	6.1280	5.8178
19	8.9501	8.3649	7.8393	7.3658	6.9380	6.5504	6.1982	5.8775
20	9.1285	8.5136	7.9633	7.4694	7.0248	6.6231	6.2593	5.9288
21	9.2922	8.6487	8.0751	7.5620	7.1016	6.6870	6.3125	5.9731
22	9.4424	8.7715	8.1757	7.6446	7.1695	6.7429	6.3587	6.0113
23	9.5802	8.8832	8.2664	7.7184	7.2297	6.7921	6.3988	6.0442
24	9.7066	8.9847	8.3481	7.7843	7.2829	6.8351	6.4338	6.0726
25	9.8226	9.0770	8.4217	7.8431	7.3300	6.8729	6.4641	6.0971

Present Value of an Uneven Series of Receipts

Our definition of an annuity includes the terms "fixed amount." In other words, annuities are made up of constant and equal receipts or payments. But often the receipts from a capital project are different and sporadic. If this is the case, in order to evaluate the economic desirability of the project (unless you have a financial calculator, spreadsheet, or software to calculate the present values of the future receipts) you must calculate each receipt or payment individually.

To illustrate the process of calculating uneven flows of receipts, let us assume that you contemplate investing $1,500 to produce an inflow of funds of $200 in the first year, $500 in the second, $400 in the third, $600 in the fourth, and $200 in the fifth. The discounted-value calculation of the future receipts with an interest rate of 12% is shown in Table 7.8. In this case, the investment is not desirable because the discounted value of the future receipts, which amounts to $1,356, is less than the $1,500 initial outflow.

Using the same example, but changing the $200 receipt in the fifth year for a $200 annuity received over six years (from year 5 to year 10), would require a slightly different procedure to calculate the present value. As shown in Table 7.9, the present value of the receipts for years 1, 2, 3, and 4 are the same as those calculated in Table 7.8. However, because the last $200 receipt is an annuity, we can use a shortcut. In the first step, the $200 receipts from years 5 to 10 (for a total of six years) have to be discounted to year four, which gives the amount of $822.28.

TABLE 7.8   CALCULATION OF THE PRESENT VALUE FOR UNEVEN SUMS

Year	Receipts	Discount Factor	Present Value
1	$ 200	.8929	$ 178
2	500	.7972	399
3	400	.7118	285
4	600	.6355	381
5	200	.5674	113
Total	$1,900		$1,356

In the second step, the $822.28 amount has to be discounted to year 0, which gives $522.56. The calculation process is shown in Table 7.9 and illustrated graphically in Figure 7.3. In total, the discounted value of the receipts amounts to $1,765.76, which is more than the original outflow. Therefore, in this case, the investment is desirable because it compares favourably to the initial $1,500 investment.

TABLE 7.9   CALCULATION PROCEDURE FOR UNEVEN SERIES OF RECEIPTS

A. PV of $ 200 in year 1 (.8929)   = $ 178.58
    PV of $ 500 in year 2 (.7972)   =   398.60
    PV of $ 400 in year 3 (.7118)   =   284.72
    PV of $ 600 in year 4 (.6355)   =   381.30
    PV of $ 200 in years 5 to 10

B. Step 1: $ 200 × 4.1114 = $ 822.28
    Step 2: $ 822.28 × .6355   =   522.56

C. PV of total receipts   = $ 1,765.76

FIGURE 7.3   GRAPHIC ILLUSTRATION OF THE PRESENT-VALUE CALCULATIONS FROM TABLE 7.9

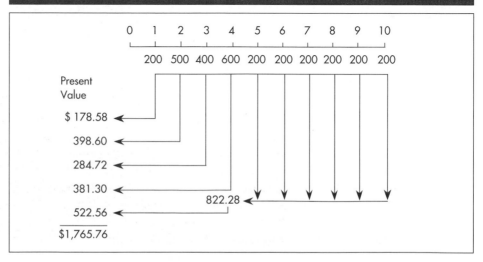

Using Interest Tables

As illustrated in Table 7.10, there are four **interest tables** in Appendix B. It is important to understand their function before using them. Tables A and C deal with compounding. If you want to find the future value of a single sum, use Table A. If you want to calculate the future value of an annuity, use Table C.

In capital budgeting, however, financial analysts use discounting tables—that is, Tables B and D. If you want to calculate the present value of a single sum, use Table B. If you want to find the present value of an annuity, use Table D.

Interest tables

Tables that show factors for multiplication to calculate compound or discount interest.

TABLE 7.10	**USING INTEREST TABLES**

These two tables are used
in capital budgeting
↓

	To Compound	To Discount
Single sum	Table A	Table B
Annuity	Table C	Table D

Working Examples

Let us review what we have seen so far in this chapter by working out four simple calculations.

Problem 1: Suppose you were to deposit $5,000 in your bank account today for a period of five years at an interest rate of 10%; to what amount will it have grown at the end of that period?

Answer: By referring to Table 7.2 or Table A, we obtain the following:

$5,000 × 1.611 = $8,055.00

Problem 2: Suppose you were offered the alternatives of either receiving $700 now or $1,000 five years from now. If the current rate of interest is 12%, which option would you go for?

Answer: By referring to Table 7.3 or Table B, we obtain the following answers:

Option 1: $700.00

Option 2: $1,000 × .56743 = $567.43

The first option is the more attractive one.

Problem 3: If you were to deposit $500 a year for the next ten years, what would be the sum of all ten deposits if the interest rate is 12%?

Answer: By referring to Table 7.5 or Table C, we obtain the following:
$500.00 × 17.549 = $8,774.50

Problem 4:   Suppose you were offered the following choices: a ten-year annuity of $1,000.00 or a $6,000.00 lump-sum payment today. If the current rate of interest is 10%, which option would you pick?

Answer: By referring to Table 7.7 or Table D, we obtain the following answer:

Option 1: $1,000.00 × 6.1446 = $6,144.60

Option 2: $6,000.00

The first option is the more attractive one.

Using Time-Value-of-Money Concepts in Investment Decisions

Let's now turn to the practical side of decision-making and examine how interest tables can help managers evaluate the economic desirability of capital expenditure projects. The remaining segments of this chapter look at the meaning of time-value yardsticks within the context of the following capital budgeting techniques:

- the future value;
- the net future value;
- the present value;
- the net present value; and
- the internal rate of return.

To describe how these techniques are used, we will turn to the $100,000 lottery example presented earlier in the chapter (Figure 7.1) and determine how much the winner should receive each year over a ten-year period in order to make the annuity equal to the lump sum. We will also use the same number in another example by assuming that a manufacturing manager is looking at the possibility of investing $100,000 to improve the efficiency of a plant, which would save $15,000 each year.

Future Value and Net Future Value

Question 1:   Should the lottery winner accept the $100,000 lump-sum payment or $15,000 a year over the next ten years?

Question 2:   Should the manufacturing manager invest $100,000 in order to save $15,000 a year during the next ten years?

Assuming that money is worth 10%, here are the answers.

If the lottery winner is given the option of receiving a $100,000 lump-sum amount now or $15,000 a year during the next ten years, the future value of both amounts is calculated as follows:

$100,000 × 2.594   (Table A) = $259,400
$ 15,000 × 15.937 (Table C) = $239,055
Net future value $ 20,345

Unquestionably, if the $100,000 were invested now in the bank at 10% over the next ten years, this amount would grow (because of time) more (to $259,400) than if the $15,000 amount were put in the bank each year (to $239,055). As shown, by the tenth year, the lump-sum payment would give an extra $20,345. Individually, both amounts are referred to as the future value, and the difference between both future amounts is referred to as the **net future value.**

Present Value and Net Present Value

On the other hand, if you want to justify which option to choose by comparing the discounted amounts, you would get a difference of $7,831 in favour of the lump-sum payment. Here is how the arithmetic works.

                        − $100,000
Present value   + $ 92,169   = or $15,000 × 6.1446 (Table D)
Net present value   − $ 7,831

As indicated, whether you bring both sums into the future (tenth year) or the present, the numbers are different, but the decision is the same—go for the $100,000 lump-sum payment.

If the manufacturing manager wants to invest $100,000 (cash outflow) to modernize the plant in order to save $15,000 (cash inflow) a year, the economics would not justify the investment. As shown above, the discounted $15,000 (or $150,000 over the ten-year period) gives a **present value (PV)** of only $92,169. At the 10% discount rate, the difference between the outflow and the inflow gives a negative $7,831 difference, which is referred to as the **net present value (NPV).** Whenever there is a negative NPV, the return on the investment is less than the rate used to discount the future cash receipts, which in this case happens to be less than 10%. When the NPV is positive, it means that the return on the invest-ment is more than the rate used to discount the future receipts.

Internal Rate of Return

Now, if both amounts were to have the same value, the lottery winner would have to receive $16,275 each year for the next ten years. This $16,275 amount is cal-culated by dividing the $100,000 amount by the factor found in Table D under column 10%, ten years (6.1446). As shown, both numbers are the same; that is,

Net future value

Difference between two sums that are compunded into the future.

Present value

The value today of a future payment or stream of pay-ments, discounted at an appro-priate rate.

Net present value (NPV)

The present value of the future cash flow of an investment, less the initial cash outflow.

the lump-sum amount is equal to the present value of the $16,275 annual receipts—the NPV is 0.

Here is how the calculation is done.

$$
\begin{array}{lll}
& -\ \$100,000 & \\
\textit{Present value} & +\ \$100,000 & = \text{or } \$16,275 \times 6.1446 \text{ (Table D)} \\
\textit{Net present value} & \underline{\underline{\$\quad 000}} &
\end{array}
$$

Now, if the plant manager wants to make a 10% return on the $100,000, plant efficiencies would also have to generate $16,275 each year. If the saving is more than this, the plant would generate more than 10%; if it is less, the return would be less. The bottom line is this: When the interest rate makes the discounted future receipts ($100,000) equal the original investment ($100,000), it is referred to as the **internal rate of return**. In this particular case, since 10% makes the future savings equal to $100,000 (the net present value equals 0), the internal rate of return on this particular investment is 10%. If the savings are more than $16,275, the plant generated a higher return. For example, if the plant were to generate $18,429 savings per year during the next ten years, the internal rate of return would be 13%, because it is this rate that makes the NPV equal to zero.

Internal rate of return (IRR)

The interest rate that equates the cost of an investment (cash outflow) to the present value of the expected returns from the investment (cash inflow).

$$
\begin{array}{lll}
& -\ \$100,000 & \\
\textit{Present value} & +\ \$100,000 & = \text{or } \$18,429 \times 5.4262 \text{ (Table D)} \\
\textit{Net present value} & \underline{\underline{+\ \$\quad 000}} &
\end{array}
$$

On the other hand, if the annual receipts were less than $16,275, the internal rate of return would be less. In the case of the manufacturing plant, the annual savings are $15,000. This means that the IRR would be less than 10% (8.1%). Here's the proof. This number is arrived at by looking at Table D, under the column 8% at ten years, where we find factor 6.7101.

$$
\begin{array}{lll}
& -\ \$100,000 & \\
\textit{Present value} & +\ \$100,651 & = \text{or } \$15,000 \times 6.7101 \text{ (Table D)} \\
\textit{Net present value} & \underline{\underline{+\ \$\quad 651}} &
\end{array}
$$

As shown, the 8% figure gives a positive $651 net present value, which means that the project generates 8% plus $651. If we were to convert this number on a percentage basis, the answer would be 0.144%. If Table D had a factor for 8.144, the present value would have been exactly $100,000, and the NPV would be zero.

FOOD FOR THOUGHT As shown in Table 7.11, using traditional accounting methods to calculate the return on this project, we divide the $15,000 amount by the $100,000 asset and obtain a 15% return (ROA). If a time-value-of-money yardstick were used, such as the IRR, the investment would give only 8.1%. In this case, the company would be losing 1.9% (after financing) each year during the next ten years instead of making a net 5.0%.

TABLE 7.11   ACCOUNTING RATE OF RETURNS VERSUS THE IRR

Calculating the accounting rate of return method (ROA)

$$\frac{\text{Receipts}}{\text{Assets}} = \frac{\$\ 15,000}{\$100,000} = 15\%$$

The Balance Sheet

ROA	15.0%		Cost of capital 10%
IRR	8.1%		

This simple illustration proves that using accounting rates of return in capital budgeting decisions can be misleading. As we will discover in the next chapter, there are different ways of calculating the accounting rates of return, and they are not the most reliable capital budgeting yardsticks. As shown in Table 7.11, time-value yardsticks are more suitable for measuring the desirability of capital projects and can be compared more accurately to the cost of capital.

How Interest Tables Came About

The concepts of compounding and discounting have been known for hundreds of years. Interest tables, however, have been around for only the past eight decades. These tables were not conceived by bankers or accountants, but by actuaries working for insurance companies. Here is how they use these tables. As shown in the upper portion of Table 7.12, if someone wished to buy a $50,000 insurance policy, that person could have been asked to pay $1,000 a year during his or her expected life span, which in this case happened to be 20 years. The insurance companies would have invested these $1,000 receipts at, say, 10% and, over the 20-year period, these sums would have a future value of $57,275. In 20 years, when the $50,000 amount was paid out (cash outflow), the company would have made a surplus of $7,275 (net future value).

In the 1950s, the industrial community decided to use the time-value-of-money idea as a capital budgeting decision-making instrument. Industrial managers said that if the time value of money was good for the insurance companies, it would also be good for the industrial companies, as both have cash outflow and cash inflow. However, there is one major difference: the time of making the cash disbursement or payment. In the case of insurance companies, the cash outflow (payment) is made in 20 years. In the case of industrial companies, the cash outflow is made at the beginning, and it is for this reason that cash receipts have to be discounted (in order to compare them to the initial investment) instead of bringing them into the future.

As shown in the lower portion of Table 7.12, the $150,000 asset that earns $20,000 a year over the next 20 years gives a $170,272 present value when using a 10% discount rate. As shown, at 10%, the net present value gives a surplus of $20,272, which means that the company would earn more than 10%. If, by inter-

TABLE 7.12 INSURANCE VERSUS INDUSTRIAL COMPANIES

Compounding

Insurance companies

Years 1 ⟶ to ⟶ 20

Yearly premiums (cash inflows) $1,000 Money is worth 10% ($1,000 × 57.275)	$ + 57,275
Death benefit (cash outflow)	$ – 50,000
Net cash flow or NFV	$ + 7,275

Discounting

Industrial companies

Years 0 ⟵ to ⟵ 20

The company invests $150,000 (cash outflow) to modernize a plant. As a result, the company's sales increase by $20,000 (cash inflows) each year.

$ – 150,000 cash outflow
$ + 170,272 present value of the savings if money is worth 10%
($20,000 × 8.5136)

$ + 20,272 net cash flow or net present value (NPV)

polation, we use a discount factor of 11.93%, the present value of the $20,000 receipts would be equal to $150,000, making the outflow equal to the inflow. In this particular case, the IRR would be 11.93%.

Using Interest Tables in Capital Budgeting

Objective 6 ▶

To calculate the financial returns by using time-value-of-money yardsticks, we need four elements:

- investment (cash outflow or disbursement);
- annual cash inflow (receipts);
- expected life span of the project; and
- cost of money (or the return that management wants to make on the investment).

Let's use one more example to calculate the NPV and the IRR of a capital project by applying interest tables. As shown on the left side of Table 13(a), the company invests $25,000 in a new capital asset and obtains $1,000 in savings each year during the next 25 years. If management wants to make 10%, the present value of the $1,000 receipts gives $9,077. Here, the NPV is a negative $15,923. This means that the IRR is negative.

TABLE 7.13a INVESTING IN A NEW ASSET

1. A company invests $25,000 in an asset.		How much must the company save each year	
2. It generates $1,000 in savings each year.		to make 10% on the asset?	
3. The expected life of the asset is 25 years.			
4. Cost of capital is 10%.			
1. Investment	− $ 25,000	−$ 25,000	Investment
2. Annual savings: $1,000			Savings per year: $ 2,754
3. Total savings: $25,000			Total savings: $ 68,850
4. Present value of savings	+ $ 9,077	+ $ 25,000	Present value of the savings
(9.0770 × $1,000)			(9.0770 × $2,754)
Net present value	− $ 15, 923	0	Net present value

If management wants to earn 10%, how much should the project generate each year over the life of the asset? As shown on the right side of Table 7.13(a), the savings should be $2,754. As indicated, this annual savings discounted at 10% gives a present value of $25,000, or an NPV of zero. Here, the internal rate of return would be 10% because it is the discount rate that makes the cash inflow equal to the cash outflow.

Now, if management wants to earn 16% (instead of 10%), the annual savings would have to be $4,100. As shown in Table 7.13(b), this annual savings gives a $25,000 present value. In this case, since 16% makes the outflow equal to the inflow, this rate would therefore be the IRR.

Now let's put things in perspective. As shown in Table 7.13(c), assuming that the treasurer of a company raises $25,000 at a cost of 10% (cost of capital on the right side of the balance sheet) and repays $2,754 a year during the next 25 years, while managers invest this sum (left side of the balance sheet) in an asset that earns $4,100 or 16% per year, the company would make 6% after paying the financing charges, for a net $1,346 per year.

TABLE 7.13b INVESTING IN A NEW ASSET

A company wants to make 16% on the $25,000 asset.
How much must the asset generate in savings or cash each year?

1. Investment	− $ 25,000
2. Annual savings: $ 4,100	
3. Total savings: $ 102,500	
4. Present value of savings	+ $ 25,000
(6.0971 × $ 4,100)	
Net present value	0

Chapter 7: Time Value of Money

TABLE 7.13c   INVESTING IN A NEW ASSET

Balance Sheet

Asset $25,000	Loan of $25,000
Saves $4,100	Repayment $2,754
Gives 16% per year	Cost of capital 10%

After financing, the company makes

6% or $1,346 per year.

❋ Decision-Making in Action

After spending several months researching how to go about planning their retirement and paying for their children's education, Steve and Lucy finally decided to meet Andrew Billingsley, a friend and personal financial advisor. Steve informed Andrew that he was very concerned about the future high cost of education and that he wanted some advice on how to plan ahead.

Steve's concern was raised when he read several articles about the spread between education inflation and cost-of-living inflation. Between 1976 and 2020, a $100 cost of living would rise to $400, while a $100 education expense would increase to $500.

Steve and Lucy are both college graduates doing extremely well. Steve works as an accountant in a government agency while Lucy is employed as a librarian at a university. Both are making a contribution to a pension fund with their respective employers that would provide a combined pension of $65,000 a year in addition to their Canada Pension Plan. They are both 30 years old and plan to retire at 55, that is, 25 years from now or in 2028.

Steve explained that he and his wife would like to make a combined $2,500 annual investment in a Registered Retirement Savings plan. Andrew examined several mortgage, bond, and equity fund performances for the last ten years after looking at the facts and the couple's interests; Andrew suggested that if they invested in an equity fund that they should expect to earn, on average, 10% over the 25-year life span.

The couple was also interested in saving money for the education of their three children, Sylvia (one year old), Phil (two years old), and Michael (six years old). They explained to Andrew that they would like to have enough money to pay for a university degree for their three children when each reached the age of 20. After reading several brochures published by Canadian banks, they learned that the cost of a university education (for four years) by the time their children reached their 20th birthday would be as follows:

- Sylvia, $58,000;
- Phil, $55,000; and
- Michael, $48,000.

Steve and Lucy indicated that they were interested in making a contribution each year for their three children. The Canadian government would match their contribution by 20% through the registered education saving plan (RESP) for a maximum of up to $400 per child. Andrew was hoping to obtain an 8% return over the life of the fund.

On the basis of the above information, we will calculate:

- how much Steve and Lucy will have in their registered retirement savings account the year they retire; and
- how much Steve and Lucy will have to save each year (after the government contribution) in order to have enough money for their children's education

by the time they each reach their 20th birthday.

The following calculations are made on yearly installments. These figures would be different if Steve and Lucy were to invest their money in these funds on a monthly or quarterly basis. Also, assume that all tax benefits are excluded from these calculations.

1. Steve and Lucy will have accumulated $245,867 if they invest a combined $2,500 a year in their RRSP.

   Calculation
   Yearly $2,500 contribution for 25 years at a 10% annual compounded growth rate.

   $2,500 × 98.347 (Table C) = $245,867

2. An annual amount of $1,119.53 will have to be invested in Sylvia's RESP account.

   Calculation
   Steve and Lucy want a $58,000 amount 19 years from now bearing an 8% interest rate.

   $58,000 ÷ 41.446 (Table C) = $1,399.41

Total contribution:	$1,399.41
Government's contribution (20%)	279.88
Steve and Lucy's contribution	$1,119.53

3. An annual amount of $1,174.90 will have to be invested in Phil's RESP account.

   Calculation
   Steve and Lucy want a $55,000 amount 18 years from now bearing an 8% interest rate.

   $55,000 ÷ 37.450 (Table C) = $1,468.62

Total contribution:	$1,468.62
Government's contribution (20%)	293.72
Stteve and Lucy's contribution	$1,174.90

4. An annual amount of $1,585.79 will have to be invested in Michael's RESP account.

   Calculation
   Steve and Lucy want a $48,000 amount 14 years from now bearing an 8% interest rate.

   $48,000 ÷ 24.215 (Table C) = $1,982.24

Total contribution:	$1,982.24
Government's contribution (20%)	396.45
Steve and Lucy's contribution	$1,585.79

Steve and Lucy would therefore have to invest a total of $6,380.22 each year in their RRSP and in their three children's RESP accounts.

Steve and Lucy's RRSPs	$2,500.00
Sylvia's RESP	1,119.53
Phil's RESP	1,174.90
Michael's RESP	1,585.79
Total	$6,380.22

Chapter Summary

Money has a time value because of the existence of interest. Because of interest, a dollar earned today would be worth more tomorrow (compounding). Conversely, a dollar earned tomorrow would be worth less today (discounting).

◀ Objective 1

In capital budgeting, inflation rates like price or cost increments are included in the financial projections. Once the projected income statements are completed, the time-value-of-money concept is used to discount all future cash inflows to the present.

◀ Objective 2

Objective 3 ▶

The element of risk has to do with uncertainties related to a project. The more uncertain the variables that affect a capital project, such as the cost of the equipment, market condition and competition, the more risky a project. If a project is highly risky, the managers will use a high discount rate to calculate the net present value of a project and determine the internal rate of return.

Objective 4 ▶

Appendix B at the end of the book presents four different interest tables. Tables A and C deal with compounding. If you want to find the future value of a single sum, use Table A. If you want to calculate the future value of an annuity, use Table C. In capital budgeting, financial analysts use discounting tables, that is, Tables B and D. If you want to calculate the present value of a single sum, use Table B. If you want to find the present value of an annuity, use Table D.

Objective 5 ▶

The four elements that must be considered in investment decisions are the cash outflow (investments), the cash inflows (receipts earned from the project), the expected life of the project, and the cost of capital raised that will be used to finance the project.

Objective 6 ▶

A knowledge of compound and discount value concepts is essential for understanding many different topics in finance and for improving the quality of capital budgeting decisions. It is important to know how to use compound and discount tables. For example, if a business invests $100,000 in a capital project and earns $40,000 a year over the next five years, the present value of the $200,000 cash inflow ($40,000 × 5) would be worth $151,632 ($40,000 × 3.790 using a 10% discount factor). The net present value would be +$51,632, or the difference between the $100,000 cash outflow and the $151,632 present value of the future cash inflows. The internal rate of return would be 28.65%, which is the interest rate used to discount all future cash inflows, so the present value equals the cash outflow.

Key Terms

Annuity	Internal rate of return (IRR)
Cash inflow	Net future value
Cash outflow	Net present value
Compound interest	Present value
Discounting	Risk
Future value	Rule of 72
Inflation	Time value of money
Interest tables	

Review Questions

1. Explain why money has a time value.

2. What is the difference between time value of money and inflation?

3. What differentiates time value of money and risk?

4. Why do you believe that cash and time are critical elements in investment decisions?

5. Within the capital budgeting framework, give a few examples to explain the difference between cash inflows and cash outflows.

6. Explain the Rule of 72.

7. What is the difference between simple interest and compound interest?

8. What is an annuity?

9. What is the meaning of net future value?

10. What is the meaning of present value?

11. What is the meaning of net present value (NPV)?

12. What do we mean by internal rate of return (IRR)?

13. What is the difference between income after taxes and cash flow?

14. How did interest tables come about?

15. Give the full names of the four interest tables.

Discussion Questions

1. Why is time value more important in gauging capital decisions than the traditional accounting methods?

2. How can the internal rate of return help managers gauge the economic value added of investment decisions when compared to cost of capital?

Testing Your Comprehension

True/False Questions

_____ 1. Money has a time value because of the existence of interest.

_____ 2. Inflation represents the level of expectations (probabilities) that something will happen in the future.

_____ 3. It is not important to consider the rate of inflation in capital decisions.

_____ 4. The risk element determines to a large extent the return that someone wants to make on an investment.

_____ 5. The $F_n = (1 + i)^n$ formula is the algebraic equation used to calculate the future value of a single sum.

_____ 6. Cash flow is more important than profit when gauging decisions on capital assets.

_____ 7. Discounting tables are used to calculate the future value of single sums or annuities.

_____ 8. Profit after taxes instead of cash is used with time-value-of-money yardsticks to justify investment decisions.

_____ 9. A dollar earned tomorrow is worth less today.

_____ 10. An annuity is a series of periodic income or payments of unequal amounts.

_____ 11. The present value of a sum received five years from now discounted at 10% is worth more than if it was discounted at 15%.

_____ 12. The present value of an undiscounted ten-year annuity is worth more today than if it was discounted.

_____ 13. Net present value is the difference between the future value of an annuity and the present value of an annuity.

_____ 14. The internal rate of return is the discount rate used to make the future value of cash receipts equal the value of a disbursement.

_____ 15. You can use annuity tables to find the discounted value of a series of equal receipts or payments.

Multiple-Choice Questions

1. Money has a time value because of the existence of:
   a. inflation
   b. risk
   c. annuities
   d. interest
   e. compounding tables

2. Cash inflow is calculated by:
   a. adding depreciation to profit before taxes
   b. adding depreciation to profit after taxes
   c. subtracting income taxes from profit before taxes
   d. subtracting operating expenses from revenue
   e. adding interest earned to income after taxes

3. To calculate the future value, one has to use:
   a. discount interest tables
   b. simple interest tables
   c. compound interest tables
   d. future interest tables
   e. inflation interest tables

4. The Rule of 72 is a quick and easy way to calculate the approximate number of years it takes for someone's investment to:
   a. double
   b. triple
   c. compound tenfold
   d. discount twofold
   e. outpace the investment

5. Investment decisions deal with two key concepts:
   a. profit after taxes and cash
   b. time and cash
   c. cash outflow and disbursements
   d. cash inflow and receipts
   e. cash and depreciation

6. An annuity can be described as a series of:
   a. periodic income or payments of unequal amounts
   b. sporadic income or payments of unequal amounts
   c. periodic income or payments of equal amounts
   d. sporadic income or payments of equal amounts
   e. irregular income or payments

7. The following has the highest value:
   a. future value of an annuity
   b. future value of a negative cash flow
   c. present value of an annuity
   d. present value of a single sum
   e. net present value of an annuity

8. Net present value is the difference between the:
   a. discounted cash inflow and the future cash flow
   b. compounded cash inflow and the future cash flow
   c. undiscounted cash inflow and the cash outflow
   d. discounted cash inflow and the cash outflow
   e. cash inflow and the discounted cash outflow

9. The internal rate of return is the discount factor that makes the:
   a. NPV positive
   b. NPV equal to zero
   c. NPV negative
   d. undiscounted cash inflow equal to the cash outflow
   e. discounted cash inflow equal to the future cash outflow

10. The following is considered a time-value-of-money yardstick:
    a. return on asset
    b. break-even point
    c. internal rate of return
    d. payback period
    e. market-value assessment

Fill-in-the-Blanks Questions

1. _____ represents the level of probable expectation that something (good or bad) will happen in the future.

2. Cash _____ represents the receipt of money generated by sales revenue less expenses.

3. The _____ interest rate is applicable on the initial principal and the accumulated interest of prior periods.

4. The Rule of 72 calculates the approximate number of years it takes for an investment to _____ when compounded annually.

5. An _____ is defined as a series of payments (or receipts) of fixed amount for a specified number of years.

6. _____ is the process of finding the present value of a series of future cash flows.

7. The value today of a future payment or stream of payments discounted at an appropriate rate is referred to as the _____ value.

8. The _____ is the difference between the present value of the future cash flow of an investment less the initial cash outflow.

9. The internal rate of return can be described as the interest rate that _____ the cost of an investment (cash outflow) to the present value of the expected returns from the investment (cash inflow).

10. Insurance companies usually deal with net _____ values.

11. The number 0.82645 looks like a _____ value factor.

12. The number −$34,300 looks like a _____ _____ net present value.

Learning Exercises

Exercise 1(a)

Joan Miller has just inherited $30,000 and has the option of investing this amount in different funds: GICs, safe mutual funds, or stock options that are more risky. Based on her analysis, the historical performance for each fund is 5%, 9%, and 12% respectively. If there are no withdrawals, how much would Joan have in these various funds at the end of 20 years?

Exercise 1(b)

You deposit $10,000 in your savings account, which pays 8% interest. If you do not make any withdrawals, how much will you have in your bank account at the end of 15 years?

Exercise 2(a)

The Millers would like to have a $30,000 education fund for their son Vincent, who is now three years old, and the same amount for their daughter Takara, who has just turned one. The Millers expect that their children will start university by the time they reach 20 years of age. How much will the Millers have to invest today (in one lump sum) if the registered education savings plan guarantees a 7% annual interest rate?

Exercise 2(b)

How much would you have to pay into an investment fund that will generate $1,000 at the end of two years, $1,500 at the end of three years, and $2,000 at the end of four years if you are earning 16% annual interest on your investment?

Exercise 3(a)

Joan Miller was given a choice on the $30,000 inheritance between receiving (1) the full payment today, or (2) a $3,000 annuity for the next 20 years and a lump-sum amount of $10,000 at the end of the tenth year. If Joan can earn 9%, which option is the most attractive?

Exercise 3(b)

You have a choice between receiving (1) a $50,000 payment today, or (2) a $7,500 annuity for the next ten years and a lump-sum amount of $20,000 at the end of the tenth year. If money is worth 10%, which option is the most attractive?

Exercise 4(a)

Len has just won $100,000 at a casino. If money is worth 10%, would it be better for Len to receive the full amount now or $15,000 each year for the next ten years?

1. What is the value of each amount ten years from now?

2. What is today's present value of each amount?

3. How much would Len have to receive each year to make the two amounts equal?

4. If Len received $15,000 each year instead of the $100,000 amount, what would be the effective interest rate or the IRR (internal of return)?

Exercise 4(b)

If money is worth 12%, would you prefer receiving $200,000 now or $30,000 each year for the next ten years?

1. What is the value of each amount ten years from now?

2. What is today's present value of each amount?

3. How much would you have to receive each year to make the two amounts equal?

4. If you receive $30,000 each year instead of the $200,000 amount, what is the effective interest rate or the IRR (internal of return)?

Cases

Case 1: The Farm Purchase

Jan Schmidt is 45 years old and has the option of buying a farm for $500,000 or investing his money in an equity fund that has earned 14% over the past seven years. After a discussion with a few investment analysts, the conclusion was that the performance of this fund could continue over the next 20 years.

If Jan buys the farm, it would generate $75,000 each year over the next 20 years. In 20 years' time, based on real estate information, the farm would be worth approximately $2 million.

1. If Jan wishes to make the same return on his investment as on the equity fund, should he buy the farm? Why or why not?

2. What is the farm's net present value with and without the sale of the farm (using 10% as the discount rate)?

3. What is the farm's internal rate of return?

Case 2: Ed's Bowling Alley

In 2004, Ed intends to invest $1,500,000 in a bowling alley. After two years of operation, he plans to invest an extra $450,000 in the business by opening a restaurant. In ten years, Ed anticipates selling the business for $3 million. Ed's cost of capital will be 11%. Ed would like to earn at least a 20% internal rate of return.

Ed can also lease a bowling alley that is located in a different city. The yearly cash flow from operations and lease payments is estimated at $200,000 (net after the lease payment) for the next ten years. Ed would also like to make 20% on this investment.

1. Is purchasing the bowling alley and restaurant a good investment?

   To answer this question, calculate the following:

   - the net present value by using the cost of capital;
   - the internal rate of return.

   Ed predicts that the business will generate the following cash inflow:

Years	Amounts
0	− $1,500,000
1	+ 200,000
2	− 450,000 (restaurant purchase)
2	+ 250,000
3	+ 300,000
4	+ 350,000
5	+ 400,000
6	+ 450,000
7	+ 500,000
8	+ 525,000
9	+ 550,000
10	+ 575,000
10	+ $3,000,000 (sale of business)

2. Is leasing the bowling alley a good decision?

3. If Ed can only do one or the other, should he go for the purchase or the lease? Why?

Capital Investment Decisions

Learning Objectives

After reading this chapter, you should be able to:

1. Comment on the reasons capital projects are critical.

2. Differentiate between compulsory investments and opportunity investments.

3. Explain the capital budgeting process.

4. Comment on the key elements used to gauge capital projects.

5. Evaluate capital investment decisions by using time-value yardsticks.

6. Assess capital investment budgeting techniques that measure risk.

7. Explain why capital projects are not approved.

Chapter Outline

OPENING CASE

By the end of 2004, the Millers were looking at several investment possibilities in order to expand their retail operations. The most viable and interesting option, one that was in line with their longer-term objective, was opening a new retail outlet. Now that they had several years of experience in the retail business and had accumulated enough cash, they were ready to move ahead with their plans.

The Millers estimated that it would cost around $350,000 to open their new retail store. Since they intended to lease a building for a ten-year period, the investment would be mainly in leasehold assets and the purchase of office equipment.

During the first year of operations, the Millers expected to invest an additional $100,000 in working capital, mostly in inventory and accounts receivable. During the second year, they expected to invest an additional $75,000 in working capital for a net investment amounting to $175,000.

The following summarizes the Miller's investment plan for their new retail store:

Year 0	Capital assets	$350,000	
Year 1	Working capital	$100,000	
Year 2	Working capital	75,000	175,000
Total capital employed			$525,000

At the end of the ten-year lease, the Millers would have the option of either expanding the store to cope with the growth or moving to a larger building. If, instead of making these changes, they were to sell their business (inventory, leasehold assets, goodwill, etc.), they estimated that they would be able to get $900,000 in cash from a potential buyer.

CompuTech's after-tax cost of capital amounts to 11.0%. This is based on funds that could be raised from lenders (short term and long term) and from shareholders.

The Millers hired a market research firm to determine the level of sales revenue that could be generated by the new store. On the basis of that information, they prepared the new store's pro-forma financial statements, to be included in the investment proposal presented to potential investors. The cash flow generated by the new store is estimated to be as follows:

Year	Cash inflow
1	$ 75,000
2	80,000
3	100,000
4	125,000
5	140,000
6–10	150,000

As shown above, the new store's cash flow during the first year is estimated at $75,000, with gradual increments between years 1 to 6. Starting in the sixth year, the Millers estimate that the cash flow will remain constant until the tenth year.

This chapter examines different time-value-of-money yardsticks that could be used by the Millers to determine the level of viability and return of their new store. In particular, the chapter focuses on three key topics:

1. the more important elements that should be taken into account when gauging the economic desirability of capital projects;

2. the time-value-of-money techniques such as net present value (NPV), the payback period, and the internal rate of return (IRR) used to measure the return on investment of capital projects; and

3. capital budgeting techniques used to assess the factor of risk inherent in capital projects.

Introduction

Capital budgeting is the process of planning, evaluating, and choosing capital expenditure projects that generate benefits (returns, profits, savings) over an extended number of years. Capital decisions are critical to the financial destiny of a company because they are irreversible, usually require a significant amount of financial resources, and can alter the future success of a business for many years. Capital projects may call for the development of a new product, a major expansion of an existing product line, the launching of a new product line, the construction of a new facility, or a significant change in direction geared to take advantage of foreseeable opportunities.

A **capital investment** (expenditure or cash disbursement) may be defined as a project that requires extensive financial resources (outflow) in return for expected flow of financial benefits (inflow) to be earned over a period of many years. A capital investment differs from an **expense investment** in that the latter generates benefits for a short period (less than one year). For example, a capital investment may represent the construction of a new plant costing $30 million (cash outflow) with an economic or physical life span of 25 years and generating

Capital investment

Project that requires extensive financial resources (cash outflow) made for the purpose of generating a return (cash inflow).

Expense investment

A fully tax-deductible cost that should produce favourable effects on the profit performance.

TABLE 8.1	PROFILE OF CAPITAL INVESTMENTS AND EXPENSE INVESTMENTS	
	Capital Investments	Expense Investments
Size of cash outlay	Large	Small
Nature of commitment	Durable	Impermanent
Accounting treatment	Capitalized	Expensed
Cash turnover	Recurrent and spread over many years	One-time and immediate
Financial impact of commitment	Significant	Minimal
Effect on financial structure	Minimal to sizeable	None

a $3 million profit (cash inflow) each year. An expense investment may consist of a $20,000 advertising cost that produces favourable effects on the profit performance during the current operating year. Table 8.1 compares capital investments and expense investments.

Why Capital Projects Are Critical

Objective 1 ➡

Capital investments are critical for a number of reasons. First, because new funds may need to be raised, the capital structure of a business can be altered significantly. Second, long-term return on a company's assets and shareholders' yield can be highly influenced by the mix of projects undertaken. It takes only one ill-conceived capital decision to reduce a firm's return (often for many years) and with it, management's credibility. Third, the future cash position of a company can be affected significantly, a vital consideration for a firm that is committed to meeting fixed-debt obligations, paying dividends, and growing (which usually means undertaking more capital investments). Fourth, once committed, a project often cannot be revised, or, can be revised only at a substantial cost.

Opportunity versus Compulsory Investments

Objective 2 ➡

Companies invest in capital projects for many reasons. A firm wishing to improve its financial performance could invest in cost-reduction programs or research and development, expand a manufacturing operation, replace obsolete equipment, install computer equipment, build a warehouse, or even buy an ongoing business. Each project varies significantly with respect to cash outlay, risk, profit levels, and time horizon. Capital projects can fall into several major categories:

- necessary investments to reduce operating costs;
- replacement investments to supplant worn-out equipment;

- market investments to improve the distribution network;

- expansion investments to increase sales volume (and profit) in existing product lines;.

- research and development investments to develop new products and new manufacturing or processing technologies;

- product improvement investments to sustain the life cycle of a product; and

- strategic investments to alter a business's mainstream activity.

These types of capital projects can be grouped into two main categories: compulsory investments, which are essential to sustain the life of a business, and opportunity investments, which are discretionary and made only if management believes they will improve the firm's long-term prosperity. Table 8.2 compares these two types of capital investments.

Compulsory Investments

Generally, **compulsory investments** are made for three reasons: contingency, legislative, and cosmetic. Those in the first category respond to a *need*. For example, a manufacturing department may have to increase its operating capacity to meet an expanded market need. Or a production manager may request that certain producing assets be replaced in order to eliminate substandard operations and maintain an acceptable level of operating efficiencies. In short, these types of investments prevent a company's rate of return from deteriorating. The second type of compulsory investment is dictated by *legislation*. For instance, the government may force businesses to invest in pollution-abatement machinery, in equipment that will meet regulatory quality control standards, or in assets affecting the safety of their employees. The third type of investments are made for *cosmetic* reasons; these include expenditures for office furniture; for protecting existing company assets (e.g., warehouses) from fire, pilferage, etc., for improving

Compulsory investment

Investment made in capital assets that does not require in-depth analytical studies.

TABLE 8.2	COMPARING COMPULSORY AND OPPORTUNITY INVESTMENTS	
	Compulsory Investments	**Opportunity Investments**
Effects	Maintain operating efficiencies	Increase momentum of the firm
Response	To a need	To an opportunity
Benefits	Immediate	Long-term
Risk	Negligible	High
Management involvement	Low-level	Top-level
Implications	Legislative, employee safety and satisfaction	Economic returns, share of market
Analytical techniques	Simple calculation	Mathematical models

Chapter 8: Capital Investment Decisions

the company image, and for making employees more comfortable (e.g., cafeteria, sports facilities).

These types of capital expenditures do not require in-depth analytical studies. Because the investments must be made for one reason or another, businesses include the required capital amounts in the company's annual capital budget and record them when the funds are disbursed. The major requirement in this process is to ensure that the firm obtains the best possible assets for the best possible price. The impact from such investments on profit position (minor expansion or modernization programs) can be measured with relative accuracy.

Opportunity Investments

Opportunity investment

Investments made in capital assets that are of a strategic nature and usually have far-reaching financial implications.

Opportunity investments, however, are far more complex and require sophisticated analysis, state-of-the art decision-making tools, and sound managerial judgment. Examples of these investments are launching a new product line, constructing a new plant, or substantially increasing manufacturing output to capture new markets. These capital projects are usually considerable and have far-reaching financial implications. The risk factor is enormous: If the venture is unsuccessful, management's reputation suffers, and there will likely be a heavy cash drain from existing operations—or, even worse, bankruptcy may result. These types of investments, however, can improve a company's competitive capability and profitability beyond current levels of performance.

Before the company commits to such investments, first it appraises the investment's chances of success as accurately as possible. Since the investment's financial return is dependent on internal and external environmental forces, the investment appraisal demands an incisive analysis of all aspects of the capital venture.

Figure 8.1 illustrates the impact investment decisions can have on a company's future. The vertical axis shows the return on investment; the horizontal axis represents the improvement profile of the return position against that of the industry over an extended number of years.

The ultimate reason for injecting funds into capital assets is to improve the return on investment—either to close the "return gap" with that of industry or to further improve the company's financial position. For example, as shown in the figure, the company's return on investment may be at 13% compared to the industry's 14%. If nothing is done (e.g., improving the productivity of its existing capital assets, injecting funds into new equipment, or doing research and development on new product lines), over the long term, the company's return may drop to 11%, while the industry's climbs to 16%; the gap widens from 1% to 5%. If the company plows funds into compulsory investments, it can hold its position at 13%, and the gap with industry will be only 3%. With additional financial resources, the firm may make opportunity investments, thus reducing the gap further. But, because of resource constraints, the firm may not still match the industry's growth. If, however, the firm is not financially bound, it could grow to a 16% level and reach both its full potential and the industry's growth.

FIGURE 8.1   GROWTH-GAP ANALYSIS

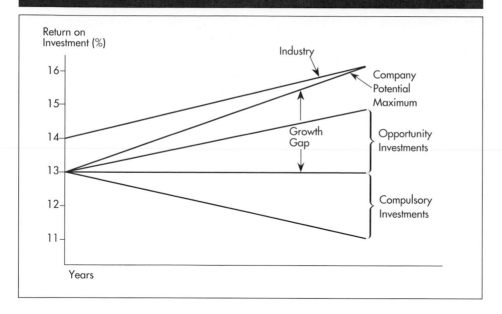

The Capital Budgeting Process

◀ Objective 3

As shown in Figure 8.2, several steps are involved in capital budgeting. The first step is to establish the corporate priorities and strategic and operational objectives within the framework of the external general and industry environments (opportunities and threats) and internal environment (strengths and weaknesses). The future can never be predicted with certainty but, with the level of information available and modern risk-analysis techniques, it is possible to deal with the

FIGURE 8.2   CAPITAL BUDGETING FRAMEWORK

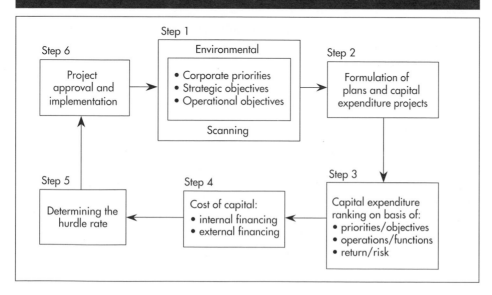

uncertainty factor in a relatively proficient manner. It is within this framework that the company mission's statement, strategic objectives, and plans are formulated.

The second step is to formulate the business plans and the capital expenditure projects. Capital projects affect a business in different ways such as improving operating efficiencies, increasing market share, etc. Management must therefore identify, select, and implement the most lucrative projects, that is, those that will best help the business achieve its strategic objectives.

The third step is to rank the capital projects on the basis of the corporate priorities and objectives, business needs (functional units), and returns:

PRIORITIES AND OBJECTIVES Most companies have priorities and a hierarchy of goals. Capital projects are therefore ranked according to how they will meet these overall priorities and strategic objectives. (Are they to increase market share, improve manufacturing efficiencies, or diversify operations?).

OPERATIONS/FUNCTIONS Capital projects must also be ranked within their respective operations (e.g., marketing, research, manufacturing, distribution).

RETURN RISK Since a healthy return is probably the ultimate objective of any business, the economic acceptability of a capital portfolio should be judged largely on this basis.

The fourth step is to fully explore the cost of alternate sources of capital. Funds are obtained from two sources: internally (e.g., through depreciation and retained earnings) and externally (e.g., from shareholders and lenders). If *internal funds* are to be used, management must decide what types of projects it intends to launch, several years before the funds are committed, so that the necessary cash can be set aside. *External funds* are generally obtained by issuing new long-term debts or shares. As discussed in Chapter 6, while the right-hand side of a balance sheet can be structured in a number of ways, it is critical to find the optimum financial structure, the one that combines the lowest cost with the least amount of risk.

The fifth step is to determine the **hurdle rate**, the level of return that each project should generate in order to be accepted as high risk, medium risk, or low risk. The hurdle rate reflects the cost of capital and an adjustment for individual project's risk. For example, if a company's cost of capital is 10% and the business is dealing with a medium-risk project, management will probably require a 25% return, which will include 15% for the project's risk. Since the capital needed to finance an investment portfolio usually exceeds the funds available, a firm needs financial criteria for selecting those projects offering the most attractive returns. Hurdle rates are determined in a number of ways, such as a company's weighted cost of financing new projects, long-term borrowing rates, ongoing internal rate of return, or even a figure chosen arbitrarily by top management. Hurdle rates are influenced by:

- level of capital funds needed;
- reputation of the company or management;

Hurdle rate

Capital budgeting technique used to rank the financial desirability of capital projects according to their cost of capital and risk.

- capital structure;
- type of issues to be offered;
- nature of projects (e.g., risk); and
- nature of industry.

Once the hurdle rate has been agreed upon and projects have been ranked on the basis of objectives, operations, and return, all that remains is the last step, selecting and implementing the projects.

Key Elements Used to Gauge Capital Projects

◀ Objective 4

A few basic capital budgeting concepts should be understood before examining the techniques used for gauging the economic desirability of capital projects. This section reviews the elements that serve as major inputs for capital project evaluation. They include cash outflow, cash inflow, economic or physical life span, and sunk costs.

Cash Outflow

When management decides to invest funds in a capital project, the decision entails an outflow of cash in terms of the initial cash outflow, working capital, and normal capital additions.

INITIAL CASH OUTFLOW When a decision is made to proceed with a capital project, such as the purchase of equipment, an initial cash outflow is recorded only once. However, cash outflow can also take place over a period of several years. For instance, a new plant could be constructed over a three-year period with cash outflow taking place over that same time span. Irrespective of the accounting treatment, all initial cash disbursements must be considered cash outflow. For example, a firm may invest $10 million to modernize a plant; from an accounting perspective, part of that amount, say $200,000, could be expensed the year the outflow takes place, while the remaining $9.8 million is capitalized and depreciated over a ten-year period. However, for capital budgeting evaluation purposes, all outflows must be shown as disbursements the year the money is spent.

Another point to consider about the initial cash outflow is that the financing of a project need not be taken into account. A company may receive 50% financing on the $10 million capital outlay. Irrespective of the amount of funds to be received from external sources, the project should be evaluated on the premise that the company uses its "own" cash or its equivalent for the entire project. Interest charges should not be considered an expense and thus should not be included in the pro-forma income statements. The intent of capital budgeting is to (1) gauge the economic returns of individual capital projects (stand-alone projects), (2) compare each competing project with the others, and (3) compare the return (i.e., internal rate of return) to the cost of capital (see the lower portion of Figure 6.1 in Chapter 6).

WORKING CAPITAL Another cash outflow to consider is working capital. Some projects, such as modernization, replacement of obsolete equipment, or installation of antipollution equipment, may not require additional working capital. However, other projects, such as the construction of a new plant or the expansion of an existing facility, may cause revenues and working capital to increase. The working capital spending usually takes place at the time the project comes onstream, usually the first and second year of operation. Incremental net working capital can take place several years after the launching of the new plant. These additions to working capital should therefore be included as cash outflow in the evaluation of the project.

NORMAL CAPITAL ADDITIONS Some capital projects may require additional capital expenditures for repairs and parts after the initial capital investment. If this is the case, these expenditures should be included as cash outflow when evaluating the capital project.

Cash Inflow

A capital project usually generates cash inflow during its entire physical life. This inflow of cash originates from several sources: net income, noncash expenses, and residual value.

NET INCOME A new project will generate additional cash because of increased sales (see Table 8.3) or produce savings resulting from more efficient operations.

NONCASH EXPENSES Since CCA (equivalent to the depreciation expense) and amortization are not a cash outflow but used solely for income tax relief purposes, the net income (or profit) figure does not reflect the true cash inflow. The calculation of net income and cash flow is shown in Table 8.3. As shown, since capital

TABLE 8.3 NET INCOME VERSUS CASH INFLOW	
	Net Income
Operating income (other cash expenses)	$ 100,000*
Capital cost allowance	50,000
Income before taxes	50,000
Income taxes (50%)	25,000
Income after taxes	25,000
Add back capital cost allowance	50,000
Cash inflow	$ 75,000

* Could include incremental profit resulting from increased sales, and excludes depreciation expense.

projects deal with cash flow and not net income, the amount incorporated in the project evaluation is $75,000 (cash) and not $25,000 (income after taxes).

RESIDUAL VALUE Since money has a time value, it is important to anticipate not only the future cash inflow of a project generated by additional sales revenue or savings but also the sale of the **residual value** of the assets at the end of the life of the project. Estimating the residual value of an asset can be done in a number of ways:

Residual value

Represents the sale of an asset or a business at the end of its physical life.

- Engineers can examine similar facilities and, based on historical experience, estimate the future residual value of the asset.
- Accountants can calculate the undepreciated book value of the assets and determine the residual value of the newly acquired assets by using several assumptions.
- Suppliers of equipment and machinery can also provide valuable assistance in estimating residual values.

Residual values can have a significant impact on the return calculation. The impact of the present value of residual assets is examined in the next section.

Economic or Physical Life of a Project

A capital investment (cash outflow) is made in exchange for future income (cash inflow). Since the **economic life** of a project plays a key role in determining the financial return of a project, this aspect of the analysis should be done prudently. In one instance, engineers, suppliers, or accountants may determine that a piece of equipment will last five years; in another instance, they may estimate 25 years. The longer the physical life of the project, the longer the cash inflow will be generated, and the more beneficial the financial return of the project will be. For example, if we refer to Chapter 7, the present value of a five-year $10,000 annuity bearing a 10% interest rate amounts to $37,908 ($10,000 × 3.7908), while the present value of a 25-year $10,000 annuity bearing the same interest rate amounts to $90,770 ($10,000 × 9.0770).

Economic life

Number of years that a capital asset or investment opportunity will last.

Also, the physical life span of a project is important in order to calculate the present value of the residual value of the asset. The time span and the interest rate also have an impact on the financial return of a project. Table 8.4 shows the

TABLE 8.4   PRESENT VALUES OF $1,000 RESIDUAL VALUE

Interest Rate (%)	Economic Life (Years)				
	5	10	15	20	25
5	783	614	481	377	295
10	621	385	239	149	92
15	497	247	123	61	30
20	402	161	65	26	10
25	328	107	35	11	4
30	269	72	19	5	1

present values of an asset that has a residual value of $1,000 with varying discount rates and economic lives.

Sunk Costs

Sunk cost

Investment cost incurred prior to making the decision to proceed with a capital project.

Sunk costs are funds that have already been spent on a project prior to making the decision to proceed with it. For instance, a firm may hire engineers to study the feasibility of investing huge sums of money in a project; those engineering costs may amount to $300,000. The recommendation may be to proceed or not to proceed with the capital project. The engineering fees are considered "sunk costs," meaning that these costs should not be taken into consideration when calculating the financial return of the project. The fact that management wants to make a decision on the project means that it has discretion (go or no go); sunk costs, on the other hand, offer no discretion. Whether the decision is positive or negative, the $300,000 amount will still have been disbursed.

Objective 5 ▶

Using Time-Value Yardsticks in Investment Decisions

The main purpose of capital budgeting is to make decisions that will maximize a company's investments. Capital budgeting compels management to answer two basic questions: First, which of the many projects emanating from various departments should be approved? Second, how many projects, in total, should be approved?

In short, capital budgeting provides a methodology that helps management rank a multitude of investment proposals in order of priorities, strategic and economic importance, and return on investment.

Rate of return is probably the most widely used guide for helping managers make decisions related to the commitment of capital investments. The purchase of securities; acquisition of new assets; investment in product development, modernization, expansion, or construction all have one common trait—they generate income in return for funds disbursed. The rate of return can, therefore, be regarded as the relationship between funds committed and funds generated. This relationship is expressed in terms of a ratio or percentage. The arithmetic itself is relatively simple, but the fact that there is a choice in selecting the numerator and the denominator when calculating the return suggests that the results can vary substantially. The denominator, for example, can be expressed in terms of the original investment, depreciated investment, average investment, or capital employed. The numerator, where profit is shown, also varies depending on the selected year of income. The formula for calculating accounting returns also varies. The countless variables and formulas used for calculating return on investment have generated a good deal of bewilderment.

This section reviews different types of capital budgeting methods available and the arguments for and against each technique. Five capital budgeting methods used for gauging and ranking capital project proposals will be discussed. They are:

1. accounting methods;
2. payback period;
3. net present value (NPV);
4. internal rate of return (IRR) or discounted cash flow (DCF); and
5. profitability index (PI).

Each of these capital budgeting methods will be discussed in terms of (1) what it is, (2) what it does, (3) how it works, and (4) the arguments for and against it. After reviewing these capital budgeting techniques, sensitivity analysis and risk analysis will be discussed.

The Accounting Methods

WHAT IT IS The **accounting methods,** also referred to as the "traditional yard-sticks," the "financial statement methods," the "accountant's methods," and the "book value rate of return," make use of data presented on financial statements to express the economic results of a capital investment.

Accounting methods
Calculation of the book value rate of return by using data presented on financial statements.

WHAT THEY DO The accounting methods give a rate of return of a capital project at a particular point in time (year) based on a book profit and a book investment.

HOW THEY WORK The rate of return calculation based on these yardsticks is relatively simple; profit is divided by an appropriate investment base. It can be calculated in one of the following ways: (1) the annual return on original investment, (2) the annual return on average investment, (3) the average book return on investment, and (4) the average return on average investment. By using the following assumptions, let's examine how each is calculated:

- Original investment $200,000
- Salvage value   nil
- Life of the project   5 years
- Method of depreciation $40,000 (straight-line)
- After-tax income or profit $60,000

1. The annual return on original investment is calculated as follows:

$$\frac{\text{Annual income}}{\text{Original investment}} \times 100 = \frac{60,000}{\$200,000} \times 100 = 30\%$$

2. The annual return on average investment is calculated as follows:

$$\frac{\text{Annual income}}{\text{Original investment}/2} \times 100 = \frac{60,000}{\$200,000/2} \times 100 = 60\%$$

* Instead of using the original or depreciated investment in the calculation, half of the investment, or the mid-point of the life of the assets (2.5 years) is used.

Chapter 8: Capital Investment Decisions

3. The average book return on investment is calculated as follows:

$$\frac{\text{Total income} - \text{Original investment}}{\text{Weighted average investment}} \times 100$$

$$\frac{\$300{,}000 - \$200{,}000}{\$600{,}000} \times 100 = 16.7\%$$

The calculation of the average investment is as follows:

Year	Original Investment	–	Accumulated Depreciation	=	Book Value
0	$200,000		—		$200,000
1	200,000		$ 40,000		160,000
2	200,000		80,000		120,000
3	200,000		120,000		80,000
4	200,000		160,000		40,000
5	200,000		200,000		—
Average investment					$600,000

4. The average return on average investment is calculated as follows:

$$\frac{\text{Total income} - \text{Original investment}}{\text{Original investment}/2 \times \text{Life of assets}} \times 100 = \frac{\$300{,}000 - 200{,}000}{\$200{,}000/2 \times 5} \times 100 = 20\%$$

The following summarizes the different rates of return obtained by using various accounting methods:

Methods of calculation	Rate of return
• Annual return on original investment	30.0%
• Annual return on average investment	60.0%
• Average book return on investment	16.7%
• Average return on average investment	20.0%

There are numerous other ways of calculating the return on investment by using the accounting methods. For the same project, there are four returns ranging from 16.7% to 60.0%. If this project had generated uneven flows of income (say, year 1, $25,000; year 2, $70,000; year 3, $80,000; year 4, $90,000; and year 5, $100,000), this would compound the combinations for calculating the different rates of return. We could obtain different returns for each year, reflecting the profit level for a particular year. When using these accounting methods for capital budgeting purposes, it is important that strict guidelines be written to ensure that all departments are consistent in their return calculations.

Arguments for accounting methods:
  • They are simple to use and easy to calculate.

- The audit is simple because the information relates to accounting data.
- Emphasis is on income or profit rather than cash flow.

Arguments against accounting methods:
- They do not take into account that money has a time value.
- They do not provide a "true" rate of return, which is essentially the exact earning rate of the dollars in use. The average book return method usually understates the rate of return, while the annual return method overstates it.
- The returns focus only on one specific year, while a project usually has a longer physical life span.
- It is meaningless to compare an accounting rate of return to other rates offered on bonds, loans, or any other figures quoted on the financial markets.
- They assume that a capital project will last for the depreciable life, when in fact this is generally not true.
- Since the time pattern of income varies from project to project, it is difficult to make effective comparisons between them.

The Payback Method

WHAT IT IS This method measures the period of time it takes for the cash outflow of a project to be totally recovered by the anticipated cash inflow; in other words, it measures how soon the initial funds disbursed are recovered by the project. The **payback period** is also known as the cash recovery period, the payoff method, or the payout method.

WHAT IT DOES This technique measures time risk, not risk conditions. It is helpful in the project-selection process and also gives a valid measure of the expected project risk. The longer it takes for the initial investment to be recovered, the greater the risk. This is critical for a company engaged in an industry where product obsolescence is a factor, and where there are abrupt technological changes. A firm engaged in a relatively stable industry will be more likely to accept projects with longer payback periods. Payback can be considered an indicator of profitability. Projects that have a short payback period should have higher earnings in the short run. However, since this method favours immediate cash inflow, it may sacrifice future cash growth.

HOW IT WORKS There are different ways of calculating the payback. The payback calculation is simple. For example, a business that invests $1.5 million in a venture that generates an annual cash inflow of $500,000 during its physical life will have a three-year payback period. The formula is:

$$P = \frac{I}{NCF}$$

Payback period

The number of years required for a capital investment to generate enough undiscounted cash inflow to just cover the initial cash outflow.

where the original investment (I) is divided by the net cash inflow (NCF). It should be noted that this formula works only when cash inflow is equally distributed annually or when the irregular annual cash inflow is averaged out. The application of this formula to the above example is as follows:

$$\text{Payback} = \frac{\$1,500,000}{\$500,000} = 3.0 \text{ years}$$

The traditional payback method, the payback reciprocal, and the discounted payback are three methods used for calculating the economic desirability of a project.

THE TRADITIONAL PAYBACK METHOD When cash inflow is irregular, the calculation of the traditional payback period is done in the following way:

Years	Annual Net Cash flow	Cumulative Cash flow
0	$(200,000)	$(200,000)
1	25,000	(175,000)
2	70,000	(105,000)
3	80,000	(25,000) ← Payback
4	90,000	65,000
5	$100,000	$165,000
Total cash inflow	$365,000	

The illustration shows that the payback period takes place between years 3 and 4, since cash flow turns positive during the fourth year. In most cases, cumulative cash flow will not equal zero at specific given years, but instead, in fractions of a year, or months. If this is the case, interpolation will have to be calculated by dividing the remaining cumulative net cash negative flow for the third year, amounting to $25,000, by the positive net cash flow for the fourth year of $65,000. This gives a fraction of a year of 0.385. The payback period therefore is 3.385 years.

Payback reciprocal

Capital budgeting technique that gives a rough estimate of the return on investment of a capital project.

THE PAYBACK RECIPROCAL Another way of calculating the payback is by finding the **payback reciprocal,** which gives a very rough estimate of the return on investment. The calculation of the reciprocal is done in two steps. First, the average net cash inflow generated by the project must be calculated. In this case, the project generates an average net cash inflow of $73,000. The calculation is as follows:

$$\frac{\text{Total net cash inflow}}{\text{Number of years}} = \frac{\$365,000}{5} = \$73,000$$

Second, the average net cash inflow is divided by the initial cash outflow.

$$P = \frac{\$73,000}{\$200,000} = 36.5\%$$

THE DISCOUNTED PAYBACK METHOD A company concerned about the element of time value will go beyond the traditional way of calculating the payback period. During the early 1980s, because of high interest rates, more businesses were taking into account the time value of money when calculating the payback period. Therefore, they calculated the present value of future cash inflows to find the number of years it takes for the initial cash outflow to be totally recovered. Using a discount factor of, say, 15% to calculate the present value of the future stream of funds, the **discounted payback** period is 4.75 years. The calculation is as follows:

Discounted payback

The number of years required for a capital investment to generate enough discounted cash inflow to just cover the initial cash outflow.

Year	Annual Net Cash Flows	Discount Factors	Present Values	Cumulative Present Values
0	$(200,000)	1.00000	$(200,000)	$(200,000)
1	25,000	.86957	21,739	(178,261)
2	70,000	.75614	52,930	(125,331)
3	80,000	.65752	52,602	(72,729)
4	90,000	.57175	51,457	(21,272) ←
5	100,000	.49718	49,718	28,446

Arguments for the payback method:

- Because it is simple to use, it may be employed as a crude screening device. Before the company embarks on extensive, complicated, and costly feasibility studies, a quick calculation can easily distinguish between profitable projects and those that will produce marginal financial results. In short, the payback can quickly separate the desirables from the undesirables.

- A firm that thrives on technological innovations would likely use this method. In this type of business, management wants to be reasonably assured that the total cost of a venture will be recovered before better products or manufacturing processes are introduced. Here, management may have no alternative but to embark on capital projects that generate high initial cash inflow and recover costs within a short time frame.

- A growth business that relies heavily on internal cash may find) payback a useful method. Management of businesses in desperate need of cash may wish to trade off longer-term yield for short-term cash. A rapidly growing firm that opts for "dynamic projects" would find this method appropriate.

- Payback focuses on factors that are more discernable or visible than five or 15-year projected figures that must be used to calculate the net present value or the internal rate of return. Even under dynamic environmental conditions, a firm equipped with good intelligence reports and forecasting techniques can, within reasonable limits, determine a project's potential initial cash outlay and the cash inflow, at least up to the payback point. Time-value yardsticks, such as the internal rate of return (to be discussed later in this chapter), must incorporate into the calculation the more distant and unpredictable cash inflow (total physical life of the assets), which, in many circumstances, are merely "calculated guesses."

Arguments against the payback method:

- This technique fails to measure the "true economic worth" of a capital expenditure project because it focuses only on çash flow earned before the payback point, and it ignores the project's total physical life span. The payback period techniques place emphasis on liquidity and not return. The issue is this: Should a firm invest for the purpose of recovering its cash as quickly as possible, or should the decision be based on return? In other words, should management inject funds into a project that offers a short payback at the expense of lucrative profits earned beyond the payback point?

- Opponents of this method say that it does not adequately compare the relative economic worth of projects, since it can encourage the deployment of capital funds toward less efficient projects rather than highly efficient ones. For example, a capital-intensive project with high initial cash outflow and start-up expenses and a 20-year physical life may show a long payback period. On the other hand, a labour-intensive project with a minimal initial cash outlay but substantially higher labour and operating costs over its physical life may show a shorter payback and probably a shorter physical life span. Because of a shorter payback, the less efficient (or labour-intensive) project may be accepted instead of the capital-intensive project that could very well be more efficient.

- The payback method does not take into consideration the time of the flow of funds even before the payback point. Although the payback method is geared to gauge liquidity, it fails even to do this job properly. Consider the following hypothetical example. Two projects with initial cash outflow of $1.6 million may show a four-year payback period.

	Cash Flow in $000's		
Years	*Project A*	*Project B*	*Cash Flow Difference*
0	$(1,600)	$(1,600)	—
1	400	200	$200
2	400	200	200
3	400	600	(200)
4	$ 400	$ 600	$(200)
Net cash flow	0	0	
Payback period	4 years	4 years	

Project A shows a superior cash flow profile because it produces $400,000 more by the end of the second year. These funds can be reinvested in lucrative endeavours. Also, if both projects cease to operate at the end of the second year, the firm would recoup 50% of the original outlay in project A and only 25% in project B. (This method is called the bailout payback period).

The Net Present Value Method (NPV)

WHAT IT IS The net present value technique measures the difference between the sum of all cash inflow and the cash outflow discounted at a predetermined interest rate, which sometimes reflects the company's weighted cost of capital or the hurdle rate.

WHAT IT DOES This method helps to establish whether a specific project will bring returns that exceed the cost of borrowing funds to undertake it. The rationale is relatively straightforward. If the net present value of a project, discounted at the company's cost of capital rate, is positive, the project may be classified as acceptable. If, on the other hand, the resulting net amount is negative, it would be economically unattractive and therefore rejected. This method is also useful for making realistic comparisons between projects. Since a common denominator (interest rate) is used in the calculation, it is easy to identify those projects that generate the most favourable results.

HOW IT WORKS There are several steps in calculating the net present value of a project: (1) determine the projected cash flow, (2) determine the expected weighted cost of capital, then (3) compute the net present value itself. Referring to the example used in the payback calculation in the section titled "The Payback Method," the present value of the $200,000 investment with a 15% discount rate gives a total of $228,446 in discounted cash inflow for a net present value of $28,446.

Years	Net Cash flow	Discount Factors	Net Present Value
0	$(200,000)	1.00000	$(200,000)
1	25,000	.86957	21,739
2	70,000	.75614	52,930
3	80,000	.65752	52,602
4	90,000	.57175	51,457
5	100,000	.49718	49,718
Net present value (NPV)			$ 28,446

Arguments for net present value:

- This method is easy to use since no trial-and-error calculations are required (unlike the internal rate of return method, which will be discussed next).

- It examines the total physical life of the assets.

- It facilitates the choice between different projects.

Arguments against net present value:

- The time-value-of-money concept is more difficult to grasp than the accounting methods such as return on assets.

- It is difficult to determine which cost of capital should be used to find the present value: Short-term or long-term? Current weighted cost of capital or next year's? Current rate of return or the short- or medium-term rate? The hurdle rate?

- The net present value method does not measure the level of risk of a project, so it is difficult to determine whether or not a project offers sufficient benefits in relation to its potential hazards. A statement like "This project gives a $28,446 net present value when discounted at 15%" is meaningless in the context of evaluating the risk of a capital project.

The Internal Rate of Return (IRR)

WHAT IT IS The internal rate of return (IRR), also known as the discounted cash flow (DCF) rate of return, the true yield, or the investors' method, can be described as the specific interest rate used to discount all future cash inflows, so that their present value equals the initial cash outflow. The financial community has used the discounting mechanism for many decades to calculate insurance premiums and bond yields. Later, the industrial community adopted it to evaluate capital projects.

WHAT IT DOES It shows the economic merits of several projects and compares their returns to other financial indicators, such as the weighted cost of capital and the company's aggregate rate of return.

HOW IT WORKS The internal rate of return is found by trial and error (if a financial calculator or a spreadsheet is not available). Once the total annual cash flow is estimated, the net present value of the cash inflow and outflow are computed using an arbitrary interest rate. The totals are then compared. If the present value of the cash inflow is lower than the cash outflow, the procedure is repeated, this time using a lower interest rate. If, however, the present value of the cash inflow is higher than the cash outflow, a higher interest rate is called for. The process continues until the total net cash flow equals zero. The required calculation for our earlier example is illustrated as follows:

Year	Net Cash Flows	At 18%		At 20%		At 22%	
		Factor	PV	Factor	PV	Factor	PV
0	($200,000)	1.00000	($200,000)	1.00000	$(200,000)	1.00000	($200,000)
1	25,000	.84746	21,186	.83333	20,833	81967	20,492
2	70,000	.71818	50,273	.69444	48,611	.67186	47,030
3	80,000	.60863	48,690	.57870	46,296	.55071	44,057
4	90,000	.51579	46,421	.48225	43,402	.45140	40,626
5	$100,000	.43711	$43,711	.40188	$40,188	.37000	$ 37,000
Net present value			$10,281		$ (670)		$(10,795)

The calculation shows that it is the 20% interest rate that equalizes (near enough) the cash flow. (By using a financial calculator or a spreadsheet, we get exactly 19.87%.) The internal rate of return on this investment is therefore 20%. Trial-and-error calculations would have to be done if the net difference is more significant.

If the cash outflow takes place at year 0, and all cash inflows are constant each year of the project, it is quite easy to figure out the internal rate of return. For example, a $200,000 initial cash outflow and a $70,000 annual cash inflow give a 22% internal rate of return. First we divide the $200,000 by the $70,000, which gives a factor of 2.8571. By referring to the present value of an annuity of $1 (see Table D in Appendix B), we can obtain the internal rate of return by finding the 2.8571 present value factor in the row opposite five years. The present value factor of 2.8571 lies between 22% (2.8636) and 23% (2.8035). In this case, the internal rate of return is 22.11%.

Arguments for internal rate of return:

- It focuses attention on the entire economic life of an investment. It concerns itself with cash flow and ignores book allocations.
- It considers the fact that money has a time value.
- It permits a company to compare the return of one project to the cost of capital (see Figure 6.1 in Chapter 6).
- It facilitates comparisons between two or more projects.

Arguments against internal rate of return:

- This method covers activities that take place during the entire life span of a project. While this may be considered a strong point, it could also be a drawback. How can one predict internal and external environmental conditions ten, 15, and 20 years ahead?
- It ignores potential "cash throw-offs"—that is, should a company assess the financial desirability of a project in a vacuum, or should it include the added income produced by the incremental cash that is generated by the project? For example, when a project generates, say, $25,000 during the first year of operation, should the interest earned on this money be considered when calculating the return of the project in question?
- The technique is relatively difficult to grasp. Operating managers understand ratios, such as the division of profit by the project investment; however, the internal rate of return calculation contains more than simple arithmetic. Concepts such as cash flow, time span, discounting, and present value—all essential components of the internal rate of return calculation—are introduced.
- This method poses some difficulty for determining the "true" financial benefits of a project. Since the investment return is expressed in terms of a percentage or a ratio, this method poses an element of delusion. For instance, a company's capital expenditure budget may contain several

Chapter 8: Capital Investment Decisions

projects in the amount of $100,000, with internal rates of return in the 25% range. Other important projects in the $1 million range with a 20% internal rate of return may be weeded out, due to the comparative low factor yield. The absolute present-value sums are not evident. Put simply, you can invest $100 at 30% and $10,000 at 25% for a one-year period and, although the return on the first project is highly attractive, the absolute dollars earned are only $30. In the second case, the yield is lower; however, the dollars earned are $2,500. This cash throw-off can be reinvested in other projects generating additional revenue.

- It assumes that the cash flow can be reinvested at the calculated rate of return.

The Profitability Index (PI)

Profitability index

Ratio of the present value of the cash inflow to the present value of the cash outflow discounted at a predetermined rate of interest.

WHAT IT IS The **profitability index**, also known as the present value index, or benefit-cost ratio, shows the ratio of the present value of cash inflow to the present value of the cash outflow, discounted at a predetermined rate of interest.

WHAT IT DOES This method helps to rank capital projects by the ratio of the net present value for each dollar to the cash outflow and to select the projects with the highest index until the budget is depleted.

HOW IT WORKS Refer to the earlier example, where the initial cash outlay is $200,000, the cost of capital is 15%, the life of the project is five years, and the cash inflow is as follows:

Years	Cash Inflow	PV Using Discount Rate of 15%
1	$ 25,000	$ 21,739
2	70,000	52,930
3	80,000	52,602
4	90,000	51,457
5	$100,000	49,718
PV		$228,446

The present value of the future cash inflow is $228,446. The PI is calculated as follows:

$$\frac{\$228,446}{\$200,000} = 1.142$$

If the index is greater than 1.0, it means that the flow of cash discounted at a predetermined discount factor (e.g., cost of capital) is more than the cash disbursement. If it is less than 1.0, it means that the incoming cash flow of the project gives less than the discounted factor. For example, if 15% was used to calculate the PI of all projects shown in Table 8.5, projects A to E generate more than 15%, and projects F to K, less.

TABLE 8.5 CAPITAL RATIONING AND THE PI INDEX

Projects	Cash Outflows	PV	PI	Aggregate PI
A	$300,000	$510,000	1.7	
B	200,000	320,000	1.6	
C	$1,700,000 600,000	840,000	1.4	1.36
D	400,000	440,000	1.1	
E	200,000	200,000	1.0	
F	200,000	160,000	0.8	
G	250,000	175,000	.7	
H	150,000	60,000	.4	
I	90,000	27,000	.3	
J	300,000	60,000	.2	
K	200,000	0	0	

This method helps to rank capital projects in a logical way because it looks at projects both in relation to budget constraints and in terms of which ones offer the highest total net present value. Table 8.5 illustrates this methodology. Let's say that a company has a maximum of $1.7 million to invest. As shown in the table, the company has 11 projects under review (A to K), each having specific cash outflow with corresponding net present values and profitability indexes. The company will give the green light to projects A to E for a total cash outlay of $1.7 million. This means that projects F to K will be deferred until the following year. The aggregate PI for all approved projects is 1.36 ($2,310,000 ÷ $1,700,000).

Arguments for and against the profitability index:

The arguments for and against the profitability index are the same as those for and against the net present value method, with one exception: The net present value expresses all dollars in absolute terms, while the PI method expresses the results in relative terms, that is, an index.

Capital Budgeting Techniques That Measure Risk

◀ Objective 6

It was mentioned earlier that time-value yardstick results are based on a project's total physical life span. This implies the need to deal with the future, to use a series of underlying assumptions as benchmarks for computing the "best possible estimates." There is one overriding weakness in this approach: It is vulnerable to the element of change. No one can predict, with any certainty, future environmental conditions, such as those related to economic, political, social, and technological factors, and, more specifically, elements affecting the industry, such as prices, competitors' aggressiveness, level of investment intentions by competitors, research and development, and labour costs. So the internal rate of return is based on the assumption that all estimates will materialize, that the price over the next five years will be x, that the cost of materials and wages will be y and z, etc. Thus, there are many chances for estimates to be off target. For example, a 15.6% internal rate of return can be increased or decreased by a change or several changes in the estimates.

More sophisticated capital budgeting techniques have been developed to help decision-makers deal with probabilities or possibilities. These yardsticks can identify a range of results based on patterns of variations, rather than using one single set of factors to generate the "best possible result" (such as the one used to calculate the internal rate of return).

Two techniques used for dealing with "range of results" are sensitivity analysis and risk analysis.

Sensitivity Analysis

Sensitivity analysis

Capital budgeting technique that involves the identification of profitability variations as a result of one or more changes in a project's base case to certain key elements of a capital project.

Sensitivity analysis involves the identification of profitability variations as a result of one or more changes in the base case related to certain key elements of a project. These could include the purchase of land, buildings and equipment; sales volume; selling price; cost of material or labour; length of the physical life of the assets; and even a change in the tax rate. To illustrate, the internal rate of return of the project mentioned earlier in the section titled "Internal Rate of Return" was 20% based on one set of estimates. If selling prices vary by 10%, construction costs by 5%, and sales volume by 10%, the effect of these changes (individually) on the base case would be as follows:

Factors	% Variation in Factor	Internal Rate of Return
Base case	—	20.0%
Selling price	−10%	16.3%
Cost of construction	+ 5%	18.8%
Sales volume	−10%	17.5%

These factors may vary either individually or in combination. It is important to note that sensitivity checks do not contain the element of probability related to individual factors. This method simply illustrates the degree of change in the base internal rate of return as a result of one or more changes related to a project.

Risk Analysis

Risk analysis

Process of attaching probabilities to individual estimates in a capital project's base case.

Risk analysis is the process of attaching probabilities to individual estimates in the base case. It was stated earlier that the process of appraising investment proposals has one weakness—the element of uncertainty. Those preparing the estimates to be included in the return calculation must know the degree of uncertainty related to their respective estimates.

Past experience alerts managers to the possible degree of error in their estimates. Therefore, management's knowledge should be used extensively to obtain the best-quality decision-making. The risk-analysis method will produce a full spectrum of return outcomes, from the most pessimistic to the most optimistic. Weighing the uncertainty factor, therefore, becomes an integral part of the project evaluation process. In this way, the sales manager, production manager, financial executive, plant engineer, cost accountant, purchasing agent, and others can all provide calculated guesses regarding the likelihood of possible outcomes in the selling price, cost of labour, cost of machinery, cost of raw material, etc. Their input can be illustrated as follows:

Sales volume (000s of units)	100	200	300	400
probabilities (%)	.05	.15	.65	.15
Selling price ($)	1.50	1.70	1.90	2.10
probabilities (%)	.05	.15	.70	.10
Cost of labour ($)	.75	.80	.85	.90
probabilities (%)	.10	.15	.60	.15
Project cost ($000s)	200	250	300	350
probabilities	.05	.10	.75	.10
Life of project (years)	10	11	12	13
probabilities (%)	.05	.10	.80	.05

As mentioned earlier, the probabilities indicated under each variable (volume, price, etc.) are provided by managers based on their experience or calculated guesses.

The results of the risk analysis calculations could read as follows:

IRR Range (%)	Number of Occurrences	% of Total	% Cumulative
5–8	4	.4	.4
8–11	30	3.0	3.4
11–14	133	13.3	16.7
14–17	323	32.3	49.0
17–20	283	28.3	77.3
20–23	167	16.7	94.0
23–26	43	4.3	98.3
26–29	17	1.7	100.0
Total	1,000	100.0	

The above means that there are four chances in 1,000 that the project's internal rate of return will fall between 5% and 8%, 30 chances in 1,000 that it will fall between 8% and 11%, etc. The report could also indicate the following:

Minimum rate of return	5.3%
Maximum rate of return	29.3%
Mean	18.1%

Probability
68.3% that the return will fall between 15.6% and 22.0%
95.5% that the return will fall between 9.0% and 23.9%
99.7% that the return will fall between 5.9% and 29.0%

This example indicates that of the 1,000 internal rate of return outcomes (an arbitrary number chosen by financial analysts) under the most pessimistic circumstances, the financial return is 5.3%, while the most optimistic calculated

Chapter 8: Capital Investment Decisions

guesses would predict a 29.3% return. Within these two extremes lies a full range of outcomes to help judge the risk factors inherent in a project.

Why Capital Projects Are Not Approved

Two factors can prevent a business from proceeding with a large number of capital projects: cash insufficiency and hurdle rate (which determines in a large measure the extent to which projects are satisfactory or viable).

Cash Insufficiency

Cash insufficiency

Not enough cash generated by a capital project to pay for fixed charges.

Cash insufficiency means that a project does not generate enough cash to pay for fixed charges. Before overloading a business with too much debt (a cheaper source than equity), management will calculate the appropriate debt-to-total-capitalization ratio. The risk factor largely determines this optimum capital mix. If a firm adds too much debt to its capital structure, future fixed charges will increase, affecting the firm's cash position. The question to answer is: Will the capital projects generate sufficient cash to meet proposed fixed commitments, or will there be a cash insufficiency?

Hurdle Rate

As mentioned earlier, hurdle rate is used to rank the financial desirability of capital projects according to their cost of capital. Essentially, capital budgeting is the process of finding the break-even point between the yield of a capital project and the weighted cost of capital. Obviously, the wider the spread between the aggregate yield or internal rate of return of the projects and the cost of capital, the better it is for the shareholders.

To find this break-even point, the aggregate internal rate of return must, of course, be known. It is also essential to pinpoint the sources (e.g., internal financing, such as retained earning, and external financing, such as bond or share issues) and cost of the capital needed to finance all capital projects.

The capital project selection system is often referred to as the capital rationing process, meaning that only the most viable projects—that is, those that exceed the hurdle rate—are approved. Figure 8.3 presents this process. As shown in the figure, the company's total capital projects requested amount to $7 million, comprising ten individual projects (A to J) and several other minor projects grouped under K. The aggregate or cumulative internal rate of return for all projects is 17.0%. Based on the company's cost of capital, management decides to set the project's hurdle rate (or cut-off rate) at 15.0%. (This rate does not necessarily reflect the cost of capital; instead, it shows the minimum acceptable rate of return.) As indicated, if the company invests beyond $5 million (dotted line), it may have to obtain an extra $2 million at a higher interest rate.

FIGURE 8.3   CAPITAL-RATIONING PROCESS

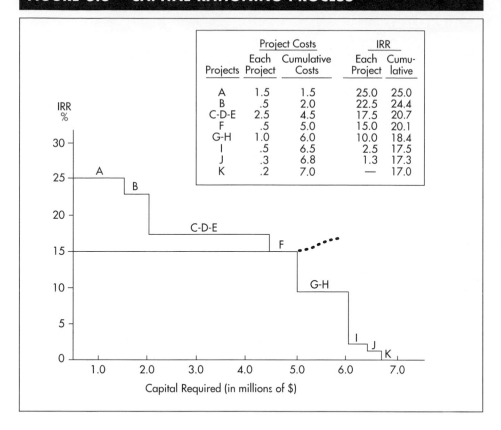

Projects	Project Costs		IRR	
	Each Project	Cumulative Costs	Each Project	Cumu-lative
A	1.5	1.5	25.0	25.0
B	.5	2.0	22.5	24.4
C-D-E	2.5	4.5	17.5	20.7
F	.5	5.0	15.0	20.1
G-H	1.0	6.0	10.0	18.4
I	.5	6.5	2.5	17.5
J	.3	6.8	1.3	17.3
K	.2	7.0	—	17.0

✳ Decision-Making in Action

Let's now turn to analyzing capital expenditure projects to see how these various capital budgeting techniques are used. Three projects will be analyzed:

- modernization;
- launching a new product; and
- constructing a new plant (New-Tech Inc.).

MODERNIZATION

Suppose a business contemplates investing $1.5 million to modernize a plant. On the basis of the following information, it is possible to determine whether a capital expenditure is worth the investment.

- The economic life of the project is estimated at ten years.

- The savings (or net cash inflow) are estimated at $300,000 per year.
- The cost of capital is 14%.

This information is sufficient to assess whether the project has some economic merit. By referring to the discount tables, we can calculate the present value of the future savings by using the 14% discount factors. If the sum of the future savings, discounted to today's value, exceeds the $1.5 million initial capital outlay, it means that the project is economically attractive. If, however, the sum of the inflow is negative, it means that the project should not proceed. As shown in Table 8.6, since the difference between the initial cash outflow and the future cash inflow is positive by $64,830, the project could very well be approved.

TABLE 8.6 CASH FLOW FORECAST FOR MODERNIZING A PROJECT

Year	Outflow	Inflows	Discount Factors @ 14%	Present Value
0	$1,500,000	—	—	($1,500,000)
1	—	$ 300,000	0.87719	263,157
2	—	300,000	0.76947	230,841
3	—	300,000	0.67497	202,491
4	—	300,000	0.59208	177,624
5	—	300,000	0.51937	155,810
6	—	300,000	0.45559	136,676
7	—	300,000	0.39964	119,891
8	—	300,000	0.35056	105,167
9	—	300,000	0.30751	92,252
10	—	300,000	0.26974	80,921
	Total Inflows			+ $1,564,830
	Net Difference			+ $ 64,830

FIGURE 8.4 GRAPHIC ILLUSTRATION OF THE YEARLY CASH INFLOWS AND OUTFLOWS

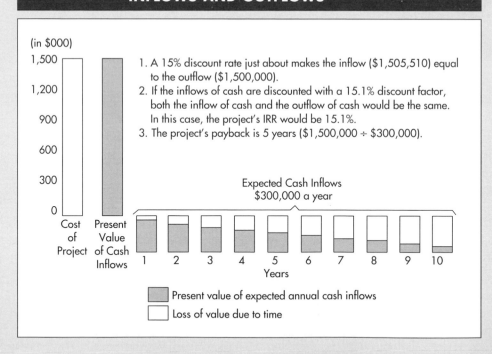

1. A 15% discount rate just about makes the inflow ($1,505,510) equal to the outflow ($1,500,000).
2. If the inflows of cash are discounted with a 15.1% discount factor, both the inflow of cash and the outflow of cash would be the same. In this case, the project's IRR would be 15.1%.
3. The project's payback is 5 years ($1,500,000 ÷ $300,000).

Figure 8.4 graphically displays the results of the present value calculations for individual years. The shaded squares show the present values of each $300,000 receipt, while the white portion of each square shows the loss in value because of time.

However, since we are dealing with an annuity situation, instead of using Table B (present value of a single sum), we can use Table D and look under column 14% (cost of capital) for ten years. By multiplying the $300,000 expected savings by the 5.2161 discount factor, we get the same number: $1,564,830 for a positive $64,830 net present value. If we used a 15% discount factor, the net present value would be $5,510. In this case the internal rate of return is 15.1%.

The following factors may reinforce or reverse our decision:

- a change in the economic life of the project;
- a change in the income tax bracket;
- a change in the initial cash outflow;
- a change in the cash inflow;
- a change in the cost of capital;
- a change in the expected return on the capital assets;
- the economic attractiveness of other projects considered by the company;
- the shortage in the amount of funds available;
- the nature of other projects. (Other projects may generate a lesser return but may be required by law—for example, antipollution equipment.)

LAUNCHING A NEW PRODUCT

Let's look now at the launching of a new product.

Table 8.7 gives detailed information about the project and is divided into four parts:

- Part A shows the various elements related to the $2.0 million cost or cash outflow of the project.
- Part B gives the project's annual pro-forma income after taxes for five years.
- Part C shows the project's annual pro-forma income statement and cash flow for five years.
- Part D gives the overview of the project's five-year cash flow forecast (the cash inflow and cash outflow for each year).

Here are the assumptions related to the project. As shown in Part A, management invests $2.0 million in the project; $150,000 in research and development (R & D), $1,350,000 in equipment, machinery, and other assets; and $500,000 in working capital. The investment in working capital consists of the following:

Accounts receivable	$600,000	cash outflow
Inventory	300,000	cash outflow
Total	900,000	
Accounts payable	400,000	cash inflow
Net working capital	$500,000	net cash outflow

Part B gives the five-year pro-forma income statement. If management wants to calculate the return outcomes of the project by using the accounting methods, it could compute the following yearly returns:

| | Yearly return on | |
	Capital Employed (%)	Capital Assets (%)
Year 1	2.5	3.3
Year 2	10.0	13.3
Year 3	18.7	25.0
Year 4	25.5	34.0
Year 5	34.5	46.0
Average return	18.2	24.3

| | Return on average investment | | Return on depreciated assets | |
	Capital Employed (%)	Capital Assets (%)	Capital Employed (%)	Capital Assets (%)
Year 1	4.0	6.7	2.9	4.2
Year 2	16.0	26.7	14.3	22.2
YEAR 3	30.0	50.0	34.0	66.6
Year 4	41.0	68.0	63.7	170.0
Year 5	55.2	92.0	138.0	+ 1000.0

Part C of Table 8.7 gives a more detailed forecast of management's pro-forma income statement and statement of cash flow. The most difficult part of a project analysis is not calculating the payback or the internal rate of return but making the forecast related to the project itself. For example, the marketing department would have to estimate the company's sales revenue, which includes both the number of units sold (or service) and the unit selling price, adjusted for inflation.

The manufacturing department would have to forecast the cost of goods sold, which includes the cost of raw materials, freight-in, and the transformation of the raw materials into finished products. This forecast also includes anticipated inflation increments over the life of the project.

Similar cost forecasts would also have to be prepared by other organizational units that are expected to be part of the project. As indicated, this forecast takes into account the capital cost allowance (the tax-deductible item) rather than depreciation to calculate the income taxes to be paid each year over the life of the project. In order to determine the yearly cash flow generated by the project, since capital cost allowance is not a cash outflow (but a tax-deductible expense), it is added back to the income after taxes.

Part D of Table 8.7 gives the actual disbursements (cash outflow) and receipts (cash inflow) of the project. There are two distinct cash disbursements: the $1.5 million related to R & D, purchase of the machinery and equipment, investment in other assets made during year 0; and the $500,000 disbursements related to working capital, which in this case are spread equally over years 1 and 2. The third line is the pro-forma cash inflow generated by the project. This line is drawn from Part C of the table. Other assumptions related to the project are that the assets have a five-year life span and that, at the end, the assets (equipment, machinery, and other assets) will be sold for $300,000, and the $500,000 in working capital will be totally recovered.

Based on the above cash flow, the project's payback period, net present value, and internal rate of return are as follows:

A. Payback period is 4.1 years.

	Annual net cash flow (000s)	Cumulative cash flow (000s)
Year 0	($1,500.0)	($1,500.0)
Year 1	50.0	(1,450.0)
Year 2	150.0	(1,300.0)
Year 3	550.0	(750.0)
Year 4	650.0	(100.0)
Year 5	$1,600.0	$ 1,500.0 ← Payback

B. Net present value (NPV) based on a 10% cost of capital

	Annual net cash flow (000s)	Discount factors	Present values (000s)
Year 0	($1,500.0)	1.000	($1,500.0)
Year 1	50.0	0.909	45.4
Year 2	150.0	0.826	123.9
Year 3	550.0	0.751	413.1
Year 4	650.0	0.683	444.0
Year 5	$1,600.0	0.621	993.6
Present value			2,020.0
Net present value (NPV)			+ $ 520.0

TABLE 8.7 EVALUATING A CAPITAL EXPENDITURE PROJECT

A. The project

Assets	
R & D	$ 150,000
Equipment/machinery	850,000
Other assets	500,000
Net working capital	500,000
Total capital employed	$ 2,000,000

B. The pro-forma income statement

Years	Income After Taxes
1	$ 50,000
2	200,000
3	375,000
4	510,000
5	690,000

C. Pro-forma income statement and cash flow

Years	1	2	3	4	5
Sales revenue	$ 1,300.0	$ 1,700.0	$ 2,415.0	$ 3,000.0	$ 3,700.0
Cost of goods sold	600.0	700.0	990.0	1,240.0	1,560.0
Gross margin	700.0	1,000.0	1,425.0	1,760.0	2,140.0
Selling and administrative expenses	350.0	400.0	500.0	600.0	650.0
Income before C.C.A.	350.0	600.0	925.0	1,160.0	1,490.0
C.C.A.	250.0	200.0	175.0	140.0	110.0
Income before taxes	100.0	400.0	750.0	1,020.0	1,380.0
Taxes (50%)	50.0	200.0	375.0	510.0	690.0
Income after taxes	50.0	200.0	375.0	510.0	690.0
Add back C.C.A.	250.0	200.0	175.0	140.0	110.0
Cash flow	$ 300.0	$ 400.0	$ 550.0	$ 650.0	$ 800.0

D. Pro-forma cash flow (000s)

Years	0	1	2	3	4	5
Assets	$(1,500)	—	—	—	—	—
Working capital	—	$(250)	$(250)	—	—	—
Pro-forma cash flow	—	300	400	550	650	800
Sale of assets	—	—	—	—	—	300
Recovery of working capital	—	—	—	—	—	500
Total cash flow	$(1,500)	$ 50	$ 150	$550	$650	$1,600

C. Internal rate of return (IRR) is 18.4%.

	Annual net cash flow (000s	Present values (000s)		
		17%	18%	19%
Year 0	($1,500.0)	($1,500.0)	($1,500.0)	($1,500.0)
Year 1	50.0	42.7	42.4	42.0
Year 2	150.0	109.6	107.7	105.9
Year 3	550.0	343.4	334.7	326.4
Year 4	650.0	346.8	385.3	324.1
Year 5	$1,600.0	729.8	699.4	670.4
Net present value (NPV)		+ $ 72.3	+ $ 19.5	− $ 31.2

Internal rate of return 18.4%

Without a financial calculator or a spreadsheet, the internal rate of return is found on a trial-and-error basis, by using the 17%, 18%, and 19% discount rates until the net present value moves from a positive to a negative. As shown above, the calculation indicates that the internal rate of return is between 18% (net present value of +$19.5 thousand) and 19% (net present value of −$31.2 thousand).

CONSTRUCTING A NEW PLANT (NEW-TECH INC.)

Let's look now at the third capital expenditure project. New-Tech Inc. is contemplating opening a new plant to manufacture pocket calculators. The cost of the project is as follows:

Land	$ 50,000
Building	200,000
Equipment/Machinery	100,000
Trucks	150,000
Total capital assets	$500,000
Net working capital	150,000
Total capital employed	$650,000

The company expects to realize $2.0 million in sales revenue during the first year of operation, which would be maintained during the life of the plant. The company's pro-forma income statement is as follows:

Sales revenue		$2,000,000
Cost of goods sold		1,700,000
Gross margin		300,000
CCA	$ 25,000	
Interest	40,000	
Other operating expenses	145,000	
Total operating expenses		$ 210,000
Profit before taxes		90,000
Income taxes		40,000
Profit after taxes		$ 50,000

The company engineer indicates that the life span of the plant is 15 years. According to the company's real estate division manager, in 15 years, the market value of the land will have increased to $150,000, and the residual value of the buildings, equipment, and trucks will be in the order of $150,000. Working capital is expected to be totally recovered at the end of the project.

The company will borrow from different sources to finance the project, and the cost of capital, according to the company's treasurer, will be 11%. Management would like to obtain at least 25% on the project (hurdle rate). If you were a member of the management committee, would you go along with this proposal?

Table 8.8 gives the payback period, the net present value, and the internal rate of return. As shown on the following page, the first step is to calculate the annual cash flow from operations. This is done by rearranging the income statement and converting the

$50,000 after-tax income into cash flow; as shown, the calculation gives an amount of $97,280. Here are some of the assumptions and the arithmetic:

Gross margin		$300,000
Less: CCA	$ 25,000	
Other expenses	145,000	170,000
Profit before taxes		130,000
Income taxes		57,720
Profit after taxes		72,280
Add back CCA		25,000
Cash flow from operations		$ 97,280

It is assumed that the $300,000 gross margin is all cash inflow. The two other expense items deducted from the gross margin are CCA (for the purpose of keeping the example simple, CCA is treated on a straight-line basis), and other operating expenses. Because the company is in the 44.4% tax bracket (from the projected income statement, $40,000 ÷ $90,000), the project itself will be taxed for $57,720 ($130,000 × 44.4%). Interest expenses are excluded from the calculation because one of the objectives of finding the "internally generated return" (internal rate of return) is to compare it with the cost of the capital— that is, funds obtained from external sources. CCA is simply used as a tax shield; it is added back to the profit after taxes, which gives a net yearly cash inflow from operations in the amount of $97,280. As shown in Table 8.8, using the cost of capital (11%) as the discount rate gives the project a positive net present value of $158,445. On the basis of this discount rate, company management would be tempted to approve the project. However, because of the risk factor, management has established a 25% hurdle rate. Using 25% as the discount rate gives the project a $228,737 negative net present value, which is far less than expected. As shown in the table, using 15% as the discount rate gives the project a negative net present value of $6,300. With a financial calculator or a spreadsheet, we obtain exactly 14.81%. The bottom line is this: The project generates a 14.8% internal rate of return, and after the cost of capital of 11% (or paying the external cost of financing the project), the company would be left with only 3.8%. This is much less than the 14.0% spread (25.0% − 11.0%) that management was hoping to realize to offset the risk associated with the project.

TABLE 8.8   NEW-TECH INC.

Year	Cash Flow	25% Factors	25% Cash Flow	11% Factors	11% Cash Flow	15% Factors	15% Cash Flow
0	$ (500,000)	1.00000	$ (500,000)	1.0000	$ (500,000)	1.0000	$ (500,000)
1	$ (150,000)	.80000	$ (120,000)	.9009	$ (135,135)	.8696	$ (130,435)
1	$ 97,280						
↕		3.85930	$ 375,432	7.1909	$ 699,530	5.8474	$ 568,835
15	$ 97,280						
15	$ 450,000	.03518	$ 15,831	.03518	$ 94,050	.1229	$ 55,300
Net present value:			$ (228,737)		+ $ 158,445		$ (6,300)

Payback period: 6.7 years

Internal rate of return: 14.8%

Chapter Summary

Objective 1 ➠   Capital budgeting is the process of planning and evaluating capital projects and deciding which will generate the best returns over an extended period. Capital projects are critical because they can alter the financial destiny of a business.

Objective 2 ➠   Capital projects fall into two groups: compulsory investments, which should be done in order to sustain the life of a business, and opportunity investments, which can be done to make the business grow.

Objective 3 ➠   The capital budgeting process includes six key steps: establishing corporate priorities and strategic objectives; formulating the plans and capital expenditure projects; ranking projects through capital budgeting methods (priorities, operations and return/risk); calculating the cost of capital; determining the hurdle rate; and project selection and implementation.

Objective 4 ➠   Capital-budgeting elements include cash outflow, such as the initial cash outlays, net working capital, and normal capital additions; cash inflow, which includes net income, noncash expenses, such as depreciation and the residual value; the establishment of the economic life of a project; and sunk costs.

Objective 5 ➠   Many different techniques are used for evaluating and ranking capital projects. There are the accounting methods, the payback method, the net present value method, the internal rate of return, and the profitability index. Time-value yardsticks are effective for measuring the financial desirability of capital projects in view of the fact that future cash inflows (savings or additional profits), when discounted at a predetermined interest rate (usually the weighted cost of capital), are compared to the initial cash outflow (initial cash disbursement).

Objective 6 ➠   More sophisticated methods are used to evaluate the element of risk; they are the sensitivity analysis and the risk analysis. Both have benefits and drawbacks.

Objective 7 ➠   Two factors can prevent a capital project from going forward: lack of cash and the hurdle rate.

Key Terms

Accounting methods	Opportunity investment
Capital investment	Payback period
Cash insufficiency	Payback reciprocal
Compulsory investment	Profitability index
Discounted payback	Residual value
Economic life	Risk analysis
Expense investment	Sensitivity analysis
Hurdle rate	Sunk costs

Review Questions

1. Why are capital projects so critical?

2. Differentiate between a capital investment and an expense investment.

3. What are compulsory investments? Give several examples.

4. What are opportunity investments? Give several examples.

5. What are the critical steps involved in the capital-budgeting process?

6. What items are usually included in the initial cash outflow?

7. Why is working capital part of cash disbursements in a capital investment, and what is its makeup?

8. Use an example to show how you would calculate the cash inflow by using the income after taxes.

9. What do we mean by residual value?

10. What do we mean by the economic life of a project?

11. Why are accounting methods not reliable yardsticks for measuring the economic desirability of capital projects?

12. Differentiate between "time risk" and "risk conditions."

13. What are the arguments for and against the payback method?

14. What does the net present value measure?

15. What are the arguments for using the net present value method of calculating the economic viability of capital projects?

16. How is the internal rate of return calculated?

17. How is the profitability index calculated?

18. What is sensitivity analysis?

19. What is risk analysis?

20. What factors prevent a business from proceeding with a large number of capital projects?

21. Why is capital cost allowance instead of the depreciation expense used in capital budgeting?

Discussion Questions

1. Do you believe that "capital budgets are neither absolute limits on investment nor are they automatically affected by project ranking on purely quantitative grounds"?

2. Why is it that cost of capital affects investment capability and risk tolerance?

Testing Your Comprehension

True/False Questions

_____ 1. A capital investment generates benefits for a short time period (less than one year).

_____ 2. Legislative investments are considered compulsory investments.

_____ 3. Opportunity investments are made to improve the return on a company's investment.

_____ 4. In capital budgeting, working capital is usually considered as cash inflow.

_____ 5. Capital cost allowance, not depreciation, is used in capital project analysis to calculate the amount of income taxes to be paid.

_____ 6. Sunk costs means funds that should have been spent on a project prior to the decision to proceed with it.

_____ 7. A good argument for using the accounting methods to measure capital projects is that cash flow, rather than profit, is used.

_____ 8. The payback method measures the period of time it takes for the cash outflow of a project to be totally recovered by the anticipated cash inflow.

_____ 9. The payback method measures risk conditions, not time risk.

_____ 10. The payback reciprocal is a capital budgeting technique that gives a rough estimate of the return on investment of a capital project.

_____ 11. The net present value is a technique that measures the difference between the sum of all undiscounted cash inflow and discounted cash outflow.

_____ 12. The internal rate of return can be described as the specific interest rate used to discount all future cash inflows, so that their present value equals the initial cash outflow.

_____ 13. An advantage of the internal rate of return is that it focuses on profit after taxes instead of cash inflow.

_____ 14. When the profitability index shows .94, it means that management should approve the project.

_____ 15. Sensitivity analysis deals with probabilities and gives hundreds of returns.

_____ 16. Risk analysis produces a full spectrum of return outcomes, from the most pessimistic to the most optimistic.

_____ 17. The hurdle rate is sometime used to calculate the net present value.

_____ 18. Cash insufficiency and the hurdle rate are the two main factors that can prevent a business from proceeding with a large number of capital projects.

Multiple-Choice Questions

1. An expense investment is:
   a. durable
   b. significant
   c. spread over many years
   d. capitalized
   e. impermanent

2. The following is an opportunity investment:
   a. building a warehouse
   b. modernizing a plant
   c. launching a new product
   d. pollution abatement equipment
   e. building a cafeteria

3. A cash outflow in capital budgeting includes spending funds on:
   a. salaries
   b. advertising
   c. travel
   d. equipment
   e. depreciation

4. Capital cost allowance is considered:
   a. a cash expense
   b. a tax relief
   c. a deduction against working capital
   d. a cash outflow
   e. an asset

5. A sunk cost is considered a cost that is:
   a. not included in a capital project
   b. included in a capital project
   c. included as an expense investment
   d. part of outgoing cash flow
   e. part of the payback calculation

6. An argument for using the accounting rate of return methods is that they:
   a. are accurate
   b. are reliable
   c. are simple to calculate
   d. provide a true yield
   e. focus on the entire life of the project

7. The payback method measures the time it takes for the cash outflow of a project to be totally recovered by:
   a. sales revenue
   b. profit after taxes
   c. profit before taxes
   d. cash inflow
   e. net cash flow

8. A disadvantage of the payback method is that it:
   a. ignores cash inflow earned before the payback point
   b. ignores cash inflow earned after the payback point
   c. is difficult to calculate
   d. measures only risk conditions
   e. does not take into account cash flow

9. The net present value technique measures the difference between the sum of all cash inflow and cash outflow discounted by the:
   a. cost of financing
   b. internal rate of return
   c. cost of capital
   d. inflation rate
   e. Bank of Canada interest rate

10. The internal rate of return is achieved when the cash outflow equals the:
    a. net future value
    b. net present value
    c. discounted income after taxes
    d. undiscounted cash inflow
    e. discounted cash inflow

11. The profitability index shows the ratio of the present value of cash inflow to the:
    a. present value of the undiscounted profit before taxes
    b. cash outflow
    c. future value of the cash inflow
    d. net present value of the cash flow
    e. discounted income after taxes

12. The hurdle rate is sometimes used to calculate the:
    a. payback period
    b. internal rate of return
    c. profitability index
    d. net present value
    e. accounting rate of return

Fill-in-the-Blanks Questions

1. A _____ investment is a project that requires extensive financial resources (cash outflow) made for the purpose of generating a return (cash inflow).

2. A _____ investment may be made for contingency, legislative, and cosmetic reasons.

3. A cash _____ is referred to as the initial disbursement made to launch a capital project.

4. In capital budgeting, the _____ _____ value represents the sale of an asset or a business at the end of its physical life.

5. A _____ cost is considered an investment cost incurred prior to making the decision to proceed with a capital project.

6. In capital budgeting, the accounting methods used to determine the return on investment of capital projects make use of data presented on _____ .

7. The _____ method calculates the number of years required for a capital investment to generate enough undiscounted cash inflow to cover the initial cash outflow.

8. The payback _____ is a capital budgeting technique that gives a rough estimate of the return on investment of a capital project.

9. The net present value technique measures the difference between the sum of all cash inflow and the cash outflow _____ _____ at a predetermined interest rate.

10. The internal rate of return can be described as the specific interest rate used to discount all future cash inflows, so that their present value _____ the initial cash outflow.

11. The _____ gives a ratio of the present value of the cash inflow to the present value of the cash outflow discounted at a predetermined rate of interest.

12. _____ analysis involves the identification of profitability variations as a result of one or more changes in the base cash related to certain key elements of a project.

13. _____ analysis is the process of attaching probabilities to individual estimates in capital project's base case.

14. Two reasons can prevent a business from proceeding with a large number of capital projects: cash insufficiency and the _____ _____ rate.

Learning Exercises

Exercise 1(a)

The Millers are considering a $200,000 expansion for their existing retail outlet. That expansion would generate $35,000 in cash each year over the next ten years. CompuTech's cost of capital is 8%. On the basis of this information, calculate CompuTech's:

1. payback period;

2. net present value;

3. internal rate of return; and

4. profitability index.

Exercise 1(b)

XYZ Inc. wants to invest $1 million in a capital project that would generate $300,000 in savings each year. The physical life of the project is ten years, and the cost of capital is 10%. By using the above information, calculate the:

1. payback period;

2. net present value;

3. internal rate of return;

4. profitability index.

Exercise 2(a)

A retailer is interested in selling a retail business to the Millers for $1 million. This includes all physical assets, the working capital, and goodwill. The Millers estimate, based on the company's historical financial statements, that the annual cash flow from the retail store would be in the $195,000 range. In 20 years, the Millers think that they could get $4 million for the store.

Should the Millers buy the retail store if they want to earn 20% on their investment?

To answer this question, calculate the:

1. payback period;

2. net present value;

3. internal rate of return; and

4. profitability index.

Exercise 2(b)

Today, you have some cash and the choice of buying a small retail store in a downtown location for $700,000. This includes all physical assets located in the retail store and the inventory. You also have the option of buying $700,000 of investment securities paying 14% interest. The annual cash flow from the retail store operations is expected to be $115,000. In 20 years you plan to retire, and you believe that the store will be sold then for $2 million.

If you wished to make the same return on your investment as you would with the investment securities, would you buy the retail store?

To answer this question, calculate the:

1. payback period;

2. net present value;

3. internal rate of return; and

4. profitability index.

Exercise 3(a)

The Millers are considering two options: to buy or to lease another retail outlet.

OPTION 1: PURCHASE

Year

0	Cost	$ 900,000
1	Additional cost	100,000
1	Cash flow from operations	150,000
2	Cash flow from operations	300,000
3	Cash flow from operations	400,000
4	Cash flow from operations	500,000
5	Cash flow from operations	600,000
5	Cash flow from sale of business	1,000,000

If the Millers want to make 30%, should they buy the retail store? To answer this question, calculate the following:

1. net present value; and

2. internal rate of return.

OPTION 2: LEASING

If the Millers lease a store in another town, the net yearly cash flow from operations and lease payments is estimated at $70,000 (net) from year 1 to year 5.

1. If they want to make 30% on their investment, should they lease the store?

2. Which of the two options should they choose?

Exercise 3(b)

You have two options: to buy or lease a video store.

OPTION 1: PURCHASE

Year

0	Cost	$300,000
1	Additional cost	80,000
1	Cash flow from operations	45,000
2	Cash flow from operations	70,000
3	Cash flow from operations	90,000
4	Cash flow from operations	105,000
5	Cash flow from operations	140,000
6	Cash flow from operations	160,000
7	Cash flow from operations	165,000
8	Cash flow from operations	170,000
9	Cash flow from operations	175,000
10	Cash flow from operations	180,000
11	Cash flow from sale of business	400,000

If you want to make 25% on your money, should you buy the video store? To answer this question, calculate the following:

1. net present value; and

2. internal rate of return.

OPTION 2: LEASING

You can lease a video store in another town. The net yearly cash flow from operations and lease payments is estimated at $45,000 (net) from year 1 to year 10.

1. If you want to make 25% on your investment, should you lease the video store?

2. Which of the two options would you choose?

Exercise 4(a)

After looking at several options, including those described in Exercises 2(a) and 3(a), the Millers were more interested in opening a new retail outlet. The investment in capital assets in the new outlet is estimated at $350,000, and an additional $175,000 in working capital (accounts receivable and inventory) is to be spent over the first two years of operations. The economic life of the project is estimated at ten years with a resale value of $900,000. The cost of capital is estimated at 11%, and the Millers would like to yield a 20% internal rate of return. CompuTech's second retail store will generate the following cash flow during a ten-year period:

Year	Cash inflow	Cash outflow
0		$350,000
1	$ 75,000	100,000
2	80,000	75,000
3	100,000	
4	125,000	
5	140,000	
6–10	150,000	
10	900,000	

1. What is CompuTech's net present value using 11% and 20%?

2. What is the retail store's payback period?

3. What is CompuTech's internal rate of return?

4. What is the profitability index?

5. Should the Millers proceed?

Exercise 4(b)

Aaron Manufacturing Inc. intends to invest $70,000 in a modernization capital project that will generate the following cash inflow during eight years:

Year	
1	$12,000
2	17,000
3	18,000
4	23,000
5	15,000
6	11,000
7	9,000
8	8,000

1. Calculate the net present value at 12% and 18%.

2. Determine the internal rate of return of the capital project.

3. If the annual cash flow were $15,000 per year for eight years, what would be the net present value at 12% and 18%?

4. What level of annual cash flow would be required to obtain a 20% internal rate of return?

5. How would the results of (1) and (2) change if there was a capital recovery of $40,000 at the end of year 8?

Exercise 5

Luster Electronics Company is analyzing two capital projects, project A and project B. Each has an initial capital cost of $12,000, and the cost of capital for both projects is 12%. The projected annual cash flow is as follows:

Year	Project A	Project B
0	–$12,000	–$12,000
1	7,000	5,000
2	4,000	3,500
3	3,500	3,000
4	3,000	2,500
5	2,300	2,000
6	2,000	1,500

1. For each project, calculate the:
   - payback period;
   - net present value;
   - internal rate of return; and
   - profitability index (using the 12% discount rate).

2. Which project or projects should be accepted if the two are independent?

3. Which project should be accepted if the two are mutually exclusive?

Exercise 6

Smith Manufacturing is subject to a 50% tax rate and a 12% hurdle rate. Company management is considering purchasing a new finishing machine that is expected to cost $200,000 and reduce materials waste by $60,000 a year. The machine is expected to have a ten-year life span and will have a zero salvage value. For the purpose of this analysis, straight-line depreciation will be used instead of the CCA.

1. Calculate the cash flow.

2. Calculate the present value, the net present value, the internal rate of return, and the profitability index.

Cases

Case 1: Excel Products Ltd.

One of Excel Products Ltd.'s strategies is to invest in new product lines. This involves periodic investments in research and development, plant, equipment, and working capital. This year, the company invested $4 million in a research and development project to develop a new product.

The managers are not sure whether they should invest an additional $9 million in capital assets for the launching of the new product line. The economic life

Chapter 8: Capital Investment Decisions

of the project is expected to be 12 years, and straight-line depreciation will be taken over the project's life span. At the end of the life of the project, it is expected that the equipment and machinery will be sold for $2 million.

Working capital will also be invested over the first three years: $2 million during the first year, $1 million during the second, and $500,000 during the third; and $2.9 million of that amount is expected to be recovered at the end of the 12 years. The marketing organization estimates that $1.2 million will be spent to promote the new product during the first year.

The company estimates that income before depreciation, promotional expenses, and income taxes will be $3 million a year during the first five years, $4 million per year for the following five years, and $5 million during the last two years.

The company's income tax rate is 46%, and cost of capital is 10%. For the purpose of this analysis, the depreciation expense will be used as the CCA tax deduction.

On the basis of the above information, calculate the company's:

1. net present value;
2. internal rate of return; and
3. profitability index.

Case 2: Koplaye Instruments Inc.

The board of directors of Koplaye Instruments Inc. is considering investing more than $5.8 million in the construction of a new plant to produce widgets for export. Although several members of the board have reservations about the project, many believe that the company will be making a wise decision.

The treasurer of the company has been able to raise funds from different sources and indicates that the company's cost of capital would be 11%.

However, the board members feel that the project is not too risky and that a 15% hurdle rate would be acceptable.

The engineers of the company present the following information and estimate the life of the project to be ten years.

	Costs (in $000s)	CCA
Cost of assets		
Land	$ 600	
Buildings	2,000	5%
Machinery/equipment	2,500	20%
Research and development	500	20%
Other assets	200	10%
Total assets	$5,800	

The marketing department indicates that there would be $300,000 invested in working capital in year 1, $250,000 in year 2, and $200,000 in year 3.

The controller provides the highlights of the project's pro-forma sales and cost data.

Year	Sales revenue (in $000s)	Cost of Goods sold (in $000s)	Other expenses (in $000s)
1	$5,000	$2,000	$ 700
2	5,500	2,200	700
3	6,000	2,400	750
4	6,500	2,600	800
5	7,000	2,800	800
6	7,500	3,000	850
7	8,000	3,200	900
8	8,000	3,200	900
9	8,000	3,200	900
10	8,500	3,400	950

The company's controller estimates that $600,000 worth of the working capital will be recovered at the end of the project. The engineers also estimate that about $2 million of the capital assets will be sold in year 10. The company's income tax rate is 46%.

With the above information, calculate the project's:

1. annual cash flow forecast during the ten-year period by using the actual CCA rates;
2. payback period;
3. net present value using the cost of capital and the hurdle rate;
4. internal rate of return; and
5. profitability index.

9

Budgeting, Financial Planning, and Controlling

Learning Objectives

After reading this chapter, you should be able to:

1. Describe the reasons for budgeting and the responsibility-centre concept.

2. Explain the budgeting process within the overall planning framework.

3. Present the different types of budgets.

4. Show how budgeting can become an effective management exercise.

5. Discuss why cost accounting is essential for managers.

6. Describe financial planning in terms of preparing pro-forma financial statements.

7. Explain the meaning of sustainable growth and how it can be calculated.

8. Evaluate the financial health of a business and how it is calculated.

9. Comment on the importance of controlling, the control system, and the different types of controls.

Chapter Outline

OPENING CASE

After spending several months going over the economics involved in opening a new retail store, the Millers were now preparing their investment proposal to be presented to several investors. In 2004 CompuTech was able to reduce its debt and purchase all assets from internally generated funds (see Exercise 5(a) in Chapter 3). The Millers were also pleased with their financial results in terms of managing their liquidity and debt structure. The financial statements also revealed that they had the ability to manage their assets (total assets turnover is 1.57 times) well and generate a reasonable return on the company's assets (12.3%). Those financial statements and financial ratios that were presented and calculated in Exercise 4 of Chapter 4 would be presented to investors.

CompuTech's break-even point, which was calculated in Exercise 5(a) of Chapter 5, also shows positive results only two years after the company started ($327,272 or 77.8% of the revenue). Furthermore, Exercise 4(a) of Chapter 8 reveals that the new retail outlet would be a viable venture; in fact, it shows an excellent internal rate of return (25.5%). Even the financing package that the Millers were considering appeared reasonable. As mentioned in the Opening Case in Chapter 6, of the $449,000 that they required for the new retail store ($350,000 in capital assets and $99,000 in working capital), 35% would be financed from internal operations, that is approximately $157,000, and 15%, or approximately $70,000, from shareholders. The business and shareholders would therefore provide 50% of the funds. The Millers would be seeking 50% of the funding requirements from lenders ($150,000 from long-term lenders and $72,000 from short-term lenders).

Everything looked positive. However, the Millers realized that they had to present to the lenders and to potential shareholders their projected financial statements about the company for the next several years as well as a detailed cash budget for 2005. They also had to prove that they had an efficient system in place to help them manage their monthly cash budget and to pay their bills as they came due. They also realized that the banks would not expect to look at the company's detailed cost structure. Still, the Millers planned to show them that they knew, through their cost accounting system, how they made informed business decisions and that they had in place an effective control system to reveal, in a precise and timely way, good or bad operating and financial results.

As part of their investment proposal, the Millers were to include the following financial reports:

- last two years' financial statements;
- personal financial statements;
- projected income statements (three years);
- projected balance sheets (three years);
- projected statement of changes in financial position or cash flows (three years);
- projected working capital requirements (one year);
- monthly cash budget (one year);
- detailed sources and uses of funds (one year);
- credit references; and
- loan repayment schedule.

In addition to the above information, the Millers were prepared to demonstrate that CompuTech would be able to manage its 90% increase in sales revenue in 2005 and would more than double income after taxes (sustainable growth). The Millers also wanted to show that the company's overall financial health position (Z-score) is excellent.

The Millers wanted to prepare a business plan to satisfy not only investors' needs but also, more importantly, their own needs. They realized that planning and budgeting were prerequisites to the success of any business and were prepared to take the time to go about their planning activity in an accomplished and professional way.

This chapter examines in detail three key topics:

1. how a business should go about preparing different types of budgets;
2. how to prepare projected financial statements; and
3. how managers should monitor their business activities through effective control systems.

Introduction

This chapter deals with three major themes: budgeting, financial planning, and controlling. Of these, budgeting is probably the most crucial. Fixing corporate objectives and priorities, determining departmental and unit goals, formulating programs and policies, developing market/product strategies, and writing detailed operational plans and procedures are all essential steps in arriving at a perfectly orchestrated planning effort. Individually, these steps can accomplish very little; they become meaningful only as part of an integrated whole. These planning efforts are translated into the common language of business—dollars—through budgeting.

Financial planning involves combining all individual operating budgets (sales, manufacturing, administration, R & D, etc.) into pro-forma or projected financial statements such as the income statement, the balance sheet, and the statement of cash flows, and ensuring that the business grows without depleting its physical, human, and financial resources.

Controlling is the feedback system designed to compare actual performance to predetermined standards, in order to identify deviations, measure their significance, and take any action required to assure that all corporate resources are being used in the most effective and efficient way possible for achieving corporate objectives.

Budgeting

Objective 1 ▶

Budgeting

Process by which management allocates corporate resources, evaluates financial outcomes, and establishes systems to control operational and financial performance.

Budgeting is the process by which management allocates corporate resources, evaluates the financial outcome of its decisions, and establishes the financial and operational profile against which future results will be measured. If managers regard budgeting simply as a mechanical exercise, or a yearly ritual performed by planning groups or accountants, they will not really grasp how the company can improve its economic performance and operating efficiencies. This section looks at budgeting by exploring the following questions:

- What part does budgeting play in planning as a whole?
- What can budgeting contribute to the decision-making process?
- What types of budgets are available?
- What information should be considered when formulating a budget?
- What are the pitfalls to avoid if budgeting is to be done effectively?

Before discussing these questions, let's examine the underlying purpose of budgeting and the importance of the responsibility-centre concept.

Reasons for Budgeting

Reasons for budgeting

Improve communication, coordination, decision-making, monitoring, and accountability.

Essentially, **reasons for budgeting** comprise translating corporate intentions into specific tasks and identifies the resources needed by managers to carry them out. To do this well requires effective communication, sound coordination, and a detailed search, by all managers, to find new ways of improving economic performance and efficiencies at the operating level. Budgeting also establishes specific financial and operational boundaries (standards, targets, and ratios) for controlling purposes.

Let's explore the key elements of this brief description and relate them to the role of budgeting within the organization as a whole.

COMMUNICATION Budgeting enforces communication in two directions. Front-line managers must communicate vertically to justify the resources they need to achieve their goals. For example, they will have to explain, in considerable detail, how their tasks will be performed, as well as the scope and volume of their activities. This process is repeated at every echelon in the organization. Thus, budgeting activates communication between superiors and subordinates, and helps affirm their mutual commitment to the firm's goals.

Horizontal communication between organizational units (receivers and providers of services) is also necessary. For example, computer or administrative services must obtain confirmation from, say, the marketing or manufacturing departments about service needs and the resources required for implementing specific projects.

COORDINATION Hundreds of different tasks are performed by an organization's various divisions. To realize the corporate profit goals, these tasks must be synchronized. Unquestionably, budgeting is essential to the creation of a unified whole. For example, budgeting helps to link the number and types of units to be marketed to elements such as number of units that should be manufactured and distributed, the funds needed for credit purposes, and the purchase of new equipment and raw materials.

DECISION-MAKING No other business plan requires more decisions than a budget. Is this particular activity really needed? If yes, how extensive should the service be? What is the most effective way of performing this task? How can we best measure the efficiency of this operation? How relevant is this task to the rest of the organization? What resources are needed to do this job, the project, or the program? How does this activity relate to the overall objectives of the company? All these questions and many more must be scrutinized and resolved before management can arrive at a perfectly balanced profit plan.

MONITORING As indicated earlier, budgeting involves setting standards (e.g., financial and operational performance indicators) that are central to management accountability. When resources are allocated to a manager, they should be accompanied by standards that stipulate, in precise terms, how efficiently they should be deployed. Standards facilitate reporting, and a well-designed reporting system helps management keep up to date on the following issues:

- Are we on target? If not, why?
- Who is responsible for the unfavourable profit performances?
- What impact will an increase in material or labour costs have on profits?
- If we are to maintain or increase profits, should certain costs be trimmed? Should prices be changed?
- What are the causes of the variances in each organizational unit?

PERFORMANCE EVALUATION AND ACCOUNTABILITY Budgeting is a key instrument in the evaluation of a manager's performance and accountability. In the light of a fixed budget, managers can be evaluated from two angles: as planners or decision-makers and as implementers or doers. Those who exceed or underspend their budgets are not necessarily bad or good managers. Nevertheless, budgeting establishes the targets that help gauge managerial performance and accountability, something that cannot be done by intuition and personal judgment alone.

Responsibility Centres

An important task of the budgeting function is to establish a planning and controlling system that enables managers to gauge an organization's operational and financial performance. The management tool that facilitates pinpointing managerial responsibility and accountability for attaining objectives and realizing plans is the **responsibility centre,** the unit headed by a manager accountable for results.

The responsibility centre concept establishes control systems that are used to gauge managerial performance. These controls include costs, revenues, and investment of funds. A responsibility centre manager may be responsible for one or all three.

The responsibility centre concept has led to responsibility centre accounting (also called profitability accounting or activity accounting), which is a system of collecting and reporting revenue and cost information by responsibility centres.

The advantages of responsibility accounting are to:

- facilitate the delegation of decision-making;
- promote the concept of management by objectives, in which managers agree on a set of goals; and
- help use the management-by-exception tool.

The structure of a company's management control system should be tied closely to the company's responsibility centres. According to the responsibility concept, all tasks, duties, or objectives should be assigned to a specific individual in an organization, and he or she should be held accountable for achieving the intended results. Any organizational chart comprises a hierarchical organization structure in which each unit is headed by a responsibility centre manager.

As shown in Figure 9.1, the manager reporting to the director is responsible for specific objectives. For example, a marketing manager may be responsible for introducing a new program by say, October 30 at an estimated cost of $100,000 to generate 150,000 units and $4 million in sales revenue. When a manager accepts the funds to launch a program, he or she is **accountable** for performing the tasks and for realizing the objectives. Here, the manager is responsible for reporting to a superior (the director) about the attainment of the objective, the realization of the plans, and the manner in which the resources were used to realize the objective.

Responsibility centres help to establish effective managerial controls that help to measure organizational units in terms of:

- costs or expenses (ongoing operating costs or capital costs);
- outputs (units produced or revenues);
- inputs (resources consumed to produce the outputs);

Responsibility centre

Organizational unit headed by a manager accountable for results.

Accountable

Manager who accepts responsibility for realizing the objectives and plans and reporting the extent of accomplishments.

FIGURE 9.1 RESPONSIBILITY AND ACCOUNTABILITY PROCESS

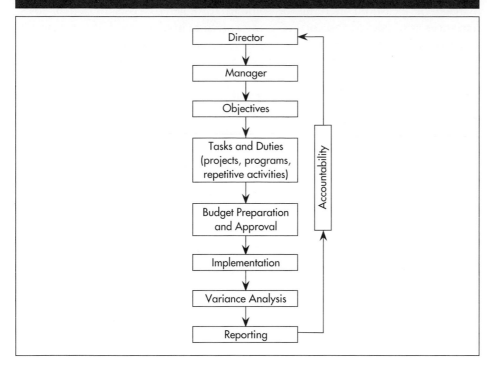

- efficiency (relationship between the outputs and the resources used to produce them);
- effectiveness (degree of success in attaining the objectives); and
- ratios to gauge the operational and financial performance.

There are four **categories of responsibility centres:** revenue centres, cost centres, profit centres, and investment centres.

The *revenue centre* is measured in terms of sales revenue generated by what it sells. There is no need here to relate inputs to outputs. These responsibility centres are found in sales organizations responsible for product lines. For example, a sales manager may be responsible for a region, a district, or a territory. A revenue centre usually has few costs (e.g., salaries, rent, lease). Revenue centre managers are responsible for sales volume, selling price, and sales revenue. In service organizations, this manager would be responsible for billing rates, billable time, and cost per hour of employee time.

The *cost centre*, also called an expense centre, measures an organizational unit's resource inputs—that is, the costs used to make a product or to provide a service. It is called "cost" because the responsibility-centre manager's performance is measured in terms of the funds spent to make a product or provide a service. These managers have no control over sales or marketing functions. It is difficult to measure profit performance for cost centres because of the problem of allocating revenue to these units.

Categories of responsibility centres

Revenue, cost, profit, and investment centres.

This type of performance measurement system is concerned only with direct costs and meeting production budgets and quotas. Under the cost centre, the manager is measured in terms of standard (budgeted) costs to actual costs. Variances are analyzed and corrective measures are implemented (if necessary) in order to make the units more efficient. Cost centres include departments such as accounting, MIS, maintenance units in a manufacturing company, legal services, human resources, and public relations.

Nonprofit organizations such as hospitals, schools, universities, and government agencies are often structured on the basis of cost centres. Although cost centres are usually small, they can be large if the managers are responsible for the administrative activities of an entire plant.

There are two categories of cost centres. The first is the *engineered-cost centre* or standard-cost centre, where it is possible to make a rough estimate of the expenses that a centre will incur in order to provide a specific service. For example, the average cost for testing samples in a laboratory may be established at $17.45, while the annual per-square-foot maintenance and cleaning costs of a building may be $5.85.

In other cases, it is impossible to make even a rough estimate of the resources required to produce a service. Here, inputs cannot be related to outputs scientifically, and the operating efficiencies cannot be measured quantitatively. These expense centres are referred to as *discretionary-cost centres.*

The *profit centre* combines both revenues (outputs) and expenses (inputs). When expenses are deducted from revenues, we obtain a standard called profit that can also be measured in terms of contribution margin, gross margin, controllable profit, and incremental profit. For profit centres, both the inputs and the outputs can be measured in dollar terms. These centres sell services or goods to customers (this may represent the major portion of a centre's revenue) or internally, to other units within a company. Examples of profit centres are auto repair centres in a department store and an appliance department in a retail store. An important advantage of a profit centre is that it enhances the delegation of authority and encourages managers to make more enlightened decisions.

The *investment centre* is identical to the profit centre except that investments are considered when measuring performance. Here, profits are compared to investments, and this relationship is an overall economic goal called return on investment (ROI). Here, management is interested not only in looking at profit levels (outputs) but also in comparing them to investments (inputs). Investment centres are widely used in large decentralized organizations. Take the example of fast food outlets like Tim Horton's or Burger King. In both instances, investments in land, buildings, and equipment are made (inputs) and the outlets are expected to generate a profit (output). If it costs $2 million (investment) to start a Tim Horton's outlet and it generates $200,000 in profit a year, the investment centre will show a 10% return.

Budgeting Process in Terms of Planning as a Whole

◀◼ Objective 2

Creating a budget is not the same as creating a plan. A budget is a component of a plan; therefore, the plan must be created first. Strategic and operational objectives must be established, along with strategic plans to accomplish them.

Figure 9.2 shows how planning and budgeting are linked to one another. The process is as follows. Top-level managers analyze the company's (1) external environment in terms of opportunities and threats and (2) existing resources (financial, human, materials) in terms of strengths and weaknesses. A document is prepared and subsequently reviewed by the management committee (corporate review, which is step 1 of the corporate-level responsibility). Simultaneously, the responsibility centres (or divisions) review past and current operating performances (step A of the division responsibility) and develop the division and sales budget (step B). These plans are reviewed and tested against the planning assumptions (steps 2 and C). If the division plans show compatibility, the next step (step 3) involves the development of the corporate strategies to assess the impact the plans may have on existing operations. The strategic plans, division plans, and sales budget are reviewed by the management committee (steps 4 and 5). If the strategies, division plans, and budgets are approved, the responsibility centre managers are given the go-ahead (step 6). The divisions then prepare the variable and overhead budgets (step D). All budgets are then consolidated into a master budget and financial plan (step E), which are reviewed by the management committee (step 7). The information contained in these plans is used as input for the following year's planning and budgeting cycle (step 8). The plans are implemented, and results are reviewed for monitoring purposes and for making changes (if necessary) to the plans and budgets (step F).

Companies do not necessarily follow these steps in the order presented, but they usually go through each one. If one step is missed, the appropriate amount of budget dollars may fail to be allocated to the correct responsibility centres, priorities, and plans.

Types of Budgets

◀◼ Objective 3

Because different types of decisions are made in organizations, managers use different budgeting methodologies. Table 9.1 shows the different types of budgets prepared by organizations and the reasons they are prepared.

These budgets can be grouped under four headings: (1) **operating budgets,** (2) complementary budgets, (3) comprehensive budgets, and (4) capital budgets. Let's examine the meaning of each.

Operating budgets

Budgets prepared by operating managers.

Operating Budgets

As shown in Figure 9.3, three types of budgets are used to formulate a master budget or projected income statement, which comprises sales budgets, manufac-

FIGURE 9.2   PLANNING-BUDGETING-CONTROLLING INTERRELATIONSHIP

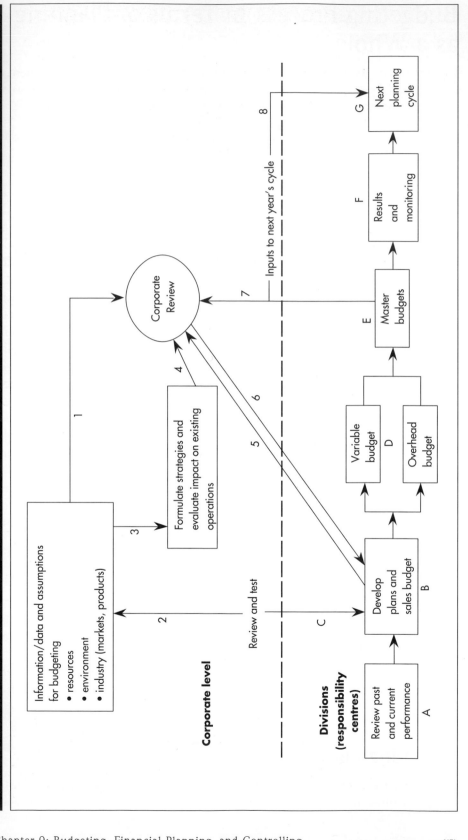

TABLE 9.1   TYPES OF BUDGETS AND PURPOSE

Type of Budgets	Purpose
1. Manufacturing budget	Production requirement (materials, labour, energy, etc.)
2. Marketing budget	Sales and advertising plans
3. Branch, division, or regional budgets	Responsibility centres
4. Product budget	ROI on specific products
5. Executive staff budget	Specialized budget (compensation and human resources)
6. Cash budget	To meet current cash obligations and obtain line of credit
7. R & D budget	Strategies upon which future sales and revenue depend
8. Capital expenditure budget	New plants, expansions, modernizations, R & D
9. Pro-forma income statement	Profit forecast
10. Pro-forma balance sheet	Financial structure forecast

FIGURE 9.3   PRO-FORMA PROFIT PLAN (MASTER BUDGET)

Sales	$1,000,000	} Sales budgets
Less:		
Manufacturing expenses: variable and direct expenses such as labour and materials	600,000	} Flexible budgets
Contribution margin	400,000	
Fixed expenses such as depreciation, insurance, and plant maintenance	100,000	} Absorption costing
Profit margin on manufacturing operations	300,000	
Overhead expenses:		
Indirect and overhead expenses such as service organizations, support functions, projects, and overhead units for:		
(1) operating units (tooling, quality control, scheduling)	50,000	Incremental budgeting or zero-based budgeting
(2) corporate units (finance, human resources, engineering)	100,000	
Total overhead expenses	150,000	
Profit	$ 150,000	

turing budgets (flexible budgets), and staff or overhead budgets (incremental or zero-based budgeting). At the start of a budget year, the master budget serves as a plan or standard. At the end, it is used as a control device to help managers gauge their performance against plans. Today, with the help of spreadsheets and customized software packages, budgeting can be used as an effective tool for evaluating "what-if" scenarios through sensitivity analysis and simulations. By incorporating different assumptions in the master budget, managers can quickly find the best courses of action to follow to optimize their financial performance.

Among the variety of budgets used in organizations, the sales budget is used by marketing departments, the flexible or variable budget is used by manufacturing departments, and incremental or zero-based budgeting is used by indirect or overhead units.

Sales budgets are prepared by the sales department and are critical because they provide the basis for formulating other segments of the master budget. The sales budget includes the number of units expected to be sold and the unit selling price, which translates into the sales revenue forecast. The sales budget is often broken down on a quarterly or even monthly basis.

Flexible or variable budgets are used by plant or production departments where costs of production (standard costs) are used as benchmarks for comparing actual results to identify price and quantity variances. The intent here is to not only verify if a production unit is living within its budget but also, more importantly, whether it is operating within pre-determined engineered standards.

Other costs, such as rent, depreciation, or insurance, are fixed. They are, however, chargeable, or absorbed by individual products or divisions. Therefore, to determine net margin on manufacturing for each product line, these fixed costs are included in appropriate units through a variable-costing mechanism. For example, under the absorption costing mechanism, if a plant produces six different products (or services) and incurs a $50,000 overhead expense such as insurance, hydro, or general maintenance, this amount will be absorbed (or charged) by each product, depending, of course, on the numbers of units produced or the amount of time it takes for each product to be manufactured. The accounting system used to allocate overhead costs will be discussed later under the heading "Cost Accounting."

Incremental budgeting or *traditional budgeting* works like this: projected new expenses for the coming year are added to the previous year's total expenses and are expressed as percentages of the previous year's total. Such a budget might look like this:

		% Increase
Last year's expenses	$350,000	
Inflation	7,000	2.0%
New activities	10,500	3.0%
Increase due to volume	14,000	4.0%
Next year's budget	$381,500	9.0%

The incremental budgeting approach has the following flaws:

- it is difficult to relate the budget to specific objectives and plans;
- past activities may be approved without being put to the test and really justified;
- corporate priorities may get lost in the shuffle; and
- the previous year's figures could have been inflated by one-time special expenses.

Zero-based budgets (ZBB) (similar to activity-based budgets) are based on the premise that every budget dollar requires justification. Unlike the traditional budgeting approach—whereby expenditures of the previous years are automatically incorporated into the new budget proposal, and only increments are scrutinized and subjected to debate—zero-based budgeting places all dollars, including last year's authorized expenditures and new requests, on an equal footing. It assumes that a responsibility-centre manager has had no previous expenditures. It is much like the reengineering process, whereby managers ask the question "If we were re-creating this organizational unit or company today, given what we know and given current technology, what would it look like?"

In the zero-based budgeting process, responsibility-centre managers prepare budget proposals called decision packages. These budget proposals are subsequently ranked against each other to compete for scarce corporate resources. Zero-based budgeting is a priority form of budgeting process whereby all budget proposals are ranked in order of importance. It is an effective tool used to analyze programs, proposals, or projects for the purpose of optimizing the use of a company's resources.

ZBB focuses on input-output relationships. It is a process that can be used by overhead organizational units such as purchasing, marketing, administration, engineering, human resources, legal services, and operations research.

The three steps involved in ZBB are:

1. the identification of the decision units (responsibility centres) in terms of their mission, activities, outputs, measurement indicators (efficiencies and effectiveness);

2. the preparation of the decision packages (budget proposals), which contain a description of the objectives, activities, programs, projects, outputs, efficiency and effectiveness standards, resource requirements (person-years, physical, budgets), risk, and time requirements; and

3. the ranking of the decision packages based on corporate priorities and strategies.

Complementary Budgets

Complementary budgets are the offspring of operating budgets and present operating budget data differently. They too can be classified into separate groups: product budgets, program budgets, item-of-expenditure budgets, and cash budgets.

Product budgets are used by marketing organizations to identify the profit performance of different products. For example, the budgets for three products may be prepared in the following way:

Complementary budgets
Budgets that complement operating budgets although data is presented differently and in more detail.

	Products		
	A	B	C
Sales revenue	$500,000	$770,000	$1,300,000
Cost of goods sold	250,000	300,000	600,000
Gross margin	250,000	470,000	700,000
Marketing budget			
Distribution	50,000	75,000	100,000
Advertising	25,000	40,000	70,000
Salaries and commissions	100,000	150,000	250,000
After-sales service	50,000	40,000	100,000
Total marketing budget	225,000	305,000	520,000
Net product margin	$ 25,000	$165,000	$ 180,000

From this budget, it is possible to find out how much money will be spent by each department (e.g., distribution, advertising, etc.) and on each product. This budget therefore gives an idea of the profitability level of each product. A business may also calculate the return on investment of each product by identifying, for each, the capital investments and the profit level (after allocating the company's overhead).

Program budgets are used mostly by nonprofit organizations, including federal, provincial, and municipal governments. Program budgeting has been called the Planning-Programming-Budgeting System (PPBS). Five basic steps are involved in this budgeting process:

- The objectives of the major activities or programs are identified.
- The benefits (or results) to be generated by each activity or program are analyzed.
- The initial outlay and the future costs for each program are estimated.
- The alternatives are examined.
- The budget is prepared on the basis of the first four steps.

Item-of-expenditure budgets are the most popular format of budget preparation. Here, resources are classified in an entirely different way. For example, expenses might break down into salaries, supplies, equipment, travel, and utilities. A typical item-of-expenditure budget follows:

Items	Amounts
Salaries and wages	$200,000
Transportation and communication	25,000
Information	12,550
Professional services	35,500
Rentals	10,000
Purchases, repairs, and upkeep	5,000
Utilities, materials, and supplies	32,000
Other expenditures	20,000
Total	$340,050

Cash budgets are used for cash planning and control. They are also used for negotiating a line of credit with commercial banks. These budgets trace, on a monthly basis, the funds that will be (1) available and (2) required. In short, cash budgets keep track of the adequate monthly cash balances that a business needs, avoiding unnecessary idle cash and possible cash shortages. As shown in Table 9.2, the cash budget is usually broken down in four sections:

1. the cash receipt section;
2. the cash disbursement section;
3. the cash surplus or deficit section; and
4. the financing section.

The cash budget is prepared in two steps. The first step requires that all future receipts from cash sales and collections are identified for each month. The second step requires that all cash disbursements for individual expense items are pinpointed. The difference between the receipts and the disbursements gives either a net cash surplus or a deficiency.

TABLE 9.2   THE CASH BUDGET

	January	February	March	April	May	June	July
1. Cash Receipt Section							
Sales	$225,000	$285,000	$290,000	$300,000	$400,000	$500,000	$600,000
Collections							
Within 30 days (10%)	22,500	28,500	29,000	30,000	40,000	50,000	60,000
In 30–60 days (40%)	80,000	90,000	114,000	116,000	120,000	160,000	200,000
In 60–90 days (50%)	142,500	100,000	112,500	142,500	145,000	150,000	200,000
Total receipts	$245,000	$218,500	$255,500	$288,500	$305,000	$360,000	$460,000
2. Cash Disbursement Section							
Cost of goods sold	$115,000	$125,000	$100,000	$150,000	$200,000	$250,000	$300,000
Payments							
Cash (30%)	34,500	37,500	30,000	45,000	60,000	75,000	90,000
30 days (70%)	70,000	80,500	87,500	70,000	105,000	140,000	175,000
Total payment	104,500	118,000	117,500	115,000	165,000	215,000	265,000
Sales and administration	52,300	50,300	50,060	50,500	38,000	56,000	55,000
Disbursements	108,000	82,000	111,500	85,860	88,000	84,000	71,000
Total disbursements	$264,800	$250,300	$279,060	$251,360	$291,000	$355,000	$391,000
3. Cash Surplus or Deficit Section							
Total receipts	$245,000	$218,500	$255,500	$288,500	$305,000	$360,000	$460,000
Total disbursement	264,800	250,300	279,060	251,360	291,000	355,000	391,000
Gain (deficit) month	$ (19,800)	$ (31,800)	$ (23,560)	$ 37,140	$ 14,000	$ 5,000	$ 69,000
4. Financing Section							
Beginning bank balance	$ 27,200	$ 7,400	$ (24,400)	$ (47,960)	$ (10,820)	$ 3,180	$ 8,180
Gain (deficit) month	(19,800)	(31,800)	(23,560)	37,140	14,000	5,000	69,000
Cumulative gain (surplus)							
deficit (loan)	$ 7,400	$ (24,400)	$ (47,960)	$ (10,820)	$ 3,180	$ 8,180	$ 77,180

Several departments must participate in the preparation of the cash budget, and it requires a certain degree of judgment. For example, the sales department provides the sales revenue figures, while the credit manager provides a breakdown of the approximate percentage of sales revenue that will be made on a cash basis, on credit, or paid within 30, 60, or 90 days. Various departmental heads also provide information on operating expenses related to purchases, wages, salaries, lease payments, etc.

The financial officer then determines the amount of cash that should be:

- kept in the bank at all times (cash at start of month);
- invested in short-term securities (surplus cash), and
- required from the bank in the form of a line of credit (outstanding loans).

The cash budget is a tool that allows for deliberate planning for the efficient acquisition of funds and for short-term investments.

Comprehensive Budgets

Comprehensive budget

A set of projected financial statements such as the income statement, the balance sheet, and the statement of cash flows.

When the controller has received all revenue forecasts and budgets from the operating managers, the accountants consolidate and prepare the pro-forma financial statements into a **comprehensive budget**. The various projected financial statements will be discussed later in this chapter under the heading "Financial Planning."

Capital Budgets

Capital budget

Budget that shows how much will be spent for the purchase of capital assets.

A **capital budget** reveals how much is required to invest in capital assets. This budget breaks down the capital assets by major category, how much funding is needed and when it is required, the location of the assets, and reasons for spending. These budgets include investments such as cost-reduction programs, research and development projects, expansion of a manufacturing operation, replacement of obsolete equipment, installation of computer equipment, construction of a warehouse, or even the purchase of an ongoing business. Capital projects or capital assets generate benefits (returns, profits, savings) over an extended number of years. Projects that are included in capital budgets are critical as they usually require a significant amount of financial resources. The capital budgeting process and the evaluation methods were examined in Chapter 8.

Rules for Sound Budgeting

Table 9.3 summarizes the most important rules to follow when preparing budgets, especially operating budgets such as sales, flexible, and overhead budgets. These rules are prerequisites for effective budgeting, and violation of any of them can easily jeopardize the budgeting process.

TABLE 9.3 TEN RULES FOR SOUND BUDGETING

Rule 1: Pinpoint authority
Make sure that reporting responsibilities are clear and managerial authority is well defined.

Rule 2: Integrate all planning activities
To be effective, budgeting must be linked in a systematic way to other planning activities, such as setting objectives, identifying corporate priorities and strategies, and establishing guidelines and management objectives.

Rule 3: Insist on sufficient and accurate information
Information is essential to decision-making, the prime purpose of budgeting. All budget aspects, from cost-benefit analyses to the establishment of performance standards, depend upon the availability of current and accurate data.

Rule 4: Encourage participation
Essentially, accountability is measuring achievement against objectives. Participation in goal-setting encourages enthusiastic efforts. Few people like to be held accountable for hitting or missing someone else's targets.

Rule 5: Link budgeting to monitoring
Budgeting is meaningless if it is not linked to monitoring. What is the point of spending endless hours formulating plans and budgets, if management does not follow up by comparing actual performance with standards?

Rule 6: Tailor budgeting to the organization's needs
How information is presented, consolidated, and reviewed is a highly individualized matter. A system that works well for one organization will not necessarily produce the same results for another. Because management style, information needs, and corporate structures differ, each must create a budgeting system that meets its own special requirements.

Rule 7: Communicate budget guidelines
To ensure economy of time and effort, remove confusion in an organization, and prevent the budgeting system from faltering, it is essential to establish and communicate premises, guidelines, and assumptions.

Rule 8: Relate costs to benefits
It is essential to appraise every unit in terms of its contribution to the organization, the benefits expected from the services it provides, and the funds it needs to perform its tasks.

Rule 9: Establish standards for all units
One reason for preparing budgets is to make sure resources are spent efficiently and effectively. To determine this, it is important to establish performance standards. Although it may be easy to establish performance standards at the production level, it is harder with overhead units (e.g., administration, research groups, or accounting operations). Nevertheless, every effort should be made to set performance goals.

Rule 10: Be flexible
Managers should be able to respond easily to changing circumstances. On the manufacturing side, budget levels change with the level of production; managers responsible for production operations will clearly not be limited to their budget ceilings if sales levels are exceeded by 10 or 20%. They respond to marketing needs. With overhead units, however, because of the absence of engineering standards, budgets often become permanently fixed. Yet it is only common sense that, during the operating year, managers responsible for overhead units should be allowed to increase or reduce their activities, and in turn their budgets, to meet new requests or priorities.

How to Make the Budgeting Exercise Effective

If a new or revised budgeting process is to be implemented in an organization, the members of the management committee should ask the following questions if they want the system to be effective and meaningful:

- What should budgeting do for this organization?
- What type of budgets and budgeting process should we have?
- How much of a new budgeting system can the organization absorb during the first year of implementation? During the second year? (It may take years to get managers technically and mentally involved in a new planning and budgeting system.)
- How should the information flow? How should our various organizational units communicate?
- What authority should be delegated to the various echelons of the organization? Where should decisions be made?
- How much time and money are we prepared to spend to get the budgeting system off to a good start?
- Who should be in charge of implementing the new planning and budgeting program?

These questions are important because they have to do with the culture of an organization, which is basically "how we do things around here." When these questions have been answered, and top-level managers are committed to making budgeting work within the context of the overall planning framework, the next steps are to (a) design the new planning and budgeting system; (b) assign responsibilities; and (c) implement the program.

Design a Permanent Budget Program

Budgeting should be regarded as a permanent process. If there are difficulties with a new budgeting system during the initial years, it should not be completely abandoned in favour of a new one. Too many changes confuse people, so it is better to meet new organizational needs by making gradual adjustments.

Assign Responsibilities

Usually a firm's planning group or controller is responsible for designing and coordinating the budget. But it is not, and should not be, the controller's responsibility to prepare the operating managers' budgets. These managers should be responsible for preparing their own budgets for funds and be fully conversant with all guidelines and procedures. It may take a fair amount of time for some managers to accept these responsibilities and to become familiar with the system, but in the long run their participation will have favourable effects on organizational productivity and morale.

IMPLEMENT Once the budgeting procedures have been carefully thought out and budgeting responsibilities are understood by all, the next step is implementation and monitoring.

How to Avoid Budgeting Pitfalls

Putting a budgeting system in operation is one thing; maintaining it as a purposeful management instrument is another. If these four rules are followed, many budgeting problems can be avoided.

KEEP THE PAPERWORK TO A REASONABLE LEVEL If managers get entangled in procedures and waste their time filling out pointless reports and compiling endless columns of numbers, the result will be a budgeting system that is being served by managers rather than helping them make better decisions. Today, with the use of spreadsheets, this rule can easily be fulfilled.

KEEP BUDGETING SUBSERVIENT TO OBJECTIVE-SETTING Budgeting is not an end in itself; it is a tool that helps managers determine how best they should deploy their resources to achieve the organization's objectives and priorities.

DO NOT TAKE PAST ACTIVITIES FOR GRANTED Because objectives and priorities change from year to year, the budgeting exercise should be flexible enough to adapt to current priorities and demands, regardless of the way things were done in the past. Each year, when managers prepare their budgets, they should justify their requests and outline how they will spend the budgeted funds in order to realize their objectives and implement their plans.

MAKE BUDGETING A TOP-MANAGEMENT PRACTICE Budgeting is the responsibility of every manager in an organization, and all (including top-level managers) must be involved in the process. If top management abdicates its budgeting responsibility, this may have adverse effects on the organization. For example, lower-level managers may lose interest in budgeting, and it may be regarded as an exercise done by accountants. On the other hand, strong support by top-level managers promotes a view of budgeting as a meaningful process.

Cost Accounting

◀◀ Objective 5

Cost accounting is a key component of the budgeting process. Usually, large organizations have a staff of cost accountants who devote all of their time to collecting and analyzing costs for the purpose of improving managerial decisions regarding future production and product strategies. Cost accounting is the process of collecting information for reporting the costs incurred related to the acquisition or production of products or services. It provides managers with information on the costs associated with buying or selling a product because the cost of each unit must be known to help determine how much it should be sold in order to make a reasonable profit. If a company is not able to sell a product at a price higher than it costs, the company does not have a viable business.

The cost accounting process involves the allocation of all cost data related to manufacturing, purchasing, and selling. The process of properly documenting variable costs and equitably allocating fixed costs helps an organization to control its costs more thoroughly and increase the transparency of managerial accountability. This next section deals with three parts of the cost accounting process: *activity-based costing, cost accounting systems*, and *variance reporting.*

Activity-Based Costing

One important branch of cost accounting that emerged during the late 1980s is **activity-based costing (ABC).** This system focuses on the analysis of overhead costs to determine whether they can be directly related to specific activities.

Organizational activities usually include two types of costs: direct and indirect. Direct costs generally consist of direct labour and direct materials that are directly incurred when making a product or providing a service. These costs increase proportionately with volume of production. Indirect costs are those that cannot be identified clearly with a single product or service.

With the growth of overhead components in a company's total cost structure, there is a danger of a growing proportion of indirect cost being allocated to products or services on an arbitrary basis rather than by being measured. Here is the difference between direct and indirect costs: employees working on the production line are considered direct costs for that particular department while the cost of heating a building is regarded as an indirect cost and would have to be allocated among different departments in the building.

Activity-based costing is the process that allocates these indirect costs to the products that caused them to be incurred. The ABC mechanism process provides managers with better information for costing and pricing decisions. The focus of activity-based costing is therefore to pinpoint the various drivers of the indirect costs to determine whether they can be related to an activity, product, or service that can be measured.

Cost Accounting Systems

To obtain the real benefits of activity-based costing, the system should provide information to managers to help them make informed decisions. The two basic **cost accounting** systems that can help managers analyze costs are job order costing and process costing.

Basically, job order costing focuses on how much it costs to produce a specific product, service, contract, or order. Process costing, on the other hand, gathers information by production departments (or cost centre) related to a continuous stream of identical products, and costs are averaged out to all the production output that takes place in the department. For example, a textile plant

Activity-based costing

Accounting system that focuses on the analysis of overhead costs to determine how they relate to different products, services, or activities.

Cost accounting

Accounting system that provides information to managers to make informed decisions.

may produce shirts with different colours and sizes. The cotton used in the production runs will be assigned to all shirts at the same cost per yard used. Irrespective of the size and colour of the shirts produced, the selling price itself does not change the cost of the cotton even if the packaging and marketing costs vary with each category of shirts. The production of similar products manufactured on a continuous basis through a series of uniform production steps is known as processes. Table 9.4 summarizes the basic differences between these two costing accounting systems.

Let's examine these costing processes in more detail.

JOB ORDER COSTING With a **job order costing** system, material, direct labour, and manufacturing overhead are charged to a specific job, shop, or customer order (a discrete order). These costs are directly related to producing a good or providing a service. For example, if a company produces a pen made of plastic, ink, and felt, the costs of these materials would be identified and be part of the direct cost related to making the pens. This costing system is best suited to situations in which products are manufactured in identifiable lots or batches or in which the products are manufactured to customer specifications. This system is widely used by custom manufacturers such as printing shops, aircraft manufacturers, and construction companies. In the service sector, organizations such as auto repair shops and professional services also use this job-costing accounting system.

Job order costing

Accounting system that helps to allocate direct costs related to producing a specific good.

Here is a simplified example of how the costs of a particular job can be calculated.

Direct materials		Direct labour	
June 14	$2,000	Week of June 14	210 hours @ $11.50
June 22	1,800	Week of June 21	130 hours @ $9.30
June 28	2,400		
Total	$6,200		

Let's assume that the factory overhead rate is set at $5.50 per direct labour hour. With this information, the costs and the selling price of a specific job including a mark-up of 35% of costs would be calculated as:

TABLE 9.4   JOB ORDER COSTING VERSUS PROCESS COSTING

	Job Order Costing	Process Costing
Who uses it	Custom manufacturing	Processing industries
Nature of the work	Jobs, contracts, orders	Physical units
Type of information recorded	Job cost sheets	Cost of production reports
The way costs are accumulated	By work orders	By departments
What the system calculates	• Inventory costing • Profit and loss of each job	Unit cost used to calculate cost of goods completed and work-in-process

a. *Cost of the job*

Direct materials		$ 6,200
Direct labour:		
210 hours @ $11.50	$ 2,415	
130 hours @ $9.30	1,209	3,624
Manufacturing overhead:		
440 hours @ $5.50		2,420
Cost of job		12,244

b. *Selling price of the job*

$12,244 + 35\% (\$12,244) = \$12,244.00 + \$4,285.40 = \underline{\underline{\$16,529.40}}$

Process costing

Accounting system that helps to allocate direct and departmental overhead costs in organizations that produce goods on a continuous basis.

PROCESS COSTING Process costing focuses on the accumulation of costs by departments or production processes. As shown in the following example, these costs are accumulated under two distinct categories: direct materials and conversion costs (sum of direct labour and departmental overhead). The unit cost is calculated by dividing the total costs charged to a responsibility centre by the number of outputs generated by that particular responsibility centre or department. Process costing is used by organizations where products or services are based on a continuous process and can be found in manufacturing organizations such as petroleum, oil refinery, textiles, chemicals, and food processing, and service-oriented institutions such as hospitals, schools, and banks.

The following gives a simplified example of how the costs for a food processing plant would be calculated. There are two departments (X and Y) involved in the processing of the food during a 30-day period (September, for example).

Actual production costs:
Direct materials used: 22,000 gallons costing $33,000
Direct labour and departmental overhead: $23,000

Actual production:
Completed and transferred to department Y: 10,000 gallons
Ending work-in-process: 12,000 gallons and 20% complete as to conversion.

(a) The accounting process starts with the calculation of the flow of physical units (gallons) on which the work was done during the period (September). As shown, all inputs (gallons) must equal all outputs (gallons).

To be accounted for:	
Added in September	22,000 gallons
Accounted for as follows:	
Completed in September	10,000 gallons
In process, end of September	12,000
Total	22,000 gallons

(b) This next step in the cost accounting process involves the calculation of output in terms of equivalent units. The total amount of work done during the month is calculated in order to determine the unit cost of production. The partially finished units are measured on an "equivalent whole-unit" basis for process-costing purposes. For example, if 200 units are 50% completed, this will be considered the equivalent of 100 completed units.

	Materials (gallons)	Converted units (gallons)
Units completed	10,000	10,000
Ending working-in-process (12,000 gallons)		
100% of materials	12,000	
20% converted	—	2,400
Equivalent units produced	22,000	12,400

(c) The next step involves the identification of all costs assigned to the department during the period (in this case, September) and, from this, the unit cost per equivalent unit is calculated. This is arrived at by dividing the total costs by the equivalent units of production during the period.

	Total cost	Equivalent production (gallons)	Unit cost
Materials	$39,600	22,000	$1.80
Conversion cost	26,040	12,400	2.10
To be accounted for	$65,640		$3.90
Ending work-in-process			
Materials	$21,600	12,000	$1.80
Conversion cost	5,040	2,400	2.10
Total work-in-process	$26,640		
Completed and transferred	39,000	10,000	$3.90
Total accounted for	$65,640		

Variance Reporting

Variance analysis compares standards to actual performance. A standard is the predetermined cost of manufacturing, servicing, or marketing a product during a specific time period. It is based on current and projected future operating conditions and is dependent on quantitative and qualitative measurements. These standards are based on engineering studies involved in time and motion studies. Actual performance is the actual cost experienced by a department for processing a quantity of outputs during a period in question.

Variance analysis
Accounting system that compares standards to actual performance.

Organizations that have managers responsible for responsibility centres such as a division, a department, a program, a product, or a territory will find the variance analysis system useful for performance evaluation and making accountability more transparent. Variance analysis can be done on a daily, monthly, quarterly, or yearly basis depending on the importance of highlighting problems quickly.

Under the variance-analysis reporting environment, the responsibility centre manager analyzes how much it will cost to produce a product (or provide a service) for every unit of output. This is subsequently compared to standard costs used as benchmarks and useful for gauging efficiencies. For example, if the standard cost to produce a widget is $6.37, and the actual cost is $6.68, the factors causing the variation will be identified in order to take the necessary remedial actions. That $0.31 difference between the actual costs and the standard costs is referred to as a variance. Variances are caused by three factors: materials, labour, and departmental overhead. Let's examine how each of these variances is calculated.

Material variance

Variance in costs between standards and actual performance due to changes in quantity of materials used or changes in the price of the materials used.

MATERIAL VARIANCE Material variance recognizes that actual material costs may vary from standard costs for two reasons: price and quantity. For instance, if a department forecasts an input of 30,000 units, the actual material cost compared to the standard would be calculated as follows:

Standard:	30,000 units @ $3.00	$90,000
Actual:	30,400 units @ $3.20	$97,280

Material Cost Variance

	Amount	In $ Variance
Quantity Variance		
Actual: 30,400 units @ standard price of $3.00	$91,200	
Standard: 30,000 units @ standard price of $3.00	$90,000	
Variance (unfavourable)		$1,200
Price Variance		
Actual: 30,400 units @ actual price of $3.20	$97,280	
Standard: 30,400 units @ standard price of $3.00	91,200	
Variance (unfavourable)		$6,080
Total material variance (unfavourable)		$7,280

The actual costs of the material compared to the standard costs for making the units varied by $7,280. Total material used exceeded the standard by 400 units while the unit price exceeded standard by $0.20 per unit.

The mix comprising the above variance of $7,280 shows what type of information should be reported to the appropriate responsibility-centre managers. The quantity variance will be brought to the attention of the processing manager while the price variance will be reported to the purchasing department.

LABOUR VARIANCE **Labour variance** is also made up of two components, time and rate. If the actual time taken to produce x number of units varies from the standard, it is referred to as *time variance*. If the actual salaries or wages paid to process a number of units vary from standard, this is referred to as *rate variance*. To illustrate, let's assume that an organization processes x number of units; the actual labour cost compared to the standard would be presented in the following way:

Standard:	10,000 hours @ $4.10	$41,000
Actual:	9,800 hours @ $4.21	$41,258

The $258 variance can be explained in the following way:

Labour Cost Variance

	In $ Amount	Variance
Time		
Standard: 10,000 hours @ standard rate @ $4.10	$41,000	
Actual: 9,800 hours @ standard rate @ $4.10	40,180	
Variance (favourable)		$ 820
Rate		
Actual: 9,800 hours @ actual rate of $4.21	$41,258	
Standard: 9,800 hours @ standard rate of $4.10	40,180	
Variance (unfavourable)		$1,078
Labour variance (unfavourable)		$ 258

Just as in the case of material variance, the labour variance would be reported to the appropriate responsibility managers.

OVERHEAD VARIANCE Plant overhead standard rate is calculated by dividing the expected plant overhead costs by the standard quantity of outputs. Included in these overhead costs are items such as purchases of indirect materials, indirect departmental wages, and maintenance. Such costs usually change with varying production output levels. Other costs, including depreciation, taxes, and insurance, are fixed and remain constant irrespective of the level of output.

In view of possible changes in total overhead costs as a result of varying output levels, it is preferable to prepare various budgets showing the costs incurred at varying production levels. Here is how this departmental overhead budget would be presented.

Labour variance

Variance in costs between standards and actual performance due to changes in the amount of time and rate used to make a product.

Overhead variance

Variance in costs between standards and actual performance due to changes in indirect costs.

Departmental Overhead Budget
In $

	\% of capacity			
	80%	*90%*	*100%*	*110%*
Direct labour (hours)	8,000	9,000	10,000	11,000
Units (standard)	24,000	27,000	30,000	33,000
Budgeted Departmental Overhead				
Variable costs				
Hydro, power, and heat	5,040	5,670	6,300	6,930
Indirect materials	2,480	2,790	3,100	3,410
Maintenance and repairs	2,000	2,250	2,500	2,750
Indirect plant wages	9,120	10,260	11,400	12,540
Total variable costs	18,640	20,970	23,300	25,630
Fixed costs				
Departmental supervision	3,250	3,250	3,250	3,250
Depreciation				
Machinery	1,750	1,750	1,750	1,750
Equipment	800	800	800	800
Insurance and taxes	1,400	1,400	1,400	1,400
Total fixed costs	7,200	7,200	7,200	7,200
Total plant overhead	$25,840	$28,170	$30,500	$32,830

Variable cost:	($23,300 ÷ 10,000 hours) =	$2.33
Fixed overhead:	($7,200 ÷ 10,000 hours) =	$0.72
Total		$3.05

As shown, the standard departmental overhead hourly rate is $3.05 ($30,500 ÷ 10,000 hours). If the department's actual production is 27,000 units (90% of capacity), the variance would be calculated as follows:

Standard:	9,000 hours @ $3.05		$27,450
Actual:	Variable departmental overhead	$22,200	
	Fixed departmental overhead	7,200	29,400
Variance (unfavourable)			$ 1,950

The $1,950 variance can be explained in the following way:

Departmental Overhead Variance
In $

Controllable costs

Actual departmental fixed overhead	$29,400	
Budgeted departmental overhead for standard units produced (90% of capacity)	28,170	
Variance (unfavourable)		$1,230

Volume

Normal capacity hours	10,000	
Standard hours for actual units produced	9,000	
Normal capacity hours not used	1,000	
Fixed overhead rate	$ 0.72	
Variance overhead (unfavourable)		720
Total departmental overhead variance (unfavourable)		$1,950

As shown, the controllable cost variance of $1,230 would be considered the departmental manager's responsibility.

Financial Planning

Objective 6

As shown in Figure 9.4, operating budgets are ultimately integrated into projected financial statements, also known as **pro-forma financial statements.** The most important financial statements that managers, owners, lenders, and other interest groups examine to gauge the overall financial performance of a business are the income statement, the balance sheet, and the statement of cash flows.

Pro-forma financial statements

Projected financial statements (e.g., income statement, balance sheet, and the statement of cash flows).

FIGURE 9.4   RELATIONSHIP BETWEEN OPERATING BUDGETS AND PRO-FORMA FINANCIAL STATEMENTS

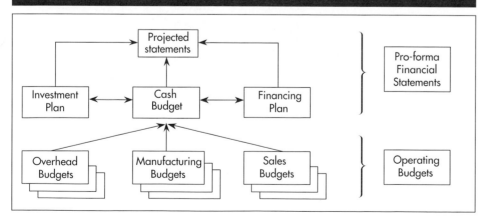

Pro-Forma Income Statement

Table 9.5 presents Eastman Technologies Inc.'s pro-forma income statement. The statement shows the company's future sales revenue, costs, and profit performance. To examine the company's expected financial performance, managers can refer to the ratios that were examined in Chapter 4 and also use the common-size ratio analyses (see Tables 4.3 and 4.4) and horizontal analyses (see Tables 4.5 and 4.6). Eastman's 2003 year-end forecast and 2004 budget year operating performance are summarized opposite.

TABLE 9.5	PRO-FORMA INCOME STATEMENT		
Eastman Technologies Inc.			
Income Statements for the Years Ended December 31			

	2004	2003	Planning Assumptions
Net sales	$3,050,000	$2,500,000	(22% increase)
Cost of goods sold	2,050,000	1,900,000	(67% of sales from 76%)
Gross margin	**1,000,000**	**600,000**	(67% increase)
Operating expenses			
Selling expenses			
Sales salaries	$ 158,000	$ 140,000	(5% of sales from 6%)
Advertising expenses	34,000	20,000	
Total selling expenses	192,000	160,000	
Administrative expenses			
Office salaries	185,000	170,000	(6% of sales from 7%)
Rent	29,000	20,000	
Depreciation	48,000	40,000	
Total administrative expenses	262,000	230,000	
Total operating expenses	454,000	390,000	(15% increase but 15% of sales from 16%)
Operating income	**546,000**	**210,000**	
Other income	23,000	20,000	
Other expenses (interest)	41,000	35,000	
	19,000	15,000	
Income before taxes	528,000	195,000	
Income taxes	264,000	97,500	
Income after taxes	**$ 264,000**	**$ 97,500**	(9% of sales from 4%)

	As % of sales	
	2004 budget	*2003 year-end*
Sales	1.00	1.00
Cost of goods sold	0.67	0.76
Gross margin	0.33	0.24
Selling expenses	0.06	0.06
Administrative expenses	0.09	0.09
Income after taxes	0.09	0.04

The pro-forma income statement summarizes the various components of sales revenue and expense projections for a specific budgeting period. However, for controlling purposes, the pro-forma income statement should be done on a quarterly or even monthly basis.

As shown in Table 9.5, significant improvements were forecast in the cost of goods sold, which has a favourable effect on the gross margin and income after taxes.

The horizontal analysis (increments between two consecutive income statements) shows the following:

	% Increase
Sales	22.0
Cost of goods sold	7.9
Gross margin	66.7
Selling expenses	20.0
Administrative expenses	13.9
Income after taxes	170.1

Table 9.6 shows Eastman's 2004 pro-forma statement of retained earnings. The company will pay $50,000 in dividends, retain $214,000 in the business, and accumulate retained earnings in the amount of $469,000.

TABLE 9.6   PRO-FORMA STATEMENT OF RETAINED EARNINGS

Eastman Technologies Inc.
Retained Earnings Statement for the
Year Ended December 31, 2004

Retained earnings (beginning balance)		$255,000
Earnings	$264,000	
Dividends	50,000	214,000
Retained earnings (ending balance)		$469,000

Pro-Forma Balance Sheet

A similar analysis can be done for the balance sheet. As shown in Table 9.7, Eastman Technologies Inc.'s pro-forma balance sheet presents the financial structure in terms of current assets, capital assets, current liabilities, long-term debt, and owners' equity, and how these elements are distributed during 2003 and 2004. As shown in the table, Eastman Technologies Inc.'s total assets increased by $279,000—that is, from $1,800,000 to $2,079,000.

The pro-forma balance sheet is formulated by starting with the balance sheet for the year just ended and adjusting it, using all activities that are expected to take place during the budgeting period. The more important reasons for preparing a pro-forma balance sheet are:

- to disclose some unfavourable financial conditions that management might want to avoid;

TABLE 9.7   PRO-FORMA BALANCE SHEET

Eastman Technologies Inc.
Balance Sheets as at December 31

Assets	2004	2003	Planning Assumptions
Current assets			
Cash	$ 45,000	$ 22,000	(Cash to sales to 1.5%
Prepaid expenses	67,000	60,000	from 0.9%)
Accounts receivable	325,000	300,000	(5-day improvement)
Inventory	230,000	218,000	(0.2 time improvement)
Total current assets	**667,000**	**600,000**	
Capital assets (at cost)	1,600,000	1,340,000	(see capital budget
Accumulated depreciation	188,000	140,000	for details)
Capital assets (net)	**1,412,000**	**1,200,000**	
Total assets	$2,079,000	$1,800,000	
Liabilities			
Current liabilities			
Accounts payable	$ 220,000	$ 195,000	(10% of COGS)
Notes payable	140,000	150,000	
Accrued expenses	30,000	20,000	
Taxes payable	90,000	80,000	
Total current liabilities	**480,000**	**445,000**	
Long-term debts	**830,000**	**800,000**	
Common shares	300,000	300,000	(no change)
Retained earnings	469,000	255,000	(see income statement
Owners' equity	**769,000**	**555,000**	and statement of retained earnings for details)
Total liabilities and equity	$2,079,000	$1,800,000	

- to serve as a final check on the mathematical accuracy of all the other schedules;
- to help managers perform a variety of financial ratios; and
- to highlight future resources and obligations.

To determine where these increments are registered, we have to examine the key elements of the assets such as accounts receivable, inventories, and capital assets as a percentage of total assets. The vertical analysis of the key components of Eastman's balance sheet is as follows:

	As % of Total Assets	
	2004 budget	2003 year-end
Current assets	0.32	0.33
Capital assets	0.68	0.67
Total assets	1.00	1.00
Current liabilities	0.23	0.25
Long-term debts	0.40	0.44
Total debt	0.63	0.69
Owners' equity	0.37	0.31
Total assets	1.00	1.00

As shown, there is little change in the ratio of total current liabilities compared to capital assets. However, when looking at the mixture of the liability and equity accounts, debt is reduced from 69%, as a percentage of total liabilities and owners' equity, to 63%.

Pro-Forma Cash Flow Statement

Table 9.8 presents Eastman's pro-forma cash flow statement. Essentially, it shows the amount of cash that will be used to finance the company's capital budget. As shown in the investing activities portion of the statement, $260,000 will be invested in capital assets. Operating activities will generate $280,000, which will be used exclusively to buy the assets and to pay the dividends to the shareholders.

Now that management has produced the operating budgets and the pro-forma financial statements, the next two key questions are:

- Is the company growing within its operating and financial capabilities?
- How healthy is the business? Will its financial health improve or deteriorate?

TABLE 9.8   PRO-FORMA CASH FLOW STATEMENT

Eastman Technologies Inc.
for the Year Ended 2004

Operating activities

	Sources	Uses
Net income from operations	$264,000	
Depreciation	48,000	
Cash	—	$ 23,000
Marketable securities	—	—
Prepaid expenses	—	7,000
Accounts receivable	—	25,000
Inventory	—	12,000
Accounts payable	25,000	—
Notes payable	—	10,000
Accrued expenses	10,000	—
Taxes payable	10,000	—
Total	357,000	77,000
Cash from operations	**280,000**	

Financing activities

	Sources	Uses
Payment of dividends	—	50,000
Long-term debt	30,000	—
Common shares	—	—
Total	30,000	50,000
Cash from financing	**(20,000)**	
Investing activities	**—**	**$ 260,000**
Total	**$387,000**	**$ 387,000**

The presentation format of this cash flow statement is different from the one presented in annual reports (e.g., Table 3.6 in Chapter 3). This format is considered as more of a management tool and lists more details under operating activities, and the cash account is listed under operating activities and not as a separate item.

Objective 7 ▶

The Sustainable Growth Rate

Most people equate growth with success, and managers often see growth as something to be maximized. Their view is simple: if the company grows, the firm's market share and profits should also increase. However, growing too quickly (if growth is not properly managed) may create problems. In some instances, growth outstrips a company's human, production, and financial resources. When that happens, the quality of decision-making tends to deteriorate under constant pressure, product quality suffers, and financial reserves often disappear. The bottom line is this: if growth is not managed, a business can literally grow broke.

There is no question that there are limits to how quickly a company should grow. Preoccupation with growth at any cost can overextend a company administratively and financially. Results can be lower profit, cash shortages, and, ironically, slower growth ultimately as managers pause to regroup and repair the damage. Some signs of trouble associated with growing too quickly are substantial increases in receivables and inventories relative to sales, declining cash flow from operations, and escalating interest-bearing debt.

In order to understand growth management, we must first define a company's **sustainable growth rate.** It is defined as the maximum rate at which a company's sales can increase without depleting financial resources. Managers must therefore look at different options when they target the company's sustainable growth rate. In many instances, management should limit growth in order to conserve financial strength.

Sustainable growth rate
Rate of increase in sales revenue a company can attain without depleting financing resources, borrowing excessively, or issuing new stock.

If a company wants to grow, it has several options:

- increase its profit margin on sales;
- reduce the payout of dividends in order to retain earnings;
- sell new equity;
- increase leverage (more debt versus equity); or
- increase the productivity of its assets.

It is possible to develop a sustainable growth equation that shows a company's optimum growth rate. The formula that can help determine the optimum growth rate is:

$$\text{Growth} = \frac{(M)\ (R)\ (1 + D/E)}{(A) - (M)\ (R)\ (1 + D/E)}$$

where:

$$M = \text{Ratio of net income to sales}$$
$$R = \text{Ratio of reinvested income to income before dividends}$$
$$D/E = \text{Ratio of total liabilities to net worth}$$
$$A = \text{Ratio of assets to sales}$$

Eastman's 2003 and 2004 sustainable growth rates are 9.9% and 38.6% respectively. The ratios used to arrive at these growth potentials are:

			2004	2003
M	=	Ratio of net income to sales	0.09	0.04
R	=	Ratio of reinvested income to income before dividends	0.81	0.51
D/E	=	Ratio of total liabilities to net worth	1.70	2.24
A	=	Ratio of assets to sales	0.68	0.72

The reason Eastman can grow faster in 2004 than in 2003 is that important favourable changes are expected. As shown, there is a significant change in the ratio of net income to sales. In 2003, the company had only $0.04 in profit for every dollar's worth of sales to invest in growth such as investments in capital assets or research and development. This ratio jumped to $0.09 in 2004.

The ratio of reinvested income to income before dividends also increased. In 2003, the company's ratio was only 0.51 (with income after taxes of $97,500 and payment of $47,500 in dividends), compared to 0.81 for 2004 (with profit after taxes of $264,000 and payment of only $50,000 in dividends). This means that the company will have more cash to reinvest in the business for growth purposes.

A similar improvement is taking place in the ratio of total liabilities to net worth. In 2003, 69% of the company's total assets were financed by debt. This figure is expected to drop to 63% in 2004. The ratio of total liabilities to net worth will also improve from 2.24 to 1.70. This improved performance gives the company more flexibility to borrow in the future.

The fourth ratio used in the formula is the total number of assets needed to support every dollar's worth of sales. As shown, in 2003, the company required $0.72 worth of assets to produce $1.00 in sales; in 2004, the company required only $0.68. This is another improvement.

Because it has shown improvements in these four ratios, the company will be able to improve its sustainable growth to 38.6%, which compares favourably to the company's expected sales revenue growth in 2004 of 22%. This means that the company is well within its organizational and financial capabilities.

Assessing the Financial Health of a Business

Objective 8 ➡

Let's turn now to measuring Eastman's financial health. In 1962, Edward Altman developed a mathematical model to help financial analysts predict the financial performance of businesses. Altman utilized a combination of traditional ratios and a sophisticated statistical technique known as discriminant analysis to construct a financial model for assessing the likelihood that a firm would go bankrupt. The model combined five financial measures utilizing both reported accounting and stock/variables to arrive at an objective overall measure of corporate health called the **financial health score** or the Z-score. For example, if the five ratios give a Z-score of 3.0 or higher, the company is in a healthy financial position or in a safe zone. If the score falls between 1.8 and 3.0, the company would be in the grey zone and could go either way. If the score is less than 1.8, the company would be in danger of bankruptcy.

Table 9.9 shows Altman's Z-score formula and Eastman's five financial ratios for the years 2003 and 2004. As shown, Eastman scored 2.34 in 2003 (grey zone) and 3.11 in 2004 (safe zone). This indicates that the company was able to take positive financial steps to make the company more viable. Here is a brief explanation for each of these ratios.

Financial health score (Z-score)

Linear analysis in which five measures are objectively weighted to give an overall score that becomes the basis for classifying the financial health of a business.

- Ratio (a): There was no change in the ratio of total assets to net working capital between the two accounting periods.

TABLE 9.9   ALTMAN'S Z-SCORE

Measuring the financial health zone of
Eastman Technologies Inc. for 2003 and 2004

Safe zone	3.0 and over
Grey zone	1.8 to 3.0
Bankrupt zone	0 to 1.8

$$Z = 1.2\,(a) + 1.4\,(b) + 3.3\,(c) + 0.6\,(d) + 1.0\,(e)$$

		2004	**2003**
$a =$	$\dfrac{\text{Working capital}}{\text{Total assets}}$	0.09	0.09
$b =$	$\dfrac{\text{Retained earnings}}{\text{Total assets}}$	0.23	0.14
$c =$	$\dfrac{\text{Earnings before interest and taxes}}{\text{Total assets}}$	0.26	0.12
$d =$	$\dfrac{\text{Equity}}{\text{Total liabilities}}$	0.59	0.45
$e =$	$\dfrac{\text{Sales}}{\text{Total assets}}$	1.47	1.39
	Z-score	3.11	2.34

- Ratio (b): The relationship between total assets and retained earnings increased substantially in 2004 over 2003 (from 0.14 to 0.23). This change is a result of an 84% increase in the retained earnings account shown on the balance sheet. This reflects a strong profit performance ($0.09 income after taxes for every dollar's worth of sales in 2004 compared to $0.04 in 2003) with a small increase in dividend payments.

- Ratio (c): The ratio of total assets to earnings before interest and taxes also increased substantially. This reflects a strong profit performance in 2004 compared to 2003.

- Ratio (d): The debt-to-equity ratio also improved in 2004 (0.59 compared to 0.45).

- Ratio (e): The total-assets-to-sales ratio also improved in 2004 (1.47 to 1.39).

Controlling

Controlling is a function of the management process that closes the management loop. What is the point of planning and budgeting if managers are not informed of the results of their efforts? We sometimes hear people say "We have things under control," meaning that all activities involved in realizing a project are well coordinated. On the other hand, if someone says that an activity is "out of control," it means that it is at the mercy of events. Establishing strategic and operational control points is crucial to ensuring that objectives and plans are realized.

The Control System

As shown in Figure 9.5, establishing an effective control system involves six steps:

Step 1: Design the subsystem.
Step 2: Establish performance indicators.
Step 3: Determine performance standards.
Step 4: Measure performance.
Step 5: Analyze variations.
Step 6: Take corrective action to resolve unfavourable situations that may arise.

DESIGN THE SUBSYSTEM The first step in establishing a control system is to determine the type of subsystem within the overall management system that would be most effective. The control subsystem should fit the culture of the organization and be one that managers and employees at all echelons will benefit from. Managers in bureaucratic organizations may prefer a *bureaucratic control* system, while democratic organizations may opt for *organic controls.* Managers should also ask questions such as How do we want the system to help us? Should the control system be more future-oriented (solve the problem before it appears) or reactive (give us information after an event takes place)? Or should we have both systems?

The system should be designed on the basis of what specific inputs (quantity and quality) are required by managers and when they need the information for analyzing their activities and making decisions. Managers will also prefer that the information output be presented in a certain way (e.g., reports or computer printouts).

ESTABLISH PERFORMANCE INDICATORS As shown in Figure 9.5, the entire control process is closely linked to the planning activity. Establishing operational and financial objectives during the planning phase allows managers to determine the type of **performance indicators** they should use for measuring accomplishments. The control process allows managers to determine how organizational units should be measured. First, managers determine the key elements or characteristics of the organizational units in terms of costs and benefits. Second, they determine which of these elements need to be measured. We are referring here to the principle of selectivity (also known as Pareto's Law), which states that often only

Performance indicators

How an organizational unit should be measured.

FIGURE 9.5 THE CONTROL PROCESS

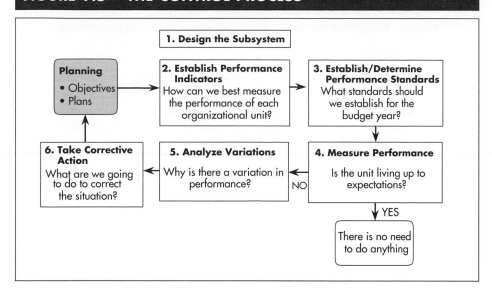

a small number of vital activities account for the largest number of outputs. If the appropriate indicators are not identified, it may be difficult for managers to measure the real organizational performance. For example, return on investment is an appropriate indicator for assessing the global company performance, cost per unit is suitable for gauging manufacturing operations, and share of market is excellent for measuring marketing performance. Table 9.10 gives examples of performance indicators (operating and financial) suitable for gauging objectives for different organizational units.

TABLE 9.10 STANDARDS FOR ASSESSING PERFORMANCE

Organizational Units	Performance Indicators	Standards	Performance	Variations
Company-wide	Return on investment (%)	17.5	17.7	0.2
Departments				
• Marketing	Share of market (%)	12.7	12.4	(0.3)
• Production	Cost per unit ($)	2.07	2.05	0.02
Organizational Units				
• Sales	Number of units sold	200,000	210,000	10,000
• Quality control	Number of tests per day per technician	6	6	—
Employees				
• Marketing	Number of customers visited per day per sales representative	3	2.5	(0.5)
• Production	Number of units produced per hour	35	38	3

Indicators can also be used to measure the performance of specific activities within a department such as marketing and production, or units such as sales and quality control. Indicators can also help to measure employee performance.

Performance standards

Quantitative measurement used as benchmarks to compare results with performance.

Categories of performance standards

There are four categories of standards: time, output, cost, and quality.

DETERMINE PERFORMANCE STANDARDS Once performance indicators are selected, the next step is to pinpoint the standards applicable for a particular time period (day, week, month, or year). These standards are established during the planning phase and serve as benchmarks for comparing results. There are four broad **categories of performance standards:** time, output, cost, and quality.

Time standards determine the length of time required to perform a specific task. For example, the length of time it takes to serve a customer at a bank or the length of time between a customer complaint and responding to it determines the quality of service offered and, thus, customer satisfaction.

Output standards measure the number of units that should be produced by individuals or groups. Managers of ticket agents for an airline company know the number of calls they can respond to on an hourly basis or the number of minutes it takes on average to provide information to their clients. For a telephone company, management knows the number of service calls technicians can respond to each day. At a university, student advisors know how many students they can meet daily.

Cost standards measure the resources required to produce goods or services. Holiday Inns or Westin Hotels know how much it costs to clean their rooms each day, Bic knows how much it costs to make a pen, and Gillette knows how much it costs to produce a can of shaving foam.

Quality standards pinpoint the level of quality needed to meet customer expectations. The "total quality management" concept focuses on quality standards that signal whether customers are receiving the expected quality products or services. For example, the services expected by guests at Holiday Inn or Journey's End may be different from those expected from the Westin Hotels or Four Seasons, and the customer expectations for a Rolex watch would be different than for a Timex. Although organizations sell products of different qualities, the critical point is to gauge the quality standards anticipated by customers and to carefully respond to their needs. Table 9.10 also gives examples of performance standards.

MEASURE PERFORMANCE Performance could be measured daily, weekly, monthly, or annually. To measure performance, managers need information that can be obtained from five sources: written reports, computer printouts, oral presentations, personal observations, and electronic media.

Written reports are used widely, particularly in large organizations. They are costly because of the time it takes to write the reports and for others to read them. To be effective tools, written reports should be brief (one page) in outline rather than narrative form, and structured to highlight the most critical information. *Computer printouts* can quickly provide all types of operating and financial data or information. Today, spreadsheet programs allow managers to enter data, which the computer calculates and presents numerically or graphically. From these printouts, managers can readily extract specific information. *Oral presentations* are effective as there is an immediate exchange of ideas during staff meetings between, say, subordinates and supervisors. Individuals communicating information at such meetings can use simple visual displays (e.g., simple line graphs, milestone charts), which are considered effective media for explaining performance and remedial action plans. To be effective, however, such meetings should be brief. Managers should establish before the meeting which reports should be presented and which should be distributed and read beforehand. Through *personal observations*, managers can visually detect the status of an operation. Management by walking about (MBWA) still is considered by many an effective management technique that can help managers make critical observations regarding the behaviour of individuals and groups, and operating activities. Today, information can be provided to managers instantly through *electronic media*. A sales manager, for example, can open his or her computer before the day starts and look at sales performance for the previous days, weeks, or months for individual sales representatives, or area or region managers.

To compare results to standards, managers must analyze information. Table 9.10 also shows how results are compared to standards. For example, the company established a target of 17.5% return on investment and achieved 17.7%, a superior performance.

ANALYZE VARIATIONS Variations between standards and results must be analyzed to determine the reasons for "off-performance" situations. Unfavourable variations do not necessarily mean mediocre performance. For example, is $10,000 over budget in manufacturing expenses unfavourable? Analysis may reveal that the manufacturing department produced more units to meet marketing needs, and thus increased corporate profits. If the advertising department spent $100,000 less than was budgeted, does this represent a favourable situation? Perhaps at first glance it may. However, after scrutiny, the manager may find that corporate revenues are $800,000 less than expected and profits $125,000 less than budgeted due to not having spent the $100,000 advertising budget. Overall, the company profit performance is down by $25,000.

Let's take another example to show the importance of properly analyzing variations. The credit department may have exceeded its salary budget by $14,000, but if credit clerks worked overtime to recover the accounts receivable more rapidly and succeeded in reducing the average collection period from 50 to 45 days, the benefits could have exceeded the $14,000 overtime cost.

It is not enough just to look at the column showing variations and judge quickly the performance of an organizational unit. Managers should investigate the reasons for the variations and determine whether they have favourable or unfavourable effects on the overall company performance.

TAKE CORRECTIVE ACTION When variations have been identified and the exact causes are known, managers then take the necessary steps to solve the problems. Managers have three options. First, there is the status quo. If a manager is on target or the variation is only minimal, he or she may decide to do nothing.

Second, a manager may wish to correct a situation. This is a likely option if the manager sees serious operating problems and wants to bring operations back in line. Third, the manager may want to change the standard. This may be appropriate if the original standard was set too high or if uncontrollable circumstances have changed the environment dramatically.

Types of Controls

Most control systems are one of three types: preventive controls, screening controls, or feedback controls (see Figure 9.6).

Preventive controls

System that helps to guide actions toward intended results.

PREVENTIVE CONTROLS Preventive controls (also known as feedforward controls, preliminary controls, steering controls, or proactive controls) take place when one wants to guide actions toward intended results. A recipe for making a cake is a classic example. The recipe will guide the cook to help him or her realize the intended results (the cake). This control system emphasizes the future; a manager knows what he or she wants, and puts in place the necessary mechanism to ensure that the intended results are achieved.

Now let's take two business situations to illustrate how preventive controls work. Before hiring bank tellers, the human resources department will identify the required qualifications to ensure that the manager hires efficient and effective tellers and maintains the employee turnover at a low level. The job description prevents staffing officers from hiring unsuitable job applicants; that is why this system is called preventive control. Similarly, in a manufacturing operation that makes products such as soft drinks, coffee, chocolate bars, or hamburgers, management will specify the quality level and the ingredients before production actually begins.

FIGURE 9.6 TYPES OF CONTROL SYSTEMS

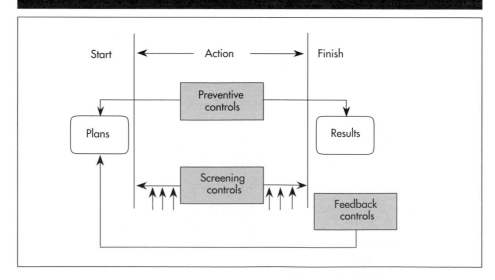

SCREENING CONTROLS **Screening controls,** also known as concurrent controls, take place during the implementation phase or as the process takes place. Some screening controls take the "yes-no" form. This means that the process can either be continued or stopped in order to take corrective actions. For example, when buying a house, a potential homeowner will say yes or no during each step of the purchase process (visit the house, negotiate the price or other terms, agree with the terms of the mortgage loan) before signing the final purchase agreement.

Screening controls can also be done by using what is called the "steering" mechanism. This means that as the process evolves, the degree of deviation is gradually brought back into line without actually stopping the process. In an automobile manufacturing plant, for example, control points are established at every critical step of the assembly line. As a car moves along the line, periodic control checks are executed to see that each job is performed according to standard before the car moves to subsequent assembly points. Steering controls reduce unnecessary manufacturing costs (e.g., having to remove the dashboard if the electrical wiring system is improperly installed).

Screening controls
System that helps to monitor performance while work is being performed.

FEEDBACK CONTROLS **Feedback controls,** also known as corrective controls or post-performance controls, are like thermostats. They place emphasis on past performance and the manager takes corrective action only when comparisons are made and the variations detected. Managers are reacting to a given situation; for example, if your bank statement shows an overdraft, you will immediately take action by rushing to the bank to make a deposit. In organizations, daily, weekly, and monthly reports work the same way: they inform managers about performance so they can take the necessary actions to correct unfavourable situations. Report cards, budget reports, and audit reports are typical feedback controls.

The objective of these three types of control systems is the same—to assist managers to gauge performance and take corrective action to reach stated objectives.

Feedback controls
System that helps to focus on variations of past performance.

✳ Decision-Making in Action

In October 2003, Dytex Ltd. was in the process of starting its annual planning process. At its monthly management committee meeting, John Lipton, CEO of the company, informed its members that, over the next several years, the economic and industry conditions appeared extremely positive. He made the point that he wanted Dytex to take advantage of this opportunity by significantly improving the company's financial performance. He stressed the importance that all managers in every division would have to take a serious look at their operating budgets and try to be creative in finding ways to improve their respective perform-

ance. He insisted that he wanted to have aggressive growth in the marketplace and improvement in operating efficiencies in all divisions, departments, and organizational units.

He asked Arlene Gibson to make a brief presentation of the company's financial statements for the years 2003 (actual) and 2004 (forecast). The income statements, the statements of retained earnings, the balance sheets, and the statements of changes in financial position including financial performance measures are presented in Table 9.11.

After the presentation, Mr. Lipton gave a rough idea of his key objectives based on the following planning assumptions:

First, we're going to be aiming for a 17% increase in sales revenue based on the premise that three of the four sectors in which our divisions compete will show growth close to 15%. With the new and improved product lines that we plan to introduce in the marketplace, coupled with some creative advertisements and innovative marketing strategies, we should not have problems in achieving that growth. Nevertheless, we will have to ensure that we have the physical, financial, and human resource means to achieve this growth rate.

Second, the return on sales over the past several years has been less than that experienced by our key competitors. In 2003, our return on sales was 4.7% and, based on our most recent forecast, we expect to show 6.1% by the end of this year. Our key competitors are showing performance in the area of 8 to 10%. In fact, we should use Gilmore Inc. as our benchmark; their return on sales is 14%. I do know that there is room for improvement in efficiencies in both cost of production and marketing, and our managers should make every effort to cut costs, improve efficiencies, eliminate waste, and be more economical in the way they operate.

Third, our divisions expect to invest substantial sums of money in capital assets in 2005: modernizations, acquisition of new assets, investment in research and development, and the expansion of two plants. During our discussions of the past several meetings and some preliminary reports that I have received from your divisional controllers, I estimate a $20 million investment in capital assets.

Fourth, I would like to have these capital projects funded mostly by internally generated cash. This cash will come from increased operating efficiencies (profit) and improvement in the way that we manage our accounts receivable and inventories. This year, there appears to be deterioration in the way that receivables and inventories are managed. With the 17% increase in sales revenue, I don't expect receivables

and inventories to increase in the same proportion. Improvements in these two working capital accounts will allow us to invest less cash in working capital accounts. Some members of the board of directors have expressed a willingness to invest more funds in Dytex. However, I would like to keep this at a minimum because we have several acquisitions in sight over the next several years, and I would like to keep our debt-to-equity ratio healthy. We will need external funds for these acquisitions.

The bottom line is this: I want to make sure that Dytex's financial position is improved during the next several years. In 2003, the company's overall financial health score was at 2.54. Based on our year-end forecast, we expect that it will reach 2.66 in 2004. I would like to see a continued improvement and reach a score of 3.00 by 2005. Also, our economic value added in 2003 was a meager $248,000 with a forecast of $707,000 by year-end. I would like to be able to show the members of the board of directors that EVA showed a sizeable gain for next year.

Now, we have three months of planning and budgeting. Arlene Gibson and her staff will be coordinating this process. They will consolidate the divisional and departmental budgets and present the pro-forma financial statements at our late-November meeting. If the financial results are in line with these broad goals, we will bring these numbers to the board members for review and approval. If not, we will have to ask our managers to redo their budgets in order to squeeze more cash from our operations.

During the November special budget sessions, Arlen Gibson presented the 2005 consolidated financial statements with key financial indicators (see Table 9.11). Also, she pointed out the following fixed payments during the planning period:

(in $000s)	2003	2004	2005
Lease payments	1,000	1,200	1,300

Mr. Lipton was pleased with the statements and indicated that he was prepared to present them to the next meeting of the board for review and approval.

TABLE 9.11   DYTEX LTD'S FINANCIAL STATEMENTS AND PERFORMANCE
MEASURES

**Income Statements
for the Period Ending December 31**

(in $000s)	2003 Actual	2004 Forecast	2005 Budget
Net sales revenue	102,000	109,000	128,000
Cost of goods sold	71,000	73,000	82,000
Gross margin	31,000	36,000	46,000
Operating expenses			
Selling expenses	11,000	12,000	13,000
Administrative expenses	10,000	10,700	11,300
Total operating expenses	21,000	22,700	24,300
Operating income	10,000	13,300	21,700
Interest income	100	150	200
Interest charges	2,000	2,300	2,500
Income before taxes	8,100	11,150	19,400
Income taxes	3,300	4,500	5,820
Income after taxes	4,800	6,650	13,580

Statements of Retained Earnings for the Periods Ending December 31

Beginning retained earnings	13,000	17,800	24,450
Net earnings for the year	4,800	6,650	13,580
Ending retained earning	17,800	24,450	38,030

TABLE 9.11 DYTEX LTD'S FINANCIAL STATEMENTS AND PERFORMANCE MEASURES (continued)

**Balance Sheets
as at December 31**

(in $000s)	2003 Actual	2004 Forecast	2005 Budget
Assets			
Current assets			
Cash/term deposits	1,100	1,450	1,600
Prepaid expenses	300	500	600
Accounts receivable	9,000	12,700	14,000
Inventory	6,000	8,000	8,500
Total current assets	16,400	22,350	24,400
Capital assets			
Gross capital assets	100,000	113,000	135,000
Accumulated depreciation	30,000	33,000	38,000
Net capital assets	70,000	80,000	97,000
Total operating expenses	86,400	102,350	121,400
Liabilities			
Current liabilities			
Accounts payable	4,000	4,100	4,700
Working capital loans	5,000	5,300	5,900
Accruals	200	500	770
Total current liabilities	9,200	9,900	13,370
Long-term debts	34,400	38,000	41,000
Total liabilities	43,600	47,900	52,370
Owners' equity			
Capital shares	25,000	30,000	31,000
Retained earnings	17,800	24,450	38,030
Owners' equity	42,800	54,450	69,030
Total liabilities and owners' equity	86,400	102,350	121,400

Chapter Summary

Budgeting is a vital element of the management planning and control process. It is the process that translates corporate intentions into specific tasks and identifies the resources needed by each manager to carry them out. The budgeting process enhances communication and coordination of different organizational units, facilitates decision-making, and provides a framework for monitoring and for performance evaluation. The management tool that facilitates pinpointing managerial responsibility and accountability for attaining objectives and realizing plans is the responsibility centre.

◄■ Objective 1

Budgeting is only part of the planning and control framework. For a budgeting process to be effective, it must be preceded by objectives and priorities set by senior management, as well as objectives set at the operating level. Budgeting must also be followed by a control mechanism. Managers should follow basic rules when they prepare their operating budgets. To avoid budgeting problems, remember these points: paper should be kept to a minimum; budgeting should be subservient to goal-setting; no activities should be taken for granted; and top management should be committed to participate actively in the budgeting process.

◄■ Objective 2

An organization may have different types of budgets, which can be grouped under three categories: operating budgets (flexible and overhead budgets), complementary budgets (product budgets, program budgets, item-of-expenditure budgets, and cash flow budgets), and comprehensive budgets (pro-forma financial statements and capital expenditure budgets). Flexible budgets are employed at the plant level, where costs of production are used as checkpoints to compare actual results and to ascertain price and quantity variances. A production budget will vary with the number of units produced. Zero-based budgeting is a management tool used by administrative or overhead units. Here, the manager of each unit reviews all activities—past, present, and projected—and evaluates them in terms of productivity versus costs.

◄■ Objective 3

To be an effective management tool, budgeting should be regarded as a permanent process. All managers should be responsible for preparing their own budget. Since specific departments play important roles in improving various components of the balance sheet and the income statement, it is critical that they prepare their budgets in a responsible way. The budgeting exercise should keep paperwork at a reasonable level. Also, it should be subservient to objectives, and past activities should be not taken for granted. To be effective, top-level managers should take an active part in budgeting process.

◄■ Objective 4

The aim of cost accounting is to provide managers with information on the costs associated with buying or selling a product or providing a service. Activity-based costing focuses on the analysis of overhead costs to determine whether they can be directly related to specific activities. There are two types of cost accounting

◄■ Objective 5

systems that help managers make effective decisions: job order costing and process costing.

Objective 6 ➤➤ Financial planning is the activity that integrates all budgets into pro-forma financial statements to determine whether the company is improving its financial performance. There are three pro-forma financial statements: the pro-forma income statement; the pro-forma balance sheet, and the pro-forma cash flow statement.

Objective 7 ➤➤ Management should also be able to manage the company's growth. This is important if the company is not to deplete its human and financial resources. The sustainable growth formula is a tool that identifies how quickly a company should grow in order to conserve financial strength. The four ratios used to calculate the sustainable growth rate are (a) ratio of net income to sales, (b) ratio of reinvested income to income before dividends, (c) ratio of total liabilities to net worth, and (d) ratio of assets to sales.

Objective 8 ➤➤ The Z-score formula, which combines five ratios, is used to assess the financial health of a business.

Objective 9 ➤➤ Controlling is the management activity that helps managers determine whether they have realized their plans and objectives. Establishing a control system involves six steps: designing the subsystem, establishing performance indicators, determining performance standards, measuring performance, analyzing variations, and taking corrective action to resolve unfavourable situations that may arise. Control systems can be grouped into three major categories: preventive controls, screening controls, and feedback controls.

Key Terms

Accountable	Material variance
Activity-based costing	Operating budgets
Budgeting	Overhead variance
Capital budgets	Performance indicator
Categories of performance standards	Performance standards
Categories of responsibility centres	Preventive controls
Complementary budgets	Process costing
Comprehensive budgets	Pro-forma financial statements
Cost accounting	Reasons for budgeting
Feedback controls	Responsibility centre
Financial health score (Z-score)	Screening controls
Job order costing	Sustainable growth rate
Labour variance	Variance analysis

Review Questions

1. What is budgeting?
2. Why is budgeting so important?
3. Explain the meaning of the responsibility-centre concept.
4. Comment on the various types of responsibility centres.
5. Explain budgeting in terms of planning as a whole.
6. What are operating budgets?
7. Differentiate between incremental budgeting and zero-based budgeting.
8. What do we mean by complementary budgets?
9. What is the purpose of a cash budget?
10. List the more important rules of sound budgeting.
11. What are some of the more important budgeting pitfalls to avoid?
12. What is the purpose of cost accounting?
13. Differentiate between job-order costing and process costing.
14. What is financial planning?
15. What do we mean by the term "sustainable growth"?
16. Explain Altman's financial health formula.
17. What is controlling?
18. Explain the various steps involved in the control system.
19. Comment on the various types of performance standards.
20. Differentiate between preventive controls and screening controls.

Discussion Questions

1. Contrast control as a "policing activity" and control as a "steering activity."
2. Since managers cannot control everything, what factors should be considered when determining which activities should be controlled?

Testing Your Comprehension

True/False Questions

_____ 1. Budgeting is the process that translates corporate intentions into specific tasks, and identifies the resources needed by managers to carry them out.

_____ 2. Budgeting should not be used to evaluate a manager's performance.

_____ 3. Responsibility-centre accounting is considered essential to the design of a good management system.

_____ 4. Zero-based budgeting is based on the premise that every budget dollar requires justification.

_____ 5. Cash budgets are used in large measure to negotiate a line of credit with commercial banks.

_____ 6. The cost accounting process involves the allocation of all cost data to manufacturing, purchasing, and selling.

_____ 7. Process costing is best suited in situations where products are manufactured in identifiable lots or batches or to meet customer specifications.

_____ 8. Increasing the profit margin is the best source of growth funds.

_____ 9. The Z-score formula is an excellent way to determine how fast a company should grow.

_____ 10. Performance indicators are established during the control phase and serve as benchmarks for comparing results.

_____ 11. A 17% return on investment can be considered a performance standard.

_____ 12. Job descriptions can be used as preventive control tools.

_____ 13. A bank statement is much like a screening control tool used during the control process.

_____ 14. The objective of the three types of control systems (preventive, screening, and feedback) is the same: to correct actions.

Multiple-Choice Questions

1. One reason budgeting is important is that it helps:
   a. formulate specific objectives
   b. improve communication
   c. formulate budget guidelines
   d. employees plan
   e. clarify strategic orientation

2. An important element of the responsibility-centre concept is:
   a. span of management
   b. sustainable growth
   c. managerial values
   d. delegation of responsibility
   e. accountability

3. An important prerequisite to the budgeting process is the preparation of the:
   a. planning assumptions
   b. master budget
   c. operational objectives
   d. pro-forma financial statements
   e. projected program budgets

4. The following is considered an operating budget:
   a. cash budget
   b. product budget
   c. program budget
   d. item-of-expenditure budget
   e. sales budget

5. Flexible budgets are usually prepared by the:
   a. sales department
   b. manufacturing department
   c. human resource department
   d. research and development department
   e. finance department

6. Variance analysis compares:
   a. objectives to goals
   b. budgets to standards
   c. standards to actual performance
   d. overhead costs to material costs
   e. process costing to job order costing

7. Job costing is an accounting system that:
   a. provides information to managers to make informed decisions
   b. helps to allocate indirect costs related to producing a specific good
   c. keeps paperwork at a reasonable level
   d. helps to allocate direct costs related to producing a specific good
   e. makes budgeting a top-management practice

8. The accounting system that helps to allocate direct and departmental overhead costs in organizations that produce goods on a continuous basis is called:
   a. process costing
   b. continuous costing
   c. cost accounting
   d. job order costing
   e. activity-based costing

9. The following help prepare the financial plans:
   a. pro-forma financial statements
   b. operational plans
   c. operating budgets
   d. strategic plans
   e. strategic objectives

10. The first pro-forma financial statement that should be prepared is the:
    a. balance sheet
    b. income statement
    c. statement of retained earnings
    d. statement of cash flows
    e. cash budget

11. The following ratio is not part of the sustainable growth formula:
    a. ratio of current liabilities to current assets
    b. ratio of net income to sales
    c. ratio of reinvested income to income before dividends
    d. ratio of total liabilities to net worth
    e. ratio of assets to sales

12. The following is the most often used element to calculate Altman's Z-score:
    a. working capital
    b. total assets
    c. shareholders' equity
    d. sales revenue
    e. retained earnings

Fill-in-the-Blanks Questions

1. _____ is the process by which management allocates corporate resources, evaluates financial outcomes, and establishes systems to control operational and financial performance.

2. There are four categories of responsibility centres: revenue, cost, profit, and _____ _____ centres.

3. Budgets can be grouped under four categories: operating, complementary, comprehensive and _____ budgets.

4. _____ budgets are used by plant or production departments where costs of production (standard costs) are used as benchmarks for comparing actual results to identify price and quantity discounts.

5. _____ budgets are used for cash planning and control.

6. _____ costing is an accounting system that focuses on the analysis of overhead costs to determine how they relate to different products, services, or activities.

7. _____ costing is an accounting system that helps to allocate direct costs related to producing a specific good.

8. _____ costing is an accounting system that helps to allocate direct

and departmental overhead costs in organizations that produce goods on a continuous basis.

9. The accounting system that compares standards to actual performance is called _____ analysis.

10. Labour variance is made up of two components, time and _____.

11. An _____ variance takes place when there is a difference in costs between standards and actual performance due to changes in indirect costs.

12. _____ financial statements are projected income statements and balance sheets.

13. The _____ growth rate shows the increase in sales revenue a company can attain without depleting financing resources, excessive borrowing, and issuing new stock.

14. The linear analysis in which five financial measures are objectively weighted to give an overall position of a business is called the _____ score.

15. _____ standards are quantitative measurements used as benchmarks to compare results with how well a business is doing.

16. The four categories of performance standards are: time, output, cost, and _____.

17. _____ controls are systems that help to guide actions toward intended results.

18. _____ controls are systems that help to monitor performance while work is being performed.

19. _____ controls are systems that help to focus on variations of past performance.

Learning Exercises

Exercise 1(a)

Identify efficiency and effectiveness indicators for the following organizational units or activities of CompuTech:

1. retail store;
2. company;
3. sales clerks;
4. security system; and
5. promotional coupons.

Exercise 1(b)

Identify efficiency and effectiveness indicators for the following responsibility centres, individuals, or organizations:

1. sales department;
2. telephone-answering service;

3. purchasing department;

4. politician;

5. rehabilitation centre;

6. student;

7. general insurance company;

8. cleaning department;

9. security department; and

10. school.

Exercise 2(a)

Identify the factors that you would take into consideration when determining the level of services for CompuTech's retail store.

Exercise 2(b)

Identify the factors that you would take into consideration when using zero-based budgeting to determine the level of services for the following responsibility centres:

- sanitation department;
- training department;
- quality control department;
- police department;
- advertising department; and
- telephone-answering service.

Exercise 3(a)

What is the profit for products A and B?

1. Sales are estimated at 4,500 units for product A and 1,500 for product B. Product A sells for $7.50 per unit, and B for $15.25 per unit.

2. The cost of goods sold for each unit are as follows:

	Product A	*Product B*
Purchase price	$2.40	$6.30
Freight-in	0.30	1.10

3. Store overhead costs are $120,000, and 8% of these costs are allocated against products A and B, based on the number of units sold.

4. Administrative overhead costs are $110,000, and 10% of these costs are allocated against these products on a revenue basis.

Exercise 3(b)

What is the profit for products A and B?

1. Sales are estimated at 20,000 units for product A and 30,000 for product B. Product A sells for $20 per unit, and B for $30 per unit.

2. The per-unit manufacturing costs for the products are as follows:

	Product A	Product B
Material A	$6.40	$9.30
Material B	2.30	3.60
Labour	0.75	1.05
Other	1.20	1.10

3. Total production overhead costs are $200,000, and 50% of these costs are allocated against products A and B, based on the number of units manufactured.

4. Administrative overhead costs such as rent, salaries, and advertising are $350,000, and 60% of these costs are allocated against these products on a revenue basis.

Exercise 4(a)

With the following information, prepare a cash budget for the months of January to April 2004.

The marketing department's sales forecast is:

November (2003)	$50,000
December	60,000
January (2004)	60,000
February	70,000
March	75,000
April	80,000

The credit manager provides the following information:

80% of sales are on a cash basis
20% are collected after 30 days

Cost of goods sold, which is 50% of sales, is incurred in the month in which the sales are made. These goods are paid for 30 days after the purchases are made. Monthly selling and administrative expenses are as follows:

Salaries	$12,000
Interest	2,500
Leasing	800
Depreciation	3,000
Advertising	1,000

Other expenses are as follows:

Taxes: $10,000 in February, $10,000 in April, and $10,000 in September.

Purchase of assets: $3,000 in January, $12,000 in February, $20,000 in March, and $3,000 in April.

The cash balance on January 1, 2004, is $3,000.

Exercise 4(b)

With the following information, prepare a cash budget for the months of January to April 2004.

The marketing department's sales forecast is:

November (2003)	$ 25,000
December	50,000
January (2004)	75,000
February	120,000
March	140,000
April	110,000

The credit manager provides the following information:

20% of sales are on a cash basis
60% are collected after 30 days
20% are collected after 60 days

Cost of goods sold, which is 50% of sales, is incurred in the month in which the sales are made. These goods are paid for 30 days after the purchases are made.

Monthly selling and administrative expenses are as follows:

Salaries	$22,000
Telephone	1,000
Depreciation	500
Rent	2,200
Hydro	1,100
Stationery	500

Other expenses are as follows:

Taxes: $3,000 in February and $3,000 in June.
Purchase of equipment in January for $24,000.
The cash balance on January 1, 2004, is $12,000.

Exercise 5(a)

By using CompuTech's year 2004 financial statements presented in Exercise 4 of Chapter 4 or in Appendix A, calculate the company's:

1. sustainable growth rate; and
2. Z-score.

Exercise 5(b)

With the following, calculate Eagle Electronics Inc.'s:

1. sustainable growth rate; and

2. Z-score.

BALANCE SHEET

Current assets		Current liabilities	
Cash	$ 100,000	Accounts payable	$ 350,000
Accounts receivable	300,000	Notes payable	100,000
Inventory	600,000	Bank loan	300,000
Total current assets	1,000,000	Total current liabilities	750,000
Capital assets	2,000,000	Long-term debts	1,000,000
		Common shares	400,000
		Retained earnings	850,000
		Total equity	1,250,000
Total assets	$3,000,000	Total liabilities and equity	$3,000,000

INCOME STATEMENT

Sales revenue	$3,000,000
Cost of goods sold	1,500,000
Gross margin	1,500,000
Operating expenses*	900,000
Operating income	600,000
Income taxes	300,000
Income after taxes	300,000
Dividends	$ 100,000
Retained earnings	$ 200,000

* Includes $100,000 of interest charges.

Cases

Case 1: Seabridge Distributors Inc.

Seabridge Distributors Inc. is a distributor of central air conditioners, purifiers, humidifiers, and dehumidifiers. It has the franchise for the distribution, installation, and servicing of products for a well-known national brand in eastern Canada.

In September 2003, Louise Lane, president of the company, asked Bill Vance, general sales manager, to prepare a monthly sales budget for 2004. Lane informed Vance of the importance of a sales budget, giving the following reasons:

1. It helps to set objectives for each sales representative and for individual product lines.

2. Manufacturers are informed at least six months ahead of time of Seabridge's short-term requirements for each product line; this assures getting products in the right quantities at the right time.

3. The bank manager is informed of Seabridge's financial requirements for each month of the budget year; the bank provides Seabridge with short-term money to finance inventories and is interested in the company's short-term repayment capability.

4. If Seabridge is to operate effectively, it should not be caught in a position of being short of products at times when demand is high. Similarly, it would be costly for the company to be left with excessive quantities of units in inventory at the end of a season.

Following this meeting, Bill Vance decided to have a meeting with his four area managers to get the ball rolling. In early October, Bill met with his managers, emphasizing the importance of sound sales budgeting and stressing that the foundation for the preparation of a sound sales budget is sales forecasting.

The four sales managers had sales territories with the following number of sales representatives.

Territory	Number of sales representatives
North	4
South	5
East	3
West	4
Total	16

At the meeting, Vance showed some slides indicating the industry's demand projections for each product line, the company's 2003 share of market, and what he hoped to achieve in 2004. The figures are shown below.

	Total market (in units) 2004	Share of market Estimated 2003	Share of market Objective 2004
Air conditioners	15,000	14%	16%
Air purifiers	2,300	12%	15%
Air humidifiers	83,000	11%	13%
Air dehumidifiers	74,000	9%	11%

He also presented the following percentage breakdown of the number of units sold each month for different products based on the previous five years.

	% of Sales by Month			
	Air conditioners	Air purifiers	Air humidifiers	Air dehumidifiers
January	—	3	1	—
February	—	2	1	—
March	2	2	—	—
April	4	4	—	—
May	10	8	—	5
June	28	22	—	33
July	44	33	—	56
August	12	8	6	6
September	—	6	12	—
October	—	6	38	—
November	—	4	28	—
December	—	2	14	—
Total	100	100	100	100

The average unit selling prices budgeted are as follows:

Air conditioners	$4,700
Air purifiers	650
Air humidifiers	515
Air dehumidifiers	450

At the end of the meeting, the concept of sales objectives was discussed at some length with the area managers. Although it had not been the company's practice to establish objectives for every sales representative, it was the consensus that in view of the company's ambition to increase its share of the market for 2004, objectives should be introduced.

1. On the basis of the information available, prepare a monthly sales budget for 2004 for individual and combined product lines.

2. Is there anything wrong with the way that the sales budget and sales objectives were introduced in this company? If so, how would you have approached the situation?

Case 2: Anderson Equipment Ltd.

One day in March 2003, John Sutherland, Industrial Commissioner for the city of South Elk, received a telephone call from Nick Faranda, president of Anderson Equipment Ltd., who wanted to see him as soon as possible.

When Sutherland arrived at Faranda's office, Faranda was sitting at his desk going over his current year's cash budget. Faranda informed Sutherland that as a result of the revised credit restrictions adopted by his bank, he was being asked to prepare an estimate of his financial requirements for the balance of the calendar year. All major customers of the bank were asked to provide this information.

Faranda also informed Sutherland that he would be having a meeting with Joanne Armstrong, lending officer responsible for handling the company's account and that he wanted to be in a position to show her his financial requirements for the rest of the calendar year. Consequently, Faranda asked Sutherland to help him prepare a budget forecast. On the basis of the information available, Faranda felt that it would not be necessary to borrow funds before July 2003. The budget would therefore be prepared for the period July 1, 2003, to January 31, 2004.

The marketing department provided the following sales forecast:

July	$ 50,000
August	100,000
September	500,000
October	650,000
November	550,000
December	400,000
January	200,000

Ten percent of sales are for cash. Forty percent of sales are collected after 30 days, and the remaining 50% after 60 days. Purchases, which are 80% of sales, are incurred in the month in which the sales are made. These goods are paid 30% in cash and 70% within 30 days. Selling and administrative expenses are $10,000 per month, plus 1% of monthly sales during the selling season, and are zero in months when there are no sales. Start-up costs in July are $30,000. Taxes for the entire operating period are paid in April and are 40% of the net income. The monthly depreciation is $10,000. The company feels that it is necessary to maintain a minimum cash balance of $25,000 during the selling season.

The cash balance on July 1 is $75,000.

1. Prepare a monthly cash budget from July 2003 to January 2004.

Case 3: United Manufacturers Ltd.

With the following financial objectives and assumptions, prepare the company's 2004:

(a) pro-forma income statement;

(b) pro-forma statement of retained earnings;

(c) pro-forma balance sheet;

(d) pro-forma statement of changes in financial position (cash flows); and

(e) financial ratios, and compare them with the 2003 financial results.

Also, calculate the company's 2004:

(a) sustainable growth; and

(b) Z-score.

Financial objectives and assumptions:

1. Related to the income statement
   - sales revenue will increase by 10.0%;
   - cost of goods sold as a percentage of sales revenue will climb to 51.5%;
   - selling expenses as a percentage of sales revenue will be improved slightly by 10.5%;
   - general and administrative expenses will drop to 5.7% of sales revenue;
   - research and development costs as a percentage of sales revenue will increase 2.0%;
   - depreciation will be $100,000;
   - amortization will be $20,000;
   - interest income will be $6,000;
   - interest charges will be $35,000; and
   - income tax rate (as a percentage of income before taxes) will be maintained at the 2003 level.

2. Related to the statement of retained earnings
   - an amount of $50,000 in dividends will be paid to shareholders.

3. Related to the balance sheet
   (a) Current asset accounts
      - cash in the bank will be 2.0% of sales;
      - accounts receivable will improve to 44.9 days; and
      - inventory will improve to 4.9 times.
   (b) Capital asset accounts
      - investment in capital assets will be $660,000; and
      - other assets will be increased by $100,000.
   (c) Current liabilities
      - accounts payable will increase to 11.31% of cost of goods sold; and
      - notes payable will decrease to $268,685.
   (d) Long-term debts
      - long-term notes will increase by $39,700.
   (e) Equity
      - shareholders will invest an additional $200,000 in the business.

UNITED MANUFACTURERS LTD.
INCOME STATEMENT
FOR THE YEAR ENDED DECEMBER 31

	2002	2003
Sales revenue	$2,900,000	$3,100,000
Cost of goods sold	1,870,000	1,880,000
Gross margin	1,030,000	1,220,000
Selling, administration, and other expenses		
Selling	325,000	330,000
Administration	220,000	210,000
Research and development	35,000	45,000
Depreciation and amortization	95,000	105,000
Total selling, admin., and other expenses	675,000	690,000
Operating income	355,000	530,000
Interest income	4,000	5,000
Interest charges	27,000	30,000
Total other income/charges	23,000	25,000
Income before taxes	332,000	505,000
Income taxes	166,000	252,500
Income after taxes	$ 166,000	$ 252,500

United Manufacturers Ltd.
Balance Sheets
as at December 31

	2002	2003
Assets		
Current assets		
Cash and investments	$ 48,000	$ 54,000
Accounts receivable	420,000	459,000
Inventory	256,000	268,000
Total current assets	724,000	781,000
Capital assets	2,719,000	2,919,000
Accumulated depreciation	595,000	700,000
Net capital assets	2,124,000	2,219,000
Other assets (intangible)	100,000	200,000
Total assets	$2,948,000	$3,200,000
Liabilities		
Current liabilities		
Accounts payable	$ 140,000	$ 131,600
Notes payable	256,000	263,900
Other current liabilities	150,000	100,000
Total current liabilities	546,000	495,500
Long-term debts	950,000	1,000,000
Total liabilities	1,496,000	1,495,000
Shareholders' equity		
Common shares	800,000	800,000
Retained earnings	652,000	904,500
Total shareholders' equity	1,452,000	1,704,500
Total liabilities and equity	$2,948,000	$3,200,000

10

Sources and Forms of Financing

Learning Objectives

After reading this chapter, you should be able to:

1. Make the distinction between financial needs and financing requirements.

2. Differentiate between internal financing and external financing.

3. Differentiate between the different types of risks-related financing options (ownership versus debt).

4. Comment on the various forms and sources of financing.

5. Identify the most important short-term lenders.

6. Discuss the sources of intermediate and long-term investors.

7. Comment on the different categories of equity financing.

8. Comment on the factors that influence businesses when choosing between buying or leasing an asset.

Chapter Outline

OPENING CASE

Now that the Millers have identified their 2005 financial needs (uses of funds) and financing requirements (sources of funds) (shown below) and have completed their investment proposal, they are ready to approach investors (short- and long-term lenders and shareholders) for the purpose of raising funds.

	Financial Needs (Uses of Funds)	*Financing Requirements (Sources of Funds)*
Working capital		
Cash	$ 4,000	
Prepaid expenses	5,000	
Accounts receivable	45,000	
Inventory	45,000	
Capital assets	350,000	
Internal sources		
Income after taxes		$ 77,000
Depreciation		80,000
Total internal sources		$157,000
Working capital financing		
Accounts payable		27,000
Term loan		20,000
Working capital loan		25,000
Total working capital financing		72,000
External sources		
Capital shares		70,000
Long-term debts		150,000
Total external sources		220,000
Total	$449,000	$449,000

As shown above, CompuTech needs $449,000 to finance its existing retail store (primarily working capital) and to open the new one. As shown, $99,000 will be needed to finance the working capital (cash, prepaid expenses, accounts receivable, and inventory) and $350,000 to open the new store.

Based on the Millers' financial projections for 2005, 35% or approximately $157,000 will be provided by internally generated funds (income after taxes and depreciation), and 16% or approximately $72,000 will be obtained from suppliers and short-term lenders. The Millers will approach banks to obtain $45,000, which is half of the $90,000 required to finance accounts receivable ($45,000) and inventory ($45,000). To help finance part of the $350,000 capital assets, the Millers will contact various investors and will try to obtain $70,000 from shareholders (e.g., friends, family members, private investors) and $150,000 from long-term lenders.

Although the Millers have identified their financing requirements, they are unsure whether these various sources are the best mix to finance the $449,000 financial needs. They analyzed various *sources* of financing and raised questions such as: Should we obtain more funds from:

- lenders or shareholders?
- short-term lenders or suppliers?
- leasing organizations?
- friends or private investors (i.e., angels)?
- banks or government institutions?

They also questioned themselves about the best *forms* of financing. For example, should we go for:

- term loans or conditional sales contracts?
- a line of credit or a revolving loan?
- secured loans or unsecured loans?
- seasonal loans or factoring our receivables?

This chapter explores typical financing issues that businesses must often consider. It focuses on three key topics:

1. identifying financial needs and financing requirements;
2. the various sources and forms of financing; and
3. how to calculate the economics of leasing versus owning an asset.

Introduction

Financing is one of senior management's most constant preoccupations. There are many ways a chief financial officer (CFO) can finance the purchase of assets, and funds can be obtained from a variety of sources and in different forms. Selecting the right source and form of financing can improve the long-term financial structure and profitability of a business.

Chapter 6, "Cost of Capital and Capital Structure," focused on how financing decisions could help optimize the use of funds provided by investors (shareholders and lenders). This chapter focuses on the sources and forms of financing; where, why, and how funds can be obtained; and the different types of financing instruments available to businesses.

The more important considerations to take into account when choosing the right form and source of financing are the:

- firm's annual debt commitments or obligations;
- cost of financing;
- risk factor arising from a slowdown (or acceleration) in economic or market conditions;
- control factor (related to existing shareholders);
- flexibility to respond to future financing decisions;
- pattern of the capital structure in the industry;
- stability of the company's earnings; and
- common shareholders' expectations.

Objective 1 ➠

Financial Needs and Financing Requirements

Financial needs

The items for which a business needs money.

The first thing a CFO must do before approaching investors is to identify what is to be financed. Here, we are talking about **financial needs.** Financial decisions involve what needs to be financed and the amount needed. Here are a few examples:

1. purchase of capital assets;
2. additional working capital (inventory and accounts receivable);
3. more investments in research and development; and
4. the launching of a new product requiring large expenditures in promotional and advertising activities.

Once the financial needs have been identified, the next step is to pinpoint where the financing will come from and the amounts required from different sources. Both the nature of the financial needs and the amount required will determine, to a large extent, the financing requirements in terms of sources and forms.

Figure 10.1 shows how the financial needs and financing requirements are related. The left side of the figure shows that the company will require $1.0 million to finance the expansion of its business activities. This could be in the form of the purchase of capital assets that will appear on the balance sheet and operating expense items (e.g., advertising, promotion, salaries for research and development) that will appear on the income statement. The composition of this $1.0 million financial need could be made up as follows:

Working capital	$ 200,000
Capital assets	600,000
Marketing costs	100,000
Research and development	100,000
Total	$1,000,000

FIGURE 10.1   FINANCIAL NEEDS AND FINANCING REQUIREMENTS

Financial Needs	Financing Requirements	
Investment Required to Fund the Growth of a Business	Amount of Financing Available Using **Internal Sources**	Amount of Financing Available Using **External Sources**
		Conventional Financing · Risk Financing Capital
$1,000,000 =	$200,000 +	$700,000 + $100,000

	Conventional Financing	Risk Financing Capital
Short term:	$100,000	$25,000
Long term:	$400,000	$25,000
Equity:	$200,000	$50,000

Before approaching lenders and shareholders, the CFO must be very precise when calculating the financial needs. Lenders want to be assured that the amounts that will be financed are backed up by reasonable and consistent assumptions. Here are a few examples of questions the CFO should ask in examining planning assumptions:

- Are the sales revenue estimates reasonable relative to the expected market growth?

- Are the levels of accounts receivable and inventory in line with the company's sales growth?

- Will the investment in capital assets produce the estimated number of units and sales revenue?

- Will the company be able to service its debt with the projected sales growth?

- Are the company expenses incurred in cost of goods sold, selling, and administration reasonable and in line with industry standards?

The right side of Figure 10.1 (debt and equity) shows the **financing requirements,** that is, the amount of cash required, and where it will come from to finance the $1.0 million expansion. This is the subject of the chapter. As shown on the following page, the $1.0 million of financial needs identified in the figure will be financed in the following way:

Financing requirements
Where the money will come from (shareholders and lenders) to finance a business.

a. Internal sources		$ 200,000
b. External sources		
Short-term debt		
• conventional	100,000	
• risk capital	25,000	$ 125,000
Long-term debt		
• conventional	400,000	
• risk capital	25,000	425,000
Equity		
• shareholders	200,000	
• risk capital	50,000	250,000
Total external sources		800,000
Total financing requirements		$1,000,000

Objective 2 ▶▶

Internal versus External Financing

Internal sources

Funds generated by a business (e.g., profit, depreciation).

As explained in the previous section, businesses can obtain financing from two principal sources: internal and external. **Internal sources** are funds generated by the business itself. For example, Table 3.3 in Chapter 3 shows the principal sources of internal financing, which include income from operations, sale of capital assets, sale of investments, and a decrease in working capital accounts. External sources comprise funds obtained from outside sources. Table 3.6, under the heading "Financing Activities," shows that the two principal sources of external financing are shareholders (equity) and lenders (loans). As indicated earlier, equity financing can be obtained from conventional shareholders and risk capital lenders. Similarly, debt financing can also be obtained from conventional lenders (e.g., banks, suppliers, insurance companies) and risk capital investors (e.g., factoring, subordinated debts). This chapter deals primarily with external financing. But first, let's examine how a business can generate its own funds internally.

Income from operations is the main common source of internal funding. To calculate the amount of funds generated by a business, we have to refer to the income statement and the statement of retained earnings. By examining Eastman Technologies Inc.'s income statement and statement of retained earnings, shown in Tables 3.7 and 3.9 respectively in Chapter 3, we obtain the following:

Net income from operations	$ 97,500
Add: depreciation (non-cash expense)	40,000
Total funds generated by the business	137,500
Less: dividends paid to shareholders	47,500
Funds retained in the business	$ 90,000

In this case, after paying taxes and dividends, $90,000 will be reinvested in the business. These funds can be used to purchase capital assets, to help finance working capital accounts, or to reduce the principal on the debt.

Working capital is also an important source of financing. Working capital accounts, such as accounts receivable and inventory, usually increase when a business grows. However, if a business is in financial difficulty, it can reduce the level of its net working capital and could generate extra funds. During the early 1980s, when interest rates reached unprecedented heights, many businesses had to cut back on their inventory and accounts receivable.

Let's examine how a business can generate funds from its accounts receivable and inventory accounts. To illustrate the calculation, let's refer to Eastman Technologies Inc.'s income statement and balance sheet, shown in Tables 2.3 and 2.5 respectively, in Chapter 2.

In 2003, Eastman Technologies had $300,000 in accounts receivable and an average collection period of 44 days. If management wants to reduce this figure to 30 days, it will have to squeeze more funds from this account without placing sales performance in jeopardy; therefore, management may implement a more aggressive credit policy. With an average daily sales performance of $6,849 and a collection period target of 30 days, accounts receivable could be reduced to $205,470 ($6,849 × 30) from $300,000. This would produce an additional one-time source of funds of $94,530.

Also, the balance sheet shows inventory at $218,000 with a turnover of 8.7 times. If management sets an inventory target of 10 times, it can achieve this by introducing more efficient purchasing practices and better inventory management control systems. The 10-times ratio reduces inventory to $190,000 ($1,900,000, which is the cost of goods sold, divided by 10) thus generating an additional one-time amount of $28,000.

Risk Analysis to Evaluate Financing Options

◀ Objective 3

Once the CFO has identified the company's financial needs, working capital ($200,000), capital assets ($600,000), marketing costs ($100,000), research and development ($100,000), and the financial requirements also identified earlier, the next step is to pinpoint the instruments (or forms) that could be used to finance the expansion program. To do so, the CFO must focus on the following questions:

1. What will be required to finance the temporary working capital, permanent working capital, and capital assets (financial needs)?

2. What are the financing options (or instruments) available to meet our needs? Financing instruments include conventional financing instruments and risk capital financing instruments.

When selecting a specific financing source, it is important to understand that each source bears different costs. Risk is the key to determining how much it costs to finance a business. There is a direct relationship between risk and return. Risk (the variability of returns, or the chance of losing on the investment) and return (what investors expect to earn) go hand in hand. As the risk of a project or business venture increases, the return (or cost of capital) that investors expect to earn on their investment to compensate for the risk will also increase.

Before examining the various forms and sources of financing, let's define the three different types of risks that businesses have to cope with. They are business risk, financial risk, and instrument risk.

Business risk is intrinsic in a firm's operations. It involves the uncertainty inherent in projecting the future operating income or earnings before interest and taxes (EBIT). The industry and economic environment in which a firm operates impose business risk. A high-tech firm, for example, faces a great deal more business risk than food processor businesses. Expected future demand and product life cycle for food are less difficult to predict than the future demand for most high-technology products. General economic cycles and changing industry conditions cause business variations. This is the single most important determinant that will influence a firm's capital structure (debt versus equity).

Financial risk has to do with financial leverage, that is, a firm's capital structure. In general, the more debt a firm employs, the greater the risk of insolvency and hence the riskier it is to finance the business. Essentially, financial risk is an additional burden of risk placed on common shareholders as a result of management's decision to use more debt. To be sure, highly leveraged firms may not have the financial strength to ride out a prolonged sales decline or an economic recession. The bottom line is this: financial risk can magnify business risk since there is a greater reliance on fixed-cost (interest) or the amount of cash required to pay for the loans.

Instrument risk is the quality of the security available to satisfy investors (e.g., secured versus unsecured loans). For example, a first-mortgage loan is less risky (because of the guarantees) than a second mortgage. Also, a conditional sales contract is less risky than financing accounts receivable through factoring.

It is also important for management to consider the interplay between business risk and financial risk and to maintain an appropriate balance between the two. For instance, a firm facing a relatively low level of business risk can be much more aggressive in using debt financing than a business operating at a relatively high level of business risk.

Also, when risks are high, the financing instruments (common shares versus risk capital) must offer a corresponding high rate of return to attract investors. Figure 10.2 shows the risk curve, which is the relationship between risk and return for different financing instruments. As shown in the figure, financing instruments, based on their specific characteristics (security, claim on cash flow, liquidity/marketability, and pricing) can be placed at different points on the risk curve.

Although equity appears to command a high return, for a growing business, it is often the most stable and appropriate source of capital. Conventional financing, which is generally provided by commercial banks, credit unions, and trust companies, tends to accept a lower return since the risk related to the invest-

Business risk
The uncertainty inherent in projecting the level of sales revenue and income.

Financial risk
The way a business is financed (debt versus shares).

Instrument risk
The quality of security available to satisfy investors.

FIGURE 10.2   FINANCING OPTIONS (RISK VERSUS RETURN)

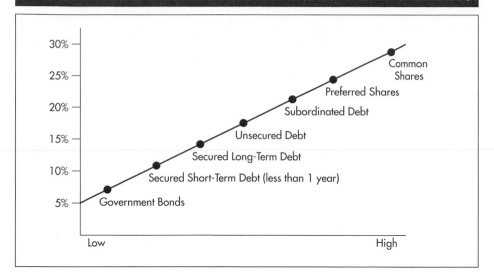

ment is low because of the collateral used to guarantee these loans. In contrast, high-risk investors tend to invest in projects with higher levels of risk and, for this reason, will demand a higher rate of return.

The rest of this chapter deals with external forms and sources of financing. The features, including the advantages and disadvantages, of each source of financing will be examined.

External Forms and Sources of Financing

As mentioned earlier, a business can obtain money from a wide range of sources and in different forms. **Sources** are institutions that provide funds and include commercial banks, investment bankers, equipment vendors, government agencies, private venture capital investors, suppliers, trust companies, life insurance companies, mortgage companies, individuals (angels), institutional investors, and shareholders. **Forms** are the financing instruments used to buy assets or to finance the growth of a business. They include short-term loans (secured or unsecured), term or installment loans, revolving loans, lease financing, mortgages, bonds, preferred and common shares, and risk capital.

Table 10.1 shows different forms and sources of external financing broken down into four categories: short-term, intermediate, long-term, and equity financing. But, before looking at the various forms and sources of short-term financing, let's examine the meaning of the matching principle, the criteria used by investors to rate borrowers, and how a business can make itself creditworthy.

◀ Objective 4

Sources of financing

Institutions or individuals (e.g., banks, private investors) that provide funds to a business.

Forms of financing

Instruments used to finance a business.

TABLE 10.1 FORMS AND SOURCES OF FINANCING

Reasons for financing	Forms	Sources
1.	**Short-term financing**	
Flexible current assets		
Cash	Line of credit	Chartered banks
	Seasonal loan	
	Revolving credit	
	Notes payable	
	Single loan	
	Trade credit	Suppliers
Accounts receivable	Accounts receivable financing	Factoring companies
Inventory	Inventory financing (general lien, floor planning, warehouse financing)	Confirming institutions
	Consignment	Suppliers
Durable current assets:	Working capital loans	Chartered banks
Accounts receivable and inventory		Trust companies
		Government agencies
2.	**Intermediate financing**	
Machinery and equipment	Term loans	Chartered banks
	Conditional sales contracts	Trust companies
	Service leases	Finance companies
	Sale and leaseback	Leasing companies
	Financial leases	
3.	**Long-term debt financing**	
Capital assets:	Leases (as above)	Leasing companies
Land, buildings, and heavy equipment	Bonds	Investment dealers
	Mortgage (secured and unsecured)	Pension, insurance, and trust companies; chartered banks
	Subordinated debts	Government agencies
		Venture capitalists/private investors
4.	**Equity financing**	
All of the above including intangible assets such as: R&D, promotional programs	Retained earnings	Reinvested earnings
	Shares (common and preferred)	Ownership investment
	Grants/contributions	Institutional investors
		Government-based corporations
		Private investors

The Matching Principle

Matching principle

Process that relates financial needs to financing requirements in terms of length of time (e.g., mortgage used to finance a house).

The basic idea of the **matching principle** is to match the maturity of the financial needs to the period of time the funds are required (financing requirements). This principle takes into consideration two factors: cost and risk.

As shown in Figure 10.3, funds are needed to finance capital assets, durable (permanent or fixed) current assets, and flexible (or variable) current assets. The matching principle stipulates that capital assets and current assets should be financed by the appropriate sources of financing: capital assets by long-term debt,

FIGURE 10.3 STRATEGIES FOR FINANCING WORKING CAPITAL

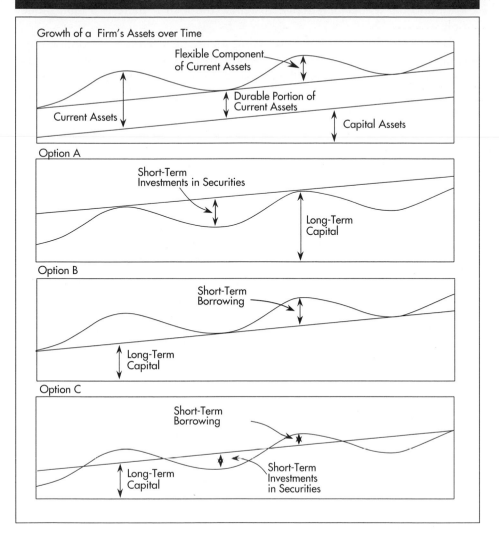

and current assets by short-term credit. As shown in the figure, the flexible component of the current assets fluctuates depending on the financial needs of a business. Durable current assets are necessary in order to operate a business, and the flexible current assets fluctuate with changing business conditions.

Three basic strategies can be used to finance current asset (or working capital) accounts. In the first strategy (option A), all current assets are financed by long-term debt; this is considered the most conservative strategy but the most costly. It is not risky because the business always has the required debt to meet its current needs. However, it is costly because any excess cash is invested in short-term securities. The return earned from the short-term investments (say, 4%) is far less than the cost of a loan (say, 10%).

In the second strategy (option B), all current assets are financed by short-term credit. This option is risky because interest rates may rise when it is time to renew a loan, and the lender may refuse to renew the loan if there is a tight money supply.

The third strategy (option C) is a compromise between the first option (conservative and more costly) and the second (risky and less expensive). In this option, the business uses a small amount of short-term credit to meet peak seasonal working capital requirements. However, during the off-season, excess cash or liquidity is stored in marketable securities. The crests above the line represent short-term financing; the troughs below the line represent holdings in short-term securities.

Criteria Used by Investors to Rate Borrowers

Investors require certain information before investing funds in a business. Some of the information will be provided by the business, and investors will obtain the rest through their own files and networking. Investors look at potential borrowers using different criteria commonly referred to as the **"C's" of credit:** character, collateral, capacity, capital, circumstances (or conditions) and coverage.

Character means two things to an investor (lender or shareholder). First, the borrower should have the required skills and abilities to manage her business professionally and be serious, dependable, and accountable. Second, the borrower should be true to her word, and appear to feel morally obligated to pay her debt, dividends, or principal according to her promise. Investors seek reputation and honesty. Credit is derived from the Latin word *credere,* meaning "to believe" or "to trust," and it implies a promise to pay. There is no question that investors are concerned with borrowers' integrity and willingness to meet their financial commitments.

Collateral is the pledge offered by a business (particularly to lenders) in exchange for a loan. It is like a form of insurance on physical assets, which will be rightly owned by the lender if a business stops operating or is liquidated. This is vital to lenders, since the absence of such security increases their risk. Businesses that have a high credit rating may obtain a loan on an unsecured basis, that is, on faith and trust; others, however, are obliged to back their borrowings with collateral.

Capacity means two things to investors. First, it means the ability of a business to generate enough cash to meet its obligations—repayment of the principal, interest, and dividends. A close examination of a business's cash flow forecast or cash budget can indicate a business's capacity to meet its financial commitments. Second, it means how capable the management team is in managing a new project or an expanded operation—essentially, managerial skills or technical ability in the areas of production, marketing, manufacturing, distribution, finance, and competence in making a business expansion or a new operation a real success.

Capital refers to a business's financial structure—the mix between the shareholders' equity and the funds provided by lenders. The more money shareholders

C's of credit

Factors (character, collateral, capacity, capital, circumstances, coverage) that investors look at to gauge the creditworthiness of a business.

have invested in their business, the more confidence the lenders will have about providing a loan.

Circumstances, or *conditions*, refer to the environment governing business's performance, specifically the status of the industry in terms of trends in demand, prices, competition, profitability, and government regulations.

Coverage refers primarily to insurance coverage. Most businesses are subject to losses arising from different sources: death of a principal owner or an important partner; damage to the business property resulting from fire, explosion, or any violent cause; embezzlement, theft, or any dishonest acts committed by a shareholder, officer, or employee; and public liability suits. Investors feel less vulnerable when businesses to which they have lent money are adequately covered by insurance.

The information regarding the "C's" of credit is usually required by investors. If appropriate information is not provided, investors will seek it elsewhere, such as from business contacts, other investors, suppliers, or credit institutions.

Making a Company Creditworthy

Making a business creditworthy is the first step for obtaining funds quickly and at a more attractive rate. Investors turn down loans or capital shares for numerous reasons, ranging from objective to subjective.

Potential borrowers should analyze their business situation from an investor's perspective when deciding to seek funds. This is important since fundraisers should anticipate investors' questions and give careful consideration to the way that they should be answered. Although specific and detailed questions vary according to a particular situation, here is a broad range of reasons why investors tend to reject investment proposals or loan applications.

1. Factors related to creditworthiness:
   - poor earnings record;
   - questionable management ability;
   - collateral of insufficient quality or quantity;
   - slow and past due in trade or loan payments;
   - poor accounting system;
   - new firm with no established earnings record; or
   - poor moral risk (character).
2. Factors related to a bank's overall policies:
   - not enough equity;
   - requested maturity of the loan too long;
   - applicant has no established deposit relationship with the bank;
   - type of loan not handled by the bank;
   - line of business not handled by the bank; or
   - loan portfolio for the type of loan already full.

Let's now turn to the different types of forms and sources of short-term, intermediate, and long-term financing.

Sources of Short-Term Financing

Short-term financing can be obtained from suppliers (trade credit or accounts payable), chartered banks (trust companies), and specialized lenders who finance current assets such as accounts receivable (factoring companies) and inventory (confirming institutions) on a secured basis.

Suppliers

Supplier credit is also known as trade financing. Almost all businesses use trade credit. When a firm (purchaser) buys goods or services from another firm (supplier), the former does not have to pay for the goods or services immediately; a debt becomes outstanding to the supplier. Invoices for materials, supplies, and services provided by suppliers are not received until some days after the materials are delivered or services performed.

This type of debt is shown on the balance sheet as accounts payable. This is a very attractive form of financing since, in most instances, buyers do not have to pay for the goods or services for a period of 30 days, or sometimes 60 days; furthermore, it is interest-free. As a business grows, supplier credit also grows. The volume orders increase, resulting in increased credit. Trade credit is offered to buyers who usually have a good credit rating. Nevertheless, trade credit may be dangerous for a business that does not know how to use this credit instrument. In some cases, businesses abuse their credit limit and have difficulty reimbursing their suppliers. This situation can easily damage a business's reputation.

Table 10.2 lists the advantages and disadvantages of supplier credit.

TABLE 10.2 ADVANTAGES AND DISADVANTAGES OF SUPPLIER CREDIT	
Advantages	**Disadvantages**
• Inexpensive source.	• Usually insufficient to bridge fully the timing difference between paying for supplies and receiving cash from sales.
• Limited documentation required.	
• Easy access.	• Very short term in nature.
• No costs.	• If company does not pay on time, the supplier might cut off future supplies, which could have adverse effects on the business.
• No controls.	
• No security.	

Chartered Banks and Trust Companies

The second most important source of short-term financing is **chartered banks** and trust companies. Banks make short-term loans that usually appear on the borrowing firm's balance sheet as seasonal loans, operating loans, or working capital loans. These loans can fluctuate as often as daily to cover expected cash shortfalls. These credit instruments are designed to finance fluctuating current assets.

Short-term loans do not come spontaneously; borrowers must specifically request them. Short-term loans are, of course, more flexible than trade credit, since the money can be spent on a wider range of business needs. Bank loans can be either unsecured or secured by some form of collateral that the bank can foreclose on if the borrower cannot pay back the loan as agreed. Unsecured loans usually have a higher cost.

CHOOSING A BANK As a firm's financial needs increase, it usually asks its banker to increase its line of credit. If the bank refuses, the firm may be forced to forgo attractive growth opportunities. Most firms try to choose a bank that is willing to provide service, advice, and counsel; assume some risks; and show some loyalty to its customers. A business owner therefore expects to develop a long-term relationship with a banker. When an owner looks for financing, it is preferable to select a commercial bank (or branch) that will be an asset, not a liability, to the business. Here are some of the more important attributes to look for when selecting a commercial bank.

Financial Counselling: It is a banker's job to stay abreast of financial developments, so one of the most valuable functions that a commercial loan officer can perform for a business is that of external financial expert. Management or owners should look for a bank where the commercial loan officers specialize in businesses of their size and type and should develop a strong relationship with the person handling the loan.

Loyalty: The loyalty of a commercial bank to its customers is very important. Certain banks, when times get a little rough, may quickly shut the door on applications for increases in line of credit (especially for smaller businesses). Other banks will work with a business as much as possible to help ride the storm.

Degree of Loan Specialization: It is important that lending arrangements be serviced by the department in the bank that specializes in the business's particular type of loan (e.g., working capital loan, revolving loan).

Understanding the Nature of the Industry: A banker who has adequate knowledge of the industry and particular financing requirements can be an invaluable resource. The banker will not have to familiarize himself with the business; taking the required time to find such a banker can help business owners receive the financial counselling they need to solve their problems.

Chartered bank

An institution responsible for receiving, lending, and safeguarding money and transactions of individuals and businesses.

Full Range of Services: Management should choose a bank that offers a full range of banking services.

Reputation: The reputation of the bank or branch in terms of counselling services and providing loans to businesses is also important. Bank loans exhibit much greater variability than other sources of business funds.

TYPES OF BANK LOANS Most bank loans are short term and self-liquidating. That is, money is lent for a business purpose such as the purchase of inventory and repaid from the proceeds of the sale of the inventory. Since firms need to buy inventory before they can sell it, they need to borrow frequently to cover seasonal shortfalls in cash flow (e.g., the pre-Christmas sales season for retailers). Then, at the end of the sales season, they can pay off the loans.

A typical bank loan might have a maturity of only 90 days. When it is repaid, the bank can lend the money to some other firms that have different cash flow patterns. Most of the fixed maturity loans (e.g., 90 days) are made at what is called discount interest, which means that the interest is deducted in advance.

About half of the outstanding loans of the chartered banks are classified as operating loans and used by businesses to finance inventories and accounts receivable. These loans are frequently renewed year after year and basically amount to quasi-permanent working capital financing. Most of the operating loans are not made on a basis of fixed maturity but, instead, on a demand basis. This means that the bank can request payment at any time. Demand loans are risky because if the bank suddenly demands repayment, the company would have no choice but to negotiate another loan with another financial institution. Also, the interest rate on this type of loan is usually not fixed, but floating. The floating rate is usually specified as prime rate plus some premium for risk. The cost of bank loans varies for different borrowers at any given time because of differences in the risk to the lender. The cost of bank loans also varies over time as economic conditions change and interest rates fluctuate. The base interest rate is the one established by the Bank of Canada. This is the rate a bank would have to pay if it borrowed from the Bank of Canada. Commercial banks must therefore charge a higher rate to their customers. The lowest rate for any given bank is the prime rate, which is the rate the banks charge their best (least-risky) customers. Other borrowers pay more, depending on the risk of the loan. A typical operating loan might have a cost stated as prime plus two, meaning that if the prime rate were 6%, the borrower would pay 8%. As the prime goes up or down, the loan rate also changes if it is floating. Usually interest is calculated each month and is deducted from the firm's bank account.

Line of credit

A formal or written agreement between a bank and a borrower regarding a loan.

Banks offer different forms of credit to their clients. First, there is the **line of credit,** which is a formal or written agreement between a banker and a borrower regarding the maximum amount of loan that will be extended to a business during a given year. For instance, a business may estimate that it will require a $20,000 loan during a four-month period (say October to January) to produce goods and to sell them on credit. Although the business may have a high credit rating and may be able to obtain as much as $50,000, the business owner will have

TABLE 10.3 ADVANTAGES AND DISADVANTAGES OF A BANK LINE OF CREDIT

Advantages	Disadvantages
• Easy and fairly quick to access.	• Increases the financial risk since cash servicing is required.
• Relatively inexpensive.	• Amount available is limited by the ceiling.
• Flexible.	• If the company experiences problems, lender is in a position to demand/cancel the line, and go for the option of realizing on the security.
• Loan revolves up and down and maximizes the use of cash.	
• Suitable for short-term temporary needs.	• Not suitable for long-term requirements where the company expects return over a long term.
• Usually, reporting requests are minimal.	• The company may not have suitable security, or financial risk may be too high.
• Interest/fees are tax deductible.	

to indicate to the loan officer the amount required and when it will be needed. The agreement (based on the cash budget) confirms that the funds to be provided will be available in the form of a temporary loan. Table 10.3 lists the advantages and disadvantages of a bank line of credit.

Second, seasonal or **self-liquidating loans** are used by businesses primarily to finance temporary or fluctuating variations in accounts receivable and inventory, which are the working capital accounts that are flexible. For instance, a business that sells ski equipment may have a specific seasonal borrowing pattern. It may need some financing in July, as inventory begins to accumulate. Once inventory is shipped to retailers in September and October, buyers start to make their payments. Seasonal loans can be secured or unsecured, and interest rates can fluctuate over time. Like a demand loan, the bank can call such loans at any time. In most cases, these loans are repaid on an installment basis (amortized over the life of the loan), but they may also be repaid in a lump sum.

Self-liquidating loan

Funds used to finance temporary or fluctuating variations in working capital accounts (e.g., accounts receivable, inventory).

Third, there is **revolving credit,** which is similar to a line of credit. In this case, the bank signs an agreement with the borrower (business) to extend credit to a maximum amount. This type of financing costs a little more because additional fees can be levied by the bank. For instance, if the bank offers a credit limit of $300,000, and the borrower uses only $200,000, the unused portion of the borrowing may be liable to a standby fee, say 0.5%, which is charged to compensate the bank for committing itself to the loan.

Revolving credit

Maximum amount of a loan a bank agrees to provide a business (borrower).

Finally, there is **interim financing,** also called bridge financing, which is a loan made available to businesses to help them finance a capital project, such as the construction of a new plant or the expansion of an existing one, until regular financing, such as a first mortgage payment, is received. This financing is called interim because it is used to bridge the time gap between the date construction begins and the time that the long-term loan is received.

Interim financing

Loan made to a business to help finance a capital project, such as the construction of a new plant, until regular financing is obtained.

Firms that are not able to obtain unsecured credit, such as a line of credit, a seasonal loan, or revolving credit, because of low credit standing (or because they want a lower interest rate) must pledge some of their assets as security in order to

Secured loan

A loan that the borrower guarantees by pledging some assets.

obtain a loan. In the case of a **secured loan**, the borrower puts up some assets such as marketable securities, equipment, machinery, buildings, land, accounts receivable, or inventory, as collateral to be claimed by the lender if the borrower does not respect the loan agreement or if the business is liquidated. Since most of the capital assets are financed by long-term loans (mortgages), short-term lenders will use accounts receivable and inventory as collateral to secure short-term loans.

An instrument frequently used by banks is *commercial paper,* or *corporate paper*. For larger firms, commercial paper is an alternative to bank loans. The maturity of commercial paper is generally very short but may go as long as one year. When the maturity date arrives, the borrower must pay; extensions are usually out of the question. Failure to pay on time will cause irreparable damage to a firm's reputation, perhaps preventing it from borrowing in the future.

Asset-Based Financing

Asset-based lending is a form of short-term risk capital financing. Just like a bank line of credit, an asset-based loan is subject to a ceiling amount based on accounts receivable and inventory margins. It also involves a security pledge on accounts receivable and inventories. However, pure asset-based loans differ from bank loans because they rely on collateral coverage rather than being linked directly to financial forecasts. Therefore, business and financial risk are less of an issue with asset-based lenders compared to conventional short-term lenders. However, pricing is higher, and interest charges may range from the prime rate plus 2% to 5% per annum.

Short-term risk capital financing is offered by factoring companies and confirming institutions.

Factoring

Selling accounts receivable to a financial institution.

FACTORING COMPANIES Under **factoring,** the business makes an outright sale of its accounts receivable to finance a business. The customer is told that the invoice has been sold and is asked to make payments directly to the finance company (the factor). This arrangement clearly increases the lender's risk. To reduce the risk, the factor virtually takes over the work of the borrower's credit department. All orders received from customers are sent to the finance company, which does a credit check. Factoring is fairly costly for businesses. Factoring involves a continuing agreement under which the factor purchases accounts receivable as they take place. The factor assumes the risk of accounts becoming uncollectable and is responsible for collections. The factor may also perform credit checks on customers. There are two general types of factoring arrangements.

First, there is *maturity factoring*. In this arrangement, the factor purchases all of the business's invoices, paying the face value less a discount or commission (typically 0.5 to 1.5% of face value). The customer is then told to pay the amount due to the factor by an agreed due date, say 30 days. The factor may charge the business interest on amounts outstanding after the due date.

Second, there is *old-line factoring*. Here, the factor performs a lending function. It will advance funds to the company based on 70% to 90% of the value of an invoice. The factor may charge interest at prime rate plus 1% to 1.5% per annum, as long as the invoice is outstanding. In this case, the company receives cash almost immediately after the sale is made.

CONFIRMING INSTITUTIONS Inventory is an asset that can serve as excellent security for short-term loans. The major factor that is taken into account by lenders before extending inventory financing is the marketability of the inventory. Work-in-process inventory, for example, is poor collateral. Raw materials may be more secure, since they can be sold to other manufacturers; finished goods, ready to be shipped to retailers, may not be as good collateral as raw materials. The level of financing obtained on inventory depends largely on the nature of the goods.

Confirming institution
Organization that finances inventory.

Inventory can be financed in a number of ways. First, it can be financed by having a *blanket coverage* or a general lien put on it, such as the one used for accounts receivable. Then the lender can claim as collateral a percentage of the business's inventory. This type of arrangement is easy to set up, but the lender takes a risk in that it does not have absolute control over the quality and quantity of the goods held in stock.

Second, there is *floor planning*. This type of financing is used primarily in the durable goods industry to finance automobile, farm, and industrial equipment dealers. In this case, each product is identified by a serial number and, when the good is sold, a portion of the proceeds is forwarded to the lender for repayment of the loan. Each time goods are replenished, the borrower must sign a new agreement that specifies the terms and conditions. Sometimes, the lender will spot-check to certify the quantity and quality of the physical assets.

Third, there is *warehouse financing*. This type of financing involves an independent third party that controls access to the goods as security for the lender. There are two basic types of warehousing arrangements. First, there is "field warehousing." Here, the inventory is located in a specified area on the borrower's property, and the warehousing agent exercises very strict control. Second, there are "public warehousing" arrangements. Here, the merchandise is located away from the borrowers' premises, probably in a public warehouse under the control of the warehouse agent.

Fourth, there is *consignment*. This means that although a seller delivers goods to a buyer, the seller remains the owner until the goods are sold to the public. Since the buyer does not purchase the goods, the seller may need to obtain short-term loans to finance the product. In this case, the buyer takes no risk. The profit margin on consigned goods is normally smaller than that on similar nonconsigned items.

Table 10.4 lists the advantages and disadvantages of asset-based financing.

TABLE 10.4 ADVANTAGES AND DISADVANTAGES OF ASSET-BASED FINANCING

Advantages	Disadvantages
• Ideal for growing, highly leveraged, and turnaround situations, because of the higher level of risk assumed by the lender.	• Not suitable for all industries; needs high levels of accounts receivable and inventories.
• No complicated financial covenants, which require monitoring and compliance. This results in less chance of default under a loan agreement.	• Increases the financial risk, due to interest servicing.
• Given the heavy reliance on the value of the collateral, it increases the opportunity for leverage.	• More expensive than conventional short-term financing.
• Lowers the need to raise equity, avoiding equity dilution.	• Onerous inventory and accounts receivable monitoring requirements, sometimes as often as daily.
• Interest is tax deductible.	

Objective 6 ➡

Sources of Intermediate- and Long-Term Debt Financing

We will differentiate intermediate financing from long-term debt financing by the length of time funds are borrowed. Intermediate financing refers to a two- to five-year loan, while long-term financing refers to five years or longer.

The next several sections deal with loans that are provided to businesses for a long term in order to finance the purchase of capital assets.

Conventional Long-Term Financing

Long-term loan

Loan to finance capital assets for a long period of time (over five years).

Term loan

Loan made to buy capital assets.

Intermediate- and **long-term loans** usually finance capital (or fixed) assets. These may be straightforward term loans, usually secured by the physical asset itself. Banks, life insurance companies, pension funds, and federal and provincial government agencies provide longer financing on capital assets.

Term loans are a principal form of intermediate-term financing used for the purchase of capital assets (usually three to seven years). However, in certain circumstances, the maturity may be as long as 15 years. A term loan involves an agreement whereby the borrower agrees to make a series of interest and principal payments on specific dates to a lender. This differs from a bank line of credit, whereby repayment is at any time (demand) or at a specified time in one lump sum. The key characteristics of a term loan are the following:

- Terms of the loan are tailored to suit the needs of the borrower.
- Security is usually in the form of a chattel mortgage on equipment or machinery.
- In addition to collateral, the lender may place specific restrictions on the operations of the business (e.g., no additional borrowings and no increase

in salaries to the officers, senior executives, and managers of the company without prior approval of the lender).

- The loan is retired by systematic repayments over the life of the loan.

A **conditional sales contract** is a written agreement between a buyer and a seller regarding the purchase of production equipment or other physical assets on a time-payment basis. Under this arrangement, the seller of the capital asset accepts a partial payment of the value of the asset as a down payment, which is usually a minimum of one-third; the rest is paid on a monthly installment basis. Legal ownership of the property is retained by the seller until the buyer has made all the required payments according to the term of the agreement, which usually runs from 12 to 36 months.

Table 10.5 lists the advantages and disadvantages of term loans and conditional sales contracts.

Bonds are long-term contracts, typically for 20 or 30 years, under which a borrowing firm agrees to make payments of interest and principal, usually semi-annually, to the holder of the bond contract. The investor buys an annuity with regular payments until the maturity date, when the principal amount is repaid. An indenture is a legal document that spells out the rights of both the bondholders and the issuing firm. A trustee, usually a trust company, represents the bondholders and ensures that the firm lives up to its obligations. The firm pays the total interest payment to the trustee as scheduled, and the trustee then pays the bondholders, who are required to clip coupons off the bond and cash them like cheques.

Bonds may be secured or unsecured. *Secured bonds* are essentially long-term promissory notes. Holders of secured bonds have prior claims over the assets and earnings (similar to first, second, and third mortgages). *Unsecured bonds* are called debentures. Only the earning power of the firm backs them up. Bonds may also be convertible into shares of the issuing company, or redeemable before the stated maturity date, at the request of either the bondholder or the firm. Many variations on this theme are possible. The firm does not know who buys the

Conditional sales contract
Agreement made between a buyer and a seller regarding the purchase of an asset (e.g., truck).

Bond
Long-term loan that can be secured or unsecured (20 to 30 years).

TABLE 10.5	ADVANTAGES AND DISADVANTAGES OF TERM LOANS AND CONDITIONAL SALES CONTRACTS	
Advantages	**Disadvantages**
• Longer repayment terms.	• Ties up asset.
• Easy access.	• Increases financial risk given the cash payments of interest and principal.
• Flexibility.	
• Tax deductibility of interest.	• Commits the business since it is subject to penalties.
• Suitable for long-term needs: permanent current assets and capital assets.	• Often includes restrictive covenants.
• Low cost relative to other long-term sources of financing.	• Business may not have suitable security to offer since the business/financial risk may be too high.
• Commits the lender for a long term.	
• Does not dilute equity.	

bonds. Thus the issuance of bonds is a very impersonal and inflexible financing method, not suitable for all firms or investors. These unsecured bondholders are similar to general creditors; they have a claim on the residual value of all assets that are left unencumbered.

Mortgage

Loan against which specific real property is used as collateral (e.g., building).

Mortgages are a pledge of a specific real estate property, such as land or buildings. Mortgages are long-term financing (e.g., 25 years). The amount of the mortgage is calculated based on the market value of the property. For example, 75% of the market value might be a common assessment, but a company can find companies that will finance up to 90% of the value of an asset. These investors frequently prefer long maturity periods. The repayment schedule is usually based on equal blended payments of interest and principal. The interest rate is fixed for a specific term and depends on the going market rate, the length of the term, and availability. This type of financing is provided by insurance companies, pension funds, chartered banks, and trust companies.

Table 10.6 lists the advantages and disadvantages of mortgage financing.

Risk Capital Long-Term Financing

Risk capital investors invest funds in equity shares and equity-related debt in relatively small or untried enterprises, thereby absorbing much of the risk that commercial lenders are unwilling to shoulder. These investors prefer dealing with companies whose products are already selling and are proven successes but who haven't yet exploited their markets.

Subordinated debt

Loan that is more risky, for which investors charge higher interest rates.

Subordinated debts are risk capital term debt whereby investors accept a higher level of risk compared to conventional sources. These instruments levy a rate of interest that typically ranges from 8% to 12%. However, the overall rate of return to the investor will be higher. Participation features could increase the rate of return and make the expected return range between 15% and 25% per year. This type of financing is good only if a business has exhausted secured financing options (e.g., term loans based on capital assets, or short-term financing based on

TABLE 10.6 ADVANTAGES AND DISADVANTAGES OF MORTGAGE FINANCING	
Advantages	**Disadvantages**
• Long-term commitment, without equity dilution.	• Fairly rigid financing instrument.
• Maturity matches the long life of the asset.	• Increases financial risk due to fixed stream of interest and principal repayments.
• Interest is tax deductible.	• If company fails to make payment, it could be subject to penalties.
• Relatively inexpensive source of long-term financing.	
• Easy to access.	
• Considers the value of the asset more than the value of the business.	
• Standard documentation requirements. Restrictive covenants will be basic.	

current assets). Subordinated debts are best suited to rapidly growing companies, expansion programs, management and leverage buyouts, and acquisitions.

Effectively, under such lending arrangements, investors structure the instrument to share in the expected success of the company. Here are a few examples:

- royalties (percentage of net cash flow generated from operation);
- participation fees;
- normal cost of common shares;
- warrants or options to purchase shares; and
- rights to convert debt into common shares.

Subordinated debt repayments can be tailored to the characteristics of individual businesses. Therefore, there is less risk of the borrower defaulting than with conventional long-term sources of financing. Sources of subordinated debts include private-sector venture capital firms, institutional investors, labour-sponsored funds, and government-sponsored corporations.

Table 10.7 lists the advantages and disadvantages of subordinated debts.

Equity Financing

◀ Objective 7

Equity is the interest an owner holds in a business. If a business is privately owned, the owners can also obtain funds from investors that specialize in small and medium-sized business loans and mortgages. In this case, owners of the privately owned business will prepare an investment proposal and will go directly to specific individuals and ask them to become shareholders of the business.

For publicly owned businesses, the process is more complicated. The owners have to prepare a prospectus and approach an investment dealer in order to raise funds from the general public through a public issue. In a public issue, the investment dealer buys the securities from the firm and sells them to the general public.

Let's turn now to the role of the investment dealer and the cost of raising funds from the general public. As mentioned earlier, long-term financing can be

TABLE 10.7 ADVANTAGES AND DISADVANTAGES OF SUBORDINATED DEBT FINANCING	
Advantages	**Disadvantages**
• Flexible and can be tailored.	• Takes time to access.
• Less expensive than equity.	• Expensive relative to other sources of short-term and long-term financing.
• Fills a financing gap and high leverage is available.	• Some cash flow servicing requirements.
• Not as much dilution as straight equity.	• Investors will take a more active role in the company than other lenders.
• Available to a variety of industries.	• Set-up costs are high.
	• Restrictive covenants often apply.
	• Does not provide the stability of equity.

obtained from two distinct sources: lenders, when money is provided in the form of a loan, such as bonds or mortgages (covered earlier) and shareholders, when funds are raised by issuing shares. Investment dealers (or investment bankers) facilitate the financing of business firms by buying (wholesale) securities issues of bonds or shares and reselling them (retail) to their clients. Investment dealers borrow the money they need to finance the issue. Usually, they get it from banks on a very short-term basis and repay their lenders when the issue sells out. This process may take a week or two, or it may all be completed in one day.

The cost of public issues of either bonds or shares is high because there are many legal details that must be taken care of. The process is lengthy, requiring approval by at least one provincial securities commission, and sometimes by several, depending on where the bonds or shares are issued. Thus, this source of funds can be used only at infrequent intervals and for large amounts of money. New firms are usually either too small to use investment dealers or find their services (which may cost as much as 10% to 25% of the funds raised) too expensive. Table 10.8 summarizes the steps involved in making a public issue.

Let's now turn to the major sources of equity funds: shareholders, risk capital investors, and government institutions.

Shareholders

Shareholders

The owners of a business (common and preferred shareholders).

Funds can be provided by **shareholders** in the form of common shares and preferred shares. The owners (shareholders) of a business provide *common share* financing. The collective and specific rights of the shareholders related to common shares are listed in Table 10.9.

TABLE 10.8 STEPS INVOLVED IN MAKING A PUBLIC ISSUE

Step 1:	The firm decides to list (or not to list) its issue on the exchange (Toronto Stock Exchange, Montreal Stock Exchange, or Vancouver Stock Exchange).
Step 2:	The firm selects one or more investment dealers to take responsibility for buying and selling the issue (the underwriter(s)).
Step 3:	A preliminary conference takes place between the issuing company and the underwriter(s) to discuss the amount of capital to be raised, the type of security to be issued, and the general terms of the issue.
Step 4:	A preliminary prospectus is prepared. The preliminary prospectus discloses important aspects of the issue and forms the basis of the agreement among all parties.
Step 5:	A public accounting firm makes an audit of the company's financial situation and prepares the required financial statements to be included in the preliminary prospectus.
Step 6:	After it is signed, the preliminary prospectus is filed with the appropriate provincial securities commission. This is followed by a waiting period (usually around 15 business days) which gives the staff of the securities commission time to go over the prospectus to evaluate the accuracy of the data and content, and to ensure that there are no deficiencies or misrepresentations in the document.
Step 7:	After clearance is given by the securities commission, the final prospectus is prepared and final clearance is given. At this point, the underwriting agreement is signed between the issuing company and the underwriter. Here, an agreement is reached about the date of the issue, the actual price that the underwriter is prepared to pay, and his or her commission.

TABLE 10.9   SHAREHOLDERS' COLLECTIVE AND SPECIFIC RIGHTS

Collective Rights

- Amend articles of incorporation
- Adopt and amend bylaws
- Elect the directors of the corporation
- Authorize the sale of capital assets
- Authorize mergers and amalgamations
- Change the amount of authorized common and preferred shares
- Alter the rights and restrictions attached to the common shares
- Create a right of exchange of other shares into common shares

Specific Rights

- Vote in the manner prescribed by the corporate charter
- Sell their share certificates to other interested parties
- Inspect corporate books (practical limitations)
- Share in residual assets of the corporation (last among the claimants)

To a company, the most attractive feature of issuing common shares is that they do not entail fixed charges. Unlike a mortgage payment, dividends are paid when income is generated. Common shares do not have fixed maturity dates and can be sold more easily than debt.

Preferred share financing has some characteristics both of common share and of debt financing. The preferred share appears in the equity section of the balance sheet. Although this type of financing is considered equity, preferred shareholders do not have the same rights as common shareholders.

Table 10.10 lists the advantages and disadvantages of equity financing.

The payout of income, control, and risk factors related to common share financing, preferred share financing, and long-term debts are listed in Table 10.11.

TABLE 10.10   ADVANTAGES AND DISADVANTAGES OF EQUITY FINANCING

Advantages	Disadvantages
• Low risk.	• They extend voting rights or control to additional shareholders.
• Dividends are paid when income is generated.	• Give the right to more owners to share in income; thus dilutes the equity interest.
• No restrictive covenants that could cause default.	• Takes time to access.
• Provides stability and permanency.	• Underwriting costs are expensive.
• Common shares do not have fixed maturity dates.	• Dividends are not tax deductible.
• Share can be sold more easily and investors realize a return on their equity in the marketplace at no cost to the company.	

TABLE 10.11   DETERMINING THE CHOICE OF LONG-TERM FINANCING

	Payout of Income	Control	Risk
Common shares	Paid after interest and preferred share dividends; by decision of the board of directors, all or a portion of the remaining funds may be retained by the business or distributed in the form of dividends.	Common shareholders have the legal right to make all major decisions and to elect the board of directors. They have the ultimate control of the corporation.	Since they have the last priority of claims in the event of liquidation, they bear the highest risk of any claimants.
Preferred shares	Dividends are paid before common dividends and are cumulative if they are not paid during a specific year.	Preferred shareholders sometimes have a right to elect some of the directors on the board of directors (minority).	They have priority over the common shareholders regarding the assets (in the event of liquidation) and earnings for payment of dividends.
Long-term debts	There is a fixed payment of interest, which is made in the form of a sinking fund.	Usually, long-term creditors do not have the right to vote. However, if the bond goes into default, the bondholders may be able to take control of the company.	Bondholders have the first claim (secured) over the assets of a company (in the event of liquidation) and earnings.

Risk Capital Investors

Risk capital investors

Individuals or institutions that provide money to finance a business that entails relatively high risk. These investors seek a high potential return.

Risk capital investors provide equity financing to small or untried enterprises, thereby absorbing much of the risk that commercial lenders are unwilling to shoulder. Commercial lenders are rarely interested in inventions requiring further research, development, and engineering. They have certain preferences about the companies they want to back. These preferences are usually based on the type, history, and status of the company and the amount of financing needed.

On the other hand, risk capital investors prefer dealing with companies whose products have potential to succeed in the marketplace or are already selling well but that lack the capital to exploit their markets. Risk capital investors generally provide equity financing or both equity and long-term debt financing (e.g., subordinated debt).

Risk capital investments are unique in the following ways:

- they apply mostly to fast-growth businesses;
- usually, several years are required before the risk capital investors can liquidate their investment or make an exit;
- during the early years there is usually no organized secondary market;
- the new firm faces a high risk of failure; and
- several infusions of capital are frequently necessary before the new enterprise becomes a "going concern."

Risk capital investments can be categorized as embryonic, start-up, development, expansion, turnaround, or buyout. *Embryonic investments* are made in firms intending to develop a new product or process up to the point where it is possible to make a prototype. *Start-up investments* are made in new firms just getting started with a new product or service in an established market. *Development investments* are made in small firms that are already in production and just about to realize profits but do not have sufficient cash flow to continue operations. *Expansion investments* are made in smaller firms in need of additional productive capacity, but without sufficient funds of their own. *Turnaround investments* are made in firms that are currently experiencing financial difficulties, but that have great potential for profitability with more capital and better management. *Buyout investments* are made in firms that are already established and have a proven and good track record but whose owners are seeking to sell out and retire. Usually some or all of the current employees are the ones who want to buy the firm but do not have the funds to do so.

Here is a profile of the general types of risk capital investors.

Angel investors are professional investors, retired executives with business experience and money to invest, or high-net-worth individuals simply looking for investment opportunities. Angels will usually invest between $25,000 and $300,000 in a venture. Many angels are sophisticated investors and will go through the formal due diligence review.

Private investors and **venture capital** firms are individuals or groups of professionals with a vast amount of experience, contacts, and business skills that can help a business become more profitable. The size of their investment can range from $25,000 to $5 million. Investors in this category have particular preferences, strategies, and investment criteria. While some private firms will be more interested in investing in the development stage, many will be interested in companies involved in the expansion, acquisition, and management/leveraged buyout stages. These investors include labour-sponsored venture funds such as Working Ventures Canadian Fund, Fonds de Solidarité, and Canadian Medical Discoveries Fund.

Institutional investors provide equity and subordinated risk capital investment to small and medium-sized businesses. They include subsidiaries of commercial banks, investment banks, certain life insurance companies, and pension funds. These companies fund investments that are less than $1 million, as well as larger ones. Canada has a wide range of such organizations including Bank of Montreal Capital, Royal Bank Capital Corporation, CIBC Wood Gundy Capital, Penfund Partners, Investissement Desjardins, Roynat, Ontario Teachers' Pension Fund, and TD Capital.

Government-backed corporations make investments in smaller, regional communities where mainstream investors are less active. For example, the Atlantic Canada Opportunities Agency (ACOA) provides support to businesses located in the Atlantic provinces. The Business Development Bank of Canada (BDC) is unique in its status because it offers a one-stop shopping service. Its mission is to help create commercially viable business projects, together with counselling, training, and mentoring assistance. It provides:

Venture capital

Risk capital supplied to small companies by wealthy individuals (angels), partnerships, or corporations, usually in return for an equity position in the firm.

- venture loans (between $100,000 to $1 million) for expansion and market development projects;

- working capital for growth funding (up to $100,000);

- patient capital, directed at knowledge-based businesses in the early stages of development, offered on a long-term basis (up to $25,000); and

- micro-business programs for training and counselling to very small companies, along with up to $25,000 for new businesses and up to $50,000 for existing businesses.

Corporate strategic investors differ from traditional venture capital companies in that their motivation extends beyond financial reasons. Their business agreements are referred to as strategic alliances or corporate partnerships. A strategic investor may have a broad range of objectives that include enhancing innovation, gaining exposure to new markets and technologies, identifying and accessing acquisition candidates, assuring sources of supply, assisting a client, initiating new ventures internally, and spinning off businesses when there are potentially profitable operations that are inappropriate for the original firm.

Government Institutions

Government financing is a direct or indirect form of financial assistance to businesses offered by a municipal, provincial, or federal agency to help businesses carry out capital expenditure projects or expansion of their activities that, without such assistance, would be delayed or even abandoned completely. Government financing (or programs) can be grouped into two broad categories: allowances for income tax purposes and direct and indirect incentives. Federal financing aid can come from nonrefundable grants, refundable incentives, conditionally refundable incentives, equity participation, direct loans, guarantee of loans, remission of tariff, export financing, cost sharing, fees for counselling purposes, training grants, and small business loans. Provincial financing aid can come from forgivable loans, direct loans (mortgage, small business loans), working capital loans, training grants, guarantee of loans, equity participation, inventory financing, leasebacks, and venture capital. Municipal financing aid can come through free land, deferred taxes, and industrial sites (e.g., infrastructure assistance).

The more important governmental financial institutions include the Export Development Corporation, the Farm Credit Corporation, the Business Development Bank of Canada, and provincial venture capital organizations.

EXPORT DEVELOPMENT CORPORATION The Export Development Corporation (EDC) is a Crown corporation that provides a wide variety of financial services, including export insurance, bonds, loans, and lines of credit to both Canadian exporters and foreign buyers. Canadian exporters can insure their export sales against nonpayment by foreign buyers for up to 90% of the value of the shipments. This insurance can cover commercial and/or political risks of insolvency, default, repudiation by the buyer, cancellation of import licences, blockage of funds, and war. Virtually any export transaction can be insured by EDC, which provides export financing at either fixed or floating rates of interest to foreign buyers of Canadian goods. The money is paid in Canada directly to the exporting company, so the export sale is a cash sale for the Canadian firm. EDC can operate either on its own account or for the government, in case the Canadian government would like to assist exports in ways that may fall outside the normal purview of the more commercial transactions normally made by EDC.

FARM CREDIT CORPORATION The Farm Credit Corporation (FCC) is a Crown corporation created in 1959 to provide domestic financial services to enable individual Canadian farmers to establish, develop, and/or maintain viable farm enterprises. The corporation also makes farm loans to groups or syndicates of farmers organized to share the use of farm machinery and specialized farm buildings and their equipment. Loans made by FCC are usually made at fixed rates of interest based on the combined overall cost of funds to FCC. These loans can be for terms of 5 to 15 years with amortization as long as 30 years.

An important innovation is the shared-risk mortgage, which was introduced in 1985. This type of loan has an interest rate that is adjusted each year. There is equal sharing between the FCC and the farmer in interest rate increases and decreases, up to the maximum allowable fluctuation of 2.5%. The normal term of the shared-risk mortgage is six years, and the loan limit is $350,000 for individuals or $600,000 for partnerships.

Another innovation is the Commodity-Based Loan Program, which began in 1986. Payments are calculated by linking the loan principal amount to a price index of one or two of the major commodities produced on the farm. If prices go up by 5%, for example, then both the principal of the loan and the periodic payments would also increase by 5%. Financial advisory services are also offered to new or existing borrowers on request.

THE BUSINESS DEVELOPMENT BANK OF CANADA The Business Development Bank of Canada (BDB) is a Crown corporation established in 1975 (under the name Federal Business Development Bank) to promote and assist the establishment and development of small and medium-sized Canadian businesses. It provides three types of services: financial (loans and loan guarantees), venture capital, and management (counselling, training, information, and financial planning). The BDB concentrates on helping new businesses that cannot obtain funds from other sources. It is, therefore, a supplemental or last-resort lender. It has tended to concentrate most of its efforts on helping companies in manufacturing, wholesale and retail trade, and tourism.

The BDB provides loans, loan guarantees, equity financing, or any combination thereof in whatever way is best suited to the needs of the firm. The BDB provides funds for start-ups, modernization, expansion, change of ownership, or other business purposes to firms unable to obtain financing from other sources on reasonable terms and conditions. Term loans can be used to finance capital assets such as buildings, land, machinery, or equipment, with the assets used as collateral. In some cases term loans can also be made to finance working capital needs.

PROVINCIAL VENTURE CAPITAL ORGANIZATIONS Most provinces have established legislation allowing private investors to set up small business development companies that act as suppliers of venture capital. In some provinces, such as Manitoba, the provincial government matches 35% of the capital raised by private investors. In Ontario, the provincial government provides a tax-free cash grant of 30% of the investor's contribution, thus reducing the risk for individual investors. Some provinces have direct financing programs for small businesses that meet certain qualifications. These programs change frequently.

THE *SMALL BUSINESS LOANS ACT* The *Small Business Loans Act* (SBLA) is a federal law intended to help new and existing small businesses obtain financing for capital asset needs from the chartered banks and other designated lenders (trust companies, credit unions, and caisses populaires) according to normal commercial procedures. The federal government guarantees the loans. The maximum amount is $100,000, and the maximum term is ten years. The interest rate is usually prime plus and fluctuates as the prime rate changes. SBLA loans are restricted to firms whose gross revenues do not exceed $2 million annually.

Objective 8 ▶

Choosing between Leasing versus Owning

Almost any physical asset can be purchased or leased. We are all familiar with residential apartment leasing, whereby a lessee (the renter) acquires the right from the lessor (owner) to inhabit the apartment in return for monthly rental payments.

Leasing is an alternative to more traditional financing for any assets, but especially for equipment that has a useful life of three to ten years. The **lessee** or user gets the full use of the assets without the bother of owning them, and frequently this can be accomplished with little or no down payment. The **lessor** is the one who lends the asset to the lessee. The three most popular forms of leases are operating leases, financial leases, and sale and leaseback.

OPERATING LEASES **Operating leases** provide not only financing but also maintenance of the asset, so they are popular for office equipment and cars as well as highly technical types of equipment, such as computers. The operating lease is an agreement between a lessee and a lessor that can be cancelled by either party upon due notice. Usually, the lease price includes services and repairs. Operating leases are not always fully amortized during the original contract period; the lessor expects to recover the rest of its costs by either leasing the asset again or selling it. If the original lessee believes that the equipment has become obsolete, it is usually possible to cancel the contract at little or no penalty cost prior to the normal expiry date of the lease period.

FINANCIAL LEASES A **financial lease** is a mutually agreed-upon commitment by the lessor and lessee under which the latter agrees to lease a specific asset over a specified period of time. A financial lease does not provide for maintenance, is

Lessee

One who pays to use an asset without owning it.

Lessor

One who lends an asset to someone (lessee).

Operating lease

A lease that is cancellable by the lessee at any time upon due notice.

Financial lease

Mutually agreed commitment by a lessor and a lessee for a specified period of time.

usually fully amortized, and does not normally include a cancellation clause. Financial leases are commonly used for such assets as airplanes, office equipment, movable offshore oil drilling rigs, medical equipment, railroad cars, and construction equipment. Lessors generally borrow 80% of the cost of the asset from a third party (or parties) on a nonrecourse basis. The loan is secured only by the lease payments and is not a general obligation of the lessor. Lease periods as long as 15 or 20 years are common. The lessor records on its balance sheet only the net investment (20%) but can deduct both interest on its debt financing and depreciation on the asset; therefore, income for tax purposes is usually negative in the early years of the lease. The lessee may get lower lease payments than would otherwise be the case, and all of its lease payments are usually tax-deductible. Virtually all financial institutions are involved in leasing, either directly or through subsidiaries.

In a financial lease, three parties are involved: the lessee, the lessor, and a lender. Here is how a typical financial lease works. The company (lessee) decides on the equipment or machinery it wants to use. The company approaches a leasing company and specifies the asset it wants and the length of time for which it will be needed. The leasing company then (1) borrows money from a lender (if necessary), (2) buys the asset from a manufacturer, and (3) leases it to the company (lessee). Usually, the lease period lasts throughout the useful life of the asset so that the leasing company does not find itself in the position of having to lease it to another company. In this lease agreement, the leasing company does not even take physical possession of the asset.

SALE AND LEASEBACK A **sale and leaseback** arrangement can be used only once, since it requires the firm to sell an asset, then lease it back. Thus, it still gets to use the asset while increasing the funds available within a particular time period. Lease payments in such arrangements are similar to mortgage payments or payments on a long-term loan. For example, a firm could sell its factory building and land to a financial institution, then lease it back. The selling firm in this case receives the full purchase price of the property, which it can use for any purpose. It is committed to making periodic payments to the financial institution, which is equivalent to paying rent.

Sale and leaseback

Arrangement made by a company to sell an asset to a lessor, then lease it back.

Lease-or-Buy Analysis

Intermediate- and long-term financing are generally used to acquire capital assets, such as buildings, machinery, and equipment. As long as the assets do the job, managers are not concerned about how assets are financed. Managers' prime interest is to see that the assets do the job at the lowest possible cost. To financial managers, however, the choice between owning or leasing has significant financial implications. Their job is to ensure not only that assets are obtained at the lowest possible cost and on the most favourable terms but also that they produce the greatest financial benefits to the owners. Although leasing has far-reaching legal and accounting implications, we will deal here only with the cost factors in comparing the choice between leasing or owning an asset. Table 10.12 presents a cost comparison between owning and leasing $1 million worth of assets. The assumptions underlying this comparative cost analysis are:

- Life of the assets is ten years.
- Duration of the lease is ten years with annual installments of $162,745 (before tax) and $81,372 (after tax) based on a 10% compounded interest charge.
- Debt agreement is 100% of assets; a ten-year repayment schedule with a 10% compounded interest charge. (Assets are rarely financed at 100% of value; however, this assumption is made only to illustrate the true economic comparison between the two options.)
- CCA is 15%.
- Income tax is 50%.
- Residual value of the asset is nil.

As shown in column 1, the annual cost of the lease is $81,372, or $162,745 × 50% (income tax rate). The second column shows the annual payment for the $1,000,000 loan. The $162,745 figure is obtained by dividing $1,000,000 by the factor 6.1446 (from Table D in Appendix B at the end of the book, column 10% and line 10 years). Columns 3 and 4 show how much will be paid each year for interest and principal. In the first year, with a $1,000,000 loan at a 10% interest rate, the interest charge will be $100,000 (column 3) and the principal repayment will be $62,745. Column 5 shows the annual capital cost allowance for the $1,000,000 capital assets. Year 1 shows $75,000 [($1,000,000 × 15%) ÷ 2], and the remaining yearly figures are calculated on a declining basis. Column 6 shows the total tax-deductible amount comprising the interest charges (column 3) and capital cost allowance (column 5). Column 7 shows the yearly tax shield. Since the company is in a 50% income tax bracket, it will benefit from an $87,500 (column

TABLE 10.12 COMPARISON OF COST OF OWNING VERSUS COST OF LEASING

| | | | | | Computing Net Cost of Owning | | | | | |
	1	2	3	4	5	6	7	8	9	10
Year	Lease Payment After Tax at 50%	Total Payment	Interest	Principal	CCA	Income Tax–Deductible Expenses	Tax Shield 50%	Net Cost of Owning	Net Advantage (Disadvantage) vs Lease	Present Value at 10%
		(3 + 4)				(3 + 5)	(6 ÷ 2)	(2 – 7)	(1 – 8)	
1	$ 81,372	$ 162,745	$100,000	$ 62,745	$ 75,000	$ 175,000	$ 87,500	$ 75,245	$ 61,278	$ 5,570*
2	81,372	162,745	93,725	69,020	138,750	232,475	116,238	46,508	34,865	28,814*
3	81,372	162,745	86,823	75,922	117,938	204,761	102,380	60,365	21,008	15,783*
4	81,372	162,745	79,230	83,515	100,247	179,477	89,739	73,006	8,367	5,714*
5	81,372	162,745	70,880	91,865	85,210	156,090	78,045	84,701	(3,328)	(2,066)
6	81,372	162,745	61,693	101,052	72,428	134,121	67,061	95,585	(14,312)	(8,079)
7	81,372	162,745	51,587	111,158	61,564	113,151	56,576	106,169	(24,796)	(12,725)
8	81,372	162,745	40,472	122,273	52,329	92,801	46,401	116,344	(34,971)	(16,315)
9	81,372	162,745	28,245	134,500	44,480	72,725	36,363	126,383	(45,010)	(19,089)
10	81,372	162,745	14,795	147,950	37,808	52,603	26,302	136,444	(55,071)	(21,232)
	$813,720	$1,627,450	$627,450	$1,000,000	$785,754	$1,413,208	$ 706,604	$920,850	$(107,125)	$(23,624)

*Favours owning ( ) Favours leasing

6 ÷ 2) tax shield. Column 8 shows the net cost of owning the asset, which is the annual payment of the loan (column 2) less the annual tax shield. Column 9 (net advantage or disadvantage versus lease) shows the net difference between the after-tax lease payment and net cost of owning. As indicated, it is preferable to lease the asset. During the ten-year period, the total cost of owning is $920,850 versus $813,720 for leasing, for a net difference of $107,120.[1] In the early years, there is a distinct cash flow advantage to owning the asset; by the fifth year, however, cash flow favours leasing.

At this point, it appears that the lease option is better. However, because of the existence of interest, both alternatives should be discounted to arrive at a more meaningful and realistic comparison. As shown in column 10 of the table, using a 10% discount factor, in this particular case, leasing is still a better option by the amount of $23,624.

Factors That Influence Lease-or-Buy Decisions

This example of comparative cost analysis does not consider all the cost factors affecting the economics of each option. Many other factors may also have to be considered. The most common include interest rate, residual value, obsolescence, risk factor, increase of financial leverage, adjunct costs, capital cost allowance rate, and discount rate.

INTEREST RATE Although the example in Table 10.12 assumes the same interest rate for both leasing and owning, this may not always be the case. It is important to compare the lessor's interest rate with prevailing lending interest rates. Some leasing firms offer specialized services, and their costs will be included in the leasing charges, thus complicating the comparison.

RESIDUAL VALUE Most assets have a residual value at the end of a lease period. If a firm owns an asset and sells it at the end of a similar period, the resulting cash inflow may be a reason to favour owning.

OBSOLESCENCE The type of equipment also influences owning versus leasing. If a piece of equipment will soon become obsolete, leasing may be the best option. Why purchase a piece of equipment with a ten-year life span when it will become obsolete to the company after four? Some will argue that the higher the obsolescence factor, the higher the cost of the lease. This is not always true, because lessors can often find other users for their equipment; not all users have the same obsolescence rate.

RISK FACTOR Leasing a piece of equipment with a high rate of obsolescence passes the element of risk to the lessors.

---

1   The difference in the totals is due to the rounding of the figures in individual columns.

Chapter 10: Sources and Forms of Financing

INCREASE OF FINANCIAL LEVERAGE Leasing is often claimed to have a double effect on financial leverage. First, more money is usually available to finance assets through a lease than its alternate source, a loan. Assets can be leased at 100%, but chattel mortgage or conditional sales contracts can be obtained at only 50% or 75%. Second, financing part of a capital asset through leasing leaves room for future financing, if an expansion is contemplated right after start-up. However, while leasing may seem to hold out the promise of greater leverage, less risk of obsolescence, and lower cost, care should be used in considering this financing option. Lenders are wise to the financial obligations of "off-balance sheet" financing and take them into account when assessing creditworthiness.

ADJUNCT COSTS Certain costs, such as legal fees, are not as high for leasing as for debt financing; these should also be considered in the cost comparison.

CAPITAL COST ALLOWANCE A change in the capital cost allowance rate may alter the decision. For example, if the CCA rate is increased from 15% to 25%, this would favour the purchase option.

DISCOUNT RATE The same discount rate is used in Table 10.12 to find the present value of owning and leasing. Since discounting reflects a risk factor, and owning may be riskier than leasing, a higher interest factor would be used to discount the owning option than leasing; this would favour the lease option.

✳ Decision-Making in Action

Ted Bentley, owner of Microplus Inc., is very encouraged about his company's expansion program and its capability for producing power modules. He feels that the market is growing rapidly and that power modules would provide Microplus Inc. with higher margins that would help improve his company's financial performance. He points out that the key to Microplus's future growth and success is to market new highly profitable power modules.

Before meeting investors, the company's controller first formulated financial projections based on the company's objectives and plans. After several months of discussions with the key members of the management team, the controller was able to prepare three-year projections for the company's income statements, balance sheets, and cash flows. The expansion program is expected to cost $1.1 million and is broken down as follows:

Financial needs		
Capital assets		$ 600,000
Working capital requirements		
Accounts receivable	$ 200,000	
Inventory	200,000	
Subtotal	400,000	
Accounts payable	100,000	300,000
Marketing costs		200,000
Total		$1,100,000*

On the financing requirements side, Microplus's bank will lend a very small amount to the company on its accounts receivable (30%) and inventories (40%). Based on the estimated purchases, the controller

*This $1.1 million financial need is netted out after supplier financing (accounts payable). Excluding supplier financing, Microplus would have to raise $1.2 million.

figured a $100,000 amount in credit outstanding with various suppliers. The bank is also prepared to finance part of the capital assets in the amount of $200,000 with annual payments bearing an annual 10% interest charge. The controller informed Ted Bentley that on the basis of the pro-forma financial statements, particularly the statement of changes in financial position, an amount of $200,000 would be available to finance the expansion through internal sources. Shareholders are also prepared to invest an extra $100,000 into the business to finance the expansion.

Ted Bentley realizes that he will be short by $460,000 in financing to meet his $1.1 million investment need. After some discussion with several financial advisors, they suggest that he should approach nonconventional investors who would be prepared to provide risk capital financing. This suggestion is based on the nature of the business (high tech) and the fast growth that is expected to take place in the industry and particularly in Microplus. Ted decided to meet two risk capital investors.

The first was the Business Development Bank of Canada, which indicated that it would provide a subordinated debt in the amount of $200,000 with collateral on the capital assets. Ted also met an individual in risk capital lending who was also interested in investing $260,000 in equity funds in Microplus. Ted Bentley was aware that although the cost of equity would be high (typically in the 25% to 40% return), it would not have to be paid by Microplus on an annual basis. The high return expected by the risk capital investor would be earned at exit through a buyout situation probably in the fourth or fifth year after the expansion.

On the basis of the above information, the following presents how Microplus's financial needs will be financed. Table 10.13 summarizes both the company's financial needs and financing requirements.

Financial needs (uses)		Financing Requirements (sources)	
Capital assets	$ 600,000	Bank	$ 200,000
Accounts receivable	$ 200,000	Bank (30% on receivables)	60,000
Inventory	200,000	Bank (40% on inventory)	80,000
Marketing costs	200,000	Suppliers	100,000
Total	$1,200,000	Internal sources	200,000
		Shareholders	100,000
		BDB	200,000
		Risk capital firm	260,000
		Total	$1,200,000

Financial requirements can be analyzed from different angles. First, using internal sources versus external sources shows the percentages provided by short-term lenders and long-term investors. As shown below, 16.7% of the financing will come from internal sources, while total external funding represents 83.3%, with short-term representing 20% and long-term 63.3% of the funding requirements.

		Amount		Percentage
Internal		$ 200,000		16.7%
External				
Short-term	$240,000			20.0%
Long-term	760,000			63.3
Sub-total		1,000,000		83.3
Total		$1,200,000		100.0%

Chapter 10: Sources and Forms of Financing

TABLE 10.13 MICROPLUS'S FINANCING REQUIREMENTS

	Internal Sources	External Sources				
	Cash Flow from Operations	Conven-tional	Risk	Conven-tional	Risk	Total
Internal						
From operations	$200,000					$200,000
External						
Conventional financing						
Short-term						
• Suppliers		$100,000				$100,000
• Accounts receivable (30%)—Bank		60,000				60,000
• Inventory (40%)—Bank		80,000				80,000
Intermediate and long-term debt financing						
1. Conventional financing—Bank		$200,000				200,000
2. Risk financing Subordinated debt—(BDB)			$200,000			200,000
Equity financing						
1. Conventional shareholders				$100,000		100,000
2. Risk capital— Institutional investors					$260,000	260,000
Total financing requirements	$200,000	$440,000	$200,000	$100,000	$260,000	$1,200,000

Another way to analyze Microplus's financing requirements is to differentiate between the amount of funds generated from debt versus equity (capital structure or financial leverage) after internal sources have been provided. As shown below, lenders (debt) provide 53.3% of the total financing package.

		Amount	Percentage
Internal		$ 200,000	16.7%
External			
Debt	$640,000		53.3%
Equity	360,000		30.0
Sub-total		$1,000,000	83.3
Total		$1,200,000	100.0%

As shown on the following page, risk capital financing accounts for 38.3% of the total financing package, with the remainder split between internal sources (16.7%) and conventional sources (45%).

	Amount		Percentage
Internal		$ 200,000	16.7%
External			
Conventional	$ 540,000		45.0%
Risk	460,000		38.3
Subtotal		$1,000,000	83.3
Total		$1,200,000	100.0%

Chapter Summary

Financial needs has to do with the acquisition of the assets needed by a business for a particular project (modernization, expansion, new plant) while *financing requirements* focuses on where the money will come from (shareholders, lenders) to buy the assets. The first thing that a company must do before approaching investors (financing requirements) is to identify its financial needs, which could be in the form of working capital, capital assets, marketing costs, and research and development.

◀◀ Objective 1

Financing can be obtained from two sources. First, *internally*, through depreciation and amortization, by using income from operations and by managing the current assets more effectively; and second, *externally*, from shareholders (through purchase of common or preferred shares) and short-term and long-term lenders.

◀◀ Objective 2

External financing can be obtained from different sources and in different forms. Each is used to finance a specific asset, different venture, or business undertaking. A business faces three types of risks. *Business risk* has to do with the uncertainty inherent in projecting future earnings of a business. *Financial risk* deals with a company's financial structure. *Instrument risk* focuses on the type of instrument that should be used to finance a business.

◀◀ Objective 3

When considering financing, businesses should attempt to match, as closely as possible, the maturity of the source of funds to the period of time for which the funds are needed. To do this, both cost and risk should be considered. Investors use different criteria for assessing the worthiness of prospective clients. The "C's" of credit are character, collateral, capacity, capital, circumstances (or conditions), and coverage. The most popular sources of *short-term financing* are suppliers, chartered banks and trust companies, and asset-based financing. Sources of *medium- and long-term financing* are also commercial banks and trust companies. In addition, there are conventional long-term investors (e.g., banks, shareholders) and risk-capital investors including government institutions. Government financing is a direct or indirect form of financial assistance to businesses offered by a municipal, provincial, or federal agency to help businesses carry out capital

◀◀ Objective 4

expenditure projects or expand their activities. The more important governmental financial institutions include the Export Development Corporation, the Farm Credit Corporation, the Business Development Bank of Canada, and provincial venture capital organizations.

Objective 5 ➥
The most popular forms of short-term financing are suppliers (for trade credit) and chartered banks that offer lines of credit, seasonal or self-liquidating loans, revolving credit, and interim financing. Other financing institutions also offer secured loans on accounts receivable and inventory. Lenders can offer asset-based loans. These include factoring on accounts receivable and general liens, floor planning, warehousing agreements, and consignment to finance inventory.

Objective 6 ➥
Intermediate and long-term financing are obtained from conventional institutions and include term loans, conditional sales contract, bonds, and mortgages. Risk capital funds can also be obtained on a subordinated debt basis whereby investors accept a higher level of risk.

Objective 7 ➥
Equity financing can be secured from shareholders and risk capital firms. These types of funds can be obtained from private or public sources. If public offerings are made, investment dealers must be used to process the issue. When considering common share, long-term debt, and preferred share financing, different factors must be taken into account: the payout of income, control, risk, and the advantages and disadvantages of each. Risk capital firms provide financing for smaller, high-risk firms. They generally provide equity financing or both equity and long-term financing. Risk capital investments can be categorized as embryonic, start-up, development, expansion, turnaround, or buyout. They include angel investors, private investors, institutional investors, and government-backed corporations.

Objective 8 ➥
Lease financing is another popular way of acquiring assets. The three major types of leases are service leases, financial leases, and sale and leaseback. Before deciding on buying or leasing assets, the cost of each option should be evaluated. The factors that will determine the choice are interest rate, residual value, obsolescence factor, risk factor, financial leverage, depreciation rate, and the discount rate.

Key Terms

Bond

Business risk

C's of credit

Chartered bank

Conditional sales contract

Confirming institution

Factoring

Financial lease

Financial needs

Financial risk

Financing requirements

Forms of financing

Government financing

Instrument risk

Interim financing

Internal sources

Lessee

Lessor

Line of credit

Long-term loan

Matching principle

Mortgage

Operating lease

Revolving credit

Risk capital investors

Sale and leaseback

Secured loan

Self-liquidating loan

Shareholders

Short-term financing

Sources of financing

Subordinated debt

Supplier credit

Term loan

Venture capital

Review Questions

1. What is the difference between financial needs and financing requirements?

2. Differentiate between internal and external financing. Give several examples.

3. Discuss the concepts of business risk, financial risk, and instrument risk.

4. How can working capital become a source of internal financing?

5. Differentiate between flexible and durable current assets.

6. Explain the meaning of "matching principle."

7. Identify the six C's of credit.

8. Explain the significance of the word "capacity."

9. How can a company become more credit-worthy?

10. Why are suppliers important sources of financing?

11. What factors should a company consider before selecting a chartered bank as a lender?

12. Differentiate between a seasonal loan and revolving credit.

13. What is commercial or corporate paper?

14. What sort of financing do factoring companies and confirming institutions provide?

15. What is the purpose of a subordinated debt?

16. What steps are involved when making a public issue?

17. Differentiate between a shareholder collective right and specific right. Identify three of each type of right.

18. Differentiate between a secured bond and an unsecured bond.

19. What is the purpose of a risk capital investor? Comment on some of them.

20. What types of capital investments do risk capitalist firms invest in?

21. How can government agencies help businesses?

22. Differentiate between an operating lease and a financial lease.

Discussion Questions

1. Is it easier for a big firm to obtain a loan than a small business? Explain.

2. Why is it important for a business to understand the nature of its assets before approaching lenders?

3. If you were to provide a term loan to a small business entrepreneur, what provisions would you include in the contract in order to protect your interest?

4. Do you believe that leasing would be as popular if income taxes did not exist? Explain.

Testing Your Comprehension

True/False Questions

F 1. Income from operations is the most common source of external financing.

T 2. Working capital can be grouped under two headings: flexible current assets and durable current assets.

F 3. The basic idea of the matching principle is to match the maturity of the internal funds needed to the period of time the funds are required.

T 4. Two of the six C's of credit include collateral and conditions.

T 5. Capacity means the ability of a business to generate enough cash to meet its debt payment.

F 6. Suppliers are excellent sources of long-term financing.

T 7. Most firms try to choose a bank that is willing to provide service, advice, and counsel; to assume some risks; and to show some loyalty to its customers.

F 8. About half of the outstanding loans of the chartered banks are operating loans used by business firms to finance equipment and machinery.

F 9. Suppliers often offer revolving credit and interim financing to customers in order to gain their loyalty.

T 10. Factoring companies finance accounts receivable.

F 11. Investment dealers facilitate short-term financing.

T 12. A major disadvantage of shareholder financing is that dividends are not tax-deductible.

T 13. Secured bonds are essentially long-term promissory notes.

___F___ 14. Venture capital companies provide financing for large, low-risk firms.

___F___ 15. Internal financing can be grouped into two broad categories: short-term financing and long-term financing.

___T___ 16. The Business Development Bank of Canada is a Crown corporation.

___F___ 17. An operating lease is the most complex of all leases.

___F___ 18. Leasing is always more advantageous than buying.

Multiple-Choice Questions

1. The following is an internal source of financing:
   a. depreciation
   b. trade suppliers
   c. shareholders
   d. venture capitalists
   e. factoring companies

2. The following is a source of financing:
   a. increase in accounts receivable
   b. decrease in inventory
   c. decrease in accounts payable
   d. increase in sales revenue
   e. decrease in the mortgage account

3. The following is a form of short-term financing:
   a. financial lease
   b. conditional sales contract
   c. bond
   d. sale and leaseback
   e. revolving credit

4. The following is not considered one of the C's of credit:
   a. capacity
   b. circumstances
   c. circumspection
   d. conditions
   e. coverage

5. The following provide financing exclusively on accounts receivable:
   a. confirming institutions
   b. commercial banks
   c. trust companies
   d. factoring companies
   e. suppliers

6. Usually, interim financing is used to finance:
   a. purchase of capital assets
   b. inventories
   c. accounts receivable
   d. research and development projects
   e. advertising and promotional programs

7. The following is not a typical form of financing activity offered by chartered banks:
   a. seasonal loans
   b. interim financing
   c. self-liquidating loans
   d. revolving credit
   e. common share financing

8. Financing used in the durable goods industry to finance automobile or farm equipment is called:
   a. warehouse financing
   b. floor planning
   c. consignment
   d. revolving credit
   e. seasonal loans

9. The following is a common shareholder specific right:
   a. amend articles of incorporation
   b. change the amount of authorized common shares
   c. share in residual assets of the corporation
   d. adopt and amend bylaws
   e. authorize the sale of physical assets

10. The following form of financing has a claim only on the residual value of assets that are left unencumbered:
    a. unsecured bonds
    b. secured bonds
    c. mortgage
    d. conditional sales contract
    e. term loans

11. The following is not considered a venture capital investment:
    a. turnaround investment
    b. start-up investment
    c. embryonic investment
    d. accounts receivable investment
    e. buyout investment

12. The Business Development Bank of Canada provides funds to firms that are:
    a. involved only in public offerings
    b. interested in locating in underdeveloped regions of Canada
    c. unable to grow
    d. exporting goods in different countries
    e. unable to obtain funds from conventional lending institutions

13. The following lease cost is a tax-deductible expense:
    a. investment costs
    b. capital cost allowance
    c. principal on loan
    d. accounts receivable expense
    e. deferred taxes

Fill-in-the-Blanks Questions

1. When a business identifies "what is to be financed" such as working capital, capital assets and marketing costs, it is referred to as _____ _____.

2. _____ has to do with where money will come from (shareholders and lenders) to finance a business.

3. External financing comprises funds provided from _____ (lenders and shareholders).

4. _____ are funds generated by a business (profit, depreciation).

5. _____ risk has to do with the uncertainty inherent in projecting the level of sales revenue and income.

6. _____ risk has to do with the way that a business is financed (debt versus equity).

7. _____ risk has to do with the quality of security available to satisfy investors.

8. _____ of financing are institutions that provide funds and include commercial banks, investment bankers, equipment vendors, etc.

9. _____ of financing are the financing instruments used to buy assets or to finance the growth of a business (e.g., short-term loans, revolving credit, bonds, etc.).

10. The process that relates financing needs to financial requirements in terms of length of time (e.g., mortgage used to finance a house) is referred to as the _____ _____ principle.

11. One of the C's of credit that is referred to as a pledge that a business offers in exchange for a loan is referred to as _____ _____.

12. One of the C's of credit that refers to a business's financial structure is called _____ _____ structure.

13. Sources of financing obtained for a period of less than one year (e.g., trade credit, line of credit) is referred to as _____ _____ financing.

14. _____ usually provide financing by selling their goods or services to customers on credit.

15. _____ financing is a loan made to a business to help finance a capital project, such as the construction of a new plant, until regular financing is obtained.

16. _____ companies are financial institutions that buy accounts receivable.

17. A _____ sales contract is an agreement made between a buyer and a seller regarding the purchase of an asset (e.g., truck)

18. A _____ debt is a loan that is more risky, for which investors charge higher interest rates.

19. _____ capitalists are individuals or institutions that provide money to finance a business that entails relatively high risk.

20. In a leasing agreement, the _____ _____ is the one who pays to use an asset without owning it.

21. In a leasing agreement, the _____ _____ is the one who lends an asset to someone.

22. An _____ lease can be cancelled by the lessee at any time upon due notice. Assets included in such leases are office equipment, cars, and computers.

23. A _____ lease is a mutually agreed-upon commitment by two parties for an extended time period. Assets included in such leases are airplanes, movable offshore oil drilling rigs, and major medical equipment.

Learning Exercises

Exercise 1(a)

1. If the Millers borrow $100,000 for five years at 9%, what would be their annual loan payments?

2. If they borrowed $500,000 for 15 years at 14%, what would be their annual loan payments?

Exercise 1(b)

1. If you borrowed $300,000 for four years at 10%, what would be your annual loan payments?

2. If you borrowed $650,000 for ten years at 12%, what would be your annual loan payments?

Exercise 2(a)

Calculate the annual payment, interest, and principal for each year on the $100,000 loan presented in Exercise 1(a).

Exercise 2(b)

Calculate the annual payment, interest, and principal for each year on the $300,000 loan presented in exercise 1(b).

Exercise 3

The Millers are asking your advice on how they should finance a second retail store that they want to open. They saved $60,000 and are now considering opening the retail store, specializing in selling and servicing computer equipment. The Millers will need cash to finance the start-up of their second store (e.g., advertising and promotion) and to purchase furniture, fixtures, and equipment, etc. They will also require funds to finance the purchase of goods for inventory.

1. Prepare a comparative analysis describing the advantages and disadvantages of the various forms of financing that could be obtained to purchase the assets and inventory, and for start-up promotional expenses.

2. What forms of financing would you suggest to the Millers? Why?

Exercise 4

On the basis of the information contained in Exercise 3, what type of sources of financing would you suggest to the Millers? Why?

Exercise 5(a)

The Millers are unsure whether they should buy or lease a truck. A five-year lease could be arranged with annual lease payments of $5,000, payable at the beginning of each year. The tax shield from lease payments is available at year-end. CompuTech's tax rate is 35%, and the company's cost of capital is 12%.

The truck would cost $25,000 and has a five-year expected life span, and no residual value is expected. If purchased, the asset would be financed through a term loan at 14%. The loan calls for equal payments to be made at the end of each year for five years. The truck would qualify for accelerated capital cost allowances written off on a straight-line basis over five years.

Calculate the cash flows for each financing alternative. Which alternative is the most economically attractive?

Exercise 5(b)

Calculate the following lease-or-buy option.

A four-year lease could be arranged with annual lease payments of $90,000, payable at the beginning of each year. The tax shield from lease payments is available at year-end. The firm's tax rate is 40%, and the company's cost of capital is 10%.

The machine costs $500,000 and has a four-year expected life, and no residual value is expected. If purchased, the asset would be financed through a term loan at 12%. The loan calls for equal payments to be made at the end of each year for four years. The machine would qualify for accelerated capital cost allowances written off on a straight-line basis over two years.

Calculate the cash flows for each financing alternative. Which alternative is the most economically attractive?

Exercise 6(a)

The Millers are faced with the decision of purchasing or leasing several computers (including a cash register) for their new store. The computers can be leased for $8,000 a year or purchased for $30,000. The lease includes maintenance and service. The salvage value of the equipment five years hence is $6,000.

The company uses the declining depreciation method to calculate the depreciation. The rate of depreciation is 35%. If the computers are purchased, service and maintenance charges (a deductible cost) would be $300 a year.

The firm can borrow the entire amount at a rate of 14% if the purchase option is exercised. The tax rate is 35%, and the company's cost of capital is 11%.

On the basis of the above, which method of financing would you choose?

Use the following capital cost allowance amounts to calculate the cost of the equipment.

Year	Amount
1	$10,050
2	6,825
3	4,436
4	2,884
5	1,875

Exercise 6(b)

Hull Manufacturing Co. is faced with the decision of purchasing or leasing a new piece of equipment. The equipment can be leased for $4,000 a year or purchased for $15,000. The lease includes maintenance and service. The salvage value of the equipment five years hence is $5,000. The company uses the declining-depreciation method to calculate the depreciation. The rate of depreciation is

30%. If the equipment is owned, service and maintenance charges (a deductible cost) would be $900 a year.

The firm can borrow the entire amount at a rate of 15% if the purchase option is exercised. The tax rate is 50%, and the company's cost of capital is 16%.

On the basis of the above, which method of financing would you choose?

Use the following capital cost allowance amounts to calculate the cost of the equipment.

Year	Amount
1	$4,500
2	3,150
3	2,205
4	1,543
5	1,081

Cases

Case 1: Grip Case Inc.

In April 2003, Miriam and Ben Friedman were thinking about starting their own business, Grip Case Inc. Their objective was to produce and market inexpensive attaché cases. It was not their intention to compete directly against expensive cases produced by companies such as Samsonite, Hartmann, Zero Halliburton, or Airway. Miriam and Ben felt that if their company produced an inexpensive case (retailing at about $50), they would sell at least 15,000 units during the first year of operation. Of course, the launching of the Grip Case Inc. would be conditional on obtaining financing from various lending institutions.

Miriam and Ben intended to approach their venture in three phases. The first phase would consist of a detailed feasibility study, including legal work for patent registration and additional work on the product design. The second phase would comprise the preparation of a detailed investment proposal required to seek the necessary financing for the purchase of the capital assets, the working capital requirements, and operating funds needed to market the products effectively. The third phase would be implementation through production and commercialization.

Attaché cases are marketed under private brands or manufacturers' brands. Private brands account for a smaller segment of the Canadian retail market. Most often, private brand cases are manufactured for retail outlets such as The Bay, Sears, Wal-Mart, etc. Manufacturers' brand names include Hartmann, Samsonite, Airway Atlantic, U.S. Luggage, and Stebco.

After examining dozens of different types of cases, Ben and Miriam found that the four most important elements of the product, with regards to consumer choice, are construction, convenience, interior, and exterior. The quality of construction of a case depends on its frame, hinges, handle, feet, latches, and locks. Convenience is determined by what the case offers, such as files and pockets. Ben and Miriam found that cases are available with a wide variety of files and pockets. How the interior of a case is divided also interests buyers. Things that buyers look for are lining, stability, and file compartments. Some attaché cases have pockets for business cards, a calculator, airline tickets, and parking-lot receipts. The exterior comes in different qualities. This factor significantly affects the retail sales price. Cases are made of leather, vinyl, or moulded plastic. Good-quality leather cases are the most expensive with a price range of between $250 and $800. Vinyl cases are priced between $75 and $250. The cheapest moulded-plastic case sells in the $70 range.

Although Ben and Miriam intended to market the three basic types of cases (attaché case, briefcase, portfolio), they wanted to market only the attaché cases during the first year of operation in order to hold down their initial investment and production costs. The type of case that they wanted to market would retail between $40 and $60. The cost of production and the amount of markup sought by the middle parties would determine the exact price. They would focus primarily on the student markets (secondary, colleges, and universities). They believed that a practical, low-priced model could meet consumers' needs. Grip Case Inc. would sell its products directly to wholesalers and/or retailers. The exact distribution network had not yet been determined.

Grip Case Inc. is to manufacture cases for private brands and sell to retail stores such as K-Mart, Wal-Mart, Zellers, discount stores, and drugstores. The company would also sell cases bearing its own brand name, "Grip Case." By selling cases at about $25 to wholesalers/retailers, and with 15,000 units, the company would be able to cover its costs and begin to make a profit during the second year of operation. The following shows Grip Case Inc.'s financial needs.

FINANCIAL NEEDS

Working capital		
Accounts receivable	$ 40,000	
Inventory	60,000	$100,000
Capital assets		
Leasehold improvements	100,000	
Equipment	70,000	
Machinery/truck	80,000	250,000
Research and development		50,000
Marketing/promotion		50,000
Total financial needs		$450,000

Grip Case Inc.'s condensed pro forma income statements for the first three years of operations are as follows:

Years	1	2	3
No. of units	15,000	20,000	25,000
Unit selling price	$ 25.00	$ 25.00	$25.00
Sales revenue	$375,000	$500,000	$625,000
Cost of goods sold	187,500	250,000	312,500
Gross margin	187,500	250,000	312,500
Administration	85,000	95,000	110,000
Selling/promotion	90,000	70,000	80,000
Depreciation/amortization	30,000	30,000	30,000
Total operating expenses	205,000	195,000	220,000
Operating income	(17,500)	55,000	92,500
Interest charges	25,000	25,000	25,000
Income before taxes	(42,500)	30,000	67,500
Income taxes	—	—	12,000
Income after taxes	($42,500)	$ 30,000	$ 55,500

Ben and Miriam had accumulated $150,000 over the past ten years and were planning to invest the entire amount in the business in the form of equity. They knew they would have difficulty obtaining debt financing but had a $250,000 house of which 40% could be used as collateral. However, they were prepared to use this option only as a last resort.

Ben and Miriam were determined to adopt a conservative strategy, growing slowly and carefully in starting their business. Rather than investing huge sums of money in expensive equipment and buying a building, they intended to purchase some used equipment and rent a building belonging to Miriam's father. If, after the first three years, the attaché case product line reached the expected level of sales, they would then consider making the other cases, that is, the briefcase and the portfolio product lines. Depending on the company's financial position three years after start-up, Ben and Miriam might lease a larger building or even build their own.

Although Ben and Miriam were still at the research stage, they had done some costing to calculate how much profit they would make for each case. At 15,000 units, the cost of production would be in the $187,500 range, for a total unit production cost of approximately $12.50. The cost breakdown is as follows: direct materials, $6.30/unit, direct labour, $2.00 (for a total of $124,500 in variable costs), and the rest ($63,000) in fixed manufacturing costs.

1. What questions do you think lenders will want to ask Ben and Miriam regarding their venture?

2. How many units would the company have to sell in the first year of operation in order to break even? When will the company break even? Is the break-even point in that year reasonable? Why or why not?

3. What type of investors or lenders should Ben and Miriam approach? Why?

4. What type of collateral would the lenders want to take into consideration?

5. How much do you believe they will be able to obtain from the different financing sources? Why?

Case 2: Baldwin Equipment Inc.

Management of Baldwin Equipment is considering increasing the productivity of its plant. Management heard from suppliers that a certain piece of equipment could entail an after-tax cash flow savings of more than $35,000 a year if it was installed in their plant. However, Jim Henderson, the controller of the company, is not sure whether the company should buy or lease the equipment.

If the asset is leased for a ten-year period, it would cost the company $45,000 a year (before tax). The company's income tax rate is 50%.

If the company buys the asset, it would cost $300,000. However, the controller indicated that the asset could be financed entirely through debt for a ten-year period at a cost of 10%. The asset's capital cost allowance is 25% (declining basis).

On the basis of this information, the controller is now considering whether to purchase or lease the equipment.

However, Jim Henderson is considering doing a sensitivity analysis regarding the two options by modifying some of the data in the base case.

On the basis of the following, calculate the effect that each individual change in the base case would have on the decision. Calculate the net change on an undiscounted and discounted basis.

Changes to the base case are as follows:

- Capital cost allowance would be increased to 40%.
- The discount rate would be increased to 15%.
- The interest on the loan would be 8%.
- The company would be able to sell the asset for $50,000 in the tenth year.

11

Working Capital Management

Learning Objectives

After reading this chapter, you should be able to:

1. Define terms such as "working capital," "net working capital," and "working capital management."

2. Comment on the importance of managing cash.

3. Identify different strategies related to managing marketable securities.

4. Discuss the importance of accounts receivable management and describe related techniques.

5. Explain the importance of inventory management and describe related techniques.

6. Show how current liabilities can be managed.

Chapter Outline

OPENING CASE

During the third year of operation, the Millers were spending more time on the management of their working capital accounts such as accounts receivable and inventory. This is quite understandable because during the early years of any business, a considerable amount of funds are invested in working capital. The following shows the evolution of CompuTech's current assets, net working capital, total assets, and sales revenue between the years 2003 and 2005.

(in $000s)	2003	2004	2005	% Increase
Current assets	105	136	235	124%
Current liabilities	52	60	132	153%
Net working capital	53	76	103	94%
Total assets	237	268	637	168%
Sales revenue	350	420	800	128%

As shown, the Millers' current assets and net working capital increased by 124% and 94% respectively between 2003 and 2005 while current liabilities show a 153% growth. Sales revenue increased by 128%. In order to improve their profit and financial performance, the Millers realize that they have to be very cautious as to how they manage their working capital accounts.

Len and Joan are beginning to realize that managing working capital accounts is more complex and time-consuming than managing capital assets. In the case of capital assets (e.g., investing in a new store), they have to go through a detailed capital budgeting process using time-value yardstick analysis in order to make their decision. However, once that decision is made, nothing much can be done; they have to live with the consequences, good or bad. On the other hand, managing working capital accounts is a daily chore and has to be done meticulously.

The Millers know that they have to sell goods and services on credit and maintain inventory in their store. These working capital accounts represent essential investments and must be made in order to generate sales. However, the Millers realize that they have to be wise in the way that they spend their cash in these unproductive but necessary accounts. As Len pointed out:

> Too much investment in accounts receivable and inventory is considered a
> drain on CompuTech's cash flow position and can even blemish the return on

our investment. The more that we have to invest in these accounts, the more we will have to borrow from short-term lenders. And of course, the larger the loan, the more interest charges CompuTech has to pay, which ultimately reduces profitability.

As shown on the previous page, part of the 153% increase in current liabilities comprises loans obtained from commercial banks.

The Millers must therefore ensure that just enough funds are invested in working capital accounts to meet their day-to-day operations and maximize profitability but not so much that such unproductive assets represent a cash drain on CompuTech. For this reason, the Millers have to manage on a continual basis each current asset and current liability to ensure that they know exactly how much cash is needed (current assets) and how much cash is required (current liabilities).

This chapter explores the importance of managing working capital accounts. In particular, it focuses on three key topics:

1. What is the goal of managing working capital, and why is it important to accelerate the cash conversion cycle?

2. How can current asset accounts such as cash, accounts receivable, and inventory be managed?

3. How can current liability accounts such as accounts payable, accruals, and working capital loans be managed?

Introduction

In Chapter 1, "working capital" (or operating capital) referred to all accounts appearing in the current accounts of the balance sheet: current assets and current liabilities. In the early years of financial management, working capital included only current asset accounts such as cash, marketable securities, accounts receivable, and inventory. These assets are essential for operating a business. Having money in the bank to pay ongoing bills; holding money in marketable securities, such as short-term investments; and maintaining accounts receivable and inventory are surely not productive assets. However, if a company is to produce goods and sell its products, a certain amount of money must be tied up in these types of accounts. It is important for a business, however, to ensure that a minimum amount of funds is tied up in these current asset accounts, just enough to ensure that it can meet its day-to-day operations and maximize profitability but not so much that such unproductive assets represent a cash drain on the business. Managing current assets is a critical factor since it represents a major portion (in many cases, about half) of a manufacturing company's total assets.

Today, working capital is defined more broadly. It includes current liabilities, such as accounts payable, notes payable, other accruals, or all loans that are due within a 12-month period (see Table 11.1 for a typical list of working capital accounts). A current liability, such as accounts payable, is interest-free. Therefore, it is worthwhile for a business to take advantage of this type of short-term liability to finance its business activities. However, a business should be careful not to jeopardize its position by not being able to meet its short-term obligations.

Net working capital is defined as the difference between current assets and current liabilities. As shown in Table 11.1, for instance, if a company's current assets total $1,420,000 and its current liabilities are $720,000, the net working capital is $700,000 (current ratio of 1.97 times).

Working capital management refers to all aspects of the management of individual current asset and current liability accounts, ensuring proper interrelationships among all current asset accounts, all current liability accounts, and other balance sheet accounts such as capital assets and long-term debts.

Working capital accounts require more time than capital assets such as land, buildings, machinery, and equipment. The level of investment in each of the working capital accounts usually changes on a day-to-day basis, and, in order to effectively manage the business, managers must always know how much money is required in each of these accounts. Mismanagement of current accounts can be costly; excess current assets means a drain on profits and can be a source of undue risk. Not enough current assets, on the other hand, may entail revenue loss since a shortage of inventory, for example, may mean that goods wanted by customers are not readily available.

This chapter explains how current asset and current liability accounts should be managed in order to maximize an organization's profitability. The accounts that will be examined in this chapter are cash, marketable securities, accounts receivable, accruals (prepaid expenses), and inventory under current assets; and accounts payable, accruals (wages and taxes), and working capital loans under current liabilities.

Net working capital

The difference between current assets and current liabilities.

Working capital management

Managing individual current asset and current liability accounts to ensure proper interrelationships among them.

TABLE 11.1 THE MEANING OF WORKING CAPITAL
Working Capital Accounts

Current Assets		Current Liabilities	
Cash	$ 25,000	Accounts payable	$ 400,000
Marketable securities	100,000	Accrued wages	50,000
Accounts receivable	500,000	Taxes payable	20,000
Prepaid expenses	40,000	Notes payable	50,000
Inventory	755,000	Bank loan	200,000
Total current assets	$1,420,000	Total current liabilities	$ 720,000

Net working capital is the difference between current assets and current liabilities.

The Meaning of Working Capital Management

◄◄ Objective 1

The **goal of managing working capital** is to accelerate the cash flow cycle in a business after sales have been made. The faster the cash circulates, the more profitable it is to the business, because it means that a company has less cash tied up in unproductive (but necessary) assets. Let's use Table 11.1 as an example. If accounts receivable and inventories were reduced by $75,000 and $100,000 respectively, the company would be able to deposit $175,000 in investment securities, say at 10%, and earn $17,500 in interest annually. Instead, company management would probably want to invest this excess cash in more productive assets such as plant modernization or new equipment, which would generate a 20% return on the assets each year, as long as the inventories and accounts receivable are kept at the new level.

There are two broad approaches for measuring the productivity of cash within a business: days of working capital (DWC) and cash conversion efficiency (CCE). The objective of the **days of working capital** measurement is to calculate the number of days of working capital a business holds in order to meet its average daily sales requirements. The lower the number of days, the more efficient a business is in managing its cash. Consider, for example, Eastman Technologies Inc., which was introduced in Chapters 2 and 3. In this case, the company shows 47.2 days of working capital. This ratio is calculated as follows:

$$\frac{(\text{Accounts receivable} + \text{Inventory}) - \text{Accounts payable}}{\text{Net sales}/365} =$$

The information used to calculate Eastman's DWC is drawn from the income statement (Table 2.3) and the balance sheet (Table 2.5):

$$\frac{(\$300,000 + \$218,000) - \$195,000}{\$2,500,000/365} = \frac{\$323,000}{\$6,849} = 47.2 \text{ days}$$

The **cash conversion efficiency** ratio measures the efficiency with which a business converts sales revenue to cash flow within its operations. The financial data used for calculating Eastman's CCE ratio is drawn from Table 3.6 (Statement of Changes in Financial Position) and Table 2.3 (Income Statement):

$$\frac{\text{Cash flow from operations}}{\text{Net sales}} = \frac{\$126,500}{\$2,500,000} = 5.1\%$$

By themselves, Eastman Technologies' cash performance ratios do not mean much unless they are compared to previous years' data and to industry standards. The sixth working capital survey prepared by *CFO* magazine appeared in the August 2002 issue. The survey lists the cash conversion efficiency ratio (CCE) and the day's working capital ratios (DWC) for many companies and industries. The results for the industries included in the survey ranged from 4% (Food Retailers & Wholesalers) to 20% (Medical & Biological Technology) for the CCE and from

Goal of working capital management
To accelerate the cash flow cycle in a business after sales have been made.

Days of working capital
The number of days of working capital a business holds to meet average daily sales requirements.

Cash conversion efficiency
Ratio that measures how quickly a business converts sales revenue to cash flow within its operations.

15 days (Food Retailers and Wholesalers) to 103 days (Industrial Diversified) for the DWC. The following gives the results of the survey for just 10 industries:[1]

	DWC	CCE
Automobiles (motor vehicles & parts)	41 days	7%
Chemicals	72	8
Electrical Components & Equipment	81	8
Food & Beverage	42	8
Food Retailers & Wholesalers	15	4
Forest & Paper Products	39	9
Health-Care Products & Services	44	9
Home Furnishings & Appliances	65	8
Industrial Diversified	103	10
Medical & Biological Technology	99 days	20%

The company that ranked first for the CCE was Microsoft, a technology company with 53%, and for DWC, it was *Hollywood Entertainment*, a retailing business with −20 days.

Managing working capital accounts means reducing costs related to working capital accounts, investing short-term excess of cash, and keeping receivables and inventory as low as possible while increasing payables. All this allows a business to do more business. Increasing sales is not the only answer to improving profitability; all accounts that are affected as a result of incremental sales must be managed efficiently and effectively.

An important criterion for measuring financial performance is return on assets (ROA). The accounts appearing under current assets are in the denominator of the ROA equation; consequently, if working capital accounts are minimized, ROA is improved.

An important concept related to the management of working capital accounts is the **cash conversion cycle,** depicted in Figure 11.1. As shown, working capital accounts can be displayed on a wheel, and the faster the wheel turns the faster and more effectively management can use the cash generated from sales. The goal is to identify the number of days it takes to perform each activity shown on the wheel. For example, if it takes 12 days for customers to make their purchase decisions, 6 days for the credit manager to approve a new customer, 19 days to process goods in the plant, and 9 days to bill customers, the objective would be to reduce the number of days for each of these activities. If, overall, it takes 95 days for cash to circulate in a business, the objective would be to reduce this to, say, 80 days. In Chapter 1, under the heading "Investing Decisions," we used financial ratios such as the average collection period and inventory turnover as tools to determine how working capital accounts, if accelerated, can improve the cash conversion cycle or the performance related to cash flow. As shown in the example on page 16, by improving the average collection period from 60 to 30 days, cash flow improved by $150,000. Similarly, if the inventory turned faster (from 4 to 5 times), the cash flow also improved by $50,000.

Cash conversion cycle

Periodic transformation of cash through working capital and capital assets and back to cash.

---

1 Tim Ryan, "We Can Work It Out: The 2002 Working Capital Survey," *CFO* magazine, August 2002, vol. 18, no. 8, p. 47.

FIGURE 11.1   THE CASH CONVERSION CYCLE

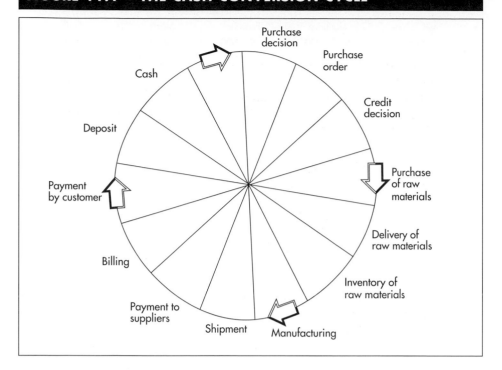

The shaded portion of Table 11.2 shows the difference between profit and cash flow and how improvement in working capital accounts can accelerate cash flow. The upper portion of the table shows the amount of profit generated each month. The middle section (Current Performance) shows the amount of cash generated by the business by collecting 10% of sales within the first month, 50% in the second month, and 40% in the third month. An amount of 50% for purchases is paid during the same month that goods are purchased, and the remaining 50% during the following month. The lower portion of the table (Targeted Performance) shows how cash flow is improved by collecting the accounts receivable more quickly and by paying the suppliers more slowly.

The following summarizes the cash balance at the end of each month as a result of managing these two working capital accounts more efficiently and the cumulative cash improvement for the four-month period.

	January	*February*	*March*	*April*
Current performance	$120,000*	$150,000	$219,000	$273,000
Targeted performance	$135,000	$195,000	$255,000	$291,000
Monthly cash flow improvement	$ 15,000	$ 45,000	$ 36,000	$ 18,000
Cumulative cash flow improvement	$ 15,000	$ 60,000	$ 96,000	$114,000

* These numbers are calculated by subtracting the beginning cash balance from the ending cash balance for individual months. For example, in January the amount is $120,000, the difference between $220,000 and $100,000.

TABLE 11.2   PROFIT VERSUS CASH FLOW

	Profit Forecast			
	January	February	March	April
Sales revenue	$ 300,000	$ 400,000	$ 440,000	$ 480,000
Purchases (50% of sales revenue)	(150,000)	(200,000)	(220,000)	(240,000)
Operating expenses	(120,000)	(150,000)	(160,000)	(170,000)
Total expenses	(270,000)	(350,000)	(380,000)	(410,000)
Profit	**$ 30,000**	**$ 50,000**	**$ 60,000**	**$ 70,000** ←

	Cash Flow Forecast (current performance)			
Beginning cash balance	$ 100,000	$ 220,000	$ 370,000	$ 589,000
Collections*				
10%—cash payment	30,000	40,000	44,000	48,000
50%—in 30 days	100,000	150,000	200,000	220,000
40%—in 60 days	80,000	80,000	120,000	160,000
Total cash available	210,000	270,000	364,000	428,000
Cash flow from operations** (profit + depreciation)	35,000	55,000	65,000	75,000
Purchases***				
50%—cash payment	(75,000)	(100,000)	(110,000)	(120,000)
50%—in 30 days	(50,000)	(75,000)	(100,000)	(110,000)
Total disbursements	(125,000)	(170,000)	(210,000)	(230,000)
Ending cash balance	**$ 220,000**	**$ 370,000**	**$ 589,000**	**$ 862,000** ←

	Cash Flow Forecast (targeted performance)			
Beginning cash balance	$ 100,000	$ 235,000	$ 430,000	$ 685,000
Collections*				
50%—cash payment	150,000	200,000	220,000	240,000
40%—in 30 days	80,000	120,000	160,000	176,000
10%—in 60 days	20,000	20,000	30,000	40,000
Total cash available	250,000	340,000	410,000	456,000
Cash flow from operations** (profit + depreciation)	35,000	55,000	65,000	75,000
Purchases***				
20%—cash payment	(30,000)	(40,000)	(44,000)	(48,000)
80%—in 30 days	(120,000)	(160,000)	(176,000)	(192,000)
Total disbursements	(150,000)	(200,000)	(220,000)	(240,000)
Ending cash balance	**$ 235,000**	**$ 430,000**	**$ 685,000**	**$ 976,000** ←

* Assumes sales at $200,000 per month for October, November, and December.
** Excludes $5,000 for depreciation expense.
*** Assumes purchases of $100,000 in November and December.

By improving the management of only two working capital accounts (accounts receivable and accounts payable), the business was able to improve its cash position by $15,000 in January, $45,000 in February, $36,000 in March, and $18,000 in April for a cumulative improvement of $114,000 ($976,000 − $862,000).

Let's now examine how individual working capital accounts can be managed.

Managing Cash

◀ Objective 2

Cash consists of holdings and short-term deposits. Paying for ongoing obligations, such as the purchase of raw materials and the payment of salaries and current bills, is a constant drain on a company's cash reservoir. However, this reservoir is constantly being replenished by cash sales of inventory and the collection of accounts receivable. Let's examine how cash flows in a business.

Cash
Holdings and short-term deposits.

The Flow of Cash

Cash management is usually assigned to a high-level manager in a business—usually the chief financial officer (CFO) or the treasurer. The goal is to ensure that cash flows into a business as quickly as possible and is used wisely. Figure 11.2 shows how cash flows in and out of a business. At the centre of the system lies the cash pool (or cash reservoir). The cash is used to pay operating expenses, that is, to pay lenders, suppliers, dividends, and taxes, to buy capital assets, and to maintain inventory and accounts receivable.

Why Maintain an Adequate Cash Pool?

The cash pool must be maintained at an appropriate level, and specific amounts must be designated for specific purposes (e.g., inventory, marketable securities, accounts receivable). Maintaining a balanced cash pool is important for four reasons. First, it enables a business to conduct its ordinary operating transactions,

FIGURE 11.2 WORKING CAPITAL FUNDS FLOW

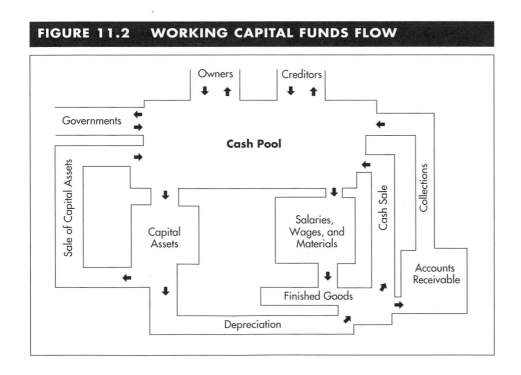

such as paying current bills (e.g., hydro, salaries, supplies, materials, and telephone) and to partially finance its inventories and accounts receivable. Second, an emergency fund is needed because of the difficulty in accurately forecasting the matching of cash receipts and cash disbursements. It can also be used as leverage for borrowing additional cash on a short-term basis. Third, it can be used for taking advantage of opportunities, such as cash discounts if bills are paid within a specified number of days. Finally, it can be used as an instrument for maintaining a credit standing with short-term lenders and suppliers.

Making Cash a Productive Asset

The main objective of cash management is to maintain a reasonable amount of cash so that profitability is not affected and payment of short-term commitments is possible. One way to increase profitability is to reduce the time lag between the date money is mailed by customers and the date it is deposited in the company's bank account to produce a return. For example, if a business can make 12% on short-term securities, and an amount of $30,000 tied up in the mail arrives 20 days late, the company misses the opportunity of making $197.26. The calculation is as follows:

$$\$30{,}000 \times 12\% \times \frac{20\text{-day delay}}{365 \text{ days}} = \$197.26$$

If a company has hundreds or thousands of such cheques arriving late, it can easily miss the opportunity of making thousands of dollars each year in interest alone.

Establishing a Minimum Cash Balance

One cash management activity involves determining exactly how much cash is needed on hand to conduct the ongoing operations of a business. In order to manage cash effectively, a firm must synchronize its cash inflows with its cash outflows on a monthly basis. Cash planning is done through the cash budget (see Table 9.2 in Chapter 9 for an example of a monthly cash budget). The cash budget allows a firm to ascertain the:

- flow of the monthly cash receipts;
- flow of the monthly cash disbursements;
- surplus or shortages of cash at the end of each month; and
- amount of cash that should be invested in short-term securities (surplus) or that will be required from the bank in terms of a loan (shortage).

The objective of cash management is to set a minimum level of cash to satisfy business needs under normal operating conditions in order to increase organizational profitability but without lessening business activities or exposing a firm to undue risk in meeting its financial obligations. Cash reserves (including marketable securities) should be sufficient to satisfy daily cash expenditures. A business needs:

- a practical minimum cash balance to operate with;
- an amount necessary to absorb any unforeseen expenditures; and
- some money to exploit profitable business opportunities (e.g., cash or special discounts on purchases, anticipation of an increase in the price of raw materials, or acquiring a specialized piece of equipment at an attractive price).

Cash needs can be estimated using the following two steps:

STEP 1 Determine the average daily cash expenditures over recent months.

STEP 2 After recognizing the special characteristics of the business, estimate the appropriate cash reserves as a specific number of days' average cash outflow.

For example, if a business spends $300,000 in cash each month, the average daily cash outflow is $10,000 ($300,000 ÷ 30). Here, the treasurer might determine that six days of cash are required to meet the average expenditures under normal business operations. If this is the case, management would need a cash balance of no more than $60,000 ($10,000 × 6 days).

Ways to Improve the Collection of Cash

There are different ways a firm can speed up cash receipts in order to make that asset productive.

CUSTOMERS' DECISIONS TO PURCHASE A customer's decision to purchase goods or services initiates the cash conversion period. Introducing the most rapid communication process to encourage a customer to place an order as quickly as possible is the first step in the cash conversion cycle (see Figure 11.1). A purchase order serves as the medium of communication. Customers should be able to transmit their orders to the company as quickly as possible.

REDUCE THE NEGATIVE FLOAT Float is defined as the time lag between the day a cheque is mailed to the firm and the time the funds are received by the firm. There are three ways to improve a negative float, that is, eliminate idle cash.

The first is electronic communications. The **wire-transfer process** (and the Internet) is an effective means of collecting payments from customers for large purchases. Because wire transfer eliminates delays caused by the postal system, the administrative structure of a business, or the cheque-clearing process, it allows a business to use the collected funds more rapidly. This process transfers money from the sender or customer's bank account into the receiver or firm's bank account in a matter of hours.

Under the electronic system, money is wired directly from a customer's bank account to a business's bank account. This system allows accounts to be debited

Float
The amount of funds tied up in cheques that have been written but are still in process and have not yet been collected.

Wire-transfer process
Means for transferring funds between customer and supplier by using the Internet or any other electronic medium.

and credited daily. At the end of each day, excess cash is invested in short-term deposits in order to generate additional earnings. Unfortunately, many businesses consider only personnel and equipment costs involved in these alternatives and overlook the one- to seven-day reduction in their cash conversion period that results from eliminating mail delays.

The electronic communication of purchase orders is generally suitable when a business has an ongoing relationship with a customer. Repeat customers usually compose the bulk of the sales; so using electronic communication for them helps a business improve its service and accelerate cash flow.

The second process involves **regional banks.** Under this process, customers pay their accounts to banks, and the payment can be transferred to the company's account more quickly than by mail delivery. Collection accounts are established at a series of commercial banks strategically located around the country, and customers are encouraged to pay their bills in their region rather than sending the payments to a central location.

The third strategy is to establish a **post office box** in an area where the firm has many customers. The lockbox system is a procedure whereby a firm rents post office boxes in different cities and entrusts their management to banks, which monitor the lockboxes periodically. The firm instructs customers in a particular region to mail their cheques to regional post office box numbers rather than directly to the firm. As soon as cheques from customers arrive, they are microfilmed, checked for completeness, and deposited in the firm's account. Although this system can be an effective means of improving the collection of cash, a business must weigh the bank's fees against the benefits that accrue from a shorter cash conversion period. Often, the profit potential of a more rapid cash flow can make the cost of the lockbox service insignificant.

The following compares the traditional payment system and the lockbox system.

Traditional Payment System

1. Invoice is sent to the customer.

2. Invoice and payment are sent to the company.

3. Company processes payment and credits customers' account.

4. Company deposits the cheque at the bank.

5. Bank processes the cheque and forwards it to the customer's bank.

6. Customer's bank debits customer's account and returns the cancelled cheque with the next bank statement.

The Lockbox System

1. Invoice is sent to the customer.

2. Invoice and cheque are sent to the company's post office lockbox.

3. Bank processes payment and credits the customer's bank account.

4. Bank advises the company of payment information.

5. Bank forwards cheque to the customer's bank.

6. Customer's bank debits customer's account and returns the cancelled cheque with the next bank statement.

Such a system can help reduce the time lag by three to four days.

Regional banks

Locations where customers pay their accounts (local bank), which are subsequently transferred to the seller's bank account.

Post office box

Location where customers pay their accounts (local post office box), which are subsequently transferred to the seller's bank account.

Managing Marketable Securities

◀■ Objective 3

One of the CFO's responsibilities is to adjust the company's cash balance on an ongoing basis, either by investing excess cash in temporary short-term securities or by securing extra cash through short-term bank borrowings.

It is more profitable for a business to invest cash in marketable securities, even if it is only for several days, than to leave it dormant in a bank account that does not generate interest. The main objective of managing marketable securities is to invest the temporary excess cash in order to increase profitability.

Funds are held in short-term marketable securities or temporary investments for three reasons:

1. to finance seasonal or cyclical operations (temporary working capital);
2. to finance known financial requirements, such as purchase of equipment or machinery; and
3. to invest funds received from the sale of long-term securities (shares or bonds).

Different types of marketable securities can be held by businesses, and the attributes of each should be examined carefully before investing. Four main attributes should be considered. First, there is *maturity*, the length of time by which the principal amount of a marketable security must be paid back to the investor. Second, there is the *denomination*, the unit of transaction for buying or selling a short-term security. Third, there is *marketability*, or the ability of an investor to sell a marketable security. Finally, there is the *yield determination*, which is the method of earning a return on the investment.

There are different types of **investment securities,** such as Canada Treasury bills, bank deposits, commercial paper, finance company paper, Eurodollar deposits, Canadian government bonds, and corporate bonds with different maturity dates and yields. Depending on the length of time a treasurer wants to place funds, he or she will have to find the most suitable type of security, that is, the one that responds most favourably to the business's needs.

Investment securities
Funds invested in short-term deposits such as treasury bills, bank deposits, etc.

Strategies for Managing Marketable Securities

Managing marketable securities for a small business is relatively easy. The only requirement is the need to match the short-term investments with the excess cash shown in the monthly cash budget. A large business, on the other hand, must determine investment strategies that will optimize the return on investment. In many cases, businesses have millions of dollars tied up in cash or near-cash accounts. It is therefore important for such businesses to determine effective investment strategies in short-term marketable securities. There are six approaches.

First, there is the *do-nothing* option. In this case, the company simply lets the excess funds accumulate in its bank account. Here, funds are not invested in short-term securities, therefore profitability is sacrificed.

Second, there is the investment of funds on an *ad hoc basis*. This approach is accomplished when investment securities are synchronized with projected cash disbursements. This method is used by firms that, because of a shortage of resources or a lack of expertise within the company, do not want to devote much time and energy to this activity.

Third, there is the *riding-the-yield approach*. Here, the treasurer examines the investment portfolio and invests in the securities that will offer the highest interest rate. For example, he or she may sell off a long-term security before maturity and purchase a short-term security simply to obtain a higher yield.

Fourth, *guidelines* can be developed. This is particularly useful if many people are involved in investing in short-term securities (e.g., in insurance companies and trust companies). Such guidelines give the securities analysts procedures to be followed systematically in order to reflect senior management's viewpoint and take into consideration both return and risk.

Fifth, *control limits* can be established, allowing the analysts to take action only when the cash balance reaches an upper or lower control limit. This approach does not specify which marketable securities should be bought or sold but states only when action should be taken.

The sixth option is the *portfolio approach*. Here, individual marketable securities are not examined as isolated investment opportunities but as part of a group of investments. In this case, both risk and returns are taken into consideration from a broader viewpoint—the portfolio perspective. There may be hundreds of different investment options, and each option is evaluated on the basis of a total investment strategy that is consistent with the financial objectives of the firm. Some securities may offer low return and low risk; others, high risk and high return.

Objective 4 ➤

Managing Accounts Receivable

Since most firms sell on credit, and for most of them credit accounts for the bulk of their sales, it is important to manage the accounts receivable effectively. The level of accounts receivable is determined in two ways: first, by the volume of sales made on credit; and second, by the time it takes for customers to pay off their accounts.

The mission of the credit manager is to:

1. set credit terms;
2. grant credit to customers;
3. bill the customers;
4. monitor payments made by customers;
5. collect accounts receivable; and
6. ensure adequate credit insurance.

Let's review each of these activities.

Set Credit Terms

It is the responsibility of the credit manager to decide what **credit terms** a firm should adopt. These terms are greatly influenced by the industry of which the firm is part. A basic element of credit terms to businesses is the length of time given to customers to pay their accounts.

Trade discounts can help a company's cash flow at the expense of earnings and may very well be a good tradeoff. For example, a business may allow a 2% discount off the original sale price of goods if a customer pays an invoice within 10 days of shipment and charges the full amount for payment within 30 days (i.e., 2/10, N/30). However, before deciding to offer trade discounts, the credit manager estimates the costs and benefits that will result. Should a firm offer its customers a policy of 2/10, N/30? Or 1/10, N/30? Or 2/10, N/45? To answer this question, the credit manager must explore the following points.

First, the manager measures the benefits. When a customer pays in accordance with the discount terms, it shortens a company's average collection period and accelerates cash flow. At the same time, the investment in receivables is reduced, as are the costs associated with carrying that investment. Cash discounts presumably benefit both parties in the transaction: The customers reduce their purchase costs when taking the discount, and the firm enjoys a better cash flow and a lower investment in accounts receivable.

Second, the credit manager calculates the effective price when offering a purchase discount. The bottom line is this: before introducing discounts into credit terms, the credit manager recognizes how such allowances affect a company's earnings.

Before changing the policy, the credit manager must go through a detailed calculation. To illustrate, let's assume that a company sells products with an average unit-selling price of $400.00. The cost of manufacturing or buying materials from suppliers is $250.00. Furthermore, in that particular industry, customers have the habit of paying 60 days after purchase. As shown below, if the cost of money is 10%, it would be more advantageous for the firm to offer the 2/10, N/30, since the profit generated when customers pay in 10 days is $146.65, compared to $145.89 if they continue to pay in 60 days. Here is the arithmetic. If the customer benefits from the 2% discount, line 1 shows that the company would receive $392.00 ($400.00 × 98%) instead of $400.00. Whether the company offers a 2% discount or not, line 2 indicates that the company would have to pay $250.00 to manufacture the product or to buy it from a supplier. Line 3 shows the credit costs for both options. The company would have to pay a $0.68 ($250.00 × 10% × 10/365) credit cost to finance the $250.00 purchase if payment is received in 10 days, and $4.11 ($250.00 × 10% × 60/365) if payment is received in 60 days. Line 4 shows that the company would make $5.37 ($392.00 × 10% × 50/365) if the $392.00 is deposited in the bank for the 50-day period and earns 10%. Based on this calculation, line 5 shows that there is an economic advantage to offering the 2% discount.

Credit terms

Conditions under which credit is extended, especially how quickly the customer is expected to pay the account.

Line		10-day payment	60-day payment
1.	Effective price	$392.00	$400.00
2.	Purchase (or manufacturing) cost	−250.00	−250.00
3.	Credit cost (10 and 60 days)	−0.68	−4.11
4.	Interest on money (50 days)	+5.37	—
5.	Net profit	$146.65	$145.89

Grant Credit to Customers

The second activity of the credit manager is the granting of credit. Two questions must be asked in the context of credit analysis: should credit be granted to a customer? If yes, how much? The criteria used by firms to rate borrowers can be summarized as the six "C's" introduced in Chapter 10: character, collateral, capacity, capital, circumstances, and coverage.

In order to shorten the cash conversion cycle, the credit decision should be made as soon as a purchase order is received. Therefore, it is important to approve in advance lines of credit for major customers. In other words, the credit manager should anticipate customers' needs before they exceed their credit limits (see Figure 11.1).

Little is lost if a customer does not use the full credit line. However, customers who do increase their purchases will find their orders delivered more promptly if credit is pre-approved. Indeed, pre-approved credit facilitates the completion of a sale and improves a firm's service capability. A faster response inevitably offers a competitive advantage.

The same approach can be used for new customers. It is preferable to check the creditworthiness of a new account in advance, before receiving a larger order. Obtaining the information for a credit check—bank checks, supplier checks—can take several days and thus lengthen the cash conversion period. Moreover, if the delay is too long, the business may risk losing the sale to a competitor with a more efficient credit-decision process.

However, reliable credit analysis should not be sacrificed for the sake of speedy approval. Even a modest increase in bad-debt losses (if some customers do not pay their bills) can offset the benefits from a lower cash-conversion period. At the same time, any element in the administrative process that delays the completion of a sale hampers the smooth flow of cash into a business.

Let's review the types of credit analysis that businesses go through when granting credit to consumers and businesses.

CONSUMER CREDIT Credit-scoring systems are often used to analyze the creditworthiness of potential customers. Under a **credit-scoring system,** the credit clerks are given specific guidelines for rating a potential customer as a good or bad risk. This system is used by businesses offering credit cards to thousands of consumers (e.g., retail stores and banks). Table 11.3 shows a typical credit-scoring system. As shown, several variables are examined, and each is given a weight. This

Credit-scoring system

System used to analyze the creditworthiness of potential customers.

TABLE 11.3 CREDIT SCORING SYSTEM

Variable	Measurement	Value	Weight	Weighted Value
Age	In years as reported	36	0.4	14.4
Marital status	Coded 1 (yes) or 0 (no)	1	20.0	20.0
Occupation	Coded 1 to 5 for different professions	4	4.3	17.2
Time in last job	In years as reported	6	0.9	5.4
Annual income	In thousands of dollars as reported	45.0	0.6	27.0
Residence	Coded 1 to 5 for different postal zones	3	4.6	13.8
Home ownership	Number of years owned as reported	4	1.2	4.8
Telephone	Coded 1 (yes) or 0 (no)	1	15.0	15.0
Total credit score				117.6

weight has been determined by taking a sample of existing customers and finding the factors that distinguish those who pay their accounts promptly from those who are slow payers. In this case, the variables include age, marital status, occupation, time in last job, annual income, residence, home ownership, and whether they have a telephone; and the credit score totals 117.6. The credit clerk will then decide, using the predetermined guidelines, what steps should be taken with each consumer. For example, the guidelines may stipulate that if the score is less than 60 points, credit will be denied; if it is between 60 and 80, the customer will be investigated further; and if it is greater than 80, credit will be granted. Under these guidelines, the consumer in our example would be granted credit.

BUSINESS CREDIT Granting credit to commercial enterprises involves a different type of analysis. Here, the firm may want to go through an analysis of the potential customer and obtain information regarding its credit standing. In certain cases, the firm will ask for a credit report, such as the one provided by Dun & Bradstreet or Standard and Poor's. Typical information provided by credit institutions is summarized in Table 11.4.

On the basis of the information obtained, the firm will specify the type of account that should be granted (open account or other arrangement), the credit period (when payment is due), the size of the discount, and the discount period.

IMPACT OF ALTERNATIVE CREDIT POLICIES Decisions about the extent of credit to be provided to customers are determined by a firm's **credit policy.** If a business has a restrictive credit policy, it will most likely sell less, have less invested in

Credit policies

Decisions about the extent of credit that should be extended to customers.

TABLE 11.4   INFORMATION SHOWN ON BUSINESS CREDIT REPORTS

Summary	Classification code for line of business, year business started, rating, principal executives (owners).
Report information	Payments, sales worth, number of employees, trends.
Payments	How business pays its bills (i.e., amounts owing, amounts past due, terms of sales, manner of payment, and supplier comments).
Finance	Financial conditions and trend of business (balance sheet and income statement).
History	Names, birthdates, and past business experience of the principals or owners, affiliations, ownership, outside interests of the principal owners.
Operations	Nature of the premises, neighbourhood, size of floor space, production facilities.

accounts receivable and inventory, and have fewer bad debts. Conversely, as a firm relaxes its credit terms, it sells more goods to a wider range of customers that include poorer credit risks; this in turn increases bad debts.

An integrated management analysis should precede any change in a firm's credit terms or policies. There is a close connection between selling and credit. Since most firms do not really have a choice of selling on credit or for cash, the most important decision for a business is when to change the credit policy of the firm over time. An ROI framework is appropriate for comparing credit alternatives because it focuses on the investment a firm makes in accounts receivable. It also allows a business to systematically consider potential sales and profits, alternative credit terms including cash discount, and bad-debt expenses. Changing credit terms therefore requires the analysis of certain links or relationships that should not be ignored when evaluating alternative credit terms and policies. The decision to extend credit consideration and carry the resulting investment in accounts receivable focuses on a tradeoff between (1) the cost of carrying the investment in accounts receivable, and (2) the benefits of a larger sales volume.

The most important links are between:

- credit terms and policy and the firm's total marketing effort;
- credit policy and the inventory level;
- credit policy and production capacity; and
- credit policy and the efficiency of the firm's operations.

To establish an appropriate credit policy, the credit manager must examine the changes in the level of profit generated as a result of a relaxed credit policy and the extra investment in accounts receivable and inventory. Table 11.5 shows how to calculate changes in profit and investment resulting from a change in credit terms. In this case, if the firm's cost of capital is 12%, it will not proceed with the proposed credit policy.

TABLE 11.5 ESTABLISHING A CREDIT POLICY

	Existing Terms	Proposed Terms
Expected volume (units)	500,000	550,000
Expected sales revenue ($10.00 per unit)	$5,000,000	$5,500,000
Expected profit before bad debts (10% of revenue)	$ 500,000	$ 550,000
Expected bad debt expense*	$ 25,000	$ 55,000
Expected profit (after bad debts)	$ 475,000	$ 495,000
Incremental profit	—	20,000
Expected collection period (days)	31	38
Average accounts receivable	$ 425,000	$ 575,000
Inventory	$ 850,000	$ 900,000
Incremental investment	—	$ 200,000

* A 0.5% factor is used for calculating bad debts for existing credit terms, and a 1.0% factor
is used for the proposed terms.

$$\text{Return on investment} = \frac{\$20,000}{\$200,000} = 10\%$$

As shown in the table, the levels of accounts receivable and inventory are affected by the proposed change in the credit policy. It is important to calculate the effect each change in credit policy has on working capital accounts.

Bill Customers

The invoice identifies the merchandise sold, the shipment date, and the amount due from the purchaser. Prompt completion and transmission of an invoice are important elements of the cash cycle for two reasons. First, few purchasers will pay for merchandise prior to the receipt of the invoice. Indeed, in most businesses, the invoice typically serves as the trigger for the payment process in the accounting system. Second, the invoice date usually initiates the payment period defined by a firm's selling terms.

Prompt completion and transmission of the invoice increases cash availability and earnings. A firm should not render a monthly statement of account to trigger customer payment. Rendering statements is a costly, time-consuming, and self-defeating administrative process. Also, allowing customers to pay in response to monthly statements, rather than to purchase invoices, adds from one to 30 days to the cash conversion cycle, as customers ignore the invoices and wait for the monthly statement. Issuing the invoice that completes a sale is the final step in the administrative process.

Chapter 11: Working Capital Management

Monitor Payments Made by Customers

Irrespective of how a credit policy is determined, once it is adopted, collection must be monitored continually to gauge the effectiveness of the policy and how well it is applied. Several approaches can be used to gauge the effectiveness of a credit policy, to monitor the payment behaviour of customers over a period of time, and to take corrective action on delinquent accounts. The most common are (1) average collection period (in days), and (2) the aging of accounts receivable.

AVERAGE COLLECTION PERIOD The average collection period is the average time it takes for customers to pay their accounts after credit sales have been made. Let's examine how this works. Assume that a business sold $3.0 million last year and the same amount this year. However, the accounts receivable increased from last year's $450,000 to this year's $500,000. This is an indication that customers paid their accounts more slowly over the last 12 months. The calculation is done as follows:

$$\text{Last year's average collection period} = \frac{\$450,000}{\$3,000,000} \times 365 = 54.7 \text{ days}$$

$$\text{This year's average collection period} = \frac{\$500,000}{\$3,000,000} \times 365 = 60.8 \text{ days}$$

The company shows a 6.1-day deterioration in the average collection period.

AGING OF ACCOUNTS RECEIVABLE While 6.1 days may seem like a small increase, the credit manager may want to examine in more detail the aging of the company's accounts receivable. The credit manager may want to spot changes in customer-paying behaviour by preparing an aging schedule showing the percentage of each month's sales still outstanding at the end of successive months. The schedule gives a picture of any recent change in the makeup of the receivables. This type of information is presented in Table 11.6. As shown, the **aging of accounts receivable** is grouped by age category and by what percentage of receivables outstanding fall in each age category.

Aging of accounts receivable

A report showing how long accounts receivable have been outstanding. It gives the percentage of receivables past due for one month, two months, or other periods.

TABLE 11.6 AGING OF ACCOUNTS RECEIVABLE
As a percentage of total receivables

% of Receivables	Last Year	This Year
Under 30 days old	60.4	54.2
between 31 and 60 days	24.4	23.8
between 61 and 90 days	7.2	10.4
between 91 and 120 days	6.5	8.3
over 121 days	1.5	3.3

Examining the aging process is an essential element of the accounts receivable analysis; it identifies specific groupings of accounts within the total component that make up an overinvestment. The aging schedule also shows how long accounts receivable have been outstanding at a given point in time.

Collect Accounts Receivable

The collection of accounts was discussed earlier in this chapter under the heading "Managing Cash." Effective credit collection begins by mailing invoices promptly. Once the invoice is mailed, the credit manager must examine, on a regular basis, the average collection period and take remedial action if targets are not realized. Several steps can be adopted to accelerate the collection of accounts from delinquent customers. First, there is the *"dunning" approach,* mailing a duplicate copy of the original invoice. Second, the credit manager can make a personal *telephone call,* which can serve as a routine, but stronger, reminder. Third, the credit manager can call on customers and initiate *constructive counselling.* Fourth, *registered letters* can be sent to delinquent accounts as notices that if payment is not received by a certain date, the firm will involve a third party (e.g., a collection agency) in the collection process. Finally, the most expensive way is to resort to formal *legal charges.*

Ensure Adequate Credit Insurance

Credit insurance provides protection against the cash drain caused by uncollectible accounts receivable. Just as a vehicle theft or a warehouse fire can disrupt a business, the inability to collect a large receivable can cut off its cash flow. Not only can credit insurance prevent a cash flow crisis, but also can lead to higher earnings. Insurance protection on accounts receivable can be secured in two ways:

1. The **indemnification policy** is insurance a business takes against the catastrophic loss in cash that might occur when a large receivable becomes uncollectible because of debtor bankruptcy, debtor composition (reorganization of debt by creditors), or any other proceedings that reflect a debtor's insolvency.

2. The **credit insurance policy** provides coverage for losses suffered from any of a firm's accounts receivable that become uncollectible. The coverage is subject to two practical limits. First, the insurance company can apply a deductible amount to each loss. Second, the insurance company can limit the maximum coverage for each debtor. Typically, those limits are tied to ratings established by national credit agencies such as Dun & Bradstreet. While premiums vary, the coverage may cost 0.25% to 0.5% of annual sales, which could be a small price to pay for survival.

With this type of insurance, a company can be more liberal in granting credit to high-risk customers. If they don't pay, the insurance company would compensate the company.

Indemnification policy
Insurance a business takes against the catastrophic loss in cash.

Credit insurance policy
Insurance to cover losses suffered from a firm's accounts receivable that become uncollectible.

Managing Inventory

The objective of inventory management is to replenish inventory or stocks in such a way that associated order and holding costs are kept to a minimum in order to enhance profitability.

Turning inventory more rapidly improves cash flow, earnings, and ROI. One more way for a firm to analyze its management effort is by calculating the annual inventory turnover rate, or the number of times a business sells, or turns, its investment in inventory in the course of a year. It is an activity indicator that relates an investment in inventory directly to sales volume (for a retail or wholesale business) or cost of goods sold (for a manufacturer).

The turnover rate calculation is significant because of its direct relationship to cash flow and profits. Thus, the faster the inventory turns over, the lower the investment in inventory. Most managers understand that moving merchandise more rapidly is the key to profitability.

To calculate the inventory turnover rate, the annual cost of goods sold or sales revenue must be divided by the average investment in inventory.

Maintaining the right level of inventory can be compared to maintaining an appropriate level of water in a bathtub. If water flows out of the tub more rapidly than into it, the tub will soon be empty. However, if more water is let in than out, the tub will overflow. The same principle applies in inventory management. On one side, inventory is used continuously to produce manufactured goods and, on the other, raw materials keep flowing into the storage area. The idea is to determine two things: (1) the proper level of investment that should be kept in inventory, and (2) how much inventory should be purchased, and at what interval, to maintain an appropriate level of stock.

A delay in shipment lengthens the cash conversion period and hinders cash flow. To avoid delays in shipment, a firm should have a well-organized shipping department that is well coordinated with the administrative process.

An inventory control system should answer two essential needs:

- It should maintain a current record of the amount of each inventory item held in stock.
- It should be able to locate that stock.

Neither element should be left to chance or memory. Accountants refer to this system as *perpetual inventory*. The sale and purchase of each item in inventory is logged on a computerized stock sheet. Then, at any time, the sheets specify the total inventory of each item held in stock; the sheet should also identify the exact location of the items. This prevents shipping delays, as employees do not have to search for stock in the warehouse. The perpetual inventory system also helps to determine the reorder points for each item on the stock ledger sheets or computerized inventory software program when the economic ordering quantity system (to be discussed later) is applied.

A periodic count of every item in stock is the first, fundamental principle of sound inventory management. The physical count serves two primary objectives:

- It enables a business to verify the accuracy of its accounting procedures that keep track of the investment in inventory. As the exact amount of each item in stock is verified, it confirms the value of the investment.
- The physical count provides the basic data necessary to perform an item analysis of the inventory.

Item analysis enables a firm to control its investment in inventory. This analysis measures the amount of investment in each item in stock against the amount actually required, based on the firm's recent sales experience. It identifies the specific source of any overinvestment in inventory.

Types of Inventory

Before examining the techniques used to make inventory decisions, let's look at the different things that are inventoried. These include office supplies such as pencils, paper, and pens and spare parts, which are used by the manufacturing operations in the event of breakdowns. However, the three most important **types of inventory** for most manufacturing operations are raw materials, work-in-process, and finished goods.

Raw material inventories consist of goods purchased for the purpose of manufacturing goods. This type of inventory is influenced by the level of production, the reliability of sources of supply, and the efficiency of scheduling purchases and production operations.

Work-in-process inventories consist of partially assembled or incomplete goods in the production cycle. Such inventories are not ready for sale.

Finished inventories consist of products that are ready to be sold and shipped to customers.

Types of inventory
Raw materials, work-in-process, and finished goods.

Inventory Decision Models

Inventory management means determining the optimal level of inventory that should be kept in stock at all times. Three models will be discussed here: material requirements planning, just-in-time inventory management, and economic ordering quantity.

MATERIAL REQUIREMENTS PLANNING **Material requirements planning (MRP)** is excellent for developing a production schedule to help coordinate and utilize resources (materials, people, and equipment) more effectively. The greater breadth and variety of product lines, together with increasingly expensive inventory, spurred management to adopt computers and use them to manage the huge amounts of production-related information in an entirely new way. By using MRP, it is possible to link individual departments in the production flow from a planning and scheduling point of view.

The MRP system that is based on anticipated shipments of finished goods uses that finished-unit schedule to derive subassembly schedules and component schedules. To develop these schedules for individual departments requires a thor-

Material requirements planning (MRP)
Method for developing a schedule to help coordinate and utilize resources in production.

ough understanding of how components feed into subassemblies, and how subassemblies in turn feed into the finished products. This information is referred to as a bill of materials for a finished end item.

When planning material requirements, it is also necessary to know the timing relationships between various departments and the production-cycle times within each department. Knowing the bill of materials for that final assembled item and those timing relationships can help managers use the schedule for final assembly. They can also derive the schedules by which subassemblies would have to be produced in preceding time periods, and by which components would have to be produced in even earlier time periods. In addition, it helps to ensure that the components and subassemblies will come together according to the final assembly schedule.

Just-in-time inventory management

An inventory management technique that obtains supplier materials just when they are needed.

JUST-IN-TIME INVENTORY MANAGEMENT Using the **just-in-time inventory** process helps to reduce inventory, speed the cash conversion cycle (see Figure 11.1), and increase profitability. In the last decade, the Japanese supply system called just-in-time (JIT) or *kanban* has received a great deal of attention. It includes frequent (even daily) deliveries of parts or supplies, which help to reduce working inventories. This system places responsibility on the supplier for "no defects," as well as responsibility for scheduled delivery of exactly the right quantity with "no excuses." Thus, safety stock and production-line float can be eliminated.

To make near-perfect coordination feasible, suppliers are encouraged or even required to locate plants very close to the customer's production line. These and other coordination activities in planning and production dramatically reduce in-process inventory, improve product quality, reduce need for inspection, and increase salable output per day.

Economic ordering quantity (EOQ)

Method that determines the optimum quantity of goods that should be ordered at any single time.

ECONOMIC ORDERING QUANTITY Another commonly used approach for determining optimal levels of inventory is the **economic ordering quantity (EOQ)** model. The main purpose of this technique is to minimize total inventory costs, consisting of ordering costs and carrying costs. Inventory decisions are influenced by the reorder point, which is the level of inventory that is held at the time a new order is placed, and the reorder quantity, which is the quantity ordered each time. Before examining the EOQ model, let's look at the different types of costs associated with inventory management. Inventory costs fall into two groups: ordering costs and holding costs.

Ordering costs

Category of costs associated with the acquisition of goods (e.g., receiving, inspecting, accounting).

Ordering costs include:

- the actual cost of the merchandise acquired;
- the administrative costs of scheduling, entering, and receiving an order;
- the labour costs of receiving, inspecting, and shelving each order; and
- the cost of accounting and paying for the order.

Since inventory acquisition costs rise as a business places more orders, the frequency of acquisitions should be kept to a minimum. Everyone recognizes the direct costs of acquiring inventory: the purchase price of the merchandise.

However, many overlook other acquisition costs, which increase the actual cost of any particular order, and the inverse relationship they have to the size of the average investment in inventory.

Two facts concerning these costs are relevant here. First, the administrative, accounting, and labour costs associated with any order are far more significant than many people realize. Indeed, the cumulative acquisition costs from numerous orders can exert a significant downward effect on earnings. Second, the cumulative acquisition costs remain relatively constant regardless of the size of the order involved.

Holding costs are the category of costs associated with holding or storing goods in inventory. It is this cost that most people associate with inventory. Included in this category would be:

Holding costs
Category of costs associated with the storing of goods in inventory (e.g., insurance, rent).

- the costs of maintaining and managing warehouses or other storage facilities;
- the costs of safety systems for guarding inventory;
- the costs of inventory shrinkage that might occur from spoilage, theft, or obsolescence; and
- the cost of company funds tied up in inventory (opportunity costs or interest charges).

Holding costs rise as the size of inventory increases and, as such, each component of these costs should be examined with a view to keeping them at a minimum.

In contrast to acquisition costs, holding costs may be viewed as variable costs in the sense that more units held in inventory result in an increase in these costs. The financial or opportunity costs increase in exact proportion to the size of the investment. However, other carrying costs also increase, although the proportions are less precise. Therefore, as investment is increased, warehouse costs also increase because the firm needs more space to store more inventory. As the investment grows, the firm will also experience rising insurance and maintenance costs, as well as an increase in expenses from deterioration or obsolescence. Estimates of holding costs ranging from 20% to 30% of the value of inventory are not uncommon. The basic economic ordering quantity equation states that the ideal reorder quantity is as follows:

$$EOQ = \sqrt{\frac{2 \times (order\ cost) \times (yearly\ demand)}{(annual\ carrying\ cost\ for\ one\ unit)}}$$

If a business sells 5,000 units of product per year, the ordering costs are $50.00 per order, and the carrying costs are $0.80 per unit per year, we find that the company should reorder 790 units each time it places an order. The calculation is as follows:

$$EOQ = \sqrt{\frac{2 \times \$50.00 \times 5,000}{\$0.80}} = 790\ units$$

TABLE 11.7 DETERMINING THE ECONOMIC ORDERING QUANTITY

Number of Orders	Order Quantity (units)	Annual Order Cost (at $50.00 per order)	Average Unit Inventory (2) ÷ 2	Average Dollar Investment (4) × $5.35	Annual Holding Costs (5) × 15%	Ordering Cost + Holding Cost (3) + (6)
1	2	3	4	5	6	7
1	5,000	$ 50	2,500	$13,375	$2,006	$2,056
2	2,500	100	1,250	6,687	1,003	1,103
5	1,000	250	500	2,675	401	651
6	833	300	416	2,226	334	634
8	625	400	312	1,669	250	650
10	500	$500	250	$ 1,337	$ 200	$ 700

Table 11.7 shows the total ordering and holding costs for ordering different quantities during the year. Column 1 shows the number of orders the company can place during the year; it ranges from one to ten orders. Column 2 presents the number of units it would have to order each time an order is made. For example, by placing five orders, the company would order 1,000 units each time. Column 3 indicates the annual cost for placing the orders. For example, ordering five times during the year would cost the company $250.00 ($50.00 × 5). Column 4 shows the average number of units that the company would have in its warehouse, depending on the number of orders it places. For instance, if only one order or 5,000 units is placed during the year, the average number of units the company would have in stock would be 2,500 (5,000 ÷ 2). Column 5 presents the average dollar investment. For example, if the holding cost per unit, which includes maintenance, spoilage, interest charges, etc., is $5.35, the average dollar investment if the company places one order per year is $13,375 (2,500 × $5.35). Column 6 shows the annual holding costs, which can be calculated in two ways. The first is to multiply 15%, which represents the annual holding cost, by the average dollar investment and obtain $2,006 ($13,375 × 15%). The second is to multiply the annual holding cost per unit of $0.80 by the average unit inventory and obtain the same answer, $2,006 (2,500 × $0.80). Column 7 shows the sum of column 3 (ordering cost) and column 6 (annual holding costs). As shown, 833 units (closest to 790) is the combination that costs the least ($634).

INVENTORY REPLENISHMENT Another extension of the EOQ is the decision related to **inventory replenishment.** Suppose the company decides to order 790 units each time it places an order. The next decision is to decide the frequency of the orders. Figure 11.3 shows the factors that are considered for replenishing inventory. They are:

Inventory replenishment

Decision related to when to order goods from supplier.

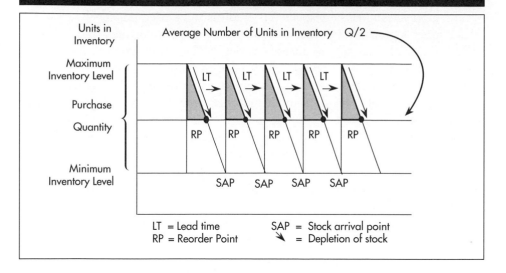

FIGURE 11.3   INVENTORY LEVELS

LT = Lead time   SAP = Stock arrival point
RP = Reorder Point   ↘ = Depletion of stock

- the minimum and maximum levels of inventory the business will want to have in stock prior to the point of placing a new order;
- the total time it takes from the purchase to the receipt of the goods (LT); and
- when the order should be placed (RP).

Managing Current Liabilities

◀ Objective 6

The management of current liabilities is also part of working capital management. Current liabilities are the credit obligations that fall due within a 12-month period. For a business, it is important to determine which assets should be financed by short-term liabilities and which by long-term sources. A business should always maximize the use of its accounts payable and accruals as sources of financing, because they are spontaneous and self-adjusting. This means that these accounts can expand and contract with changes in the levels of sales. When more sales are made, accounts payable increase in roughly the same proportion. Similarly, when more people are on the payroll, wages and salaries payable increase.

The main objective of managing payables and accruals is to provide the business with a spontaneous source of financing at no cost. Some of the more popular sources and forms of short-term financing were discussed in Chapter 10.

This section deals with sources of working capital financing. Leverage is the extent to which a firm's assets are supported by debt. We will deal here with short-term leverage: the funds that can be derived from suppliers (accounts payable), various accruals, and working capital loans obtained from commercial banks. This section will examine the benefits of leverage and how this type of financing can help realize higher earnings.

Accounts Payable

Several guidelines must be respected if credit is to be used effectively. First, the sales budget is prepared in order to determine when the raw materials financing will be required. Second, the manufacturing budget is established in order to ascertain salary and wage payments. Third, suppliers that offer the best products and services are selected, determining the credit terms that best meet the company's needs. Finally, the decision is made regarding when and how invoices should be paid.

Managing accounts payable requires a good relationship between the company and its suppliers. This means that when bills arrive, they should be paid according to the agreement, on the appropriate date. This allows a firm to maintain a good credit standing with its suppliers and ensures that they will continue to sell goods and provide services to it.

However, nothing prevents a firm from taking advantage of cost-free funds, such as accounts payable. It is a matter of deferring the payment of the accounts' bills, and ensuring, at the same time, that the suppliers maintain confidence in the firm as a "slow, but sure, payer."

A supplier contributes financing to a firm any time account credit consideration is extended. This trade credit allows a business to defer cash payment for a purchase in accordance with the supplier's selling terms. Conceptually, trade credit provides the same benefits to a business as any other form of leverage: It increases a company's cash capability and enables it to satisfy objectives that might remain out of reach in the absence of external financing. However, it is more closely connected with the cash flow cycle than any other form of financing; therefore, its use calls for deliberate cash planning that focuses on the following four points:

- the link between trade credit and cash capability;
- benefits the firm can derive from an alternative supplier's selling terms;
- the relationship between trade credit and the cash flow process with the help of the average payment period calculation and the period that contributes positively to cash flow; and
- good working relations with suppliers.

LINK BETWEEN TRADE CREDIT AND CASH CAPABILITY Trade credit is a significant source of financing for most businesses and, if it is properly administered within the planning and purchasing functions, can help a business increase its cash capability and obtain interest-free, permanently revolving loans in the form of an infinite series of single-payment loans.

The goal of accounts payable management is to provide as much spontaneous financing as possible at zero cost to a business. A major advantage of trade credit is the flexibility it gives a business. It is at management's discretion to determine whether a cash discount should be taken or not, or whether it should stretch its accounts payable beyond the credit period. "Leaning on credit" involves postponement of payment beyond the credit period. The opportunity cost of leaning on credit is a possible deterioration of a company's credit rating.

Credit is directly related to purchasing and is not an isolated activity; it is part of a comprehensive process that touches on the effective scheduling of products and services for sale to customers. In order to determine the amount of trade credit a business requires, management must know how many units it needs to buy and when to buy them. The key activities related to purchasing are as follows:

- preparation of a sales budget;
- preparation of a production budget;
- determining what and when to purchase;
- determining which suppliers to use;
- determining what credit terms to accept;
- receiving purchases and ensuring quality; and
- determining when and how to pay invoices.

BENEFITS DERIVED FROM ALTERNATIVE SUPPLIER SELLING TERMS Delaying disbursements generates more cash capability in a firm and increases profitability. The maximum cash disbursement period comes from two complementary management practices:

- liability management; and
- float management.

In either instance, the objective remains the same—the retention of all cash in a business as long as possible. A business should not pay its bills before they become due. This is the guiding principle of liability management. Of course, a business should never abuse a creditor's consideration, nor should it exceed the requirements set by the suppliers' required payment terms. But, if management experiences a tight cash flow, it can delay cash disbursements beyond the credit terms.

In some industries, such as electronics and printing, the practice of stretching payables is common. In other industries, such as steel and food commodities, failure to observe supplier terms can eliminate any future credit consideration. Certainly, management should know where it stands before deferring any payment beyond its due date.

As indicated earlier, extending the average payable period, which is the relationship between trade credit and the cash flow process, increases cash capability and earnings. Average payable period measures the average length of time each dollar of trade credit is used. A common characteristic of trade credit is that it is spontaneous (i.e., self-adjusting). As sales expand, a business necessarily purchases more materials and parts, hence payables increase. Trade credit involves the acquisition of materials, parts, and supplies needed, and a delay between the date of their acquisitions and the date of payment to the creditors increases the company's cash capability and earnings.

To calculate the average payable period and to find how it contributes to positive cash flow, accounts payable is divided by the average daily purchases. For example, if the accounts payable shown on a balance sheet are $300,000, and the average daily purchases are $10,000, the average payment period is 30 days. Thus, each dollar of trade credit consideration contributed to a business remains in the bank account for 30 days before being returned to the supplier in the form of a cash payment. If the average payment period is extended to 45 days, accounts payable increase to $450,000 ($10,000 × 45 days), which gives an extra $150,000 in cash.

Two important factors should be considered here:

- Payments to suppliers should not be extended to a point where relationships and goodwill are damaged.
- Cash discounts should be considered before making payments.

RELATIONSHIP BETWEEN TRADE CREDIT AND CASH FLOW A trade discount can help increase profitability at the expense of cash flow; therefore, it is a matter of calculating the tradeoff. Many businesses offer various types of trade discounts if a supplier wants to increase its cash flow position. A business can reinvest its accelerated cash flow rapidly and thus increase profitability. The earnings that the supplier loses from today's discounts could benefit it more in the future.

When a company decides to offer a trade discount, it may mean that its average collection period is long (45, 60, or even as high as 90 days). If this is the case, a company may offer trade discounts to get its customers to pay faster. This has two benefits:

- accelerated cash flow;
- increase in profitability.

If a supplier offers a trade discount, the business should take advantage of it, as long as the cost of borrowing from the bank is less than the supplier discount. Here is the effective cost of various early-payment discounts when annualized:

Discounts allowed for payment in ten days	Annualized cost to the supplier
0.5%	9%
1%	18%
2%	37%

This means that if a supplier offers a 2% discount, net 30-day payment option, the 2% discount translates into a 37% annual borrowing cost. Figure 11.4 shows how this percentage was calculated.

GOOD WORKING RELATIONSHIP WITH SUPPLIERS A favourable working relationship with suppliers has a direct influence on a firm's cash capability. A good working relationship affects both the amount and the terms of the credit consideration a business receives. One may argue that making a major purchase from any supplier involves considerations that proceed beyond any potential credit consideration. However, price structures, product lines, delivery schedules, and service capabilities remain relevant.

FIGURE 11.4   WORKING RELATIONSHIP WITH SUPPLIERS

$$\text{Annualized interest cost} = \left(\frac{\text{Discount percentage}}{100 - \text{Discount percentage}}\right) \times \left(\frac{365}{\text{Credit limit} - \text{discount period}}\right) =$$

$$\left(\frac{2\%}{(100\% - 2\%)}\right) \times \left(\frac{365}{30 - 10}\right) =$$

$$\left(\frac{2\%}{98\%}\right) \times \left(\frac{365}{20}\right) = 37.2\%$$

Most businesses eventually establish ongoing relationships with their major suppliers; once such relationships are established, a business should seek to develop and maintain the maximum potential cash capability from each supplier's credit consideration.

Two management practices contribute to good supplier relations: First, practice consistent payment patterns. Erratic payments upset even the most patient suppliers. So long as they know when to expect payment for purchases, even if persistently late, they can feel comfortable with the relationship.

Second, keep the lines of communication open. The more a supplier knows about a business, the more it can respond to the company's needs. After all, the business's purchases presumably are profitable sales for the supplier. The better the supplier responds to a business's needs, the more it can improve its own bottom line.

Opening lines of communication can help a business in two ways. First, by informing suppliers of projected requirements for credit considerations, management may obtain an increased line of credit. In this way, a business can lay the groundwork for approval by giving suppliers the information that will facilitate the credit decision process. Second, it can help a business slip unscathed through a cash flow problem.

Accruals

Accruals such as salaries and taxes payable are similar to trade credit in that they are spontaneous sources of financing. They differ from trade credit in that they are much less a decision variable; that is, a business is relatively constrained in what it can do to influence accruals as a source of financing. However, some techniques can be used to improve cash flow and profitability.

SALARIES AND WAGES PAYABLE Some managers may not realize that they, together with their fellow employees, are a source of financing to their firm. Indeed, all employees help finance their firm since they are not paid for their services on a day-by-day basis. Instead, they are paid at the end of the week, every two weeks, or perhaps at the end of the month.

For firms operating seasonal businesses, wages and salaries payable represent a spontaneous and flexible source of financing. During the busiest part of the year, when more employees are hired in the production process, the amount of financing available from wages and salaries payable increases. From a management perspective, there is not much flexibility with this source of financing. However, some leeway exists when a firm may choose to pay its employees (including management) less frequently—for example, monthly rather than semi-monthly. But, because there are laws that dictate how frequently employees must be paid, there is a limit to the amount of additional financing that can be obtained this way.

Also, a business may pay its employees by draft rather than by negotiable cheque, thus delaying payment even further. Employees receive their cheques just as quickly, but the funds will remain on the balance sheet for a longer period until the bank draft works its way back to the business's bank, and the cash account is decreased. This procedure creates additional zero-cost financing for the business.

TAXES PAYABLE Taxes payable are also a potential free source of financing. Taxes that are owed to various governments constitute another accrual that becomes part of short-term financing. Property taxes and income taxes (provincial and federal) do not become due at the moment they are incurred; rather, their payment is delayed until a later date.

Taxes payable are a free source of financing since governments often do not charge interest on outstanding balances. However, if management must accumulate funds in a special chequing account in anticipation of a future tax payment, there is an opportunity cost since those funds cannot be used for anything else.

Because the timing of tax payment is specified by government agencies, including Canada Customs and Revenue Agency, there is little that a business can do to manipulate this free source of short-term financing. An exception would occur if management deliberately decided to delay tax payments beyond the due date, even though a known penalty would result. There have been reported cases in other countries where firms have deliberately avoided paying taxes to their government, recognizing that the penalties for late tax payments were less than the interest rates charged by banks and other lenders on comparable amounts of financing.

However, penalties or interest charges made by certain governments (including Canada's) are not tax-deductible expenses. If this is the case, it may be more economically attractive to pay the taxes on the due date.

Capital Cost Allowance

If the capital cost allowance for the purchase of capital assets is higher than the internal depreciation rate, management should take advantage of it, since it represents an interest-free government loan. The acquisition of an asset affects the bottom line in two ways: depreciation and capital cost allowance. As explained in Chapter 2, depreciation is the internal rate used by a business and represents the estimated decrease in the book value of capital or long-lived assets, computed annually (usually with the straight-line method). For accounting purposes, depreciation is treated as an expense that appears on the income statement.

Capital cost allowance (CCA) is Canada Customs and Revenue Agency's equivalent of depreciation. Irrespective of the method of depreciation used to calculate the income of a business, Canada Customs and Revenue Agency establishes a set of percentages for different groups of assets that must be used to determine the amount of taxes to be paid by a business.

Given that the CCA rate is usually higher than the internal rate of depreciation, and that CCA is used to calculate the taxes a firm should pay, the higher tax (CCA) deduction will allow the company to defer paying its taxes. Here is how the arithmetic works. If a business buys a truck for $50,000 and Canada Customs and Revenue Agency allows a 40% CCA rate (declining basis), while the internal rate of depreciation is 10% (straight line), the company would pay $5,000 less in taxes in the first year. Since this amount has to be paid at a later date (say two or three years from now), management may wish to put the money in the bank at 10% and earn $500 (before taxes) in interest from the bank. The CCA amount for the first year is $10,000 [($50,000 × 40%)] ÷ 2 and the depreciation amount is $5,000 ($50,000 × 10%).

Working Capital Loans

Most companies will need some sort of **working capital loan**. In order not to waste its time and that of lenders, management should always be sure to match the sources of financing to the appropriate assets. (This topic was also covered at some length in Chapter 10.)

Working capital loans
Short-term loans made for the purpose of financing working capital accounts (e.g., inventory, accounts receivable).

As mentioned earlier, leverage is another term used for money borrowed from bankers. Since bank credit is a significant element in cash flow management, it is important to choose the type of loan that will maximize the firm's profitability and cash capability.

Basically, management should use short-term credit (that with a maturity of one year or less) to finance seasonal current assets and long-term credit to finance permanent assets—current and capital. It is important to match the maturities of sources and the maturities of uses of funds. Also, since there are so many different forms and sources of financing, managers must ensure that that they approach a lender that will meet their specific need, such as a short-term loan, term or installment loan, or revolving loan.

✳ Decision-Making in Action

When Bill Webber, controller of Pickford Electronics Inc., attended the annual financial planning meeting with his management group, he observed that the company's profitability could be improved if all working capital accounts moved faster. He continued his explanation by stating that if the turnover of Pickford's accounts receivable and inventory moved faster, and accounts payable slower, the company would improve its profitability, have more cash to work with, and be in a much better financial position.

Bill was not an operating manager and could not do anything to improve the company's cash performance. However, he made the point that all division and branch managers should be more cautious in the way that the cash flow of the company was managed. As he pointed out, extra cash could be reinvested into the company and help Pickford grow at a faster pace. Janice Simmons, the general manager, thought that the point should be discussed further to determine how this cash flow idea could be implemented.

After several meetings, Janice and Bill agreed that all managers should become sensitive to the importance of cash flow management and be given some training that would help them find solutions to improve the company's cash conversion cycle. During one of the management meetings, Janice pointed out that a portion of the future budgeting and financial planning meeting should be devoted to the function of cash management.

It was therefore decided that all managers at Pickford would be required to attend a two-day course on the topic of working capital management, given by an expert in the field. This course would be given to groups of 15 managers at a time over a two-month period.

After the training sessions, Janice convened all managers to a meeting and had Bill Webber explain the financial targets to be incorporated in Pickford's financial plan, namely the days of working capital and the cash conversion efficiency ratio. Bill pointed out that if all current asset and current liability accounts were improved, a responsibility shared by all managers, these two financial targets could be improved. He also indicated that once the operating budgets, the projected income statement, and the balance sheet were completed, he would present to the managers the improvements in the various working capital accounts, and particularly, the results related to the days of working capital and the cash conversion efficiency targets. He also added that if the cash flow objectives were not met, all operating budgets and plans would have to be redone until the targets were achieved.

A month later, Bill Webber presented a summary of the year-end 2003 and 2004 financial targets. Both he and Janice were pleased with the results as he pointed out that the cash flow from operations for the years 2003 and 2004 showed a $99,000 increase, that is 50%. The makeup of the cash flow is as follows:

Cash flow	2003	2004	Change
Income after taxes	$127,000	$179,000	$52,000
Depreciation/amortization	80,000	97,000	17,000
Change in net working capital	− 10,000	+ 20,000	30,000
Net operating cash flow	$197,000	$296,000	$99,000

As shown, the overall cash flow improvement was due to an increase in three operating activity accounts: income after taxes, depreciation/amortization, and a change in net working capital. The following paragraphs show how each cash flow item is calculated. As shown below, the income after tax improvement was due to two factors. First, sales revenue increased by 15%, and return on sales jumped from 8.5% to 10.4%.

Income statement	2003	2004	% change
Sales revenue	$1,500,000	$1,725,000	15.0%
Cost of goods sold			
Purchases	735,000	784,000	6.7
Manufacturing expenses	315,000	337,250	7.1
Subtotal	1,050,000	1,121,250	6.8
Gross margin	450,000	603,750	34.2
Other expenses and taxes	323,000	424,750	31.5
Income after tax	$ 127,000	$ 179,000	40.9%
Return on sales	8.5%	10.4%	

The return on sales improvement is due mainly to improvements in cost of goods sold. Here is the vertical analysis for the key expense items shown on the income statement for 2003 and 2004.

Vertical Analysis	2003	2004
Sales revenue	100.0%	100.0%
Cost of goods sold	70.0	65.0
Gross margin	30.0	35.0
Other expenses including taxes	21.5	24.6
Income after taxes	8.5%	10.4%

The net change in working capital accounts in 2003 shows a net increase over 2002 in working capital (and a decrease in cash flow) of $10,000 and a decrease in 2004 in working capital (and an increase in cash flow) of $20,000. The favourable cash flow performance in 2004 is due in large measure to the acceleration in the cash conversion cycle; that is, a faster payment in accounts receivable, an improved inventory turnover, and a slowdown in the payment of accounts payable.

Working Capital Accounts	2002	2003	2004
Accounts receivable	$150,000	$155,000	$150,000
Inventory	120,000	125,000	120,000
Subtotal	270,000	280,000	270,000
Accounts payable	110,000	110,000	120,000
Net working capital	$160,000	$170,000	$150,000
Net change in working capital		+$ 10,000	–$ 20,000

Note: An increase in net working capital means a negative affect on cash flow; a decrease signifies a positive effect.

As shown, Pickford invested an additional $10,000 in working capital in 2003 and plans to reduce it by $20,000 in 2004. Bill Webber indicated that the favourable cash flow performance would help the company significantly decrease its days of working capital from 41.4 days to 31.7 days and increase its cash conversion efficiency ratio from 13.1% to 17.2%.

By using a flip chart, Bill Webber explained how these working capital accounts would be improved and the impact on the company's cash flow position.

He indicated that the net working capital between 2003 and 2004 is expected to drop by $20,000 (from $170,000 to $150,000) despite the fact that the average daily sales will show an increase of $616 or 15%. This change will improve the days of working capital by 10 days (from 41.4 days to 31.7 days). Bill Webber further explained this improvement with the following calculations:

Days of working capital

2003

$$\frac{\text{Net working capital}}{\text{Average daily sales}} = \frac{\$170,000}{\$4,110} = 41.4 \text{ days}$$

Average daily sales = $4,110 ($1,500,000 ÷ 365)

2004

$$\frac{\text{Net working capital}}{\text{Average daily sales}} = \frac{\$150,000}{\$4,726} = 31.7 \text{ days}$$

Average daily sales = $4,726 ($1,725,000 ÷ 365)

As Bill pointed out, net working capital dropped from $170,000 to $150,000 due to improvements in the average collection period in accounts receivable and inventory turnover, and the extension of the average daily payables. He gave the following explanation for each.

AVERAGE COLLECTION PERIOD The average collection period improved from 37.7 days to 31.7 days because of a change in the policies of the collection procedures. Here is the calculation:

2003

$$\frac{\text{Accounts receivable}}{\text{Average daily sales}} = \frac{\$155,000}{\$4,110} = 37.7 \text{ days}$$

2004

$$\frac{\text{Accounts receivable}}{\text{Average daily sales}} = \frac{\$150,000}{\$4,726} = 31.7 \text{ days}$$

INVENTORY TURNOVER The inventory turnover improved from 8.4 times to 9.3 times despite the 6.8% increase in cost of goods sold. This inventory turnover's favourable performance is caused by a reduction in inventory level in the amount of $5,000 or 9.6%. This is due to a better method in the way the raw materials are purchased and the acceleration in the manufacturing process. This is calculated as follows:

2003

$$\frac{\text{Cost of goods sold}}{\text{Inventory}} = \frac{\$1,050,000}{\$125,000} = 8.4 \text{ times}$$

2004

$$\frac{\text{Cost of goods sold}}{\text{Inventory}} = \frac{\$1,121,250}{\$120,000} = 9.3 \text{ times}$$

AVERAGE PAYABLE PERIOD The average payable period increased slightly from 55 days to 56 days. Bill explained that this small improvement was due to the fact that the purchasing department was able to negotiate better prices and credit conditions with several of Pickford's key suppliers. Here is the calculation:

2003

$$\frac{\text{Accounts payable}}{\text{Average daily purchases}} = \frac{\$110,000}{\$2,014} = 55 \text{ days}$$

Average daily purchases = $2,014 ($735,000 ÷ 365)

2004

$$\frac{\text{Accounts payable}}{\text{Average daily purchases}} = \frac{\$120,000}{\$2,148} = 56 \text{ days}$$

Average daily sales = $2,148 ($784,000 ÷ 365)

The cash conversion efficiency ratio also improved as a result of the 50.2% increase in operating cash flow (from $197,000 to $296,000) compared to the 15% increase in sales revenue.

Cash conversion efficiency ratio

2003

$$\frac{\text{Operating cash flow}}{\text{Sales revenue}} = \frac{\$197,000}{\$1,500,000} = 13.1\%$$

2004

$$\frac{\text{Operating cash flow}}{\text{Sales revenue}} = \frac{\$296,000}{\$1,725,000} = 17.2\%$$

Bill Webber concluded his presentation by saying that if a major effort had not been made in improving the working capital accounts, the company would have probably have had to invest an additional 15% or $25,000 instead of having a $20,000 reduction in these accounts. As a result, Pickford will be able to use this incremental $45,000 cash flow amount for investment purposes, for its expansion program, and for buying capital assets.

Chapter Summary

Working capital comprises all accounts appearing under the headings "Current Assets" and "Current Liabilities" in the balance sheet. These accounts include accounts receivable and inventory (current assets) and accounts payable and short-term loans (current liabilities). Net working capital is the difference between the total of current assets and the total of current liabilities. If a company's balance sheet shows $200,000 in current assets and $100,000 in current liabilities, it means that its net working capital is $100,000. *Working capital management* involves the management of all current asset and current liability accounts. Since these types of accounts vary on a day-to-day basis, managing this current portion of business activities is time-consuming. The objective of working capital management is to manage individual current accounts, ensure a proper balance between all asset accounts and all liability accounts, and balance relationships with other balance sheet items such as capital assets and long-term debt.

◀◀ Objective 1

Managing current assets includes cash, marketable securities, accounts receivable, and inventory. The essence of managing cash is to ensure an adequate reservoir of cash to enable a business to conduct its ordinary operating activities, handle emergencies, and take advantage of specific opportunities. The preparation of a cash budget helps management find what level of cash is needed and when. There are two ways a firm can speed up cash receipts: by changing the paying habits of customers and by reducing the negative float.

◀◀ Objective 2

Managing marketable securities consists of investing surplus cash in profit-making investments, such as Treasury bills, bank deposits, or bonds. The six different approaches used for managing marketable securities are (a) do nothing, (b) ad hoc, (c) riding the yield, (d) guidelines, (e) control limits, and (g) portfolio. It is a matter of selecting the one that best responds to the needs of a business.

◀◀ Objective 3

Managing accounts receivable involves six activities: setting credit terms, granting credit to customers, billing, monitoring payments made by customers, applying the necessary measures to maintain or reduce the average collection period, and obtaining proper credit insurance. Some of the techniques used for managing accounts receivable include (a) the trade discount net 30-day analysis, (b) the credit-scoring system, (c) credit report analysis, (d) monitoring the aging of accounts receivable, and (e) credit insurance analysis.

◀◀ Objective 4

Managing inventory consists of replenishing stocking points in such a way that associated order and holding costs are kept at a minimum. Keeping inventory low helps to improve profitability. Three methods used to manage inventory are material requirements planning (MRP), just-in-time (JIT), and the economic order quantity (EOQ).

◀◀ Objective 5

Management of current liabilities consists of using current debt, such as accounts payable, accruals, and working capital loans, as effective sources of financing.

◀◀ Objective 6

Key Terms

Aging of accounts receivable
Cash
Cash conversion cycle
Cash conversion efficiency
Credit insurance policy
Credit policies
Credit terms
Credit-scoring system
Days of working capital
Economic ordering quantity (EOQ)
Float
Goal of working capital management
Holding costs

Indemnification policy
Inventory replenishment
Investment securities
Just-in-time inventory management
Material requirements planning (MRP)
Net working capital
Ordering costs
Post office box
Regional bank
Types of inventory
Wire transfer process
Working capital loans
Working capital management

Review Questions

1. What do we mean by net working capital?

2. What is the goal of working capital management?

3. What does the days of working capital measure? Why is it important?

4. What does the cash conversion efficiency ratio measure? Why is it important?

5. What do we mean by the cash conversion cycle? Show how it works.

6. With an example, differentiate between cash flow and profit.

7. How can accelerating the flow of cash improve ROI?

8. What are the different approaches that can be used to improve the cash collection period?

9. Differentiate between the process related to the lockbox system and the traditional payment system.

10. Explain the various strategies related to managing marketable securities.

11. Comment on the different functions of the credit manager.

12. Differentiate between "average collection period" and "aging of accounts receivable."

13. What types of insurance can a firm use to protect its accounts receivable?

14. Explain the various types of inventories that a company has to carry at all times.

15. What do we mean by "material requirements planning" within the management of inventory?

16. Explain how the economic ordering quantity method works.

17. Identify several ordering costs and several holding costs.

18. How can accounts payable be a source of financing?

19. How can accruals be a source of financing?

20. What are working capital loans?

Discussion Questions

1. Why is it more difficult to manage working capital accounts than capital asset accounts?

2. Who is responsible for managing the working capital accounts? Discuss.

Testing Your Comprehension

True/False Questions

___F___ 1. Net working capital is the difference between the cash account and current liability accounts.

___T___ 2. The goal of managing working capital is to accelerate the amount of cash circulating in the business after sales have been made.

___F___ 3. The concept related to the management of capital asset accounts is referred to as the cash conversion cycle.

___T___ 4. Cash management is usually assigned to a high-level manager such as the chief financial officer or the treasurer.

___F___ 5. There is no difference between profit and cash flow.

___F___ 6. Cash planning is done through the preparation of an operating budget.

___F___ 7. One way to reduce the negative float is by using the just-in-time inventory management process.

___T___ 8. The lockbox system is an effective system used for accelerating collections in order to reduce the negative float.

___T___ 9. Marketable securities are similar to cash.

___T___ 10. Giving trade discounts to customers can help a company's cash flow at the expense of profitability.

___F___ 11. The average collection period is a technique used to analyze the aging of the accounts receivable.

___T___ 12. Insurance protection on accounts receivable can be secured by a confident credit policy.

___T___ 13. Turning inventory more rapidly improves ROI.

___F___ 14. The economic ordering quantity technique is referred to as *kanban* and is a system that was conceptualized by Japanese firms.

___F___ 15. The cost of purchasing merchandise is considered a holding cost.

___F___ 16. Managing accounts payable requires a good relationship between the company and its customers.

___T___ 17. The equivalent of a 2% discount, net 30-day payment translates into a 36% annual borrowing cost.

___T___ 18. Accruals such as salaries and taxes payable are similar to trade credit in that they are spontaneous sources of financing.

___F___ 19. CCA allowance is usually lower than the internal depreciation rate.

___T___ 20. Leverage is another term for money borrowed from bankers.

Multiple-Choice Questions

1. Net working capital is the difference between current assets and:
   a. current cash
   b. the cash conversion cycle
   c. long-term liabilities
   d. liquidity
   e. current liabilities

2. Working capital management refers to all aspects dealing with the management of:
   a. current asset accounts
   b. current liability accounts
   c. current asset and current liability accounts
   d. capital asset accounts
   e. all current accounts with the exception of cash

3. Cash reserves include:
   a. accounts receivable
   b. accruals
   c. inventory
   d. marketable securities
   e. prepaid expenses

4. The time lag between the day a cheque is mailed to the firm and the time the funds are available to the firm is referred to as:
   a. dunning
   b. float
   c. cash conversion cycle
   d. the yield approach
   e. *kanban*

5. The amount received on a $400 invoice by a company that offers a 2% net 30-day credit policy would be:
   a. $ 392
   b. $ 360
   c. $ 398
   d. $ 378
   e. $ 382

6. A strategy used for collecting accounts receivable is:
   a. *kanban*
   b. just-in-time
   c. lockbox
   d. dunning
   e. economic billing system

7. The economic ordering quantity is usually used for managing:
   a. raw materials inventory
   b. work-in-process inventory
   c. finished inventory
   d. average inventory
   e. just-in-time inventory

8. A cost associated with ordering is:
   a. warehousing
   b. insurance
   c. receiving
   d. interest charges
   e. spoilage

9. The following is an accrual expense:
   a. salaries
   b. salaries payable
   c. capital cost allowance
   d. depreciation expense
   e. rental charges

Fill-in-the-Blanks Questions

1. Accounts appearing on the current asset and current liability portion of the balance sheet are referred to as operating capital or _____ _____ accounts.

2. _____ is the difference between current assets and current liabilities.

3. The goal of working capital management is to accelerate the _____ cycle in a business after sales have been made.

4. The objective of the days of working capital measurement tool is to calculate the number of days of working capital a business holds in order to meet its average _____ sales requirements.

5. The _____ ratio measures how fast a business converts sales revenue to cash flow within its operations.

6. _____ consists of holdings and short-term deposits.

7. The amount of funds tied up in cheques that have been written but are still in process and have not yet been collected is called _____ _____.

8. _____ banks are locations where customers pay their accounts, which are subsequently transferred to the seller's bank account.

9. _____ securities are funds invested in short-term deposits such as treasury bills, bank deposits, etc.

10. The mission of the credit manager is to set _____ terms, grant credit to customers, bill the customers, and monitor payments made by customers.

11. The _____ calculation measures the number of days it takes for customers to pay their accounts.

12. The _____ of accounts receivable is a report that shows how long accounts receivable have been outstanding and gives, for example, the percentage of receivables past due for one month, two months, or other periods.

13. The _____ policy is insurance a business takes against the catastrophic loss in cash that might occur when a large receivable becomes uncollectible because of debtor bankruptcy.

14. There are basically three types of inventories: raw materials, _____, and finished goods.

15. The _____ is a method used for developing a schedule to help coordinate and utilize resources in production.

16. _____ inventory management is a technique that obtains supplier materials just when they are needed.

17. The _____ is a method that determines the optimum quantity of goods that should be ordered at any single time.

18. _____ costs is a category of costs associated with the storing of goods in inventory (e.g., insurance, rent).

19. _____ costs is a category of cost associated with the acquisition of goods.

20. To calculate the average payable period and to find how it contributes to positive cash flow, accounts payable is divided by the average daily _____.

Learning Exercises

Exercise 1(a)

By using the information contained in CompuTech's 2004 financial statements:

(a) Make a list of the working capital accounts

(b) Calculate CompuTech's net working capital

Net capital assets	$132,000
– Accounts payable	20,000
Purchases	205,000
Salaries (selling)	55,000
– Accounts receivable	45,000
– Term loan	40,000
Capital shares	100,000
– Marketable securities	5,000
Depreciation	40,000
– Cash	16,000
Travelling	3,000
– Inventory	65,000
– Prepaid expenses	5,000

Exercise 1(b)

With the following information:

(a) Make a list of the working capital accounts

(b) Calculate the net working capital

Buildings	$100,000
Cash	5,000
Accounts receivable	25,000
Accounts payable	40,000
Inventory	50,000
Cost of goods sold	150,000
Land	500,000
Accrued wages	10,000
Prepaid expenses	12,000
Goodwill	50,000

Exercise 2(a)

With the following information, calculate CompuTech's days of working capital for the years 2003 and 2004.

	2003	2004
Income after taxes	$ 25,000	$ 33,000
Depreciation	38,000	40,000
Accounts receivable	35,000	45,000
Cash	10,000	16,000
Marketable securities	5,000	5,000
Prepaid expenses	5,000	5,000
Term loan	35,000	40,000
Inventory	50,000	65,000
Accounts payable	17,000	20,000
Sales revenue	$350,000	$420,000

Exercise 2(b)

With the following information, calculate the company's days of working capital for the years 2003 and 2004.

	2003	2004
Income after taxes	$ 176,000	$ 225,000
Depreciation	55,000	70,000
Accounts receivable	360,000	385,000
Inventory	450,000	490,000
Accounts payable	400,000	440,000
Sales revenue	$2,200,000	$2,500,000

Exercise 3(a)

With the information contained in Exercise 2(a), calculate CompuTech's cash conversion efficiency ratio for the years 2003 and 2004. To do these calculations, assume that in 2002 CompuTech's net working capital was $40,000.

Exercise 3(b)

With the information contained in Exercise 2(b), calculate the company's cash conversion efficiency ratio for the years 2003 and 2004. To do these calculations, assume that in 2002 the company's net working capital was $350,000.

Exercise 4(a)

CompuTech can make 12% by investing its money in a long-term investment. If the Millers receive an amount of $10,000 20 days sooner, how much would the company make?

Exercise 4(b)

A business can make 15% by investing its money in bonds. If the treasurer receives an amount of $20,000 30 days sooner, how much would the company make?

Exercise 5(a)

CompuTech sells on terms of net 30 days and is considering a change to net 45 days. The Millers want to invest the extra funds in their new retail store, hoping that this will generate a return on assets greater than 25%. The expected effect of the change in credit is summarized below.

	Net 30 Today	Proposed	Net 45 Change
		(in $000's)	
Sales	$420	$450	$30
Net operating income	33	43	10
Accounts receivable	45	65	20
Total assets	268	330	62

Should the Millers make the change?

Exercise 5(b)

A company sells on terms of net 30 days and is considering a change to net 60 days. The firm wants to invest in projects that generate a return on assets greater than 20%. The expected effect of the change in credit is summarized below.

	Net 30 Today	Proposed	Net 60 Change
		(in $000's)	
Sales	$1,000	$1,200	$200
Net operating income	100	120	20
Accounts receivable	82	197	115
Total assets	500	630	130

Would you make the change?

Exercise 6(a)

CompuTech sells goods with an average retail sales price of $250.00 to industrial accounts. These accounts usually pay 65 days after the date of purchase. If CompuTech's cost of borrowing is 11%, should the Millers offer 1/10, N/30 to these accounts? Cost of sales for each unit is $110.00.

Should the Millers change their credit collection policy?

Exercise 6(b)

A firm sells goods with an average retail sales price of $550.00. Customers usually pay 60 days after the date of purchase. If the cost of borrowing is 12%, would it be preferable for the company to offer 1/10, N/30? Cost of producing the goods per unit is $125.00.

Should the company change its credit collection policy? Why or why not?

Exercise 7(a)

CompuTech is planning to change its credit policy. The product is characterized as follows:

Current selling price	$10.00 per unit
Average cost	$7.50 per unit
Current annual sales	4,000 units
Current terms of sale	net 30 days

The company wishes to extend its credit period to terms of net 60 days. Allowing for the reaction of competitors, it is anticipated that such a move would produce the following results:

1. Sales are expected to increase to 5,000 units.

2. Bad-debt losses are expected to increase by $2,000 per year.

The marginal cost per unit for the increased number of units to be produced would be $6.50. The company's after-tax rate is 35%, and its required minimum rate of return on such investments is 16% after tax.

Would you recommend that the Millers change the company's credit policy?

Exercise 7(b)

A company is planning to change its credit policy. On the basis of the following information, would you recommend that the company proceed?

The product is characterized as follows:

Current selling price	$5.00 per unit
Average cost	$4.50 per unit
Current annual sales	360,000 units
Current terms of sale	net 30 days

The company wishes to extend its credit period to terms of net 60 days. Allowing for the reaction of competitors, it is anticipated that such a move would produce the following results:

1. Sales are expected to increase to 420,000 units.

2. Bad-debt losses are expected to increase by $6,000 per year.

The marginal cost per unit for the increased number of units to be produced would be $3.00. The company's after-tax rate is 40%, and its required minimum rate of return on such investments is 15% after tax.

Would you recommend that the company change its credit policy?

Chapter 11: Working Capital Management

Exercise 8(a)

The Millers are thinking of marketing one of their products more aggressively. Current sales are 2,000 units per year and are expected to increase by 25%. Current carrying costs are estimated at $0.23 per unit, and order costs are estimated at $1.50. The Millers want to minimize their inventory costs.

Calculate CompuTech's current economic ordering quantity.

Exercise 8(b)

A company decides to market its products more aggressively. Current sales are 60,000 units per year and are expected to increase by 20%. Current carrying costs are estimated at $0.50 per unit, and order costs are estimated at $10.00. The firm wants to minimize its inventory costs.

Calculate the company's current economic ordering quantity.

Exercise 9(a)

The Millers have decided to increase their advertising to push one of their product lines. Current sales are 2,500 units per year, and they are expected to increase by 60% next year. Current carrying costs are estimated at $0.10 per unit, and the order costs are estimated at $3.50.

The Millers want to minimize their inventory costs.

1. What is the economic ordering quantity?

2. What is the optimal number of orders per month once the new sales level is reached?

Exercise 9(b)

A company has decided to market its products more aggressively. Current sales are 30,000 units per year, and they are expected to increase by 50% next year. Carrying costs are estimated at $0.20 per unit, and the order costs are estimated at $7.00.

The firm wants to minimize its inventory costs.

1. What is the economic ordering quantity?

2. What is the optimal number of orders per month once the new sales level is reached?

Exercise 10(a)

CompuTech buys $205,000 worth of goods each year.

The Millers think that it would be possible to delay paying their bills up to 50 days without jeopardizing their relationship with suppliers. At the moment, the company's accounts payable are $20,000.

If the company defers paying its bills to 50 days, how much financing would the company be able to obtain from that source?

Exercise 10(b)

A company buys $2 million worth of goods each year. The treasurer of the company thinks that it would be possible to delay paying its bills up to 45 days without jeopardizing its relationship with suppliers. At the moment, the company's accounts payable are $165,000.

If the company defers paying its bills to 45 days, how much financing would the company be able to obtain from that source?

Exercise 11

A company's accounts payable amount to $500,000, and annual purchasing costs for materials from suppliers are $10,000,000. A new purchasing policy states that they should be paid in 30 days.

How much cash would the company generate if it follows the 30-day policy? What if the firm negotiates a 40-day, or even a 60-day, payment term?

Case

Kent Imports Ltd.

Albert Cunningham began his career as a manufacturers' representative in the medical equipment business. His lines included products imported from several European manufacturers. Albert's business gradually evolved into Kent Imports Ltd., a wholesaling business that purchased medical equipment from European manufacturers and sold to retailers through a sales organization. By purchasing shipments of medical equipment in large quantities from European manufacturers, Kent Imports was able to negotiate favourable prices and reduce shipping costs substantially. Furthermore, the company was able to assure delivery to customers because orders could be filled from a Toronto warehouse rather than from a European location. In 2000, Albert retired and turned over his business to his son David. At that time, sales had reached $13 million a year and profits were in excess of $400,000.

By late 2002, David could see that sales for the year were going to be below $12 million and that income after taxes would be in the $200,000 range. He decided to hire a marketing manager who would boost sales more quickly.

David contacted an executive placement firm, which recommended Ross Belman. Belman had a record of frequent job changes but had produced very rapid sales increases in each position that he had occupied. He stayed with Kent Imports Ltd. for only 15 months (leaving in November 2003). In that short period of time, Belman was able to increase sales from $12 million to over $18 million. Furthermore, profit soared by 273% during that year. Even when Belman announced his resignation to take another position with a larger company, David felt the decision to hire him had been a good one.

David contacted the executive placement firm once again. This time the firm recommended Helen Tang, a young woman who was currently a district sales manager for another import manufacturer. Helen was very interested in the job because it would give her greater marketing responsibilities. Helen asked David what policy changes Ross Belman had implemented to increase sales so dramatically. David explained Belman's belief that merchandise availability was the key to medical equipment import sales. Belman had insisted on increases in the amount of inventory carried by Kent Imports and had encouraged medical equipment retailers to carry more by extending more generous credit terms. Specifically, he established an unofficial policy of not pressing for collection as long as the merchandise was still in a store's inventory. The sales representatives—who were paid a commission at the time of sale—were given the responsibility of reporting what inventory the stores actually held. In addition, Belman implemented a change in credit standards so that the company could approve more new stores for credit. He felt that the old policy was biased against these new retail stores because they did not have a track record. Willingness to sell to this group had accounted for nearly half of the total sales increase.

Helen asked if this policy had weakened the company's accounts receivable, particularly the cash flow position. David responded by saying that he had been monitoring the average collection period very closely and there had been only a very slight change. Helen told David that although she was very interested in the position, she could not make a decision until she had looked at the company's financial statements. David was hesitant to show this information to an outsider, but he finally agreed to let her look at the income statements and balance sheets in the office. Helen did her own analysis of the company's financial statements in addition to determining to what extent the working capital policies actually helped improve Kent Imports' overall financial performance.

1. Do you agree with David Cunningham that the quality of the working capital accounts (accounts receivable and inventory) showed only a slight change?

2. Comment on the company's overall financial performance for the years 2002 and 2003 particularly as it relates to the (1) liquidity ratios, (2) debt/leverage ratios, (3) asset-management ratios, and (4) profitability ratios.

3. Have the company's days of working capital and cash conversion efficiency ratio improved during the time Ross Belman was the marketing manager?

4. Did David do the right thing hiring Ross Belman?

(In $000s)	2002		2003	
Sales revenue		$11,800		$18,600
Cost of goods sold		8,500		13,200
Gross margin		3,300		5,400
Operating expenses				
Selling expenses	$1,100		1,620	
Administration expenses	1,500		2,100	
Depreciation	200		300	
Total operating expenses		2,800		4,020
Operating income		500		1,380
Interest charges		200		320
Income before taxes		300		1,060
Income taxes		110		350
Income after taxes		$ 190		$ 710

KENT IMPORTS LTD.
BALANCE SHEETS
AS AT DECEMBER 31

(In $000s)	2002	2003
Current assets		
Cash	$ 160	$ 240
Prepaid expenses	100	70
Accounts receivable	1,600	2,100
Inventory	2,100	3,600
Total current assets	$3,960	$6,010
Capital assets (gross)	2,900	3,700
Accumulated depreciation	800	1,100
Capital assets (net)	2,100	2,600
Total assets	$6,060	$8,610
Current liabilities		
Accounts payable	$ 850	$1,400
Bank loan	310	1,100
Total current liabilities	1,160	2,500
Long-term debts	1,300	1,800
Total debts	2,460	4,300
Shareholders' equity		
Common shares	1,500	1,500
Retained earnings	2,100	2,810
Total shareholders' equity	3,600	4,310
Total liabilities and equity	$6,060	$8,610

Note: In 2001, the company's net working capital was $2,700,000.

12

Business Valuation

Learning Objectives

After reading this chapter, you should be able to:

1. Differentiate between market value and book value.

2. Discuss the various valuation models.

3. Comment on the meaning of scanning the environment.

4. Explain how to go about documenting planning assumptions.

5. Show how to restate the income statement and the balance sheet.

6. Present the various ways of price-tagging an ongoing business.

7. Calculate the market value of publicly traded companies.

Chapter Outline

OPENING CASE

After three years of operation, CompuTech Inc. was doing extremely well in terms of meeting its financial goals. The Millers were now moving their business into another phase of its development, that of opening several retail stores. Their retail concept had caught on with the general public, and the earnings generated by CompuTech were better than competing firms'.

The Millers had two options in terms of growth. First, to grow slowly by opening a retail outlet (perhaps every two years) by using internally generated funds over the next ten years. The second option was to approach a risk capital investor who would be interested in investing in the business. This option would help them grow more rapidly. It is a strategy that would enable the Millers to open five retail outlets in 2006 and more in 2007. However, this strategy would require equity participation in CompuTech Inc. by a venture capitalist. In that case, the Millers would have to share business ownership.

They discussed this option with their advisors Bill Murray and May Ogaki and both agreed that this course of action was a viable one. Bill made the following points:

> Private investors are very demanding and require a substantial return on their investment. The investment proposal will have to be complete and clearly demonstrate several key points. First, these investors want to see evidence that the investment opportunity generates a return commensurate with the risk— usually 25% to 40% compounded and adjusted for inflation. Second, they seek a good management team. Since most risk capital investors claim that management is the single most important aspect of a business opportunity, they regard reputation and quality of the team as key. Third, they will be looking for a viable exit strategy and options to realize their investment. Since these types of investors usually want to cash in their shares somewhere between three and seven years after making their investment, they want to be assured that you will have thought about how to comply with their wishes. This may require going public or selling their shares to another buyer. They might even want you to buy back the shares. Fourth, these investors will want to monitor and control their investment by having a voice on your board of directors, suggesting who should sit on your board and its composition, receiving monthly financial statements, having a say in hiring key managers, etc.

May Ogaki added the following points regarding the strategy for approaching private investors:

> You have to understand that these types of private investors often reject investment opportunities because entrepreneurs do not understand the needs, requirements, and specialization of a particular investor. If you approach the

wrong investor, you run the risk of being rejected. The best approach to con-
tacting private investors is to ensure that they will be able to provide the
amount of capital that you require. Also, be certain that they are familiar with
the industry that you are in and, most important, that they are located in your
region. This is particularly important if they want to take an active part in your
business. Another key criterion when selecting a private investor is to pick
one who is a leader in the investment community and able to give you sound
advice about your business. This type of deal should provide benefits to both
sides: you offer a good investment opportunity in terms of a return and the
investor offers the capital you need to realize your dream.

The Millers realized that the investment proposal would have to be very con-
vincing if they were to attract venture capital funds. The proposal would have to be
very clear in providing information about the financing needs, financial requirements,
investment potential, and management capabilities.

This chapter looks at three key topics:

- What type of information should be incorporated in an investment proposal?

- How can financial statements be restated to help gauge the real market value of
  a business?

- How can investors go about determining the real value of a business opportunity?

Introduction

Throughout this book, we have talked about book value: what a business owns
and owes, or the value of a business's assets and liabilities. There was no mention
of the market value of a business—how much it would be worth if it were sold as
an "ongoing business."

As an example, the book value of a house bought in Toronto during the early
1970s for $40,000 would be less than what the owner could sell it for today. When
the house was purchased, the value of the land could have been, say, $5,000 and
the house itself, say, $35,000. Today, because the house has lost some value
because of wear and tear (depreciation), it could now be worth only $15,000 "on
the books." However, because the house appreciated in value over the years, the
market value of that house and land, or their real worth, could be around
$400,000. This example illustrates the point that there is a difference between the
value of assets shown in the books and the real value of these assets if they were
put up for sale on the market.

If we examine Eastman Technologies Inc.'s 2003 balance sheet, shown in
Table 2.5 of Chapter 2, we see that the company's total assets amount to
$1,800,000 and total liabilities to $1,245,000 ($445,000 in current liabilities and
$800,000 in long-term debts). In this case, Eastman's "book value," being the dif-
ference between the asset and liability components of the balance sheet, is
$555,000. If the owners were to sell Eastman at book price, they would sell the

assets for what they are worth on the books ($1,800,000), transfer to the new owners the liabilities ($1,245,000), and ask for a $555,000 cheque. Certainly, if Eastman's owners were to sell the business, they would not sell it for book value but for what it is worth on the market. They would therefore assess the true market value of the business, as a going concern, and sell it for a price that (like that of the house) would probably be different from what is shown on the books.

As shown in Figure 12.1, this chapter explores various topics dealing with the process of buying an ongoing business, more specifically, market valuation. We will begin by looking at the meaning of price-level accounting and current-value accounting, that is, the difference between book value and market value. We will then turn to valuation methods that organizations and investors use to determine the value of businesses. The rest of the chapter looks at how to put a price tag on privately owned ongoing businesses. In particular, the process includes scanning the environment, documenting the planning assumptions, restating financial statements, and three methods used to price-tag ongoing businesses: asset valuation, net present value, and industry multipliers. The chapter ends with a brief examination of price-tagging publicly owned businesses.

Objective 1 ▶

Market Value versus Book Value

Book value

The accounting value of an asset (the original cost minus total depreciation deductions made to date). This is shown on the financial statements as a firm's assets.

Market value

The price at which an item, business, or asset can be sold.

To businesspersons, it may not make much sense to report information on financial statements that does not really reflect the "true" or "real" market value of assets. For example, Table 12.1 presents a balance sheet showing the house that was purchased in 1970. The table indicates that after some 30 years, the $40,000 house, after allowing for depreciation, would have a $15,000 value on the books. As shown in the table, however, the "real value" of the house is $400,000. If the owner wants to borrow, say, $200,000, his or her balance sheet would look absurd (upper portion of Table 12.1) because the liability side of the balance sheet would be $185,000 more than the **book value** of the house. However, as shown on the lower portion of the table, if the **market value** of the house were shown on the balance sheet, the owner's financial structure would be more appropriate. Now,

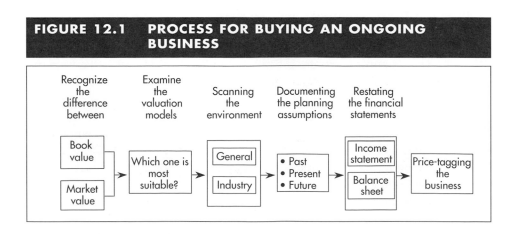

FIGURE 12.1   PROCESS FOR BUYING AN ONGOING BUSINESS

Recognize the difference between / Examine the valuation models / Scanning the environment / Documenting the planning assumptions / Restating the financial statements

Book value / Market value → Which one is most suitable? → General / Industry → • Past • Present • Future → Income statement / Balance sheet → Price-tagging the business

the owner could have done different things with the $200,000 mortgage money. It could have been:

- deposited in the bank account;
- used to make major alterations to the house;
- used to buy other assets such as a cottage, a car, or a trailer;
- used to make a one-year first-class trip around the world.

If the homeowner picked the fourth option, that mortgage money would have simply been spent and not shown on the asset side of the balance sheet. If that had been the case, the balance sheet would have shown $15,000 on the asset side and $200,000 on the liability side, similar to the amounts shown in Table 12.1.

Because of the difference between book values and market values, some individuals would challenge the validity of the traditional accounting practices and ask the following question: do financial statements prepared according to traditional accounting principles fairly present the financial position of a company in a period of inflation? Many would say no! For this reason, over the past decades, accountants have attempted to deal with this issue in order to present information on financial statements in a more sensible way. They have come up with two suggestions: price-level accounting and current-value accounting.

Price-level accounting means that the numbers on financial statements are restated in terms of current purchasing power. Thus, if an asset such as a building were purchased five years ago for $1,000,000 at a time when yearly inflation was 4%, the value of the building would therefore be reported as $1,217,000.

Current-value accounting is based on what it would currently cost a business to acquire an asset with the same capability or capacity as the one it currently owns. In the above example, if the asset were to be purchased today at a cost of say, $1,200,000, that would be the value reported on the balance sheet.

Take the example of Eastman Technologies Inc.'s 2003 balance sheet, shown in Table 2.5. The balance sheet shows the owners' equity to be $555,000. This is known as the book value and is based on the original or historical purchase price of all assets, adjusted for depreciation (total $1,800,000), less the amount of money owed to lenders, which amounts to $1,245,000.

Price-level accounting

Accounting method used to restate assets on financial statements in terms of current purchasing power (inflation).

Current-value accounting

Accounting method used to restate assets on financial statements in terms of what they would be worth if purchased today.

TABLE 12.1 BOOK VALUE VERSUS MARKET VALUE

Balance Sheet (based on book value)

House:			
Original cost	$40,000		
Depreciation	25,000		
Net book value	$15,000	New mortgage	$200,000

Balance Sheet (based on market value)

House:			
Market value	$400,000	New mortgage	$200,000

As previously stated, if Eastman's owners were to sell their business for book value, they would sell the assets for what they are worth in the books, transfer the liabilities to the new owners, and ask for a $555,000 cheque. However, the company could be worth more than $555,000 for two reasons. First, Eastman's assets listed on the balance sheet are historically based. This means that if the company purchased, in 2000, a piece of machinery for $100,000, the transaction provides an objective measure of the asset's value, which is what is shown on the company's balance sheet. However, this 2000 value may not have much relevance today. In fact, the asset could be worth more (particularly if it was land).

Second, the assets of the company could generate excellent earnings. These earnings are not reflected in the balance sheet. However, if the earnings produce a 20% or 25% annual return, anyone wanting to sell such a business would certainly take the level of earnings of these assets into consideration.

Some may argue that accountants should disregard the purchase price of capital assets and use a more meaningful current value in financial statements. The problem with this is that for many assets, objectively determinable current values do not exist. Therefore, accountants have opted for objective historical cost values over subjective estimates of current value.

Also, the government of Canada would also have serious reservations about having company officials re-appraising capital assets higher than historical values. The reason is simple: the original $100,000 used to calculate the capital cost allowance would be increased and consequently reduce the amount of income taxes that the company would pay to the government. Furthermore, what government organization would be responsible for policing the activity of determining whether assets shown on balance sheets reflect the true market value? Also, balance sheets would have to be adjusted each year to reflect inflation or the changing prices of the capital assets. How would these changes be reflected on the right side of the balance sheet?

To solve the valuation problem, some 20 years ago the Canadian Institute of Chartered Accountants recommended that all Canadian enterprises whose securities are traded in the public market disclose in their annual reports, whenever appropriate, supplementary information about the effects of changing prices. In other words, if the value of a building is shown in the books at $600,000 (after depreciation) and the market value is $1,200,000, the annual report would comment on this difference through an appropriate footnote.

Objective 2 ➡

Valuation Models

Different models can be used to value businesses. So far, we have talked about the book value and the market value. In Chapter 8, we examined the present value and the discounted cash flow methods to determine the value of an investment in capital assets (i.e., NPV and IRR). The time-value-of-money approach can also be used for business valuation purposes. Depending on the reason for valuing a business, organizations use different approaches.

In his book *Techniques of Financial Analysis*,[1] Erich Helfert identifies several valuation models. There is the **economic value**, which has to do with the ability or capacity of an asset to produce a stream of after-tax cash flows. For example, a person who invests $100,000 in Canada Savings Bonds does so in order to earn future cash receipts in the form of interest payments. However, the person may invest $100,000 in a capital asset for additional savings through productivity or for increased sales revenues. The investor would therefore compare the worth of the future receipts (cash inflows) to the original investment (cash outflows). The economic-value approach is a future-oriented concept based on the principles of tradeoff and risk. For example, how much would one expect to earn from Canada Savings Bonds—4% or 5%—or in a revenue-generating business asset—15%, 20%, or 25%? The investor would also examine the risk factor related to that particular investment. For example, the investor might be prepared to accept a 7% economic return on the relatively risk-free Canada Savings Bonds investment or 25% in a revenue-generating business venture that is riskier. Risk is the price tag on the sought-after economic return. The economic-value concept therefore looks at future cash flow expectations and the relative risk associated with the investment.

Economic value
Valuation method used to determine the ability or capacity of an asset to generate cash.

The second approach is based on market value, the worth of an asset traded on the market between a buyer and a seller without duress. The stock market is a classic example of market value. At a particular point in time, some buyers would be prepared to buy (and others to sell) a share for what each party believes it is worth. By using this approach, the buyer and the seller are able to arrive at a mutually acceptable value for the commodity in question. A consensus is built between the two parties, where the value of a commodity is therefore subject to individual preferences and the psychological climate that exists at the time of the transaction.

Both the economic-value method and the market-value approach deal with theoretical values, based exclusively on estimates. Unless the commodity is actually transferred between two parties, the market value is considered hypothetical. Consequently, one can establish a minimum and a maximum value of a commodity if a seller considers trading it on the market on a particular date.

We have already mentioned the third approach, the book value method, which deals with the worth of an asset recorded on the balance sheet, based on generally accepted accounting principles. Book value can be described as the historical value of an asset represented by its purchase price (original cost of the asset) less the accumulated depreciation.

The **liquidation value** shows the worth of specific assets when sold separately. Liquidation means that a business must sell an asset under duress in order to obtain some cash. The liquidation value does not reflect the real worth of an asset or a business. In most cases, it is substantially below the economic value, the market value, and even the book value of an asset.

Liquidation value
Worth of an asset if sold under duress.

---

1. Erich A. Helfert, *Techniques of Financial Analysis*, 6th edition (Homewood, Ill.: Richard D. Irwin, Inc. 1987), pp. 337–42.

Cost of acquiring a new asset to replace an existing asset with the same functional utility.

The **replacement value** or reproduction value is the cost of replacing an existing capital asset with an identical asset. This is a good approach for measuring the worth of an ongoing business because it is based on engineering estimates and judgments. However, this approach is flawed since it does not take into consideration the real worth of the management team, the reputation of the business, the strength of the organization, and the value of its products. Furthermore, it is difficult to equate the value of assets of an ongoing plant with so-called "equivalent assets." For example, what appears to be a "duplicate asset" may, in fact, have a higher or lower rate of productivity. With the passage of time, most physical assets are subject to some technological and physical wear and tear.

Collateral value

An assessment by lenders of the value of a particular asset taken as a guarantee for credit.

To secure their loans or other types of credit, lenders use the **collateral value** approach. This method is based on the premise that maximum credit will be allowed to a particular business against identifiable assets. Generally, in order to allow for a margin of safety, lenders will set a lower value than the asset's market worth.

Assessed value

Method used by municipal governments for determining the level of property taxes.

Municipal governments use the **assessed value** approach for property taxation. The rules used to determine the assessed value vary widely between municipalities and do not necessarily reflect market values. The prime purpose of the assessed value is to levy tax revenues. Such values have little connection with other market values.

Economic value is the "price" that is placed on a business as an ongoing entity. For example, you will surely pay more for a retail store that is operating (ongoing) than for the physical assets of a similar business that is on the brink of declaring bankruptcy. For the ongoing business, you would have to pay for the goodwill, which includes the customers, reputation, patents, employees, image, etc. This approach compares the cash outflow to future cash inflows. The final section of this chapter will explore how to calculate values of ongoing businesses through time-value-of-money yardsticks such as the internal rate of return and the net present value approach.

Before looking at the process of putting a price tag on an ongoing business, let's examine several steps that an investor will want to go through. They include scanning the environment, documenting the planning assumptions, and restating the financial statements.

Objective 3 ➡

Scanning the Environment

Scanning the environment

Method used during the planning process for the purpose of pinning down planning assumptions or premises.

As shown in Figure 12.1, the first thing to look at in the valuation process is the nature of the industry in which a business operates and the competition it faces. This is commonly referred to as **scanning the environment.** If the business operates in an extremely volatile and competitive environment, this affects its viability and profitability. Its risk is higher and the cash and earnings generated by the business may be more difficult to predict.

Scanning the environment means formulating assumptions on which the purchase decision will be based. Here, we are talking about assessing the general and industry environments and formulating planning assumptions that could be expressed in quantitative and qualitative terms. *Quantitative factors* such as the

GNP, labour rates, market demand, supply capability, imports, unemployment rate, and prevailing interest rates help to profile the conditions under which the business operates and to prepare the detailed operating plans related to marketing, manufacturing, research and development, engineering, and production.

Qualitative factors examine additional important perspectives such as government regulations and controls, labour activities, consumer preferences, and so on. The general environment includes economic, political, social/ethical, technological, and international conditions. Industry conditions include such factors as the profile of the consumers, number and power of suppliers, the competitive climate (rivalry among competing sellers), the threat of substitute products, potential entry of new competitors, and growth patterns. The main objective of scanning the environment is to pin down the "opportunities" and "threats" facing the business.

Documenting the Planning Assumptions

◀◀ Objective 4

The next step is to document the planning assumptions (or premises) that will help prepare the pro-forma financial statements. Investors will want to examine a company's past performance, determine whether the existing resources will be adequate to realize the new owners' strategic intentions, and also look at the company's pro-forma financial statements (i.e., income statement and balance sheet), which will be discussed later in this chapter.

Past Performance

Looking at the track record of a business (for, say, the previous four or five years) is always important for investors. A history of healthy past performance supports the decision to purchase. A company's track record can be gauged in terms of overall performance, operating performance, and market performance.

Overall performance is a measure of how a company has used its resources in the past. Useful ratios to gauge overall performance may be grouped under two headings: those measuring financial conditions, such as current ratio, acid test ratio, and debt ratios; and those measuring profitability, such as return on sales and return on equity.

Operating performance is a measure of managerial and technical competence. This is important in determining to what extent the existing management team is able to make the business profitable. Pertinent information on managerial performance relates to the major organizational functions. For example, under marketing—product acceptability, distribution efficiencies, sales performance; under manufacturing—operating expenses, cost of raw material, utilization of plant capacity, capital assets turnover, inventory turnover, and accounts receivable turnover; and under human resources—labour turnover, quality of the workforce, and general working conditions.

Market performance is a measure of a firm's position within its industry. Did it lose, maintain, or improve its market position? Was it able to manage its busi-

Overall performance

Ratios used to measure how well a business is deploying its resources.

Operating performance

Method used for gauging the efficiency and effectiveness of management at the operating level (e.g., marketing, production).

Market performance

Method used for gauging the efficiency and effectiveness of management within the industry in which it operates.

ness under adverse environmental or industry conditions? How? Why? By how much? A number of firms compile industry data against which historical company performance can be compared. For example, Dun & Bradstreet Canada, Standard & Poor's, and several commercial banks disclose, through written reports or Web sites, pertinent industry ratios based on financial and taxation statistics. Dun & Bradstreet Canada provides in its Canadian Industry Norms and Key Business Ratios very comprehensive and essential financial data on company and industry key ratios related to solvency, efficiency, and profitability. Standard & Poor's Compustat Services provides online information related to industry and company financial performance. Examples of this type of information are presented in Chapter 4 in Table 4.8.

Present Capability

If a business is purchased, its present capability is analyzed to objectively review the company's strengths and weaknesses and determine what needs to be done in order to carry out the new strategic and operational plans. It is also appropriate to specify how any deficiencies could be resolved. If, for instance, market share and profitability have been declining steadily, the new investors may strive to reverse this trend by introducing new products, modifying some existing products, and changing production processes to eliminate waste and inefficiencies.

The purchase of a business may call for different direction and orientation of the resources. Therefore, the analysis of present capability focuses on the following questions: Can the resources be extended? By how much? What new resources must be added in order to make the business more profitable? How will existing and new resources be integrated? Is there a need to redefine the company's mission, objectives, and priorities? The new owners may have to plan in detail the new business's capabilities in the following areas:

- human resources (technical and managerial);
- financial resources;
- machinery, equipment, and facilities;
- sources of raw material (suppliers);
- know-how (techniques, programs, systems);
- internal relations (employees);
- external relations (union, image, financial community, community relations, government relations, associations); and
- organizational structure.

Future Cash Needs and Profitability

This segment of the analysis is the most time-consuming and demanding. It is difficult because, unlike analyzing past performance and diagnosing existing operating functions (e.g., marketing, production, research and development, etc.), looking into the future involves establishing a series of assumptions underlying the purchase decision. The point of the analysis is not only to justify the purchase but also to determine how much the business is really worth and what plans will be required to make the business achieve its strategic, operational, and financial objectives.

Restating the Financial Statements

◀◀ Objective 5

The key documents investors examine when buying a business are its financial statements: the income statement and the balance sheet. On the balance sheet, investors look at the book value of a company's assets and how much the business owes to creditors on these assets. By examining each item individually, investors can put a price tag on each asset to determine how much each is "actually worth," or its market value.

However, looking at the balance sheet is not enough. The investor will also examine the income statement to determine the company's existing and, most important, potential earning power. The true value of a business is directly related to its ability to generate earnings, and the income statement is the dominant document for arriving at this number. However, the earnings the existing owners are able to generate may be different from what the new owners will be able to realize. Therefore, as with the balance sheet, assessing the individual components of the income statement is essential to determine, for example, if more sales revenue can be generated, and if there could be improvements in operating efficiencies in order to improve the bottom line. Each expense account on the income statement is examined to determine whether cost savings could be realized through economy, downsizing, and increased productivity.

Financial ratios are used to analyze financial statements to assess a company's liquidity, debt/coverage, asset management, and profitability performance. Typical questions that investors ask include:

- Have these financial statements been audited?
- Is the business carrying too much debt?
- What is the real worth of the physical assets?
- Is the company profitable?
- Are the operating costs reasonable? Inflated? Out of line?
- Is the business carrying too much accounts receivable compared to sales revenue? Too much inventory compared to the cost of goods sold? What is the real worth of these assets?
- How much is the reputation of the business worth?

After reviewing a company's financial statements, the investor will formulate planning assumptions for each item included in the financial statements in order to help produce the pro-forma income statement and balance sheet.

Let's now examine how each element shown on the income statement and the balance sheet can be restated to determine the real worth of a business.

Restating the Income Statement

Looking at only one year's income statement does not give enough information to gauge the full meaning of a company's operating performance. The company's historical financial and operating performance must be analyzed in some detail for several years to determine how consistent a company is in generating revenues and earnings and how each cost element has performed in the past. Specific things to look for are the following: Has sales revenue been on the increase? Are the operating expenses, such as cost of goods sold and selling and administration expenses, consistent from year to year? If we were to buy this company, would we be able to increase sales revenue? Reduce costs? If so, how would we be able to achieve such improvements?

Let's assume that an investor wants to purchase Eastman Technologies Inc. The potential investor would want to analyze the company's existing income statement and, by exploring some of the questions mentioned earlier, could restate the numbers. In other words, every account on this statement would be examined in terms of how the business would operate under the new owner.

Eastman Technologies Inc.'s 2003 actual income statement and pro-forma statement are shown in Table 12.2.

SALES REVENUE In 2003, Eastman Technologies Inc. sold $2,500,000 worth of goods, and the new owners estimate $4,000,000, a 60% increase, for 2004. The new owner's marketing plan would determine how this growth will be realized. The so-called "marketing variables," which include selling, advertising, promotion, distribution, product, market finance, and market definition, have a direct influence on that all-important figure in the pro-forma income statements—sales revenue. Miscalculating the number of units to be sold and the selling price could severely affect profitability.

Predicting the mood of the consumer calls for a thorough investigation of wants or needs. The marketing plan usually includes the following:

- marketing philosophy;
- description of the market (size, trends);
- objectives (volume, price, share of market, and product mix);
- consumer profile;
- a list of the more important customers that will buy from the company (Who are they? Where are they located? Are they wholesalers? Retailers? Government organizations?);
- marketing functions (strengths and weaknesses);
- product description (features, patents, packaging, market test results, etc.);
- marketing programs (sales promotion, sales organization, distribution, credit, warehousing facilities);
- competitive advantage;
- selling costs as a percentage of sales;
- advertising and promotional budget;

TABLE 12.2 RESTATING THE INCOME STATEMENT

Eastman Technologies Inc.
Income Statement for the Years Ended December 31
Actual and Buyer's Restated Estimates

	Actual 2003		Buyer's Restated Estimates, 2004	
Net sales	$ 2,500,000	1.00	$4,000,000	1.00
Cost of goods sold	1,900,000	.76	2,400,000	.60
Gross margin	**600,000**	**.24**	**1,600,000**	**.40**
Operating expenses				
Selling expenses:				
Sales salaries	$140,000	0.05	$245,000	0.06
Advertising expenses	20,000	0.01	85,000	0.02
Total selling expenses	160,000	0.06	330,000	0.08
Administrative expenses:				
Office salaries	170,000	0.06	190,000	0.05
Rent	20,000	0.01	30,000	0.01
Depreciation	40,000	0.02	150,000	0.03
Total administration expenses	230,000	0.09	370,000	0.09
Total operating expenses	390,000	0.16	700,000	0.18
Operating income	**210,000**	**0.08**	**900,000**	**0.23**
Other income	20,000	0.01	32,000	0.01
Other expenses (interest)	35,000	0.01	194,000	0.06
Net	15,000	0.01	162,000	0.05
Income before taxes	195,000	0.08	738,000	0.18
Income taxes	97,500	0.04	369,000	0.09
Income after taxes	**$ 97,500**	0.04	**$ 369,000**	0.09

- service arrangements;
- pricing strategies; and
- warranties on products.

COST OF GOODS SOLD Based on a marketing plan, each expense item included in the expense accounts shown on the income statement is examined carefully. For example, even though the cost of goods sold shows one figure, the new buyers would want to examine the many different costs that are included in the $1,900,000 to determine whether efficiencies can be obtained through purchasing, freight, and manufacturing. Most expenses are incurred at the manufacturing level, through plant expenses, manufacturing costs, maintenance, raw material purchases, insurance, cost of inventory, utilities, and wastage.

This plan focuses on efficiencies and shows production at competitive prices. Manufacturing's prime objective is to make a product that meets the needs of marketing (its selling agent) at the best possible price. The total manufacturing concept should incorporate the most modern techniques, equipment use, material handling, storage, inventory control, traffic, record keeping, and costing. Production scheduling should be integrated with sales.

Calculating the break-even points for several future years of operation could highlight the relationship between revenue and costs (fixed and variable) and is considered a valid yardstick to determine level of risk. Several sensitivity checks can estimate the margin of safety regarding a price or volume drop, or an increase in operating expenses with no corresponding change in selling price.

Planning assumptions related to cost of goods sold and manufacturing expenses deal with the following:

- production operation (job-shop or mass production);
- plant layout;
- production runs (capacity and forecast of utilization rate);
- fixed and variable cost estimates (break-even point);
- list of equipment (auto equipment, trucks, vehicles);
- raw material costs and reliability;
- maintenance costs;
- government regulations (health, security);
- economics of a two- or three-shift schedule; and
- quality control procedures.

As shown in Table 12.2, vertical analysis helps to determine to what extent the new owners would be able to improve manufacturing efficiencies. Under the present owners, cost of goods sold as a percentage of sales is 76% (or $0.76 for each $1.00 worth of sales), and the new owners project a $0.16 improvement, down to 60% (or $0.60 for each dollar's worth of sales). Because of this exceptional improvement in cost of goods sold, the gross margin would jump from 24% to 40%.

SELLING EXPENSES The assumptions related to selling expenses can be covered in the marketing plan and reflect the planning assumptions related to sales and advertising. As shown in the table, despite the 60% increase in sales revenue, selling expenses will be increased by 106%, reflecting the emphasis that the new owners may put on selling their products and services. As shown, selling expenses as a percentage of sales increase from 6% to 8%.

ADMINISTRATIVE EXPENSES As shown in the table, administrative expenses include office salaries, rent, and depreciation. There is a 61% increase in these expenses, which is equivalent to the sales revenue increment. Because of this, total administration expenses as a percentage of sales are maintained at 9%. Individually, office salaries increased by 12%, rental charges by 50%, and depreciation expense by 275%; the latter increase is due to the significant increase in capital assets.

Total operating expenses, which include both selling and administration, increased by 79%, and as a percentage of sales, they increased from 16% to 18%. Because of the significant improvement in sales revenues and costs of goods sold, operating income increases by 328%; as a percentage of sales, it improves from 8% to 23%.

Other income and interest expenses show a substantial increase. The interest expense reflects a huge increase in liabilities to finance the purchase of the assets.

THE BOTTOM LINE As a result of the changes in the revenue and expense accounts, the income after taxes reaches $369,000, which represents a 278% increase. As a percentage of sales, income after taxes increases from 4% to 9%. This means that in 2004, for every $1.00 of sales, the company will make $0.09 in after-tax income, compared to $0.04 in 2003.

The acquisition of the business by the new owners will therefore make the business more profitable. The new owners are expected to earn $369,000 in profit after taxes and $519,000 in cash flow (income after taxes plus depreciation).

Now that we know the potential earning power of the business, the next question is: Based on the income statement projections, how much is the business worth? Restating the balance sheet will give us this information.

Restating the Balance Sheet

Table 12.3 shows Eastman Technologies Inc.'s present owners' balance sheet and the buyer's estimated value of individual assets and liabilities. The buyer's estimated market value represents the new owner's pro-forma balance sheet. For this reason, items such as accounts receivable, inventory, net capital assets, and retained earnings reflect what the investor would really buy from the present owners and how these assets would be financed. Let's look at the various components of the balance sheet.

CURRENT ASSETS Based on the market value, the worth of the current assets is estimated at $502,000. The value of both cash ($22,000) and prepaid expenses ($60,000) shows their actual worth. Based on a detailed audit of the company's accounts receivable and inventory accounts, they have been reduced to $250,000 and $170,000 respectively.

CAPITAL ASSETS Capital or fixed assets, which include land, buildings, equipment, and machinery, are valued at $3,000,000 for an increase of 123% over the book value of the seller's assets. Presumably, both the investor and the seller asked their respective real estate agents and engineers to estimate the market value of the individual assets shown on the balance sheet. Since we are dealing with the opening balance sheet, there is no accumulated depreciation. At the end of the first fiscal year, however, this account would show an amount of $150,000 (drawn from the income statement) for the use of the capital assets.

TABLE 12.3 RESTATED BALANCE SHEET

Eastman Technologies Inc.
Balance Sheets as at December 31
Actual and Buyer's Restated Estimates

	Actual 2003		Buyer's Restated Estimates, 2004	
Assets				
Current Assets				
Cash	$ 22,000	0.01	$ 22,000	0.01
Prepaid expenses	60,000	0.03	60,000	0.02
Accounts receivable	300,000	0.17	250,000 ✓	0.06
Inventory	218,000	0.12	170,000 ✓	0.04
Total current assets	**600,000**	0.33	**502,000**	0.13
Capital assets (at cost)	1,340,000	0.74	3,000,000 ✓	0.77
Accumulated depreciation	140,000	0.08	—	0.00
Capital assets (net)	**1,200,000**	0.67	**3,000,000**	0.77
Goodwill	—	—	**400,000** ✓	0.10
Total assets	$ 1,800,000	1.00	$ 3,902,000	1.00
Liabilities				
Current liabilities				
Accounts payable	$ 195,000	0.11	$ 195,000 ✓	0.05
Notes payable	150,000	0.08	150,000	0.04
Accrued expenses	20,000	0.01	20,000	0.01
Taxes payable	80,000	0.04	80,000	0.02
Total current liabilities	**445,000**	0.25	**445,000**	0.11
Long-term debts	**800,000**	0.44	**2,000,000**	0.51
Total liabilities	1,245,000	0.69	2,445,000	0.63
Common shares	300,000	0.17	1,457,000	0.37
Retained earnings	255,000	0.14	—	—
Owners' equity	**555,000**	0.31	**1,457,000**	0.37
Total liabilities and equity	$ 1,800,000	1.00	$ 3,902,000	1.00

✓ Denotes items that are taken into consideration for the purchase of the business.

GOODWILL Goodwill is a special asset that appears on a balance sheet when a business is sold. It represents the value of the reputation, faithful customers, and good name of the existing company. It is the excess paid for a business over the fair market value of the assets less the liabilities just prior to the purchase. In the case of Eastman, the new owners might pay $400,000 for the name and reputation. Like capital assets, this $400,000 can be amortized over a period of years, and the amortization expense (just like depreciation) would be included in the buyer's income statement.

CURRENT LIABILITIES All items reported under current liabilities are brought forward from the seller's balance sheet to the new owner's opening balance sheet. In Table 12.3, current liabilities amount to $445,000.

LONG-TERM DEBTS As shown in the table, the buyers will borrow $2,000,000 to purchase the current and capital assets.

COMMON SHARES Common shares represent the amount of cash that the buyers would have to put up in order to buy the business. An amount of $1,457,000 would be invested in the business by the new owners and represents 31% of the total liabilities and owners' equity.

Price-Tagging an Ongoing Business

◀◀ Objective 6

Now that we have created the projected income statement and opening balance sheet, we can determine how much the business is worth as a going concern. Three techniques will be used to make that calculation: asset valuation, net present value, and industry multipliers.

Asset Valuation

The **asset valuation** method is to look at the buyer's restated balance sheet (Table 12.3) and select the items that the buyer is interested in purchasing. These items are shown in Table 12.4. The only assets that are of interest to the new owners are accounts receivable, inventory, capital assets, and goodwill. As shown, the buyer will probably keep the accounts payable (sometimes accrued expenses) since they are used to finance current assets such as accounts receivable and inventory. Based on the re-appraised value, the buyer will purchase the seller's working capital for an amount of $225,000.

> **Asset valuation**
>
> Methodology used to restate the numbers appearing on financial statements.

   The other assets include capital assets such as the land, buildings, equipment, machinery, and tools. These assets would be listed in detail at book price and market price. The value of these assets is $3 million. The other asset that the buyer will purchase is the goodwill. As shown, this is valued at $400,000.

TABLE 12.4 COST OF THE BUSINESS	
Accounts receivable	$ 250,000
Inventory	170,000
Total current assets	420,000
Less: accounts payable	195,000
Net working capital	225,000
Capital assets	3,000,000
Goodwill	400,000
Purchase price	$ 3,625,000

Chapter 12: Business Valuation

As shown in Table 12.4, the seller is asking $3,625,000 for the business. The question is this: Based on the pro-forma income statement, is the asking price worth it? The potential buyers could invest $3,625,000 in investment securities at 10% a year (before tax) and earn $362,500 a year. If they buy the business instead, they should expect larger earnings because of the risk factor.

Net Present Value Method

The net present value method is based on the time-value-of-money concept and takes into account cash inflows and cash outflows. This topic was covered in Chapters 7 and 8. As shown in Table 12.5, the net present value is calculated by taking into account both the cost of capital and the hurdle rate. The seller's asking price is $3,625,000. This is the amount of cash that the buyer would have to pay and includes working capital, capital assets, and goodwill.

The next step is to determine the amount of cash that would be generated over the life of the project. From the buyer's income statement shown in Table 12.2, the cash inflow is estimated at $519,000. This is made up of the income after taxes of $369,000 plus depreciation of $150,000. If we assume that the owner will want to keep the business for a period of ten years, after which he or she will want to sell it for, say, $6,000,000, the net present value of the purchase, using a 10% cost of capital discount rate, is a positive $1,877,287. This means that the buyer would earn 10% on the investment plus $1,877,287 over the ten-year period.

If cost of capital were used as the rate for approving the purchase, the buyer would certainly buy the business. However, because of the risk involved, if the

TABLE 12.5	NPV BASED ON COST OF CAPITAL AND HURDLE RATE	
	Cost of capital 10%	Hurdle rate 20%
Purchase price (outflow)	− $3,625,000	− $3,625,000
Cash inflows		
Cost of capital $519,000 × 6.1446	+ 3,189,047	
Hurdle rate $519,000 × 4.1925		+ 2,175,907
Sale of business		
Cost of capital $6,000,000 × .38554	+ 2,313,240	
Hurdle rate $6,000,000 × .16151		+ 969,060
Net present value	+ $ 1,877,287	− $ 480,033

buyer's hurdle rate on the investment is 20%, the net present value would be negative, that is, −$480,033. In this case, the buyer would earn less than the expected 20%. She would probably not buy the business for the $3,625,000 asking price. However, if the buyer insists on making a 20% return, a counter-offer of $3,144,967 ($3,625,000 − $480,033) could be made—which, in this case, would make the cash outflow equal to the cash inflow. At that price, the IRR would be 20%. On the other hand, if the buyer still purchases the business for the $3,625,000 asking price, an internal rate of return of only 17.2% would be made.

Industry Multipliers

The other approach to putting a price tag on a business is the use of **industry multipliers.** Here, the buyer or seller would refer to a list of multipliers that applies to a particular industry. Although many individuals use multipliers, some (particularly buyers) refrain from using them because they focus too much on gross sales, rather than income after taxes. Critics argue that it's not the top line—but the bottom line—that counts.

Industry multipliers

A standard used to determine the value or worth of a business.

Table 12.6 presents a list of typical industry multipliers. Although some of them are accurate in some industries, they should still be used with caution because they tend to simplify, to a large extent, the worth of a business. Nevertheless, these multipliers can be used as a complementary tool to obtain a rough estimate of an asking price. Using these multipliers with another technique such as NPV may result in roughly the same asking price. If that's the case, the valuation price would be an approximate estimate.

Because of a wide variation in gross sales from year to year, it may be wise to calculate the asking price by using the company's last three or four years' income statements. One may also want to average out the last three years' gross sales revenue to calculate the asking price.

In the case of Eastman Technologies Inc., a price-earnings multiple can also be used to determine the value of the company. A price-earnings multiple is equal to the inverse of a capitalization rate. For example, if the investor wants to use an 11% capitalization rate, the price-earnings multiple would be 9.1 (100 ÷ 11%) If the investor wants to use 13%, the price-earnings multiple would be 7.7 (100 ÷ 13%). To determine the company's market value by using the price-earnings multiple, the investor would therefore have to determine the appropriate capitalization rate and multiply this rate by maintainable after-tax cash flow, which in the case of Eastman is $519,000 ($369,000 + $150,000). If the investor wants to use a 13% capitalization, the value of the business would be $3,996,300 ($519,000 × 7.7).

If the investor buys, say, 40% ownership of the business, he or she would be entitled to only 40% of the $3,996,300, or $1,598,520.

TABLE 12.6 INDUSTRY MULTIPLIERS

Industry	Multiplier
Travel agencies	.05 to .1 × annual gross sales
Advertising agencies	.75 × annual gross sales
Collection agencies	.15 to .2 × annual collections + equipment
Employment agencies	.75 × annual gross sales
Insurance agencies	1 to 2 × annual renewal commissions
Real estate agencies	.2 to .3 × annual gross commissions
Rental agencies	.2 × annual net profit + inventory
Retail businesses	.75 to 1.5 × annual net profit + inventory + equipment
Sales businesses	1 × annual net profit
Fast food (nonfranchise)	.5 to .7 × monthly gross sales + inventory
Restaurants	.3 to .5 × annual gross sales, or .4 × monthly gross sales + inventory
Office supply distributors	.5 × monthly gross sales + inventory
Newspapers	.75 to 1.5 × annual gross sales
Printers	.4 to .5 × annual net profit + inventory + equipment
Food distributors	1 to 1.5 × annual net profit + inventory + equipment
Building supply retailers	.25 to .75 annual net profit + inventory + equipment
Job shops	.5 × annual gross sales + inventory
Manufacturing	1.5 to 2.5 × annual net profit + inventory
	.75 × annual net profit + equipment + inventory (including work in progress)
Farm/heavy equipment dealers	.5 × annual net profit + inventory + equipment
Professional practices	1 to 5 × annual net profit
Boat/camper dealers	1 × annual net profit + inventory + equipment

Source: Richard W. Snowden, *Buying a Business* (AMACOM: New York, 1994), pp. 150–151.

Market Value of Publicly Traded Companies

Objective 7 ➡

To calculate the value of publicly traded companies, analysts must use the number of common shares issued and the share market price. Here, in order to calculate the market value of the shareholders' equity, we have to multiply the number of outstanding common shares by the share price on the last day that the shares were traded on the stock market.

Let's assume that Eastman Technologies Inc. is a publicly traded company and has 30,000 shares outstanding. With a $555,000 net worth, that means that the book value of each share outstanding would be $18.50 ($555,000 ÷ 30,000). However, if the shares were traded at, say, $25.00, the market value of the company, or the equity portion of the balance sheet, would be $750,000 ($25.00 × 30,000). In this case, the ratio of the market value to the book value would be 1.35 times.

✳ Decision-Making in Action

Robin Pedwell, CEO of Amoco Sauna Inc., is considering launching a new product line on the Canadian market by the early part of 2004. The company is in the process of completing a prototype beauty care product—a compact, portable, and multifunctional facial sauna. If Amoco is successful in Canada, Pedwell would then market the product line in the U.S. and European markets.

The development of the multifunctional facial sauna began in 2001, when the company's marketing research department studied the market opportunities for health and beauty care products. The favourable market results encouraged Pedwell to design and develop a new line of products—a "family of products"—for health and beauty care. The leading product, called "Beauty Facial Sauna," was a portable, hand-held, steam-generating apparatus.

The only obstacle to Pedwell's dream was a shortage of the cash he needed to complete his research in 2003 on the facial sauna and to market the new product line in the early months of 2004. Because of the nature of the business venture, he was aware that conventional lenders would not be interested in financing his project. He realized that his only option was to obtain funds from high-risk capital investors. He was aware that obtaining funds from these types of investors would be a very difficult, time-consuming process, and also very expensive.

Therefore, Pedwell approached a long-time friend and financial advisor with excellent connections in the high-risk capital markets, Norm Woodstock. He would help Pedwell develop an investment proposal and develop a strategy on how to approach high-risk investors. Woodstock first suggested determining the value of the business as a going concern several years after the launching of the new product line. In other words, he asked: What will Amoco's financial statements look like several years from now? Woodstock knew that high-risk investors are particularly interested in investing money in highly successful ventures, those that offer very high returns (somewhere in the 25% to 35% range). Also, these types of investors want to ensure that they have a clear option about how they would go about making their exit from the company by selling their shares four to five years after their initial investment. An exit strategy could take the form of a public offering or the possibility that Pedwell himself would buy back the investors' share.

Before going through the detailed calculation and preparing the investment proposal, Woodstock analyzed Amoco's financial statements and indicated to Pedwell the different methods that could be used to determine the value of his company. Woodstock pointed out four methods: the book value, the liquidation value, the going-concern value, and the discounted cash flow (DCF) method.

Woodstock pointed out that the DCF method is the most suitable method to determine the real value of Amoco. However, he decided to calculate the value of the business by using all methods just to get some idea about Amoco's different economic values.

BOOK VALUE As Woodstock pointed out to Pedwell, the book value of Amoco is the company's net worth or shareholders' equity, based on generally accepted accounting principles. Simply subtracting the liabilities from the book value of Amoco's assets gives the economic value called shareholders' equity or net worth. Illustration 1 shows Amoco's book value for the year-end 2003. As shown, the estimated book value of the company is estimated at $700,000.

LIQUIDATION VALUE Woodstock explained that the liquidation value would be useful only if Amoco were sold in order to satisfy its creditors. By using this approach, tangible assets such as land usually have a liquidation value close to their market value. Inventories and accounts receivable, on the other hand, are usually valued at less than that shown in the books. Woodstock also added that in order to determine the liquidation value, all of Amoco's assets would be assigned a distressed value while all debts would be listed at book value. As he pointed out, most assets sold under duress are discounted from their book value. The difference between the distressed value of the assets and the actual or book value of the liabilities is considered the liquidation value. This value would not reflect Amoco's real worth.

In most instances, a liquidation value is substantially less than the market value and book value. This method would be used only if Amoco were in serious financial trouble and had to liquidate its assets to pay the creditors. As shown in Illustration 1, Amoco's liquidation value is estimated at $245,000. The book value of the company's assets is reduced by $455,000 or 28% while the liabilities (both current and long-term) remain the same at the $900,000 level.

ILLUSTRATION 1

Estimated Balance Sheet For year-end December 31, 2003	Book Value	Liquidation Value
Assets		
Current assets		
Accounts receivable	$ 300,000	$ 125,000
Inventory	200,000	200,000
Other current assets	150,000	100,000
Total current assets	650,000	425,000
Total net capital assets	900,000	700,000
Other assets	50,000	20,000
Total assets	$1,600,000	$1,145,000
Liabilities and owners' equity		
Total current liabilities	$ 600,000	600,000
Total long-term debts	300,000	300,000
Total liabilities	900,000	900,000
Total owners' equity	**700,000**	**245,000**
Total liabilities and owners' equity	$1,600,000	$1,145,000
	Book value	Liquidation value

GOING-CONCERN VALUE Woodstock indicated that the going-concern value was a more relevant approach for determining a price tag for an ongoing business because it was related to Amoco's ability to produce a stream of after-tax cash flows. This method would show the pro-forma income statements after the new sauna product line was introduced in Canada. This forecast would require the help of many managers in the company involved in marketing, production, research and development, administration, accounting, etc. Woodstock indicated that a high-risk investor would base his or her investment decision on sales revenue, marketing and manufacturing costs, income after taxes, and cash flow estimates. Most important, the investor would want to be confident about the reliability of all revenue and cost estimates contained in the income statement.

As Woodstock pointed out, typical nonrisk investors are prepared to accept a 5% return if money is invested in relatively risk-free investments such as Canada Savings Bonds. However, high-risk investors, those prepared to invest in companies such as Amoco, expect to earn a return between 25% and 35%. Woodstock further explained that the level of risk is the price tag that helps determine a sought-after economic return. Therefore, the going-concern value has the ability to look at future cash flow expectations and the relative risk associated with an ongoing business.

Illustration 2 presents Amoco's income statement for 2004, the year that Amoco expects to launch the new product line. As shown, Amoco anticipates earning $450,000 in income after taxes and $550,000 in after-tax cash flow ($450,000 + $100,000). If a potential investor wants to earn 20%, Amoco's going-concern value would be $2,750,000 ($550,000 ÷ 20%). The $550,000 amount represents the maintainable, perpetual, or indefinite cash flow that Amoco expects to generate. A capitalization rate is a discount rate used to find the present value of a series of future receipts. In this particular instance, a 20% capitalization rate is the required rate of return expected by risk capital investors from Amoco. Woodstock indicated that this rate is based on a number of subjective factors and conditions at the time of valuation.

If the risk capital investors found Amoco's venture extremely risky and wanted to earn 30%, the cash flow receipts of $550,000 would give a $1,833,000 ($550,000 ÷ 30%) present value. Illustration 2 shows that the higher the capitalization rate (30% versus 20%) the lower the present value ($1,833,000 versus $2,750,000).

ILLUSTRATION 2

Amoco Sauna Inc.
Pro-Forma Income Statement
for 2004

(In $000s)			
Sales revenue		$5,000	
Total cost of goods sold		2,960	
Gross margin		2,040	
Operating expenses			
Total selling expenses	800		
Total administrative expenses	500		
Total operating expenses		1,300	
Operating income		740	
Other income/charges		90	
Income before taxes		650	
Income taxes		200	
Income after taxes		450	
Add back depreciation and amortization		100	
After-tax cash flow from operations		$ 550	$ 550
Divided by capitalization rate		20%	30%
Going-concern value		**$2,750**	**$1,833**

Chapter 12: Business Valuation

Discounted Cash Flow Method The most appropriate approach for calculating the value of Amoco is the discounted cash flow (DCF) method. The primary benefit of the DCF method is that it allows for fluctuations in future cash flows over a period of time.

The following lists the four steps involved in calculating Amoco's value by using the DCF method. Each step is explained in the next several pages.

Step 1: Calculate Amoco's yearly after-tax cash flow.

Step 2: Calculate Amoco's projected residual value.

Step 3: Calculate Amoco's estimated market value.

Step 4: Calculate the investor's before- and after-tax return.

Step 1: Calculate Amoco's Yearly After-tax Cash Flow. The first step for calculating Amoco's market value is to determine its after-tax cash flow forecast for the years 2004 to 2008. As mentioned earlier, these estimates are based on Amoco's management team and business-related experts in the field of sauna products.

Amoco hopes to have completed the research activities of the sauna's new product line by the end of 2003 and be ready for market distribution in Canada by early 2004. If the product line is well accepted in Canada (which is what Pedwell expects), Amoco would then be ready to launch the product line in the U.S. market. As shown in Illustration 3, the cash flow from operations generated by Amoco jumps from $550,000 (the detailed calculation for this figure is shown in Illustration 2) in 2004 to $1,450,000 in 2008. This represents a $900,000 growth over a four-year period for a whopping 164% increase.

After adding the investments in capital assets and incremental working capital to the after-tax cash flow from operations, Amoco shows a negative $850,000 cash flow in 2004 and positive cash flows between years 2005 and 2008 (from $200,000 to $950,000). As shown, a 20% discount rate to be considered by investors for this type of venture is used to determine the present value of the projected cash flows. This discount factor reflects the risk associated with Amoco's new product line. As shown, the projected present value cash flow loses more value proportionately to the undiscounted net cash flow (NCF) as it reaches the end of the forecast period. This is due to the fact that smaller discount factors are used in later years to reflect the loss of value as a result of time. The present value of the cash flow for each year is then added to determine the net present value (NPV). The net present value for the five-year forecast, using a 20% discount rate, is $324,000.

ILLUSTRATION 3

In 000's of $	2004	2005	2006	2007	2008
Cash flow from operations	550	800	900	1,200	1,450
Capital investments	−1,200	−400	−400	−300	−300
Incremental W.C.	−200	−200	−200	−200	−200
Subtotal	−1,400	−600	−600	−500	−500
NCF	−850	+200	+300	+700	+950
Factor @ 20%	.83333	.69444	.57870	.48225	.40188
Present value	− 708	+ 139	+ 174	+ 337	+ 382
NPV	**+ $324**				

The above shows that after making the initial $1.4 million investment, Amoco's venture will still produce a positive net cash flow to the extent of $324,000 during the five-year period.

By taking into account only the above five-year cash flow forecast, the business venture would gen-erate an internal rate of return of 36.9%. If the company's last year's $950,000 was maintained indefinitely and capitalized by using 18% (this will be discussed in Step 2 under "Calculate Amoco's Projected Residual Value"), this would give an additional inflow of cash in the amount of $5.3 million. If this amount were incorporated in the return calculation, the company's internal rate of return would jump to 78.6% with a $2.1 million NPV using a 20% discount rate.

As pointed out by Woodstock, this is a very lucrative venture if the projected cash flow is realized. The only obstacle is to convince risk capital investors of the feasibility of realizing these cash flow estimates.

Step 2: Calculate Amoco's Projected Residual Value. This step determines the residual value of a business. This is important to risk capital investors since they want to compare the amount of money that they will invest in the business to what the business will be worth once it reaches maturity. In the case of Amoco, Pedwell is looking for $600,000 from private investors. He will have to demonstrate that the investment will multiply many-fold and earn a return that will offset the risk. This is explored in this second step.

At the end of the forecast period, in 2008, Amoco will likely remain viable and continue to generate $950,000 in net cash flow for an indefinite period of time. The residual value is the present value of projected after-tax maintainable cash flow expected beyond 2008. As shown in Illustration 3, the maintainable cash flow from operations for 2008 is $1,450,000. Also, capital spending for each year after 2008 is estimated at $300,000 in addition to a $200,000 increase in working capital resulting from the anticipated introduction of the sauna product line in the U.S. market and possibly the European market. It is assumed here that Amoco will maintain its level of operations based on the 2008 performance (a realistic estimate according to Pedwell).

When calculating the residual value, a capitalization rate must be determined. Using capitalization is similar to discounting a maintainable cash flow in perpetuity. To calculate this figure, the maintainable after-tax cash flow amount of $950,000 is divided by an acceptable capitalization rate. In this case, the capitalization rate used for Amoco is 18% instead of the previous 20%. The difference between the discount rate and the capitalization rate is that the latter is adjusted for inflation, growth, and risk. By using this capitalization rate, the value of Amoco in 2007 would be $5.3 million ($950,000 ÷ 18%). Furthermore, the

present value of this amount will be discounted to 2003, the year that the investor will advance the $600,000 to Amoco, by using a 20% discount rate. Amoco's present value of the residual value totals $2,121,030 ($5,277,777 × .40188). Here is how it is calculated:

(In $000s)	2008
Cash flow	$1,450
Investments	−500
Net cash flow	950
Capitalization rate @ 18%	$5,277,777
Present value factor @ 20%	.40188
Prevent value of the residual value	$2,121,030

Step 3: Calculate Amoco's Estimated Market Value. This step in the valuation process involves the calculation of Amoco's estimated fair market value. As shown below, Amoco's fair market value is estimated at $2,445,030 and reflects Amoco's five-year after-tax discounted cash flow of $324,000 (step 1) and the estimated residual value of $2,121,030 (step 2).

Present value of cash flow from operations	$ 324,000
Present value of the residual value	2,121,030
Estimated fair market value	$2,445,030

Step 4: Calculate the Investor's Before- and After-tax Return. This last step in the process involves the calculation of the investor's return on investment on a before- and after-tax basis. Pedwell will seek a $600,000 amount from a risk capital investor. This cash will be used to finalize the research and development on the sauna product line and help to fund a marketing program to launch it in Canada.

This investment will be required by the middle of 2003. Here, capitalization will also be used to determine Amoco's residual value. But first, the total value at exit must be determined by multiplying the maintainable after-tax cash flow by a multiple. Here, the multiple is equal to the inverse of a capitalization rate. In this case, a 12.5% capitalization rate is used, which equals 8.0 (100 ÷ 12.5%) price-earnings multiple. As shown in Illustration 4, by using the 8 times multiple, the value at exit is estimated to be $7,600,000

($950,000 × 8 times). Since it is assumed that the risk capital investor has a 40% equity participation in the company, this means that $3,040,000 in gross proceeds will be paid to him or her in 2008.

As shown in Illustration 4, by using a 38.3% discount rate, the present value of the $3,040,000 would be equivalent to the $600,000 investment made by the risk capital investors.

ILLUSTRATION 4

(In $000s)	2003	2004	2005	2006	2007	2008
Before-tax return						
Initial investment	−600	—	—	—	—	—
Total value at exit						
After-tax cash flow	—	—	—	—	—	950
Multiple	—	—	—	—	—	8.0
Total value at exit	—	—	—	—	—	7,600
Investor's share (40%)	—	—	—	—	—	3,040
Initial investment	-600					
Total cash flows	+600					3,040
Net present value	00					
Before tax IRR on investment	**38.34%**					

The discount rate would therefore be considered the investor's before-tax internal rate of return (IRR) on investment. As shown in Illustration 5, similar calculations would have to be done to calculate the investor's IRR on an after-tax basis.

ILLUSTRATION 5

In 000's of dollars	
Gross proceeds received on exit	$3,040
Initial investment	−600
Capital gain on investment	2,440
Taxable portion (75%)	1,830
Investor's tax payable (50%)	915
Gross proceeds received on exit	$3,040
Investor's tax payable	915
Net after-tax proceeds paid to investor	$2,125

(In $000s)	2003	2004	2005	2006	2007	2008
After-tax return						
Initial investment	−600	—	—	—	—	—
Total value at exit						
After-tax cash proceeds to investor	—	—	—	—	—	2,125
Total cash flows						
Initial investment	−600					
Total cash flows	+600					2,125
Net present value	00					
After-tax return on investment	**28.78%**					

Assuming that the after-tax cash flow is $2,125,000 at exit, the investor's after-tax IRR on investment would be 28.8%. Here, by using a 28.8% discount rate, the present value of the $2,125,000 received in 2008 would be equivalent to the $600,000 investment made by the risk capital investor today. This discount rate would therefore be considered the investor's after-tax internal rate of return (IRR).

The return on investment by the investor would be earned only when he or she sells shares at the planned exit in year 2008. The exit could be made in one of the following ways:

- initial public offering;
- sale of all the shares of the company;
- sale of the investor's shares to a third party; or
- buyback of the investor's shares by Pedwell.

Chapter Summary

The *book value* of a business is what a business is worth on the books—that is, the difference between total assets and total liabilities. *Market value* is what a business is worth to a buyer as an ongoing entity. Because financial statements do not necessarily reflect the true market value of a business, accountants have attempted to resolve this issue through price-level accounting and current value accounting.

◄◄ Objective 1

Different valuation models exist. They include economic value, market value, book value, liquidation value, replacement value, collateral value, assessed value, and going-concern value.

◄◄ Objective 2

When buying a business, it is important to scan the environment and to document the planning assumptions in order to construct a pro-forma income statement and pro-forma balance sheet.

◄◄ Objective 3

Documenting the planning assumptions means examining a company's past performance, determining whether the existing resources will be adequate to realize the new owner's strategic intentions, and also looking at the restated company's pro-forma financial statements: the income statement and the balance sheet.

◄◄ Objective 4

Objective 5 ➡ A new owners' financial statements should be restated (income statement and balance sheet) to reflect what the new owners see in terms of sales revenue, cost of goods sold, operating expenses, and balance sheet accounts (assets, liabilities and shareholders' equity).

Objective 6 ➡ Price-tagging a business can be done through the *asset valuation method*, which is the difference between the market value of the assets of an ongoing business and its liabilities; the *net present value method*, which takes into consideration cash outflow (purchase price of the business) cash inflow (profit plus depreciation) and the potential resale value of the business at a later date; and *industry multipliers*, which reflect a percentage of the sales revenue.

Objective 7 ➡ To calculate the value of publicly traded companies, one has to multiply the number of common shares issued and the share market price.

Key Terms

Assessed value

Asset valuation

Book value

Collateral value

Current-value accounting

Economic value

Industry multipliers

Liquidation value

Market performance

Market value

Operating performance

Overall performance

Price-level accounting

Replacement value

Scanning the environment

Review Questions

1. Differentiate between market value and book value.

2. What do we mean by price-level accounting?

3. What do we mean by current value accounting?

4. Identify the most commonly used valuation models.

5. Explain the following valuation models:
   - market value
   - liquidation value
   - collateral value
   - assessed value

6. Why is it important for buyers of a business to scan the environment?

7. What are planning assumptions? Why are they important?

8. What do buyers look for when they assess the past performance of a business?

9. What financial ratios are useful for appraising a business?

10. How would you go about restating the income statement of a business?

11. How would you go about restating the balance sheet of a business?

12. What is goodwill?

13. What do we mean by asset valuation?

14. How can the net present value method help buyers to put a price tag on a business?

15. What are industry multipliers? What are their primary weaknesses?

16. What technique is used to put a price tag on the market value of publicly traded companies?

17. What do we mean by "maintainable cash flow"?

18. What is a residual value?

19. Discuss the meaning of "estimated fair market value."

20. What do we mean by "capitalization rate" and "earnings multiple"?

Discussion Questions

1. Are the methods and techniques used for valuing a small business the same as those for a large business? Why or why not?

2. Valuation techniques are essentially assessment tools that attempt to quantify the available objective data. Yet such quantification will always remain subjective in part. Explain.

3. Why is it that valuing a business for sale or purchase is one of the most complex tasks an analyst can undertake?

Testing Your Comprehension

True/False Questions

_____ 1. Because of the significant difference between book values and market values, some individuals challenge the validity of the traditional-value accounting practices.

_____ 2. Current-value accounting means that numbers on financial statements would be restated in terms of current purchasing power.

_____ 3. Inflation is what would be taken into account when dealing with price-level accounting.

_____ 4. Assets listed on a balance sheet are historically based.

_____ 5. The Canadian Institute of Chartered Accountants is the organization that recommends that all Canadian enterprises whose securities are traded in the public market disclose in their annual reports, whenever appropriate, supplementary information on the effects of changing prices.

_____ 6. The liquidation value of a business relates to the ability of a business to produce after-tax cash flows.

_____ 7. The market-value approach is a technique used to analyze the worth of an asset traded on the market between a buyer and a seller without duress.

_____ 8. The key financial statements used when buying a business are the statement of retained earnings and the statement of changes in financial position.

_____ 9. The factors that affect the cost of goods sold number on the income statement are the selling price and the share of the market.

_____ 10. Goodwill is a special asset that appears on a balance sheet when a business is sold.

_____ 11. The difference between total assets and total liabilities is equity, which is the amount of cash that the buyer of a business has to put up in order to buy the business.

_____ 12. Net present value is one of several methods used by buyers for evaluating the worth of a business.

_____ 13. Industry multipliers make use of NPV to put a price tag on a business.

_____ 14. Some people refrain from using industry multipliers because the approach focuses too much on gross sales, rather than income after taxes.

_____ 15. To calculate the value of publicly traded companies, analysts would have to use the number of common shares issued and the share market price.

Multiple-Choice Questions

1. Price-level accounting means that numbers on financial statements would be restated in terms of:
   a. book value of assets
   b. current purchasing power
   c. historical value
   d. seller's price
   e. net present value

2. Adjustments in financial statements, that is, the difference between market value and book value, can be reported in annual reports through:
   a. surveys
   b. purchase price of an asset + inflation
   c. market values
   d. restated values
   e. footnotes

3. The economic-value model used for evaluating a business is based on the:
   a. ability or capacity of an asset to produce a stream of after-tax cash flows
   b. historical performance of a business to generate profit
   c. industry in which the company is performing
   d. ability of management to bargain for the price of a business
   e. capacity of an asset to generate sales revenue

4. The following is not a valuation model:
   a. market value method
   b. collateral value method
   c. planning assumption value method
   d. liquidation value method
   e. replacement or reproduction value method

5. Market performance is used to rate a firm's position:
   a. within the general environment
   b. within the industry
   c. with regard to its historical performance
   d. with regard to its anticipated future performance
   e. with regard to its financial statements

6. A key document used for examining a company's financial performance is the:
   a. statement of retained earnings
   b. balance sheet
   c. statement of expenses
   d. cash purchases statement
   e. trial balance

7. The following is an important segment that has to be restated on the income statement:
   a. accounts receivable
   b. gross fixed assets
   c. operating expenses
   d. goodwill
   e. working capital accounts

8. Goodwill is the excess paid for a business over the:
   a. fair market value of the assets
   b. inflated value of the assets
   c. debt a company owes against the assets
   d. depreciated value of the assets
   e. seller's asking price

9. Cash flow from operations is calculated by:
   a. adding depreciation to income before taxes
   b. adding capital cost allowance to income before taxes
   c. adding depreciation to income after taxes
   d. subtracting all expenses from sales revenue
   e. subtracting income taxes from income before taxes

10. To put a price tag on a business, some will use industry multipliers that focus on:
    a. profit before taxes
    b. cost of sales
    c. profit after taxes
    d. cost of doing business
    e. sales revenue

11. One method commonly used to determine the value of publicly traded companies is the ratio of:
    a. book value to historical value
    b. market value to book value
    c. total market value of the assets to total liabilities
    d. total common shares outstanding to sales revenue
    e. total common shares outstanding to profit after taxes

Fill-in-the-Blanks Questions

1. The accounting value of an asset (the original cost minus total depreciation deductions made to date) is referred to as the _____ _____ value.

2. The _____ value is the price at which a business or asset can be sold.

3. _____ accounting is the method used to restate assets on financial statements in terms of current purchasing power (inflation).

4. _____ accounting is a method used to restate assets on financial statements in terms of what they would be worth if purchased.

Chapter 12: Business Valuation

5. The _____ value shows the worth of specific assets when sold under duress.

6. To secure their loans or other types of credit, lenders use the _____ value approach, which is a method based on the premise that maximum credit will be allowed to a particular business against identifiable assets.

7. _____ valuation is a method used to restate the numbers appearing on financial statements.

8. _____ performance is a method used for gauging the efficiency and effectiveness of management within the industry in which it operates.

9. _____ is a special asset that appears on a balance sheet when a business is sold.

10. When buying a business, three major types of assets are purchased: working capital, capital assets, and _____ assets.

11. Industry _____ are standards used to determine the value or worth of a business.

12. To calculate the value of publicly traded companies, analysts have to use the numbers of common shares issued and the share _____.

13. The difference between the total assets and total liabilities presented on the balance sheet is known as _____.

14. The _____ rate is a discount rate used to find the present value of a series of future receipts.

15. A _____ value of a business is a more relevant approach for determining a price tag for an existing business because of its ability or capacity to produce a stream of after-tax cash flows.

16. A _____ multiple can be used to determine the value of a company.

17. In order for the purchase price of an ongoing business to be acceptable, the net present value should be _____.

18. To determine a company's ability to generate cash as an ongoing concern, it is important to produce the pro-forma _____ _____.

19. The two more important investments or cash outflows made by businesses as going concerns are capital assets and incremental _____ _____.

20. When determining whether to buy a business or not, venture capitalists always want to know how much return they will receive on their investment. The financial criteria used to gauge the return is the _____ _____.

Learning Exercises

Exercise 1(a)

With the following information, prepare CompuTech's:

- Balance sheet for the year ending December 31, 2005.
- Revised balance sheet if the Millers were to liquidate the business.

By liquidating the assets, the Millers would probably obtain 70% of the accounts receivable amount shown on the balance sheet for the year ending December 31, 2005, no more than 50% for the inventory, and 30% for the net capital assets. Len hopes to obtain at least $20,000 in goodwill by liquidating the business.

Accounts	Amounts
Sales revenue	$800,000
Accounts payable	47,000
Accumulated depreciation	158,000
Accounts receivable	90,000
Leasing charges	10,000
Cash	20,000
Capital shares	170,000
Cost of goods sold	406,000
Marketable securities	5,000
Working capital loan	25,000
Retained earnings	135,000
Long-term debts	200,000
Inventory	110,000
Gross capital assets	560,000
Salaries	135,000
Prepaid expenses	10,000
Term loan	60,000

1. What is CompuTech's book value? 305,000

2. What is CompuTech's liquidation value? (58,000)

3. Would the Millers have enough money to pay all their creditors? deficit 58,000

4. If the Millers' business cannot cover all its liabilities, what will they have to do? No, because of deficit

Exercise 1(b)

John Hepworth, the sole proprietor of John's Variety, is having some difficulty with his retail store. He's concerned about the possibility of having to close it. He knows that the value of his business as a going concern is not high because of the minimal level of profit that his store has shown over the past two years.

He's now thinking seriously about getting out of the business by liquidating his assets and paying his creditors in full. His bank manager informed him that if he liquidates his assets, he would probably obtain 65% of the accounts receivable amount shown on his balance sheet for the year ending December 31, 2004, no more than 40% for his inventory, and 60% for his net capital assets.

John was hoping to obtain at least $50,000 in goodwill. With the information listed below, prepare the following:

Chapter 12: Business Valuation

- John's balance sheet for the year ending December 31, 2004.
- John's revised balance sheet if he were to liquidate his business.

Accounts	Amounts
Sales revenue	$3,000,000
Inventory	200,000
Capital shares	150,000
Accumulated depreciation	200,000
Selling expenses	130,000
Cash	10,000
Marketable securities	50,000
Retained earnings	385,000
Accounts payable	150,000
Accrued expenses	50,000
Taxes payable	25,000
Other current assets	25,000
Long-term debts	350,000
Capital assets (at cost)	900,000
Accounts receivable	300,000
Working capital loan	175,000

1. What is John's book value?

2. What is John's liquidation value?

3. Will John have enough money to pay all his creditors?

4. If John's business cannot cover all his liabilities, what will he have to do?

Exercise 2(a)

With the following information, calculate the after-tax cash flow from CompuTech's operations.

Accounts	Amounts
Sales revenue	$800,000
Income taxes	42,000
Selling expenses	135,000
Cost of goods sold	406,000
Administrative expenses	110,000
Interest charges	30,000

A depreciation amount of $80,000 is included in selling expenses and administrative expenses.

1. Calculate the value of the business as a going concern by using the following capitalization rates: 15% and 25%.

2. By using a 30% discount rate, calculate the present value of the business if it had a 15-year life span.

3. If an investor were to invest $300,000 in the business, how much cash should the business generate each year during a five-year period if the investor wants to earn 25%?

Exercise 2(b)

With the following information, calculate the after-tax cash flow from operations.

Accounts	Amounts
Sales revenue	$3,000,000
Interest charges	100,000
Income taxes	175,000
Cost of goods sold	1,800,000
Selling expenses	400,000
Administrative expenses	$ 300,000

Depreciation expenses of $200,000 and amortization expenses of $100,000 are included in the cost of goods sold and other operating expenses.

1. Calculate the value of the business as a going concern by using the following capitalization rates: 10%, 20%, 30%, and 40%.

2. By using a 20% discount rate, calculate the present value of the business if it had a five-year life span and a ten-year life span.

3. If an investor were to invest $400,000 in the business, how much cash should the business generate each year during a ten-year period if the investor wants to earn 30%?

Exercise 3(a)

The Millers are looking at the possibility of opening three new retail stores for CompuTech. Len will be approaching a risk capital investor, Oscar Eden, hoping to obtain a $200,000 amount in equity participation. This amount represents 20% of the company's equity share.

When Len had his first meeting with Oscar, he presented the following financial projections:

	Cash flow from operations	Investments	Working Capital
Year 0	—	$200,000	—
Year 1	$200,000	200,000	$100,000
Year 2	300,000	300,000	100,000
Year 3	500,000	300,000	50,000
Year 4	600,000	50,000	25,000
Year 5	900,000	50,000	25,000

Chapter 12: Business Valuation

During the conversation Len and Oscar agreed that 15% should be used as a discount rate to calculate the present value of the company's cash flow and also as a capitalization rate. Oscar pointed out that he hoped at the end of five years, when he would want to make his exit, the company would be worth at least five times its last year's cash flow.

1. What is CompuTech's net present value?

2. What is CompuTech's internal rate of return using only the five-year projections?

3. What is CompuTech's present value of the residual value?

4. What is CompuTech's fair market value?

5. What is Oscar Eden's internal rate of return on his investment?

Exercise 3(b)

Trevor Johnson, CEO of Eastern Electronics Inc. is looking at the possibility of marketing a new product line. Trevor will be approaching a risk capital investor, Bill Miller, hoping to obtain a $500,000 amount in equity participation. This amount represents 30% of the company's equity share.

When Trevor had his first meeting with Bill Miller, he presented the following financial projections:

	Cash flow from operations	Investments	Working capital
Year 1	$ 300,000	$800,000	$300,000
Year 2	500,000	300,000	200,000
Year 3	800,000	200,000	100,000
Year 4	900,000	100,000	50,000
Year 5	1,300,000	100,000	50,000

During the conversation between Trevor and Bill, both agreed that 20% should be used as a discount rate to calculate the present value of the company's cash flow and also as a capitalization rate. Bill pointed out that he hoped that at the end of five years, when he would want to make his exit, the company would be worth at least six times its last year's cash flow.

1. What is the company's net present value?

2. What is the company's internal rate of return using only the five-year projections?

3. What is the company's present value of the residual value?

4. What is the company's fair market value?

5. What is Bill Miller's internal rate of return on his investment?

Exercise 4(a)

By using 11% as CompuTech's cost of capital and the following estimates, calculate the following values for one of the company's retail stores:

1. the yearly present values; and

2. the cumulative net present values.

In 000's	Year 1	Year 2	Year 3	Year 4	Year 5
Projected income after taxes	$80	$90	$100	$110	$120
Projected capital cost allowance	$ 6	$ 8	$ 9	$ 10	$ 11
Projected incremental investment in working capital	$ 2	$ 3	$ 2	$ 1	$ 1

Exercise 4(b)

By using 10% as the company's cost of capital and the following estimates, calculate the following values for a manufacturing plant:

1. the yearly present values;

2. the cumulative net present values.

In millions	Year 1	Year 2	Year 3	Year 4	Year 5
Projected income after taxes	$3.0	$3.4	$3.9	$4.3	$4.8
Projected capital cost allowance	$1.1	$1.2	$1.3	$1.4	$1.5
Projected incremental investment in working capital	$0.6	$0.5	$0.6	$1.0	$0.5

Exercise 5(a)

Len and Joan Miller want to go public and are considering selling shares. CompuTech's balance sheet for 2005 is as follows:

CompuTech Inc.
Balance Sheet as at December 31, 2005

Current assets	$235,000	Current liabilities		$132,000
Capital assets	402,000	Long-term debts		200,000
		Common shares	170,000	
		Retained earnings	135,000	
		Total equity		305,000
Total assets	$637,000	Total liabilities and equity		$637,000

Assume that CompuTech Inc. has 20,000 shares outstanding, which are currently trading at $35.50.

1. What is the book value of the shares?

2. What is the market value of the shares?

3. What is the ratio of the market value to the book value?

Exercise 5(b)

The shareholders of Zimtex Electronics Inc. are considering selling their shares. The company's balance sheet is as follows:

Current assets	$ 300,000	Current liabilities		$ 150,000
Capital assets	800,000	Long-term debts		400,000
		Common shares	200,000	
		Retained earnings	350,000	
		Total equity		550,000
Total assets	$1,100,000	Total liabilities & equity		$1,100,000

The company has 25,000 shares outstanding, which are currently trading at $42.50.

1. What is the book value of the shares?

2. What is the market value of the shares?

3. What is the ratio of the market value to the book value?

Cases

Case 1: Lewin Foods Inc.

Helen Campbell and several business friends are considering buying Lewin Foods Inc., a privately owned company. Helen has just received the financial statements from the present owner and is trying to calculate the bid that should be made to the owners of the company.

Helen realizes that the financial statements do not provide enough information to make a decision. So she hires several real estate agents, engineers, and accountants to help her determine the value of the land, machinery, equipment, and working capital.

Lewin Foods Inc.'s financial statements are as follows:

LEWIN FOODS INC.
INCOME STATEMENT
FOR THE PERIOD ENDING DECEMBER 31, 2003

Net sales		$5,600,000
Cost of goods sold		3,400,000
Gross margin		2,200,000
Operating expenses		
Selling expenses	$750,000	
Administrative expenses	440,000	
Depreciation	100,000	
Total operating expenses		1,290,000
Operating income		910,000
Other income/charges		35,000
Income before taxes		875,000
Income taxes (42%)		367,000
Income after taxes		$ 508,000

Although the company is generating $508,000 in income after taxes and $608,000 in cash flow, Helen and her team estimate that they could increase sales substantially and reduce costs. After much deliberation, the management team estimates that it could increase the income after taxes to $850,000 and cash flow to $975,000.

LEWIN FOODS INC.
BALANCE SHEET
AS AT DECEMBER 31, 2003

Assets

Current assets		
Cash	$ 200,000	
Prepaid expenses	60,000	
Accounts receivable	765,000	
Inventory	1,200,000	
Total current assets		$2,225,000
Capital assets (at costs)	3,000,000	
Accumulated depreciation	1,200,000	
Capital assets (net)		1,800,000
Total assets		$4,025,000

Liabilities

Current liabilities

Accounts payable	$ 600,000	
Notes payable	400,000	
Taxes payable	200,000	
Total current liabilities		$1,200,000

Long-term debts

Mortgage	500,000	
Long-term notes	600,000	
Total long-term debts		1,100,000

Shareholders' equity

Common shares	300,000	
Retained earnings	1,425,000	
Total shareholders' equity		1,725,000
Total liabilities and equity		$4,025,000

The various consultants and auditors reported to Helen that the accounts receivable are worth $650,000, or about 85% of what is currently shown on the company's balance sheet. The value of the inventory, however, is not in as good shape. The auditors indicate that only $800,000 would be worth buying; it represents approximately 67% of what is shown on Lewin's balance sheet. Helen is prepared to take over all of the accounts payable.

The estimates regarding capital assets are as follows:

Land	$ 200,000
Buildings	800,000
Equipment	1,400,000
Machinery	600,000
Total	$3,000,000

During his conversation with Helen, Mr. Lewin, owner of Lewin Foods Inc., indicates that an amount of $700,000 in goodwill would have to be included in the selling price.

Because of the risk, Helen and her partners feel that they should earn at least a 25% internal rate of return on the business. The partners would be prepared to keep the business for 15 years and would hope to sell it for $8 million.

Funds raised to purchase the business would be obtained from various sources at a cost of 12%.

1. Would you buy the business?

2. If so, how much would you offer Mr. Lewin if you wanted to make a 25% internal rate of return?

Case 2: National Photocell Inc.

In early 2004, Bill MacMillan, one of the shareholders of National Photocell Inc., was completing a proposal for the expansion of his research-oriented business into a commercial supplier of photochemical equipment.

MacMillan felt his proposal was sound. However, he was concerned that the business might have difficulty in raising funds, as the project would require a high level of financial support, particularly from high-risk capital investors.

Only a few firms, all with their own specialized production, characterized the photochemical equipment industry. There was little direct product competition, and many opportunities existed for new product innovations. Companies in the industry were typically small, with sales generally less than $3 million per year. MacMillan's revenue forecast is shown on the Income Statements (see Illustration 1). As shown, sales revenue jumps from $1.0 million in 2005 to $8.0 million by 2010. The forecast period also shows that the income after tax flow adjusted for investments in capital assets and incremental working capital will show substantial increments from $70,000 in 2005 to $667,000 in 2010. However, National Photocell expects to show a negative cash flow in 2006 in the amount of $536,000.

MacMillan felt that the company would require approximately $1.5 million in financing to set up production, marketing, and training of personnel and for equipment purchases. Investment in capital assets for production start-up would take place in 2005 and continue in 2006. Other funds would be used for working capital, with the heaviest investment in accounts receivable and inventory, which would also be required in 2005.

MacMillan felt that traditional lenders would be willing to finance about $500,000 of the new financial needs. This would help finance the purchase of the capital assets and some working capital. The remaining $1.0 million would be raised from equity. About 60% of the new equity capital would be provided by existing shareholders and 40% by private investors. As shown on the balance sheets (Illustration 2), the inflow of common shares would take place in 2005.

National Photocell Inc. would operate on a three-year cycle: high growth during the first two years, and consolidation and planning for future growth during the third year. Marketing efforts will focus on North America for the first two years and then shift to a focus on Europe.

MacMillan believed these financial needs and financing requirements were very accurate and realistic. Nevertheless, he knew that he would have to prepare a very effective and comprehensive investment proposal in order to attract one or two investors to finance the business. He fully understood that risk capital investors are interested in ventures that offer:

- a good business opportunity, one that generates a high return;
- an excellent management team;
- a feasible exit strategy; and
- the ability to monitor and control their investment.

MacMillan was prepared to explain to potential investors how National Photocell could meet their needs. The most important factor would be the potential return that the investors expect to earn on this venture when they exit the business. He knew that the investors would want to reap their investment by 2010. He also knew that the business had to demonstrate a superior return performance so the the investors could earn a high return, something in the order of 30% to 40%.

ILLUSTRATION 1
National Photocell Inc.
Pro-Forma Income Statements
For the period ending December 31

(In $000s)	2005	2006	2007	2008	2009	2010
Sales revenue	$1,000	$2,500	$3,500	$5,000	$7,000	$8,000
Cost of goods sold	700	1,750	2,380	3,350	4,620	5,200
Gross margin	300	750	1,120	1,650	2,380	2,800
Operating expenses						
Selling expenses	100	250	420	650	910	1,040
Administrative expenses	56	140	214	301	462	520
Total operating expenses	156	390	634	951	1,372	1,560
Operating income	144	360	486	699	1,008	1,240
Interest charges	30	125	110	105	105	95
Income before taxes	114	235	376	594	903	1,145
Income taxes	34	71	132	220	361	458
Income after taxes	80	164	244	374	542	687
Add back depreciation	50	100	110	120	125	130
Cash flow from operations	130	264	354	494	667	817
Capital investments	40	600	200	200	200	100
Incremental working capital	20	200	100	100	100	50
Subtotal	60	800	300	300	300	150
Net cash flow	$ 70	$– 536	$ 54	$ 194	$ 367	$ 667

ILLUSTRATION 2
National Photocell Inc.
Pro-Forma Balance Sheets
As at December 31

(In $000s)	2005	2006	2007	2008	2009	2010
Assets						
Current assets						
Cash	$ 20	$ 25	$ 40	$ 100	$ 250	$ 650
Prepaid expenses	50	55	75	80	105	120
Accounts receivable	150	380	500	750	965	1,250
Inventory	170	430	644	803	1,200	1,407
Total current assets	390	890	1,259	1,733	2,520	3,427
Capital assets (cost)	2,800	3,400	3,600	3,800	4,000	4,100
Accumulated depreciation	300	400	510	630	755	885
Capital assets (net)	2,500	3,000	3,090	3,170	3,245	3,215
Total assets	$2,890	$3,890	$4,349	$4,903	$5,765	$6,642
Liabilities						
Current liabilities						
Accounts payable	$ 75	$ 150	$ 170	$ 190	$ 200	$ 240
Working capital loan	100	400	400	350	450	500
Accrued expenses	30	80	70	80	90	90
Taxes payable	35	45	50	50	50	50
Total current liabilities	240	675	690	670	790	880
Long-term debts	1,100	1,500	1,700	1,900	2,100	2,200
Total liabilities	1,340	2,175	2,390	2,570	2,890	3,080
Shareholders' equity						
Common shares	1,400	1,400	1,400	1,400	1,400	1,400
Retained earnings	150	315	559	933	1,475	2,162
Total shareholders' equity	1,550	1,715	1,959	2,333	2,875	3,562
Total liabilities and shareholders' equity	$2,890	$3,890	$4,349	$4,903	$5,765	$6,642

On the basis of the following assumptions, answer the questions below:

- The discount rate used to calculate the net present value is 20%.
- The capitalization rate used to calculate the capitalized value of National Photocell is 18%.
- The times multiple ratio to calculate the total value at exit in 2009 is 8.5.
- The taxable portion of the capital gain on investment is 75%.
- The company's income tax rate is 50%.

1. What will the company's book value be by 2010?
2. What is the company's net present value from 2006 to 2010?
3. What is the company's capitalized value?
4. What is the company's fair market value?
5. What is the company's internal rate of return during the five-year period (2006 to 2010)?
6. What is the company's internal rate of return using the estimated fair market value?
7. What is the risk-capital investor's internal rate of return on the investment on (a) a before-tax basis? (b) an after-tax basis?
8. Give your overall impression about the company's financial projections by using the liquidity ratios, the debt/coverage ratios, the asset-management ratios, and the profitability ratios.
9. Do you think that the risk-capital investors will be interested in this venture? Why or why not?

Appendix A

CompuTech Inc.
Financial Statements

Income Statements
Statements of Retained Earnings
Balance Sheets
(for the years 2003 to 2005)

CompuTech Inc.
Income Statements
For the period ending December 31
(in thousands of $)

	2005	2004	2003
Sales revenue	800	420	350
Cost of goods sold			
Purchases	400	205	175
Freight in	6	4	2
Total cost of goods sold	406	209	177
Gross margin	**394**	**211**	**173**
Selling expenses			
Salaries	75	55	45
Commissions	5	3	2
Travelling	5	3	2
Advertising	10	5	3
Depreciation	40	20	20
Total selling expenses	135	86	72
Administrative expenses			
Salaries	60	38	30
Leasing	10	7	5
Depreciation	40	20	18
Total administrative expenses	110	65	53
Total operating expenses	245	151	125
Operating income	**149**	**60**	**48**
Interest income	—	—	—
Interest charges	30	14	10
Income before taxes	119	46	38
Income taxes	42	13	13
Income after taxes	**77**	**33**	**25**

CompuTech Inc.
Statements of Retained Earnings
For the period ending December 31
(in thousands of $)

	2005	2004	2003
Retained earnings (beginning of year)	58	25	0
Net earnings for the year	77	33	25
Sub-total	135	58	25
Dividends	0	0	0
Retained earnings (end of year)	135	58	25

CompuTech Inc.
Balance Sheets
As at December 31
(in thousands of $)

	2005	2004	2003
Assets			
Current assets			
Cash	20	16	10
Marketable securities	5	5	5
Prepaid expenses	10	5	5
Accounts receivable	90	45	35
Inventory	110	65	50
Total current assets	235	136	105
Capital assets			
Gross capital assets	560	210	170
Accumulated depreciation	158	78	38
Total net capital assets	402	132	132
Total assets	**637**	**268**	**237**
Liabilities			
Current liabilities			
Accounts payable	47	20	17
Term loan	60	40	35
Working capital loan	25	—	—
Total current liabilities	132	60	52
Total long-term debts	200	50	60
Total liabilities	332	110	112
Shareholders' equity			
Capital shares	170	100	100
Retained earnings	135	58	25
Total shareholders' equity	305	158	125
Total liabilities and shareholders' equity	**637**	**268**	**237**

Appendix B

Interest Tables

Table A: Future Value of a Single Sum

INTEREST FACTORS $F_n = P(1 + i)^n$ FOR CALCULATING F,
FUTURE VALUE OF A SUM

Year	1%	2%	3%	4%	5%	6%	7%	8%
1	1.010	1.020	1.030	1.040	1.050	1.060	1.070	1.080
2	1.020	1.040	1.061	1.082	1.103	1.124	1.145	1.166
3	1.030	1.061	1.093	1.125	1.158	1.191	1.225	1.260
4	1.041	1.082	1.126	1.170	1.216	1.262	1.311	1.360
5	1.051	1.104	1.159	1.217	1.276	1.338	1.403	1.469
6	1.062	1.126	1.194	1.265	1.340	1.419	1.501	1.587
7	1.072	1.149	1.230	1.316	1.407	1.504	1.606	1.714
8	1.083	1.172	1.267	1.369	1.477	1.594	1.718	1.851
9	1.094	1.195	1.305	1.423	1.551	1.689	1.838	1.999
10	1.105	1.219	1.344	1.480	1.629	1.791	1.967	2.159
11	1.116	1.243	1.384	1.539	1.710	1.898	2.105	2.332
12	1.127	1.268	1.426	1.601	1.796	2.012	2.252	2.518
13	1.138	1.294	1.469	1.665	1.886	2.133	2.410	2.720
14	1.149	1.319	1.513	1.732	1.980	2.261	2.579	2.937
15	1.161	1.346	1.558	1.801	2.079	2.397	2.759	3.172
16	1.173	1.373	1.605	1.873	2.183	2.540	2.952	3.426
17	1.184	1.400	1.653	1.948	2.292	2.693	3.159	3.700
18	1.196	1.428	1.702	2.026	2.407	2.854	3.380	3.996
19	1.208	1.457	1.754	2.107	2.527	3.026	3.617	4.316
20	1.220	1.486	1.806	2.191	2.653	3.207	3.870	4.661
21	1.232	1.516	1.860	2.279	2.786	3.400	4.141	5.034
22	1.245	1.546	1.916	2.370	2.925	3.604	4.430	5.437
23	1.257	1.577	1.974	2.465	3.072	3.820	4.741	5.871
24	1.270	1.608	2.033	2.563	3.225	4.049	5.072	6.341
25	1.282	1.641	2.094	2.666	3.386	4.292	5.427	6.848

Year	9%	10%	11%	12%	14%	16%	18%	20%
1	1.090	1.100	1.110	1.120	1.140	1.160	1.180	1.200
2	1.188	1.210	1.232	1.254	1.300	1.346	1.392	1.440
3	1.295	1.331	1.368	1.405	1.482	1.561	1.643	1.728
4	1.412	1.464	1.518	1.574	1.689	1.811	1.939	2.074
5	1.539	1.611	1.685	1.762	1.925	2.100	2.288	2.488
6	1.677	1.772	1.870	1.974	2.195	2.436	2.700	2.986
7	1.828	1.949	2.076	2.211	2.502	2.826	3.185	3.583
8	1.993	2.144	2.305	2.476	2.853	3.278	3.759	4.300
9	2.172	2.358	2.558	2.773	3.252	3.803	4.435	5.160
10	2.367	2.594	2.839	3.106	3.707	4.411	5.234	6.192
11	2.580	2.853	3.152	3.479	4.226	5.117	6.176	7.430
12	2.813	3.138	3.498	3.896	4.818	5.936	7.288	8.916
13	3.066	3.452	3.883	4.363	5.492	6.886	8.599	10.699
14	3.342	3.798	4.310	4.887	6.261	7.988	10.147	12.839
15	3.642	4.177	4.785	5.474	7.138	9.266	11.974	15.407
16	3.970	4.595	5.311	6.130	8.137	10.748	14.129	18.488
17	4.328	5.054	5.895	6.866	9.276	12.468	16.672	22.186
18	4.717	5.560	6.544	7.690	10.575	14.463	19.673	26.623
19	5.142	6.116	7.263	8.613	12.056	16.777	23.214	31.948
20	5.604	6.728	8.062	9.646	13.744	19.461	27.393	38.338
21	6.109	7.400	8.949	10.804	15.668	22.575	32.324	46.005
22	6.659	8.140	9.934	12.100	17.861	26.186	38.142	55.206
23	7.258	8.954	11.026	13.552	20.362	30.376	45.008	66.247
24	7.911	9.850	12.239	15.179	23.212	35.236	53.109	79.497
25	8.623	10.835	13.586	17.000	26.462	40.874	62.669	95.396

Year	22%	24%	26%	28%	30%	32%	34%	36%
1	1.220	1.240	1.260	1.280	1.300	1.320	1.340	1.360
2	1.488	1.538	1.588	1.638	1.690	1.742	1.796	1.850
3	1.816	1.907	2.000	2.097	2.197	2.300	2.406	2.515
4	2.215	2.364	2.520	2.684	2.856	3.036	3.036	3.421
5	2.703	2.932	3.176	3.436	3.713	4.007	4.320	4.653
6	3.297	3.635	4.002	4.398	4.827	5.290	5.789	6.328
7	4.023	4.508	5.042	5.630	6.275	6.983	7.758	8.605
8	4.908	5.590	6.353	7.206	8.157	9.217	10.395	11.703
9	5.987	6.931	8.005	9.223	10.605	12.167	13.930	15.917
10	7.305	8.594	10.086	11.806	13.786	16.060	18.666	21.647
11	8.912	10.657	12.708	15.112	17.922	21.199	25.012	29.439
12	10.872	13.215	16.012	19.343	23.298	27.983	33.516	40.038
13	13.264	16.386	20.175	24.759	30.288	36.937	44.912	54.451
14	16.182	20.319	25.421	31.691	39.374	48.757	60.182	74.053
15	19.742	25.196	32.030	40.565	51.186	64.359	80.644	100.713
16	24.086	31.243	40.358	51.923	66.542	84.954	108.063	136.969
17	29.384	38.741	50.851	66.461	86.504	112.139	144.804	186.278
18	35.849	48.039	64.072	85.071	112.455	148.024	194.038	253.338
19	43.736	59.568	80.731	108.890	146.192	195.391	260.011	344.540
20	53.358	73.864	101.721	139.380	190.049	257.916	348.414	468.574
21	65.096	91.592	128.169	178.406	247.064	340.450	466.875	637.261
22	79.418	113.574	161.492	228.360	321.184	449.394	625.613	866.675
23	96.890	140.831	203.480	292.300	417.539	593.200	838.321	1178.680
24	118.205	174.631	256.385	374.144	542.800	783.024	1123.350	1603.000
25	144.210	216.542	323.045	478.905	705.640	1033.590	1505.290	2180.080

Table B: Present Value of a Single Sum

INTEREST FACTORS $P = F\left[\dfrac{1}{(1+i)^n}\right]$ FOR CALCULATING P,

PRESENT VALUE OF A SUM

N	1%	2%	3%	4%	5%	6%	7%	8%
1	0.99010	0.98039	0.97007	0.96154	0.95238	0.94340	0.93458	0.92593
2	.98030	.96117	.94260	.92456	.90703	.89000	.87344	.85734
3	.97059	.94232	.91514	.88900	.86384	.83962	.81630	.79383
4	.96098	.92385	.88849	.85480	.82270	.79209	.76290	.73503
5	.95147	.90573	.86261	.82193	.78353	.74726	.71299	.68058
6	.94204	.88797	.83748	.79031	.74622	.70496	.66634	.63017
7	.93272	.87056	.81309	.75992	.71068	.66506	.62275	.58349
8	.92348	.85349	.78941	.73069	.67684	.62741	.58201	.54027
9	.91434	.83675	.76642	.70259	.64461	.59190	.54393	.50025
10	.90529	.82035	.74409	.67556	.61391	.55839	.50835	.46319
11	.89632	.80426	.72242	.64958	.58468	.52679	.47509	.42888
12	.88745	.78849	.70138	.62460	.55684	.49697	.44401	.39711
13	.87866	.77303	.68095	.60057	.53032	.46884	.41496	.36770
14	.86996	.75787	.66112	.57747	.50507	.44230	.38782	.34046
15	.86135	.74301	.64186	.55526	.48102	.41726	.36245	.31524
16	.85282	.72845	.62317	.53391	.45811	.39365	.33873	.29189
17	.84438	.71416	.60502	.51337	.43630	.37136	.31657	.27027
18	.83602	.70016	.58739	.49363	.41552	.35034	.29586	.25025
19	.82774	.68643	.57029	.47464	.39573	.33051	.27651	.23171
20	.81954	.67297	.55367	.45639	.37689	.31180	.25842	.21455
21	.81143	.65978	.53755	.43883	.35894	.29415	.24151	.19866
22	.80340	.64684	.52189	.42195	.34185	.27750	.22571	.18394
23	.79544	.63416	.50669	.40573	.32557	.26180	.21095	.17031
24	.78757	.62172	.49193	.39012	.31007	.24698	.19715	.15770
25	.77977	.60953	.47760	.37512	.29530	.23300	.18425	.14602

N	9%	10%	11%	12%	13%	14%	15%	16%
1	0.91743	0.90909	0.90090	0.89286	0.88496	0.87719	0.86957	0.86207
2	.84168	.82645	.81162	.79719	.78315	.76947	.75614	.74316
3	.77218	.75131	.73119	.71178	.69305	.67497	.65752	.64066
4	.70843	.68301	.65873	.63552	.61332	.59208	.57175	.55229
5	.64993	.62092	.59345	.56743	.54276	.51937	.49718	.47611
6	.59627	.56447	.53464	.50663	.48032	.45559	.43233	.41044
7	.54703	.51316	.48166	.45235	.42506	.39964	.37594	.35383
8	.50187	.46651	.43393	.40388	.37616	.35056	.32690	.30503
9	.46043	.42410	.39092	.36061	.33288	.30751	.28426	.26295
10	.42241	.38554	.35218	.32197	.29459	.26974	.24718	.22668
11	.38753	.35049	.31728	.28748	.26070	.23662	.21494	.19542
12	.35553	.31863	.28584	.25667	.23071	.20756	.18691	.16846
13	.32618	.28966	.25751	.22917	.20416	.18207	.16253	.14523
14	.29925	.26333	.23199	.20462	.18068	.15971	.14133	.12520
15	.27454	.23939	.20900	.18270	.15989	.14010	.12289	.10793
16	.25187	.21763	.18829	.16312	.14150	.12289	.10686	.09304
17	.23107	.19784	.16963	.14564	.12522	.10780	.09293	.08021
18	.21199	.17986	.15282	.13004	.11081	.09456	.08080	.06914
19	.19449	.16351	.13768	.11611	.09806	.08295	.07026	.05961
20	.17843	.14864	.12403	.10367	.08678	.07276	.06110	.05139
21	.16370	.13513	.11174	.09256	.07680	.06383	.05313	.04430
22	.15018	.12285	.10067	.08264	.06796	.05599	.04620	.03819
23	.13778	.11168	.09069	.07379	.06014	.04911	.04017	.03292
24	.12640	.10153	.08170	.06588	.05322	.04308	.03493	.02838
25	.11597	.09230	.07361	.05882	.04710	.03779	.03038	.02447

N	17%	18%	19%	20%	21%	22%	23%	24%
1	0.85470	0.84746	0.84034	0.83333	0.82645	0.81967	0.81301	0.80645
2	.73051	.71818	.70616	.69444	.68301	.67186	.66098	.65036
3	.62437	.60863	.59342	.57870	.56447	.55071	.53738	.52449
4	.53365	.51579	.49867	.48225	.46651	.45140	.43690	.42297
5	.45611	.43711	.41905	.40188	.38554	.37000	.35520	.34111
6	.38984	.37043	.35214	.33490	.31863	.30328	.28878	.27509
7	.33320	.31392	.29592	.27908	.26333	.24859	.23478	.22184
8	.28478	.26604	.24867	.23257	.21763	.20376	.19088	.17891
9	.24340	.22546	.20897	.19381	.17986	.16702	.15519	.14428
10	.20804	.19106	.17560	.16151	.14864	.13690	.12617	.11635
11	.17781	.16192	.14756	.13459	.12285	.11221	.10258	.09383
12	.15197	.13722	.12400	.11216	.10153	.09198	.08339	.07567
13	.12989	.11629	.10420	.09346	.08391	.07539	.06780	.06103
14	.11102	.09855	.08757	.07789	.06934	.06180	.05512	.04921
15	.09489	.08352	.07359	.06491	.05731	.05065	.04481	.03969
16	.08110	.07078	.06184	.05409	.04736	.04152	.03643	.03201
17	.06932	.05998	.05196	.04507	.03914	.03403	.02962	.02581
18	.05925	.05083	.04367	.03756	.03235	.02789	.02408	.02082
19	.05064	.04308	.03669	.03130	.02673	.02286	.01958	.01679
20	.04328	.03651	.03084	.02608	.02209	.01874	.01592	.01354
21	.03699	.03094	.02591	.02174	.01826	.01536	.01294	.01092
22	.03162	.02622	.02178	.01811	.01509	.01259	.01052	.00880
23	.02702	.02222	.01830	.01509	.01247	.01032	.00855	.00710
24	.02310	.01883	.01538	.01258	.01031	.00846	.00695	.00573
25	.01974	.01596	.01292	.01048	.00852	.00693	.00565	.00462

N	25%	26%	27%	28%	29%	30%	31%	32%
1	0.80000	0.79365	0.78740	0.78125	0.77519	0.76923	0.76336	0.75758
2	.64000	.62988	.62000	.61035	.60093	.59172	.58272	.57392
3	.51200	.49991	.48819	.47684	.46583	.45517	.44482	.43479
4	.40960	.39675	.38440	.37253	.36111	.35013	.33956	.32939
5	.32768	.31488	.30268	.29104	.27993	.26933	.25920	.24953
6	.26214	.24991	.23833	.22737	.21700	.20718	.19787	.18904
7	.20972	.19834	.18766	.17764	.16822	.15937	.15104	.14321
8	.16777	.15741	.14776	.13878	.13040	.12259	.11530	.10849
9	.13422	.12493	.11635	.10842	.10109	.09430	.08802	.08219
10	.10737	.09915	.09161	.08470	.07836	.07254	.06719	.06227
11	.08590	.07869	.07214	.06617	.06075	.05580	.05129	.04717
12	.06872	.06245	.05680	.05170	.04709	.04292	.03915	.03574
13	.05498	.04957	.04472	.04039	.03650	.03302	.02989	.02707
14	.04398	.03934	.03522	.03155	.02830	.02540	.02281	.02051
15	.03518	.03122	.02773	.02465	.02194	.01954	.01742	.01554
16	.02815	.02478	.02183	.01926	.01700	.01503	.01329	.01177
17	.02252	.01967	.01719	.01505	.01318	.01156	.01015	.00892
18	.01801	.01561	.01354	.01175	.01022	.00889	.00775	.00676
19	.01441	.01239	.01066	.00918	.00792	.00684	.00591	.00512
20	.01153	.00983	.00839	.00717	.00614	.00526	.00451	.00388
21	.00922	.00780	.00661	.00561	.00476	.00405	.00345	.00294
22	.00738	.00619	.00520	.00438	.00369	.00311	.00263	.00223
23	.00590	.00491	.00410	.00342	.00286	.00239	.00201	.00169
24	.00472	.00390	.00323	.00267	.00222	.00184	.00153	.00128
25	.00378	.00310	.00254	.00209	.00172	.00142	.00117	.00097

Table C: Future Value of an Annuity

INTEREST FACTORS $W = R \left[\dfrac{(1 + i)^n - 1}{i} \right]$ FOR CALCULATING W,

FUTURE VALUE OF AN ANNUITY

N	1%	2%	3%	4%	5%	6%	7%	8%
1	1.000	1.000	1.000	1.000	1.000	1.000	1.000	1.000
2	2.010	2.020	2.030	2.040	2.050	2.060	2.070	2.080
3	3.030	3.060	3.091	3.122	3.153	3.184	3.215	3.246
4	4.060	4.122	4.184	4.246	4.310	4.375	4.440	4.506
5	5.101	5.204	5.309	5.416	5.526	5.637	5.751	5.867
6	6.152	6.308	6.468	6.633	6.802	6.975	7.153	7.336
7	7.214	7.434	7.662	7.898	8.142	8.394	8.654	8.923
8	8.286	8.583	8.892	9.214	9.549	9.897	10.260	10.637
9	9.369	9.755	10.159	10.583	11.027	11.491	11.978	12.488
10	10.462	10.950	11.464	12.006	12.578	13.181	13.817	14.487
11	11.567	12.169	12.808	13.486	14.207	14.972	15.784	16.646
12	12.683	13.412	14.192	15.026	15.917	16.870	17.889	18.977
13	13.809	14.680	15.618	16.627	17.713	18.882	20.141	21.495
14	14.947	15.974	17.086	18.292	19.599	21.015	22.551	24.215
15	16.097	17.293	18.599	20.024	21.579	23.276	25.129	27.152
16	17.258	18.639	20.157	21.825	23.658	25.673	27.888	30.324
17	18.430	20.012	21.762	23.698	25.840	28.213	30.840	33.750
18	19.615	21.412	23.414	25.645	28.132	30.906	33.999	37.450
19	20.811	22.841	25.117	27.671	30.539	33.760	37.379	41.446
20	22.019	24.297	26.870	29.778	33.066	36.786	40.996	45.762
21	23.239	25.783	28.677	31.969	35.719	39.993	44.865	50.423
22	24.472	27.299	30.537	34.248	38.505	43.392	49.006	55.457
23	25.716	28.845	32.453	36.618	41.430	46.996	53.436	60.893
24	26.974	30.422	34.427	39.083	44.502	50.816	58.177	66.765
25	28.243	32.030	36.459	41.646	47.727	54.864	63.249	73.106

N	9%	10%	11%	12%	14%	16%	18%	20%
1	1.000	1.000	1.000	1.000	1.000	1.000	1.000	1.000
2	2.090	2.100	2.110	2.120	2.140	2.160	2.180	2.200
3	3.278	3.310	3.342	3.374	3.440	3.506	3.572	3.640
4	4.573	4.641	4.710	4.779	4.921	5.066	5.215	5.368
5	5.985	6.105	6.228	6.353	6.610	6.877	7.154	7.442
6	7.523	7.716	7.913	8.115	8.536	8.977	9.442	9.930
7	9.200	9.487	9.783	10.089	10.731	11.414	12.142	12.916
8	11.029	11.436	11.859	12.300	13.233	14.240	15.327	16.499
9	13.021	13.580	14.164	14.776	16.085	17.519	19.086	20.799
10	15.193	15.937	16.722	17.549	19.337	21.322	23.521	25.959
11	17.560	18.531	19.561	20.655	23.045	25.733	28.755	32.150
12	20.141	21.384	22.713	24.133	27.271	30.850	34.931	39.581
13	22.953	24.523	26.212	28.029	32.089	36.786	42.219	48.497
14	26.019	27.975	30.095	32.393	37.581	43.672	50.818	59.196
15	29.361	31.773	34.405	37.280	43.842	51.660	60.965	72.035
16	33.003	35.950	39.190	42.753	50.980	60.925	72.939	87.442
17	36.974	40.545	44.501	48.884	59.118	71.673	87.068	105.931
18	41.301	45.599	50.396	55.750	68.394	84.141	103.740	128.117
19	46.019	51.159	56.940	63.440	78.969	98.603	123.413	154.740
20	51.160	57.275	64.203	72.052	91.025	115.380	146.628	186.688
21	56.765	64.003	72.265	81.699	104.768	134.840	174.021	225.026
22	62.873	71.403	81.214	92.503	120.436	157.415	206.345	271.031
23	69.532	79.543	91.148	104.603	138.297	183.601	244.487	326.237
24	76.790	88.497	102.174	118.155	158.659	213.977	289.494	392.404
25	84.701	98.347	114.413	133.334	181.871	249.214	342.603	471.981

N	22%	24%	26%	28%	30%	32%	34%	36%
1	1.000	1.000	1.000	1.000	1.000	1.000	1.000	1.000
2	2.220	2.240	2.260	2.280	2.300	2.320	2.340	2.360
3	3.708	3.778	3.848	3.918	3.990	4.062	4.136	4.210
4	5.524	5.684	5.848	6.016	6.187	6.362	6.542	6.725
5	7.740	8.048	8.368	8.700	9.043	9.398	9.766	10.146
6	10.442	10.980	11.544	12.136	12.756	13.406	14.086	14.799
7	13.740	14.615	15.546	16.534	17.583	18.696	19.876	21.126
8	17.762	19.123	20.588	22.163	23.858	25.678	27.633	29.732
9	22.670	24.713	26.940	29.369	32.015	34.895	38.029	41.435
10	28.657	31.643	34.945	38.593	42.620	47.062	51.958	57.352
11	35.962	40.238	45.031	50.399	56.405	63.122	70.624	78.998
12	44.874	50.895	57.739	65.510	74.327	84.321	95.637	108.438
13	55.746	64.110	73.751	84.853	97.625	112.303	129.153	148.475
14	69.010	80.496	93.926	109.612	127.912	149.240	174.065	202.926
15	85.192	100.815	119.347	141.303	167.286	197.997	234.247	276.979
16	104.935	126.011	151.377	181.868	218.472	262.356	314.891	377.692
17	129.020	157.253	191.735	233.791	285.014	347.310	422.954	514.661
18	158.405	195.994	242.586	300.252	371.518	459.449	567.758	700.939
19	194.254	244.033	306.658	385.323	483.973	607.473	761.796	954.278
20	237.989	303.601	387.389	494.213	630.165	802.864	1021.810	1298.820
21	291.347	377.465	489.110	633.592	820.214	1060.780	1370.220	1767.390
22	356.444	469.057	617.278	811.998	1067.280	1401.230	1837.100	2404.650
23	435.861	582.630	778.771	1040.360	1388.460	1850.620	2462.710	3271.330
24	532.751	723.461	982.251	1332.660	1806.000	2443.820	3301.030	4450.010
25	650.956	898.092	1238.640	1706.800	2348.800	3226.850	4424.380	6053.010

Table D: Present Value of an Annuity

INTEREST FACTORS $B = R\left[\dfrac{1 - (1 + i)^{-n}}{i}\right]$ FOR CALCULATING B,

PRESENT VALUE OF AN ANNUITY

Year	1%	2%	3%	4%	5%	6%	7%	8%
1	0.9901	0.9804	0.9709	0.9615	0.9524	0.9434	0.9346	0.9259
2	1.9704	1.9416	1.9135	1.8861	1.8594	1.8334	1.8080	1.7833
3	2.9410	2.8839	2.8286	2.7751	2.7232	2.6730	2.6243	2.5771
4	3.9020	3.8077	3.7171	3.6299	3.5459	3.4651	3.3872	3.3121
5	4.8535	4.7134	4.5797	4.4518	4.3295	4.2123	4.1002	3.9927
6	5.7955	5.6014	5.4172	5.2421	5.0757	4.9173	4.7665	4.6229
7	6.7282	6.4720	6.2302	6.0020	5.7863	5.5824	5.3893	5.2064
8	7.6517	7.3254	7.0196	6.7327	6.4632	6.2098	5.9713	5.7466
9	8.5661	8.1622	7.7861	7.4353	7.1078	6.8017	6.5152	6.2469
10	9.4714	8.9825	8.5302	8.1109	7.7217	7.3601	7.0236	6.7101
11	10.3677	9.7868	9.2526	8.7604	8.3064	7.8868	7.4987	7.1389
12	11.2552	10.5753	9.9539	9.3850	8.8632	8.3838	7.9427	7.5361
13	12.1338	11.3483	10.6349	9.9856	9.3935	8.8527	8.3576	7.9038
14	13.0038	12.1062	11.2960	10.5631	9.8986	9.2950	8.7454	8.2442
15	13.8651	12.8492	11.9379	11.1183	10.3796	9.7122	9.1079	8.5595
16	14.7180	13.5777	12.5610	11.6522	10.8377	10.1059	9.4466	8.8514
17	15.5624	14.2918	13.1660	12.1656	11.2740	10.4772	9.7632	9.1216
18	16.3984	14.9920	13.7534	12.6592	11.6895	10.8276	10.0591	9.3719
19	17.2261	15.6784	14.3237	13.1339	12.0853	11.1581	10.3356	9.6036
20	18.0457	16.3514	14.8774	13.5903	12.4622	11.4699	10.5940	9.8181
21	18.8571	17.0111	15.4149	14.0291	12.8211	11.7640	10.8355	10.0168
22	19.6605	17.6580	15.9368	14.4511	13.1630	12.0416	11.0612	10.2007
23	20.4559	18.2921	16.4435	14.8568	13.4885	12.3033	11.2722	10.3710
24	21.2435	18.9139	16.9355	15.2469	13.7986	12.5503	11.4693	10.5287
25	22.0233	19.5234	17.4131	15.6220	14.0939	12.7833	11.6536	10.6748

Year	9%	10%	11%	12%	13%	14%	15%	16%
1	0.9174	0.9091	0.9009	0.8929	0.8850	0.8772	0.8696	0.8621
2	1.7591	1.7355	1.7125	1.6901	1.6681	1.6467	1.6257	1.6052
3	2.5313	2.4868	2.4437	2.4018	2.3612	2.3216	2.2832	2.2459
4	3.2397	3.1699	3.1024	3.0373	2.9745	2.9137	2.8550	2.7982
5	3.8896	3.7908	3.6959	3.6048	3.5172	3.4331	3.3522	3.2743
6	4.4859	4.3553	4.2305	4.1114	3.9976	3.8887	3.7845	3.6847
7	5.0329	4.8684	4.7122	4.5638	4.4226	4.2883	4.1604	4.0386
8	5.5348	5.3349	5.1461	4.9676	4.7988	4.6389	4.4873	4.3436
9	5.9852	5.7590	5.5370	5.3282	5.1317	4.9464	4.7716	4.6065
10	6.4176	6.1446	5.8892	5.6502	5.4262	5.2161	5.0188	4.8332
11	6.8052	6.4951	6.2065	5.9377	5.6869	5.4527	5.2337	5.0286
12	7.1607	6.8137	6.4924	6.1944	5.9176	5.6603	5.4206	5.1971
13	7.4869	7.1034	6.7499	6.4235	6.1218	5.8424	5.5831	5.3423
14	7.7861	7.3667	6.9819	6.6282	6.3025	6.0021	5.7245	5.4675
15	8.0607	7.6061	7.1909	6.8109	6.4624	6.1422	5.8474	5.5755
16	8.3125	7.8237	7.3792	6.9740	6.6039	6.2651	5.9542	5.6685
17	8.5436	8.0215	7.5488	7.1196	6.7291	6.3729	6.0472	5.7487
18	8.7556	8.2014	7.7016	7.2497	6.8399	6.4674	6.1280	5.8178
19	8.9501	8.3649	7.8393	7.3658	6.9380	6.5504	6.1982	5.8775
20	9.1285	8.5136	7.9633	7.4694	7.0248	6.6231	6.2593	5.9288
21	9.2922	8.6487	8.0751	7.5620	7.1016	6.6870	6.3125	5.9731
22	9.4424	8.7715	8.1757	7.6446	7.1695	6.7429	6.3587	6.0113
23	9.5802	8.8832	8.2664	7.7184	7.2297	6.7921	6.3988	6.0442
24	9.7066	8.9847	8.3481	7.7843	7.2829	6.8351	6.4338	6.0726
25	9.8226	9.0770	8.4217	7.8431	7.3300	6.8729	6.4641	6.0971

Year	17%	18%	19%	20%	21%	22%	23%	24%
1	0.8547	0.8475	0.8403	0.8333	0.8264	0.8197	0.8130	0.8065
2	1.5852	1.5656	1.5465	1.5278	1.5095	1.4915	1.4740	1.4568
3	2.2096	2.1743	2.1399	2.1065	2.0739	2.0422	2.0114	1.9813
4	2.7432	2.6901	2.6386	2.5887	2.5404	2.4936	2.4483	2.4043
5	3.1993	3.1272	3.0576	2.9906	2.9260	2.8636	2.8035	2.7454
6	3.5892	3.4976	3.4098	3.3255	3.2446	3.1669	3.0923	3.0205
7	3.9224	3.8115	3.7057	3.6046	3.5079	3.4155	3.3270	3.2423
8	4.2072	4.0776	3.9544	3.8372	3.7256	3.6193	3.5179	3.4212
9	4.4506	4.3030	4.1633	4.0310	3.9054	3.7863	3.6731	3.5655
10	4.6586	4.4941	4.3389	4.1925	4.0541	3.9232	3.7993	3.6819
11	4.8364	4.6560	4.4865	4.3271	4.1769	4.0354	3.9018	3.7757
12	4.9884	4.7932	4.6105	4.4392	4.2785	4.1274	3.9852	3.8514
13	5.1183	4.9095	4.7147	4.5327	4.3624	4.2028	4.0530	3.9124
14	5.2293	5.0081	4.8023	4.6106	4.4317	4.2646	4.1082	3.9616
15	5.3242	5.0916	4.8759	4.6755	4.4890	4.3152	4.1530	4.0013
16	5.4053	5.1624	4.9377	4.7296	4.5364	4.3567	4.1894	4.0333
17	5.4746	5.2223	4.9897	4.7746	4.5755	4.3908	4.2190	4.0591
18	5.5339	5.2732	5.0333	4.8122	4.6079	4.4187	4.2431	4.0799
19	5.5845	5.3162	5.0700	4.8435	4.6346	4.4415	4.2627	4.0967
20	5.6278	5.3527	5.1009	4.8696	4.6567	4.4603	4.2786	4.1103
21	5.6648	5.3837	5.1268	4.8913	4.6750	4.4756	4.2916	4.1212
22	5.6964	5.4099	5.1486	4.9094	4.6900	4.4882	4.3021	4.1300
23	5.7234	5.4321	5.1668	4.9245	4.7025	4.4985	4.3106	4.1371
24	5.7465	5.4509	5.1822	4.9371	4.7128	4.5070	4.3176	4.1428
25	5.7662	5.4669	5.1951	4.9476	4.7213	4.5139	4.3232	4.1474

Year	25%	26%	27%	28%	29%	30%	31%	32%
1	0.8000	0.7937	0.7874	0.7813	0.7752	0.7692	0.7634	0.7576
2	1.4400	1.4235	1.4074	1.3916	1.3761	1.3609	1.3461	1.3315
3	1.9520	1.9234	1.8956	1.8684	1.8420	1.8161	1.7909	1.7663
4	2.3616	2.3202	2.2800	2.2410	2.2031	2.1662	2.1305	2.0957
5	2.6893	2.6351	2.5827	2.5320	2.4830	2.4356	2.3897	2.3452
6	2.9514	2.8850	2.8210	2.7594	2.7000	2.6427	2.5875	2.5342
7	3.1611	3.0833	3.0087	2.9370	2.8682	2.8021	2.7386	2.6775
8	3.3289	3.2407	3.1564	3.0758	2.9986	2.9247	2.8539	2.7860
9	3.4631	3.3657	3.2728	3.1842	3.0997	3.0190	2.9419	2.8681
10	3.5705	3.4648	3.3644	3.2689	3.1781	3.0915	3.0091	2.9304
11	3.6564	3.5435	3.4365	3.3351	3.2388	3.1473	3.0604	2.9776
12	3.7251	3.6060	3.4933	3.3868	3.2859	3.1903	3.0995	3.0133
13	3.7801	3.6555	3.6381	3.4272	3.3224	3.2233	3.1294	3.0404
14	3.8241	3.6949	3.5733	3.4587	3.3507	3.2487	3.1522	3.0609
15	3.8593	3.7261	3.6010	3.4834	3.3726	3.2682	3.1696	3.0764
16	3.8874	3.7509	3.6228	3.5026	3.3896	3.2832	3.1829	3.0882
17	3.9099	3.7705	3.6400	3.5177	3.4028	3.2948	3.1931	3.0971
18	3.9279	3.7861	3.6536	3.5294	3.4130	3.3037	3.2008	3.1039
19	3.9424	3.7985	3.6642	3.5386	3.4210	3.3105	3.2067	3.1090
20	3.9539	3.8083	3.6726	3.5458	3.4271	3.3158	3.2112	3.1129
21	3.9631	3.8161	3.6792	3.5514	3.4319	3.3198	3.2147	3.1158
22	3.9705	3.8223	3.6844	3.5558	3.4356	3.3230	3.2173	3.1180
23	3.9764	3.8273	3.6885	3.5592	3.4384	3.3254	3.2193	3.1197
24	3.9811	3.8312	3.6918	3.5619	3.4406	3.3272	3.2209	3.1210
25	3.9849	3.8342	3.6943	3.5640	3.4423	3.3286	3.2220	3.1220

Glossary

Accountable: Manager who accepts responsibility for realizing the objectives and plans and reporting the extend of accomplishments.

Accounting: Process of recording and summarizing business transactions on a company's financial statements.

Accounting cycle: Steps involved in processing financial transactions for preparing financial statements.

Accounting equation: Assets = Liabilities + Equity *or* Assets – Liabilities = Equity

Accounting methods: Calculation of the book value rate of return by using data presented on financial statements.

Accrual method: Accounting method that considers sales when made and expenses when incurred, regardless of when the transactions take place.

Activity-based costing: Accounting system that focuses on the analysis of overhead costs to determine how they relate to different products, services, or activities.

Administrative expenses: Expenses that are not directly related to producing and selling goods or services.

Aging of accounts receivable: A report showing how long accounts receivable have been outstanding. It gives the percentage of receivables past due for one month, two months, or other periods.

Amortization: A tax-deductible expense that applies to intangible assets such as goodwill and trademarks.

Annuity: A series of payments (or receipts) of fixed amount for a specified number of years.

Assessed value: Method used by municipal governments for determining the level of property taxes.

Asset valuation: Methodology used to restate the numbers appearing on financial statements.

Asset-management ratios: A calculation that evaluates how efficiently managers use the assets of a business.

Assets: Resources that a business owns to produce goods and services (e.g., cash, accounts receivable, buildings).

Auditor's report: Report prepared by an independent accounting firm that is presented to a company's shareholders.

Average collection period: The number of days customers take to pay their bills.

Balance sheet: Financial statement that shows a "snapshot" of a company's financial condition (assets, liabilities, and equity).

Benchmarking: Process of searching for the best practices by comparing oneself to a competitor's excellent performance.

Benchmarks: Excellent industry norms to which one's own financial ratios can be compared.

Bond: Long-term loan that can be secured or unsecured (20 to 30 years).

Book value: The accounting value of an asset (the original cost minus total depreciation deductions made to date). This is shown on the financial statements as a firm's assets.

Bookkeeping: Activity that involves collecting, classifying, and reporting accounting transactions.

Break-even chart: Graphic that shows the effect of change in both revenue and costs on profitability.

Break-even point: Level of production where sales revenue equals total costs.

Break-even wedge: Method that helps managers determine the most appropriate way of structuring operating costs (fixed versus variable).

Budgeting: Process by which management allocates corporate resources, evaluates financial outcomes, and establishes system to control operational and financial performance.

Business risk: The uncertainty inherent in projecting the level of sales revenue and income.

C's of credit: Factors that banks consider to gauge the creditworthiness of a business: character, collateral, capacity, capital, circumstances, coverage.

Capital assets: Balance sheet accounts such as land, buildings, equipment, and machinery.

Capital assets turnover: Measures how intensively a firm's capital assets are used to generate sales.

Capital budget: Budget that shows how much will be spent for the purchase of capital assets.

Capital cost allowance: A tax deduction that Canadian tax laws allow a business to claim for the loss in value of capital assets due to wear and tear and/or obsolescence.

Capital investment: Project that requires extensive financial resources (cash outflow) made for the purpose of generating a return (cash inflow).

Capital structure: The permanent financing sources used to buy capital assets.

Cash: Holdings and short-term deposits.

Cash break-even point: Number of units or sales revenue that must be reached in order to cover total cash fixed costs (total fixed costs less depreciation).

Cash budget: A treasury function that determines the cash flow of business at the micro level to determine the level of liquidity.

Cash conversion cycle: Periodic transformation of cash through working capital and capital assets and back to cash.

Cash conversion efficiency: Ratio that measures how quickly a business converts sales revenue into cash within its operations.

Cash flow: Sum of the income after taxes plus depreciation.

Cash inflow: The receipt of money generated by sales revenue less expenses.

Cash insufficiency: Not enough cash generated by a capital project to pay for fixed charges.

Cash method: Accounting method of recording business transactions when sales are made and expenses incurred.

Cash outflow: Cash disbursements for the purchase of assets.

Categories of performance standards: There are four categories of standards: time, output, cost, and quality.

Categories of ratios: Balance sheet ratios, income statement ratios, combined ratios.

Categories of responsibility centres: Revenue, cost, profit, and investment centre.

Characteristics of long-term financing sources: Factors to consider when raising funds from long-term sources are payout, risk, voting rights, cost of capital, tax cost, and cost of issue.

Chart of accounts: A set of categories by which accounting transactions are recorded.

Chartered bank: An institution responsible for receiving, lending, and safeguarding money and transactions of individuals and businesses.

Collateral value: An assessment by lenders of the value of a particular asset taken as a guarantee for a loan.

Combined leverage: Financial technique used to calculate both operating and financial leverage.

Committed fixed costs: Costs that must be incurred in order to operate a business.

Common-size ratios: Method of reducing (1) all numbers on the balance sheet to a percentage of total assets and (2) all numbers on the income statement to a percentage of sales revenue.

Common-size statement analysis: Method of converting (1) all numbers on the balance sheet to a percentage of total assets and (2) all numbers on the income statement to a percentage of sales revenue.

Complementary budgets: Budgets that complement operating budgets whereby data is presented differently and in more detail.

Compound interest: Interest rate that is applicable on the initial principal and the accumulated interest of prior periods. Compounding is the process of determining the final value of payments when compound interest is applied.

Comprehensive budgets: Projected financial statements such as the income statement, the balance sheet, and the statement of cash flows.

Compulsory investment: Investments made in capital assets that do not require in-depth analytical studies.

Conditional sales contract: Agreement made between a buyer and a seller regarding the purchase of an asset (e.g., truck).

Confirming institution: Organization that finances inventory.

Consecutive balance sheets: Balance sheets from consecutive periods show whether a change in each account is a source or a use.

Contribution margin: The difference between sales revenue and variable costs.

Controllable costs: Costs for which operating managers are accountable.

Controller: Person responsible for establishing the accounting and financial reporting policies and procedures of a business.

Cost accounting: Accounting system that provides information to managers to make informed decisions.

Cost of borrowed funds: Effective after-tax cost of raising funds from different sources (lenders and shareholders).

Cost of capital: The cost of borrowing funds from investors (creditors and shareholders) to finance a business.

Cost of common shares: Includes dividends paid to shareholders, flotation costs, and growth rate.

Cost of debt: Interest charges less income taxes.

Cost of financing: How much it costs (%) a business to finance all assets shown on a company's balance sheet

Cost of goods sold: Cost incurred in making or producing goods that are sold.

Cost of preferred shares: Includes fixed dividends paid to shareholders and the flotation costs.

Cost of retained earnings: Includes dividends and growth rate.

Cost-volume-profit analysis: Tool used for analyzing how volume, price, product mix, and product costs relate to one another.

Credit: Accounting entries recorded on the right side of an account.

Credit insurance policy: Insurance to cover losses suffered from a firm's accounts receivable that become uncollectible.

Credit policies: Decisions about the extent of credit that should be extended to customers.

Credit terms: Conditions under which credit is extended, especially how quickly the customer is expected to pay the account.

Credit-scoring system: System used to analyze the creditworthiness of potential customers.

Current assets: Balance sheet accounts such as cash, accounts receivable, and inventory.

Current liabilities: Debts that a business must pay within one year (i.e., accounts payable).

Current ratio: Gauges general business liquidity.

Current-value accounting: Accounting method used to restate assets on financial statements in terms of what they would be worth if purchased.

Days of working capital: The number of days of working capital a business holds to meet average daily sales requirements.

Debit: Accounting entries recorded on the left side of an account.

Debt/coverage ratios: Measures the capital structure of a business and its debt-paying ability.

Debt-to-equity ratio: Measures the proportion of debt used compared to equity to finance all assets.

Debt-to-total-assets ratio: Measures how much debt a business uses to finance all assets.

Deferred taxes: Future tax liability resulting from the difference between depreciation and capital cost allowance.

Demassing: Recession-driven technique to remove management layers from organizational charts to cut costs.

Depreciation: Estimated decrease in the value of capital assets due to wear and tear and/or obsolescence.

Direct costs: Materials and labour expenses that are directly incurred when making a product.

Discounted payback: The number of years required for a capital investment to generate enough discounted cash inflow to cover the initial cash outflow.

Discounting: The process of finding the present value of a series of future cash flows.

Discretionary fixed costs: Costs that can be controlled by managers.

Double-entry bookkeeping: System for posting financial transactions so that the accounting equation remains in balance.

Du Pont Financial System: Presentation of financial ratios in a logical way to measure return on investment (ROI).

Earnings per share: Measures how much net income is available to each outstanding share.

Economic life: Number of years that a capital asset or investment opportunity will last.

Economic ordering quantity (EOQ): Method that determines the optimum quantity of goods that should be ordered at any single time.

Economic value: Valuation method used to determine the ability or capacity of an asset to generate cash.

Economic value added (EVA): Tool that measures the wealth a company creates for its investors. It is calculated by deducting a company's cost of capital from its net operating profits after taxes (NOPAT).

Efficiency: The relationship between profits (outputs) generated and assets employed (inputs).

Expense investment: A fully tax-deductible cost that should produce favourable effects on the profit performance.

External financing: Funds obtained from investors (long-term lenders and shareholders).

Factoring: Selling accounts receivable to a financial institution.

Feedback controls: System that helps to focus on variations of past performance.

Financial benchmarks: Financial performance ratios that can be calculated by using dollar figures shown on financial statements (income statement and balance sheet) for the purpose of pinpointing excellent financial performance.

Financial health score: Linear analysis where five measures are objectively weighted to give an overall score that becomes the basis for classifying the financial health of a business.

Financial lease: Mutually agreed commitment by a lessor and a lessee for a specified period of time.

Financial leverage: Financial technique used to determine the most favourable capital structure (debt versus equity).

Financial management: Activity involved in raising funds and buying assets in order to obtain the highest possible return.

Financial needs: The items for which a business needs money.

Financial ratio: Comparison or relationship between numbers shown on financial statements.

Financial risk: The way that a business is financed (debt versus shares).

Financial statements: Financial reports, which include the income statement, the statement of retained earnings, the balance sheet, and the statement of changes in financial position.

Financial structure: Shows the way a company's assets are financed by the entire right-hand side of the balance sheet (short-term and long-term financing).

Financing activities: That portion of the statement of changes in financial position that shows how much cash was provided (or used) from external sources (e.g., sale of shares, borrowing or repaying a mortgage, payment of dividends).

Financing decisions: Decisions related to borrowing from lenders and shareholders.

Financing mix: Proportion of funds raised from lenders and shareholders.

Financing requirements: Where the money will come from (shareholders and lenders) to finance a business.

Fixed costs: Costs that remain constant at varying levels of production.

Fixed-charges coverage ratio: Measures to what extent a business can service all its fixed charges (e.g., interest, leases).

Float: The amount of funds tied up in cheques that have been written but are still in process and have not yet been collected.

Forms of financing: Financing instruments used to buy assets (e.g., term loan).

Funds flow: The procurement (source) or allocation (use) of funds.

Future value: The amount to which a payment or series of payments will grow by a given future date when compounded by a given interest rate.

Generally accepted accounting principles (GAAP): A broad set of rules delineating how various transactions will be reported on financial statements.

Goal of working capital management: To accelerate the cash flow cycle in a business after sales have been made.

Government financing: Funds obtained (directly or indirectly) from government institutions to finance a business.

Gross margin: Difference between sales revenue and cost of goods sold.

Hard financial benchmarks: Financial targets that can be applied to any business or industry to gauge financial performance.

Holding costs: Category of costs associated with the storing of goods in inventory (e.g., insurance, rent).

Horizontal statement analysis: Shows percentage change of accounts on two consecutive financial statements.

Hurdle rate: Capital budgeting technique used to rank the financial desirability of capital projects according to their cost of capital.

Income: The excess of revenues over expenses.

Income after taxes: Difference between operating income and other expenses (e.g., interest charges), including income taxes.

Income statement: Financial statement that shows a summary of revenues and expenses for a specified period of time.

Indemnification policy: Insurance a business takes against a catastrophic loss in cash.

Indirect costs: Costs that are necessary in the production cycle but that cannot be clearly allocated to specific products or services.

Industry multipliers: A standard used to determine the value of a business.

Inflation: A price rise characteristic of periods of prosperity.

Instrument risk: The quality of security available to satisfy investors.

Intangible assets: Items that are not tangible but represent some value to a business (e.g., trademarks, patents).

Interest tables: Numbers found in compound or discount interest and annuity tables.

Interim financing: Loan made to a business to help finance a capital project, such as the construction of a new plant, until regular financing is obtained.

Internal financing: Funds obtained from retained earnings, depreciation, and a reduction in working capital accounts.

Internal rate of return (IRR): The specific interest rate used to discount all future cash inflows so that their present value equals the initial cash outflows.

Internal sources: Funds generated by a business (e.g., profit, depreciation).

Inventory replenishment: Decision related to when to order goods from supplier.

Inventory turnover: The number of times a year a company turns over its inventory.

Investing activities: That portion of the statement of changes in financial position that shows how much cash was provided (or used) to buy or sell assets (e.g., purchase or sale of a building).

Investing decisions: Decisions related to the acquisition of assets (current and capital).

Investment securities: Funds invested in short-term deposits such as treasury bills, bank deposits, etc.

Investments: Assets such as bonds and shares purchased from other businesses.

Job-order costing: Accounting system that helps to allocate direct costs related to producing a specific good.

Journalizing: Process of recording transactions in a journal (e.g., sales journal, salaries journal).

Just-in-time inventory management: An inventory management technique that obtains supplier materials just when they are needed.

Labour variance: Variance in costs between standards and actual performance due to changes in the amount of time and rate used to make a product.

Lessee: One who pays to use an asset without owning it.

Lessor: One who leases an asset to someone (lessee).

Leverage: Technique used to determine the most suitable operating and financial structure that will help amplify financial performance.

Liabilities: The debts of a business.

Line of credit: A formal or written agreement between a bank and a borrower regarding a loan.

Liquidation value: Worth of an asset if sold.

Liquidity: Ability of a firm to meet its short-term financial obligations.

Liquidity ratios: Measure the ability of a firm to meet its cash obligations.

Long-term debts: Debts that are not due for at least one year.

Long-term loan: Loan to finance capital assets for a long period of time (over five years).

Marginal cost of capital: The increased level of average cost resulting from having borrowed new funds at higher rates than those previously borrowed.

Market performance: Method used for gauging the efficiency and effectiveness of management within the industry in which it operates.

Market value: The price at which an item, business, or asset can be sold.

Market-value ratios: Measurement tools to gauge the way investors react to a company's market performance.

Matching principle: Process of selecting the most appropriate financing source when buying an asset.

Material requirements planning (MRP): Method for developing a schedule to help coordinate and utilize resources in production.

Material variance: Variance in costs between standards and actual performance due to changes in quantity of materials used and changes in the price of the materials used.

Mortgage: Loan obtained against which specific real property is used as collateral (e.g., building).

Net change in noncash working capital accounts: The cash flow provided (or used) by working capital accounts such as accounts receivable, inventory, and accounts payable.

Net future value: Difference between two sums that are compounded into the future.

Net present value (NPV): The present value of the future cash flow of an investment, less the initial cash outflow.

Net sales: What a business earns for the sale of its products and/or services.

Net working capital: The difference between current assets and current liabilities.

Noncontrollable costs: Costs that are not under the direct control of operating managers.

Nonoperating section: Section of the income statement that shows income or expenses that are not directly related to the principal activities of a business (e.g., interest income, extraordinary expenses, nonrecurring items).

Operating activities: The portion of the statement of changes in financial position that shows how much cash was provided (or used) from internal sources (e.g., income after taxes, depreciation).

Operating budgets: Budgets prepared by operating managers.

Operating decisions: Decisions related to accounts appearing on the income statement (e.g., sales revenue, cost of goods sold, selling expenses).

Operating income: Difference between gross margin and operating expenses.

Operating lease: A lease that can be cancelled by the lessee at any time upon due notice.

Operating leverage: Financial technique used to determine to what extent fixed costs are used relative to variable costs.

Operating manager: Person in charge of organizational units such as marketing, manufacturing, or human resources, and responsible for making operating and investing decisions.

Operating performance: Method used for gauging the efficiency and effectiveness of management at the operating level (e.g., marketing, production).

Operating section: Section of the income statement that shows a company's gross margin and operating income.

Opportunity cost: The income sacrificed by not pursuing the next best alternative.

Opportunity investment: Investments made in capital assets that are of a strategic nature and usually have far-reaching financial implications.

Ordering costs: Category of costs associated with the acquisition of goods (e.g., receiving, inspecting, accounting).

Overall performance: Ratios used to measure how well a business is deploying its resources.

Overhead variance: Variance in costs between standards and actual performance due to changes in indirect costs.

Owners' section: Section of the income statement that shows the amount of money left to the shareholders (i.e., income after taxes).

Payback period: The number of years required for a capital investment to generate enough undiscounted cash inflow to just cover the initial cash outflow.

Payback reciprocal: Capital budgeting technique that gives a rough estimate of the return on investment of a capital project.

Performance indicator: How an organizational unit should be measured.

Performance standards: Quantitative measurement used as benchmarks to compare results with performance.

Planned downsizing: Systematic way of cutting overhead costs.

Post office box: Location where customers pay their accounts (local post office box), which are subsequently transferred to the seller's bank account.

Posting: Process of transferring recorded transactions from the journals to the appropriate ledger accounts (e.g., sales revenue, accounts receivable).

Present value: The value today of a future payment or stream of payments, discounted at an appropriate rate.

Preventive controls: System that helps to guide actions toward intended results.

Price/earnings ratio (P/E): Indicates how much investors are willing to pay per dollar of reported profits.

Price-level accounting: Accounting method used to restate assets on financial statements in terms of current purchasing power (inflation).

Process costing: Accounting system that helps to allocate direct and departmental overhead costs in organizations that produce goods on a continuous basis.

Productivity measures: Methods of measuring organizational performance (i.e., return on assets).

Profit break-even point: Number of units or sales revenue that must be reached in order to cover total costs plus a profit objective.

Profit margin on sales: The operating efficiency of a business.

Profitability index: Ratio of the present value of the cash inflow to the present value of the cash outflow discounted at a predetermined rate of interest.

Profitability ratios: Measure the overall effectiveness of a business.

Pro-forma financial statements: Projected financial statements (e.g., income statement, balance sheet).

Prosperity: The ability of a business to grow smoothly.

PV ratio: Profit-volume ratio; the contribution margin expressed on a per-unit basis.

Quick ratio: Shows the relationship between the more liquid current assets and all current liabilities.

Ratio analysis: Helps readers of financial statements assess the financial structure and performance of a business.

Ratio measures: Liquidity, debt/coverage, asset-management, profitability, and market value.

Reasons for budgeting: Improve communication, coordination, decision-making, monitoring, and accountability.

Regional banks: Locations where customers pay their accounts (local bank), which are subsequently transferred to the seller's bank account.

Relevant costs: Cost alternatives that managers can choose from to operate a business.

Relevant range: Costs (fixed and variable) that apply to a certain level of production.

Replacement value: Cost of acquiring a new asset to replace an existing asset with the same functional utility.

Residual value: Represents the sale of an asset or a business at the end of its physical life.

Responsibility centre: Organizational unit headed by a manager accountable for results.

Retained earnings: Amount of money kept by a company after paying dividends to its shareholders.

Return: Adequate funds to finance a company's growth.

Return on equity: The yield shareholders earn on their investment.

Return on sales: Measures a company's overall ability to generate profit from each sales dollar.

Return on total assets: The performance of assets employed in a business.

Revenue break-even point: Sales revenue that must be reached in order to cover total costs.

Revolving credit: Maximum amount of a loan a bank agrees to provide a business (borrower).

Risk: Represents the level of probable expectations (good or bad) that something will happen in the future.

Risk analysis: Process of attaching probabilities to individual estimates in capital project's base case.

Risk capital investors: Individuals or institutions that provide money to finance a business that entails relatively high risk. These investors seek a high potential return.

Rule of 72: Calculation that shows the approximate number of years it takes for an investment to double when compounded annually.

Rules of sources of funds: A source of funds takes place when there is a decrease in an asset account or an increase in a liability or equity account.

Rules of uses of funds: A use of funds takes place when there is an increase in an asset account or a decrease in a liability or equity account.

Sale and leaseback: Arrangement made by someone to sell an asset to a lessor, then lease it back.

Scanning the environment: Method used during the planning process for the purpose of pinning down planning assumptions or premises.

Screening controls: System that helps to monitor performance while work is being done.

Secured loan: A loan that the borrower guarantees by pledging some assets.

Self-liquidating loan: Funds used to finance temporary or fluctuating variations in working capital accounts (e.g., accounts receivable, inventory).

Self-regulated financial benchmark: Financial targets that are determined by a business's own policies, practices, and other financial measures.

Selling expenses: Cost incurred by a marketing organization to promote, sell, and distribute its goods and services.

Semi-variable costs: Costs that change disproportionately with changes in output levels.

Sensitivity analysis: Technique that shows to what extent a change in one variable (e.g., selling price, fixed costs) impacts on the break-even point.

Shareholders: The owners of a business (common and preferred shareholders).

Shareholders' equity: Funds provided in a business by its shareholders (i.e., shares, retained earnings).

Short-term financing: Sources of financing obtained for a period of less than one year (e.g., trade credit, line of credit).

Soft financial benchmarks: Most financial benchmarks fall in this category and should be used with some degree of interpretation.

Solvency: Ability to service or pay all debts (short and long-term).

Source of funds: Cash that is obtained from different sources (e.g., obtaining a loan, selling an asset).

Sources of financing: Institutions (e.g., banks, private investors) that provide funds to a business.

Stability: Relationship between debt and shareholders' equity.

Statement of changes in financial position: Financial statement that shows where funds come from and where they went.

Statement of retained earnings: Financial statement that shows the amount of income retained in a business since it was started.

Subordinated debt: Loan that is more risky, for which investors charge higher interest rates.

Sunk costs: Investment costs that have been incurred prior to making the decision to proceed with a capital project.

Supplier credit: Financing obtained from suppliers (accounts payable).

Sustainable growth rate: Rate of increase in sales revenue a company can attain without depleting financing resources, excessive borrowing, or issuing new stock.

Term loan: Loan made to buy capital assets.

Time value of money: Rate at which the value of money is traded off as a function of time.

Times-interest-earned ratio: Measures to what extent a business can service its interest on debt.

Total assets turnover: Measures how intensively a firm's total assets are used to generate sales.

Treasurer: Person responsible for raising funds and regulating the flow of funds.

Trend analysis: Analyzing a company's performance over a number of years.

Trial balance: Statement that ensures that the general ledger is in balance (debit transactions = credit transactions).

Types of inventory: Raw materials, work-in-process, and finished goods.

Unit break-even point: Number of units that must be sold in order to cover total costs.

Use of funds: Cash that is disbursed or expended for buying or paying something (e.g., paying a mortgage, buying a car).

Variable costs: Costs that fluctuate directly with changes in volume of production.

Variance analysis: Accounting system that compares standards to actual performance.

Venture capital: Risk capital supplied to small companies by wealthy individuals (angels), partnerships, or corporations, usually in return for an equity position in the firm.

Wire transfer process: Means for transferring funds between customer and supplier by using the Internet or any other electronic medium.

Working capital: Total current assets and total current liabilities.

Working capital loans: Short-term loans made for the purpose of financing working capital accounts (e.g., inventory, accounts receivable).

Working capital management: Managing individual current asset and current liability accounts to ensure proper interrelationships among them.

Index

Program budget, 348
Prospectus, 420
Prosperity, 12
Provincial financing aid, 424
Provincial tax rates, 63
Provincial venture capital organizations, 426
Public corporation, 63
Public issue, 419–420
Public warehousing, 415
Publicly owned companies, 223
PV, 273
PV ratio, 183

Quaker Oats, 219
Quality standards, 372
Quality work, 21
Quantity variance, 358
Quick ratio, 130–131

Raising funds, 225
Rate variance, 359
Ratio analysis, 129–140
    asset-management ratios, 134–136
    debt/coverage ratios, 131–134
    defined, 122
    limitations, 155–156
    liquidity ratios, 129–131
    market-value ratios, 138–139
    overview, 140
    profitability ratios, 137–138
    why used, 122–127
Ratio measures, 129
Raw materials, 57, 469
R&D budget, 345
Reasons for budgeting, 338–340
Regional banks, 458
Relevant costs, 184–185
Relevant range, 184
Replacement value, 506
Reproduction value, 506
Residual value, 299
Responsibility accounting, 340
Responsibility centre, 340–342
Results-oriented budgeting techniques, 22
Retail store break-even chart, 193, 194
Retained earnings, 54, 59, 224, 228–229
Return, 123
Return on equity, 138
Return on investment (ROI), 154
Return on sales, 137
Return on total assets, 138
Return risk, 296–297

Revenue break-even point, 188
Revenue centre, 341
Revolving credit, 413
Riding-the-yield approach, 460
Risk, 223, 224
    business, 404
    capital budgeting, 311
    financial, 404
    instrument, 404
    lease-or-buy decisions, 429
    long-term financing, 422
    return, 296–297
    time value of money, 259
Risk analysis, 312–314, 403–405
Risk capital investors, 422–424
Risk capital long-term financing, 418–419
ROI, 154
Royal Bank Capital Corporation, 423
Roynat, 423
Rule of 72, 263
Rules of sources of funds, 94
Rules of uses of funds, 94

Salaries and wages payable, 477–478
Sale and leaseback, 427
Sales budget, 346
Sales volume, 214
SBLA loans, 426
Scanning the environment, 506–507
Screening controls, 375
Seasonal loan, 413
Secured bonds, 417
Secured loan, 414
Self-liquidating loan, 413
Self-regulated financial benchmarks, 149
Selling expenses, 52
Semi-variable costs, 178
Sensitivity analysis, 190, 312
Service centre break-even chart, 192–193
Shared-risk mortgage, 425
Shareholder rights, 421
Shareholders, 420
Shareholders' equity, 48, 59
Short-term financing, 406, 410–416
    asset-based financing, 414–416
    chartered banks/trust companies, 411–414
    defined, 416
    factoring, 414–415
    inventory financing, 415
    suppliers, 410

Short-term loans, 411–414
Short-term risk capital financing, 414–415
Short-term solvency, 125
Simplification, 21
Six Sigma, 22
Small business deduction, 64
Small Business Loans Act (SBLA), 426
Soft financial benchmarks, 147
Solvency, 125
Source of funds, 13, 88, 93, 94
Sources of financing, 405, 406
Stability, 12
Standard & Poor's, 508
Standard & Poor's Compustat Services, 149, 508
Standard-cost centre, 342
Standards, 339, 357
Standby costs, 177
Start-up investments, 423
Statement of cash flows. *See* Statement of changes in financial position
Statement of changes in financial position, 47, 48, 84–116
    defined, 96
    financing activities, 99
    investing activities, 100
    operating activities, 98–99
    pro-forma, 365–366
    source of funds, 88, 93, 94
    use of funds, 88, 93, 95
Statement of earnings. *See* Income statement
Statement of financial condition. *See* Balance sheet
Statement of operations. *See* Income statement
Statement of retained earnings, 47–48, 54
Steering controls, 374
Straight-line method of depreciation, 65–66
Strategic benchmarks, 146
Subordinated debt, 418–419
Sum-of-the-years'-digits method, 66
Sunk costs, 300
Supplier credit, 410
Supplier relations, 476–477
Sustainable growth rate, 366–368

T-accounts, 44
Tax cost, 224–225
Taxation
    business losses, 64

Photograph Credits

p. 3: 32327BME/Business Meetings CD165/© 2002 Stockbyte
p. 35: PhotoDisc/Getty Images
p. 85: Keith Brofsky/PhotoDisc/Getty Images
p. 119: Comstock
p. 173: 32329BME/Business Meetings CD165/© 2002 Stockbyte
p. 211: PhotoDisc/Getty Images
p. 255: Anne Bradley/Nelson photo
p. 289: PhotoDisc/Getty Images
p. 335: 32332BME/Business Meetings CD165/© 2002 Stockbyte
p. 397: 32319BME/Business Meetings CD165/© 2002 Stockbyte
p. 447: David Buffington/PhotoDisc/Getty Images
p. 499: 32393BME/Business Meetings CD165/© 2002 Stockbyte